www.wadsworth.com

www.wadsworth.com is the World Wide Web site for Wadsworth and is your direct source to dozens of online resources.

At *www.wadsworth.com* you can find out about supplements, demonstration software, and student resources. You can also send email to many of our authors and preview new publications and exciting new technologies.

www.wadsworth.com
Changing the way the world learns®

Personality

Contemporary Theory and Research

THIRD EDITION

Valerian A. Derlega
Old Dominion University

Barbara A. Winstead
Old Dominion University

Warren H. Jones
University of Tennessee

THOMSON
WADSWORTH

Australia • Canada • Mexico • Singapore • Spain
United Kingdom • United States

Editor: *Michele Sordi*
Assistant Editor: *Jennifer Wilkinson*
Editorial Assistant: *Chelsea Junget*
Marketing Manager: *Chris Caldeira*
Marketing Assistant: *Laurel Anderson*
Advertising Project Manager: *Tami Strang*
Project Manager, Editorial Production: *Paula Berman*
Art Director: *Vernon T. Boes*
Print/Media Buyer: *Doreen Suruki*

Permissions Editor: *Joohee Lee*
Production Service and Compositor: *Scratchgravel Publishing Services*
Photo Researcher: *Laura Molmud*
Copy Editor: *Patterson Lamb*
Cover Designer: *Cheryl Carrington*
Cover Image: *Norton Simon Museum, Gift of Dr. Kati Breckenridge, 2000*
Text and Cover Printer: *Webcom Limited*

Printed in Canada

1   2   3   4   5   6   7   08   07   06   05   04

For more information about our products,
contact us at:
**Thomson Learning Academic Resource Center
1-800-423-0563**

For permission to use material from this text or
product, submit a request online at
http://www.thomsonrights.com.
Any additional questions about permissions
can be submitted by email to
thomsonrights@thomson.com.

Library of Congress Control Number: 2003116809

ISBN 0-534-59871-4

Thomson Wadsworth
10 Davis Drive
Belmont, CA 94002-3098
USA

Asia
Thomson Learning
5 Shenton Way #01-01
UIC Building
Singapore 068808

Australia/New Zealand
Thomson Learning
102 Dodds Street
Southbank, Victoria 3006
Australia

Canada
Nelson
1120 Birchmount Road
Toronto, Ontario M1K 5G4
Canada

Europe/Middle East/Africa
Thomson Learning
High Holborn House
50/51 Bedford Row
London WC1R 4LR
United Kingdom

Latin America
Thomson Learning
Seneca, 53
Colonia Polanco
11560 Mexico D.F.
Mexico

Spain/Portugal
Paraninfo
Calle Magallanes, 25
28015 Madrid, Spain

Brief Contents

Contents

CHAPTER 3   Genetic and Environmental Influences   63
David C. Rowe and Edwin J. C. G. van den Oord

CHAPTER 6   Motives   156

Barbara A. Woike and Dan P. McAdams

CHAPTER 9   **Self-Concept, Self-Esteem, and Identity   246**
Roy F. Baumeister

CHAPTER 10   Self-Awareness and Self-Consciousness   281

Stephen L. Franzoi and Mark H. Davis

CHAPTER 11   Personality and Control   309

Jerry M. Burger

CHAPTER 12   Sex and Gender   332

Richard A. Lippa

Preface

Personality: Contemporary Theory and Research is a unique textbook in presenting areas of current personality research written at a level that can be understood by undergraduates. In preparing this book, we invited psychologists who are experts in particular areas of personality to contribute chapters. The goal in each chapter is to present an overview of an area (including a history of constructs, definitions, methodological issues, and a review of research topics within the area). In most chapters, authors also give a detailed description of a particular research program (of their own work, whenever possible) to illustrate how research in personality is conducted.

We have been pleased to find an enthusiastic audience for our approach to teaching contemporary research in personality in the earlier editions of this textbook. In this third edition, you will find most of the authors who contributed to the second edition with updated materials and references. We have expanded the book's coverage by including new chapters on personality structure by Robert R. McCrae and on culture and personality by A. Timothy Church and Fernando A. Ortiz. Richard A. Lippa has also contributed a new chapter on sex and gender, Barbara A. Woike (with Dan P. McAdams) has rewritten the chapter on motives, and Edwin J. C. G. van den Oord has revised the chapter on genetic and environmental influences that was single-authored by David C. Rowe in the first and second editions. (We regretted to learn that Dr. Rowe was gravely ill when we contacted him about a revised chapter and he recommended Dr. van den Oord. David Rowe's death in 2003 is a significant loss to psychology and to personality research.) We hope this third edition continues to serve courses with the aim of focusing on personality research.

The book is divided into two major sections. Part One deals with basic issues in personality, including fundamental questions in personality psychology, personality measurement, genetic and environmental influences, biological approaches, personality development, and motives. The chapters on basic issues summarize major traditions of research in personality and up-to-date accounts of work in these areas. Part Two deals with topics in personality that are influential, including personality structure; the psychological unconscious; self-concept, self-esteem, and identity; self-awareness and self-consciousness; control; sex and gender; emotions; moral character; culture; stress and illness; relationships; and disorders of personality.

Besides providing coverage of important issues and topics in personality research, the chapters show the relevance of personality processes in explaining human behaviors. The chapters include Activity Boxes that provide students with an illustration of how the material discussed in the chapter can be applied to them. Each chapter also includes Discussion Questions to assist students in reviewing the material.

This text is an introduction to personality that focuses on current theory and research, and it makes a distinctive contribution by adopting this approach. *Personality: Contemporary Theory and Research* is suitable for undergraduates in junior- and senior-level courses in which the goal is to introduce students to major concepts and research. The book is also suitable as a graduate-level text focusing on empirical research in personality.

We want to thank the authors of the individual chapters who enthusiastically and graciously took on this responsibility. We are grateful to the editorial staff of Wadsworth Publishers, particularly Michele Sordi who encouraged us to develop this third edition of the text. We also thank Chelsea Junget at Wadsworth for her ready assistance in the production of the book. Finally, we thank the following reviewers for their comments: David DiLalla, Southern Illinois University; Lisa Lockhart, Texas A&M University, Kingsville; and Marc Setterlund, Alma College.

About the Editors

Valerian J. Derlega is professor of psychology at Old Dominion University in Norfolk, Virginia. His research interests focus on social and personality variables involved in coping with stress, especially living with the human immunodeficiency virus (HIV). Dr. Derlega is co-author (with Kathryn Greene, Gust Yep, and Sandra Petronio) of the book *Privacy and Disclosure of HIV in Interpersonal Relationships: A Sourcebook for Researchers and Practitioners*. He has also published research articles and chapters on self-disclosure in personal relationships and on gender and sexual orientation.

Barbara A. Winstead is professor and chair of psychology at Old Dominion University in Norfolk, Virginia. Her research interests include gender and relationships, social support, and coping with multiple roles. She is co-author (with Jessica Griffin) of "Friendship Styles," published in the *Encyclopedia of Women and Gender*, volume one. She is also the author of research articles and books on social support and gender and relationships.

Warren H. Jones is professor of psychology at the University of Tennessee in Knoxville. His interests broadly span the areas of personality and social psychology but have focused mainly on the impact of personality in interpersonal situations. In addition to publishing numerous articles and chapters on the topics of shyness, loneliness, guilt, trust, betrayal, and forgiveness, he has also published several edited volumes on the topics of personality and/or relationships. In addition, he has served as the editor of the *Journal of Personality and Social Psychology* and the *Psi Chi Journal of Undergraduate Research*.

About the Contributors

Roy Baumeister received his Ph.D. in 1978 from Princeton. He has published several hundred articles, chapters, and books on psychological processes, including the books *Evil: Inside Human Violence and Cruelty, Losing Control: How and Why People Fail at Self-Regulation, The Social Dimension of Sex,* and *The Cultural Animal: Human Nature, Meaning, and Social Life.* In 2003 he was awarded the prestigious Eppes professorship at Florida State University, where he is helping to build a rapidly growing Ph.D. program in personality and social psychology. He also travels around the world giving lectures, and he likes to play guitar and windsurf.

Stephen Briggs is provost and vice president for academic affairs at the College of New Jersey, where he is responsible for strategic planning, program development, and academic operations. He earned his undergraduate degree in psychology at Wake Forest University and his Ph.D. in personality psychology at the University of Texas at Austin in 1982. He has held previous academic positions at the University of Tulsa (Oklahoma) and Rollins Collins (Florida). His research interests involve the experience and expression of personality traits as they relate to one's emerging sense of self. Although time for research and writing is scarce in his current position, Briggs finds that his background in personality psychology serves him well as he works with people of all kinds and as he tackles complicated problems using the analytical skills of a research psychologist.

Jerry M. Burger is professor of psychology at Santa Clara University. He is the author of *Desire for Control: Personality, Social and Clinical Perspectives* and the textbook *Personality,* now in its sixth edition. His current research interests include personal control, social influence, and preference for solitude.

Jonathan Cheek received his Ph.D. from Johns Hopkins University and has been teaching personality psychology at Wellesley College since 1981. His research interests are shyness and self-concept. His hobby is appreciating and collecting Haitian art.

A. Timothy Church received his Ph.D. in psychology from the University of Minnesota and is a professor at Washington State University. From 1982 to 1984 he was a visiting professor at De La Salle University in the Philippines. His primary research interests include cross-cultural personality structure and assessment and alternative perspectives on the study of personality and culture.

He is currently associate editor for the *Journal of Cross-Cultural Psychology* and consulting editor for the *Journal of Personality and Social Psychology* and the *Journal of Research in Personality.*

Laurie L. Couch is associate professor of psychology at Morehead State University in Morehead, Kentucky. Her interests involve investigations of how personality and social cognition operate in interpersonal relationships. In particular, she continues to study experiences of trust and betrayal in romantic relationships from both quantitative and qualitative perspectives. Most recently her work has been investigating the role of personality qualities like trust in the experience of betrayal, the process of coping with betrayal, the cognitive processes involved in the experience of betrayal, and the mental and physical health risks associated with betrayal.

Richard J. Davidson is William James and Vilas Research Professor of psychology and psychiatry at the University of Wisconsin-Madison where he directs the Laboratory for Affective Neuroscience and the Keck Laboratory for Functional Brain Imaging and Behavior. His research focuses on the neural substrates of emotion. A major focus of recent research is on interactions between the prefrontal cortex and the amygdala in the regulation of emotion in both normal individuals and patients with affective and anxiety disorders.

Mark H. Davis is professor of psychology at Eckerd College in St. Petersburg, Florida. He is the author of over 40 articles and chapters in the area of social psychology as well as a book, *Empathy: A Social Psychological Approach*. In addition, he is the editor of *Annual Editions: Social Psychology*. He received his Ph.D. in psychology from the University of Texas and his B.A. in psychology and political science from the University of Iowa.

Nicholas Emler is currently professor of social psychology at the University of Surrey, England, and also holds a professorial appointment at the Université de Paris V, Rene Descartes. He has previously been professor of social psychology at the London School of Economics, Oxford University, and the University of Dundee in Scotland. He has been a consulting editor of the *Journal of Personality and Social Psychology* and chief editor of the *European Journal of Social Psychology*. His research has addressed various themes in moral psychology; current interests include delinquency, reputation, the development of political commitments, and leadership.

Stephen L. Franzoi is professor of psychology at Marquette University in Milwaukee, Wisconsin. He is the author of over 40 articles and chapters in the area of social psychology as well as two books, *Social Psychology* and *Psychology: A Journey of Discovery*. In addition, he is associate editor of *Social Problems*. He received his Ph.D. in psychology from the University of California at Davis and his B.S. in sociology and personality psychology from Western Michigan University.

Warren H. Jones is professor of psychology at the University of Tennessee in Knoxville. His interests broadly span the areas of personality and social psychology, but have mainly focused on the impact of personality in interpersonal situations. In addition to publishing numerous articles and chapters on the topics of shyness, loneliness, guilt, trust, betrayal, and forgiveness, he also has published several edited volumes on the topics of personality and/or relationships. In addition, he has served as the editor of the *Journal of Personality and Social Psychology* and the *Psi Chi Journal of Undergraduate Research*.

Kathleen A. Lawler is professor of psychology at the University of Tennessee in Knoxville, Tennessee. She is a health psychologist, interested in the physiology of emotional states and factors that predict optimal health across the life span. Her current work is focused on the physiology of forgiveness and spirituality, and the relationship of these factors to health.

Mark R. Leary is professor and chair of psychology at Wake Forest University (Winston-Salem, North Carolina). He obtained his Ph.D. from the University of Florida in 1980 and held positions at Denison University and the University of Texas at Austin before moving to Wake Forest in 1985. His interests focus primarily on how people's concerns with social evaluation, approval, and acceptance affect their thoughts, emotions, and behavior. Within this broad area, he has published nine books and approximately 150 articles and chapters on topics such as social anxiety, self-presentation, reactions to interpersonal rejection (such as hurt feelings and anger), and self-esteem. He is also interested in work that bridges the gap between social and personality psychology on one hand and clinical and counseling psychology on the topic. He served for ten years as an associate editor of the *Journal of Social and Clinical Psychology* and was the founding editor of *Self and Identity*, a new journal that publishes research dealing with self-processes.

Richard A. Lippa is professor of psychology at California State University, Fullerton. He was a National Science Foundation Graduate Fellow at Stanford University, where he received his doctorate in psychology. He has published numerous research articles on gender, masculinity, and femininity, and the recent book, *Gender, Nature, and Nurture* (2002). For more information about Dr. Lippa's research interests, see his Web page (http://psych.fullerton.edu/rlippa/), where you can participate in a number of Internet surveys on masculinity, femininity, and personality.

James E. Maddux is a professor in the department of psychology at George Mason University in Fairfax, Virginia. He received his Ph.D. in clinical psychology in 1982 from the University of Alabama. His main areas of interests are the interface of social and clinical psychology, health psychology, self-efficacy theory, and conceptions of mental health and disorder. He is the editor of the *Journal of Social and Clinical Psychology*. He is co-author (with David F. Barone and C. R. Snyder) of *Social Cognitive Psychology: History and Currrent*

Domains and co-editor (with Barbara A. Winstead) of *Psychopathology: Current Theory, Research, and Issues.*

Marina F. Martin is a graduate student in the master's degree program in psychology at the University of Tennessee. She received her B. A. degree in psychology from Tennessee Wesleyan College in Athens, Tennessee. Her area of interest is the physiology of stress and the relationship of stress to chronic illness.

Dan P. McAdams is professor of psychology and of human development and social policy at Northwestern University. He teaches courses on personality theory and research, adult development and aging, and the narrative study of lives. He has conducted research on the topics of intimacy and power motivation, generativity in midlife, the concepts of suffering and redemption in human lives, and the role of life stories in personality development across the life course. He is the 1989 winner of the Henry A. Murray Award from the American Psychological Association for excellence in personality research and the study of lives.

Robert R. McCrae received his undergraduate degree in philosophy from Michigan State University, and 1976 his doctorate in personality psychology from Boston University. Since then he has worked as a full-time researcher, mostly at the National Institute on Aging. His research has focused on personality structure and assessment and the application of trait psychology to an understanding of health, well-being, and aging. With Paul T. Costa, Jr., he is author of the Revised NEO Personality Inventory.

Rowland Miller is professor of psychology at Sam Houston State University in Huntsville, Texas. His dissertation at the University of Florida won the American Psychological Association and Psi Chi's Newman Award for Excellence in Research, so he's a proud Florida Gator. He studies embarrassment and close relationships and has authored or coauthored three books, including *Intimate Relationships* (3rd ed.).

Clare E. Mundell received her Ph.D. in clinical psychology from George Mason University in 2000 and is in private practice in Chapel Hill, North Carolina, specializing in psychoanalytic psychotherapy with adults. She is a psychoanalyst-in-training at the UNC-Duke Psychoanalytic Institute. Prior to entering private practice, Dr. Mundell was a clinical assistant professor of psychology at the University of North Carolina at Chapel Hill and served as staff psychologist at John Umstead Hospital in Butner, North Carolina. Her areas of research interest include psychotherapy with psychotic patients, psychoanalytic psychotherapy, and mental health policy.

Michael Nash is professor of psychology at the University of Tennessee and editor emeritus of *The International Journal of Clinical and Experimental Hypnosis.* He received his Ph.D. from Ohio University in 1983 and completed his clinical internship in the Yale University School of Medicine Department of Psychiatry in the same year. He has published two books, one on the research foundations of hypnosis and another on the topic of psychoanalysis, both co-authored with Dr. Erika Fromm. He has authored over 70 publications in scientific journals on the topics of human memory, dissociative pathology, sex abuse, psychotherapy, and hypnosis. He is a Diplomate in clinical psychology, and is the recipient of numerous awards, including the Morton Prince Award, for his scientific and clinical writing..

Fernando A. Ortiz is a doctoral student in counseling psychology at Washington State University and a research assistant on the Culture and Personality Project. His primary research interests include Mexican ethnopsychology and cross-cultural research. A native of Mexico, he first became interested in cultural differences and personality while working with culturally diverse populations in the California mental health system.

David Rowe graduated magna cum laude from Harvard University in 1972 and earned his Ph.D. in behavior genetics from the University of Colorado in 1977. His research fields were behavioral genetics and evolutionary psychology. He published over 160 articles/book chapters plus two books, and received several honors. He was a pioneer in studying the effects of genes on the environment, and his book *The Limits of Family Influence* has greatly influenced contemporary thinking about parenting. Dr. Rowe passed away in 2003.

Edwin van den Oord graduated cum laude from the University of Amsterdam in 1991 and two years later received his Ph.D. degree in psychiatric and behavioral genetics from Erasmus University in Rotterdam, the Netherlands. He has over 50 publications in peer reviewed journals and has won several awards. His current research interests include statistical genetics and the interplay of genotypes and environment.

Rebecca L. Volz is a 2002 graduate of the University of Tennessee, with a B. A. degree in psychology. She plans to attend a graduate program in clinical psychology, with a focus either on health or family psychology.

Tricia Waters is assistant professor of psychology at Colorado College. She received her Ph.D. in psychology, with a concentration in personality development, from Boston University. Her research interests include false self behavior and the psychology of women.

Barbara A. Woike is an assistant professor at Barnard College, an undergraduate women's institution affiliated with Columbia University in New York City. As a personality psychologist, she teaches courses in personality theory and research, motivation and emotion, and health psychology. She has published numerous articles on the implicit and explicit motivation distinction and the influence of these motives on memory processes.

Basic Issues in Personality

PART 1

1 | The Scientific Study of Personality

MARK R. LEARY

CHAPTER OUTLINE

Jot down the names of five people whom you know well—friends, parents, brothers or sisters, teachers, employers, co-workers—and add your own name to the list too. Look over your list of names for a moment and think about ways in which these six people differ from one another. Think beyond obvious physical differences, such as age and appearance, to how they tend to think, feel, and behave. Are some people on your list more outgoing and friendly than others? Do some of them usually appear cheerful, whereas others tend to be dour, if not depressed? Are one or two of these people always late, whereas others are usually punctual? Do some of them dread speaking in front of groups, whereas others actually enjoy being in the spotlight? Do you get the sense that certain of these people are reasonably well adjusted and able to cope with whatever happens but others fall apart easily over minor problems and hassles? Are some of them dominant, independent types, whereas others are conforming and submissive? Who are the open-minded people on your list, and who are more closed-minded?

Now think for a moment about what these people have in common. In what ways are they similar in how they tend to think, feel, and behave? Do they all prefer to be accepted rather than rejected by other people? Do they all have at least one or two friends? Do they all smile when they're happy but frown when they're sad? Do they all occasionally make excuses for their undesirable behaviors? Do they all identify themselves as either a man or a woman?

As you answered these questions about the differences and similarities among these individuals, you were thinking primarily about aspects of their personalities—their tendencies to think, feel, and behave in particular ways. Some of these personality characteristics—such as the tendency to be outgoing, open-minded, or depressed—distinguish some of the people on your list from others, whereas other characteristics, such as a desire for social acceptance, are probably shared by all of them. But all of the characteristics involve aspects of these individuals' personalities.

PERSONALITY: A DEFINITION

To begin, we should be explicit regarding what psychologists mean when they use the term *personality*. In everyday language, people often use the word to refer to something like social skill or charisma, as when we say someone "has a lot of personality." But behavioral researchers use the term in a somewhat different sense.

Personality can be defined as *the system of enduring, inner characteristics of individuals that contributes to consistency in their thoughts, feelings, and behavior*. This simple definition conveys a great deal about personality, so we need to examine its three main components closely.

Personality Is Enduring

First, personality involves characteristics of individuals that are relatively enduring. Aspects of a person's personality are stable over time. Psychologists distinguish between states and traits on the basis of the stability or consistency of a person's responses. A *state* is transient and short lived, the person's current re-action in the present situation. If I ask, "How nervous do you feel right now?" your answer reflects your current state of nervousness or anxiety. A *trait*, on the other hand, is relatively stable and lasting, the person's general tendency to react in a particular way. If I ask, "How nervous do you typically feel?" your answer reflects your standing on the trait of nervousness.

Any particular trait may be thought of as an indication of a person's tendency or predisposition to experience a particular relevant state. A person who scores "high" on a trait tends to experience the corresponding state more frequently and in a wider array of situations than a person who is "low" on the trait (Fleeson, 2001). For example, if you score high on a measure of trait anxiety, you are likely to experience the state of anxiety more often than if you score low on trait anxiety.

Noting that personality is enduring does not mean that people's personalities cannot change; they can, and they do. Perhaps you are more outgoing now than you were as a child. But changes in personality usually occur gradually over an extended period of time.

Personality Is Intrapersonal

The second defining feature of personality refers to inner, "intrapersonal" characteristics. Since the earliest days of psychology, behavioral scientists have recognized that how people think, feel, and behave depends on the interplay of two distinct sets of factors. On one hand, behavior is affected by things that lie outside the individual. We respond to stimuli and events in our world, such as aspects of the physical environment, the type of social situation we are in, and the characteristics and behavior of other people who are present. At the same time, however, our behavior is affected by attributes and processes within us. We respond on the basis of our goals, motives, needs, self-concept, feelings, and other intrapersonal factors (intrapersonal means "inside the person").

Kurt Lewin (1935) concisely captured the joint contributions of external and internal factors in the formula:

$$B = f(P,E), \text{ or}$$
*B*ehavior is a function of the *P*erson and the *E*nvironment.

A complete understanding of human behavior requires that behavioral researchers examine both of these sets of factors. Yet, from the beginnings of behavioral science, researchers have disagreed about whether external, situational factors or internal, intrapersonal factors play the more important role in behavior, and different psychological specialties have tended to focus on one set of determinants or the other. While not denying that external factors affect behavior, personality psychologists focus primarily on the study of inner, intrapersonal psychological characteristics and processes.

Personality Involves Behavioral Consistency

These enduring, inner characteristics and processes lead to a certain degree of consistency in how people respond across various situations. To understand what this means, imagine what you would be like if you did not possess a personality. Without a personality, your behavior would be a product of the immediate situation in which you found yourself. We might be able to predict your behavior by examining the stimuli and events going on around you, but we would not find it useful to consider your traits, motives, self-concept, or other inner psychological characteristics. As a result, we would see little coherence or consistency in your behavior across different situations. Your thoughts, feelings, and behavior would change dramatically as the situation changed. In fact, other people would be unable to describe what you are like because they would not observe any consistency in your behavior.

Your inner psychological characteristics—your personality—are partly responsible for your tendency to behave similarly across different situations. As you move from one situation to another, you carry with you a set of characteristics—traits, goals, physiological reactions, and so on—that lead to a certain amount of consistency in your behavior. Psychologists have debated the degree to which people respond consistently across different situations, but little doubt exists that, when viewed over time, people show consistency that is attributable to their personalities (Epstein, 1983).

Furthermore, personality involves not only a person's characteristics but also how those characteristics are organized and integrated. People's personalities display a certain degree of unity or coherence in that the various parts function as a unified whole. As a system, personality involves not only certain components (such as traits and motives) but also an organizational structure and the processes by which the system functions and develops (Mayer, 1993).

FUNDAMENTAL QUESTIONS IN PERSONALITY PSYCHOLOGY

The relatively enduring, intrapersonal characteristics and processes that are of interest to personality psychologists account for both the idiosyncratic differences that distinguish one person from another (individual differences) and the common features of human nature that virtually everyone shares (psychological universals). Personality psychology focuses on both the stable psychological differences and the stable psychological similarities among people.

Individual Differences

Historically, personality psychologists have been interested primarily in *individual differences*—personality characteristics and processes that differ across people. Human beings are remarkably variable in their personalities. Any psychological attribute we might think of can be viewed along a continuum; some people are "low" on the characteristic, some people are "moderate," and other people are "high" (see Figure 1.1).

Figure 1.1 | The trait continuum.

Very low   Low   Average   High   Very high

Consider the trait of agreeableness for example. If we measured people's scores on the trait of agreeableness—how friendly, kind, warm, and helpful they tend to be—people's scores would spread out along an agreeableness continuum ranging from low to high. Some people are very, very low in agreeableness; in fact, they are irritable, critical, suspicious, and downright nasty. As we move up the continuum through the moderate range, we find people who are more and more agreeable. At the high end of the continuum are people who are exceptionally good-natured, helpful, trusting, and agreeable. Put simply, people demonstrate considerable individual differences in agreeableness (see Figure 1.2).

Figure 1.2 | The trait of agreeableness.

Importantly, scoring low or high on a trait does not mean that the person always manifests the relevant state. For example, scoring high in agreeableness does not indicate that a person is always agreeable. Nor is someone who scores low in agreeableness always disagreeable. In fact, no matter where people stand on a trait—low, average, or high—they display a great deal of variability in the states they experience (Fleeson, 2001). Even people high in agreeableness are sometimes disagreeable, and those who are low in agreeableness may be quite pleasant. The difference between people who score low versus high on a trait lies in the frequency with which they manifest the relevant state.

Personality psychologists have been very interested in understanding individual differences in personality. In particular, researchers in the field of personality psychology have been interested in three central questions about individual differences in personality: (1) What are the basic components of personality and how are they related to one another? (2) How do these components develop and change within the individual? (3) How do these inner psychological characteristics relate to behavior? Let us examine each of these fundamental questions.

Personality Components   The first task in understanding any complex system, such as personality, is to identify and understand its components. What are the basic components of personality? How many fundamental personality characteristics (traits, needs, motives, or whatever) are there, and what are they? Faced with a very large number of characteristics that are interrelated in complex ways, personality psychologists have devoted a great deal of attention to the nature and structure of personality.

The scientific study of personality requires the use of reliable and valid measures of these components, and personality psychologists have developed, tested, and refined thousands of personality measures. Many of these measures were developed solely for use in behavioral research, but others were constructed for use by psychologists who work in applied settings, such as personnel psychologists who use such measures to help businesses select employees and clinical psychologists who use them to assess the personalities of their troubled clients.

In their efforts to understand the content and structure of personality, researchers rely heavily on *factor analysis*—a statistical technique that allows them to identify the basic dimensions (or factors) that underlie a large set of measures. Although individual differences in personality can be described using thousands of different words in the English language, factor analysis allows researchers to look beyond these superficial differences to uncover the fundamental personality characteristics that distinguish one person from another. As we will see in later chapters, personality psychologists now believe that personality can be reasonably well described in terms of only five basic traits, the so-called "big five" personality factors—extraversion, emotional stability (or neuroticism), agreeableness, openness, and conscientiousness.

Personality Development and Change   Personality researchers have also been interested in where individual differences in personality come from—the processes that lie behind personality development and change. Why are some people more talkative, achievement-oriented, lonely, confident, expressive, guilt-ridden, or creative than others? Many theories have been offered to explain why people's personalities differ. Freud's psychoanalytic theory, for example, was an effort to explain individual differences in terms of childhood experiences. Other theories trace personality to biological predispositions, patterns of reinforcement and punishment, or the development of cognitive belief systems.

After many years of focusing primarily on the development of personality in childhood, personality researchers turned more recently to the ways personality changes during adulthood. Although the seeds of personality are sown early in life, people's personalities sometimes change markedly during adolescence and early adulthood. However, after the age of about 30, central aspects of personality tend to change relatively little (McCrae & Costa, 1990).

Personality Processes and Behavior   A large amount of work in personality psychology has been devoted to understanding the relationship between personality and behavior. Many researchers have been interested simply in the ways personality manifests itself in how people think, feel, and behave. For example, what difference does it make, behaviorally speaking, whether a person has low self-esteem or high self-esteem? Do people who have low versus high self-esteem tend to feel and act differently and, if so, under what circumstances do such behavioral differences appear? A great deal of research has explored the relationship between personality on the one hand and thought, feeling, and behavior on the other.

Furthermore, researchers have been interested in the processes that underlie these behavioral differences. Simply demonstrating that people who score differently on a measure of personality, such as self-esteem or extraversion, behave differently is only the first step toward understanding how personality operates. For example, we not only want to know how people with low versus high self-esteem behave differently but also why these behavioral differences occur.

Psychological Universals

Variation in human personality is truly remarkable; we see individual differences everywhere we look. Yet, if we step back and look at human behavior more globally, we also see many patterns of thought, emotion, and behavior that are common to most, if not all normal human beings regardless of their background or culture. For example, all people have an inherent need to belong; few otherwise normal individuals would rather be scorned, rejected, and ostracized than embraced, accepted, and loved (Baumeister & Leary, 1995). Similarly, people in all cultures have leaders, become embarrassed (and blush), and live in groups. In addition, certain fears—of the dark, snakes, and death, for example—seem virtually universal, and particular patterns of mate selection are so widespread that they appear to emerge from some fundamental aspect of human nature. (For example, around the world, it is far more common for women to marry men older than themselves than it is for men to marry older women.) These kinds of similarities suggest that, despite the many differences in their individual personalities, all people possess certain inner, enduring characteristics in common, suggesting that they come into the world preprogrammed to respond in certain ways (Barkow, Cosmides, & Tooby, 1992).

Identification of Universals   Personality psychologists, along with specialists in cross-cultural psychology, evolutionary psychology, and anthropology, have tried to identify aspects of human behavior that are universal. This has been a formidable task, and much disagreement exists regarding not only which aspects of personality are universal but also the criteria by which we should decide what is universal and what is not.

One area that has received particular attention involves emotions and emotional expression. Clearly, all human beings have the capacity to experience emotion, but do people in all cultures experience the same basic emotions and express them in essentially the same ways? Some researchers suggest that facial expressions are universal for six basic emotions—happiness, surprise, sadness, fear, disgust, and anger (Ekman, 1993)—whereas others dispute these findings (Russell, 1994). The question is not a minor one, for in order for us to understand the links between personality and emotion, we must know something about the structure and origin of emotional experience itself.

Sources of Universality   Once universals in human personality are discovered, the question arises of why such similarities exist in people around the world. Two general answers to this question are possible. The evolutionary perspective proposes that behavioral tendencies that increased the likelihood of survival and reproduction were passed along from generation to generation and became part of human nature. Early hominids whose nervous systems led them to behave in ways that increased their ability to survive and reproduce passed along to their offpring the genetic blueprints for nervous systems that were associated with these reproductive advantages. For example, parents who became emotionally attached to their children were more likely to have children who reached maturity and had their own children than parents who felt no attachment for their offspring. Over evolutionary time, the tendency for people to form family attachments presumably became stronger as the parents with the neurological predisposition toward attachment had more surviving children than the parents who did not have this predisposition.

In considering the evolutionary basis of human personality, keep in mind that the evolutionary processes responsible for human anatomy and physiology occurred over millions of years. During most of this time, our humans and prehuman ancestors lived in small, hunting-gathering-scavenging clans on the African savanna. Thus, whatever psychological predispositions *Homo sapiens* possesses today evolved in response to the living conditions that existed during prehistory. Certain evolutionary adaptations that were once beneficial may be irrelevant or even disadvantageous in modern society.

A second explanation for universality is that people naturally learned over time that certain patterns of behavior were useful in helping them deal with certain challenges that are common to all human beings. Once learned, such behaviors were passed on from one generation to the next through culture rather than through genes. For example, people in all cultures create containers, such as baskets and bowls, in which they carry things. But it seems likely that this universal behavior is a cultural creation rather than a biological one (see Activity Box 1.1).

Activity Box 1.1   **Personality and Common Sense**

Through our direct experience with other people, most of us have developed certain beliefs—our own personal theories—about personality. Some of these assumptions are true, but others are undoubtedly false. Regardless, they affect how we feel and behave. Below are listed several common beliefs about personality. Which are true and which are false?

TRUE   FALSE

_____ _____   1. Compared to people of normal intelligence, geniuses tend to be odd and maladjusted.

_____ _____   2. Birth order—whether a child is born first, second, or later in a family—is related to his or her personality.

_____ _____   3. Most people who make notable contributions to society—scientists, writers, composers, and the like—make their greatest contributions in old age.

_____ _____   4. Aggressive people tend to have low self-esteem.

_____ _____   5. Personality does not change much after age thirty.

_____ _____   6. People who are optimistic tend to be physically healthier than people who are pessimistic.

_____ _____   7. Low self-esteem causes people to have psychological problems.

_____ _____   8. People can be easily classified into categories or types.

_____ _____   9. People are not strongly influenced by the hidden, subliminal messages in advertisements, popular songs, and self-help audio tapes.

_____ _____ 10. Most people have a pretty good idea of how they are perceived by other people.

Answers can be found at the end of the chapter.

HOW IMPORTANT IS PERSONALITY?

Although virtually all psychologists agree with Lewin's claim that behavior is a function of both the person and the environment, they differ in the importance they place on personality in understanding human behavior. Whereas personality psychologists insist that personality processes account for a great deal of behavior, some behavioral researchers suggest that situational influences are more important and that personality is, at best, a minor influence. And, to make matters more confusing, both sides of the argument can point to data that support their positions. So, how important is personality for understanding people's behavior?

The Strength of the Situation

Like many things in psychology, the answer to this question is "it depends." First, the importance of personality in human behavior depends, in part, on the *strength* of the situation in which a person finds himself or herself. A "strong" situation is one that has a great deal of structure and many converging cues indicating how the person should act. A "weak" situation is a relatively unstructured one with few external cues to guide behavior (Ickes, 1982).

Imagine going to an athletic event (e.g., a baseball, basketball, or football game) and hearing the loudspeaker blare, "Please stand for the playing of our national anthem." As the opening notes of the "Star-Spangled Banner" begin, the crowd rises. This is a very "strong" situation. We may observe slight variations in what people do once standing—some sing along and some don't, for example—but the distinctive personalities of the spectators bear little relationship to whether they stand or not. The situation is in control.

Compare this to going to the beach where the situation is much weaker than in the previous example. Some people are playing volleyball, some are reading, some are talking, some are strolling alone, some are searching for seashells, some are basking in the sun, and so on. And, even those who are engaging in the same behavior may be doing so in different ways. Some of the volleyball players are competing energetically, whereas others seem indifferent to winning. Some of the people are talking more loudly than others. Some of the sunbathers are nearly naked, whereas others' swimsuits are more modest. Because the situation is relatively "weak," people's personalities take over. Extraverts and introverts at the beach may behave differently, for example. As a result, we can infer a great deal more about people's idiosyncratic personalities from watching them in a weak situation (such as at the beach) than by observing them in a strong situation (such as during the playing of the national anthem).

Individual Differences in Responsivity to the Situation

The importance of personality to behavior also depends on the degree to which a person is responsive to situational influences. Some people are more affected by situational factors than are others. For those who are highly responsive to situational cues, personality factors may be of relatively little importance in their behavior. In contrast, for people who are less responsive to the immediate situation, personality looms large in how they think, feel, and behave. For some people, behavior is more a function of the environment; for others, behavior is more a function of their personality (Lamphere & Leary, 1990).

Researchers have identified several personality characteristics that relate to the degree to which people are or are not responsive to situational cues. Many years ago, Witkin and his colleagues identified such a trait, which they called *field independence-field dependence* (Witkin, Dyk, Faterson, Goodenough, & Karp, 1962). As originally defined, field independence-dependence involved the degree to which a person is able to perceive part of a visual field independently of its surroundings. In essence, field-dependent people tend to see things globally, whereas field-independent people perceive things in terms of their component parts. Field-dependent people see the forest; field-independent people see the trees.

Although the construct of field independence-dependence was interesting as a purely perceptual phenomenon, research began to show that individual differences in field independence-dependence were related to broader aspects of personality functioning. Compared to field-independent people, field-dependent people seek more information from other people about what they should do, are more likely to conform to social norms, are less autonomous, and pay greater attention to social stimuli (Bastone & Wood, 1997; Karp, 1977; Messick, 1994). One study even showed that field-independent police officers performed better in dangerous, high stimulation situations, presumably because they were not as distracted by the activity and noise around them (Vrij, van der Steen, & Koppelaar, 1995). These and other findings suggest that field-dependent people are more strongly affected by their environments, whereas field independents behave more in line with their personalities.

Self-monitoring is another personality variable that is related to the degree to which people are influenced by the situation in which they find themselves (Snyder, 1974). High self-monitors are more sensitive and responsive to situational cues regarding how to behave than are low self-monitors. Research has shown that the behavior of high self-monitors is more variable across situations than the behavior of lows because highs react more to the immediate social context (Snyder, 1987). We could say that low self-monitors, like field-independent people, "have more personality" in the sense that their behavior is more a function of their own personal attributes than the behavior of high self-monitors.

Traitedness

For many years, most psychologists assumed that every individual could be classified as falling somewhere along a variety of trait dimensions. That is, if we examine any particular personality characteristic—extraversion, agreeableness, self-monitoring, achievement motivation, and so on—everyone could be rated as low, moderate, or high on that characteristic. Put differently, we have assumed that every personality characteristic is applicable to everyone. However, the assumption that all traits apply to everybody is now being questioned.

As we have seen, the concept of personality implies that a person's behavior will show a certain degree of consistency across different situations. Consider the trait of conscientiousness—the degree to which a person is dependable, responsible, and careful as opposed to undependable, unreliable, and negligent. Presumably, everyone falls somewhere along the continuum of conscientiousness: some people tend to be very conscientious, some people are moderately conscientious, and some people are not conscientious at all. This is not to say that people act the same way all of the time; the situation may exert a strong influence on how conscientiously a person behaves. But, given that conscientiousness is a fundamental trait, we should see some consistency in everybody's behavior along this dimension.

However, this commonsense assumption may not be valid. Evidence suggests that not all traits are relevant to everyone's personality (Bem & Allen, 1974). That is, the trait continuum of conscientiousness may be relevant to describing some people's personalities, whereas it may not apply to other people at all. People for whom conscientiousness is relevant to understanding their personality will display consistencies in how conscientious (or nonconscientious) they are across different situations. Such individuals are said to be *traited* in conscientiousness. People for whom conscientiousness is less relevant to understanding their personality will display little consistency in how conscientious (or nonconscientious) they behave across different situations. These individuals, who would be described as *untraited* in conscientiousness, essentially lack the trait of conscientiousness-nonconscientiousness altogether.

Research shows that people who are traited on a particular characteristic behave more consistently across situations. In addition, their behavior correlates highly with other measures of the trait; for example, we can predict how conscientiously they will act by knowing how they score on a self-report measure of conscientiousness. In contrast, untraited people show a great deal of variability in their behavior vis-à-vis the trait, and their behavior does not correlate with their scores on other relevant measures; we cannot predict how conscientiously they will act by knowing how they score on a measure of conscientiousness (Baumeister, 1991; Baumeister & Tice, 1988; Britt, 1993). Thus, whether personality is "important" to understanding behavior also depends on whether the person is traited on a particular characteristic

APPROACHES TO PERSONALITY RESEARCH

People have been interested in personality for thousands of years, probably since human beings first developed a sufficient degree of consciousness to wonder why people act as they do. The writings of many ancient civilizations include references to personality, although the Greeks may have been the first to systematically develop explanations of personality differences. (Greek thinkers, for example, tried to explain personality differences in terms of how much of certain bodily fluids, such as blood, bile, and phlegm, a person possessed.) Most early efforts to understand personality were based on casual observation, logic, or religious doctrine rather than systematic investigations.

Only in the past hundred years or so have we begun to examine personality in a scientific manner. The scientific study of personality can be traced to two scholarly developments in the late nineteenth century. Personality psychology was the child of two very different parents, and this mixed lineage can still be seen in the field today.

The Two Parents of Personality Psychology

One of the parents of personality psychology was medicine, specifically the medical specialties that today we call neurology and psychiatry. Some physicians of the late 1800s became interested in patients who had physical problems that had no apparent physiological basis. Among them were Jean Charcot, Pierre Janet, and Sigmund Freud, each of whom made important contributions to understanding these so-called hysterical disorders by focusing on their psychological causes and treatment. Their work created a great deal of interest in the psychological processes that underlie certain medical and emotional problems. Freud and many of his followers went on to develop complex theories of the human personality to account for a variety of physical and behavioral problems.

These early psychiatrists relied primarily on the case study method for developing and testing their ideas about personality. The case study method involves the systematic, in-depth study of a single individual—in this instance, essentially everything the psychiatrists could find out about the life histories of their troubled patients. Later, as psychologists also began to do counseling and psychotherapy, they too used clinical case studies as a basis for speculating about personality and behavior.

The other parent of personality psychology was scientific psychology, founded by Wilhelm Wundt in 1879. Wundt proposed that the methods of investigation used in other sciences could be applied to the study of behavior and the mind. Among his many contributions to behavioral science, Wundt established the first laboratory devoted exclusively to studying psychological phenomena. Although Wundt himself did not deal extensively with personality, other researchers in his laboratory were interested in understanding individual differences among the subjects who participated in their experiments (Tyler, 1963). Soon, other researchers in Europe and the United States were applying scientific methods to the study of behavior, thought, and emotion.

Personality psychology as a distinct subfield of psychology emerged in the 1930s, chiefly through the work of Gordon Allport (1937) and Henry Murray (1938). Although Allport and Murray differed in their theoretical perspectives, they shared the view that new approaches were needed to study human personality, and each made many theoretical and methodological contributions to the field.

The basic research methods that were developed and refined by the early scientific psychologists, both in personality psychology and other areas of behavioral science, are still used in personality psychology today. They involve variations of four basic approaches to research—the correlational approach, experimental approach, quasi-experimental approach, and case study approach (for full discussions of these approaches, see Leary, 2001).

The Correlational Approach

The correlational approach is used to describe the relationships that exist between two or more naturally occurring variables. For example, we would use a correlational approach to determine whether children who sleep-walk are also more likely to wet the bed at night (i.e., whether there a relationship between bed-wetting and sleep-walking) or to identify personality variables that predict achievement in college. The correlation method was originally developed by the eminent British scientist, Sir Francis Galton, to study similarities among family members, but it was quickly adopted by other researchers to examine the relationships among personality characteristics as well as the relationships between personality and behavior. Much of what we know about personality was obtained using correlational techniques.

The correlational approach to research involves a family of interrelated statistical analyses (with esoteric names such as Pearson correlation, partial correlation, regression analysis, path analysis, structural equation modeling, and factor analysis). Although differing in specifics, these analyses provide statistical information regarding the nature of the relationships between variables. The basic statistic that appears in virtually all correlational research, the *correlation coefficient*, expresses information about the direction and strength of the relationship between two variables. You will encounter correlation coefficients throughout this book, so be sure you understand how to interpret them here.

The direction of a correlation can be either positive or negative depending on whether the variables are directly or inversely related to one another. For example, depression and anxiety are positively correlated: people who score high in depression also tend to score high in anxiety, and people who score low on depression tend to score low in anxiety. When variables correlate positively, scores on the two variables tend to go up and down together. Self-esteem and shyness, in contrast, are negatively correlated: people with high self-esteem tend to score low on measures of shyness, whereas low self-esteem is associated with higher shyness. A negative correlation indicates that low scores on one variable are associated with high scores on the other variable, and vice versa.

The strength of a correlation coefficient is expressed on a scale from .00 to 1.00. A correlation of .00 indicates that the variables are not at all related; increasingly larger coefficients reflect stronger relationships. A correlation of 1.00 (either +1.00 or −1.00) reflects a "perfect" correlation in which the variables are so strongly related that people's scores on one variable can be predicted perfectly from knowing their scores on the other variable. (Perfect correlations are very rare.)

To provide an example of the usefulness of the correlation approach, we turn to research on authoritarianism. In the aftermath of World War II, Adorno, Frankel-Brunswik, Levinson, and Sanford (1950) became interested in identifying personality characteristics that were associated with the blind obedience to authority that occurred during the holocaust in Nazi Germany. How could so many seemingly normal people obey authority figures who told them to exterminate millions of people? These researchers identified a constellation of personality attributes that they named the authoritarian personality.

In the years since their research was published, hundreds of studies have been conducted to examine features of authoritarianism, and most of these have used a correlational approach. For example, scores on measures of the authoritarian personality correlate positively with prejudice toward members of minority groups and with endorsement of conservative political candidates, and correlate negatively with the degree to which people can tolerate ambiguous situations (Altemeyer, 1988; Peterson, Doty, & Winter, 1993).

Walker, Rowe, and Quinsey (1993) studied the relationship between authoritarianism and sexual aggression toward women. They correlated the scores of 204 men on a measure of authoritarianism with several measures of attitudes toward women. They found that authoritarianism correlated +.36 with respondents' hostility toward women, +.51 with the degree to which respondents accepted interpersonal violence, and +.18 with the likelihood that respondents said they would force a woman to have sex. These correlation coefficients show a positive association between the authoritarian personality and aggressive attitudes toward women. As scores on authoritarianism increase, so does hostility toward women, acceptance of violence, and endorsement of forced sex. (You will encounter authoritarianism again in Chapter 3 when we examine heredity factors that underlie attitudes.)

We must be very careful when interpreting correlations because we cannot make definitive statements about causality on the basis of correlational data. Because the correlational approach measures variables as they occur naturally, we have no way of knowing for certain why the relationship between the variables exists. Does one variable actually *cause* the other one, or are they related because of the influence of some third variable? A correlation tells us that the variables are correlated with one another, but without controlling other factors that might influence the relationship between them, we can not say for certain why the correlation exists.

Even so, personality researchers often use a procedure called *partial correlation* to test the plausibility of hypotheses about why two correlated variables might be related. A partial correlation expresses the relationship between two variables while statistically removing the influence of one or more other variables. If removing the influence of other variables does not change the correlation between two variables, then those other variables cannot be causing the two variables to be correlated. If, however, removing the influence of other variables lowers or eliminates the correlation between two variables, it is plausible that those variables are somehow responsible for the correlation between them. Even so, our conclusions are only tentative because we are dealing with correlational data.

For example, Campbell and Foster (2002) were interested in understanding why people who score high in narcissism—the tendency to hold inflated views of one's importance and desirability—are less committed to their romantic relationships than people who score low in narcissism. The researchers reasoned that narcissists may be less committed to a relationship because they believe that, by virtue of their importance and desirability, there are many other people who would be happy to have a relationship with them. Thus, they do not need to worry much about their current relationship falling apart. To test this hypothesis, Campbell and Foster studied 119 undergraduate students, measuring participants' narcissism, commitment to their relationship partners, and beliefs regarding the availability of alternative romantic partners. The data showed that, as expected, narcissism and commitment were negatively correlated; that is, narcissists did indeed have significantly less commitment to their partners. Furthermore, narcissism correlated positively with the belief that the participants had other viable alternatives to their present relationships. To test the hypothesis that the people high in narcissism have lower commitment because they think they have more alternatives, the researchers calculated the partial correlation between narcissism and commitment while statistically removing ("partialing out") the effects of alternatives. When beliefs about relationship alternatives were statistically removed, the partial correlation between narcissism and commitment was no longer significant, suggesting that their beliefs about alternative partners were responsible for the narcissism-commitment link. Again, because these are correlational data, we cannot conclude for certain that narcissists are less committed to relationships because they think they have more alternatives, but the data are certainly consistent with that explanation.

The Experimental Approach

Whereas the correlational approach examines relationships among variables as they occur naturally, the experimental approach to personality research involves artificially varying or manipulating certain variables (the *independent variables*) to study the effects of these changes on thought, emotion, physiological reactions, or overt behavior (the *dependent variables*). In personality psychology, experimental research is used to study the effects of situational variables on internal psychological processes and to understand how people who score differently on some personality characteristic react differently to experimentally manipulated situations.

An example of a study that used the experimental method to study the effects of situational variables on internal personality processes was conducted by Lewicki (1985) to examine nonconscious processes. When participants arrived for the experiment, they met an experimenter who treated them rudely or in a neutral fashion. (This was the independent variable.) They then went to another room where they were asked to choose to work with one of two other experimenters, one of whom resembled the first experimenter in appearance while the other did not. Participants who had been treated rudely by the first experimenter showed a stronger tendency to avoid the experimenter who looked like her than did participants who had been treated neutrally. This preference occurred even though the participants were unaware that their choice had been influenced by the similarity between the first and second experimenter, thus suggesting that their decision was affected by nonconscious processes. In this experiment, the effects of an independent variable manipulated by the experimenter (being treated rudely versus neutrally) on dependent variables (preference and liking for a similar-looking person) were studied.

Personality researchers also use the experimental approach to examine how people who score differently on some feature of personality react differently to particular situations. I mentioned earlier that most behavior is a product of aspects of the situation and aspects of the individual's personality. To the extent that this is true, much can be gained by examining the effects of situational and personality variables in the same study. Strictly speaking, studies that examine the effects of manipulated situational variables and measured personality variables simultaneously involve features of both the correlational method (in that measures of preexisting personality variables are used) and the experimental method (in that aspects of the situation are experimentally manipulated). This hybrid experimental-correlational combination is sometimes called a moderator-variable, mixed, or expericorr design.

One of my students conducted such a study to test the hypothesis that women who are predisposed toward eating disorders restrict their food intake as a way of feeling a sense of control (Rezek & Leary, 1990). In this study, women's scores on a measure of eating disorders were obtained. Then the women were placed in a laboratory situation in which they were led to experience a low or high degree of control (perceived control was the independent variable), and how much the women ate during what they thought was a taste-testing experiment was measured (amount of food eaten was the dependent variable). Results showed that women who were predisposed toward eating disorders ate significantly less when they were led to feel a low degree rather than a high degree of control. In contrast, women without a tendency toward eating disorders did not eat differently as a function of whether they experienced low or high control. These data supported the idea that low perceived control leads women prone to eating disorders to eat less than they otherwise would. By combining a manipulated independent variable (low versus high control) with a measured personality variable (low versus high tendency toward eating disorders), this design showed how people with different personalities respond differently to different situations.

The Quasi-experimental Approach

Sometimes, personality researchers are interested in studying the effects of a situational variable that, for either practical or ethical reasons, they cannot manipulate in an experiment. In such instances, they use a quasi-experimental approach. In a quasi-experimental study, the researcher lacks full control over the variables of interest and, thus, cannot manipulate the independent variable or control other variables. Instead, the researcher studies the effects of events that occur naturally.

For example, Crocker, Sommers, and Luhtanen (2002) were interested in how being accepted or rejected for admission into graduate school affected the self-esteem of undergraduate students who were applying to graduate programs. The researchers could not conduct a true experiment to answer this question because doing so would require that they experimentally manipulate whether the students were accepted or rejected by graduate programs, which would create obvious logistical and ethical problems. Instead, they obtained a sample of students who were waiting to hear the outcome of their applications to graduate school and measured the students' self-esteem twice a week (plus on every day that they heard from a graduate program). This was a quasi-experimental design because the event of interest—being accepted or rejected by a graduate school—occurred naturally rather than being manipulated by the researcher. Because it was a quasi-experimental design, the researchers could not determine who would receive acceptances or rejections, nor could they control the myriad other variables that might affect self-esteem as they could have in a true experiment. Nonetheless, Crocker et al. were able to show that acceptances and rejections affected self-esteem only among students whose self-esteem was based on academic performance. For students who did not root their self-esteem in academic pursuits, responses from graduate schools had no effect on self-esteem.

A special case of the quasi-experimental approach is the longitudinal design. Personality researchers use longitudinal designs to study the effects of the passage of time on personality variables or on the relationship between personality and behavior. In the simplest longitudinal designs, researchers simply measure the relationship between two or more variables at two or more points in time and examine changes that occur.

For example, Raine, Reynolds, Venables, and Mednick (2002) tested the hypothesis that children who score high in stimulation-seeking would gradually become more intelligent than those low in stimulation-seeking because children high in stimulation are more likely to explore their surroundings, interact with other children, and converse with adults. The researchers measured IQ and stimulation-seeking for 1,795 three-year-old children living on the island of Mauritius in the Indian Ocean. Eight years later, when the children were 11 years old, they were retested. Children who scored high in stimulation-seeking at age 3 scored an average of 12 points higher in IQ at age 11 than the children who were low in stimulation-seeking.

Case Study Approach

I noted that many early personality researchers relied heavily on case studies—in-depth investigations of particular individuals—to investigate personality. Not only did Freud and the early psychiatrists base their work on case studies, but Allport (1937) and Murray (1938) explicitly advocated studying the lives of specific individuals as a way of understanding personality. Although most contemporary personality researchers rely primarily on correlational, experimental, and quasi-experimental approaches, the case study approach continues to be used by many personality psychologists today.

Case studies have three primary uses in personality psychology (McAdams & West, 1997). First, case studies are used to exemplify particular traits or processes by showing how they manifest in a particular, real individual. Case studies provide concrete examples of abstract concepts and theories. Second, case studies can facilitate the discovery of new insights about personality. Delving into one person's personality in depth may demonstrate principles, show relationships, or raise questions that the investigator had not previously considered. For example, carefully studying a number of middle-age adults could help a researcher formulate a general model of adult development (Frenkel, 1936).

Third, case studies can be used to test theories. For example, comparing the predictions of a particular theory with the unfolding of a specific person's life can show where theoretical predictions do and not match what happens in reality. In addition, case studies of several individuals can be compared to one another to determine the degree to which certain theoretical processes or relationships can be seen in the lives of several individuals, thereby checking the generalizability of a theory. Although many personality psychologists are skeptical about the usefulness of case studies for testing theories, advocates of case studies maintain that the viability of any theory in personality psychology lies in the degree to which it can explain the realities of individual lives.

PERSONALITY THEORIES

One of the central goals of personality psychology, as of any science, is to develop theories that explain the phenomena of interest. Hundreds, if not thousands, of theories have been proposed to explain aspects of personality. Some of these theories, such as Freud's psychoanalytic theory and Bandura's self-efficacy theory, are grand and comprehensive, attempting to explain a great deal about personality and human behavior within a single theory. Other theories—such as the learned helplessness theory of depression (Abramson, Seligman, & Teasdale, 1978) and the sociometer theory of self-esteem (Leary & Downs, 1995)—focus on processes that are specific to a particular aspect of personality (such as depression or self-esteem).

One thing that makes the study of personality both fascinating and frustrating for many students is that psychologists cannot seem to agree among themselves about the most useful ways to conceptualize and explain personality. Many competing theories exist, and theorists often make little effort to link their views with those of others. Given that the field is peppered by so many different theoretical perspectives, students are understandably confused regarding how to determine the *best* theory to explain a particular phenomenon.

Often, these disagreements can be resolved empirically—that is, by collecting data that shows one theory to be superior to another. In fact, this is the primary purpose behind conducting scientific research. But sometimes, a researcher's preference for a particular theory is based more on his or her personal assumptions about human nature and the causes of human behavior than on the results of research studies. A psychoanalytic theorist, for example, assumes that unconscious processes are important, whereas a behaviorist assumes that behavior is largely affected by patterns of reinforcement in the environment. These theoretical controversies are not easily resolved by collecting data because they involve meta-theoretical assumptions that often cannot be directly tested.

Although an oversimplification, it is useful to distinguish five major meta-theoretical approaches to thinking about personality—the psychodynamic,

Table 1.1 | Major Meta-Theoretical Perspectives on Personality

Psychodynamic Perspective

Emphasis is on: unconscious processes that underlie personality

Primary determinants of behavior involve: childhood experiences; unconscious conflicts

Central constructs include: id, ego, superego, repression, fixation, Oedipus complex

Key proponents: Freud, Jung, Adler, Horney

Learning Perspective

Emphasis is on: how personality is learned

Primary determinants of behavior involve: conditioning processes

Central constructs include: stimulus-response, reinforcement, classical conditioning, operant conditioning

Key proponents: Watson, Thorndike, Hull, Skinner

Humanistic Perspective

Emphasis is on: the natural progression of psychological growth

Primary determinants of behavior involve: actualizing tendency

Central constructs include: phenomenology, unconditional positive regard, self-actualization

Key proponents: Rogers, Maslow

Cognitive Perspective

Emphasis is on: how people process information about themselves and their worlds

Primary determinants of behavior involve: cognitive processes

Central constructs include: schema, attribution, goal, self-regulation

Key proponents: Kelly, Rotter, Bandura, Mischel

Biological Perspective

Emphasis is on: anatomy and physiology of the nervous system, including genetic and evolutionary influences

Primary determinants of behavior involve: activity in the brain and other areas of the nervous system

Central constructs include: neurotransmitters, cortical arousal, heritability

Key proponents: Eysenck, Plomin, D. Buss

learning, humanistic, cognitive, and biological perspectives. These approaches differ in their fundamental assumptions regarding the primary determinants of human personality and behavior. Table 1.1 presents these five approaches and their fundamental assumptions.

As you can see in Table 1.1, these perspectives differ markedly in their assumptions about human beings. Is our personality the result of unconscious processes (psychodynamic), reinforcement history (learning), natural tendencies for personal growth and fulfillment (humanistic), beliefs and ways of thinking (cognitive), or anatomy and physiology (biological)?

We should avoid the tendency to assume that one of these meta-theoretical approaches must be correct, whereas the others are wrong. The chances are good that all of these approaches can contribute to our understanding of certain aspects of personality, and the chances are equally good that each overstates its case. A complete understanding of personality must acknowledge the merits of each approach while recognizing that each also has its weaknesses. Some perspectives may explain certain phenomena better than others but explain other phenomena less well. The purpose of conducting research is to determine which theoretical approaches are most useful in answering particular questions about personality and to identify the appropriate range of application of each theory.

Although students are sometimes frustrated by so many theories, scientists regard theoretical controversies such as these as healthy for a discipline. In fact, Feyerabend (1970), a noted philosopher of science, suggested that science is best served not by having a single theory that everyone agrees on but by having competing theories. He argued that having several competing theories should not be regarded as a "preliminary stage of knowledge which will at some time in the future be replaced by the One True Theory" (p. 321). The presence of competing theories tends to stimulate a great deal of creative and enlightening research as proponents of each perspective try to demonstrate the superiority of their approach.

THE DISCIPLINE OF PERSONALITY PSYCHOLOGY

Personality psychology is a broad and growing field. Our understanding of personality has been advanced not only by researchers trained specifically in personality psychology but also by those in social, developmental, educational, clinical, counseling, health, physiological, and industrial-organizational psychology, among others. Furthermore, researchers in other behavioral and social sciences, such as psychiatry, behavioral genetics, anthropology, communication, and sociology, have added to our knowledge of personality as well.

Advances in personality psychology have also come through attempts to develop valid ways to assess personality for practical reasons. For example, personnel and industrial-organizational psychologists have worked to develop better ways to assess and evaluate the personalities of job applicants and employees. Educational and school psychologists have developed ways to assess not only intellectual traits but also aspects of personality that facilitate or impede learning. Forensic psychologists have devoted a great deal of effort to assessing the personalities of defendants, criminals, and prisoners. Likewise, clinical and counseling psychologists have constructed personality measures to help them identify people's emotional and behavioral problems.

People who are interested in becoming personality psychologists must pursue graduate education in personality psychology or another field that involves investigating the enduring inner characteristics of individuals that constitute their personalities. After obtaining a graduate degree, such individuals may conduct research on personality; teach personality and related topics in colleges and universities; design personality measures for business, government, or psychological practice; and conduct personality assessments.

SUMMARY

Personality is the system of enduring inner characteristics of individuals that contributes to consistency in behavior. Personality psychology is the area of behavioral science that attempts to describe and understand both those aspects of the human personality that differ among people (individual differences) and those that are common to everyone (psychological universals). Personality psychologists are interested in identifying the major components of personality, understanding how personality develops and changes over time, and examining the relationships between personality processes and behavior.

Behavior is affected both by the situations in which people find themselves and by their individual personalities. A person's behavior in a particular context is more likely to be a function of his or her inner personality when the situation is weak rather than strong, when the individual tends not to be highly responsive to situational cues (e.g., field independents and low self-monitors behave more consistently with their inner personalities than field dependents and high self-monitors), and when the person is untraited on characteristics that are relevant to the situation.

Personality psychology developed around the turn of the 20th century, influenced by advances in psychiatry and scientific psychology. Early psychiatrists, such as Sigmund Freud, used the case study methodology to understand the personalities of their patients. Early scientific psychologists, in contrast, used correlational, experimental, and quasi-experimental research strategies to study personality. Contemporary personality psychology reflects the influence of both psychiatry and psychology.

Personality theories can be classified roughly into five general perspectives that differ in their fundamental assumptions about human behavior. The psychodynamic approach emphasizes the influence of unconscious processes, the learning approach focuses on people's histories of reinforcement and punishment, the humanistic approach stresses people's natural tendencies toward personal growth and fulfillment, the cognitive approach examines people's beliefs and ways of thinking, and the biological approach studies the anatomy and physiology of the nervous system. These approaches are not necessarily mutually exclusive but can each contribute to our understanding of personality.

The human personality is an exceptionally complex system, and despite a century of research and thousands of research studies, many questions remain. Yet, year by year, behavioral scientists make slow but steady progress toward understanding more and more about personality.

DISCUSSION QUESTIONS

1. As Lewin noted, virtually all behavior is a function of both environmental, situational forces acting upon the individual from the outside and intrapsychic, personality processes operating inside the individual. For each of the behaviors listed below, speculate regarding five situational factors and five personality factors that might affect the behavior.
   a. Feeling anxious while giving a speech
   b. Falling in love
   c. Becoming the leader of a group
   d. Being depressed
   e. Helping someone in an emergency situation
   f. Telling a racist joke
2. Which of the following phenomena do you think reflect human psychological universals that evolved because of their adaptive value? In each case, justify your answer.
   a. Fear of heights
   b. Test anxiety
   c. House-building
   d. Embarrassment
   e. Drinking alcohol
   f. Religious beliefs
3. Compared to other people, do you think that you are more or less responsive to situational influences? Explain your answer.
4. Explain the contributions of the following individuals to the study of behavior: Freud, Wundt, Allport, Murray.
5. Be sure that you understand the differences among correlational, experimental, quasi-experimental, and case study approaches to studying personality. Then, tell which of these four approaches would be most appropriate for answering each of the following questions:
   a. Are women more prone to depression than men?
   b. Did stress-related disorders increase after the terrorist attacks on September 11, 2001?
   c. What led Michael Jordan to return to professional basketball after retiring from the Chicago Bulls?
   d. What effect does working under time pressure have on the blood pressure of people who are low versus high in achievement motivation?
   e. Do people with low self-esteem have lower professional aspirations than people with high self-esteem?
   f. Is going away to college associated with increased feelings of loneliness?

ANSWERS TO ACTIVITY BOX 1.1 QUIZ

1. False. On the contrary, people with very high intelligence tend, on the average, to be better adjusted than people with average intelligence (Tyler, 1963).

2. True. Researchers have discovered reliable differences between firstborn and later-born children, although these differences are not always what the general public assumes (Ernst & Angst, 1983).

3. False. The bulk of the contributions of "great" people occur when they are in their 40s (Simonton, 1994).

4. False. People who are prone to violence—those who engage in child abuse, domestic violence, gang warfare, and the like—appear to think highly of themselves (Baumeister, Smart, & Boden, 1996).

5. True. After age 30, most people do not change very much (Costa & McCrae, 1994).

6. True. Optimists are healthier than pessimists (Scheier & Carver, 1993).

7. False. Evidence does not support the idea that low self-esteem *causes* psychological problems (although it is true that people with low self-esteem tend to have more problems) (Leary, Schreindorfer, & Haupt, 1995).

8. False. Most personality psychologists do not talk about different "types" of people because "type" implies that people can be neatly classified into categories or boxes. It is more useful to think of personality variables as continua.

9. True. The effects of subliminal stimuli are *very* weak (Greenwald, Spangenberg, Pratkanis, & Eskenazi, 1991).

10. False. On the contrary, most of us do not have a very good idea of how other specific individuals see us (DePaulo, Hoover, Kenny, Webb, & Oliver, 1987).

SUGGESTED READINGS

Craik, K., Hogan, R., & Wolfe, R. N. (1993). *Fifty years of personality psychology*. New York: Plenum. This book was published to celebrate the 50th anniversary of the publication of two highly influential personality texts: *Personality: A Psychological Interpretation* by Gordon Allport, and *Psychology of Personality* by Ross Stagner, both published in 1937.

Hogan, R., Johnson, J. A., & Briggs, S. R. (1997). *Handbook of personality psychology*. San Diego: Academic Press. The 36 chapters in this book explore personality psychology from all angles, including personality theory, measurement, development, biological underpinnings, cultural influences, and emotional and motivational processes.

Pervin, L. A., & John, O. (1999). *Handbook of personality: Theory and research* (2nd ed.). New York: Guilford Press. The second edition of this handbook contains 28 chapters by leading personality psychologists that cover virtually the entire field of personality psychology.

Journal of Personality. Published by Blackwell Publishing.

Journal of Personality and Social Psychology: Personality Processes and Individual Differences. Published by the American Psychological Association.

Journal of Research in Personality. Published by Academic Press.

Personality and Social Psychology Bulletin. Published for the Society for Personality and Social Psychology by Sage Publications.

Personality and Individual Differences. Published for the International Society for the Study of Individual Differences by Pergamon.

Personality and Social Psychology Review. Published for the Society for Personality and Social Psychology by Sage Publications.

SUGGESTED WEB SITES

www.spsp.org
This is the home page of the Society for Personality and Social Psychology—the largest professional association for personality psychologists.

www.personality-project.org
This web site, maintained by Dr. William Revelle of Northwestern University, provides information about personality psychology and extensive links to other sites that are relevant to the study of personality.

www.personalityresearch.org
This web site, titled "Great Ideas in Personality," focuses on scientific research programs in personality psychology.

www.issid.org/issid

This is the web site of the International Society for the Study of Individual Differences, whose purpose is to investigate the major dimensions of individual differences in the context of experimental, physio-logical, pharmacological, clinical, medical, genetic, statistical, and social psychology, and to study the determinants, causes and concomitants of individual differences.

INFOTRAC® COLLEGE EDITION SEARCH TOPICS

Personality	Psychological universals	Quasi-experiment
Trait	Correlation	Case study
Individual differences	Experiment	Personality theory

REFERENCES

Abramson, L. Y., Seligman, M. E. P., & Teasdale, J. D. (1978). Learned helplessness in humans: Critique and reformulation. *Journal of Abnormal Psychology, 87,* 49–74.

Adorno, T. W., Frankel-Brunswik, E., Levinson, D. J., & Sanford, R. N. (1950). *The authoritarian personality.* New York: Harper and Brothers.

Allport, G. W. (1937). *Personality: A psychological interpretation.* New York: Holt, Rinehart and Winston.

Altemeyer, B. (1988). *Enemies of freedom: Understanding right-wing authoritarianism.* San Francisco, CA: Jossey-Bass.

Barkow, J. H., Cosmides, L., & Tooby, J. (1992). *The adapted mind.* New York: Oxford University Press.

Baumeister, R. F. (1991). On the stability of variability: Retest reliability of metatraits. *Personality and Social Psychology Bulletin, 17,* 633–639.

Baumeister, R. F., & Leary, M. R. (1995). The need to belong: Desire for interpersonal attachments as a fundamental human motivation. *Psychological Bulletin, 117,* 497–529.

Baumeister, R. F., Smart, L., & Boden, J. M. (1996). Relation of threatened egotism to violence and aggression: The dark side of high self-esteem. *Psychological Review, 103,* 5–33.

Bastone, L. M., & Wood, H. A. (1997). Individual differences in the ability to decode facial expressions. *Psychology: A Journal of Human Behavior, 34,* 32–36.

Baumeister, R. F., & Tice, D. M. (1988). Metatraits. *Journal of Personality, 56,* 571–598.

Bem, D. J., & Allen, A. (1974). On predicting some of the people some of the time: The search for cross-situational consistencies in behavior. *Psychological Review, 81,* 506–520.

Britt, T. W. (1993). Metatraits: Evidence relevant to the validity of the construct and its implications. *Journal of Personality and Social Psychology, 65,* 554–562.

Campbell, W. K., & Foster, C. A. (2002). Narcissism and commitment in romantic relationships: An investment model analysis. *Personality and Social Psychology Bulletin, 28,* 484–495.

Costa, P. T., Jr., & McCrae, R. R. (1994). "Set like plaster?" Evidence for the stability of adult personality. In T. Heatherton & I. Weinberger (Eds.), *Can personality change?* (pp. 21–40). Washington, DC: American Psychological Association.

Crocker, J., Sommers, S. R., & Luhtanen, R. K. (2002). Hopes dashed and dreams fulfilled: Contingencies of self-worth and graduate school admissions. *Personality and Social Psychology Bulletin, 28,* 1275–1286.

DePaulo, B. M., Kenny, D. A., Hoover, C., Webb, W., & Oliver, P. (1987). Accuracy of person perception: Do people know what kinds of impressions they convey? *Journal of Personality and Social Psychology, 52,* 303–313.

Eckman, P. (1993). Facial expression and emotion. *American Psychologist, 48,* 384–392.

Epstein, S. (1983). A research paradigm for the study of personality and emotions. In M. M. Page (Ed.), *Personality: Current theory and research* (pp. 91–154). Lincoln: University of Nebraska Press.

Ernst, C., & Angst, J. (1983). *Birth order: Its influence on personality.* Berlin: SpringerVerlag.

Feyerabend, P. K. (1970). How to be a good empiricist: A plea for tolerance in matters epistemological. In B. Brody (Ed.), *Readings in the philosophy of science* (pp. 319–342). Englewood Cliffs, NJ: Prentice-Hall.

Fleeson, W. (2001). Toward a structure- and process-integrated view of personality: Traits as density distributions of states. *Journal of Personality and Social Psychology, 80,* 1011–1027.

Frenkel, E. (1936). Studies in biographical psychology. *Character and Personality, 5,* 1–35.

Greenwald, A. G., Spangenberg, E. R., Pratkanis, A. R., & Eskenazi, I. (1991). Double-blind tests of subliminal self-help audiotapes. *Psychological Science, 2,* 119–122.

Ickes, W. (1982). A basic paradigm for the study of personality, roles, and social behavior. In W. Ickes & E. S. Knowles (Eds.), *Personality, roles, and social behavior* (pp. 305–341). New York: SpringerVerlag.

Karp, S. A. (1977). Psychological differentiation. In T. Blass (Ed.), *Personality variables in social behavior* (pp. 135–178). Hillsdale, NJ: Erlbaum.

Lamphere, R. A., & Leary, M. R. (1990). Private and public self-processes: A return to James' constituents of the self. *Personality and Social Psychology Bulletin, 16,* 717–725.

Leary, M. R. (2001). *Introduction to behavioral research methods* (3rd ed.). Boston: Allyn & Bacon.

Leary, M. R., & Downs, D. L. (1995). Interpersonal functions of the self-esteem motive: The self-esteem system as a sociometer. In M. Kernis (Ed.), *Efficacy, agency, and self-esteem* (pp. 123–144). New York: Plenum.

Leary, M. R., Schreindorfer, L. S., & Haupt, A. H. (1995). The role of low self-esteem in emotional and behavioral problems: Why is low self-esteem bad? *Journal of Social and Clinical Psychology, 14,* 297–314.

Lewicki, P. (1985). Nonconscious biasing effects of single instances on subsequent judgments. *Journal of Personality and Social Psychalogy, 48,* 563–574.

Lewin, K. (1935). *A dynamic theory of personality: Select papers.* New York: McGraw-Hill.

Mayer, J. D. (1993). A system-topics framework for the study of personality. *Imagination, Cognition, and Personality, 13,* 99–123.

McAdams, D. P., & West, S. G. (1997). Introduction: Personality psychology and the case study. *Journal of Personality, 65,* 757–783.

McCrae, R. R., & Costa, P. T., Jr. (1990). *Personality in adulthood.* New York: Guilford.

Messick, S. (1994). The matter of style: Manifestations of personality in cognition, learning, and teaching. *Educational Psychologist, 29,* 121–136.

Murray, H. A. (1938). *Explorations in personality.* New York: Oxford University Press.

Peterson, B. E., Doty, R. M., & Winter, D. G. (1993). Authoritarianism and attitudes toward contemporary social issues. *Personality and Social Psychology Bulletin, 19,* 174–184.

Raine, A., Reynolds, C., Venables, P. H., & Mednick, A. A. (2002). Stimulation seeking and intelligence: A prospective longitudinal study. *Journal of Personality and Social Psychology, 82,* 663–674.

Rezek, P. J., & Leary, M. R. (1990). Perceived control, drive for thinness, and food consumption: Anorexic tendencies as displaced reactance. *Journal of Personality, 59,* 129–142.

Russell, J. A. (1994). Is there universal recognition of emotion from facial expression? A review of the cross-cultural studies. *Psychological Bulletin, 115,* 102–141.

Scheier, M. F., & Carver, C. S. (1993). On the power of positive thinking: The benefits of being optimistic. *Psychological Science, 2,* 26–30.

Simonton, D. K. (1994). *Greatness: Who makes history and why.* New York: Guilford.

Snyder, M. (1974). Self-monitoring of expressive behavior. *Journal of Personality and Social Psychology, 30,* 526–537.

Snyder, M. (1987). *Public appearances/private realities: The psychology of self-monitoring.* New York: Freeman.

Tyler, L. E. (1963). *Tests and measurements.* Englewood Cliffs, NJ: Prentice-Hall.

Vrij, A., van der Steen, J., & Koppelaar, L. (1995). The effects of street noise and field independence on police officers' shooting behavior. *Journal of Applied Social Psychology, 25,* 1714–1725.

Walker, W. D., Rowe, R. C., & Quinsey, V. L. (1993). Authoritarianism and sexual aggression. *Journal of Personality and Social Psychology, 65,* 1036–1045.

Witkin, H. A., Dyk, R. B., Faterson, H. F., Goodenough, D. R., & Karp, S. A. (1962). *Psychological differentiation.* New York: Wiley.

Personality Measurement

STEPHEN R. BRIGGS

2

Chapter 1 traced the heritage of modern personality psychology back to the late 1800s, to the detailed medical case histories of psychiatric patients by Freud and others, and to the experimental laboratory studies of behavioral scientists. We learned how the field of personality has coalesced around three central questions regarding individual differences in personality:

- The question of *structure*—What are the basic components or dimensions of personality and how are they related to one another?
- The question of *ontogeny*—What are the origins of an individual's personality, and how do these attributes emerge and change over time?
- The question of *prediction*—What can we infer about future behavior given what we know now about an individual's enduring psychological and physiological characteristics?

In this chapter, we will examine more closely how researchers study the specific questions that interest them. As you no doubt know by now, psychological researchers are careful and serious with respect to issues of method, measurement, and terminology. The concepts that you will study in this chapter have specific, technical meanings. Some of the ideas may be familiar to you—for example, the concepts of *validity* and *reliability*—but because they are abstract and multifaceted, most students find that it takes time to become adept with them. These concepts have broad applicability in the conduct of research. Be alert to their varied meanings. Compare and contrast different uses of these constructs so that you come to appreciate their value and versatility.

FRAMING QUESTIONS

Research begins with a question. Part of the intrigue of research, and part of the art, is in asking the right question. Because we are naturally curious—that being one of the universal traits rooted in our collective personality—we speculate about things spontaneously. We wonder about the rhythms and upheavals in the world around us, the natural as well as the cultural. We take things apart to see if we can put them back together again, and perhaps make them better. And we are intrinsically interested in the people around us, especially those who share our everyday lives. All of us attempt to understand others and anticipate how they will act. How will my roommate react if the rest of us leave without her? Will the instructor be lenient if I turn this assignment in late? Why did Ross lash out at Joey when it was Rachel who really hurt him? Through our conjectures and intuitions we attempt to interpret the patterns we observe in social life.

As you would expect, our questions often derive from practical concerns. Questions of this sort, posed at a broader level of applicability, are of considerable interest to decision makers in industry, government, and education. One of the important traditions in personality research involves understanding and predicting a person's reactions and behavioral tendencies. Why does this talented and accomplished employee keep attempting to discredit her peers? What constellation of traits, beliefs, motives, and experiences compels her to belittle and undermine others? Could this recurrent pattern be a precursor to a deeper act of disloyalty? How will this person handle intense stress? Or, more generally still, what kind of person is best able to endure the stress of being an air traffic controller? What kind of person is likely to steal from his employer? Which applicant has the best potential as a teacher or a salesperson? Who is likely to sustain an early heart attack? Which incoming freshmen should be paired as roommates? Each of these questions focuses in part on the personal qualities or characteristics of an individual that enhance or diminish the likelihood of some outcome. To answer such questions, a researcher must work diligently through several steps:

1. Specify the *outcome* (the pattern of behavior or events) that the researcher is attempting to understand or predict.
2. Identify the kinds of *predictors* (e.g., personality traits) that may influence the outcome.
3. Develop assessment procedures that will reveal or make evident the relationship between the outcome measures and the predictive variables.
4. Communicate the acquired information to decision makers in a useful manner.

Once you have a general question in mind, it is necessary to frame the question more formally and in such a way that it can be answered systematically using the tools and resources available. Consider, for example, a recent study conducted by an expert outside of the field of personality psychology. Jim Collins, formerly on the faculty at the Stanford School of Business, operates a management research laboratory in Boulder, Colorado, that specializes in understanding the performance of enduring great companies. His book with Jerry Porras, *Built to Last*, focused on what it takes to build a great company from the ground up. A more recent book, *Good to Great*, examines an equally straightforward question: "Can a good company become a great company and, if so, how?"

To answer this question, Collins and his team of researchers first tackled the question of specifying the outcome they wanted to explain—good companies that had become great. They defined a good-to-great company as one with "fifteen-year cumulative stock returns at or below the general stock market, punctuated by a transition point, then cumulative returns at least three times the market over the next fifteen years," with gains independent of (i.e., above and beyond) its market sector. From a pool of 1,435 Fortune 500 companies in the years 1965 to 1995, eleven were selected. Seventeen other companies were selected to serve as comparisons, good companies with similar potential and resources that either never achieved a transition point or achieved one but failed to maintain the trajectory. The team then studied these 28 companies (11 targets and 17 comparisons) using all available published materials dating back 50 years, supplemented by numerous interviews, to look at financial health, business strategy, markets and competitors, products and services, technology, location, organizational structure, corporate culture, leadership, and much more. As you have no doubt observed, Collins and his team initiated their study by carefully tackling the first two steps listed above. They specified the outcome carefully and then identified characteristics that might influence or predict the outcome.

As they analyzed this data set over several years, Collins and his team identified a set of factors that "showed up as a change variable in 100 percent of the good-to-great companies and in less than 30 percent of the comparison companies during the pivotal years" (p. 12). The factor that surprised Collins's team most was the one involving leadership. In part, this finding came as a surprise because Collins himself had given "the research team explicit instructions to *downplay* the role of top executives so that we could avoid the simplistic 'credit the leader' or 'blame the leader' thinking common today." Collins was looking for a "deeper, more scientific understanding about what makes great companies tick" rather than a nonspecific appeal to corporate leadership (pp. 21–22). What was particularly unexpected, however, was the kind of leader who emerged, for it was not the celebrity CEO we hear about most often and would expect to be leading the charge at the nation's top-performing companies.

Colman Mockler is a case in point. CEO of Gillette, the consumer products giant, from 1975 to 1991, Mockler was a quiet man who was unfailingly gracious and genteel. He maintained remarkable balance in his life, rarely working evenings or weekends. He was devoted to his family and his church. He liked to work with his hands on projects around the house. Yet, those who thought that this kindliness might mean Mockler was soft or indecisive were sorely mistaken. Three times he fought off hostile takeover bids by determined raiders. In the first instance, Mockler could easily have capitulated; Gillette shareholders would have reaped an immediate 44% gain on their stock, and Mockler and his executives would have earned millions from cashing in their own shares and golden parachutes. However, Mockler believed wholeheartedly that Gillette was poised to dominate the consumer products market and so had staked the company's future on huge investments in radically new, unproven, but technologically advanced shaving systems. Because he was unreservedly committed to the success of this strategy, Mockler led the effort to call thousands of individual investors, one by one, in order to win the proxy battle. Mockler's bet paid off, and the new technologies transformed the marketplace when they were introduced as the Sensor and Mach3 razors. Gillette went on to cumulative stock returns that were an amazing 7.9 times greater than market's healthy average from 1980–1995.

According to Collins and his team, Mockler was typical of the CEOs of all 11 of these great companies. They labeled these CEOs "level 5 leaders." They described these leaders as "a study in duality: modest and willful, humble and fearless. . . . In contrast to the very I-centric style of the comparison leaders, we were struck by how the good-to-great leaders didn't talk about themselves. . . . They'd talk about the company and the contribution of other executives as long as we'd like but would deflect discussion about their own contributions. It wasn't just false modesty. Those who worked with or wrote about the good-to-great leaders continually used words like *quiet, humble, modest, reserved, shy, gracious, mild-mannered, self-effacing, understated, did not believe his own clippings*, and so forth" (pp. 22, 27). At the same time, these level 5 leaders demonstrated an "unwavering resolve to do whatever must be done to produce the best long-term results, . . . no matter how big or hard the decisions." They "set the standard of building an enduring great company [and] will settle for nothing less" (pp. 36, 39).

For our purposes, it is intriguing to consider this cluster of personality characteristics that Collins and his team culled from their research materials and that seem to relate to a CEO's ability to effect sustained improvement in a company. If we wanted to refine and test this idea of a level 5 leader, how would we set about measuring it? Could we set up a screening protocol that would enable a corporation to identify potential candidates for leadership development? In general, how do we move from a good idea to a good measure?

DEFINING CONCEPTS

Measurement is useful in part because it proceeds hand-in-hand with thinking clearly about a concept. Everyday communication is possible because people agree more or less about the meanings of words. But the extent of agreement is far from perfect. For example, when I say that Colman is modest and willful, the positive characteristics that I have in mind may be different from the negative images these words initially create for you. Words and concepts are colored by an individual's own experiences and biases. The connotative richness of our everyday vocabulary occasionally results in misunderstandings and conflict, which is part of the price we pay for a language that is dynamic and malleable. Scientific communication, however, requires greater precision and agreement than everyday discourse. *Conceptualization* is the process by which we work to define exactly what we mean when we use a specific term. Thus, if we want to know whether hostile people experience more health problems, before we can even study the question, much less agree on an answer, we need to agree on what we mean by these four concepts—hostile people, health problems, more, and experience.

Agreeing on what a concept means often involves pointing to particular examples or *indicators*. In the case of health problems, we might specify the presence of any of the following as a sign of ill health: cardiovascular disease, elevated blood pressure, headaches, peptic ulcers, cancer, disorders of the immune system, or elevated LDL cholesterol levels. Notice, however, that this list of indicators includes both diseases and risk factors and that it is far from exhaustive. Should we include colds, toothaches, allergies, black eyes, and broken limbs on the list? In the same way, we can specify various indicators that signify what we mean by hostile: reacting aggressively to frustration, verbally insulting and picking on people, maligning others' motives, ignoring others, and flying off the handle with little provocation. Again, these indicators are far from complete, but they begin to flesh out what we mean by this particular concept.

The process of conceptualization involves defining a set of indicators that is not only reasonably clear but representative as well. A single example or two will rarely do justice to the richness of a concept. Capturing the meaning of the concept of hostility means systematically mapping its terrain by specifying its

---

Activity Box 2.1   **Measuring Conscientiousness**

As we observe ourselves and others in the course of everyday life, we often notice that people differ in terms of what they do and how they do it. Some people respond to criticism with anger and sarcasm, others are earnest and concerned, whereas still others are distraught. As we recognize certain tendencies, we tend to label the response: that person reacted spitefully, or candidly, or calmly. The adverb describes the specific reaction rather than the person typically. However, if we notice that a particular individual often reacts in a certain way, we may also want to label the person using a comparable adjective: we say that the person is generally spiteful, candid, or calm. Once we have noticed a tendency in some people, we can examine others to assess whether they also have this tendency. We begin to think of the tendency as a characteristic that is possessed to a greater or lesser extent. Does this person have the trait of spitefulness, candidness, or calmness? This progression from adverb to adjective to noun involves an increasing level of abstraction;

we move from describing behavior to describing people to describing an idea.

Personality psychologists are often interested in a familiar concept. For example, a researcher may decide to study the concept of conscientiousness. Each of us has a general understanding of this term, and we can point to those around us who are more or less conscientious. But can we be precise in our definition? The task of the researcher is to specify behaviors that adequately define the idea or concept: What list of behaviors would indicate the presence or absence of this trait?

To test your ingenuity as a researcher, try drawing up a list of ten specific, observable behaviors that could be used to measure the trait of conscientiousness in the average college student. What behaviors in class, in the dorm, in the library, in the cafeteria, and so on, would serve as legitimate and convincing measures of conscientiousness?

---

behavioral, emotional, cognitive, and physiological aspects. Any set of indicators must be selected carefully with an eye toward the breadth of the concept we are attempting to convey. This process—defining a concept clearly and systematically—is often more complicated than it sounds (see the Activity Box 2.1), but it is the meat-and-potatoes work of the research psychologist.

MEASURING VARIABLES

Measurement is the process by which numbers are used to acquire and express information about an object, person, or event. We can measure the net assets of a company, the weight of an athlete, or the duration of a temper tantrum. Notice that we do not measure an object or event per se, but rather one or more of its various attributes or characteristics—such as its worth, weight, or duration. In the social sciences, these attributes are called *variables*. For example, age, race, eye color, height and weight, intelligence quotient (IQ), modesty, willfulness, cheerfulness, marital status, and income are all attributes that can be used to describe people. For each of these variables, an individual can be assigned a *value*. In many cases values are based on a particular *unit of measurement*. For weight, the unit of measurement might be pounds, and one value (150 pounds) can be compared with other values (250 pounds) using various mathematical operations (i.e., addition subtraction, multiplication, and divi-

Table 2.1 | Four Types of Scales

Type of Scale	Defining Characteristic	Function of the Scale	Mathematical Properties	Familiar Examples
Nominal	Objects are sorted into mutually exclusive categories based on an attribute	To compare group membership; to classify	No mathematical functions; numbers used as names	Zip codes; Dewey decimal system
Ordinal	Objects are logically ordered (from high to low) based on an attribute	To compare rank order; to assign position	Greater than or less than	Class rank; ratings of top 20 teams in college basketball
Interval	Objects are ordered and spaced at equal intervals as defined by a unit of measurement	To compare amount; to count	Add and subtract	SAT scores; IQ scores; temperature in centigrade degrees
Ratio	Objects are ordered and spaced at equal intervals with a unit of measurement for which zero indicates absence of the attribute	To compare ratios or proportions	Multiply and divide	Miles per hour; temperature in kelvin degrees

sion). However, units of measurement are generally arbitrary. Why choose pounds instead of kilograms? Why is a foot 12 inches long, and exactly how long is an inch? What matters most is that different observers agree about the unit of measurement. Thus, an inch, an ounce, and a second are all defined with some exactness, the accuracy being ensured by national and international regulatory standards (e.g., seconds are calibrated precisely by an atomic clock at the Naval Observatory in Washington, D.C.). IQ scores are much less precisely defined—what exactly is an IQ point?—but psychologists have labored to develop standard items and procedures that will yield reliable results, and this process of standardization has established IQ tests as useful tools.

Not all variables, however, can be defined in terms of a unit of measurement. In the case of eye color, for example, we can distinguish blue from brown, and for the purposes of recording observations, we can arbitrarily assign blue as the number 1 and brown as the number 2. But what is the unit of measurement? Is brown twice as big, or twice as long, or twice as important as blue? In this case we are using numbers, like words, to classify objects with respect to some variable. However, the numbers are not values that can be compared mathematically. Thus, there are several classes of variables that differ in terms of what a specific value represents. Table 2.1 describes four kinds of variables.

Variables are useful to the extent that they truly represent the concepts we set out to study, yet many intriguing and important concepts turn out to be difficult to measure in any satisfying way. Some psychologists argue that the qualities of mind, character, and personality that describe an individual in the fullest and deepest sense may by their very nature preclude rigorous definition or measurement. For example, how can we truly assess someone's courage in the face of adversity or the depth of personal integrity? From this perspective, knowledge about people that is truly meaningful always transcends numbers.

Other researchers counter that as long as we can agree a concept exists—which means we can point to and agree on at least one indicator of it—then we can also find a way to measure the concept (based on that one indicator if nothing else). This camp asserts that psychology will advance as a science only if variables are defined and measured with precision. This point of view is captured in a famous quote by Lord Kelvin, the British physicist who established the Kelvin scale for temperature.

> When you can measure what you are speaking about, and express it in numbers, you know something about it; but when you cannot measure it, when you cannot express it in numbers, your knowledge is of a meager and unsatisfactory kind: it may be the beginning of knowledge, but you have scarcely, in your thoughts, advanced to the stage of science, whatever the matter may be. (Cited in Kaplan, 1964, p. 172)

This chapter is about measurement, so we need to assume for now that we can in fact study concepts that are of consequence. Nevertheless, we should not mindlessly adopt this point of view. Numbers and statistics do not have magical properties. Advances in measurement are important as means to an end, but we need always to keep the end in sight. That end has to do with the question we are asking. Careful measurement is useful to the extent that it helps us to answer the question we have in mind.

Measurement is the logical consequence of conceptualization. As we move from a rough concept at the outset, to a more careful working definition, and then to a set of specific indicators, the appropriate means by which to measure that concept become clearer. Measurement implies that we have established a systematic and standardized manner by which to define a variable. Advances in measurement result in increasingly subtle discriminations and correspondingly more precise descriptions that in turn allow for a more complete understanding of how one variable (e.g., physical health) relates to and changes as a function of some other variable (e.g., hostility). Thus, in an important way, measurement is the foundation on which an empirical science is built, but it in turn arises from the bedrock of conceptualization and theory.

LOOKING FOR CONVERGENCE

Whereas personality variables may seem more complex and abstract than some other individual characteristics (such as body size, physical health, or musical ability), the general measurement strategy is the same. Probably the single overarching principle is that of *convergence*, gathering evidence from multiple vantage points and looking for agreement. The idea is to gather information from different perspectives—a friend, a supervisor or teacher, a parent, oneself—using different kinds of methods—subjective impressions versus objective measurements—in order to examine whether these different perspectives and methods yield similar answers. Consider, for example, how to describe a person's physique.

One strategy might be to ask an individual to describe herself or to provide relevant information. People have a considerable store of knowledge about their bodies. Of course, they also have a vested interest in how such information is portrayed. We would not necessarily want to assume the accuracy of a self-reported description. Another strategy might be to ask other people to describe the target person. Presumably others might provide a more objective description of one's appearance, although they would have access to less information; for example, observers might be fooled by clever tailoring. Some close friends may have more information than a first-time observer, but those observers might also be somewhat more likely to describe their friend charitably.

An alternative strategy would be to employ more standardized measures such as height and weight. But these figures alone provide a limited picture; they do not readily distinguish muscle from fat. We could add, therefore, measures of circumference, muscle density, and proportion of body fat to flesh out the description of one's body type. Incorporating these additional measures underscores the point of this example. No one source of data can provide a complete picture. A woman may describe herself as somewhat overweight, her coworkers may say she looks great, her weight may be average for her height, and her percentage of body fat may be above normal. Together these different pieces of information, although not entirely consistent, present us with a balanced description. Our confidence in a description increases as the perspectives and methods of measurement become more varied and as the various lines of evidence converge. Any single source of data is susceptible to a variety of limitations, but by adopting *multiple modes of measurement*, biases and errors can often be canceled out or minimized. In the same way, our confidence in measuring a personality variable increases as we use several different sources and methods.

The use of multiple modes of measurement to build up converging lines of evidence is a standard approach in most of the noteworthy studies in personality psychology. In major longitudinal studies, researchers have typically collected a comprehensive set of variables at periodic intervals in order to examine the expression and experience of personality characteristics over time. In other studies, researchers have developed an extensive set of measures focusing on just a few key concepts. One approach to an intensive study of this sort is known as an *assessment center*. In this procedure, participants engage in a collection of individual and team exercises that are designed to assess specific personality characteristics in a semi-realistic setting (Task Force on Assessment Center Standards, 1989).

The roots of the assessment center enterprise can be traced back to an intensive effort launched by the United States government at the outset of World War II to identify and recruit men and women for special service in the Office of Strategic Services (OSS). As the United States lurched headlong into World War II following the surprise bombing of Pearl Harbor, the president and Congress created the OSS as a special wartime agency to conduct a variety of tactical and covert operations. The functions of the OSS, which was the forerunner of today's Central Intelligence Agency (CIA), included gathering information about the enemy's activities and strengths, analyzing this information to identify areas of vulnerability, aiding and training resistance movements, and conducting guerrilla operations behind enemy lines.

Soon after its inception, the OSS was busily and somewhat haphazardly recruiting hundreds of agents. As these recruits were trained and deployed, the need for a more rigorous screening process became apparent. To meet this need, an assessment staff of psychologists and psychiatrists was established in late 1943. The task assigned to the OSS assessment staff was to eliminate the unfit and to predict which recruits would be useful to the OSS by developing a set of procedures that would reveal the personalities of the recruits. Their work was complicated by the great variety of assignments, from historians and linguists to undercover agents and saboteurs. Despite these problems and the hurried development of the testing procedures, the assessment staff was able to process 5,391 individuals in less than two years, and their work was vital to the wartime effort. The OSS assessment staff went to great lengths to gather information about each candidate in a variety of contexts or situations and from the vantage point of multiple observers. In fact, they developed an elaborate procedure for acquiring an enormous amount of information about each candidate in a limited period of time. Their approach to the study of personality had a significant impact on postwar research and is worth studying in depth, in part because similar strategies were adopted subsequently by university and corporate laboratories around the country (for example, see the longitudinal study at AT&T, Bray, 1982), and in part because it illustrates the concurrent use of multiple methods and observers.

The OSS Assessment Project

At the outset, the OSS assessment staff had only vague descriptions of the functions that men—and virtually all of the recruits were men—would be expected to perform overseas. Many of the covert operations were still in the planning stages or were being performed behind enemy lines where even the officer in charge had only limited knowledge about the requirements of the job. Thus, it was impossible to assess men in relation to a specific, well-defined job or desired task. Instead, the assessment staff decided to assess men in relation to a cluster of general qualifications that were thought to be necessary for effective functioning in a wide variety of OSS activities.

Over a period of time, the assessment staff identified seven major personality variables that branch chiefs and administrative officers judged essential for completing assignments in their units:

1. *Motivation:* war morale and interest in OSS activities
2. *Energy and initiative:* level of effort and activity

3. *Effective intelligence:* ability to select strategic goals and attain them efficiently— practical, resourceful, original, and discerning
4. *Emotional stability:* steady, able to endure stress
5. *Social relations:* ability to get along with others, team player
6. *Leadership:* social initiative, ability to elicit cooperation, accepts responsibility, organizational ability
7. *Security:* discreet, cautious, able to keep secrets, can bluff and mislead

In addition to these personality dispositions, potential recruits were also evaluated as to level of ability (athletic skills, observational and analytic skills, and propaganda skills), potential involvement (front lines versus support staff), authority, and responsibility.

Station S, which stood for *Secret* (really!), was the primary OSS assessment school. Located in Fairfax County, Virginia, Station S was a fine country estate with a large main house and a number of other smaller structures that were situated on several acres of varied terrain. Every few days a canvas-covered Army truck carrying a group of 18 OSS candidates arrived for a three-day stopover. Candidates were recruited in a variety of ways; some were military personnel, others were civilians. Most had only a vague understanding of the nature of the OSS or the specific assignment for which they were being considered.

Students at Station S were required to hide their true identity for security reasons. The assessment staff capitalized on this requirement by instructing each student to create and maintain a cover story during his stay at Station S. He was to hide from the staff and other students his real birthplace, educational history, military rank, occupation, and current residence. Only at special times during their stay (which were called X conditions) were they allowed to break their cover story. The rest of the time the students were to guard painstakingly their true identity because the assessment staff would attempt to catch them off guard.

For three or four days, the candidates were subjected to an intense and exhausting series of missions, tests, problems, interviews, and games. The staff worked hard to create an atmosphere of friendly competition and camaraderie. From the moment a group disembarked, however, the assessment staff was collecting data that would become grist for the assessment mill.

Consider, for example, how the assessment staff gathered information about a candidate's capacity for leadership. The staff defined it as "a man's ability to take the initiative in social situations, to plan and organize action, and in so doing to evoke cooperation" (U.S. Office of Strategic Services, 1948, p. 301). The staff also distinguished between leadership assertion and leadership efficiency. By assertion they meant the candidate's drive to assume the position of leader, and by efficiency, how well a leader functioned when thrust into that role by colleagues or circumstances. The leadership variable was assessed using seven different procedures. Three of these involved situational tests in which a team of candidates was confronted with a standard problem or task and the staff observed how the team performed and who exerted leadership. Two other tests were designed to reveal leadership in the context of verbal interaction. A candidate's leadership ability was also rated by his peers (the other candidates) and by a staff member who had interviewed the candidate and who had access to the results of a variety of personality inventories. This multi-method approach to measurement was essential to the logic of the assessment school. At some point, of course, the diverse and independent sources of data had to be reconciled and interpreted to provide a summary report and recommendation. We will look at how this integration was achieved after we first look more closely at how leadership was measured using specific procedures.

Recall from our earlier discussion that measurement is the logical end product of conceptualization. To measure leadership, we move first from a vague concept to a working definition and then to a set of specific indicators. These indicators become our *operational definition* of leadership, that which spells out in concrete terms exactly how this particular concept or variable is going to be "operationalized" or measured. Adopting a set of procedures provides a standardized and systematic way of measuring leadership. Of course, any set of indicators is necessarily constrained, which means that from the outset we have invested in a measure of the concept—in this case, leadership—that we know is, to some extent, limited and incomplete.

The Brook Situation   One of the situations confronting a team of candidates on the first day of testing involved moving several large objects and members of the team across a shallow, quiet stream with banks about eight feet apart. On one bank was a log, on the other bank a heavy rock. Both sides of the brook had trees. Scattered on the ground along the bank where the candidates stood were several boards, none long enough to reach the other bank, three lengths of rope, a pulley, and a barrel with both ends knocked out. The candidates were given the following instructions:

> Use your imagination. Before you, you see a raging torrent so deep and so fast that it is quite impossible to rest anything upon the bottom of the stream. The banks are sheer, so it will be impossible for you to work except from the top of them.
>
> You are on a mission in the field, and having come to this brook you are faced with the task of transporting this delicate range finder, skillfully camouflaged as a log, to the far bank, and of bringing that box of percussion caps, camouflaged as a rock, to this side. In carrying out this assignment, you may make use of any materials you find around here. When the job is done, all of you, as well as any material you have used, are to be back on this side.
>
> This is a group problem. We would suggest that you first discuss your method of procedure. When you have decided upon your plan and are ready to go to work, let us know so that we may time you, for in the actual execution of this problem you will be working against time. (U.S. Office of Strategic Services, 1948, pp. 95–96)

All solutions to this problem involved getting one or more team members to the other side of the brook by building a bridge with the boards and rope (the rope could be used to bind several boards together) or by roping a branch on the far side of the bank and rigging an overhead cable, or by swinging across to the opposite bank on a rope tied to a high branch of a tree on the near bank. The objects could then be transferred in a similar manner. Groups were allocated one hour to solve this problem. Some groups were unable to accomplish the mission in this time period whereas one team completed the task in just four minutes.

Leadership in this context emerged in a variety of ways. Specific indicators included a candidate's ability to propose and implement a successful strategy, to organize the group into an effective working team, to combine ideas from several sources, and to minimize friction and maximize cooperative effort. A man who took the lead initially was not necessarily the same man who directed things at the end. Sometimes the candidate who guided the discussion would lose his leadership to someone who was more gifted athletically. Or perhaps the role would be reassigned when an idea failed or a better plan was proposed. The leader was not always the most assertive individual; sometimes a group might reject a member who attempted to dominate decision making in favor of a less forceful member whose ideas were more practical.

The actions and interactions that occurred at the brook were recorded by a staff member and observed by several others. Each candidate was rated independently by the staff members and these ratings were always discussed prior to arriving at a final rating for leadership.

The Construction Task   Also on the first day, each candidate had an individual appointment behind the barn. The candidate's task was to direct two helpers in constructing a wooden frame structure. But the problem was not as innocent as it seemed. The two assistants—Kippy and Buster—were actually members of the assessment staff posing as hired farmhands. Their assignment was to annoy and obstruct the candidate to the best of their ability but without disobeying any direct orders. Kippy generally acted in a passive, sluggish manner and would do little to help unless specifically instructed, whereas Buster was surly and cantankerous, full of impractical suggestions and quick to criticize.

Originally conceived of as a test of leadership, the construction task allowed each candidate to be scored in terms of whether he controlled the situation, outlined the task and explained his reasoning adequately, earned the respect of his helpers, listened to their suggestions, motivated them to work, and minimized friction and hostility. Again, the leadership variable was rated by several independent observers and later combined into a summary evaluation. Although leadership skills emerged in this context, Kippy and Buster performed their roles so effectively that no candidate ever completed the construction task and most never got very far. Their behavior was designed to frustrate the candidates, perhaps provoking a rash response, and thus the task came to be seen more as a test of emotional stability than a measure of leadership. This redefinition of the task points to how our understanding of a measure can evolve as we gather information about it. We will return to this important issue—the valid meaning of a measure—later in the chapter.

Leaderless Group Discussion   Each team met to discuss an open-ended question: What are the major postwar problems facing the United States, and (if you have time) along what lines do you think they should be solved? The team was to arrive at a consensus and then have one member present its conclusions. Leadership was rated in terms of whether a candidate was able to keep the discussion on track, command the respect of the others by virtue of his contributions, facilitate the participation of all group members, and guide the discussion toward a conclusion by summarizing points and positions and detecting agreement.

Debate   Late in the evening in the second day, all of the candidates were divided into two teams for a debate. The groups had 20 minutes to prepare their positions, and the staff observed the preparations as well as the debate itself. Although similar to the group discussion, the debate differed in that the audience was larger, the issue more competitive, and the participants better acquainted. Perhaps most important of all, however, was that prior to the debate a free bar was opened for the remainder of the evening. The abundance of alcohol undoubtedly accentuated the emotional intensity of the issue being discussed, and the debate often revealed another side of a candidate's leadership abilities.

Assigned Leadership Tasks   Many of the tasks at Station S began without a leader, and the staff watched to see who emerged on top. In these contexts, however, it was not always apparent whether other men might also have acted effectively as leader if they had been assigned the task. Thus, a series of situations was designed such that members of the group would alternate as leader. Typically, a candidate was assigned a problem that seemed particularly relevant to him (e.g., moving a team across a mined road or repairing a damaged bridge under enemy fire). In this way, the staff was able to assess each candidate's ability to organize his team, develop strategy, respond to emergencies, and maintain his role.

Sociometric Ratings   Each candidate at Station S was asked to rate the other candidates in his class. Candidates responded to 11 questions about the other men. Two of the questions were directly relevant to leadership ability: "Whom would you recommend as supervisor of a group dealing with problems of planning and organization?" and "If you were a member of a group on a dangerous mission, whom would you prefer to have as your leader?" Candidates answered these questions by nominating classmates. They could nominate as few or as many other classmates as they wanted. These *sociometric ratings* were introduced to the class both as a way of helping the staff assess the other candidates and as a way of evaluating each candidate's ability to judge others accurately. This introduction was designed to enhance the quality of the ratings.

The Interview   The single most important component of the OSS assessment strategy was the clinical interview, because the interviewer would eventually write the first draft of the personality profile that would accompany the final evaluation of the candidate. Using insights gleaned from the interview session, the interviewer integrated the various bits of information derived from the situational tasks, the batteries of self-report tests and personality inventories, and the sociometric ratings by peers.

Each candidate met alone for an hour and a half with a senior member of the staff under X conditions (the candidate was free to reveal his true identity and history and could set aside for the moment his cover story). The interview session was used to explore the candidate's life history including relationships with family members and friends, school and athletic achievements, medical illnesses, romances, wishes and fears, hopes and aspirations, and opinions and beliefs. The interviewers were generally not as interested in the exact truthfulness of a candidate's account as they were in how he interpreted and presented his past. For example, it would have been difficult for the staff to assess the veracity of a candidate's description of how he and his father got along, but regardless of accuracy, how a candidate spoke of this relationship was revealing. Did he describe his father affectionately, or was he bitter and hostile? Was he distant and reserved in his description or glowing and unrealistic? Similarly, interviewers were as attentive to how a candidate reacted to the interview situation as they were to the content of what was said. Was the candidate withdrawn or at ease, evasive or frank, flexible or rigid? What did he want to talk about, and what made him edgy? The interviews followed no single protocol; they varied considerably depending on the clinical intuition of the interviewer.

In this context, perceptions about a candidate's leadership potential were deduced from his previous accomplishments, his reactions to probing questions by an authority figure, his hobbies and interests, his motivation, and the general strength and resiliency of his character as interpreted by an experienced psychologist or psychiatrist. Although the picture of the candidate that developed during the interview generally formed the basis for the personality profile included in the final report to the candidate's recruiting officer, this picture was not independent of the other information gathered at the assessment school because the interviewer had already observed the candidate in a variety of test situations and also had access to his scores on a variety of personality tests. Thus, this session enabled the interviewer to test, refine, and consolidate an impression that was already partially formed.

Putting the Pieces Together

On the final day of each assessment session, the staff met as a whole to decide about the fitness of each of the candidates. This process involved integrating a wealth of material into a single description or personality profile. The method for doing this revolved around the primary dimensions of evaluation: the seven personality variables and the three ability variables. Using the case of leadership as an example, observers present for a particular task (e.g., the Brook Situation) rated candidates immediately following the task using a 6-point scale:

0	1	2	3	4	5
Very inferior	Inferior	Low average	High average	Superior	Very superior
7%	18%	25%	25%	18%	7%

The percentages refer to the number of candidates who would ideally fall into each category over the full term of the project. Raters were encouraged to use all points on this scale according to the correct proportion in order to prevent scores from clumping together. The raters met together that same day to compare notes. Whenever discrepancies occurred, the raters worked to understand the nature of the disagreement and to resolve it. In this way, a single rating was recorded for a candidate for each task, and this rating reflected the consensus of the observers who were present.

Ratings on each task and each personality variable were posted on a large board using color-coded thumbtacks (which was how things worked before spreadsheets). By the final staff conference, complete information about a candidate was displayed using separate columns for the primary rating variables and subcolumns for the separate situations. At a glance, a staff member could ascertain a candidate's average rating across the seven leadership tasks and could also check for any obvious inconsistencies.

During the staff conference, the interviewer would read the candidate's personality profile and one of the other observers would characterize the situational ratings of the candidate. The rest of the staff would then comment on and critique these findings and would offer their own insights, observations, and anecdotes. The group would confer about that candidate until all issues and discrepancies had been resolved and a final recommendation had been reached. In many cases, this consensus was achieved quickly and easily. Sometimes, however, a consensus was reached only after heated discussion and freely expressed disagreement. Nevertheless, agreement was almost always attained without resorting to a mechanical tallying of votes.

The OSS assessment project is an important landmark in the history of personality assessment. This massive undertaking exceeded any previous attempts to study a large group of individuals in depth. Many distinguished psychologists contributed to its success. Although we could profitably examine many aspects of this project in greater detail, for now three points warrant emphasis:

1. The OSS staff began the assessment enterprise by identifying the relevant personality variables and devising ways to assess these variables. Conceptualization led to a working definition that in turn suggested specific indicators or operational measures.
2. The OSS staff measured each personality variable in several different situations and incorporated several different methods. Using different indicators to converge on a specific personality variable provided evidence about the coherence of these indicators and helped to ensure that no one indicator was overinterpreted or overemphasized.
3. The OSS staff worked as a group to observe and describe a candidate's personality. Multiple observers provided another form of convergence that helped to ensure the accuracy of the ratings and acted to minimize biases associated with any one viewpoint or observer.

These three points are inherent in the logic of measurement, and they must be attended to in doing research of any type, personality measurement included. The first of these points, the process of conceptualization and operationalization, we covered earlier in this chapter. Points two and three, which have to do with validity and reliability, we will look at more thoroughly in the remaining pages.

CLASSIFYING METHODS FOR MEASURING PERSONALITY

Over the years, investigators have concocted many ingenious ways of assessing personality constructs. Nevertheless, the term *personality measure* is sometimes confounded with one particular method: the self-report inventory. Questionnaires of this sort are used so extensively that it is easy to understand how this approach has become virtually synonymous (even in professional journals!) with personality measurement. But there are multiple strategies for assessing personality, and it would be unfortunate and self-defeating for researchers to limit themselves to a single mode of measurement. The purpose of this section is to review some of the various ways in which personality can be assessed and to organize these approaches within a conceptual framework. Our discussion will follow loosely a system developed by Donald Fiske (1971). (Fiske—then a lieutenant in the U.S. Navy—was part of the OSS Assessment Staff and was one of the principal authors of the book that chronicles the work at Station S. He passed away in 2003 after a long and distinguished academic career.)

The system we will examine differs in several respects from the one presented by Fiske, but it defines the basic modes (or categories) using the same primary factors: the source of the data (who or what produces it) and the role the source plays in producing the data. The classification system is described in Table 2.2. The rows of the table list the defining factors, and the columns identify seven different modes. Distinctions among the modes will become apparent as we briefly examine each.

Mode 1 is the self-report questionnaire in which respondents are asked to endorse the accuracy of self-descriptive items. For instance, consider the following typical query: "I work best under pressure." The questionnaire may use a *true–false* format or a graduated scale (e.g., from *1 = strongly disagree* to *5 = strongly agree*). Respondents presumably select a particular response after considering thoughtfully their past behavior and store of self-memories. Because no other observer can access these private vaults or amass knowledge that is comparable, the self-report of an individual provides a unique perspective. However, one cannot assume that the information obtained from a self-report inventory is necessarily accurate or insightful. Consider some of the limitations of the self-report method. Respondents might do any of the following:

1. Misconstrue the meaning of an item (does this item imply that I prefer to work under pressure or that I can't work well without pressure?)
2. Hurry to finish the questionnaire and become careless
3. Not cooperate and choose deliberately to distort answers
4. Lack insight into their own motives, feelings, and actions
5. Wish to present themselves in a favorable light

These last two problems in particular have troubled researchers who use self-report instruments (Paulhus, 1986). The one problem (number four) involves *self-deception:* some people do not have much insight into their own personalities. The other issue concerns *impression management:* people often put forward an idealized view of themselves. Self-reports provide an important

Table 2.2 | Classifying the Methods for Measuring Personality

	Mode 1	Mode 2	Mode 3	Mode 4	Mode 5	Mode 6	Mode 7
Description	Trait inventories	State experiences	Ability tests	Subjective ratings	Objective ratings	Behavioral measures	Physiological measures
Source of the data	Self	Self	Self	Other	Other	Instrument	Instrument
Time frame	Past	Current	Current	Past	Current	Current	Current
How the source functions	Interprets	Perceives	Judges	Interprets	Interprets or transcribes	Records mechanically	Records mechanically
Nature of the task	Describe yourself	Describe your experience	Answer correctly	Describe this person	Describe this person	Record behavioral response	Record physiological activity
Type of variable	Ordinal or interval*	Ordinal or interval*	Ordinal, interval, or ratio	Ordinal or interval*	Ordinal or interval*	Interval or ratio	Interval or ratio
Typical variables	Traits, attitudes, beliefs	Feelings, preferences	Perceptual or social judgements	Traits, complex behaviors	Traits, behaviors	Simple behavioral responses	Cortical or autonomic response
Typical examples	MMPI, CPI NEO-PI; adjective lists	Mood surveys, preference surveys	Accuracy test, rod & frame, problem solving	Ratings by peers or supervisors	Clinical interviews or ratings	Reaction time	EEGs, heart rate, blood pressure

*The rating instruments typically used in Modes 1, 2, 4, and 5 are based on aggregates of items. Because the individual items may not contribute equally to the overall score, the scores are often not truly at equal intervals. Although it is more appropriate, therefore, to describe these variables as ordinal, researchers typically treat them as interval variables when doing statistical analyses, an assumption that typically works out acceptably.

resource for personality researchers, but one that can be deciphered correctly only in concert with other sources of information.

The second mode of measurement also relies on an individual's self-description, but the focus is on current experiences rather than previous history. For example, a cola taste test ("Do you prefer cola A or cola B?") asks a respondent to report an immediate preference and does not require an interpretation of how the respondent acts or feels typically. There is less need for inference and less opportunity for the report to be influenced by the constructive process of memory. In other words, the question involves a *state* experience rather than a *trait* tendency.

Recall from chapter 1 that traits refer to personal characteristics that are stable, long-lasting, and internally caused, whereas states describe features that are temporary, brief, and linked to external circumstances. Trait concepts enable people to predict how individuals will act now or in the future based on how they have acted before; state concepts describe actions that are influenced by and may be predicted from a particular context (Chaplin, John, & Goldberg, 1988). Trait tendencies are more central to the study of personality than are state experiences, and therefore mode 2 measures are not used as often as some of the other modes (e.g., modes 1, 4, or 6). Nevertheless, trait tendencies generally involve an increased likelihood of certain state experiences (Fleeson, 2001). For instance, people who have the trait of anxiety are more likely than most to experience anxious mood states.

Although the report of a state experience requires less interpretation and self-knowledge than the report of a trait tendency, it is still susceptible to some of the same problems. Respondents still possess privileged information and they may attempt to portray themselves in a favorable light (by choosing an answer or reporting a mood that seems more socially acceptable) or be uncooperative and attempt to impede the research.

The third mode of measurement again relies on a respondent's self-report. In this case, however, the task is to answer an item correctly. Items of this sort are analogous to problems in a puzzle book or an ability game. Although most psychologists distinguish between items that measure personality and those that measure ability (e.g., IQ tests), there are measures that combine elements of both. For example, recall from chapter 1 that the trait of *field independence* is defined as a person's ability to act independently of situational cues. Originally, this trait was assessed using a visual apparatus—the rod-and-frame test—that required an individual to look into a closed box and make perceptual judgments while ignoring the visual context (Witkin et al., 1954). Later researchers attempted to assess field independence using measures related to social context rather than perceptual context.

Tests of social intelligence—such as having to discern a person's viewpoint or having to identify correctly the meaning of social cues and facial expressions—are also relevant to the measurement of certain personality variables (e.g., empathy and dominance). Recall from the OSS project that the assessment staff introduced the sociometric ratings as a test of social intelligence—the candidate's ability to judge the other candidates perceptively. This approach has been developed in sophisticated ways in recent years (Funder, 1999). Tests of this sort are more objective than the self-report measures of modes 1 and 2 in that some answers are more correct than others. Thus, these measures rely less on self-interpretation or self-insight and minimize the potential for impression management (although occasionally a respondent may deliberately attempt to score poorly on a test.) Because of this greater objectivity, some researchers have attempted to construct self-report of personality measures using an ability approach (e.g., Willerman, Turner, & Peterson, 1976), but success has been elusive and this approach has not been widely adopted.

Modes 4 and 5 both originate from the perspective of an observer. They differ primarily in the extent to which the observer is knowledgeable and objective. Mode 4 is the counterpart to mode 1; the observer's task is to decide whether an item accurately describes the target person. This interpretation is presumably grounded in the many observations of the target that the rater has accumulated over time and in a variety of contexts. Thus, this approach assumes that the observer is a knowledgeable informant. Friends, one's spouse, a roommate, or a co-worker could all serve appropriately in this capacity. The closer the relationship, the richer the observational base. However, as the degree of intimacy increases, so also does the likelihood that the rater will feel compelled to describe the target favorably. One's companions and chums by definition are not impartial bystanders. A common example of this mode is a checklist of trait adjectives used on a letter of reference. Potential employers almost always require personal references, but they are not often helpful because the people who are best able to provide useful information are the very people who are inclined to aid and abet the prospective employee. Because this mode of measurement relies on the same type of interpretive judgments as self-reports, it is subject to many of the same constraints and biases.

To minimize biases of this sort, researchers often recruit impartial observers—individuals who have had no contact with the target person prior to the period of observation. Ratings of this sort (mode 5) are based solely on information derived from a controlled observational setting or other available records. Much of the data collected during the OSS assessment project involved this strategy of measurement: ratings by observers during the various tasks and situations, ratings from the clinical interview, and sociometric ratings. Unlike ratings by knowledgeable informants (mode 4), impartial observers offer a reasonable degree of objectivity. They should be less reluctant to assign unfavorable marks. For example, most employers interview job applicants rather than rely solely on personal references. The interviewer's evaluation is presumably more dispassionate than the ratings provided by a self-selected reference. Nevertheless, this approach also has its limitations. Most important, the observers' knowledge is necessarily restricted by the context and time frame of the observations. An interviewer must form an impression based on a short, highly constrained conversation. Even the intense, three-day schedule of testing at Station S provided only a narrow range of observational opportunities. Objective raters usually derive inferences from information that is insufficient and superficial. In addition, objective observers are subject to some of the same rating biases as observers who are well acquainted with a target.

Two common forms of rater bias are *leniency* and *halo*. Leniency is the tendency to give generally positive ratings. That friends are lenient in their ratings should not be overly surprising. Consider, however, that students tend to rate most all of their professors as above average in teaching effectiveness. Leniency from impartial strangers probably derives from a general tendency to think kindly about others and to avoid being seen as negative or critical. Recall that the OSS assessment staff attempted to offset this bias by instructing raters to assign a certain percentage of ratings into each of six categories (see the section entitled "Putting the Pieces Together").

Halo involves a blurring of conceptual distinctions. When an individual has a particularly conspicuous personal trait, this characteristic may bias an observer's ratings more generally. For example, if a woman is invariably hostile toward others and bitter about life, the negative feelings elicited by her antagonism may influence ratings of other aspects of her personality that are presumably independent (e.g., her work habits or intellectual ability). Halo refers, therefore, to a generally favorable or unfavorable rating of an individual that is rooted in a single salient aspect of his or her personality.

One way to avoid rating biases such as leniency and halo is to employ the observer primarily as a transcriber rather than as an interpreter. For example, rather than ask an observer to rate a target person's shyness, the observer might count the number and duration of speaking turns during a conversation or record the duration of directed gazing or the frequency of verbal reinforcers (Garcia, Stinson, Ickes, Bissonnette, & Briggs, 1991). The researcher seeks to minimize the interpretive responsibilities of the observer by providing explicit instructions about when and how to measure a specific behavior. In this approach, the observer performs a machine-like function; in fact, if possible, the human observer in this case would be replaced with an automated device.

Modes 6 and 7 involve this transition from human observer to mechanical instrument. In both cases, the premium is on precise measurement and a standardized procedure or mechanism. Responses are measured in terms of frequency (how often?), latency (how soon?), duration (how long?), rapidity (how often per unit of time?), and intensity (how strong?). Interpretation and subjective ratings are eliminated as much as possible. Barring equipment failure or miscalibration, the researcher is justifiably confident about the accuracy and objectivity of the data record.

But this sense of precision can be misleading. After all, the researcher still must link these automated recordings to a personality construct and this requires a fair amount of interpretation. Is the latency of a response on a preference test (i.e., how soon the respondent answers the question) a valid measure of impulsivity? Is increased muscle tension for certain facial muscles equivalent to a feeling of anger or sadness? Are increased heart rate and blood pressure valid measures of anxiety? Claims of this sort may be conceptually intriguing, but they are hardly straightforward. Thus, no method of measurement can avoid the dilemma of interpretation, although *who* provides the interpretation (an observer or the researcher) and at *what point* (when the rating is made or when the research is designed) varies across the seven modes.

The chief distinction between modes 6 and 7 involves the type of response being measured. In Mode 6, the participant in a research study responds to some event in a relatively controlled and observable way, perhaps by pushing a button or flipping a switch. A machine (e.g., a computer) is used to record this observable response. For example, in one well-known approach to the study of aggression (Buss, 1961), participants thought they were delivering electric shocks to another person as part of a teaching exercise. The level of shock delivered—the particular button pushed—was interpreted as a behavioral measure of aggressiveness. In mode 7, the instrument records ongoing physiological activity (e.g., heart rate, muscular tension, or brain activity) that is primarily private and may even be apprehended only vaguely by the person himself or herself. In mode 7, the instruments record activity that is often unobservable otherwise.

Taken together, the seven modes of measurement provide researchers with a diverse and adaptable set of tools. Different instruments are applicable to different types of problems, and choosing the appropriate instrument is always crucial to the success of a research project. There is no perfect tool or best method. Instead there are always trade-offs: the ease of data collection versus the richness of the data set, an observer who is knowledgeable versus one who is objective, an observer's interpretation of a complex behavior versus a researcher's interpretation of the psychological meaning of a simple response. Given these trade-offs, many researchers hedge their bets by selecting more than one measure of a personality variable. In order to balance the trade-offs, conventional wisdom also advocates selecting measures from more than one mode. The advantages of a multipronged approach were discussed earlier in the chapter, and one statement is worth repeating: *Our confidence in a description increases as the perspectives and methods of measurement become more varied and as the various lines of evidence converge; any single source of data is susceptible to a variety of problems, but by adopting multiple modes of measurement, biases and errors can often be canceled out or minimized.*

EVALUATING MEASURES

Researchers routinely construct new measures of personality. Of course, some of these measures are better than others. The adequacy of a psychological measure is defined primarily in terms of two fundamental principles of measurement: *reliability* and *validity*.

Reliability

To be useful, a measure must be accurate and dependable. The degree of precision necessary, however, depends on the task at hand. If the purpose is to know the temperature outside (is it cold enough for a coat?), a reading that is accurate to within a few degrees will surely suffice. But when measuring a person's temperature (does the child have a fever?), the acceptable range of error is far smaller. Some microelectronic and nanotechnology applications may require temperature readings that are highly precise. For temperature, weight, length, speed, and a host of other variables, the accuracy of a measure can be evaluated in relation to an exacting standard. Thus, in the early 1900s meters were calibrated against a rod of platinum-iridium kept in a vault at the International Bureau of Weights and Measures in Sevres, France. Today the meter is defined as 1,650,763.73 vacuum wavelengths of monochromatic orange light emitted by a krypton atom of mass 86. This definition is accepted in specialized fields of science requiring exact precision and standardization of length; it provides values that are designated as *true* or perfectly accurate.

Assessing the reliability of psychological constructs, however, is complicated considerably by the fact that the constructs are more abstract and less rigorously defined. There are no internationally established standards against which to compare constructs such as intelligence, leadership, shyness, or conscientiousness. Nevertheless, a comparable measurement model is applied so that personality measures are said to be reliable to the extent that they produce values that reflect a hypothetical *true score;* the more they miss this fictional mark, the greater is their error. But how can one measure proximity to or deviation from a fictional standard?

To estimate reliability, researchers compare various measures or measurements with one another. This approach is analogous to several people trying to decide which of several watches is accurate. In the absence of an external standard, two watches that agree provide some degree of confidence as to the actual time. If the watches do not agree, it is impossible to know which of them is inaccurate. One solution to this dilemma is to consult additional watches. The more watches that agree, the greater the likelihood that the watches that agree are accurate. Five watches, independently set, yet all in close agreement, provide a reasonable degree of certainty. If the watches do not agree exactly, calculating an average across the five should provide a good working estimate of the actual time, assuming that they are not all inaccurate in the same way (too slow or too fast). Averaging a number of imprecise measurements to obtain a more accurate estimate is a common practice in personality research and is called the principle of *aggregation* (Epstein, 1983). This is the rationale for including many items on a personality questionnaire rather than just one. The more items you use to measure a trait, the more likely you are to approximate that trait reliably. The principle is equally true for other modes of measurement; thus, aggregating ratings across observers (modes 4 or 5) or aggregating physiological recordings over time (mode 7) will increase the reliability of these measures.

Therefore, in the realm of personality measurement, reliability is estimated by collecting information at more than one time point, from more than one observer, using more than one version of the instrument, or collecting more than one sample of behavior. These various approaches lead to several different types of reliability:

1. *Test-retest reliability:* Does a measure yield the same value from one moment to the next; is it stable over time? (Example: If I step on this same scale two minutes from now, will it show the same weight?)

2. *Interobserver agreement:* Does a measure yield the same value from one observer to the next; do observers use an instrument in the same way? (Example: Will one English instructor reading my term paper assign the same grade as another reading the same paper?)
3. *Parallel forms:* Does a measure yield the same value as a comparably constructed instrument; is it interchangeable with an alternate form of the instrument? (Example: Would I score the same on different versions of the SAT?)
4. *Internal consistency:* Do the parts of a measure function similarly; are different items or behaviors interrelated? (Example: Is item A on a conscientiousness scale as closely related to the other 20 items on the test as item B?)

Each of these approaches to the assessment of reliability assumes a somewhat different working definition for the concept of reliability. In other words, reliability itself is a construct that can be defined and measured in multiple ways. Although conceptually related, these various measures of reliability do not necessarily yield the same results. Thus, just as it is important to measure a psychological concept in more than one way, it can also be important to measure a *psychometric* concept in more than one way.

Validity

In addition to being accurate, a good measure ought to be useful. Validity has to do with whether using a measure in a particular way to meet a particular need is appropriate. Because there are different kinds of uses for personality measures, it is possible to specify different kinds of validity. Thus, it is technically improper to ask whether a personality measure is generally valid (or useful) because a measure is valid only with respect to some specific use. It is more correct to ask whether there is any evidence to support using a measure in a specific way (to predict success as a leader) or to make a specific kind of inference (that this person is conscientious or shy). In this sense, validity is analogous to a kind of "truth in advertising." In the context of personality measurement, three kinds of validity are usually distinguished (Cronbach & Meehl, 1955).

Criterion Validity   Does a measure predict performance or success on some relevant outcome measure or criterion? Do students who score high on the SATs or ACTs do better in college than those who score low? Did the candidates who were rated highly at the OSS school make better agents and operatives than those who were rated poorly? In both cases the measures are used to screen candidates on the assumption that they can predict future (or even current) behavior. Is this a valid inference?

Content Validity   Does a measure adequately represent all aspects of the variable being studied? Does the final examination in a course systematically sample from all of the material contained in the lectures and the text? Did the seven factors of personality measured in the OSS Assessment Project adequately represent the dimensions that would be important for success in a covert opera-tive? In both cases the assessment procedure is designed to cover the domain of interest in a comprehensive and methodical fashion. Is this a valid inference?

Construct Validity   Does a measure assess the concept or construct that it purports to measure? Does an intelligence test really measure the construct of intelligence? Did the Brook Situation really provide information about an individual's leadership abilities? Recall that the Construction Task, which was originally designed as a test of leadership ability, was later judged to be more a measure of emotional stability. But is this a valid inference? How do we know for sure that this task actually measures either construct?

Construct validity is a difficult concept to grasp as well as a difficult concept to measure for reasons that are not unlike the problem we encountered with reliability. Constructs are abstractions; leadership, conscientiousness, shyness, and other psychological constructs are theoretical ideas rather than tangible objects. We can point to examples of these constructs but we cannot grab hold of the construct itself. Thus, we can establish a working or operational definition (of what leadership is), and we can proceed to measure the construct using specific indicators (taking charge in the Brook Situation or being rated as a leader by one's peers), but how can we be certain that these indicators (or measures) actually assess the theoretical construct of leadership? Any one measure of leadership might be flawed. However, if several different measures all converge on the same answer, then we can be more confident about our measures and about our decision. In other words, we have once again returned to the issue of convergence.

In the OSS Assessment Project, the construct of leadership was assessed in seven different ways. Did these seven different measures provide similar answers? Table 2.3 shows the correlation coefficients among the various measures. Recall from chapter 1 that a *correlation coefficient* is a statistical index of the relationship between two variables that can be interpreted in terms of direction and size. A positive correlation means that the two variables are directly related (e.g., height and weight); higher scores on one measure are associated with higher scores on the other as well. A negative correlation means that the variables are inversely related; higher scores on one measure are associated with lower scores on the other. The size of a correlation ranges from 0 to 1.0. As the size approaches 1.0, the relationship becomes stronger—changes in one variable are closely linked to changes in the other. As the size approaches 0, the two variables become increasingly unrelated or independent.

The correlations in Table 2.3 are all positive and mostly in the .3 to .5 range. This indicates that the various measures are at least moderately related, and it increases our confidence that something like leadership is being measured. Of course, many of these ratings were made by the same team of observers on the OSS Assessment Staff, so perhaps the moderate agreement is partly due to a tendency for the raters to be consistent with themselves. If an observer believes that a candidate showed leadership in the Brook Situation, that observer might be more inclined to perceive similar leadership characteristics in that candidate in other contexts. When various measures are related to one another and they all derive from the same mode of measurement, the positive correlation may be due

Table 2.3 | Intercorrelations Among the Measures of Leadership

	Brook Situation	Construction Task	Discussion	Debate	Assigned Leadership Tasks	Sociometric Ratings	Clinical Interview
Brook Situation	—	.37	.47	.41	.42	.41	.57
Construction Task	.37	—	.30	.33	.33	.24	.44
Discussion	.47	.30	—	.56	.37	.41	.48
Debate	.41	.33	.56	—	.39	.52	.47
Assigned Leadership Tasks	.42	.33	.37	.39	—	.37	.53
Sociometric Ratings	.41	.24	.41	.52	.37	—	.54
Clinical Interview	.57	.44	.48	.47	.53	.54	—

to the method and not the construct. This artifact is called *method variance*. One way to avoid this confound is to use other modes of measurement; in this case, the sociometric peer ratings would be an example. Disentangling constructs from methods is an important part of establishing a measure's construct validity (Campbell & Fiske, 1959). As we will see in the next section, using multiple methods to measure multiple trait constructs simultaneously provides us with a strategy for disentangling methods and traits.

CLASSIFYING CONCEPTS AND MEASURES

Researchers in the field of personality have studied hundreds of variables using literally thousands of self-report inventories, observational rating forms, and behavioral indices. A researcher who initiates a new study is faced with the daunting prospect of having to choose from this jumble of variables and measure the traits that are best suited for his or her specific project. Of course, these many variables and measures are not equally important or independent. Many overlap in substantial ways. It would be advantageous to know how these various constructs and measures are related to one another; in other words, it would be helpful to have a *taxonomy* of personality trait variables.

A taxonomy is a systematic and orderly classification of variables according to their presumed natural relationships. In biology, Linné studied the morphological features of animals and plants and classified them into groups or categories (e.g., phylum, genus, and species). In chemistry, Mendeleyev observed regularities in the properties of various elements as a function of their atomic numbers and charted the Periodic Table. In the field of personality, researchers have studied attributes of people in an attempt to identify a set of primary or fundamental dimensions of personality.

The most methodical and extensive efforts to develop categories of personality variables have been based on the study of words that people use to describe others and themselves; this is called the *psycholexical* approach to the study of personality taxonomy (Goldberg, 1981; John, Angleitner, & Ostendorf, 1988). This approach will be presented in some depth in chapter 7 by McCrae.

In the psycholexical approach to taxonomy, each observer rates the extent to which a set of trait adjectives, typically 20 to 100 terms, is similar or dissimilar to one or more "target" individuals. For example, a study might involve 100 men, each of whom is rated on 60 adjectives by his wife. This *matrix of observations* (60 ratings for each of 100 men) is then analyzed in terms of whether certain adjectives are used similarly and can therefore be grouped or clustered together. Intuitively, we might expect people who are described as quiet also to be described as shy and perceptive but not as outgoing or assertive. These intuitions can be evaluated empirically by calculating pairs of correlation coefficients. Terms that are used similarly by most raters will show large positive correlations, whereas antonyms will be negatively correlated. Two terms that have little in common will have a correlation of near zero.

Each adjective can be correlated with every other adjective to form a *matrix of correlations*. In the example of 100 men rated by their wives on 60 adjectives, each of the adjectives can be correlated with each of the other adjectives to form a 60 × 60 matrix of correlations: Adjective 1 would be correlated with adjectives 2, 3, 4, and so on out to adjective 60, then adjective 2 would be correlated with adjectives 3, 4, 5, and so on out to adjective 60, and so it would go for all 60 terms. This matrix would contain 1,770 nonredundant correlation coefficients. Perhaps it would be possible to make sense out of this massive matrix of correlations if one studied it long enough, but fortunately there are ways to mathematically evaluate and simplify this set of data through a procedure called *factor analysis*. Although this procedure involves rather elaborate statistical algorithms, the logic of it is reasonably straightforward. Factor analysis attempts to identify a small number of hypothetical factors or dimensions that will account for the relationships among a larger number of items (in this case, the adjectives). Each factor will be defined by its relationship with a subset of adjectives. Some adjectives will be highly related to a factor and some will not. The strength of the relationship between an adjective and a hypothetical factor is described by a *factor loading* that is similar to a correlation coefficient.

Consider, for example, the *matrix of factor loadings* presented in Table 2.4. These findings are derived from peer ratings of a large group of men and women who have participated in a research project that began in the late 1950s (McCrae & Costa, 1987). The column on the left lists pairs of adjectives that raters used to describe friends who are serving as participants in the Baltimore Longitudinal Study of Aging. In this case, the factor analytic results suggest that this list of adjectives could be described more simply in terms of five basic factors. Factor 1 is defined primarily by the first four adjective pairs: sociable–retiring, affectionate–reserved, talkative–quiet, and warm–cold. These adjective pairs all

Table 2.4 | Factor Loadings of Adjective Pairs in a Sample of Peer Ratings by Friends (*N* = 738)

| Adjective Pairs | s | Factors | | | |
	I	II	III	IV	V
Sociable–retiring	**.71**	.08	.08	−.14	.08
Affectionate–reserved	**.65**	.25	−.15	−.08	.12
Talkative–quiet	**.64**	−.19	.00	.01	.06
Warm–cold	**.57**	**.54**	.06	−.05	.09
Softhearted–ruthless	.27	**.70**	.11	.12	−.01
Forgiving–vengeful	.11	**.70**	.16	−.15	.07
Selfless–selfish	−.02	**.65**	.22	−.07	.04
Good-natured–irritable	.34	**.61**	.16	−.17	.09
Careful–careless	−.07	.11	**.72**	−.08	−.01
Reliable–undependable	.04	.23	**.68**	.14	.05
Well-organized–disorganized	−.02	−.05	**.68**	.14	.05
Hardworking–lazy	.17	.03	**.66**	−.07	.14
Calm–worrying	−.05	.20	−.05	**−.79**	.01
At ease–nervous	.08	.21	.05	**−.77**	.06
Relaxed–high-strung	−.04	.34	.02	**−.66**	.01
Secure–insecure	.16	−.07	.39	**−.63**	.08
Original–conventional	.12	.08	−.04	−.06	**.67**
Creative–uncreative	.09	.11	.25	−.08	**.56**
Imaginative–down-to-earth	.03	−.10	−.12	.16	**.54**
Broad interest–narrow interests	.20	.18	.27	−.15	**.52**

Loadings above .4 are printed in **bold.** Positive loadings signify a positive relationship with the adjective on the left; negative loadings indicate a relationship with the adjective on the right.

have large loadings on the first factor (greater than .55), whereas most of the other adjective pairs have loadings of less than .20 on this factor. In the same way, each of the other factors is defined by a set of four pairs of adjectives. Although each factor represents a hypothetical entity, that entity can be defined in part by the items that are highly related to it. These high factor loadings share something in common that is not shared with the near-zero loadings. It is up to each investigator to decide how to interpret what the high loading items share in common. Notice that in a few cases (e.g., warm–cold and good-natured–irritable) the adjective pairs load above .3 on two different factors. These dual loadings suggest that the adjective pairs are related to and help to define both Factor 1 and Factor 2.

The five basic factors represented in Table 2.4 have emerged repeatedly from analyses of peer ratings in a variety of samples: air force officers and cadets, fraternity brothers, Peace Corps trainees, and spouses. These five factors can also be replicated in self-ratings using adjectives and in personality questionnaires (Briggs, 1992). These five factors (sometimes called the "Big Five") are generally assigned the following labels:

1. Extraverted or Socially Surgent Versus Introverted
2. Agreeable or Likable Versus Antagonistic
3. Conscientious Versus Negligent
4. Emotionally Stable Versus Emotionally Unstable or Neurotic
5. Inquiring Intellect or Open to Experience Versus Closed to Experience

The importance of this five-factor structure, and the evidence supporting its stability and universality, will be reviewed in chapter 7 by McCrae.

Reducing the enormous number of trait descriptors in the English language to a small number of useful dimensions is an important achievement in the search for a taxonomy of personality variables. These five factors provide us with a basic framework for describing how people think about others and themselves. This framework qualifies as a significant advance for several reasons (Briggs, 1989). First, it provides a structure for researchers to use when constructing rating scales and self-report measures of personality; it helps to ensure that the domain of personality trait terms will be sampled broadly and systematically, and thereby serves to enhance the content validity of these measures. Second, it allows us to locate the seemingly endless supply of new constructs and measures in relation to what is already known; it clarifies the relations between what is new and what is established, and it exposes areas of needless redundancy. Third, it enables us to generate more precise hypotheses when attempting to relate personality variables to other constructs and measures. And finally, it suggests that these five dimensions deserve special attention in the continuing search for the mechanisms underlying individual differences in personality.

Although this five-factor model of the structure of personality ratings has emerged reliably across a number of studies and methods, it is also important to examine how these dimensions stand up when different modes of measurement are compared and contrasted. For example, Costa and McCrae (1985) have developed the NEO Personality Inventory, which measures the five basic factors along with a number of more narrowly defined constructs. To evaluate the validity of their measure and the five-factor model more generally, they have collected a variety of kinds of information on the individuals participating in the Baltimore Longitudinal Study of Aging mentioned earlier. The correlations presented in Table 2.5 compare self-reports on the NEO Personality Inventory with ratings by spouses and with the average rating of several peers on a parallel version of the inventory.

The correlation coefficients in this table represent two important kinds of validity coefficients. The ones in bold that run diagonally through the table are called *convergent validity coefficients;* the rest of the correlations are *discriminant validity coefficients.* Convergent validity means that the correlation

Table 2.5 | Correlations of Self-Reports with Spouse and Peer Ratings Using the Five-Factor Model

	Self-reported Factors				
Spouse Ratings	I	II	III	IV	V
I Extraversion	**.53**	.18	−.01	.09	.07
II Agreeableness	.14	**.60**	.03	.03	.09
III Conscientiousness	−.23	.15	**.57**	−.05	−.06
IV Neuroticism	.03	.18	−.01	**.53**	−.10
V Openness	−.11	.00	−.06	−.07	**.59**
Average of Peer Ratings					
I Extraversion	**.47**	.02	.02	−.04	−.25
II Agreeableness	−.25	**.30**	−.12	−.12	.03
III Conscientiousness	−.02	.08	**.43**	−.14	.08
IV Neuroticism	−.02	.11	.14	**.42**	−.02
V Openness	.13	.02	−.13	.03	**.57**

Convergent validity coefficients are printed in **bold**. Correlations in upper half of table are based on $N = 144$; for the lower half, $N = 255$ to 267.

coefficient is assessing the relationship between two variables that are conceptually the same (e.g., both scales measure Extraversion) even though one is a self-report and the other a peer or spouse rating. In contrast, the discriminant validity coefficients reported in this table measure different constructs (e.g., the correlation between Extraversion and Agreeableness) using either the same or different observers. Ideally, the convergent validity coefficients should be large relative to the discriminant validity coefficients. This holds true for each type of comparison. Self-reported Extraversion correlates .53 with the spouse's rating and .44 with the average rating across several peers, but is relatively uncorrelated with the spouse's ratings of the other four dimensions (the next highest correlation is −.23 with Conscientiousness) or with the average ratings of several peers for the other four dimensions (the highest correlation is −.25 with Agreeableness). This same pattern holds across the various scales and observers and suggests that individuals and informed observers agree about what is meant by these five personality dimensions as measured by the NEO Personality Inventory.

The use of multiple methods or modes (self, spouse, and peer rating) to measure multiple traits (the five factors) in a single study is an especially incisive strategy for disentangling constructs and methods of measurement. The matrix of correlation coefficients produced in a study of this kind is called a *multitrait-multimethod matrix* (Campbell & Fiske, 1959), and it provides an important means by which to establish the construct validity of a measure. In other words, the multitrait-multimethod matrix provides an important tool for ascertaining whether a construct measures what it purports to measure, as demonstrated through convergence with dissimilar measures of that same construct and divergence with similar measures of different constructs.

THINKING ABOUT PERSONALITY MEASUREMENT

Psychology as a science is characterized by two, broad strategies of research: *experimental* and *correlational* (Cronbach, 1957). The experimental approach emphasizes manipulation and control. The experimenter is interested primarily in changes that he or she has produced. The experimenter studies how manipulating a particular variable or treatment condition (the *independent* variable) changes behavior, attitudes, thoughts, or feelings (the *dependent* variable or outcome measure). In its most straightforward form, the experiment contrasts participants in a treatment condition with those in a control condition. Ideally the participants in the two conditions would be exactly the same before the treatment. Any individual variation that exists naturally prior to the manipulation is a potential problem that should be avoided or minimized.

Ironically, it is this individual variation that is of primary interest to the correlational researcher. The correlationist emphasizes the variation that occurs normally among individuals, between groups, between the genders, and across species. The correlational approach does not necessarily rely on the correlation coefficient as its statistical index, and another common name for this approach is *differential* psychology.

Personality research by and large is located in the correlational tradition. Personality variables involve "naturally" occurring, enduring differences among people, and there is no way to manipulate characteristics of this sort experimentally. Furthermore, it would be unethical to study personality as a dependent variable—that is, to manipulate a person's life experiences to determine their impact on his or her personality—except perhaps in the case of psychotherapy in which an individual wishes for certain changes to occur. Many important questions can only be studied looking over the course of a person's life (Block, 1971; Caspi, 1998; Caspi & Roberts, 1999). Thus, in the science of personality, the emphasis is more on careful measurement than on rigorous manipulation. Researchers study individual differences in relation to the three important kinds of questions mentioned early in this chapter.

- The question of *structure*—What are the basic components or dimensions of personality and how are they related to one another?
- The question of *ontogeny*—What are the origins of an individual's personality, and how do these attributes emerge and change over time?
- The question of *prediction*—What can we infer about future behavior given what we know now about an individual's enduring psychological and physiological characteristics?

Remember that measurement is a means to an end, and that it is useful only in proportion to what it allows us to understand or accomplish. The subsequent chapters in this book focus on a variety of issues related to the study of enduring personality characteristics. The information presented is grounded on the principles of conceptualization and measurement that have been introduced in this chapter. At times, it may be easy to overlook the fact that the various concepts and ideas are always tied to specific measures that may or may not be adequate. In evaluating the various ideas and arguments, it is important to examine the measures with a critical eye. Question the assumptions! Do the researchers establish the reliability and validity of their measures? Have they used multiple modes of measurement?

Within the field of personality, researchers often disagree with regard to such fundamental issues as the appropriate mode of measurement (e.g., self-report or behavioral indices), the unit of analysis (e.g., traits or motives as the variables), and the level of analysis (e.g., broad or narrow). Some researchers even argue that the approach taken in this chapter is misguided and unhelpful because it focuses on how individuals differ from one another rather than on patterns of responses that occur within an individual (Lamiell, 1997; Runyan, 1997). As you learn more about these competing ideas and approaches, you will have to decide for yourself which of them make the most sense and which offer the most compelling evidence.

SUMMARY

Formal methods for assessing personality arose out of practical concerns such as identifying individuals who would be productive, who would handle stress well, or who would get along with others in a group. The goal of personality assessment is to identify a relevant variable or personal characteristic, to define it unambiguously, and to devise a way to measure it that is consistent with the definition. The process of defining a characteristic is called conceptualization, and the process of choosing appropriate measures is called operationalization. Both processes push researchers toward clarity and precision as they define their concepts in terms of tangible indicators. Typically, the researcher assigns a number or value to represent an individual's standing on a particular variable in terms of a standard unit of measurement.

Personality characteristics are generally complex, and no one method or measure can represent adequately the richness and diversity of these concepts. Any particular indicator will be subject to specific flaws, biases, and shortcomings. The best way around these limitations is to use multiple indicators involving different methods and perspectives. The more varied the methods and perspectives, the more likely it is that problems and weaknesses will be balanced out and the concept measured in a full and fair manner. Common modes of measurement include self-report trait inventories, subjective or objective ratings by peers, measures of behavior, and physiological measures. A multi-method, multiperspective approach to measurement enables a researcher to examine whether the concept looks the same from different angles. If diverse measures agree, the researcher has more confidence in the results. Convergence among measures is one way of demonstrating that the various indicators are in fact measuring the desired concept.

The adequacy of a measure is evaluated in several ways. Reliability indexes estimate how much error has occurred when an individual is assigned a particular value on a measure. The higher the reliability, the more accurate are the assigned values. A measure is said to be valid to the extent that there is evidence to support a particular claim or inference. Convergent validity involves showing meaningful correlations among measures that should be related conceptually. Discriminant validity involves showing the absence of a relationship between measures that are conceptually distinct. Construct validity requires evidence that an indicator (or set of indicators) actually measures a specific concept or construct. Criterion validity requires evidence that an indicator will predict scores on a particular criterion or outcome measure.

Although the number of potential personality variables is enormous, researchers have studied the words people use to describe others and themselves in order to develop a systematic way to classify personality traits. The most widely accepted taxonomy of personality descriptors is the five-factor model that was derived from factor analyses of peer ratings. A matrix of observations by peers is summarized in terms of a matrix of correlations among the observations, which in turn is reduced to a matrix of factor loadings. Each hypothetical factor is defined by its relationship (or correlation) with the originally observed variables. This model of the major factors of personality is statistically derived and has emerged consistently in a variety of samples. These five factors provide a useful means by which to describe the major categories of personality traits.

Being able to measure aspects of an individual's personality enables researchers to test their ideas. Hypothesis testing is central to the process of scientific inquiry, and thus personality measurement provides the basis for the scientific study of personality.

DISCUSSION QUESTIONS

1. Jim Collins describes "level five leaders" as a "study in duality: modest and willful, humble and fearless." Suppose you are working for consulting firm and a company asks you to provide its senior executives with feedback regarding whether they are on their way to becoming level five leaders. What process would you follow? What kinds of measures would you attempt to develop? How would you deal with this idea of "duality"?

2. Studies have shown that conscientiousness is a consistent predictor of job performance (Barrick & Mount, 1991). Based on your analysis of the concept of conscientiousness (from Activity Box 2.1), how might conscientiousness be related to important dimensions of job performance such as oral communication, planning, delegation, supervision, decisiveness, initiative, adaptability, tenacity, and tolerance for stress (Thornton, 1992)?

3. Two of the standard exercises in an Assessment Center are a Leaderless Group Discussion (participants meet as a group without any assigned roles and discuss some issue of common concern) and an In-Basket Exercise (participants have to process a collection of materials, some urgent and

some routine, that have accumulated in the in-basket of a manager who is away from the office). Are these exercises valid measures of personality? If so, for which traits? How could you demonstrate the validity of these measures to an independent observer (e.g., an administrative law judge)?

4. Why is *convergence* a critical concept in establishing the validity of a measure? What are some examples of convergence? How is convergence related to a multitrait-multimethod matrix?

5. Chapter 1 introduced several well known and thoroughly studied personality concepts: authoritarianism, narcissism, and field independence. What are some specific, observable indicators for each of these concepts? How do you think each of the concepts fits into the five factor model?

SUGGESTED READINGS

Briggs, S. R. (1992). Assessing the five factor model of personality description. *Journal of Personality, 60*, 253–293. A closer examination of the various methods for assessing the five factor model of personality, with an evaluation of the strengths and weaknesses of these different approaches.

De Raad, B., & Perugini, M. (Eds.). (2002). *Big Five assessment.* Gottingen, Germany: Hogrefe & Huber Publishers. A comprehensive look at assessment issues related to the five-factor model.

Fiske, D. W. (1971). *Measuring the concepts of personality.* Chicago: Aldine. A classic and still useful introduction to the study of personality by one of the key participants in the OSS Assessment Project. Fiske provides a broad-minded look at personality measurement, posing questions and discussing issues in a refreshingly down-to-earth manner.

Hough, L. M., & Oswald, F. L. (2000). Personnel selection: Looking toward the future—remembering the past. *Annual Review of Psychology, 51*, 631–644. The authors provide a review of the recent literature connecting personality predictors to job performance.

John, O. P., & Srivastava, S. (1999). The big five trait taxonomy: History, measurement, and theoretical perspectives. In L. A. Pervin & O. P. John (Eds.), *Handbook of personality: Theory and research* (pp. 102–138). New York: Guilford. A careful history of the development of the five-factor model and the lines of research that converged on this solution.

Ozer, D. J. (1999). Four principles for personality assessment. In L. A. Pervin & O. P. John (Eds.), *Handbook of personality: Theory and research* (pp. 671–686). New York: Guilford. This chapter provides a deeper analysis of construct validity and offers four principles for constructing and evaluating personality measures.

West, S. B., & Finch, J. F. (1997). Personality measurement: Reliability and validity issues. In R. Hogan, J. Johnson, & S. R. Briggs (Eds.), *Handbook of personality psychology* (pp. 143–146). San Diego: Academic Press. This brief but thoughtful chapter provides a deeper look at the fundamental principles involved in personality assessment. It provides an excellent collection of references for further reading and study.

SUGGESTED WEB SITES

http://pmc.psych.nwu.edu/personality.htm

The personality project web site is maintained by William Revelle, a personality psychologist at Northwestern University, offers a comprehensive set of links to other sites. The site includes a list of readings on assessment and on personality taxonomies.

http://vrnet.ori.org/

The international personality item pool web site is a "scientific collaboratory" maintained by Lew Goldberg at the Oregon Research Institute. The web site provides access to personality items and measures that are in the public domain.

http://trochim.human.cornell.edu/

Bill Trochim, a public policy researcher at Cornell University, maintains a web site for social research methods. It includes a number of interesting sections, the most relevant of which is labeled research methods tutorials. This section has tutorials on measurement, construct validity, reliability, and the multitrait-multimethod matrix.

http://www.socialpsychology.org/ptexts.htm

The social psychology network, maintained by Scott Plous at Wesleyan University, provides a list of links to personality textbooks.

http://www.uic.edu/depts/psch/conference/mission.htm

The web site for the Association for Research in Personality (ARP), a new scientific organization for scholars whose research contributes to the understanding of personality structure, development, and dynamics.

http://www.jimcollins.com

Jim Collins, author of *Built to Last* and *Good to Great* maintains this web site to provide additional resources for those interested in his research on enduring great companies.

INFOTRAC COLLEGE EDITION SEARCH TOPICS

Conceptualization

Convergence

Reliability

Validity

Aggregation

Predictor

Outcome

Correlation

Factor analysis

Multitrait-multimethod matrix

REFERENCES

Barrick, M. R., & Mount, M. K. (1991). The big five personality dimensions and job performance: A meta-analysis. *Personnel Psychology, 44,* 1–26.

Block, J. (1971). *Lives through time.* Berkeley, CA: Bancroft.

Bray, D. W. (1982). The assessment center and the study of lives. *American Psychologist, 37,* 180–189.

Briggs, S. R. (1989). The optimal level of measurement for personality constructs. In D. Buss & N. Cantor (Eds.), *Personality research for the 1990s* (pp. 246–260). New York: Springer-Verlag.

Briggs, S. R. (1992). Assessing the five factor model of personality description. *Journal of Personality, 60,* 253–293.

Buss, A. H. (1961). *The psychology of aggression.* New York: Wiley.

Campbell, D. T., & Fiske, D. W. (1959). Convergent and discriminant validity by the multitrait-multimethod matrix. *Psychological Bulletin, 56,* 81–105.

Caspi, A. (1998). Personality development across the life course. In N. Eisenberg (Ed.), *Handbook of child psychology* (pp. 311–388). New York: Wiley.

Caspi, A., & Roberts, B. W. (1999). Personality continuity and change across the life course. In L. A. Pervin & O. P. John (Eds.), *Handbook of personality: Theory and research* (pp. 300–326). New York: Guilford.

Chaplin, W. F., John, O. P., & Goldberg, L. R. (1988). Conceptions of states and traits: Dimensional attributes with ideals as prototypes. *Journal of Personality and Social Psychology, 54,* 541–557.

Collins, J. C. (2001). *Good to great.* New York: HarperBusiness.

Collins, J. C., & Porras, J. I. (1994). *Built to last.* New York: HarperBusiness.

Costa, P. T., Jr., & McCrae, R. R. (1985). *The NEO Personality Inventory manual.* Odessa, FL: Psychological Assessment Resources.

Cronbach, L. J. (1957). The two disciplines of scientific psychology. *American Psychologist, 12,* 671–684.

Cronbach, L. J., & Meehl, P. E. (1955). Construct validity in psychological tests. *Psychological Bulletin, 52,* 281–302.

Epstein, S. (1983). Aggregation and beyond: Some basic issues in the prediction of behavior. *Journal of Personality, 51,* 360–392.

Fiske, D. W. (1971), *Measuring the concepts of personality*. Chicago: Aldine.

Fleeson, W. (2001). Toward a structure- and process-integrated view of personality: Traits as density distributions of states. *Journal of Personality and Social Psychology, 80*, 1011–1027.

Funder, D. C. (1999). *Personality judgment*. San Diego: Academic Press.

Garcia, S., Stinson, L., Ickes, W., Bissonnette, V., & Briggs, S. R. (1991). Shyness and physical attractiveness in mixed-sex dyads. *Journal of Personality and Social Psychology, 61*, 35–49.

Goldberg, L. (1981). Language and individual differences: The search for universals in personality lexicons. In L. Wheeler (Ed.), *Review of personality and social psychology* (Vol. 2, pp. 141–165). Beverly Hills, CA: Sage.

John, O. P., Angleitner, A., & Ostendorf, F. (1988). The lexical approach to personality: A historical review of trait taxonomic research. *European Journal of Personality, 2*, 171–203.

Kaplan, A. (1964). *The conduct of inquiry: Methodology for behavioral science*. San Francisco: Chandler.

Lamiell, J. T. (1997). Individuals and the differences between them. In R. Hogan, J. Johnson, & S. R. Briggs (Eds.), *Handbook of personality psychology* (pp. 117–141). San Diego: Academic Press.

McCrae, R. R., & Costa, P. T., Jr. (1987). Validation of the five-factor model of personality across instruments and observers. *Journal of Personality and Social Psychology, 52*, 81–90.

Paulhus, D. L. (1986). Self-deception and impression management in test responses. In A. Angleitner & J. S. Wiggins (Eds.), *Personality assessment via questionnaire: Current issues in theory and measurement* (pp. 143–165). Berlin: Springer-Verlag.

Runyan, W. M. (1997). Studying lives: Psychobiography and the conceptual structure of personality psychology. In R. Hogan, J. Johnson, & S. R. Briggs (Eds.), *Handbook of personality psychology* (pp. 41–69). San Diego: Academic Press.

Task Force on Assessment Center Standards. (1989). Guidelines and ethical considerations for assessment center operations. *Public Personnel Management, 18*, 457–471.

Thornton, G. C. III. (1992). *Assessment centers in human resource management*. Reading, MA: Addison-Wesley.

U.S. Office of Strategic Services. (1948). *Assessment of men: Selection of personnel for the office of strategic services*. New York: Rinehart.

Willerman, L., Turner, R. G., & Peterson, M. (1976). A comparison of the predictive validity of typical and maximal personality measures. *Journal of Research in Personality, 10*, 482–492.

Witkin, H. A., Lewis, H. B., Hertzman, M., Machover, K., Meissner, P. B., & Wapner, S. (1954). *Personality through perception*. New York: Harper and Row.

Genetic and Environmental Influences

3

DAVID C. ROWE

EDWIN J. C. G. VAN DEN OORD

CHAPTER OUTLINE

When they were reunited at age 39 years, the famous "Jim twins"—Jim Lewis and Jim Springer, identical twins separated at birth and raised by different families—discovered a trail of amazing coincidences. Comparing their lives, they learned of their common interest in woodworking; of their common experiences in school, such as liking math and disliking spelling; of their similar jobs as part-time security guards; and of a common medical problem, migraine headaches. A string of name coincidences also connected the pair; they had married first wives named Linda and second wives named Betty; they named their sons James Alan and James Allen; and their dogs, Toy. They had vacationed on the same three-block long beach in Florida. A search by one of the twins led to their reunion. At the very least, these coincidences are uncanny; at most, they are an indication of how heredity (and coincidence) can make people born with identical genetic constitutions alike, despite rearing in different families, unknown to one another. These twins are among 44 pairs currently enrolled in Thomas Bouchard's study of twins raised apart (Tellegen, Lykken, Bouchard, Wilcox, Segal, & Rich, 1988). They join several hundred adult Swedish twins raised in different families, but with various degrees of separation (Pedersen, McClearn, Plomin, & Friberg, 1985), in a modern investigation of the lives of twins who were reared apart. The purpose of this chapter is to explore the evidence surrounding the idea that personality and intellectual traits have partly genetic origins. Later in the chapter, we will return to a study of twins raised apart to learn what it can teach us about hereditary influences on traits and to place the results in the broader context of the field of *behavioral genetics*.

HISTORY

Behavioral genetics is a scientific discipline, with roots in psychology, genetics, biology, and related fields, that explores the empirical evidence on the *nurture* (meaning environment) versus *nature* (meaning heredity) debate. The term *nature–nurture debate* refers to an argument that is older than the discipline of psychology itself—a debate over whether personality traits result from genetic constitution or from environmental influence, or, if from some combination of them, how they combine and in what amounts. Even in antiquity people had some evidence for the "nature" side—namely, the regularity with which dogs could be bred for a variety of temperamental traits. Nothing particular in handling or conditions of rearing seemed to distinguish a retriever from a sheepdog, but it was clear that these behavioral tendencies ran in the dogs' bloodlines and that they could be further modified by mating the right sets of parents. Nevertheless, human personality traits might be environmental in origin: the importance of child rearing as a molder of personality appears in scholarly writings from the Renaissance to the present.

FRANCIS GALTON: FOUNDER OF BEHAVIORAL GENETICS

Behavioral genetics did not arise as a distinguishable scientific discipline until the mid-1800s. Francis Galton was directly responsible for founding behavioral genetics. An inventive man with diverse interests, he identified and labeled pressure bars in meteorology and created the correlation coefficient statistic to quantify familial resemblances for physical and behavioral traits. He invented the questionnaire-method of collecting data, and he anticipated that it might become something of an annoyance if overused. He traveled through Africa during the time of European exploration and wrote a best-seller entitled *The Art of Travel*, giving practical advice to Europeans who might want to venture into the then mysterious continent of Africa.

His contribution to behavioral genetics was to frame the question about genetic influences in terms of individual differences and to propose practical methods by which the nature–nurture question could be studied scientifically. Galton's interest was, foremost, in human differences in intellectual ability. Fancher (1985) has speculated that Galton's fascination with this question may have had a source in a personal frustration. Despite being something of a child prodigy, as an undergraduate at the prestigious Cambridge University Galton was unable to attain the top score on a rigorous examination in mathematics on which all students were ranked. Although probably disappointed, Galton did not lose the opportunity to observe that an enormous range of individual differences existed in mathematical performance: the gap between the top place finishers and the remainder of students was often huge. Galton—possibly from his personal efforts—thought that even with the most grueling training mathematical ability, like physical strength, could only be improved to a certain limit. Beyond that, the remaining individual differences would reflect inborn differences in intellectual capacity and talent.

Galton made several clever proposals for demonstrating the suspected hereditary influence on intellectual abilities. His first design was a *family study* of "eminence"—great accomplishment in a field of human endeavor. The family study method involves tracing personality traits through blood relatives. Because relatives are genetically alike, they should show some resemblance for biologically inherited traits. In his book *Hereditary Genius*, Galton (1869) listed the names of people in the *pedigrees*—the family trees—of chosen individuals who were eminent as judges, statesmen, commanders, literary men, men of science, poets, artists, and clergy (his own younger half-cousin, Charles Darwin, was included). Galton noted the percentage of these immediate relatives of eminent people who themselves had eminent accomplishments. Figure 3.1 presents one such family pedigree from Galton's book. He then compared this percentage with the percentage of all Englishmen (men only because 19th-century biographies and newspaper accounts of famous individuals were most often about men) who were eminent. The latter figure was quite low; Galton estimated that no more than 250 in each million Englishmen had made such an outstanding accomplishment as to be "eminent," a standing perhaps equal to that of people featured in *Time* cover stories today. Among fathers, brothers, and sons of eminent men, however, as many as 31% to 48% of these relatives were themselves eminent. Eminence was passed on in families Galton decided, and he regarded this as the solid proof he needed of biological inheritance of intellectual and temperamental traits.

Galton was, however, aware of a problem with the family method—namely, the confounding of hereditary and family environmental treatments. Biological relatives usually shared greater wealth and social advantage than

Figure 3.1 | Pedigree of a family from Francis Galton's *Hereditary Genius.*

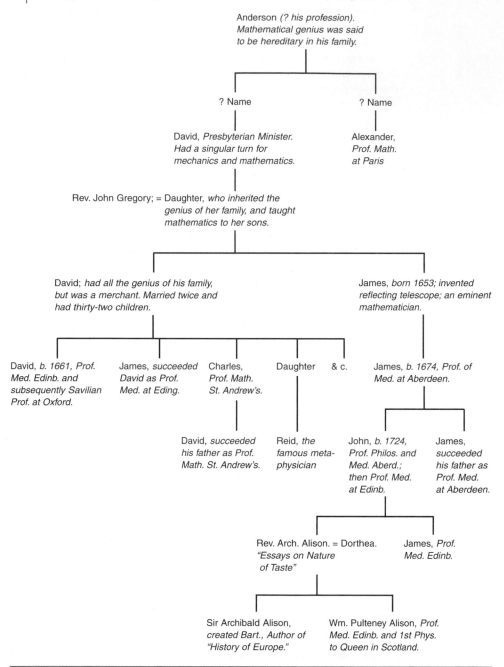

Anderson *(? his profession).*
Mathematical genius was said
to be hereditary in his family.

? Name

? Name

David, *Presbyterian Minister.*
Had a singular turn for
mechanics and mathematics.

Alexander,
Prof. Math.
at Paris

Rev. John Gregory; = Daughter, *who inherited the*
genius of her family, and taught
mathematics to her sons.

David; *had all the genius of his family,*
but was a merchant. Married twice and
had thirty-two children.

James, *born 1653; invented*
reflecting telescope; an eminent
mathematician.

David, *b. 1661, Prof.*
Med. Edinb. and
subsequently Savilian
Prof. at Oxford.

James, *succeeded*
David as Prof.
Med. at Eding.

Charles,
Prof. Math.
St. Andrew's.

Daughter

& c.

James, *b. 1674, Prof. of*
Med. at Aberdeen.

David, *succeeded*
his father as Prof.
Math. St. Andrew's.

Reid, *the*
famous meta-
physician

John, *b. 1724,*
Prof. Philos. and
Med. Aberd.;
then Prof. Med.
at Edinb.

James,
succeeded
his father as
Prof. Med.
at Aberdeen.

Rev. Arch. Alison. = Dorthea.
"Essays on Nature
of Taste"

James, *Prof.*
Med. Edinb.

Sir Archibald Alison,
created Bart., Author of
"History of Europe."

Wm. Pulteney Alison, *Prof.*
Med. Edinb. and 1st Phys.
to Queen in Scotland.

other Englishmen. Therefore, they may have acquired the traits to make their outstanding intellectual and social accomplishments from these favorable family environments. Galton replied with the invention of yet another method to study the nature–nurture question: the adoption study method. He proposed looking at the eminence of the adopted sons of Italian Roman Catholic clergy. They had social advantages but none of the biological advantages of his English comparison group. In accord with his belief, the adoptees were not eminent; environmental advantage did not appear to be the key to eminence. Galton admitted, however, that his Italian kinships had not been studied with the same thoroughness as the English ones.

The last method Galton invented was the twin study method. He noted that there were two kinds of twins—twins who appeared physically alike at birth and twins who were physically different. Based on questionnaires and biographical materials, he discovered that the twins who were unalike at birth had remained unalike both in personality and appearance in adulthood; in other words, rearing environments were unable to overcome their initial differences. In contrast, he found enduring personality similarity for the physically alike twins. This was the first twin study using the research design of comparing identical and fraternal twins.

In his will, Galton made his final contribution to behavioral genetics. He left money to the University of London to establish a chair in eugenics. A succession of distinguished scientists have occupied this chair, including Karl Pearson, who perfected Galton's correlation coefficient (hence, "Pearson correlation"), and Ronald A. Fisher, the outstanding statistician and geneticist. The word *eugenics* (meaning well born) describes another of Galton's intellectual legacies. Galton argued that the human race could be improved by encouraging intellectually bright and able people to marry and have large families. With graver consequences, he also advocated restricting the reproduction of the less able. In Europe's darkest hours of World War II, the Nazis took eugenics well beyond its original meaning with their philosophy of racial superiority and with their program of extermination carried out primarily against the Jewish people but also against Gypsies and other groups in German society. This history of the abuse of genetics—in which genetic principles were distorted to serve political aims—is a sadly tragic one. Scientists and citizens have a responsibility to oppose inaccurate or oversimplified renderings of scientific principles, be they genetic or environmental such as the use of Lysenko's theory in the former Soviet Union assuming that the heredity of organisms could be changed by changing the environment, and to oppose their abuse in the political arena.

MODERN BEHAVIORAL GENETICS: FOUNDATIONS

Modern behavioral genetics has gone far beyond Galton's beginnings. Workers in the field today, like Galton, are interested in the genetic bases of personality traits. As he did, they use the family, twin, and adoption study methods to separate genetic and family-environmental influences on behavior. At the same time, some new aims are apparent. Using the techniques of molecular genetics and new advances in statistics, researchers are trying to find the specific genes that influence behavior.

Another direction taken by human behavioral geneticists is analyzing environmental influences. One theme of this chapter is that without making provision for genetic influences, one cannot properly gauge environmental ones. Theories in psychology can be flawed if genetic influences are misinterpreted as environmental. An example is that many researchers have attributed children's authoritarianism, a personality trait characterized by a belief that authority and tradition are always right, to the social influence of parental role models. We will see later that this is an unfounded attribution.

The balance of this section will present some fundamental concepts in the study of the nature–nurture question. We can then explore the contribution of heredity to normal traits and abnormal traits, and also to trait variation often interpreted as environmental.

Single Gene Versus Polygenic Traits

Although many discoveries in genetics were made in the first half of the 20th century, one of the greatest bearing was made in 1953 by James Watson and Francis Crick. In a two-page paper published in *Nature*, they announced the structure of the DNA (deoxyribose nucleic acid) molecule, the bearer of heredity. Although we cannot review the details of molecular genetics here, we note that a gene can be viewed as a segment of DNA that has a biological function. In this segment, four biochemical bases (thymine, adenine, cytosine, and guanine) are arranged in a sequence analogous to letters in a word. This genetic code or word is translated into protein molecules that affect cellular processes. Although it was once thought that one gene coded for only one protein, we know now that the situation is much more complex. Nevertheless, this way of thinking about the gene is generally correct, and it is useful for understanding behavioral genetics.

A gene always consists of a pair of DNA segments called *alleles*. One allele is inherited from one's mother, the other from one's father. For a behavioral geneticist, the less interesting genes are those whose alleles are the same in all individuals. The more interesting ones are those that are *polymorphic*—that is, genes whose alleles vary among individuals so that genetic effects can vary among people. Although more than one gene is involved in eye pigmentation, the principles of Mendelian genetics can be illustrated by a simplification of eye color inheritance. Assume that a B allele produces brown eye-pigment and a b allele, blue pigment. The genetic constitution of a person for this single gene with two alleles would permit three possibilities: BB, Bb, and bb. In other words, the person may have brown eyes (BB, Bb), as an allele B gene can produce enough brown pigmentation to color the whole eye, or blue pigmentation (bb). The possibilities for a child will naturally depend on the genetic constitution of the parents. For example, the marriage of two brown-eyed individuals (BB × BB) can produce only brown-eyed children, whereas the marriage of two brown-eyed individuals with mixed genetic constitutions (Bb × Bb) can produce children with brown or blue eyes. In genetics the term *genotype* refers to the genetic constitution of an individual; the term *phenotype* refers to the trait that is actually observed and measured in some way. From this example, we note that different genotypes (BB, Bb) can give rise to the same phenotype (brown color).

Single defective genes typically produce extreme behavioral abnormality. For example, Tay-Sachs syndrome is caused by a single gene and produces severe mental retardation and aberrant behaviors such as self-mutilation (Wessells & Hopson, 1988, p. 337). Medical scientists have classified over 500 biochemical disorders that have single-gene origins. These single gene traits, however, are not usually of interest to psychologists, who deal with trait variation in a "normal" range.

Apportioning Trait Variation

We must therefore understand genetic and environmental influences on these polygenic personality traits. As an illustration, though, let us first consider a physical trait—height—that is known to be a polygenic trait. Height is affected by many genes that probably determine the level of growth hormone, the number of cell receptors for this hormone, and many other related biochemical events. Variation or differences among individuals in phenotype (height in this case) are the result of differences in the genotype (e.g., aabbcc to AABBCC and all possible combinations in between) plus differences in environmental factors that influence height (e.g., diet). Heritability is a statistic defined as V_g/V_p, where V_g is the genetic variance and V_p is the phenotypic variance. It is basically the proportion of the variation or individual differences in the phenotype that can be attributed to genetic effects. If the genetic contribution is small relative to the total variation that is also affected by environmental factors, then we say that the trait has a low heritability. If genes are an important source of the phenotypic differences, then we say that the trait has a high heritability.

Figure 3.2 illustrates this idea. The height of children was imagined to be manipulated in two ways: either by varying diets to include primarily "junk" foods or healthful foods or by picking parents who differ greatly in height—NBA basketball players versus jockeys. As this example illustrates, the parent–child resemblance produced by heredity would have a great effect, whereas little height difference would be found among children with different diets. This example, although exaggerated to make a point, is not far from the truth. The heritability of height in America is about 90%, so that most height differences result from the effects of different parental heights and genetic recombination (i.e., the particular set of genes a child has received from each parent). Little variation is explained by family differences in nutrition or by other nonfamily environmental factors.

Some cautions apply to interpreting the heritability statistic (Plomin, DeFries, & McClearn, 1990):

1. Heritability will depend on the population of people included in a particular study. When the range of genetic differences among people (relative to the total variation) is greater, the heritability tends to be high, because people drawn from above and below the population mean will have different genotypes. On the other hand, when the range of environmental variation

Figure 3.2 | Family dietary versus parental heights "manipulations" of children's heights.

is large, then the heritability tends to be low. Hence, a study including a range from poverty-stricken families to rich ones would tend to find a lower heritability for IQ than one including just middle-class families. Conversely, the more American social policies successfully equalized environmental opportunities for children's education, the more their remaining IQ differences would be genetic in etiology. Ironically, a more egalitarian American society probably would mean a higher heritability for IQ.

2. Heritability is an inexact number. Studies involve samples, not everyone. So the numbers deduced from them are usually imprecise. For instance, one opinion poll will show that 56% of the voters favor John Doe; another one, that 55% of the voters favor him. We may presume that Mr. Doe will win the election, although we do not know exactly what percentage of all people favor him. The same kind of sampling imprecision is found in the heritability statistic when sampling variation is the major source of difference among studies.

3. Heritability does not apply to a single person. A heritability of 70 does not mean that 70% of a single person's height was due to heredity. Heritability, however, can be used to estimate a person's *genotypic value* (his or her genetic potential for a trait) from information on how both the mother and the father scored on a trait (see behavioral genetic texts; Hay, 1985; Plomin, DeFries, & McClearn, 1990).

4. Heritability is a descriptive statistic and does not give much information about the mechanisms and processes that affect personality development.

Genetic Resemblance Between Relatives

Biological relatives share more or fewer of their genes. Parent and children and siblings share about half their genes. Parent and grandchild share about one-quarter. Cousins share about one-eighth. Therefore, for genetically influenced traits, brothers and sisters or parents and children will be more alike than "kissing cousins" and other, more distant relatives. The laws of genetics also state that neither parents-children nor siblings will be perfectly alike. For example, the sibling of a schizophrenic child has about a 10% risk of schizophrenia himself. That is a greater risk than to people in general because only about 1% of people in the American population would be diagnosed as schizophrenic. On the other hand, 90% of siblings of a schizophrenic child are themselves nonschizophrenic. In part, this reflects the process of inheritance, because one sibling may have inherited the genes disposing toward schizophrenia from a parent, whereas the luckier child may not have inherited them. It is important to recognize that genetic laws predict certain values of the parent-child or sibling phenotypic correlation but not exactly the same phenotypes for family members (except for identical twins for a completely congenital trait such as eye color).

Shared (or Common) and Nonshared Environment

Behavioral genetics also makes a partitioning of environmental influences into those that affect individual differences in a population and also operate to make family members alike (the shared influences) and those that affect individual differences in a population and operate to make family members unalike (the nonshared influences). Literally thousands of scientific studies have been

Table 3.1 | Common-Family and Within-Family Environmental Variables

Variable	Common Family	Within Family
Social class	P	
Parental religion	P	
Parental values	P	
Child-rearing styles	P	S
Father absence	P	
Maternal employment	P	
Neighborhood	P	
Family size	P	
Birth order		P
Perinatal trauma		P
Peer groups	S	P
Teachers	S	P

Note: P = predominant emphasis; S = secondary emphasis.

Source: From "Resolving the Person–Situation Debate" by D. C. Rowe, in *American Psychologist*, Vol. 4, No. 31, pp. 218–227. Copyright © 1987 by the American Psychological Association. Adapted with permission.

devoted to shared influences such as social class and intact versus divorced households (see Table 3.1). These influences can be regarded as shared because siblings' exposure to them would be about equal. Their effect is to produce a correlation between siblings or between parent and child.

Unlike shared ones, nonshared influences involve factors making siblings (or parent-child pairs) different. An example of a nonshared influence is birth order. Because siblings have different birth orders, environmental effects associated with the order of birth will operate to make siblings different from one another. Rowe and Plomin (1981) have categorized nonshared influences as accidental events, perinatal traumas, family constellation (e.g., birth order, birth spacing), sibling mutual interaction, unequal parental treatments, and influences outside the family (e.g., when siblings have different teachers). Such nonshared influences will usually reduce the sibling or parent-child trait correlation. As we will see later, nonshared environmental influences appear to play a role about equal with that of heredity in the determination of nonintellectual personality traits.

Discovering the Sizes of Genetic and Environmental Effects

Structural equation modeling is a statistical procedure that is often applied for estimating genetic and environmental effects. It involves "fitting" equations that include genetic and environmental parameters to data from different family types. A parameter is simply an unknown number, like x or y in an algebraic equation. In a basic genetic model, the unknowns are heritability and the shared environmental effect. The process of "fitting" is one of picking the best values of the unknowns to reproduce the data correlations.

Although genetic models are usually much more complex, the following simple example should help to clarify these ideas. The resemblance of adoptive siblings is due entirely to the shared environment of their adoptive homes. We find adoptive siblings when adoptive parents successively adopt two children. Each adoptive child then has a different set of biological parents. Because they have different parents, their hereditary constitution is dissimilar; a more exact way of saying this is that their hereditary constitution is uncorrelated. If we know their IQ correlation, we can write the following equation:

$$r_{IQ} = c^2$$

where r_{IQ} is the adoptive siblings' IQ correlation (their resemblance for intelligence) and c^2 a common environment parameter. In other words, the equation means that their IQ resemblance is entirely due to sharing a family environment.

Monozygotic (MZ) twins, so-called identical twins, are the result of the division of a single fertilized egg cell and thus possess identical genetic heredity. Dizygotic (DZ) twins, so-called fraternal twins, are each the product of different fertilized egg cells and so bear the same genetic resemblance to one another as ordinary siblings. MZ twins, when raised in the same family, have an IQ resemblance resulting from two influences: shared family environment, like the adoptive siblings' IQs, and heredity. Because MZ twins possess exactly the same genetic constitution, we can write another equation:

$$r_{IQ} = h^2 + c^2$$

where h^2 is the hereditary parameter and c^2 is, as before, common family environment.

Using these two equations, we can solve for h^2 and c^2. For example, if the MZ twin correlation were .81 and the adoptive sibling correlation were .26, we arrive at an estimate of $c^2 = .26$ and $h^2 = .55$. In other words, 55% of the variation in IQ scores in this hypothetical study was due to genetic variation; 26% was due to the effects of family environment. Other values of the correlations, however, could give nonsensical results. For example, if the MZ twins correlated .41 and the adoptive siblings correlated .47, then the estimate of heritability would be –.06. Because the heritability cannot be less than zero, one would have to conclude either that the heritability was zero or that the model was wrong for some reason (e.g., contrast effects in MZ twins such that they competed with one another and became dissimilar as a result).

Searching for Specific Genes

In contrast to single gene disorders where in many cases the responsible gene has been identified, finding genes has proven to be difficult for polygenic traits that are affected by multiple genes with small effects as well as environmental factors. To find genes, biological material needs to be collected. Most often this is blood but sometimes also a small amount of mucosa cells obtained by scraping the inner cheek with a cotton swab. The DNA is then extracted from this biological material and stored in freezers. There are several approaches that can be used next. Possibly the most successful method until now has been the *candidate-gene approach*. In this approach genes are selected a priori based on their biological function and the possible relevance of this function for the phenotype under consideration. These genes are then measured or "genotyped" in a sample of individuals to test whether there are differences in traits among individuals with different genotypes.

The disadvantage of the candidate gene approach is that knowledge about genes' biological functions is (very) limited for most polygenetic traits. Alternative approaches have therefore been tried. One systematically scans all human DNA located on the chromosomes to look for genes that affect a trait. Chromosomes are threadlike DNA "packages" that are present in the nucleus of every cell. Humans have 23 pairs of chromosomes, together sometimes referred to as the *genome*. The chromosomes that form a pair resemble each other. For instance, one allele of a gene is located on one chromosome of a pair and the other allele on the other chromosome of a pair. Although for over 99% of different individuals the DNA is the same, in absolute terms there are still many locations on the chromosomes where there are variations among individuals (that are polymorphic). When included in a genome scan, these polymorphic loci are called markers. They "mark" a certain physical location. In *linkage studies* the markers are typically evenly spaced across the chromosomes. It is then determined from which parental chromosome each allele of the marker was inherited. Because children do not just inherit the marker but the whole chromosomal region in which the marker is located, the whole genome can be scanned with as few as 400 markers. A marker may show a significant result when relatives who share segments of the same parental chromosomes are also more similar phenotypically. In that situation it is suspected that one or more genes must lie in the region tagged by the marker. However, because the region is large, further work needs to be done to determine the chromosomal location of the causal gene(s) more precisely.

A problem with linkage studies is that they have a low statistical power to detect genes with small effects. That is, a region that contains a causal gene will often remain undetected because the statistical test that uses the marker to examine whether a causal gene is located in that region is not significant. This may be the reason that although they identified many of the genes responsible for single gene disorders, linkage studies have not been very successful in identifying genes for polygenic traits. So-called *association studies* have more statistical power to detect genes with small effects. Usually a simple test is performed to examine whether there are differences in traits among individuals with different genotypes. A significant result can be found even if the marker is not the causal gene. This is because if the marker and causal gene lie very close to each other on the chromosome, they will be transmitted together for thousands of generations and are basically linked and inherited as a unit. This phenomenon is called *allelic association* or *linkage disequilibrium*. Thus, the two alleles co-occur and are associated together more frequently than expected by chance. Traditionally association studies have been used for fine mapping. That is, if a region or gene is suspected to contribute to a trait, markers can be placed within this region or gene to obtain a more precise location of the causal gene. Currently the possibility of scanning the whole genome using an association design is being considered. This may require over 500,000 markers (Kruglyak, 1999; Zwick, Cutler, Lin, & Chakravarti, 2002). It is not possible to do such an enormous amount of genotyping yet. However, genotyping technologies are evolving rapidly, and with the increasing amount of information that becomes available about the human genome, at some point in the future it may also be possible to make an a priori selection of markers to be included in these scans.

New approaches are constantly being developed to detect genes for complex traits. One example is the DNA microarray technology also referred to as the DNA "chip." This technology focuses on specific tissues. A single chip can measure which genes, among the thousands whose effects can in principle be measured by the chip, are expressed in that tissue. One limitation is that genes underlying human behaviors are most likely expressed in the brain. Because it is not possible to sample brain tissue, these studies have to be performed using postmortem brains. Alternatively, brains of mice, that share about 80% to 85% of their DNA with humans, are often used. Another limitation is that the technology is still expensive. As a result the sample sizes are generally very small. This presents an enormous data analysis problem. Imagine that you would have a data set with thousands of variables (the measured expression levels of the thousands of genes) collected for a set of three cases (abnormal tissue) and three controls (normal tissue). How would you find for which of the thousands of variables there is a difference between the group of three cases and the group of three controls? Nevertheless, micorarrays provide a nice illustration of the rapidly developing research tools for identifying genes underlying polygenetic traits.

MODERN BEHAVIORAL GENETICS: FINDINGS AND IMPLICATIONS

In the century since the publication of Galton's *Hereditary Genius*, there has been a gradual accumulation of studies of normal personality traits, intellectual traits, and psychopathology. Remarkable features of these data are their consistency and replicability; adoptive studies completed in the 1920s have found essentially the same results as those completed in the past decade, except that IQ heritability from recent studies is lower. Moreover, these studies together are beginning to point to some fairly general conclusions. We will now turn to highlighting behavioral genetic knowledge about personality traits.

Normal (Nonintellectual) Personality Traits

The domain of normal personality traits is a broad one. A number of different classification schemes have been put forward in this domain, but we lack a single, unified scheme endorsed by most psychologists. Some agreement has been reached, however, that at least five dimensions of personality exist in personality rating data where knowledgeable raters describe the traits of friends and acquaintances (i.e., the "big five" of neuroticism, extraversion, openness to experience, agreeableness, and conscientiousness; McCrae & Costa, 1986).

Self-report studies can make do with no fewer than three broad dimensions of personality, such as Hans Eysenck's system of Neuroticism (i.e., anxiety, depression), Extraversion (i.e., sociability, impulsiveness), and Psychoticism (i.e., lack of empathy, cruelty; Eysenck, 1953; Eysenck & Eysenck, 1968). These broader dimensions, like Eysenck's "big three" dimensions just listed, are formed of some combination of more specific and narrow traits. The number of such specific trait dimensions may be large; for instance, Cattell identified 16 subordinate dimensions of personality (Cattell, 1982). At this level, the best form of trait description may depend on one's purpose, as well as on the structure of personality itself.

Although we could survey many kinds of evidence, one of the most easily interpreted studies is the comparison of identical twins raised apart and together. At the start of this chapter, we considered the case of the "Jim twins" whose life histories were so similar. From a single pair of MZ twins, however, one cannot separate chance similarities from real ones. With a group of MZ twins, on the other hand, one can compute the twins' correlation coefficient for a personality trait, and the statistical significance of this correlation would show that the pairs' resemblance is more than just a chance matching. MZ twins raised apart, because they were adopted into different families, lack the shared environmental experiences of siblings or twins raised in the same family. Even if the families were occasionally somewhat alike, they were surely more unalike than an upbringing under one roof with the same mother and father. For MZ twins raised apart, we can expect their trait correlation is mostly due to their shared heredity. Hence, we can write the equation

$$r_{trait} = h^2$$

where h^2 is heritability. For MZ twins raised together, common family environment is potentially an additional source of twins' trait resemblance. The equation for twins raised together is

$$r_{trait} = h^2 + c^2$$

where c^2 is the family environmental effect.

A sample of 44 MZ twins raised apart has been collected at the University of Minnesota (Tellegen, Lykken, Bouchard, Wilcox, Segal, & Rich, 1988). These pairs come from both the United States and England. Half had been separated before one year of age; most of the remainder, in the preschool years. The separation time (number of years from separation to first contact) averaged 34 years. These twins were compared with a sample of 217 twins reared together in Minnesota. Both members of each twin pair completed the Multidimensional Personality Questionnaire independently.

Both the MZ twins reared apart and those reared together showed remarkable similarity in their personality test scores for 11 different personality traits (see Table 3.2). An estimate of the effect of sharing a family environment on personality resemblance can be made by solving for c^2. Table 3.2 reveals that the values of c^2—simply the MZ-apart correlation subtracted from the MZ-together correlation—were about half negative and half positive. The average value of c^2 across the 11 trait scales was only .03. In a more extensive analysis

Table 3.2 | Twin Correlations for Monozygotic Twins Reared Apart and Together and Their Genetic and Environmental Interpretations

	Twin Group and Interpretation		
	MZ Twins Together: Environment Plus Heredity	MZ Twins Apart: Heredity Only	Difference: Shared Environment Only
Multidimensional Personality Questionnaire Scales	r-Together	r-Apart	$(r\text{-T} - r\text{-A})$
Well-being	.58	.48	.10
Social potency	.65	.56	.09
Achievement	.51	.36	.15
Social closeness	.57	.29	.28
Stress reaction	.52	.61	−.09
Alienation	.55	.48	.07
Aggression	.43	.46	−.03
Control	.41	.50	−.09
Harm avoidance	.55	.49	.06
Traditionalism	.50	.53	−.03
Absorption	.49	.61	−.12
Number of twin pairs	217	44	—
Mean correlation	.52	.49	.03

Source: From "Personality Similarity in Twins Reared Apart and Together" by T. J. Bouchard, et al., in *Journal of Personality and Social Psychology,* Vol. 54, p. 1035. Copyright © 1988 by the American Psychological Association. Adapted with permission from the publisher and author.

combining these data with data from two more samples, DZ twins raised apart and together, Tellegen et al. (1988) found that the common family environment effect was statistically significant only for Social Closeness (see the .28 environmental effect in Table 3.2) that measures sociability or the extent to which the respondent likes to interact with other people.

Loehlin (1992) applied behavior genetic models to data on the "big five" personality trait dimensions. All five personality traits were highly heritable. The next largest component of variation was always nonshared environment (plus any measurement error). The smallest was the shared environment for siblings. Over the five dimensions, this last component accounted for a mere 2%–11% of the total trait variation (Loehlin, 1992, p. 67). For no personality trait examined by Loehlin did evidence exist that children learned it by imitating their parents; that is, another environmental component, one that represented any potential effect of parents' traits on offsprings' traits, always could take a value of zero in Loehlin's models of personality.

The reason for these estimates of genetic and environmental influence can be illustrated by using one large adoption study of extraversion (Eaves, Eysenck, & Martin, 1989) that was covered by Loehlin's review. In the Eaves et al. study, the correlation for extraversion between mother and biological child was .21. Because children share only half their genes with their mothers, this value should be doubled to estimate the heritability of extraversion (h^2 = .42). Now, if children acquired an extraverted personality by imitating their mothers, then mothers' extraversion should correlate with that of adoptive as well as biological children; but it did not (mother–adoptive child, r = −.02, statistically nonsignificant). Both adoptive siblings and biological siblings share a family environment during childhood. However, trait resemblance was again stronger for the biologically related family members (biological siblings, r = .25, N = 418) than it was for biologically unrelated siblings reared under one roof (adoptive siblings, r = −.11, N = 58). Thus in this pattern of correlations, we can see why in Loehlin's more complex statistical methods, personality traits were found to be heritable and only weakly influenced by shared environmental influences.

These results reveal a rather puzzling truth about personality. The average heritability of personality traits is substantial—about 50% based on the average of the above correlations for MZ twins raised apart—but the effect of family environments on most traits is a very weak one. The real environmental effect appears to reside in nonshared environmental influences. They account for the differences among identical twins (the fact that the MZ twin correlation is about .50 less than a perfect 1.0). Such nonshared influences may involve parenting in that parents can treat children (siblings) in the same family differently, but more probably they involve many kinds of environmental influences that are external to the family.

There are a couple of ways of thinking about the inheritance of personality. One is that if you were raised in a different family, with parents who used different child-rearing methods, who had different values, and who modeled different kinds of behaviors, you would be remarkably like the person you are now. Another is that children raised in the same family (exposed to one family environment) tend to be very different if their heredity is dissimilar. We know this because, as illustrated above, personality correlations for adoptive (i.e., biologically unrelated) siblings are very low or zero (see Rowe, 1994).

This result is so counter to everyday intuitions that it is hard to understand or accept. One reason is that we notice familial similarities in personality and tend to attribute them to the family environment. However, this attribution neglects the heredity that parent and child (or siblings) share. The second is that we have strong emotional reactions to events in our families, and it is hard not to believe that they affect us. These data do not disprove an impact; but they do show that the impact is not one to make parents and children alike. We can perhaps accept the result more readily if we realize that personality traits depend in part on how the brain is structured and how it operates. The unprecedented discoveries of neuroscience show that moods and emotions depend on neurotransmitters and on other brain biochemicals. It is probably through influencing brain function that heredity makes MZ twins who were raised apart alike, despite their different life histories. And such genetically regulated brain function is probably equally important for our own personality development. Activity Box 3.1 presents another example of a personality trait—authoritarianism—showing a surprising level of genetic influence.

The search for specific genes has resulted in a number of candidates that may affect personality traits. A first example involves the 5-HTT gene that affects the regulation of the chemical serotonin, which helps transmit messages in the brain. Serotonin has been implicated in anxiety in humans and animals, and it also plays a role in widely used antidepressant and antianxiety therapeutic agents as well as drugs of abuse (e.g., cocaine). The initial positive finding involved a candidate gene study of an allele in the 5-HTT gene known to affect serotonin levels. In two independent samples, results suggested that this allele accounted for 3% to 4% of total variation in anxiety-related personality traits (Lesch et al., 1996). Although there have also been negative findings, a number of independent studies have also replicated the effects of this allele of the 5-HTT gene. Another set of genes associated with personality involves the dopamine system. Dopamine affects brain processes that control movement, emotional response, and ability to experience pleasure and pain. In 1996 two studies reported an association between an allele of the dopamine D4 receptor (DRD4) gene that is known to have a biological function with the personality trait of novelty seeking (Benjamin et al., 1996; Ebstein et al., 1996). The significance of this allele for novelty seeking is, however, still controversial because replication studies have not been consistent.

Intellectual Traits

More than any other trait, the inheritance of IQ (i.e., general problem-solving ability and knowledge) has sparked bitter controversy and endless debate. In the early 1970s, this debate flared over the role of heredity in racial differences in mean IQ scores—an issue that has subsided in the 1990s. The practical use of IQ and IQ-correlated aptitude tests in the placement of children into classes for the educationally handicapped or gifted, in the selection of students into prestigious universities, and in the assignment of employees to particular jobs gives them a practical importance that is greater than most other personality tests (Gottfredson, 1997). When dollars and real-world decisions are at stake, a debate over IQ testing takes on some urgency. In this chapter, we will not discuss the research literature on the fairness of IQ tests to minorities and poor children (see Jensen, 1980). Instead, we will focus on the inheritance of IQ scores and, complementarily, on family environmental influences on them.

Table 3.3 shows the IQ correlations for different pairs of biological and nonbiological relatives based on a summary of 111 studies (Bouchard & McGue, 1981). The pattern of correlation is clear: The more closely two people are biologically related, the greater is their IQ correlation. Some comparisons can be challenged. For example, some scholars have attributed the greater IQ resemblance of MZ than DZ twins to unequal treatments, whereby MZ

Activity Box 3.1   **Family Correlations for Authoritarianism**

Many people believe that social attitudes originate in a child's imitating or adopting parental attitudes. We consider here one social attitude, authoritarianism, an attitude characterized by a rigid acceptance of authority and tradition and by a lack of acceptance of any form of nonconformity or difference. This social attitude could be learned at one's parents' knees. Is it?

The first step of this activity box is to complete the authoritarian personality questionnaire. If you can, ask a brother, sister, or parent to complete it also. Follow the scoring instructions under the questionnaire.

Average scores range from 100 to 120; scores below 100 are more nonauthoritarian; and scores over 120 are more authoritarian. If you have tested other family members, determine whether you and they scored alike—within 10 points of one another.

The second issue is what influence produces this social attitude. We suggest that you first try to list all the family environmental reasons that family members score alike on this questionnaire. Next, list all the *genetic* reasons you think family members might score alike.

Sandra Scarr (1981) found results suggesting that family environment may not be so important in shaping this social attitude. She compared familial correlations in nonadoptive families (in other words, ordinary families) and adoptive families (in which members were not related by blood). The table that follows summarizes her results.

	Nonadoptive: Environment Plus Heredity	Adoptive: Environment Only	Difference: Heredity Only
Father child	.37	.14	.23
Mother child	.41	.00	.41
Sibling	.36	.14	.22

You can see that most of the family resemblance is located in the nonadoptive families. Discuss what this implies about the inheritance of authoritarianism.

Scarr also discovered that a high IQ was negatively correlated with authoritarianism (a person with a higher IQ score tended to score lower on an authoritarianism scale). She interpreted this result to mean that people tend to reason to their own beliefs about authoritarianism—so that family environments are less important in creating acceptance of this social attitude than a person's own thinking processes. What do you think?

Questionnaire

Answer each question, entering the number value of your response in the space provided. For items marked (8–), subtract the number value of your response from 8 before entering it. For example, if you answered question 2 this way—agree a little (5)—you would enter (3). Your total score is the sum of your entries.

1 = I disagree very much
2 = I disagree pretty much
3 = I disagree a little
4 = No opinion

5 = I agree a little
6 = I agree pretty much
7 = I agree very much

Activity Box 3.1 *(continued)*

	___	1. It is essential for learning or effective work that our teachers or bosses outline in detail what is to be done and how to do it.
(8–)	___	2. One of the most important things children should learn is when to disobey authorities.
	___	3. People ought to pay more attention to new ideas, even if they seem to go against the grain of American life.
	___	4. Most people don't realize how much our lives are controlled by plots hatched in secret places.
	___	5. Most of our social problems could be solved if we could somehow get rid of the immoral, crooked, and feebleminded people.
	___	6. Human nature being what it is, there will always be war and conflict.
(8–)	___	7. It is highly unlikely that astrology will ever be able to explain anything.
	___	8. What youth needs most is strict discipline, rugged determination, and the will to work and fight for family and country.
	___	9. No weakness or difficulty can hold us back if we have enough willpower.
	___	10. If it weren't for the rebellious ideas of youth, there would be less progress in the world.
(8–)	___	11. Most honest people admit to themselves that they have sometimes hated their parents.
(8–)	___	12. Books and movies ought to give a more realistic picture of life, even if they show that evil sometimes triumphs over good.
	___	13. Every person should have complete faith in a supernatural power whose decision he obeys without question.
(8–)	___	14. The artist and the professor are probably more important to society than the businessman and the manufacturer.
(8–)	___	15. The findings of science may some day show that many of our most cherished beliefs are wrong.
(8–)	___	16. An urge to jump from high places is probably the result of unhappy personal experiences rather than anything inborn.
	___	17. Nowadays more and more people are prying into matters that should remain personal and private.
(8–)	___	18. In spite of what we read about the wild sex life of people in important places, the real story is about the same in any group of people.
	___	19. No sane, normal, decent person could ever think of hurting a close friend or relative.
	___	20. Sex crimes, such as rape and attacks on children, deserve more than mere imprisonment; such criminals ought to be publicly whipped or worse.
Total	___	

Source: Based on *The Authoritarian Personality* by T. W. Adorno, et al. Copyright © 1950 by the American Jewish Committee. Reprinted by permission of HarperCollins Publishers, Inc. And from *Measures of Personality and Social Psychological Attitudes*, ed. J. P. Robinson, et al., reprinted by permission from Elsevier.

twins receive more equal IQ-relevant treatments than DZ twins and so become more alike in IQ. Although this argument is plausible on its face, evidence suggests that greater treatment similarities of MZ twins (such as dressing alike or sharing a room) fail to make them more alike in IQ (Loehlin & Nichols, 1976). Note the correlation of .72 for MZ twins raised apart (excluding Cyril Burt's

Table 3.3   Kinship Correlations for IQ

Kinship	Correlation	Number of Pairings
MZ twins reared together	.86	4,672
MZ twins reared apart	.72	65
DZ twins reared together	.60	5,546
Siblings reared together	.47	26,473
Siblings reared apart	.24	203
Single parent–child reared together	.42	8,433
Single parent–child reared apart	.22	814
Half-siblings	.31	200
Cousins	.15	1,176
Adopted/natural siblings	.29	369
Adopted/adopted siblings	.34	369
Adoptive parent–adopted child	.19	1,397
Spouses	.33	3,817

Source: From "Familial Studies of Intelligence: A Review," by T. J. Bouchard, Jr., and M. McGue, 1981, *Science, 212,* Figure 1, p. 1056. Copyright 1981 by the American Association for the Advancement of Science. Reprinted with permission of the authors and publisher.

MZ twins-apart data, which have been controversial; Hearnshaw, 1979). Others have argued that MZ twin similarity is an artifact of their similarity of physical appearance. The weakness of this argument is that physical appearance correlates only poorly, or not at all, with most behavioral traits (e.g., are redheads smarter than blondes?). The argument also has been directly refuted by empirical work testing the assumption of appearance effects (Hettema, Neale, & Kendler, 1995; Matheny, Wilson, & Dolan, 1976; Plomin, Willerman, & Loehlin, 1976; Rowe, Clapp, & Wallis, 1987). Rather, the greater similarity of MZ twins for IQ and other behavioral traits appears to be due to their genetic similarity. Moreover, although various nongenetic explanations could be constructed for one relationship or another in Table 3.3, the total pattern of IQ associations provides convincing evidence of genetic influence. Recent estimates have placed the heritability of IQ from 40% to 80%.

The field of developmental behavioral genetics is concerned with genetic influences over the period of biological maturation and aging, that is, over the life span (Plomin, 1983). This field concentrates on the potential of genetic factors to explain both change and constancy in development. The within-person stability of IQ is moderate, with correlations of about .70 between late childhood and adulthood. One reason we know that genes are important developmentally is that the IQ of an adult person—namely, a biological parent—will correlate with the IQ of a child—namely, this parent's adopted-away child (Plomin, & DeFries, 1985). The only physical link between these two persons is their shared heredity. The IQ of the adult, however, represents effects of genes in a 15- to 25-year-old person; the IQ of the child represents the action of copies of the same genes at 1 to 3 years of age. Thus, the correlation shows us that some of the same genes can produce IQ at both ages, the originals in the parent and their active copies in the child. Even late in life, heredity exerts a profound influence on IQ test scores. Jarvik, Blum, and Varma (1972), in a study of elderly twins, found that elderly MZ twins' IQs remained very similar. One of the highest estimates of IQ heritability comes from a study of older (mean age, 66 years) adult twins that included MZ and DZ twins reared apart (Pedersen, Plomin, Nesselroade, & McClearn, 1992). This study yielded a heritability estimate for IQ of .80.

Genetic inheritance also can create changes in personality traits (Rowe, 1987). Genetic changes can occur because genes turn on and off during development. Newly active genes may favor one person's IQ more than another person's IQ at a particular age. Ronald Wilson (1978) had the insight to pursue genetic determinants of change in a long-term study in which twins took IQ tests throughout infancy and childhood. He found that children's IQs shifted with age, with some children improving and others falling behind. More interesting, he discovered that the whole profile of IQ change was heritable. This point is illustrated by Figure 3.3, which compares two twin pairs, one MZ and the other DZ. The IQ scores of the MZ twins changed in tandem; the growth curves for the two DZ individuals were different. The complex patterns of IQ change, which vary widely from one twin pair to another, seem most easily interpreted genetically, because the patterns are unique to each twin pair, but they are more similar in MZ twins than in DZ twins. In addition, genetic influence appears to create spurts and lags in physical growth and development (Fischbein, 1977a; 1977b).

Although a variety of intellectual performances are heritable, one of the most heritable of all intellectual traits is vocabulary. It may come as a surprise that vocabulary is the most heritable trait, because it should be self-evident that people are not born with specific genes representing different words in the English language. If words must be learned, then how can they be inherited?

The answer to this seeming paradox is that the structure of the brain must influence how easily words are learned. For most words, children have a variety of opportunities to learn them. A child might learn "penguin" from a TV science program, from a teacher who reads aloud to the class, from a cartoon strip, or from other family members. For an exposure to be effective, however, a child must disengage the word from its context and recognize its referent, a process that is easier for a concrete noun like "penguin" than an abstract one like "justice." Also, the word must be placed in long-term memory and there integrated meaningfully with other concepts. Information processing views of intelligence indicate that even less complex mental operations, such as letter recognition time and working memory capacity, are crucial for a high IQ (Vernon, 1987). A simple perceptual process called *inspection* time also relates to IQ. In an inspection time task, two stimuli (e.g., lines of different length, tones of different pitches) are presented for progressively shorter durations (Deary, 1996). The ability to discriminate them at ever briefer presentation times correlates robustly with IQ; that is, a brief presentation time that leads a person with lower IQ into making errors in discrimination is still enough for a person

Figure 3.3 | IQ profiles for monozygotic and dizygotic twins.

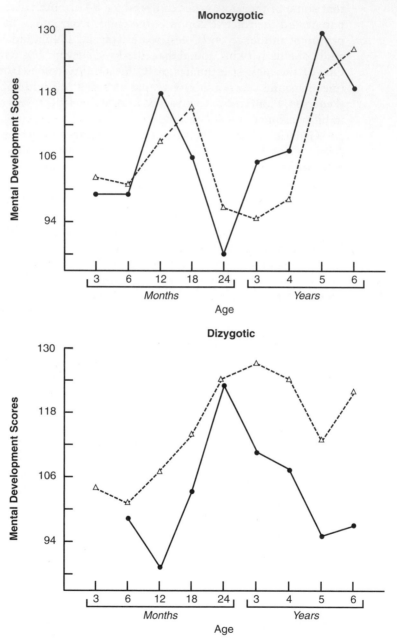

Source: From "Synchronies in Mental Development: An Epigenetic Perspective," by R. S. Wilson, 1978, *Science, 202,* p. 942. Copyright 1978 by the American Association for the Advancement of Science. Reprinted with permission of the publisher.

with high IQ to answer correctly. From these brief examples, we can understand that processes of word acquisition can be the genetically dependent component of vocabulary knowledge. Although vocabulary tests can be culturally biased, they are, within a particular culture, an excellent means of assessing heritable components of intellectual performance.

Although IQ is a fairly stable trait after the middle school years, it does change somewhat between early childhood and adolescence. Early in childhood, some children may appear brighter than others because a good home environment has given them a "head start." The correlation for the combined adopted/natural and adopted/adopted siblings pairings is about .30, meaning that 30% of IQ variation can be attributed to differences among families in intellectual stimulation in the home (see Table 3.3). The effects of these early family environments, however, are for the most part not enduring ones. They are seen in early childhood because biologically related siblings (e.g., a family has adopted one child, and then adopted a second child) are alike in IQ. For these ages, good home environments appear to raise the IQ of adoptive siblings. However, Scarr and Weinberg (1978) were surprised to discover that by late teenage years and the early 20s, these older adoptive siblings were unlike in their IQs, that is, *they were no more similar than children raised in different families*. A more recent review of kinship correlations has verified that genetic effects tend to increase with age, whereas shared environmental ones tend to decrease (McGue, Bouchard, Iacono, & Lykken, 1993). Family environmental effects are not static; they may be important early in life, but they may fade in influence later in life when other environmental influences—such as schools, peer groups, and work—come into prominence. Furthermore, the active selection of micro-environments, like a child's decision to use a library, may account for the fading influence of the family environment:

> For the young child, intellectual experience is largely determined by others. . . . During adulthood, however, experience is largely self-directed and reflects, in part, inherited abilities, interests, and dispositions so that the correlation between genotype and experience is largely actively generated. (McGue et al., 1993, p. 73)

There are well-replicated findings relating genes to cognitive disabilities. For instance, association studies have found that the APOE-epsilon 4 allele increases the risk of late-onset dementia—Alzheimer's disease (Corder et al., 1993). Furthermore, several linkage studies provided evidence that a region on chromosome 6 contains a gene for reading disability (Cardon et al., 1994). Very little attention has been paid to finding genes for cognitive ability and IQ. There are some exceptions (Plomin et al., 1994) but these studies have not yet resulted in replicated associations between genes and IQ.

Finally, good educational systems and cultural progress may benefit everyone. Flynn (1987) has obtained some evidence that IQ levels have increased historically. His observation was that students given an IQ test written in the 1920s or 1930s do better on it today than did the students who were given the same test originally. When a student is asked to take an IQ test, perhaps he should ask to be compared with the 1920 test norms! In the words of President John Kennedy, "rising tides" of democratic social progress may raise all boats—children's IQs—yet they do not eliminate individual differences in IQ.

Abnormal Traits

In the *DSM-IV-R*, the manual of psychiatric diagnoses of the American Psychiatric Association (1994), criteria are given for diagnosing a number of different types of psychopathology, including the major mental illnesses of schizophrenia and manic depressive psychosis, anxiety disorders, and a number of personality disorders. The psychiatric association emphasizes "all or none" diagnostic categories. However, at least some of the commoner varieties of these psychiatric categories may represent extreme forms of normally (i.e., bell-shaped curve) distributed behavioral tendencies (Van den Oord, Pickles, & Waldman, 2003). Statistical theory has shown that the sum of an infinite number of effects of this type will result in a normal distribution, regardless of the individual distributions of the component effects. In most cases this theorem applies with considerable precision when 50 *independent* effects (Hoel, 1984) are considered, and it is often a fair approximation with as few as 10. As a consequence, normal distributions can be expected for phenotypes that are affected by many genes and environmental factors, each of which has a small effect. Although it may in some cases be misleading to view psychopathology as "all or none," much research has come from this viewpoint. We mention in this section a few results on the inheritance of psychopathology, while admitting that the surface of this subject has barely been scratched.

The typical genetic study of abnormal traits is a proband study. Such studies first involve the identification of *probands*—individuals known to have some form of psychopathology. Second, relatives of the proband are then found and checked to see whether they are also affected. The concordance of relatives is the percentage of relatives of the proband who are affected. For example, a study of schizophrenia might identify 41 biological parents who had received a diagnosis of schizophrenia (the probands). Next, their children, if they had been given up for adoption, would be located and diagnosed using criteria similar to those used for the parents. If seven of these adoptive children were diagnosed as schizophrenic, then the concordance would be 17% (7/41).

Until 1966, considerable disagreement existed over the inheritance of schizophrenia. This disagreement was largely resolved with the first adoption study of schizophrenia. Heston (1966) discovered that children of schizophrenic parents, when adopted early and raised apart from their schizophrenic biological parents, developed the illness at about the same rate as children raised with their biological parents. In both groups of children, the concordance was about 10%. Adoption studies completed after this pioneering one supported the idea that most of the family risk is a biological one (DeFries & Plomin, 1978). Furthermore, the majority of schizophrenics (90%) lack schizophrenic biological parents (Gottesman, 1991). This latter finding agrees with a biological-threshold model of genetic effects on schizophrenia, but not with the prevalent idea that experiences in families of schizophrenics were needed to generate the disorder. Old notions such as the "schizophrenigenic mother" have been ruled out. Adoption studies also produce considerable evidence for genetic risk in many other psychiatric diagnoses, such as manic depressive psychosis and, in childhood, diagnoses related to hyperactivity (conduct disorder, attention span problems).

Some intriguing results have been found for one behavioral problem: adolescent delinquency. Two researchers combined data from three adoption studies of adolescent delinquency (Cadoret, Cain, & Crowe, 1983). They looked at the interactive effects of environmental risk—namely, depression, sibling conflict, or divorce in the adoptive families—with biological risk. The latter referred to diagnoses of alcohol abuse or criminal behavior in the biological parent of the adoptees. Only when a child was exposed to the combined risk was he or she at an increased risk of committing delinquent acts. Such interaction effects are encouraging because they suggest that improving family environments may reduce levels of delinquent behavior. Work on adult criminality, however, tends to show stronger genetic influences (Cloninger & Gottesman, 1987).

Most of the gene-finding efforts in behavioral genetics focus on abnormal behavior. Some of the genes are the same as those studied in relation to personality. For instance, using the candidate gene approach, several studies found that dopamine genes, such as DRD4 that may play a role in sensation seeking, also affected attention-deficit hyperactivity disorder (ADHD). ADHD is a common behavioral disorder in children and adolescents that is characterized by symptoms of hyperactivity and inattentiveness. The regulation of dopamine has been implicated as a cause of ADHD. In addition, ADHD is typically treated by stimulants such as methylphenidate (Ritalin), a dopamine reuptake inhibitor. This possible role of DRD4 therefore also seems to be plausible from a biological perspective.

Other genes are unique for abnormal traits. A good example is the alcohol dehydrogenases (ADHs) genes that metabolize ethanol. There is strong evidence that the ADH2-2 allele decreases the risk of alcohol dependence (Whitfield, 1997). However, because this allele is much more frequent in Asians, it is probably more important as a protective factor for alcoholism in Asians than in other ethnic groups.

A final example involves the human dystrobrevin binding protein 1 gene (*DTNBP1*) and schizophrenia. A linkage study presented evidence in support of genes related to schizophrenia in a region on chromosome 6 (Straub et al., 1995). Several genes were located in this region but follow-up association studies suggested that only the markers in *DTNBP1* affected schizophrenia (Straub et al., 2002). The first replication studies in independent samples look promising but more work needs to be done. Furthermore, because the relationship between this gene and the biological processes involved in schizophrenia is entirely speculative, follow-up studies will need to examine the biological pathways.

HOW HEREDITY CAN BE DISGUISED IN ENVIRONMENTAL CONCEPTS

Social class, child-rearing styles, parental attitudes, and other concepts measured in psychological studies, although usually thought of as environmental, can in fact be an expression of heredity (Plomin, 1994). Parental social class provides a good example. It is associated with a range of environmental differences; for example, poor people are less likely than wealthy people to have books and an enriching home environment, to be able to afford adequate nutrition, to have good neighborhood schools, to live in low-crime communities, and so on. The social class of individuals in any generation, however, is partly the result of individual differences in personality. Intelligence, achievement, sociability, persistence, and many other traits will contribute to the social standing a child will reach as an adult. This process of social mobility implies that people at different social class strata in American society will probably differ genetically in those genes influencing these personality traits that, in turn, have contributed to their falling or rising in social status in comparison to their parents' statuses. Even siblings, although they have about the same childhood advantage in life, often as adults will fall into different social class strata because of inherited personality differences. Hence, social class is a confounded variable: a higher social class is associated with both environmental advantages and with genetically transmissible traits.

We make a mistake, then, if we assume that social class effects are entirely environmental. For example, the higher IQs of upper-class children will have resulted partly from their environmental advantages, but also from their IQ-relevant heredity. The controversial book *The Bell Curve* (Herrnstein & Murray, 1994) took this finding to the other extreme and argued that social class differences were primarily genetic in origin. Although some of the arguments that are used in this book do have a scientific basis, the behavior genetic data do not support this extreme view nor would such results dictate or preclude particular social policies. An adoption study can break apart the relative size of the two influences, but in a typical family study they would be completely indistinguishable. Given this, students should be aware of the limitation of family studies of environmental effects and seek additional information from behavioral genetic studies of the same topic. Heredity and environment are not in competition; but for the development of a particular trait, it is important to know their relative influence.

Furthermore, environments and heredity can become correlated (related). First, there may be a passive matching of heredity and environment when parents transmit genetic traits that are reinforced by the family environment. Aggressive parents, for instance, might create chaotic home environments and at the same time genetically pass aggressive tendencies on to their children. The children could become even more aggressive as a result. Second, there may be a reactive correlation between heredity and environment in which genetic traits tend to elicit a particular environmental response. An attractive woman and a handsome man experience just this kind of gene—environment correlation when they are showered with social attention. Third, genetic dispositions may guide a person to pick particular environments over others. The tough, fearless, aggressive bully is more likely to hang out at a neighborhood street corner than is a timid boy, and bright kids may use the public libraries more than kids who find reading to be a chore. The ability of genes to make our environments may explain why MZ twins, when raised apart, are still able to experience so much of the world in the same way.

EVOLUTIONARY PSYCHOLOGY AND BEHAVIOR GENETICS

Behavior genetics is not the only approach to behavior based on human genetics. A second approach has been variously called "evolutionary psychology" or "sociobiology." Evolutionary psychology emphasizes the evolution of "psychological mechanisms—information-processing devices, decision rules, and so on—in conjunction with contextual input into those mechanisms" (Buss, 1995, p. 1). Sociobiology examines the evolution of various forms of social behavior and its genetic basis (Wilson, 1975). Other names for similar disciplines such as Darwinian anthropology are sometimes also used (Turke, 1990). They all share, however, the application of evolutionary theory toward understanding the etiological roots of behavior.

Evolutionary theory is familiar to most students as the scientific explanation for the origin of life on earth. The basic principles of evolution are mutation—the source of new genes in a population—and selection, the survival and reproductive success of those individuals in a population with the most adaptive traits (Dawkins, 1987, 1989). Most mutations are harmful or neutral (i.e., of little effect on survival and reproduction). However, some mutations are advantageous.

Consider for example, color vision. Anyone who has seen both black and white television and color TV knows that the latter offers a far greater discrimination of the world. In many mammals, perhaps in a majority, only two color sensitive pigments are in the eyes (green and blue, Jacobs, 1995). The third pigment (red) evolved in the primate line, perhaps 30 to 45 million years ago (Zegura, 1995). One adaptive benefit of the improved color vision allowed by trichomy (3 pigments) vision may have been the ability to see fruits, which may go unnoticed except for their colors. It also may have helped old world monkeys distinguish among friends and enemies (consider the brightly colored faces in some monkey species). As color vision confers greater visual acuity, it is unsurprising that color vision has been reinvented in several animal species. Indeed, in new world monkeys, the evolution of color vision is continuing, with some species possessing the gene for red-sensitive pigment and others not. Nocturnally active monkey species actually lose color vision, which may be without adaptive worth in their worlds of diminished light. Overall, in a Darwinian "struggle for existence," it is better for some primates, including humans, to see with greater acuity. In general, mutations that confer advantageous traits leading to survival and reproduction will spread throughout a population, changing a species' characteristics, and more rarely, creating a new species.

For understanding human behavior, however, principles that are elaborations of the idea of natural selection are most important. The first is the principle of sexual selection (Daly & Wilson, 1983; Symons, 1979). Animals not only compete against those animals that desire to eat them, weather that is too cold or too hot, a scarcity of food, and many other aspects of "nature"; they also compete against one another for finding mates and raising young. It is this latter form of competition that is called sexual selection. In sexual selection, males compete against one another for the opportunity to mate with females.

In many species, the male plays little role in the upbringing of his offspring and also has the opportunity to mate with more than one female. The male's lack of parental investment intensifies the competition among males to have as many matings with females as possible. The "winner" of this competition spreads his genes more widely than those of other males, making his traits predominate in later generations. In contrast, in most mammalian species, females devote more physical resources and time to raising their offspring; they carry a pregnancy to term, lactate to provide milk, and often help to protect the young. A desire for sexual promiscuity is not a survival benefit to most females; rather, the pressure of natural selection on females is to choose to mate with the male carrying the best genetic traits.

The second extension of natural selection is the principle of kin selection (Hamilton, 1964). Kin selection occurs because close relatives are especially alike genetically. A rare gene that the reader possesses is more likely to be found in a parent, brother, or sister than to be possessed by unrelated people. The genetic similarity of blood relatives is why the matching of tissues for transplantation is most likely to succeed when the tissue donor is a biological relative rather than a stranger. Because biological kin share genes, rare genes that promote altruistic behavior—behavior that benefits another person at some cost to the altruist's chances of survival and reproductive success—are most likely to make that altruism specific to biological kin. In a sense, the altruistic gene benefits itself, because a copy of that gene is fairly likely to be found in a brother or sister, but not in a nonrelative. The principle of kin selection explains the puzzle of altruism in otherwise selfish organisms. The willingness of a bird to pretend to have a broken wing to attract a predator away from its young, of a ground squirrel to make an alarm call if its sisters are nearby (but to remain silent if no biological relative is close), and of an ant to sacrifice itself in warfare against other ants are all examples of the principle of kin selection at work.

Although the explanation of human behavior requires acknowledging our complex cognition and culture, the principles of evolutionary theory, sexual and kin selection, can illuminate many human behaviors. A full discussion of the application of these ideas to human behavior is beyond the scope of this chapter, but recommendations for further sources are given later. For purposes of illustration, however, consider Buss's (Buss et al., 1992) evolutionary prediction, verified by his studies, that men become more jealous than women in response to thoughts of sexual infidelity by their partners, whereas women become more jealous than men to thoughts of emotional attachment to another. In general, a man would lose everything from a reproductive standpoint if his partner's child was not his own biological child (i.e., if he were cuckolded). Men may have evolved (through the biological effects of their genes) to respond strongly against any sign of sexual infidelity in a partner. On the other hand, women should be (relatively) more concerned than men about the loss of their partner's emotional and material investment in their children. For women, abandonment may be a stronger psychological trigger for emotion than sexual infidelity.

As evidence for the evolved nature of jealousy, Buss cited its cross-cultural universality, especially the universality of violence in response to sexual infidelity. If sexual jealousy were strongly culturally conditioned, one might expect to find some cultures without it; but no such cultures exist. Even among Eskimos, where under some special circumstances wives were shared, a leading cause of murder was sexual jealousy and the subsequent murder of a spouse (Buss et al., 1992). That sexual jealousy is species typical of humans, as well as present in many other animal species, makes an evolved origin more likely than a cultural one. Despite this, all cultures do not treat sexual jealously equally, some allowing it to exonerate a man for murder, others imposing the law on both spouses evenhandedly. Although behaviors have a genetic basis, their various manifestations may show an interaction of genes and culture.

The Darwinian approach to behavior just sketched may be contrasted with behavior genetics. Both share a concern about the genetic bases of behavior, but they approach the issue in quite dissimilar ways. When applying Darwinian evolutionary ideas to human behaviors, the emphasis is on the average behavior in a population. Most men show sexual jealousy if they discover a cheating wife; most women, sexual jealousy if they discover their husband is leaving them for another lover. However, the intensity of the emotion, as with all behaviors, varies among individuals. Some men show excessive vigilance of their wives, when unfounded suspicions of infidelity become a motive for abusive treatment. For the most part, this range of behavioral response goes unanalyzed in the Darwinian approach, whereas it is grist for the mill of a behavior genetic study. Furthermore, the Darwinian approach is equally concerned with genes that do not vary (which can contribute to an average response) and with genes that vary (which create individual variation). The behavior geneticist targets solely the latter. Although the fields differ in their methodological approaches (phylogenic histories vs. twins and adoptees), historical roots (Charles Darwin vs. Francis Galton), and favorite behaviors of study (sex differences vs. IQ and personality), they may be intellectually closer to one another than is commonly recognized. The average response of the organism, the focus of the sociobiologist, is what is modified by existing and new genetic variability, the focus of the behavior geneticist. The two approaches complement one another more than they conflict.

POSTSCRIPT

The results of behavioral genetic studies are clear—everywhere, we find evidence of genetic influences on human personality traits. People are not the same; partly, they are different because of inborn differences regulated by genetic inheritance. Due to advances in molecular biology we have now started to actually identify the specific genes that are responsible for these complex, multigene traits. Many questions remain, however, such as optimizing the methodology for finding genes and filling the gap in knowledge that exists between the complexities of personality description and physiology. Although the specific, biological bases for many personality traits are unknown, other chapters in this book document the remarkable progress that is being made.

The other, surprising result of behavioral genetics is that family environments are less important than was previously thought. One family can produce an aggressive child and a timid child, a sociable child and a shy child, or a bright child and a dull one. The reason is that siblings may differ from one another genetically, and these genes may influence their behavioral traits. Parent-child resemblance for behavioral traits is often noticed. This resemblance may be more the product of genes shared by parent and child than of any shared family nurture.

The weak effect of family environments on developmental outcomes and personality does not mean that family environment is not important to individuals nor does it deny that a strong emotional bond between parent and child may exist. However, the most influential environmental influences tend to be those that make family members different from each other. Strong environmental influences also lie outside the family (Van den Oord & Rowe, 1999). Because cultural changes occur rapidly, whereas genetic changes do not, trait changes that occur in recent historical times, such as an increase in IQ or in the prevalence of antisocial personality disorder, cannot have a genetic basis. The diffusion of new technologies also creates change more rapidly than could any system of biological inheritance. The role of peers in the diffusion of behavioral and material innovations should be a topic for those students interested in the broader influence of the cultural environment (Harris, 1995).

Even today genetic issues remain sensitive. A fatalistic view that we could do nothing about genetic effects, and a distaste arising from the misuse of genetics in support of racist and eugenic policies may explain some of the sensitivity of the subject. Genetic results, such as those summarized in this chapter, may also worry people concerned about egalitarian values. If people are really different, then they cannot be equal in the sense that each of us, given the proper opportunity, could with the same ease find a second derivative or dominate a group discussion. Concern for equality, however, must be melded with recognition of human differences. Even the champion of equality and human rights, John Locke, recognized that people were born with different temperamental traits (Loehlin, 1983). Behavior genetics studies such individual differences. Labels such as "inequal" do not follow from genetic theory, but are made by people who evaluate these individual differences using their normative standard. By accounting for individual differences, behavior genetics advocates a greater recognition of and respect for individuality. If we can use the range of variation in personality to make a more exciting, varied, and productive society—there is no need to devalue personality differences.

SUMMARY

A debate as old as psychology itself, and still profoundly important today, has focused on the relative effects of nature (meaning genetic heredity) and nurture (meaning all sorts of environmental influences) on personality differences. The conceptual and methodological tools for resolving this debate are contained in the field of behavioral genetics.

This chapter first covered the history of behavioral genetics, and in particular, the creative and inventive man, Francis Galton, who first saw how questions about heredity and environmental influences could be answered. In the next section, the chapter delved into the conceptual foundations and method-ological tools of the field, including the idea of apportioning individual differ-ences to genetic and environmental causes and finding the specific genes that af-fect behavior. The third section reviewed data from family, twin, and adoption studies, and molecular studies. Three domains of behavior were surveyed briefly: normal personality traits, intellectual traits, and abnormal psychologi-cal traits. The last section introduced the approach of sociobiology, the appli-cation of concepts from evolutionary theory to the investigation of all species' behavior, including that of humans.

The chapter arrived at two conclusions. First, genetic variation can explain a substantial part of variation in psychological traits. Second, with the possible exception of extreme situations such as maltreatment, the fact that shared en-vironmental influences are weak and nonshared environmental influences sub-stantial contradicts the popular belief that the family environment can mold traits in a desirable direction.

DISCUSSION QUESTIONS

1. Even today behavior genetic studies remain controversial. Are there fun-damental differences between genetics versus other scientific disciplines that raise unique ethical concerns?
2. Could knowledge about contemporary theory help to find the genes un-derlying personality traits?
3. Could you think of an evolutionary explanation for why personality is af-fected by genes or is this simply a coincidental by-product of evolution?
4. Behavior genetic studies have shown that "environmental" variables such as socioeconomic status or social support are affected by genetic influences. Only genetic studies can disentangle genetic and environmental effects. Would it be fair to argue that for a better understanding of the environ-ment we therefore need genetically informative designs?
5. Could specific genes found for personality help to refine contemporary the-ory of personality?

SUGGESTED READINGS

Benjamin, J., Ebstein, R. P., & Belmaker, R. H. (2002). *Molecular genetics and the human personal-ity*. Washington, DC: American Psychiatric Publish-ing. A nice summary of the state-of-the-play.

Daly, M., & Wilson, M. (1988). *Homicide*. New York: Aldine De Gruyter. Murder from an evolution-ary perspective? Not only is this possible, but the de-tails are worked out in Daly and Wilson's insightful book.

Galton, F. (1865). *Heredity genius: An inquiry into its laws and consequences*. London: Macmillan

(Cleveland: World Publishing, 1962). Galton's fam-ily study of eminence shows the historical founda-tions of behavioral genetics.

Gottesman, I. I. (1991). *Schizophrenia genesis: The origins of madness*. New York: W. H. Freeman. A reader-friendly tour of the role of genetic and envi-ronmental influences in the genesis of a severe form of mental illness, schizophrenia.

Leahy, A. M. (1935). Nature–nurture and intelli-gence. *Genetic Psychology Monographs Supple-ment, 16,* 235–308. Alice Leahy's classic study produced evidence for the heritability of IQ and for the genetic mediation of some effects thought to be environmental. Written with forcefulness and clarity, this article shows an understanding of the issues that was ahead of its time.

Loehlin, J. C., Lindzey, G., & Spuhler, J. N. (1975). *Race differences in intelligence.* San Francisco: W. H. Freeman. Sponsored by the Social Science Research Council, this book evaluates the question of heritable racial differences in IQ with an evenhandedness and thoroughness of analysis that sheds light on the question instead of adding more heat to an already overheated debate.

Plomin, R. (1994). *Genetics and experience: The interplay between nature and nurture.* Thousand Oaks, CA: Sage. Genetic influences in environmental measures? This statement sounds contradictory, but it is not, as explicated in Plomin's book on genes and experience.

Rowe, D. C. (1994). *The limits of family influence: Genes, experience, and behavior.* New York: Guilford. Do families mold personality and intellectual traits? Rowe does not believe so. The public and many social scientists, however, do. The book presents evidence from behavior genetic studies that avoid the conflation of genetic and environmental influences. The reader can decide who is right.

Wilson, E. O. (1975). *Sociobiology: The new synthesis.* Cambridge: Harvard University Press. Receive your first lesson in the Darwinian, evolutionary approaches to behavior from the biologist and naturalist, E. O. Wilson, who jump-started the whole field.

SUGGESTED WEB SITES

http://www.bga.org/
Site of the Behavior Genetics Association.

http://www.ornl.gov/hgmis/
Information about the Human Genome Program.

http://www.genome.gov/glossary.cfm
Talking glossary to help nongeneticists understand the terms and concepts used in genetic research.

INFOTRAC COLLEGE EDITION SEARCH TOPICS

Behavior genetics	Linkage	Evolutionary psychology
Shared environment	Linkage disequilibrium	Polygenic

REFERENCES

Adorno, T. W., Frenkel-Brunswik, E., Levinson, D. J., & Sanford, R. N. (1950). *The authoritarian personality.* New York: Harper.

American Psychiatric Association. (1994). *Diagnostic and statistical manual of mental disorders. (DSM-IV-R).* Washington, DC: APA.

Benjamin, J., Li, L., Patterson, C., Greenburg, B. D., Murphy, D. L., & Hamer, D. H. (1996). Population and familial association between the D4 dopamine receptor gene and measures of novelty seeking. *Nature Genetics, 12,* 81–84.

Bouchard, T. J., Jr., & McGue, M. (1981). Familial studies of intelligence: A review. *Science, 212,* 1055–1059.

Buss, D. M. (1995). Evolutionary psychology: A new paradigm for psychological science. *Psychological Inquiry, 6,* 1–30.

Buss, D. M., Larsen, R., Westen, D., & Semmelroth, J. (1992). Sex differences in jealousy: Evolution, physiology, and psychology. *Psychological Science, 3,* 251–255.

Cadoret, R. J., Cain, C. A., & Crowe, R. R. (1983). Evidence for gene-environment interaction in the development of adolescent antisocial behavior. *Behavior Genetics, 13,* 301–310.

Cattell, R. B. (1982). *The inheritance of personality and ability.* New York: Academic Press.

Cardon, L. R., Smith, S. D., Fulker, D. W., Kimberling, W. J., Pennington, B. F., & DeFries, J. C. (1994). Quantitative-trait locus for reading disability on chromosome 6. *Science, 266,* 276–279.

Cloninger, C. R., & Gottesman, I. I. (1987). Genetic factors in the etiology of criminal behavior. In S. A. Mednick, T. E. Moffitt, & S. A. Stack (Eds.),

The causes of crime: New biological approaches (pp. 92–109). Cambridge: Cambridge University Press.

Corder, E. H., Saunders, A. M., Strittmatter, W. J., Schmechel, D. E., Gaskell, P. C., Small, G. W., Roses, A. D., Haines, J. L., & Pericak-Vance, M. A. (1993). Gene dose of apolipoprotein E type 4 allele and the risk of Alzheimer's disease in late onset families. *Science, 261,* 921–923.

Daly, M., & Wilson, M. (1983). *Sex, evolution and behavior* (2nd ed.). Boston: Prindle, Weber, & Schmidt.

Dawkins, R. (1987). *The blind watchmaker: Why the evidence of evolution reveals a universe without design.* New York: W. W. Norton.

Dawkins, R. (1989). *The selfish gene* (2nd ed.). Oxford: Oxford University Press.

Deary, I. J. (1996). Intelligence and inspection time: Achievements, prospects, and problems. *American Psychologist, 51,* 599–608.

DeFries, J. C., & Plomin, R. (1978). Behavioral genetics. *Annual Review of Psychology, 29,* 473–515.

Eaves, L. J., Eysenck, H. J., & Martin, N. G. (1989). *Genes, culture and personality.* London: Academic Press.

Ebstein, R. P., Novick, O., Umansky, R., Priel, B., Osher, Y., Blaine, D., Bennett, E. R., Nemanov, L., Katz, M., & Belmaker, R. H. (1996). Dopamine D4 receptor D4DR exon III polymorphism associated with the human personality trait novelty-seeking. *Nature Genetics, 12,* 78–80.

Eysenck, H. J. (1953). *The structure of personality.* London: Methuen.

Eysenck, S. B. G., & Eysenck, H. J. (1968). The measurement of psychoticism: A study of factor stability and reliability. *British Journal of Social and Clinical Psychology, 7,* 286–294.

Fancher, R. E. (1985). *The intelligence men: Makers of the I.Q. controversy.* New York & London: W. W. Norton.

Fischbein, S. (1977a). Onset of puberty in MZ and DZ twins. *Acta Geneticae Medicae et Gemellologieae, 26,* 151–158.

Fischbein, S. (1977b). Intra-pair similarity in physical growth of monozygotic and of dizygotic twins during puberty. *Annals of Human Biology, 4,* 417–430.

Flynn, J. R. (1987). Massive IQ gains in 14 nations: What IQ tests really measure. *Psychological Bulletin, 101,* 171–191.

Galton, F. (1869). *Hereditary genius: An inquiry into its laws and consequences.* London: Macmillan.

Gottesman, I. I. (1991). *Schizophrenia genesis: The origin of madness.* New York: W. H. Freeman.

Gottfredson, L. S. (1997). Why g matters: The complexity of everyday life. *Intelligence, 23,* 79–132.

Hamilton, W. D. (1964). The genetical evolution of social behavior I and II. *Journal of Theoretical Biology, 7,* 1–52.

Harris, J. R. (1995). Where is the child's environment? A group socialization theory of development. *Psychological Review, 102,* 458–489.

Hay, D. A. (1985). *Essentials of behavior genetics.* Oxford: Blackwells.

Hearnshaw, L. (1979). *Cyril Burt: Psychologist.* Ithaca, NY: Cornell University Press.

Herrnstein, R. J., & Murray, C. (1994). *The bell curve: Intelligence and class structure in American life.* New York: Free Press.

Heston, L. L. (1966). Psychiatric disorders in foster home reared children of schizophrenic mothers. *British Journal of Psychiatry, 112,* 819–825.

Hettema, J. M., Neale, M. C., & Kendler, K. S. (1995). Physical similarity and the equal-environment assumption in twin studies of psychiatric disorders. *Behavior Genetics, 25,* 311–326.

Hoel, P. G. (1984). *Introduction to mathematical statistics.* New York: Wiley.

Jacobs, G. H. (1995). Variations in primate color vision: Mechanisms and utility. *Evolutionary Anthropology: Issues, News, and Reviews, 3,* 196–205.

Jarvik, L. F., Blum, J. E., & Varma, A. O. (1972). Genetic components and intellectual functioning during senescence: A 20-year study of aging twins. *Behavior Genetics, 2,* 159–171.

Jensen, A. R. (1980). *Bias in mental testing.* New York: Free Press.

Kolata, G. (1986). Manic depression: Is it inherited? *Science, 232,* 575–576.

Kruglyak, L. (1999). Prospects for whole-genome linkage disequilibrium mapping of common disease genes. *Nature Genetics, 22,* 139–144.

Lesch, K. P., Bengel, D., Heils, A., Sabol, S. Z., Greenberg, B. D., Petri, S., Benjamin, J., Muller, C. R., Hamer, D. H., & Murphy, D. L. (1996). Association of anxiety-related traits with a polymorphism in the serotonin transporter gene regulatory region. *Science, 274,* 1527–1531.

Loehlin, J. C. (1992). *Genes and environment in personality development.* Newbury Park, CA: Sage.

Loehlin, J. C. (1983). John Locke and behavior genetics. *Behavior Genetics, 13,* 117–121.

Loehlin, J. C., & Nichols, R. C. (1976). *Heredity, environment, and personality: A study of 850 sets of twins.* Austin: University of Texas Press.

Matheny, A. P., Jr., Wilson, R. S., & Dolan, A. B. (1976). Relations between twins' similarity of appearance and behavioral similarity: Testing an assumption. *Behavior Genetics, 6,* 343–351.

McCrae, R. R., & Costa, Jr., P. T. (1986). Clinical assessment can benefit from recent advances in personality psychology. *American Psychologist, 41,* 1001–1003.

McGue, M., Bouchard, T. J., Jr., Iacono, W. G., & Lykken, D. T. (1993). Behavioral genetics of cognitive ability: A life-span perspective. In R. Plomin & G. E. McClearn (Eds.), *Nature, nurture, and psychology* (pp. 59–76). Washington, DC: American Psychological Association.

Pedersen, N. L., McClearn, G. E., Plomin, R., & Friberg, L. (1985). Separated fraternal twins: Resemblance for cognitive abilities. *Behavior Genetics, 16,* 407–419.

Pedersen, N. L., Plomin, R., Nesselroade, J. R., & McClearn, G. E. (1992). A quantitative genetic analysis of cognitive abilities during the second half of the life span. *Psychological Science, 3,* 346–353 .

Plomin, R. (1983). Developmental behavioral genetics. *Child Development, 54,* 253–259.

Plomin, R. (1994). *Genetics and experience: The interplay between nature and nurture.* Thousand Oaks, CA: Sage.

Plomin, R., & DeFries, J. C. (1985). *Origins of individual differences in infancy: The Colorado Adoption Project.* New York: Academic Press.

Plomin, R., DeFries, J. C., & McClearn, G. E. (1990). *Behavioral genetics: A primer.* New York: W. H. Freeman.

Plomin, R., McClearn G. E., Smith, D. L., Vignetti, S., Chorney, M. J., Chorney, K., Venditti, C. P., Kasarda, S., Thompson, L. A., Detterman, D. K., Daniels, J., Owen, M., & McGuffin, P. (1994). DNA markers associated with high versus low IQ: The IQ quantitative trait loci (QTL) project. *Behavior Genetics, 24,* 107–118.

Plomin, R., Owen, M. J., & McGuffin, P. (1994). The genetic basis of complex human behaviors. *Science, 264,* 1733–1739.

Plomin, R., Willerman, L., & Loehlin, J. C. (1976). Resemblance in appearance and the equal environments assumption in twin studies of personality traits. *Behavior Genetics, 6,* 43–52.

Rowe, D. C. (1987). Resolving the person-situation debate: Invitation to an interdisciplinary dialogue. *American Psychologist, 42,* 218–227.

Rowe, D. C. (1994). *The limits of family influence: Genes, experience, and behavior.* New York: Guilford.

Rowe, D. C., Clapp, M., & Wallis, J. (1987). Physical attractiveness and the personality resemblance of identical twins. *Behavior Genetics, 17,* 191–201.

Rowe, D. C., & Plomin, R. (1981). The importance of nonshared (E_1) environmental influences in behavioral development. *Developmental Psychology, 17,* 517–531.

Scarr, S. (1981). *Race, social class, and individual differences in IQ.* Hillsdale, NJ: Lawrence Erlbaum.

Scarr, S., & Weinberg, R. A. (1978). The influence of "family background" on intellectual attainment. *American Sociological Review, 43,* 674–692.

Straub, R. E., Jiang, Y., MacLean, C., Ma, Y., Webb, B. T., Myakishev, M. V., Harris-Kerr, C., Wormley, B., Sadek, H., Kadambi, B., Cesare, A., Gibberman, A., O'Neill, F. A., Walsh, D., & Kendler, K. S. (2002). Genetic variation in the 6p22.3 gene DTNBP1, the human ortholog of mouse dysbindin, is associated with schizophrenia. *American Journal of Human Genetics, 71,* 337–348.

Straub, R. E., MacLean, C. J., O'Neill, F. A., Burke, J., Murphy, B., Duke, F., Shinkwin, R., Webb, B. T., Zhang, J., Walsh, D., & Kendler, K.S. (1995). A potential vulnerability locus for schizophrenia on chromosome 6p24-22: Evidence for genetic heterogeneity. *Nature Genetics, 11,* 287–293.

Symons, D. (1979). *The evolution of human sexuality.* New York: Oxford University Press.

Tellegen, A., Lykken, D. T., Bouchard, T. J., Jr., Wilcox, K. J., Segal, N. L., & Rich, S. (1988). Personality similarity in twins reared apart and together. *Journal of Personality and Social Psychology, 54,* 1031–1039.

Turke, P. W. (1990). Which humans behave adaptively, and why does it matter? *Ethology and Sociobiology, 11,* 305–339.

Van den Oord, E. J. C. G., Pickles, A. P., & Waldman, I. D. (2003). Normal variation and abnormality: An empirical study of the liability distributions underlying depression and delinquency.

Journal of Child Psychology and Psychiatry, 44, 180–192.

Van den Oord, E. J. C. G., & Rowe, D. C. (1999). A cousin study of associations between family demographic characteristics and children's intellectual ability. *Intelligence, 27,* 251–266.

Vernon, P. A. (Ed.). (1987). *Speed of information processing and intelligence.* Norwood, NJ: Ablex.

Watson, J. D., & Crick, F. H. C. (1953). Molecular structure of nucleic acids: A structure for deoxyribose nucleic acid. *Nature, 171,* 737–738.

Wessells, N. K., & Hopson, J. L. (1988). *Biology.* New York: Random House.

Whitfield, J. B. (1997). Meta-analysis of the effects of alcohol dehydrogenase genotype on alcohol dependence and alcoholic liver disease. *Alcohol and Alcoholism, 32,* 613–619.

Wilson, E. O. (1975). *Sociobiology: The new synthesis.* Cambridge, MA: Belknap Press/Harvard University Press.

Wilson, R. S. (1978). Synchronies in mental development: An epigenetic perspective. *Science, 202,* 939–948.

Zegura, S. L. (1995). The nascent zone of evolutionary change, red Burgundies, and other formative experiences. *South African Journal of Science, 91,* 437–442.

Zwick, M., Cutler, D., Lin, S., & Chakravarti, A. (2002). An empirical estimate of the number of SNPs required for a whole genome association study. *American Journal of Human Genetics, 71,* 219 (Abstract 278).

4 | Personality: Biological Perspectives

RICHARD J. DAVIDSON

CHAPTER OUTLINE

Inferences about personality have traditionally been made on the basis of self-reports and action. The use of biological measures in the study of personality has been comparatively less prevalent, although many theorists have assumed that core personality traits were somehow rooted in underlying biology. For example, Gordon Allport (1966), one of the founders of modern personality psychology, explicitly suggested that traits were subserved by underlying biological processes. He (Allport, 1966) asserted that "traits are cortical, subcortical or postural dispositions having the capacity to gate or guide specific phasic reactions. It is only the phasic aspect which is visible; the tonic is carried somehow in the still mysterious realm of neurodynamic structure" (p. 3). The assumption that core personality traits are products of underlying biological dispositions was one shared by a number of early influential workers including Freud and Pavlov. In his *Project for a Scientific Psychology*, Freud (1895/1966) suggested that individuals may differ in certain neuronal properties that would in turn account for psychological differences. Pavlov (1928) introduced the concept of strength of the nervous system and indicated that pronounced individual variability exists in this property. His work laid the foundation for an important tradition of research on the underlying biological substrates of introversion/extraversion (e.g., Eysenck, 1972).

These early theorists argued for the general importance of examining the underlying biological substrates of personality. They believed that personality traits were entities in the mind that were associated with and supported by specific patterns of biological activity. By examining these biological processes, these early theorists believed, a more direct measure of traits could be obtained. This enterprise, however, contains a number of thorny conceptual and methodological issues that merit some attention before we illustrate some of the more substantive areas.

CONCEPTUAL ISSUES IN THE STUDY OF THE BIOLOGICAL BASES OF PERSONALITY

Three Approaches to the Use of Biological Measures in the Study of Personality

There are three ways in which biological measures have most often been used in the study of personality. The first way has been to complement measures obtained from other domains. For example, a psychologist might be interested in studying introverts and extraverts. In addition to examining how such groups differ in their behavior and self-reports, scientists have also asked how such groups might differ in their physiology. The British psychologist Hans Eysenck (1967) explored this issue in considerable detail and reported a number of interesting physiological differences between such groups. For example, he reported that introverts and extraverts differ in global cortical arousal with extraverts showing less arousal than introverts. He argued that the decreased arousal in the extraverts was actually a key factor that motivated such individuals to engage in extraverted behavior. Such behavior, Eysenck believed, served to increase their arousal to more optimal levels. On the other hand, introverts were found to show heightened global cortical arousal. Introverted behavior was thought to decrease their cortical arousal to more optimal levels. Thus, these differences in arousal were believed to be causal in producing the types of behavior that are characteristically associated with extraverts and introverts. Unfortunately, this model has been criticized as overly simplistic by some researchers (e.g., Gray, 1972).

A second way in which physiological information has been used in the study of personality is to examine relations among self-report and behavioral and physiological measures of a hypothetical construct. For example, imagine an experiment in which we give a self-report measure of anxiety to a large group of participants and select those who score low in anxiety for intensive study. If we present a moderately stressful stimulus to these participants, we will likely find that some will show relatively little arousal in physiological measures that are thought to reflect anxiety, while other participants will show heightened arousal on such measures. Remember that both of these groups reported little anxiety on the self-report measure that was administered. Thus, in one group, the physiological measures seem concordant with the self-report measures and in the other group, the physiological measures are discordant with the self-report measures. Which measure are we to believe? I wish to suggest that *both* measures are providing essential information and that what is most important in this example is the degree to which such measures are concordant or discordant.

The example described above is not entirely hypothetical. My colleagues and I, and others, have studied the type of person who reports himself or herself to be low in anxiety but responds both physiologically and behaviorally in ways that suggest heightened anxiety. We performed an experiment (Weinberger, Schwartz, & Davidson, 1979) in which participants who scored very low on an anxiety scale were differentiated into two groups on the basis of a second self-report measure of repressive defensiveness. Those participants who scored low on both the anxiety measure and the measure of repressive defensiveness were considered to be truly low anxious subjects. The participants who scored low on the anxiety measure but high on the measure of repressive defensiveness were considered to be "repressors." We presented neutral and emotional phrases in response to which subjects were requested to say the first word or phrase that came to mind. We found that in response to the emotional phrases the repressors showed more arousal in several autonomic measures compared to the truly low anxious subjects. In fact, the level of arousal displayed by the repressors was comparable to (and in some cases, even higher than) that displayed by a group of high anxious participants who were also tested. This experiment illustrates the utility of measuring physiological activity in addition to self-report and action to provide a more complete account of personality. In this experiment the relation of the physiological measures to other measures of personality was most important.

The two types of approaches to the use of biological indices in personality research illustrated above both involve the use of physiological activity as *dependent* (or *outcome) variables*. In other words, groups are classified on the basis of some independent variable such as scores on a paper-and-pencil test and a study is performed to determine how such groups might differ on a physiological variable. The third way in which biological measures have been used in the study of personality has been as *independent* (or *predictor) variables*. In this strategy, subjects are not classified into groups on the basis of a traditional personality instrument such as a paper-and-pencil measure or a projective measure. Rather, this approach entails the classification of subjects on the basis of a physiological measure. Relations are then examined between subjects' scores on the physiological measure and relevant behavioral and/or self-report measures. Some scientists who have used this latter strategy have argued that by selecting subjects on the basis of biological measures, one is not necessarily constrained by the existing categories that have developed within personality psychology. It is possible that individual differences in certain physiological measures will be discovered that do not have close analogs in traditional personality psychology. The categories of individual differences that may emerge from using biological measures in this fashion may more closely reflect "natural" individual variation. At the present time, such arguments are speculative, though there is an increasing corpus of research performed within this tradition. In a very recent review, Kosslyn et al. (2002) demonstrated the utility of focusing on individual differences in biological functioning to illuminate psychological phenomena ranging from individual differences in basic cognitive functions such as mental imagery to more traditional domains of personality and affective style.

Correlate or Substrate?

When physiological measures are examined in relation to behavior or personality traits, it is useful to ask whether the measure is conceptualized as a substrate of the trait in question or as a correlate. In general, substrates can be considered an actual component of the trait while correlates are merely associated events that co-occur with the trait. If the physiological measure is taken to be a correlate of the trait, then experimental modification of the measure will not in any way alter the trait in question. For example, a number of researchers have examined individual differences in various measures of skin conductance (e.g., see Boucsein, 1992, for review). Skin conductance primarily reflects the degree of sweating on the skin and is usually measured from surface of the palms or fingers. In all likelihood, it is safe to conceptualize skin conductance differences between groups as *correlates* of an individual difference in behavior. If we were to peripherally block the skin conductance response with a locally applied pharmacological agent, we would not alter the trait in question. Other physiological measures are assumed to reflect more "basic" differences between groups and are conceptualized as substrates of traits, rather than correlates. For example, some cardiac and respiratory changes associated with anxiety may, in certain circumstances, reflect substrates of this trait. In other words, if these autonomic processes were altered by a peripheral pharmacological agent, the construct of interest (i.e., anxiety) would also likely change. A specific example of this may be seen in people suffering from social phobia who have been found to show heightened arousal in certain autonomic systems. One of the treatments for this condition is the administration of a beta-blocker that blocks the expression of these autonomic changes and has been found to significantly attentuate anxiety in some studies (see Price, Goddard, Barr, & Goodman, 1995, for review). One of the most commonly used beta-blockers to treat social phobias (atenolol) is one that has the important property of not crossing the blood-brain barrier. This is significant because it allows us to conclude that the changes in behavior associated with the administration of this drug are due primarily to the changes in peripheral autonomic activity and are not by-products of central changes. Thus, the autonomic changes that accompany this condition are properly conceptualized as substrates of the disorder, since altering the physiology changes the trait of interest. Similarly, other work suggests that altering autonomic function pharmacologically also affects memory for affect-laden information with drug-induced attenuation of autonomic function associated with poorer memory for emotional information (Packard & Cahill, 2001).

It is useful to be explicit about one's conception of whether a particular physiological measure that is being recorded is to be regarded as a substrate or correlate. If the physiological measure reflects a substrate, it may be informative with respect to the underlying psychobiology of the personality trait in question. In other words, we can potentially learn about the biological mechanisms that give rise to the trait. This type of information would be useful in advancing our understanding of basic brain/behavior relations. When we measure a correlate, such information may have enormous practical utility in the prediction of behavior. However, since correlates are not directly related to underlying biological substrates, the contribution of such information to understanding the biological bases of personality is necessarily less direct.

Does Substrate Imply Cause?

When biological substrates of personality are identified, students often assume that their presence implies a heritable cause. It is critical to underscore the fact that such an assumption is unwarranted. The identification of biological substrates of particular personality traits implies nothing about their distal cause. The issue of causality is an entirely separate issue. It certainly may be that the trait in question has heritable contributions, but this is not necessarily so. Biological differences among people occur for many reasons, only one of which is genetic.

We know from extensive data in animals that the environment can significantly alter brain function and even structure. There are two fundamental ways in which experience can shape brain function and structure (Greenough & Black, 1992). *Experience-expectant mechanisms* appear to have evolved in cases in which the information to be acquired is common to all young members of a species. For example, the presence of everyday visual and auditory input constitutes the types of experiential events that drive experience-expectant mechanisms. Experience-expectant plasticity (i.e., changes in brain structure in response to experience) involves the literal molding of brain synapses in response to species-typical early environmental input. It is the other form of plasticity, experience-dependent, that is more relevant to our understanding of personality since this form is driven by events that are idiosyncratic for each individual. According to Greenough and Black (1992), the critical requirement for *experience-dependent plasticity* is learning and memory formation that will clearly vary greatly across individuals.

The fact of experience-dependent plasticity and its documented effects on brain development and synapse formation underscore the need to exercise great caution in making inferences about the distal causes (in this case, whether the biological differences are a consequence of genetic or environmental factors) of biological differences. The brain is the most plastic organ in the body and is built to change in response to experience. It is likely that many of the biological characteristics that will be featured below as salient in our understanding of affect-related individual differences are complex products of genetic predispositions and experience. When the proper methods for quantifying the extent of genetic contribution to complex behavioral traits is used, rarely do the findings suggest that more than 50% of the variance is attributable to genetic factors (Plomin, Owen, & McGuffin, 1994).

METHODOLOGICAL CONSIDERATIONS IN THE STUDY OF THE BIOLOGICAL BASES OF PERSONALITY

Psychometric Considerations

Most of the psychometric considerations that apply to the measurement of personality with paper-and-pencil tests also apply to the study of individual differences in physiological measures. An important concern is the reliability of the measure. If individual differences in a physiological measure are examined, it is important that the measure be stable, that is, show adequate test-retest reliability. Often, physiological measures are used as correlates of personality traits with little attention paid to psychometric considerations. If a particular measure is not stable, it will be less likely to relate to other individual difference measures that show adequate test-retest stability.

The validity of the physiological measure must also be demonstrated. In many ways, most of the research on physiological correlates of personality is an attempt to demonstrate the validity (both concurrent and predictive) of the physiological measures in question. For example, in Kagan's research (Kagan, Reznick, & Snidman, 1988) on the biological bases of childhood shyness, he and his colleagues are exploring the degree to which early measures of autonomic activity predict later behavioral manifestations of shy and wary behavior. The physiological measures are used to enhance the construct validity of the temperamental dimension under study. In addition, the research establishes the predictive validity of the physiological measures that were obtained.

Resting or Task-Related Measures?

Another important methodological issue that is specific to the use of physiological measures concerns the situations during which they should be obtained. Here the basic choice is between resting measures and task-related measures.

We can record most physiological measures during a baseline condition as well as in response to specific challenges. For example, we can compare introverts and extraverts on baseline measures of heart rate and brain activity. And we can obtain the same measures in response to specific tasks designed to challenge participants in particular ways. There is no simple rule of thumb to use as a general guide in making this decision. It is certainly conceivable that differences between two groups of participants will be uncovered only if physiology is recorded in response to specific challenges. This is not unlike the cardiac stress test that is used in the diagnosis of cardiac problems. Some patients' cardiac problems are not revealed in resting measures of cardiac function. Only when their systems are challenged do differences become apparent. On the other hand, as I will illustrate below, there are certainly some physiological indices that meaningfully vary across individuals in the resting state. It is often the case that an investigator will record physiology during both a baseline period and in response to specific challenges.

In certain experimental contexts, the measurement of *baseline* physiology is really not possible. The very act of measurement is itself a challenge to the participant, particularly if the measurement procedure is complex and novel and especially in young children. For example, in studies of individual differences in temperament in young children, the process of placing electrodes on the surface of the body and recording physiology is itself a stressful challenge, particularly for subjects who are temperamentally wary to begin with. Thus, for these participants, it is not really possible to obtain a measure of pure "baseline" physiology. The physiological measures one obtains during a baseline period will inevitably reflect the interaction of the child's temperamental qualities and the stress of the measurement situation. The only way to minimize such influences is to acclimate the subject to the testing environment and have him or her return to the lab for a second testing session when the laboratory situation will be more familiar. One can then either use the data from the second session only or compare the data from the first and second sessions. Such a procedure is commonly used in sleep research, when researchers will have participants come to the sleep laboratory for two nights, with real data collected only during the second night because of the issues noted above in acclimating to a novel environment. While the challenge of placing electrodes on the body surface is novel, the stress of other, modern neuroimaging methods is considerably more significant. For example, functional magnetic resonance imaging can be used to measure small local changes in blood oxygenation level (which is correlated with neuronal activation) throughout the brain while a participant performs a task (Cohen, 1996; D'Esposito, 2000). Such images provide unprecedented spatial and temporal resolution for the examination of brain function. However, this technique requires the participant to enter the bore of an MRI scanner, where his or her head remains immobilized with a bite bar. The participant must lie very still for long periods of time inside an enormous medical instrument. This context, for some participants, is clearly anxiety provoking. To address this problem, we have created a simulator room. The shell of an old MRI scanner has been set up and resembles in virtually every detail the real scanner. The head holder and bite bar are identical to the one we use in the actual scanner. We have recorded the sounds the MRI scanner produces and play these to prospective research participants in the simulator. We present the tasks in the simulator that will be used in the actual scanner to acclimate participants to the environment and reduce their anxiety. Some participants find the procedure too anxiety provoking and never make it to the real scanner. In this way, we can maximize our data yield when using such expensive technology.

Some Commonly Used Physiological Measures in the Study of Personality

Most of the physiological variables used in personality research fall under the rubric of what would be called "psychophysiological measures." Such measures are recorded from surface electrodes on the subject's body and are therefore totally noninvasive. This makes them ideally suited for studies of normal personality when it would be difficult to justify the use of invasive measures. Although psychophysiological measures are the most commonly used, a number of other types of biological measures have also been used. These other measures vary in the degree to which they are invasive. Below I list several different psychophysiological measures and briefly illustrate how they have been used in personality research. Also offered are several examples of the ways other types of biological measures have been used.

Electrodermal Measures   Electrodermal activity refers to the measurement of the electrical activity of the skin. There are several different types of electrodermal measurement (see Fowles, 1986; Boucsein, 1992; Dawson, Schell, & Filion, 2000, for detailed discussions of this response system). The ones most commonly used in personality research are based upon skin conductance (or its inverse, skin resistance). Skin conductance refers to the conductivity of the skin to a very small external current that is applied between two electrodes, usually on the palmar surface of the hand or fingers. The primary contributor to the variations in skin conductance is the degree of sweat in the sweat glands and on the surface of the skin: the more sweat, the greater the conductivity.

Researchers most commonly measure three different attributes of skin conductance. These three attributes are all somewhat intercorrelated, although they are thought to reflect partially independent response properties. The three attributes of skin conductance are skin conductance level (SCL), skin conductance response (SCR) to an external stimulus, and spontaneous skin conductance responses (SSCR). The last measure is usually the number of responses above a minimal threshold that occur in the absence of any defined external stimulus during a particular period of time.

Individual differences in all three types of measures have been studied in relation to different personality characteristics. For example, some investigators have studied individual differences in the rate at which the SCR to simple sensory stimuli habituates. A number of researchers have reported that extraverts habituate more rapidly than introverts (e.g., Crider & Lunn, 1971). Other investigators have reported that speed of habituation of the SCR is more related to anxiety or neuroticism (e.g., Coles, Gale, & Kline, 1971; see review by O'Gorman, 1983). Differences between depressed and nondepressed subjects in different aspects of electrodermal activity have also been studied. Depressed subjects consistently show lower SCL and smaller SCRs than nondepressed subjects (see Henriques & Davidson, 1989, for review). Fowles and Kochanska (2000) have demonstrated the important interaction between individual differences in electrodermal reactivity and maternal parenting style in the prediction of the development of conscience in children. They found that electrodermal reactivity at age 4 predicted conscience for children raised by mothers who used gentle discipline.

Measures of Cardiovascular Activity   Heart rate and other measures of cardiovascular activity have been used in studies of personality for many years. A number of different indices of cardiac function have been measured. The most commonly used measures of cardiac activity are heart rate and heart rate variability. Other measures of cardiovascular function have been developed to provide additional information that is not readily available from simple measures of heart rate and heart rate variability (see Cacioppo, Uchino, & Bernston, 1994; Brownley, Hurwitz, & Schneiderman, 2000). In his studies of childhood shyness, Kagan and his colleagues (Kagan et al., 1988) have reported that shy or inhibited children have higher resting heart rates and less heart rate variability compared with uninhibited children. Those children who showed a stable temperamental disposition of wariness or inhibition from 21 months to 7.5 years had higher heart rate at every age measured. In this study, the original classification of the groups was made at age 21 months. In studies with adults, heart rate has also been used to examine individual differences. Hodes, Cook, and Lang (1985) reported that subjects with higher heart rates acquired a conditioned fear more readily than subjects with lower heart rates. Heart rate has also been found to be elevated among subjects with depression (Henriques & Davidson, 1989). As with most autonomic measures, there are both sympathetic and parasympathetic nervous system contributions to heart rate. Individual differences in the activity levels in each branch of the autonomic nervous system cannot be disentangled using heart rate alone. Other techniques, such as impedance cardiography and spectral analysis of heart rate have been used to quantify activity in the separate sympathetic and parasympathetic components of cardiac control. Cacioppo and his colleagues (Cacioppo, Uchino, & Bernston, 1994) have established that there are reliable individual differences in these differing components of heart rate control, which themselves are independent. Individuals with greater sympathetic activity in response to a laboratory stressor also have higher levels of cortisol—a stress-related hormone—and decreased levels of certain immune measures (Cacioppo, 1994) that may help to explain the mechanism by which stress may be deleterious for health in certain individuals who are particularly vulnerable.

Measures of Brain Electrical Activity   Measures of brain electrical activity are ideally suited for studies of personality since they provide potentially useful information about central nervous system *substrates* of personality and they are noninvasive and relatively easy to record (See Davidson, Jackson, & Larson,

2000). Both spontaneous brain activity (EEG) and event-related potentials (ERPs) or evoked potentials (EPs) have been used in personality research. EEG refers to the ongoing background activity of the brain. It is usually measured under resting conditions or while a participant performs a task. ERPs refer to brain activity that is specifically time-locked to some external event. ERPs are usually measured by averaging brain electrical activity for a short period of time just after a stimulus is presented. The activity that is specifically related to the event will be enhanced and the activity that is random with respect to the event will diminish. The averaging procedure is essentially a way to improve the signal-to-noise ratio of the measure. Both methods are useful in different contexts. Measurement of regional EEG activity can provide information on patterns of activation in different cortical regions. The use of EEG in personality research will be illustrated in the next section. ERPs have been used in a number of different ways in studies of individual differences.

One of the earliest applications of event-related potential (ERP) measures to the domain of personality was the study of individual differences in "augmentation/reduction." Augmentation/reduction refers to the degree to which a person tends to either augment or reduce the impact of sensory stimulation. This dimension of personality was first described by Petrie (1967/1978) in her book on individual differences in pain responsivity. Although Petrie did not use ERPs to measure augmentation/reduction, she described a number of fascinating differences between groups of people who were selected on the basis of their response to differing levels of sensory stimulation. The participants were selected by use of a behavioral measure of this dimension which she developed.

The essential principle of the measure was to determine participants' perception of the width of wooden blocks that they rubbed with their fingers. Reducers were those participants who perceived the blocks to be thinner than they actually were, while augmenters were those who perceived the blocks to be wider than they actually were. She found that participants who were reducers were more tolerant of pain and less tolerant of sensory monotomy. Augmenters, on the other hand, were less tolerant of pain but were more tolerant of sensory monotony. Petrie also reported that drugs used to reduce pain, such as aspirin, tended to make augmenters more like reducers on her measure.

The logic behind the assessment of augmentation/reduction using ERPs is simple. If a participant shows increases in the amplitude of the evoked response to a stimulus with increases in intensity, that participant is said to be an augmenter. Alternatively, if a participant shows little change or an actual decrease in amplitude of the same component of the evoked response as stimulus intensity increases, the participant would be classified as a reducer. Buchsbaum and Silverman (1968) were among the first to report on this method to assess augmentation/reduction. They randomly presented visual stimuli differing in intensity to participants while the participants' brain electrical activity was measured from a number of scalp sites. They derived separate ERPs to the light flashes of each intensity level and computed the slope of the amplitude/intensity function for each participant. This slope reflects how steeply the amplitude of the response changes as a function of increases in stimulus intensity. Participants with very large slopes would be considered augmenters; those with small slopes or negative slopes would be considered reducers. The researchers reported a correlation of 0.63 between their evoked potential method of assessing augmentation/reduction and the behavioral procedure used by Petrie. Subsequent research using the evoked potential procedure for measuring this characteristic has uncovered important genetic contributions to this trait (see Buchsbaum, Haier, & Johnson, 1983, for review). In addition, augmentation/reduction has been linked to sensation seeking (e.g., Zuckerman, 1983). Augmenters, compared to reducers, are higher in sensation seeking.

Other Biological Measures   In addition to the psychophysiological measures described above, a number of other types of biological measures have been used in research on individual differences. An important class of measures is made up of those used to provide information about regional brain activation. These are similar in purpose to EEG measures, but they differ with respect to their spatial resolution. Spatial resolution refers to the precision with which such methods can accurately reflect brain activity in very localized regions. Techniques with good spatial resolution are those that reflect very localized activity. Two methods that provide very accurate spatial information that are just now beginning to be used in individual difference research are positron emission tomography (PET; Cherry & Phelps, 1996) and functional magnetic resonance imaging (fMRI; Cohen, 1996; Davidson & Irwin, 1999). PET provides a method by which biochemical processes can be imaged throughout the brain. The specific biochemical process is determined by the tracer that is given to the participant. The tracer is a molecule that is tagged with a radioactive tracer. It is the distribution of the radioactively tagged molecule that is imaged with the PET scanner. Two of the most commonly used PET tracers enable the imaging of glucose metabolism and blood flow, respectively. Glucose is the main nutrient of the brain, and when neurons are active they metabolize more glucose. Individuals who are depressed have been found to have lower levels of glucose metabolism in the left prefrontal cortex (Baxter et al., 1989; George, Ketter, Parekh, Horwitz, Herscovitch, & Post, 1995). Blood flow is a measure that is usually highly correlated with glucose metabolism. When neurons are active, they require more oxygen, which is supplied by increasing the blood flow to that region. Certain tracers can be used that are sensitive to small, local variations in blood flow.

One of the unique qualities of PET is that it can be used to image neurotransmitter function in addition to measures that reflect activation (such as glucose metabolism and blood flow). Tracers can be administered that bind to particular receptor subtypes and provide quantitative estimates of the density of specific neurotransmitter receptors throughout the brain. Using such a technique, Farde and his colleagues (Farde, Gustavsson, & Jönsson, 1997) have reported that on a paper-and-pencil measure of "detachment" that reflects the tendency to avoid involvement with other people, individuals who scored in the extremely detached direction had lower densities of the dopamine-2 receptor in the basal ganglia, a brain region involved with motivated action. The correlation they reported between the PET measure of receptor density and the personality scale was $r = -.68$, a remarkably strong association, indicating that individual differences in emotional detachment are closely associated with less density of dopamine receptors in this specific brain region. It is likely that this technique will be used with increasing frequency in the future.

Davidson and Irwin (1999) have documented some of the ways in which fMRI is now being used to make inferences about individual differences in activation patterns in specific neural circuits. These studies are finding strong associations between such individual differences and behavioral and self-report measures of personality. For example, as noted by Davidson and Irwin (1999), participants with greater amygdala reactivity to negative versus neutral pictures report higher levels of dispositional negative affect on a simple self-report measure.

In addition to methods for the assessment of regional brain activation, other biochemical methods involving assays of either blood or saliva have been used in the study of individual differences. Individual differences have been studied in the levels of a number of different biochemicals. For example, several studies have been performed that have examined the personality correlates of individual differences in an enzyme—monoamine oxidase (MAO)—that regulates certain neurotransmitters in the brain (e.g., Buchsbaum et al., 1976). Other studies have used a measure that reflects overall activity in the hypothalamic-pituitary-adrenal axis in the study of individual differences. Cortisol levels in the saliva have been used for this purpose and have been found, for example, to be elevated in wary, inhibited children compared with uninhibited children (Kagan et al., 1988).

AN EMPIRICAL EXAMPLE OF THE BIOLOGICAL APPROACH TO PERSONALITY: CEREBRAL ASYMMETRY AND AFFECTIVE STYLE

Although functional differences between the two cerebral hemispheres of the brain in the control of emotional behavior have been noted for over 50 years (e.g., Alford, 1933; Goldstein, 1939), relatively little systematic study of this problem occurred prior to the 1980s. In the past 20 years, there has been a dramatic increase in research on this topic. Furthermore, this accumulating body of work encompasses a wide variety of methodological approaches. For example, neurological, psychiatric, and normal populations have all been studied extensively, and a range of assessment techniques have been used. These include self-report and behavioral indices of emotion, and behavioral, electrophysiological, and hemodynamic (measures that reflect local changes in brain blood flow, e.g., PET and fMRI) indices of regional brain activity (for reviews, see, e.g., Davidson, 1995; Davidson & Sutton, 1995; Davidson, 2000). In addition to this large corpus of new data in humans, animal findings consistent with the human data have been obtained, and promising animal models of the lateralization of emotion have been developed (for reviews, see, e.g., Denenberg & Yutzey, 1985; Glick & Shapiro, 1985; see Davidson, Kalin & Shelton, 1993, and Kalin, Larson, Shelton, & Davidson, 1998, for empirical examples).

One of the most significant extensions of basic research on laterality and emotion has been the study of relations between individual differences in particular indices of asymmetry and affective reactivity. After reviewing some relevant background literature, a brief overview of some of our own recent findings in this area is presented.

The literature on laterality and emotion supports two broad conclusions about the differential role of the two cerebral hemispheres in emotion. The first concerns the specialization of the *posterior* regions of the right hemisphere for the perception of emotional information. The second broad conclusion is that the *anterior* regions of the two hemispheres are differentially specialized for the experience and spontaneous expression of certain positive and negative emotions, with the left hemisphere playing a more active role for positive emotions and the right hemisphere for negative emotions (see Davidson, 2000; Davidson, Jackson, & Kalin, 2000, for reviews). It is this latter specialization that is the central concern of the studies described.

Evidence from several sources supports the conclusion about the emotional specialization of the anterior regions of the hemispheres. Studies on the affective correlates of unilateral brain damage indicate that damage to the left anterior region is more likely to result in depressive symptomatology compared with comparable right hemisphere damage. In one of the first systematic studies to compare the emotional consequences of left- versus right-sided brain damage, Gainotti (1972) reported that left-lesioned patients had significantly more negative affect and depressive symptomatology than right-lesioned patients. Subsequent studies support this conclusion (e.g., Robinson, Kubos, Starr, Rao, & Price, 1984; Sackeim, Weinman, Gur, Greenberg, Hungerbuhler, & Geschwind, 1982).

Electrophysiological studies on nonlesioned populations point toward a similar conclusion. Such studies have typically used measures of brain electrical activity to make inferences about patterns of regional activation. We and others (e.g., Ahern & Schwartz, 1985; Tucker, Stenslie, Roth, & Shearer, 1981) have reported in several studies that certain forms of negative affect are accompanied by selective activation of the right anterior region whereas positive affect is accompanied by selective activation of the left anterior region (e.g., Davidson, Ekman, Saron, Senulis, & Friesen, 1990). A strong linkage between anterior regions of the cerebral hemispheres and affective experience is additionally consistent with evidence of the extensive neuroanatomical reciprocity between prefrontal and anterior temporal regions of the cerebral cortex and limbic circuits known to be directly involved in the control of motivation and emotion (e.g., Kelly & Stinus, 1984; Nauta, 1971). Studies in depressed patients, who are best characterized as showing an absence of positive affect, indicate that they have reduced activation in the left prefrontal region based on both electrophysiological (e.g., Henriques & Davidson, 1989) and PET (e.g., Baxter et al., 1989; Drevets et al., 1997) studies.

INDIVIDUAL DIFFERENCES IN ANTERIOR ASYMMETRY AND AFFECTIVE REACTIVITY

We have conducted a number of studies in normal and clinical populations on individual differences in anterior activation asymmetry. Anterior activation asymmetry refers to the relative difference in activation between the left and right cerebral hemispheres in the anterior brain regions. In most of the studies conducted to date, activation has been inferred from measuring brain electrical activity. The amount of brain activity between 8 and 13 cycles per second (known as alpha activity) in the adult (and somewhat slower in the infant) is inversely related to activation. Thus, the *less* alpha activity there is, the greater the amount of activation. We therefore measure differences in the amount of alpha activity in the anterior regions of the cerebral hemispheres. More recently, using PET, we can measure asymmetric differences in regional cerebral glucose metabolism or regional cerebral blood flow in specific regions of the prefrontal cortex and in the structures with which the prefrontal cortex is interconnected. These anterior brain regions, consisting predominantly of the anterior temporal and prefrontal regions, have extensive connections with other brain systems that lie below the cerebral hemispheres and have been directly implicated in the control of certain aspects of emotion (see Figure 4.1). In this section, I will summarize the findings from those studies that have focused on individual differences in anterior asymmetry in normal adults and infants, since this work is most relevant to the theme of this chapter. For extensions of this approach to psychopathology, the interested reader should consult Davidson (1994a; 2000).

We have conducted several studies indicating that patterns of baseline asymmetry can indeed *predict* affective reactions at a later point in time. These *baseline* patterns of brain asymmetry are measured during the resting state and tend to be fairly stable over time. Thus, an individual can be assessed on the direction and magnitude of his or her anterior asymmetry and this measure can be considered to be a traitlike characteristic of the person (Tomarken, Davidson, Wheeler, & Kinney, 1992). We have performed several studies in both adults and in infants demonstrating that measures of baseline prefrontal activation

Figure 4.1   Major areas of the cerebral cortex.

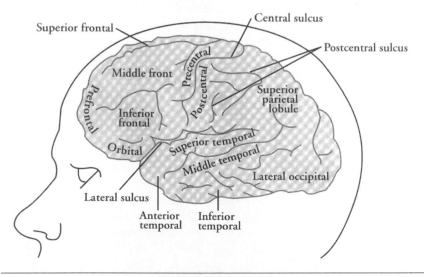

asymmetry predict subsequent affective reactions. Those individuals with greater right-sided prefrontal activation respond more intensely to stimuli designed to elicit negative affect, while individuals with greater left-sided prefrontal activation respond more intensely to stimuli designed to elicit positive affect (see, e.g., Tomarken, Davidson, & Henriques, 1990; Wheeler, Davidson, & Tomarken, 1993). In these studies, we first measured baseline brain activity in our participants. Then either later in the same session or during another session, participants viewed short video clips designed to elicit positive and negative emotion. We assessed reactivity to these short film clips by having participants rate the intensity of their positive and negative affect immediately following each of the clips. Across the three studies reported in Tomarken et al. (1990) and Wheeler et al. (1993) the pattern of results was highly consistent and indicated that participants' reactivity to the film clips was significantly predicted by prior measures of baseline prefrontal asymmetry. Our analyses further revealed that these predictions could not be accounted for by differences in the mood of our participants during the recording of brain activity. We assessed participants' mood during the time measures of brain activity were taken and found that the measures of prefrontal asymmetry still predicted reactivity to the film clips after removing the variance accounted for by baseline mood. We also computed measures of generalized affective reactivity by summing across both positive and negative emotions in response to the positive and negative film clips to ascertain whether our measures of baseline brain function might simply be predicting a trait of generalized emotional reactivity. Our analyses indicated that this was not the case. Prefrontal asymmetry specifically predicted the valence of emotional reactivity but did not predict generalized reactivity across valence. This is important since it indicates that our measures are not simply reflecting a generalized arousal process but rather reflect a bias in the valence of emotional responding. In these and other studies, we have also compared our measures of prefrontal asymmetry with measures of asymmetry derived from other brain regions recorded at the same time (e.g., from the parietal region in the posterior scalp area). These comparisons reveal that activity from the prefrontal region specifically predicts emotional reactivity. Brain activity from the posterior brain regions typically shows no systematic relation to the valence of emotional responding.

In addition to studies that have examined relations between individual differences in baseline measures of prefrontal asymmetry and reactivity to emotional stimuli, we have also examined relations between such individual differences in brain activity and scores on self-report measures of dispositional mood and personality. For example, we found that participants classified on measures of brain function as extreme left-frontally activated report more dispositional positive affect and less dispositional negative affect than their right-frontally activated counterparts (Tomarken et al., 1992b). Sutton and Davidson (1997) also demonstrated a strong relation between individual differences in prefrontal activation asymmetry and scores on a self-report measure of behavioral inhibition and activation (Carver & White, 1994). Behavioral activation reflects the tendency to experience strong positive affect or behavioral approach when specific goal-oriented situations are encountered. Behavioral inhibition reflects the tendency to experience strong negative affect or inhibition when perceived threats are encountered. For example, an individual who scored high on Behavioral Inhibition would endorse the following item: "Criticism or scolding hurts me quite a bit." Subjects with greater left-sided prefrontal activation reported more relative behavioral activation compared with inhibition relative to subjects with right-sided prefrontal activation.

Such individual differences in prefrontal activation asymmetry are observable within the first year of life and predict reactions to age-appropriate emotional challenges. Davidson and Fox (1989) measured resting EEG asymmetry from 14 female 10-month-old infants prior to their exposure to a brief episode of maternal separation. The episode was 60 seconds in duration unless the infant was judged by the experimenter to be extremely upset, at which point the episode was terminated. The focus was on individual differences in response to this stressor since several researchers have noted the pronounced differences among infants of this age in response to maternal separation (e.g., Shiller, Izard, & Hembree, 1986; Weinraub & Lewis, 1977). Moreover, infants' response to maternal separation at this age period is one component of a constellation of behaviors that are associated with individual differences in vulnerability to distress. This is a dimension of temperament for which impressive longitudinal stability has been demonstrated (for a review, see Kagan, 1984).

From the videotaped record of the session, we coded infants' responses to the maternal separation challenge. Examination of these responses revealed that 7 infants cried and 7 did not cry. An infant was classified as a noncrier only if he or she showed no evidence of crying for the entire duration of the maternal separation episode. The classification of an infant as a crier or noncrier was done prior to any EEG analysis and was therefore completely blind.

In accord with our previous findings, we predicted that infants who responded with distress to maternal separation would show more relative right frontal activation during a baseline assessment of EEG than infants who were not distressed by the situation. The results indicated that infants who cried in response to maternal separation did in fact show greater right-frontal and less left-frontal activation at rest than the noncriers. Consistent with our previous findings in adult subjects, parietal asymmetry recorded at the same time as the frontal asymmetry measures failed to discriminate between groups. To examine the consistency of the group difference in frontal asymmetry on an individual subject basis, we computed a laterality difference score for each subject. Higher numbers on this metric indicate more relative left-sided activation. As shown in Figure 4.2, every crier fell below the mean score for the noncriers and every noncrier fell above the mean score for the criers. Moreover, all but one of the criers had absolute right-sided frontal activation.

One concern that might be raised about these findings is that the difference in asymmetry between the two groups might simply reflect differences in preexistent mood; perhaps the criers were in a more irritable mood at the time of the resting baselines. To obtain data relevant to this issue, we coded infants' facial behavior during the resting baseline. On all facial signs of emotion, those infants who subsequently cried in response to maternal separation failed to differ from those who did not cry. While certainly not definitive, these findings do

Figure 4.2   Comparison of frontal asymmetry laterality scores among infants
who cried or did not cry during maternal separation.

Frontal asymmetry laterality scores (the higher the number on the y-axis, the greater the left prefrontal and less right prefrontal activation at rest; conversely, the lower the number on the y-axis,
the greater the right prefrontal and less left prefrontal activation at rest) for individual infants are
split by which infants subsequently cried or did not cry in response to a brief episode of maternal
separation. Note that all of the criers fell below the mean of noncriers and all of the noncriers fell
above the mean of the criers.

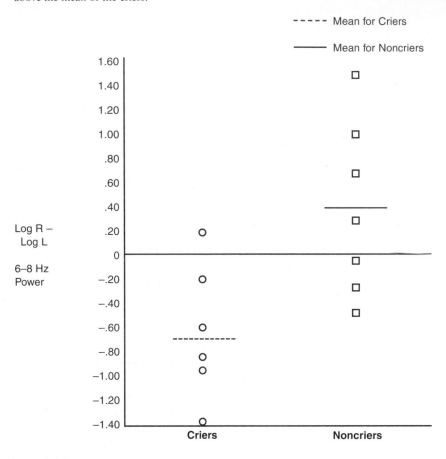

suggest that the two groups of infants were not in a different emotional state at
the time that the EEG measures were recorded.

In sum, I have presented evidence from several studies conducted in my
laboratory in which we examined relations between individual differences in
baseline measures of prefrontal activation asymmetry and various attributes of
emotional reactivity and emotion-related personality. These studies converge
on the idea that there are stable individual differences in asymmetric prefrontal
activation and that such differences predict a wide range of important behavior. In each of the studies, measures were also taken of brain activity in pos-

terior cortical regions and activation patterns in these brain regions were unrelated to the affective constructs, underscoring the specificity of the relations with prefrontal function. Our data lead us to conceptualize individual differences in prefrontal asymmetry as a diathesis that biases an individual to respond in a valence-specific manner upon presentation of the requisite stimulus.

One possible conceptualization of the effects of such individual differences is that they represent differences in *thresholds* for affective responsivity. According to such a view, individuals with relative right anterior activation would require a less intense stimulus to elicit the same amount of negative affect that would be produced by a much more intense stimulus in an individual with left-frontal activation. On the other hand, in an individual with left-frontal activation, a less intense positive stimulus would be required to produce the same level of positive emotion as would be produced by a more intense positive stimulus in a subject with right-frontal activation. This conceptualization is consistent with recent evidence that individual differences in emotion or temperament are linked to altered thresholds for perception of, or responses to, affective stimuli (for a review, see Derryberry & Rothbart, 1984). Our interpretation is also consistent with research in nonhuman animals indicating that activation of neural structures known to regulate important aspects of emotion does in fact produce lower thresholds for significant stimuli. It is also possible that individual differences in prefrontal asymmetry are associated with the duration of affective responding such that subjects with increased left prefrontal activation respond to positive incentives with a longer duration response. When such responses cumulate chronically, they lead to differences in dispositional mood and personality. Some recent evidence from our laboratory is consistent with the idea that individual differences in prefrontal asymmetry are associated with differences in the duration with which an emotion lasts. For example, in response to a negative event, some people show a persisting reaction whereas others are able to recover more quickly. We have referred to such differences in the duration of emotional responding as *affective chronometry* (Davidson, 1994b).

The research described above illustrates how individual differences in one biological variable, anterior brain asymmetry, is related to affective reactivity. In the adult studies, the relation between the physiological measure of interest and measures of affective reactivity and personality were obtained. In the infant study, subjects were classified on the basis of a behavioral measure (crying in response to maternal separation) and differences between groups were then examined in anterior asymmetry. Many questions remain to be answered in this line of research including the degree to which such measures of anterior asymmetry relate to the subsequent development of psychopathology and the underlying biological mechanisms that result in individuals with extreme asymmetry patterns showing biased affective reactivity. For example, do individuals who are particularly prone to depression and anxiety disorders show accentuated right-anterior activation when they are children, prior to any overt expression of psychopathology? On the other hand, there are quite a few individuals exposed to very stressful environments when they are young and yet do not develop any psychopathology. These individuals who are relatively invulnerable to stressful life events may be those with left-anterior activation, since it is this pattern that we have predicted should result in heightened thresholds for experience of negative affect (see e.g., Tomarken & Davidson, 1994). Unfortunately, we currently do not have the answers to these important questions but can look forward to future research in this area for new insights about these very significant issues. Although much has been learned over the past decade about the biological bases of personality, many questions remain. One of the most exciting developments is the promise afforded by the new techniques for functional brain imaging that are just now beginning to be applied to questions regarding the substrates of personality. We can expect that the next decade will produce even more exciting discoveries in this very fertile area of interdisciplinary study. Readers may want to complete the test of anterior brain asymmetry presented in Activity Box 4.1. It measures individual differences in hemispheric activation based on the direction of someone's eye gaze in response to a series of reflective questions.

SUMMARY

This chapter reviews some of the major conceptual and methodological issues in the study of biological bases of personality. Three approaches to the use of biological measures in personality research are identified: (1) use of such measures as an additional correlate of a personality construct; (2) use of such measures to examine individual differences in the relations among response systems that may all reflect different aspects of a single personality construct; and (3) use of such measures as independent variables by which to classify individuals. The question of whether to regard physiological indices of personality as correlates or substrates of the trait of interest is also discussed. A number of commonly used physiological measures in personality research are described. Following this overview, an example of a biological approach to personality from the author's own research is presented. Individual differences in baseline measures of brain asymmetry from the anterior regions of the hemispheres are shown to be related to affective reactivity in both infants and adults.

DISCUSSION QUESTIONS

1. Describe the three ways in which biological measures have most often been used in the study of personality.
2. When physiological measures are studied in relation to behavior or personality traits, what does it mean that the measure is conceptualized as a substrate of the trait or as a correlate?
3. Is there a simple rule of thumb for deciding to use physiologica measures during a baseline condition versus in response to specific challenges?
4. What are commonly used physiological measures in the study of personality?
5. What is the concept of cerebral asymmetry and how is it related to affective style?
6. What is the association between infants' responses to a brief episode of maternal separation and the biological variable of prefrontal activation asymmetry?

Activity Box 4.1   Measuring Your Hemisphericity

Hemisphericity refers to individual differences in hemispheric activation. As noted in the accompanying chapter, individual differences in anterior hemispheric activation asymmetry are related to differences in the manner in which people react to emotional situations. One way in which individual differences in hemispheric activation have been assessed is to measure the direction of a person's gaze following a reflective question. In a right-handed person, if the eyes move to the left, it has been found to be associated with right-sided activation and if the eyes move to the right, it signifies left-sided activation (e.g., Gur & Reivich, 1980). Below are 10 questions which you can have a friend ask you. These questions have been taken from the study of Schwartz, Davidson, and Maer (1975). The interested reader should consult this paper for additional details. Have your friend note the direction of your first eye movement following the presentation of the question. If on 7 or more of the questions you move your eyes to the same direction, you can infer that you are showing more activation on one side of your brain than another. If the direction of your eye movements is to the left, then you are showing right-sided activation. If the direction of your eye movements is to the right, then you are showing left-sided activation. Remember that this is only valid for right-handed individuals. People who are left-handed have a more complicated pattern of hemispheric specialization and without additional testing, it is not possible to unambiguously interpret their eye movement responses.

QUESTIONS

1. Tell me how you feel when you are anxious.
2. Visualize and describe the most upsetting photograph you have seen.
3. Imagine that you are relaxing in hot sulfur baths looking westward over the Pacific Ocean in California on a clear, sunny day. Your friend is peacefully resting with his back toward your right side. Approximately what direction is your friend looking out over?
4. Make up a sentence using the words "shock" and "anger."
5. When you visualize your father's face, what emotion first strikes you?
6. Tell me how you feel when you are frustrated.
7. Picture and describe the most joyous scene you have recently been in.
8. Imagine that you are a veterinarian and must make a long and deep incision upon a dog. You must cut a straight line from the dog's left eye to his right, front shoulder. Visualize making the incision and tell me what parts of his face you would cut through.
9. Make up a sentence using the words rhapsody and pleasure.
10. Visualize and describe the most beautiful photograph you have recently seen.

You should note that this is not at all a conclusive measure of hemisphericity. Many factors unrelated to hemispheric activation affect a person's direction of lateral gaze following questions of this kind. You should also be aware of the fact that most people do not show consistent eye movements to one or another direction. They show eye movements in different directions as a function of the question content. If you happen to be a person who does show consistent eye movements to the left or right, you can decide whether you feel that you are more vulnerable to positive or negative affect. Research suggests that those who consistently move their eyes to the left should be more likely to experience negative affect while individuals who move their eyes to the right should be more likely to experience positive affect.

SUGGESTED READINGS

Davidson, R. J. (2000). Affective style, psychopathology and resilience: Brain mechanisms and plasticity. *American Psychologist, 55,* 1196–1214. This article presents a broad overview of research from Dr. Davidson's laboratory over the past decade on relations between prefrontal and amygdala function and personality and psychopathology.

Davidson, R. J., Pizzagalli, D., Nitschke, J. B., & Putnam, K. M. (2002). Depression: Perspectives from affective neuroscience. *Annual Review of Psychology, 53,* 545–574. This article presents a comprehensive overview of modern research on abnormalities in the neural circuits underlying emotion and emotion regulation in persons with mood disorders.

Ekman, P., & Davidson, R. J. (1994). *The nature of emotion.* New York: Cambridge University Press.

This book poses 12 fundamental questions about the nature of emotion, many of which relate directly to biology and personality. Different scholars have written short essays responding to each of these questions.

Pizzagalli, D., Shackman, A. J., & Davidson, R. J. (2003). The functional neuroimaging of human emotion: Asymmetric contributions of cortical and subcortical circuitry. In K. Hugdahl & R. J. Davidson (Eds.), *The asymmetrical brain* (pp. 511–532). Cambridge, MA: MIT Press. This chapter presents a detailed overview of recent work from my laboratory and other laboratories on the hemispheric substrates of emotion and their relation to personality and psychopathology.

SUGGESTED WEB SITE

http://tezpur.keck.waisman.wisc.edu
Describes research programs being conducted at the W. M. Keck Laboratory for Functional Brain Imaging and Behavior at the University of Wisconsin–Madison. The laboratory is a state-of-the-art facility

focusing on affective and cognitive neuroscience research with brain imaging. The site includes summaries of research about the connection between the brain and emotions.

INFOTRAC COLLEGE EDITION SEARCH TOPICS

Correlates
Substrates

Cerebral asymmetry
Affective reactivity

Affective chronometry

REFERENCES

Ahern, G. L., & Schwartz, G. E. (1985). Differential lateralization for positive and negative emotion in the human brain: EEG spectral analysis. *Neuropsychologia, 23,* 745–756.

Alford, L. B. (1933). Localization of consciousness and emotion. *American Journal of Psychiatry, 12,* 789–799.

Allport, G. W. (1966). Traits revisited. *American Psychologist, 21,* 1–10.

Baxter, L. R., Schwartz, J. M., Phelps, M. E., Mazziota, J. C., Guze, B. H., Selin, C. E., Gerner, R. H., & Sumida, R. M. (1989). Reduction of prefrontal cortex glucose metabolism common to three types of depression. *Archives of General Psychiatry, 46,* 243–252.

Boucsein, W. (1992). *Electrodermal activity.* New York: Plenum.

Brownley, K. A., Hurwitz, B. E., & Schneiderman, N. (2000). Cardiovascular psychophysiology. In J. T. Cacioppo, G. Bernston, & L. Tassinary (Eds.), *Principles of psychophysiology* (2nd ed., pp. 224–264). New York: Cambridge University Press.

Buchsbaum, M. S., & Silverman, J. (1968). Stimulus intensity control and the cortical evoked response. *Psychosomatic Medicine, 30,* 12–22.

Buchsbaum, M. S., Coursey, R. D., & Murphy, D. L. (1976). The biochemical high-risk paradigm: Behavioral and familial correlates of low platelet monamine oxidase activity. *Science, 194,* 339–341.

Buchsbaum, M. S., Haier, R. J., & Johnson, J. (1983). Augmenting and reducing: Individual differences in evoked potentials. In A. Gale & J. A. Edwards (Eds.), *Physiological correlates of human behaviour: Vol. 3. Individual differences and psychopathology* (pp. 117–138). London: Academic Press.

Cacioppo, J. T. (1994). Social neuroscience: Autonomic, neuroendocrine and immune responses to stress. *Psychophysiology, 31,* 113–128.

Cacioppo, J. T., Uchino, B. N., & Bernston, G. G. (1994). Individual differences in the autonomic origins of heart rate reactivity: The psychometrics of respiratory sinus arrhythmia and preejection period. *Psychophysiology, 31,* 412–419.

Carver, C. S., & White, T. L. (1994). Behavioral inhibition, behavioral activation and affective responses to impending reward and punishment: The BIS/BAS scales. *Journal of Personality and Social Psychology, 67,* 319–333.

Cherry, S. R., & Phelps, M. E. (1996). Imaging brain function with positron emission tomography. In A.W. Toga & J. C. Mazziotta (Eds.), *Brain mapping: The methods* (pp. 191–221). San Diego, CA: Academic Press.

Cohen, M. S. (1996). Rapid MRI and functional applications. In A.W. Toga & J. C. Mazziotta (Eds.), *Brain mapping: The methods* (pp. 223–255). San Diego, CA: Academic Press.

Coles, M. G. H., Gale, A., & Kline, P. (1971). Personality and habituation of the orienting reaction: Tonic and response measures of electrodermal activity. *Psychophysiology, 8,* 54–63.

Crider, A., & Lunn, R. (1971). Electrodermal lability as a personality dimension. *Journal of Experimental Research in Personality, 5,* 145–150.

Davidson, R. J. (1994a). Asymmetric brain function, affective style and psychopathology: The role of early experience and plasticity. *Development and Psychopathology, 6,* 741–758.

Davidson, R. J. (1994b). The role of prefrontal activation in the inhibition of negative affect. *Psychophysiology, 31,* S7.

Davidson, R. J. (1995). Cerebral asymmetry, emotion and affective style. In R. J. Davidson & K. Hugdahl (Eds.), *Brain asymmetry,* (pp. 361–387). Cambridge, MA: MIT Press.

Davidson, R. J. (2000). Affective style, psychopathology and resilience: Brain mechanisms and plasticity. *American Psychologist. 55,* 1196–1214.

Davidson, R. J., & Fox, N. A. (1989). Frontal brain asymmetry predicts infants' response to maternal separation. *Journal of Abnormal Psychology, 98,* 127–131.

Davidson, R. J., & Irwin, W. (1999). The functional neuroanatomy of emotion and affective style. *Trends in Cognitive Science, 3,* 11–21.

Davidson, R. J., Jackson, D., & Larson, C. (2000). Human electroencephalography. In J. T. Cacioppo, G. Bernston, & L. Tassinary (Eds.), *Principles of psychophysiology* (2nd ed., pp. 27–52). New York: Cambridge University Press.

Davidson, R. J., & Sutton, S. K. (1995). Affective neuroscience: The emergence of a discipline. *Current Opinion in Neurobiology, 5,* 217–224.

Davidson, R. J., Ekman, P., Saron, C., Senulis, J., & Friesen, W. V. (1990). Approach/withdrawal and cerebral asymmetry: Emotional expression and brain physiology, I. *Journal of Personality and Social Psychology, 58,* 330–341.

Davidson, R. J., Jackson, D. C., & Kalin, N. H. (2000). Emotion, plasticity, context and regulation: Perspectives from affective neuroscience. *Psychological Bulletin, 126,* 890–906.

Davidson, R. J., Kalin, N. H., & Shelton, S. E. (1993). Lateralized response to diazepam predicts temperamental style in rhesus monkeys. *Behavioral Neuroscience, 107,* 1106–1110.

Dawson, M. E., Schell, A. M., & Filion, D. L. (2000). The electrodermal system. In J. T. Cacioppo, G. Bernston, & L. Tassinary (Eds.), *Principles of psychophysiology* (2nd ed., pp. 200–223). New York: Cambridge University Press.

Denenberg, V. H., & Yutzey, D. A. (1985). Hemispheric laterality, behavioral asymmetry and the effects of early experience in rats. In S. D. Glick (Ed.), *Cerebral lateralization in nonhuman species* (pp. 109–133). New York: Academic Press.

Derryberry, D., & Rothbart, M. K. (1984). Emotion, attention and temperament. In C. E. Izard, J. Kagan, & R. B. Zajonc (Eds.), *Emotion cognition and behavior* (pp. 132–166). New York: Cambridge University Press.

D'Esposito, M. (2000). Functional neuroimaging of cognition. *Seminars in neurology, 20,* 487–498.

Drevets, W. C., Price, J. L., Simpson, J. R., Jr., Todd, R. D., Reich, T., Vannier, M., & Raichle, M. (1997). Subgenual prefrontal cortex abnormalities in mood disorders. *Nature, 386,* 824–827.

Eysenck, H. J. (1967). *The biological basis of personality*. Springfield, IL: Charles C. Thomas.

Eysenck, H. J. (1972). Human typology, higher nervous activity, and factor analysis. In V. D. Nebylitsyn & J. A. Gray (Eds.), *Biological bases of individual behavior* (pp. 165–181). New York: Academic Press.

Farde, L., Gustavsson, J. P., & Jönsson, E. (1997). D2 dopamine receptors and personality. *Nature, 385,* 590.

Fowles, D. C. (1986). The eccrine system and electrodermal activity. In M.G. H. Coles, E. Donchin, & S. W. Porges (Eds.), *Psychophysiology: Systems, processes and applications* (pp. 51–96). New York: Guilford.

Fowles, D. C., & Kochanska, G. (2000). Temperament as a moderator of pathways to conscience in children: The contribution of electrodermal activity. *Psychophysiology, 37,* 788–795.

Freud, S. (1895/1966). *Project for a scientific psychology*. In J. Strachey (Ed. and Trans.), *The standard edition of the complete psychological works of Sigmund Freud* (Vol. 1, pp. 281–397). London: Hogarth Press.

Gainotti, G. (1972). Emotional behavior and hemispheric side of lesion. *Cortex, 8,* 41–55.

George, M. S., Ketter, K. A., Parekh, I., Horwitz, B., Herscovitch, P., & Post, R. M. (1995). Brain activity during transient sadness and happiness in healthy women. *American Journal of Psychiatry, 152,* 341–351.

Glick, S. D., & Shapiro, R. M. (1985). Functional and neurochemical mechanisms of cerebral lateralization in rats. In S. D. Glick (Ed.), *Cerebral lateralization in nonhuman species* (pp. 157–183). New York: Academic Press.

Goldstein, K. (1939). *The organism*. New York: Academic Press.

Gray, J. A. (1972). The psychophysiological nature of introversion-extraversion: A modification of Eysenck's theory. In V. D. Nebylitsyn & J. A. Gray (Eds.), *Biological bases of individual behavior* (pp. 182–205). New York: Academic Press.

Greenough, W. T., & Black, J. E. (1992). Induction of brain structure by experience: Substrates for cognitive development. In M. R. Gunnar & C. A. Nelson (Eds.), *Minnesota symposium on child psychology:* Vol. 24. *Developmental behavior neuroscience* (pp. 155–200). Hillsdale, NJ: Erlbaum.

Gur, R. C., & Reivich, M. (1980). Cognitive task effects on hemispheric blood flow in humans: Evidence for individual differences in hemispheric activation. *Brain and Language, 9,* 78–92.

Henriques, J. B., & Davidson, R. J. (1989). Affective disorders. In G. Turpin (Ed.), *Handbook of clinical psychophysiology*. London: Wiley.

Hodes, R. L., Cook, E. W., & Lang, P. (1985). Individual differences in autonomic response: Conditioned association or conditioned fear? *Psychophysioloqy, 22,* 545–560.

Kagan, J. (1984). *The nature of the child*. New York: Basic Books.

Kagan, J., Reznick, J. S., & Snidman, N. (1988). Biological bases of childhood shyness. *Science, 240,* 167–171.

Kelly, A., & Stinus, L. (1984). Neuroanatomical and neurochemical substrates of affective behavior. In N. A. Fox & R. J. Davidson (Eds.), *The psychobiology of affective development*. Hillsdale, N.J.: Erlbaum.

Kosslyn, S. M., Cacioppo, J. T., Davidson, R. J., Hugdahl, K., Lovallo, W. R., Spiegel, D., & Rose, R. (2002). Bridging psychology and biology. The analysis of individuals in groups. *American Psychologist, 57,* 341–351.

Nauta, W. J. H. (1971). The problem of the frontal lobe: A reinterpretation. *Journal of Psychiatric Research, 8,* 167–187.

O'Gorman, J .G. (1983). Habituation and personality. In A. Gale & J. A. Edwards (Eds.), *Physiological correlates of human behaviour: Vol. 3. Individual differences and psychopathology* (pp. 45–61). London: Academic Press.

Packard, M. G., & Cahill, L. (2001). Affective modulation of multiple memory systems. *Current opinion in neurobiology, 11,* 752–756.

Pavlov, I. P. (1928). *Lectures on conditioned reflexes. Vol. 1.* New York: International Publishers.

Petrie, A. (1978). *Individuality in pain and suffering* (2nd ed.). Chicago: University of Chicago Press.

Plomin, E., Owen, M. J., & McGuffin, P. (1994). The genetic basis of complex human behaviors. *Science, 264,* 1733–1739.

Price, L. H., Goddard, A. W., Barr, L. C., & Goodman, W. K. (1995). Pharmacological challenges in anxiety disorders. In F. E. Bloom & D. J. Kupfer (Eds.), *Psychopharmacology: The fourth generation of progress* (pp. 1311–1324). New York: Raven Press.

Robinson, R. G., Kubos, K. L., Starr, L. B., Rao, K., & Price, T. R. (1984). Mood disorders in stroke patients: Importance of location of lesion. *Brain, 107*, 81–93.

Sackeim, H. A., Weinman, A. L., Gur, R. C., Greenberg, M., Hungerbuhler, J. P., & Geschwind, N. (1982). Pathological laughter and crying: Functional brain asymmetry in the expression of positive and negative emotions. *Archives of Neurology, 39*, 210–218.

Schwartz, G. E., Davidson, R. J., & Maer, F. (1975). Right hemisphere lateralization for emotion in the human brain: Interactions with cognition. *Science, 190*, 286–288.

Shiller, V. M., Izard, C. E., & Hembree, E. A. (1986). Patterns of emotion expression during separation in the strange situation. *Developmental Psychology, 22*, 378–383.

Sutton, S. K., & Davidson, R. J. (1997). Prefrontal brain asymmetry: A biological substrate of the behavioral approach and inhibition systems. *Psychological Science, 8*, 204–210.

Tomarken, A. J., & Davidson, R. J. (1994). Frontal brain activation in repressors and nonrepressors. *Journal of Abnormal Psychology, 103*, 339–349.

Tomarken, A. J., Davidson, R. J., & Henriques, J. B. (1990). Resting frontal brain asymmetry predicts affective responses to films. *Journal of Personality and Social Psychology, 59*, 791–801.

Tomarken, A. J., Davidson, R. J., Wheeler, R. E., & Kinney, L. (1992b). Psychometric properties of resting anterior EEG asymmetry: Temporal stability and internal consistency. *Psychophysiology, 29*, 576–592.

Tucker, D. M., Stenslie, C. E., Roth, R. S., & Shearer, S. L. (1981). Right frontal lobe activation and right hemisphere performance decrement during a depressed mood. *Archives for General Psychiatry, 38*, 169–174.

Weinberger, D. A., Schwartz, G. E., & Davidson, R. J. (1979). Low anxious, high anxious and repressive coping styles: Psychometric patterns and behavioral and physiological responses to stress. *Journal of Abnormal Psychology, 88*, 369–380.

Weinraub, M., & Lewis, M. (1977). The determinants of children's responses to separation. *Monographs of the Society for Research in Child Development, 42* (Serial No. 172).

Wheeler, R. E., Davidson, R. J., & Tomarken, A. J. (1993). Frontal brain asymmetry and emotional reactivity: A biological substrate of affective style. *Psychophysiology, 30*, 82–89.

Zuckerman, M. (1983). Sensation seeking: A biosocial dimension of personality. In A. Gale & J. A. Edwards (Eds.), *Physiological correlates of human behaviour: Vol. 3. Individual differences and psychopathology* (pp. 99–115). London: Academic Press.

5 | Personality Development

PATRICIA L. WATERS

JONATHAN M. CHEEK

CHAPTER OUTLINE

The psychology of personality development addresses a very basic yet complex question: How did you become the person you are today? This is no idle philosophical musing. Views of personality development have a profound impact on how children are raised, how schools are run, and how government and social policy decisions are made. They also shape the approach therapists use when trying to help a person change and grow.

As you have seen in the two preceding chapters, contemporary researchers are devoting a great deal of attention to the genetic and biological bases of personality. Traditional personality theorists did not have access to this recently emerging body of research. Some of them assumed that biology was of fundamental importance, whereas others preferred to focus on the influence of the social environment on personality development. In fact, the history of psychology is characterized by dramatic disagreements about the innate nature of human nature and the processes of psychological development. In this chapter we examine the major theoretical approaches to personality development and link them to contemporary research topics.

Scientists usually agree that a good theory should be as simple as possible while still accounting for the phenomenon being explained. The preference for a theory requiring the fewest assumptions is called the law of parsimony. You probably have to think only a moment to realize that a simple theory most likely cannot account successfully for the variety and complexity of human personalities. Even simple assumptions about the innate nature of the infant will become complicated as they attempt to account for the change and growth that accompanies human development. Nevertheless, an overview of the basic assumptions of the major historically important theories of personality is a useful starting point.

OVERVIEW OF MAJOR THEORIES

You already have your own personal theory of personality. Because humans are social animals we need to think about other people and our relationships with them. Your views might be very explicit and well thought out. Or they might be a set of implicit assumptions that guide the ways you think about yourself and other people. In either case, you might want to compare your own views to the basic assumptions described in Table 5.1.

As you can see, theorists vary in their root assumptions. Freud (1856–1939) believed that humans are innately selfish, subject to the will of powerful instincts; that human behavior was largely motivated by intrapsychic conflicts—unconscious processes that dictate human behavior. Early experience, he believed, provides the subject matter of these conflicts.

The American behaviorist, John B. Watson (1878–1958) regarded Freud's theory as unscientific and needlessly pessimistic. Watson opposed the idea that inborn instincts shape personality and argued that learning experiences formed enduring habits of behavior. He also rejected the idea of the unconscious and the value of introspection about internal dynamics. Instead, he believed that behavior was shaped by the environment (external determinism) and the indi-

Table 5.1 | Overview of Basic Assumptions of Major Theoretical Approaches in Personality Psychology

Theorists	Innate Quality of Human Nature; at Birth, Infants Are Inherently . . .	Inner/Outer Causes of Behavior	Free Will/ Determinism	Importance of Infant and Early Childhood Experiences
Psychoanalytic (Freud)	selfish (sex and aggression motives)	inner/unconscious	determinism	high
Behaviorism (Watson, Skinner, social learning theorists)	neutral (blank slate)	outer/environmental	determinism	medium
Humanistic (Rogers)	good (self-actualization motive)	inner/conscious	free will	low
Sociocultural and biosocial (Adler, Horney)	a mix of positive and negative motives	mix of inner and outer	mix	medium to varied

vidual's learning history, and he was relatively optimistic about the possibility of unlearning bad habits and learning new good ones.

A third school of personality theory, humanistic psychology, is exemplified by another American, Carl Rogers (1902–1987). Rogers opposed Freud by asserting that the innate nature of human behavior is constructive and trustworthy. He opposed behaviorists such as Watson and Skinner by emphasizing internal causes of behavior such as the self-actualization motive. He regarded environmental pressures (conditions of worth) as a potential source of maladjustment and believed that an infant, if given unconditional positive regard, would grow into a healthy and future-oriented individual.

Biosocial/cultural theorists (such as Adler [1870–1937]) tend to believe that extreme positions in arguments about good versus bad human nature, inner versus outer causes, and so on, fail to capture the complexities of personality (that these are false dichotomies). As contemporary research has become sophisticated, these more complex theories are becoming increasingly influential, as we shall see.

First, let's turn to a discussion of how the basic assumptions of the psychoanalytic, behaviorist, and humanistic theories have been elaborated as each theory tries to account for the processes of personality development, beginning with Freud and more recent examples of the psychoanalytic tradition.

FREUD AND THE PSYCHOANALYTIC TRADITION

Nearly every aspect of the field of psychology, and much of our everyday understanding of human personality, has been influenced by Freud's ideas. Freud provided the first and perhaps the most comprehensive theory of personality development. The very words he created to describe his observations have found their way into common use. References to "egotism" and slips of the tongue, for example, are testimony to the pervasiveness of his influence. In this overview we will focus on three areas of psychoanalytic theory that will help illustrate some of Freud's many contributions to our understanding of personality development: (1) the tripartite structure of the mind, (2) the psychosexual stages of development, and (3) the operation of defense mechanisms.

The Tripartite Structure of the Mind

Freud (1933) divided the adult mind into three parts: the id, ego, and superego. The id comprises raw instincts such as hunger, sex, and aggression. It is ruled by the *pleasure principle*, which seeks immediate gratification of instinctual urges. Thus the id is unremitting in its pursuit of pleasure and avoidance of "unpleasure" (anxiety). The id is the source of all mental energy: It fuels the ego and the superego. However, the id operates on an unconscious, irrational level. The conscious ego differentiates from the id in early infancy. The ego operates on both conscious and unconscious levels. It is governed by the *reality principle* and it engages in a process of reality testing to bring satisfaction to the id. For example an id instinct alerts the infant that he or she is hungry; however, the ego tests reality—mouthing objects until an appropriate food supply is found.

The superego develops in the phallic stage of psychosexual development and is the embodiment of familial and cultural values. The superego introduces a conscience, or mechanism of punishment, into the system as well as providing an ego ideal. Like the id, the superego operates on a largely unconscious, irrational level. Thus it tends to consist of unrealistic extremes of "good" and "bad" that have not benefited from the tempering effect of the conscious mind. The superego draws its energy from the id. Yet it seeks to control the id by acting as a brake on the id's impulsive antics.

Freud's theory is based on the notion of internal, unconscious forces locked in conflict. The demands of the id and superego are fundamentally at odds: The id says, "Do it NOW"; the superego says, "NEVER do it"; and the ego is left to mediate the debate. The ego serves three demanding taskmasters: the id, the superego, and reality. The ego must balance the competing demands of these three. The ego provides the id with its only link to reality. One of the chief tasks of the ego is to create a diversion that will appease the id and alleviate the anxiety associated with frustration of instinctual impulses (see the discussion of defense mechanisms later in this chapter).

The Psychosexual Stages

Freud's training as a medical doctor resulted in a view of personality development that is closely tied to biological and maturational processes. Thus, in part, Freud built the psychosexual stages around physiological features, such as the sucking instinct (early oral stage), the eruption of teeth (late oral stage), and the achievement of muscular control (anal stage). Freud's emphasis on instincts, particularly his theory of infantile sexuality, has been a source of much controversy.

Freud's infant is all id. He described infantile sexuality as polymorphously perverse: All areas of the body are experienced as sexually pleasing. Freud believed that at each stage, instinctual needs seek a new outlet. He described personality development as a progressive shift from the polymorphous perversity of the newborn to focused zones of eroticism at each of the psychosexual stages. In Freud's view, patterns of frustration and satisfaction of instinctual (libidinal) urges at each stage contribute to the permutations we observe in adult personality.

Oral Stage   In the *oral stage*, the mouth is the primary erogenous zone. In the early phase (up to approximately 8 months) gratification is found in feeding and the pleasurable oral stimulation of sucking and swallowing. In the later months of the oral phase (during teething) the infant derives pleasure from biting and chewing.

According to Freud, satisfaction of oral impulses contributes to the individual's sense of trust and independence. However, frustration or excessive gratification during the oral stage may increase the traumatic impact of weaning and produce a *fixation* on oral issues. In describing fixation Freud likened the ego to an army: Becoming fixated at a certain stage is like leaving troops behind on a distant outpost (i.e., in the oral stage). The net effect is a weakening of the army (the ego). Fixations typically result from thwarted attempts to achieve gratification of an impulse, and have consequences for later personality development (see Table 5.2). For example, frustration of urges to bite and chew in the latter half of the oral stage may contribute to an oral pessimistic style generally expressed in the belief that one's efforts are in vain. In contrast, excessive gratification of needs for sucking and swallowing in the early oral phase promotes unrealistic optimism—an assumption that all things are right with the world—based upon the early experience that one need only ask in order to receive (Kline, 1984).

Fixations in the early or late phases of the oral stage have been associated with other personality characteristics as well as seemingly mundane habits: chewing pencils, smoking cigarettes, and showing a preference for soft, milky foods as opposed to hot, spicy foods (Kline, 1984). Interpersonal styles such as high sociability, and even the desire to acquire knowledge, have been attributed to fixation in the early phase of orality.

Anal Stage   In the *anal stage*, the infant's attention shifts from the mouth to the anal region, as sphincter control becomes both a physiological possibility and a cultural mandate. Just as stimulation of the mouth is exciting to the 1-year-old, a delight in defecation is typical in the toddler. Freud believed that the gratification of anal impulses resulted in healthy feelings of self-control and mastery over one's environment.

In many cultures, toilet training during the anal stage represents the first of society's numerous attempts to control instinctual impulses. As with the oral stage, the anal stage is subdivided into two phases: Libidinal pleasure is focused in the expulsion of feces in the early phase and in retention in the later phase. Personality characteristics such as obstinacy, parsimony, excessive

Table 5.2 | Theoretical Relationship Between Freud's Psychosexual Stages and Personality Characteristics

Stage Name	Focus of Libido	Satisfying Behaviors	Outcome of Gratification	Consequences of Fixation
Early oral	mouth	sucking, swallowing	trust	gullibility, passivity, oral optimism
Late oral	mouth	biting, chewing	independence	oral pessimism, manipulativeness, sarcasm
Early anal	anus	expulsion of feces	self-control	obstinacy, cruelty, messiness
Late anal	anus	retention of feces	mastery	conscientiousness, punctuality, cleanliness
Phallic	genital organs	sexual curiosity, self-examination, and manipulation	sexual identity, superego formation (healthy conscience)	problems with authority figures, sexual maladjustment
Latency	—	—	—	—
Genital	genital organs and sublimation	sexual intercourse, intimacy, sublimation in work and art	capacity for unselfish love, fulfilling work, delay of gratification	—

conscientiousness, orderliness, and cleanliness have all been linked to a preoccupation with issues of retention. Conversely, Freud associated fixation in the early, expulsive phase with cruelty, messiness, and destructiveness (Kline, 1984).

Phallic Stage   You may have noticed that children between the ages of 3 and 5 often like to "play doctor." This is one of many expressions of the shift in focus from the anal zone to the genitals. Another is children's sudden "love affair" with their opposite-sex parent. Until the phallic stage, both boys and girls view their mother as the primary object of their love and resent the father's competition for their mother's affection. In boys this is expressed in the *Oedipus complex* as the unconscious desire to possess the mother and depose the father. However, sons fear retaliation by fathers (castration anxiety), and thus they identify with their fathers as a defense against anxiety and as a vicarious source of instinctual gratification. In identifying with the same-sex parent the child internalizes cultural and familial restrictions (such as against incest) and develops a superego that is part ego ideal (comprising the positive identifications with parental and cultural), and part conscience (comprising the restrictive identifications with parental and cultural norms).

In girls, the realization that their genitals are different from boys' produces penis envy. In Freud's view, daughters become disenchanted with their mothers for depriving them of a penis and turn their affections toward a new love object—fathers. However, to possess the father, the daughter risks total loss of her mother's love. Freud contended that this was not as strong a prohibition as the fear of castration in boys. However, to defend against the threatened loss of love, daughters identify with their mothers.

According to Freud, the relatively weaker prohibition against incestuous longings in the female results in a weaker superego. However, numerous criticisms have been raised against Freud's perception of female development. For example, Horney (1967) asked whether penis envy in girls might not have a counterpart called "womb envy" in boys. Others have questioned Freud's emphasis on anatomy as destiny, suggesting that penis envy might better serve as a metaphor for power envy (Miller, 1976).

Latency Stage   During latency, sexual instincts are dormant, as the child undergoes a solidification of the superego formed during the phallic stage.

Genital Stage   During the phallic stage, the child essentially abandons hope of possessing the opposite-sex parent as a love object and replaces that loss with identification with the same-sex parent. With the onset of puberty, sexual intimacy becomes a possibility and the individual seeks a new object of affection. Nearly all of us have observed friends or family members who have married someone who resembles their opposite-sex parent. Freud used the phrase "object finding is object refinding" to describe the unconscious tendency to seek a sexual partner who is reminiscent of the lost one of childhood. The focus during the genital stage is on finding a new love object and learning to sublimate successfully other id impulses into productive channels (such as work, sports, and hobbies)—striking a balance between love and work.

Defense Mechanisms

Recall that Freud viewed the infant psyche as a collection of polymorphously perverse and murderously aggressive id impulses seeking gratification. The goal of socialization is to gain control of these impulses. The individual achieves this by exercising the superego (conscience) and invoking a system of defenses against anxieties caused by frustration of the id or the conscious awareness of painful memories. Individuals do this in unique ways depending on their history of satisfaction and frustration at each stage of development. This history of frustrations or overgratifications (fixations), combined with the superego, form the individual's *character structure*. The dynamics of this character structure are visible in the defense mechanisms. Sigmund Freud's daughter, Anna Freud, provided a more complete elaboration of the defense mechanisms (Freud, A., 1958). A few of these are described in the following paragraphs:

Repression protects the ego from consciously experiencing the anxiety of unacceptable thoughts. These thoughts can range from taboo id wishes to painful memories. The ego keeps these thoughts in the unconscious—away from conscious awareness—where they continue to exert an influence over behavior.

Displacement is the replacement of one form of satisfaction of id impulses with another. For example, playing defensive tackle on a football team is an acceptable form of displacement for murderous aggression. When displacement takes a socially productive form it is called *sublimation*.

Projection is ascribing unacceptable, anxiety-producing facts about the self to someone or something else. For example, "I can't dance" might be converted to "He is a terrible dance partner" or "This music has no beat."

Reaction formation is the repression and transformation into its opposite of an objectionable thought. For example, a man who is drawn to sexual perversions may become a television evangelist preaching the wickedness of the flesh.

ATTACHMENT RESEARCH—A NEOANALYTIC PERSPECTIVE

In spite of the criticism and controversies surrounding many aspects of Freud's theory, he succeeded in focusing attention on the crucial role of emotional development during infancy and early childhood. In stressing the importance of the ego from birth, *ego psychologists* have posited a less pessimistic view of infancy than Freud envisioned. In their view, the infant is not a mass of unconscious id impulses, but rather a social creature, with an innate urge to merge with others. This revised conceptualization can be seen in Erikson's (1963) reinterpretation and extension of Freud's psychosexual stages into a psychosocial model of development that includes relationships formed during adolescence and adulthood. Winnicott (1960) described the newborn-caregiver relationship as a state of "fusion" in which mother and child experience such intense feelings of connection and attachment that the very boundary between them seems blurred.

Studies of early attachment patterns in other primates revealed that when given a choice between a wire "mother" with a bottle attached to it and a cloth "mother," the infant monkey sought out the wire mother only to satisfy hunger needs, but clung to the cloth mother for prolonged periods of time, presumably to satisfy needs for contact comfort (Harlow, 1958). Perhaps the most compelling evidence for the primacy of attachment in infancy has been drawn from observing the effects of maternal deprivation. In a study of the effects of institutionalization on young orphans, Spitz (1945) discovered higher infant mortality rates among infants whose physical needs had been met but whose needs for nurturance had been overlooked. Thus the availability of attachment figures affects the infant's survival on a profound level in a way Freud did not explore. The child's ability to "thrive" is placed in jeopardy in situations of caregiver deprivation.

Attachment theory stresses the importance of the infant's experience of "felt security" (Bowlby, 1969). Felt security arises out of parents' sensitivity and responsiveness to infants' signals of distress, happiness, fatigue—in sum, the infants' "affective" cues. The quality of the caregiver-infant relationship has implications for the child's ability to explore freely the physical and social environment.

Indeed, many theorists argue that early attachment patterns may set the tone for basic personality styles including the individual's regulation of emotion in a variety of social settings (Kobak & Sceery, 1988). Through their observations of mothers and infants in the Strange Situation, Ainsworth and her colleagues identified three styles of caregiver-infant attachment patterns: Secure, Anxious/Avoidant, and Anxious/Resistant Attachments (see Ainsworth, Blehar, Waters, & Wall, 1978, for a review). Table 5.3 provides an overview of differences in approach to interpersonal relationships among children who had a secure or insecure (anxious/avoidant or anxious/resistant) attachment with their mother.

When placed in an unfamiliar situation *securely attached* children demonstrate more freedom of movement and exploration, using their mother as a "secure base" of operations (Ainsworth, Bell, & Stayton, 1974). Mothers of securely attached children tend to be sensitive to the needs and wishes of their toddlers; at the same time they encourage their children's active exploration of the environment. As toddlers, securely attached children engage in social interactions with greater enthusiasm and delight and show greater persistence in solving cognitive problems. Similarly, when they are 4 to 5 years old, children who had been classified previously as securely attached, demonstrated greater ego resilience and flexibility in their interactions with other preschoolers (Arend, Gove, & Sroufe, 1979), and tended to smile more and interact with greater emotional expressiveness than their peers with different attachment histories (Waters, Wippman, & Sroufe, 1979). Preschool teachers' observations suggest that securely attached children not only demonstrate more positive (and less negative) emotions, but seem to handle negative emotion in others with greater ease (Sroufe, Schork, Motti, Lawroski, & LaFreniere, 1984). Among 6-year-olds, children with a history of secure attachment are more curious in social situations and have higher levels of self-esteem than their peers (Main, Kaplan, & Cassidy, 1985). In interactions with mothers, secure 6-year-olds are more relaxed, responsive, and willing to initiate positive interactions than their peers with other attachment histories (Main & Cassidy, 1988). Thus, enthusiasm and flexibility in problem-solving situations and greater freedom to explore the environment combine with greater social competence and higher levels of self-esteem to form a highly adaptive picture for the securely attached child.

Like those in the securely attached group, infants with *Anxious/Avoidant* attachments have little difficulty separating to explore the environment and show relatively little avoidance of strangers while in the presence of their mothers. However, their interactions are marked by relatively little affective sharing and when distressed they are as easily consoled by a stranger as by their mother (see Table 5.3). Upon reunion with their mothers after a brief separation period, infants with anxious/avoidant attachments generally ignore or turn away from their mothers, but may intermittently seek proximity (Sroufe, 1983).

As preschoolers, anxious/avoidant children tended to be ego-overcontrolled. In their approach to others they are relatively constrained and conforming and

Table 5.3 | Interpersonal Styles of Children with Different Attachment Histories

| | Secure | Insecure | |
		Anxious/Avoidant	Anxious/Resistant (Ambivalent)
Toddler	Easily soothed upon reunion with mother; seeks proximity to mother	Upon reunion with mother looks or pulls away, ignores, or mixes proximity-seeking with avoidance; as easily soothed by stranger as by mother	Upon reunion with mother mixes proximity-seeking and resistance (hits, cries); cries, seeks contact prior to separation; inconsolable
3½-year-old	Greater persistence in problem solving; greater enthusiasm and affective sharing with peers; greater peer competence and ego strength than other attachment groups	Less peer competence and ego strength than "secures"; less freedom in exploring environment	Less peer competence and ego strength than "secures"; may passively resist exploring environment
4- to 5-year-old	Moderate ego control (flexibilty in peer interactions); handles emotions of peers with greater ease, greater curiosity than other attachment group	Tends toward ego overcontrol (constrained); avoids contact with peers; low expression of emotion	Tends toward ego undercontrol (high expression of distress, fear, anger); inappropriate affect in peer interactions (impulsive, helpless)
6-year-old	In doll play, accepting, tolerant of others' imperfections; upon reunion, relaxed, responsive to parent (initiates positive interactions)	In doll play, defensive, dismissive of attachment; upon reunion, maintains distance from parent (ignores, continues to play)	In doll play, overt anger, hostility; upon reunion, may exaggerate dependency/intimacy, or spurn parent in overt or covert way (leaning against, then jerking away)

tend to avoid ambiguous or inconsistent situations (Arend, Gove, & Sroufe, 1979). Often lacking spontaneity in social situations, they are less demonstrative in displaying emotion than their securely attached peers (Sroufe, 1983). As 6-year-olds, anxious/avoidant children are dismissive of attachments in toy play (Cassidy, 1988) and maintain distance when reunited with their mother after a brief separation. This distance-seeking may be expressed subtly; the child may simply continue to be engrossed in toy play, ignoring the mother's reappearance (Main & Cassidy, 1988).

Infants with *anxious/resistant* attachments have the greatest difficulty separating to explore their surroundings and tend to be wary in the presence of strangers and in novel situations. Anxious/resistant infants appear to lack confidence in others. In times of distress, neither the mother nor a stranger can provide ready relief. Upon reunion infants with anxious/resistant attachments may react with extreme passivity or show angry ambivalence, alternating proximity-seeking with aggressive emotional expressions such as kicking, hitting, or pushing away (see Table 5.3).

At preschool age, these children continue to demonstrate a general wariness in exploring the environment and tend toward ego-undercontrol. For example, they tend to react to stressful situations with a very high degree of emotional expressiveness, have difficulties delaying gratification, and are typically more distractible with interests and enthusiasms that are generally short-lived (Block & Block, 1980). As 6-year-olds, anxious/resistant children display more angry/hostile emotions in toy play (Cassidy, 1988) and respond to reunions with parents after a brief separation by mixing exaggerated bids for dependency with angry expressions of rejection, first leaning against the parent, then jerking away (Main & Cassidy, 1988).

Internal Working Models

We have described some of the ways in which differences in caregiver-infant attachment patterns may be expressed in children's behavior in peer and school settings, but how does this process work? Many theorists believe that the child's experience of early attachment forms an *internal working model* that is integrated into the personality and invoked as a guide for behavior in subsequent social interactions (Bowlby, 1988; Main, Kaplan, & Cassidy, 1985; Kobak & Sceery, 1988). As the phrase "internal working model" suggests, early attachment experiences are taken in, or internalized by the child, but are subject to change and elaboration as a result of new experience. Thus, they are considered to be "working" or in progress. Finally, they provide a general guide or template, a "model," for interpersonal interaction. The notion of internal working models remains inferential. That is, researchers have not asked children how they structure their approach to others but have drawn inferences based upon the continuities observed between children's interactions with their primary caregivers and their interactions with peers and strangers.

The Continuity of Internal Working Models

Studies that have followed infants into the childhood years suggest that anxiously attached infants are more vulnerable to problems in peer relationships during childhood than their securely attached peers, and that these difficulties negatively impact the development of social competence (Erickson, Sroufe, & Egeland, 1985; Renken, Egeland, Marvinney, Mangelsdorf, & Sroufe, 1989). While the early evidence for continuity of internal working models is compelling, longitudinal studies that extend beyond childhood will help clarify the relative stability or variation in an individual's interpersonal approach over the life course and thus "test" the significance of early attachments for personality development.

Researchers interested in internal working models and patterns of attachment have begun to explore the relationship between adults' perceptions of their attachment with their own parents and their current attachment to their infants. Main and colleagues (1985) have identified secure, avoidant, and resistant attachment patterns using adults' retrospective accounts of their early attachment histories as the basis for determining their "state of mind" with respect to early attachment (George, Kaplan, & Main, 1984). Interestingly, mothers' responses on the Adult Attachment Interviews (AAI) were significantly correlated with their infants' behavior in the strange situation. For example, those women who reported a history of avoidant attachment to their mother had children who similarly demonstrated an avoidant attachment.

In a meta-analysis of numerous studies examining links between parents' attachment representations (based on the AAI) and parents' own attachment to their infants, Van Ijzendoorn (1995) observed consistent relationships between parental (primarily maternal) AAI accounts and the quality of attachment to their children. Maternal attachment representations tended to be related more strongly to children's attachment styles than were paternal attachments. However, the older the child, the weaker the connection became between adult attachment and security of parent-child attachment (van Ijzendoorn, 1995). This meta-analysis suggests that patterns of attachment may be transferred across generations in the family.

In recent years, the use of retrospective methods such as the Adult Attachment Interview to gain access to information about the stability of attachment relations over time and across generations has come under scrutiny (Fox, 1995). Fox has suggested that factors such as *current* psychological status of the interviewee, and personality characteristics (such as temperament) may have more impact on the way individuals respond to the Adult Attachment Interview than the actual quality of their early relationships with their caregivers. Indeed, until longitudinal work proceeds to the point that adolescents who were observed in the strange situation as infants can be classified on the basis of their responses to the Adult Attachment Interview, the question of stability of attachment patterns will remain largely inferential.

Attachment and Intimacy

The implications of a persistent attachment style extend beyond the family and early peer group. Researchers studying later periods of personality development have used a variety of methods, ranging from retrospective self-reports to ratings by friends, to assess the coherence of attachment patterns across time and situations (Hazan & Shaver, 1987; Kobak, Cole, Ferenz-Gillies, Fleming, & Gamble, 1993; Kobak & Sceery, 1988). Do we apply an internal working model of attachment, developed during our childhood relationships with primary caregivers, to our adult relationships with close friends or romantic partners?

Some studies have examined the link between adolescents' current relationships with parents and peers whereas others have used the AAI as a retrospective indicator of adolescents' early attachment relationships. In general, adolescents whose current or retrospective reports indicate a secure attachment were more socially adept and better adjusted than those reporting insecure attachments (Finnegan & Perry, 1993; Kobak & Cole, 1994).

Activity Box 5.1	**Measuring Adult Attachment Patterns**

Most measures of attachment in adulthood rely on semistructured interviews or questionnaires. Here are a number of items similar to those used on actual scales (Hazan & Shaver, 1987). Check only the items that accurately describe your feelings or your general view about the course of romantic love over time.

_____ 1. The kind of head-over-heels romantic love depicted in novels and movies doesn't exist in real life.

_____ 2. It's easy to fall in love. I feel myself beginning to fall in love often.

_____ 3. Intense romantic love is common at the beginning of a relationship, but it rarely lasts forever.

_____ 4. I find it relatively easy to get close to others and am comfortable depending upon them (and having them depend on me).

_____ 5. I am somewhat uncomfortable being close to others; I find it difficult to trust them completely, difficult to allow myself to depend on them. Often, love partners want me to be more intimate than I feel comfortable being.

_____ 6. I find that others are reluctant to get as close as I would like. I often worry that my partner doesn't really love me or won't want to stay with me.

Items such as the first three are designed to assess your "mental model" (or internal working model) of relationships. Individuals with avoidant attachment patterns, for example, tend to endorse items similar to 3, whereas "secures" endorse items like item 1 less often than either "avoidants" or "anxious/ambivalents." "Anxious/ambivalents" select items similar to 2 more often than any other group.

Hazan and Shaver (1987) were also interested in whether individuals could easily identify themselves as "secure," "avoidant," or "anxious/ambivalent" on the basis of a brief description. They asked participants to select the description that best matched their experiences and feelings in relationships. Excerpts from those descriptions are represented in items 4–6 (for complete descriptions, see Hazan & Shaver, 1987). Item 4 is most descriptive of a "securely" attached individual. Statements in item 5 best represent the opinion of individuals with avoidant attachments, and item 6 best describes the opinion of those with anxious/ambivalent attachment patterns.

These items are meant to represent the _types_ of questions used to identify attachment patterns and should not be viewed as a reliable assessment of your attachment style. The determination of attachment pattern is based on numerous items, and researchers now tend to use two continuous scales, described in Brennan, Clark, and Shaver (1998), because they are more precise than the types of measures used in earlier research on this topic.

Source: Adapted from Hazan and Shaver (1987). Used by permission.

Hazan and Shaver (1987) investigated potential links between adults' attitudes toward attachment and the quality of their attachments to intimate partners. Using a paper-and-pencil measure (see Activity Box 5.1), they observed that the incidence of each of the three attachment styles appears to be roughly the same in adulthood as in infancy: Slightly over half (56%) of the adults in Hazan and Shaver's study (1987) were classified as "securely attached." The remaining adults were nearly evenly distributed between "anxious/ambivalent" (resistant) (20%) and "avoidant" (24%) classifications. These proportions are similar to those obtained in infant research. For example, Campos, Barrett, Lamb, Goldsmith, and Stenberg (1983) identified 62% of the infants in his sample as "secure," 15% as "anxious/ ambivalent," and 23% as "avoidant."

Personality characteristics associated with each of the three attachment classifications in childhood appear to be consistent with descriptions of adults from the three attachment groups. Securely attached adults expect close relationships to endure and find others trustworthy. They tended to view themselves as likeable and were described by others as emotionally expressive (Hazan & Shaver, 1987; Kobak & Sceery, 1988). These patterns closely parallel the higher social competence and freedom of emotional expression noted earlier among securely attached children (Arend, Gove, & Sroufe, 1979).

In an earlier study, Kobak (1985) noted that peers' evaluations of avoidant and anxious/ambivalent adults described them as less socially adept than secure adults. However, only the anxious/ambivalents described themselves as less socially competent. Main and her colleagues (1985) have suggested that avoidant individuals may deny the importance of attachments, favoring "compulsive self-reliance," in a pattern reminiscent of the ego over-control of anxious/avoidant infants. Avoidant college students tended to be afraid of closeness and to doubt the existence or the durability of romantic love. Moreover, these individuals did not consider romantic love to be necessary for happiness.

In contrast, college students in the anxious/ambivalent attachment group described love as a preoccupation viewing intimate relationships as "painfully exciting." You may recall that anxious/resistant preschoolers tended to be ego-undercontrolled (i.e., highly spontaneous, but unable to sustain interest and enthusiasm). Similarly, ambivalent college students had a personality style that enables them to fall in love more easily and more frequently than their peers, but they express difficulty in finding true love. They tend to be plagued by self-doubt and were at ease disclosing feelings of insecurity (Hazan & Shaver, 1987; Kobak & Sceery 1988).

The notion that our style of developing and maintaining attachments becomes integrated into the core of our personalities continues to be a topic of debate (Fox, 1995; Rutter, 1979). However, the parallels between mother-infant attachment patterns, peer interaction styles, and adult attachment styles suggest preliminary support for the importance of internal working models of attachment in personality formation. This topic will undoubtedly receive increasing attention from researchers in the years ahead.

BEHAVIORISM AND SOCIAL LEARNING THEORY

John B. Watson (1878–1958) set out to change the definition of psychology from the study of mental life to the science of behavior. He wanted to exclude not only Freud's unconscious but also to omit any reference to the conscious mind, which he considered to be an unscientific philosophical abstraction. Instead, he proposed that the prediction and control of observable behavior should be the primary goal of psychology. Watson argued vehemently against

Table 5.4 | Hierarchy of Learning

Theorist	Type of Learning	Characteristics
Watson	classical conditioning	passive, association learning
Skinner	instrumental conditioning	active response selection through reinforcement and chaining of series of responses
Bandura	observational learning	modeling and vicarious reinforcement
Bandura and Mischel	learning rules and symbols	concepts, strategies, expectancies

the idea that instincts and heredity influence personality development, suggesting that behavior patterns are learned entirely through experience with the environment. Even the word *personality* seemed too mentalistic to him, so he suggested that it be replaced by the term "habit system" (Watson, 1930).

Behaviorism is not a theory of personality but a general theory of behavior that rejects all explanations of the internal processes of the person. The preferred research method for behaviorism is laboratory experimentation that studies other animals as well as humans. As we saw in Table 5.1, Watson assumed that human infants are a "blank slate" at birth, and whether they become adults with good or bad habits will be determined by their environment. He tried to apply the law of parsimony in his theory by explaining most adult behavior as the result of a long history of the simplest kind of learning—classical conditioning (see Table 5.4).

Classical conditioning is simple association learning. You may recall the famous example of Pavlov's dogs. After the sound of a tone (the conditioned stimulus) was paired several times with the presentation of meat powder (the unconditioned stimulus), the dog responded by salivating when only the sound of the tone was presented. In his book advising parents how to raise their children, Watson (1928) explained how classical conditioning is crucial for human emotional development. An infant has no innate fear of a furry animal such as a rabbit but does fear unexpected loud noises. By pairing a loud noise with presentation of a rabbit, Watson classically conditioned fear of the rabbit, and this learning generalized so that the infant feared other, similar objects such as a fur coat. Watson concluded that over the years, such experiences accumulate into a complex set of emotional habits.

Watson believed that emotional dependency was the worst habit a person could develop. Therefore, he advised mothers never to kiss their infants but to shake their hands and treat them as objectively as possible (just as a scientific behaviorist would!). He wanted to avoid "love conditioning" so that the child could grow up to be an efficient, self-reliant adult. Research on attachment contradicts Watson's now outdated advice, but it is worth noting that his child care manual was influential in the 1930s. Meanwhile, Watson's attempt to explain adult behavior through a history of classical conditioning came to be seen as too simplistic, and later behaviorists shifted the focus to more complex types of learning.

B. F. Skinner (1904–1990), the most famous behaviorist of the 20th century, concentrated on instrumental or operant conditioning (see Table 5.4). Rejecting the idea of free will, Skinner concluded that behavior is a function of its consequences. Humans and other animals are active organisms. Any particular response or behavior pattern that is rewarded will be selectively strengthened and whatever is ignored or punished will tend to be eliminated. By successively chaining a series of instrumental conditioning tasks, Skinner (1953) has demonstrated that even pigeons can learn remarkably complex behaviors. Instrumental conditioning can be applied in child-rearing practices, as in research showing that consistent punishment resulted in inhibition of aggression among elementary school boys (Parke & Devr, 1972). Skinnerian schedules of reinforcement also have been applied successfully in the treatment of autistic and mentally retarded children. However, the explanation of complex human behavior, such as learning to drive a car or speak a language, required psychologists to look at higher levels on the hierarchy of learning.

Albert Bandura (1925–) helped to pioneer the transition from traditional behaviorism to social learning theory (see Table 5.4). He studied the role of observational learning in the acquisition of human behavior. For example, when children saw a model being reinforced for acting aggressively, they behaved more aggressively than did children who saw a model punished for aggressive behavior (Bandura, 1965). This process is called *vicarious reinforcement*, the way we learn from watching the consequences of other people's behavior. What we observe we learn, but behavior that we think will be positively reinforced is the most likely to be performed.

Bandura (1997) more recently has extended his theory to focus on the most advanced, cognitive type of learning. Internalized goals, plans, strategies, and expectancies permit self-regulation of complex behavior. For example, Walter Mischel (1984) demonstrated that specific mental representations of potential rewards helped children to delay gratification in a laboratory test. Individuals use information such as repeated success or failure as a guide to adjust their behavior. A key determinant of self-regulated behavior is *perceived self-efficacy*—what the individual believes he or she is capable of accomplishing. Personal successes and failures, encouragement from others, and adequate role models are a few of the variables influencing the nature of the individual's perceived self-efficacy. Bandura now emphasizes self-efficacy expectancies as a central feature of personality. On the basis of their perceived self-efficacy, individuals develop a set of expectations for the self, which have direct consequences for their behavior. For example, one cigarette smoker's *self-efficacy expectancies* may cause him or her to say, "I'd like to quit smoking, but it's hard. I've tried before and I don't think I can." Another smoker might say, "I'd like to quit smoking and I know if I really put my mind to it, I can." The expectation of success or failure influences the individual's persistence and, ultimately, shapes the outcome of his or her efforts.

Cognitive social learning theory has come a long way from the external determinism of Watson's radical behaviorism, but Bandura and Mischel have tended to focus on situationally specific cognitive strategies in a way that puts them at odds with those personality theorists who emphasize biological temperament and enduring traits. Nevertheless, the growing influence of cognitive social learning theory is demonstrated by its recent use as the preferred personality theory in a new model of cultural biology developed by neuroscientists Steven Quartz and Terrence Sejnowski (2002).

ROGERS AND HUMANISTIC PSYCHOLOGY

In the mid-1940s to the 1950s, Carl Rogers introduced a new perspective on personality development. Considered to be the founder of humanistic psychology, Rogers held an essentially optimistic view of human motivation and human nature. He believed that a central, organizing or "master" motive guides human behavior—the actualizing tendency. The actualizing tendency is the natural human urge "to actualize, maintain, and enhance the experiencing organism" (Rogers, 1951, p. 487).

In contrast to Freud, Rogers believed in the innate goodness and basic integrity of human beings. Therefore, he suggested that the direction of the actualizing tendency is positive and growth promoting for the individual. In Rogers's view, the individual thrives when this propensity toward actualization is allowed to flourish and suffers when external influences exert excessive controls or restrictions. Therefore, he also opposed the external determinism of behaviorism.

Rogers takes an experiential approach to development. That is, he believes that the course of development is largely contingent upon the person's ability to interpret his or her unique experiences without distortion. While he suggests that "persons have a basically positive direction," Rogers concedes that human beings sometimes act in ways that are undesirable (Rogers, 1961, p. 27). He attributes undesirable acts to distortions and defensiveness resulting from the conflict between a person's inner experience and tendency toward actualization, and the need to be held in positive regard by others.

In an ideal world, the need for positive regard would be satisfied, initially, by parents' unfailing expressions of acceptance, sympathy, warmth, and care for the child. In this state of parental "unconditional positive regard," children learn to trust their feelings and experiences and rely on their evaluations of these experiences to guide future actions. In Rogers's view this process brings individuals closer to fulfilling their innate potential. As children mature, unconditional positive regard from others is internalized as unconditional positive *self*-regard. Positive self-regard, in turn, fosters a healthy self-concept that allows individuals to trust in their own experience and act on the basis of that trust. In reality, most families extend "conditional positive regard" to their children. That is, the parents' acceptance of the child is partially dependent (conditional) upon the child's behaving appropriately. In situations in which conditional positive regard is prevalent, "conditions of worth" are understood between the parent and child. For example, Amy knows that if she hits her little brother, her mother may get very angry and tell her she is bad. At the same time, Amy may really feel like hitting her little brother. Perhaps he's been teasing her all day. Confronted with the choice between hitting him (which would please her) and satisfying the conditions of worth (which would preserve her mother's acceptance and love), Amy experiences a classic conflict: "Shall I do what I want, or what I should do?"

Rogers suggests that in most instances, children conform to the conditions of worth and act on the basis of "shoulds" because the need for positive regard is very strong. However, he views the urge to satisfy the need for positive regard as the most serious *obstacle* to the course of actualization. Why? In order to satisfy conditions of worth, the individual often denies or distorts his or her experience. Thus, the price of conforming to conditions of worth, according to Rogers, is alienation from one's true self.

In the example of conditional positive regard noted earlier, Amy had only a few options to resolve the conflict. She could act as her evaluation of her experience dictated, and hit her little brother. But that would produce a withdrawal of positive regard and be damaging to her developing self-concept ("I am a bad person because I wanted to hit my brother"). Or, she could distort her evaluation of the experience, "I LOVE my little brother and would never do anything to hurt him," and thus win her mother's conditional positive regard at the expense of alienating her genuine feelings.

In an ideal situation Amy's mother would continue to express unconditional positive regard, by acknowledging the validity of the child's feelings and by making a distinction between the child's feelings and the appropriateness of the child's behavior. She might suggest that "Sometimes we all get very angry" and although it is understandable that Amy wants to hit her little brother sometimes, she's pretty sure that the little brother does not want to be hit and he has a right to his feelings, too.

The Fully Functioning Person

According to Rogers, treating a child with unconditional positive regard provides the foundation for healthy personality development. Acknowledging children's right to evaluate their experiences in their own way and providing a democratic, mutually respectful family atmosphere are the keys to producing "fully functioning persons." In the fully functioning person, the self-concept is built on trial and error evaluations of personal experience. Because they have developed unconditional positive self-regard, fully functioning individuals tend to trust their own judgment and have little need to distort or defend against experience. Thus, they are typically able to correct their mistakes, since they perceive them clearly and without distortions, and they are notably free of the anxiety and confusion that plague individuals who operate on the basis of "conditions of worth."

Contemporary Research Applications

Unconditional Positive Regard and the True Self   In recent years researchers have observed connections between parental "conditions of worth" and distortions in the ability to express the "true self," which adolescents describe as the "real me," my "true feelings," and as "behaving the way I want to behave and not how someone else wants me to be" (Harter, 2002). Adolescents described distortions of the true self, or *false-self behavior*, as "putting on an act," "being phony," and "expressing things you don't really believe or feel" (Harter, Marold, & Whitesell, 1992; Harter, Marold, Whitesell, & Cobbs, 1996). In a series of studies, Harter and her colleagues observed that adolescents' perceptions of their parents' supportiveness (conditional versus unconditional support) influenced their willingness to engage in false-self behavior. Adolescents who experienced their parents' support as *conditional* (i.e., contingent upon their ability to meet parental expectations) were more likely to engage in false-self behavior than were adolescents who viewed their parents' support as unconditional (noncontingent positive regard).

An even stronger link was observed between the conditionality of parents' support and adolescents' sense of *hopefulness* about garnering the support of others in the future. Those who received conditional support from their parents were likely to feel hopeless and resort to false-self behavior, presumably as a strategy to win their parents' approval and support. In contrast, those who received unconditional support from parents maintained confidence (hopefulness) about their ability to draw support in the future and engaged in true-self behavior more readily (Harter, Marold, Whitesell, & Cobbs, 1996). This work refines Rogers's assertion that parental conditions of worth may contribute to the development of a false self by suggesting that it is not only parents' conditional support but adolescents' reactions to that support that contributes to false-self behavior.

Some theories of self-concept development predict that false-self behavior, such as suppressing expression of one's true opinions and feelings, should be more apparent in girls than in boys, beginning in early adolescence. Recent research on levels of "voice" (authentic self-expression) has found, however, that adolescent females and males do not differ in expressing their opinions to parents, teachers, classmates, and friends (Harter, Waters, & Whitesell, 1997). The interesting differences found in this line of research occur *among* female high school students—girls who were traditionally feminine in terms of gender-role stereotypes reported lower levels of voice, and thus higher levels of false-self behavior, than girls who had a nontraditional, androgynous gender orientation (Harter, Waters, Whitesell, & Kastelic, 1998). (See Chapter 12 for more about contemporary research on sex and gender.)

Child-rearing Styles and Instrumental Competence   Contemporary research also appears to support, with some modifications, Rogers's view that ideal parenting involves democratic family processes as well as unconditional warmth and acceptance. For example, Baumrind (1967) found that children who scored high on instrumental competence (self-assertive, independent, socially responsible) tended to have parents whose child-rearing practices combined nurturance and warmth with a modicum of discipline and clear parent-child communication strategies.

Baumrind identified three parenting styles—Permissive, Authoritarian, and Authoritative—that produce distinctly different developmental outcomes. *Permissive* parents tend to exert low levels of control and place few maturity de-

Table 5.5 | Baumrind's Three Parenting Styles

	Authoritarian	Authoritative	Permissive
Control/discipline	high	high	low
Clarity of parent-child communication	low	high	high
Maturity demands	high	high	low
Nurturance/warmth	low	high	high

mands upon their children. At the same time, they are high on nurturance and warmth (what Rogers might call unconditional positive regard), and their communications with their children are characterized as very clear (see Table 5.5). Thus, the permissive household is typified by the fewest external impingements upon the child. Despite this atmosphere of nurturing acceptance, however, children of permissive parents tend to be less self-reliant and self-controlled and more dependent upon their parents than their peers with authoritative parents.

In the *authoritarian* household, parenting practices are the reverse of permissive: The clarity of parent-child communications is low, there is little nurturance, and parental control and maturity demands upon the child are high (see Table 5.5). As Rogers might have suggested, this family environment does little to promote the child's actualizing tendency: Children of authoritarian parents are often lacking in vitality and self-assertion, frequently shy and withdrawn, and often low in achievement motivation. Children raised permissively tend to engage in activities with greater vitality and a more positive mood than children raised in authoritarian households. However, apart from these differences, children of permissive and authoritarian parents behave in remarkably similar ways, exhibiting greater dependence on their parents and less self-control in their interactions with others.

As in the case of Amy's mother, above, *authoritative* parents combine warmth, nurturance, and clear communication strategies with relatively high levels of discipline and control (see Table 5.5). Authoritative parents expect their children to act in mature ways, and their children respond accordingly. Children raised authoritatively tend to be self-assured, independent, highly motivated to achieve, and socially responsible—in essence, their "tendency toward actualization" is apparent.

Consistent with Rogers's view, nurturance, warmth, and acceptance are clearly vital to children's healthy personality development. It is less apparent that this acceptance must be "unconditional." Indeed, Baumrind's data suggest that an optimal child-rearing style couples warmth with clearly stated, realistic demands. Is unconditional positive regard antithetical to these demands? How might you combine the two?

Unconditional Positive Regard and the Development of Creativity   According to Rogers, an environment that fosters creativity provides (1) *psychological safety*, in which the individual experiences unconditional worth and no external evaluations are imposed, and (2) a sense of *psychological freedom*, in which the individual engages in "unrestrained symbolic expression" (Harrington, Block, & Block, 1987). In such a nonevaluative atmosphere, Rogers suggests, individuals develop the internal prerequisites for constructive creativity.

In recent years, efforts have been made to apply empirical testing to Rogers's assertions about the constituents of a creativity-fostering environment. Using data from their longitudinal study, Harrington, Block, and Block (1987) developed three indices measuring the extent to which parents' child-rearing techniques conformed to Rogers's descriptions of creativity-fostering environments. These indices were compared with a composite of children's creative potential drawn from assessments conducted during preschool and 7 to 11 years later, during early adolescence. Parents who used Rogerian-style child-rearing practices with their preschoolers (such as warmth, support, and encouragement of children's independence) produced early adolescents who were higher on measures of creative potential than their peers. Even after accounting for initial differences in the intellectual abilities and creative potentials of the preschoolers, a history of Rogerian-style child-rearing increased the creativity of young adolescents. Children raised in more restrictive (authoritarian) or more chaotic (permissive) environments, in contrast, showed less creative potential as preadolescents.

THE BIOSOCIAL AND SOCIOCULTURAL TRADITION

In reviewing theory and research we have examined some key differences between the psychoanalytic, behavioral, and humanistic approaches to personality development. Alfred Adler, Harry Stack Sullivan, Karen Horney, and other interpersonally oriented theorists shifted attention away from the individual's preoccupation with selfish instinct gratification (Freud's id) as the primary motive of human action, and toward the influence of social relationships and the broader cultural context.

Adlerian Individual Psychology

Adler defined his theory as "Individual Psychology" and described an individual's striving for superiority as "the fundamental fact of life." However, as his ideas developed, he asserted that individual psychology was inextricably linked to social psychology: We are all in and of a social sphere and, as such, our strivings are not for ourselves alone, but for the perfection of society. We are born with the propensity for *social interest*—striving for cooperation with others toward the establishment of a superior society—and pathology is defined, in part, by a lack of social interest. Ideally, mothers encourage their children to develop their natural propensity for social interest by acting as the children's first link to the social world. In Adler's view the mother assists the child in extending this interest to others. The role of the father in Adler's view is to foster feelings of self-reliance and courage and to stress the need for establishing a career choice.

Adler believed that feelings of inferiority are a natural consequence of being a small, helpless infant. Children are aware of their parents' size and relative strength and much of their activity is centered around compensating for the feelings of inferiority that this engenders. Thus in Adler's view, striving for superiority, excellence, and mastery is a natural propensity that can be enhanced or constrained depending on the circumstances of the child's life, especially his or her family environment.

In Adler's view, inferiority feelings have the potential to wreak havoc or inspire greatness in an individual's life. Depending upon how the child interprets them, inferiority feelings become the source for all human striving or the root of psychopathology. In optimum settings, the child uses feelings of inferiority as an impetus to grow and change. However, inferiority feelings may become accentuated, leading the child to feel overwhelmed and ineffectual, and creating an *inferiority complex*.

Inferiority complexes have a number of causes, most of which can be attributed to treatment of the child in the first five years of life. Adler identified three primary sources: (1) pampering, (2) neglect, and (3) organ inferiority. Pampering exacerbates feelings of inferiority by depriving the child of opportunities to develop his or her independence and initiative. In a pampered situation, the anticipation of the child's every need means that the child has few opportunities to overcome initial feelings of helplessness. An inferiority complex arises as the child feels overwhelmed by his or her perceived inadequacies and is unable to develop strivings for excellence and mastery.

In instances of neglect, children are also prone to develop an inferiority complex but for largely the opposite reasons: Believing themselves to be unloved and unlovable, neglected children may have little recourse but to renounce the necessity of love, often becoming hostile and/or withdrawn. Recall that, in Adler's view, it is the parents' role to nurture the child's social interest. Without this guidance, social interest gives way to self-centered strivings, resulting in a style of life that markedly lacks the capacity for concern for others. Compassion is replaced by the more mercenary "What can I get out of this situation?"

Adler identified physical or organic deficiencies as another risk factor in the development of an inferiority complex. Children born with cerebral palsy, for example, may have normal or superior mental capacities, but because their delivery systems are impaired, such talents may be underestimated. In such instances, a physiological impairment develops into a psychological one, with intensified feelings of inferiority impairing the individual's ability to strive for achievement.

The development of *organ inferiority* in response to a physiological impairment, or an *inferiority complex* in response to early childhood experiences, is not an inevitability. Although Adler believed that one's basic goals and personality characteristics are developed by the age of 5, he acceded to the possibility of growth and change through concerted effort. Adler placed the true responsibility for striving and achieving superiority in the hands of the individual. "It is not the child's experiences which dictate his actions, it is the conclusions which he draws from his experiences" (Adler, 1958, p. 123).

Other external factors influence the child's personality. The constellation of the family may have a profound impact on the development of achievement motives, career choice, and interpersonal skills. Adler suggested that the firstborn child is likely to fall prey to pampering and thus have an increased chance of developing an inferiority complex. The birth of a sibling can prove to be a very painful dethroning and may further exacerbate the eldest child's feelings of inferiority. Personality characteristics of firstborns may reflect this early history: Adler suggested that among firstborns there are higher instances of maladjustment with peers, neurotic tendencies, even criminality and alcoholism (Adler, 1958). On the other hand, they may assume a parental role with younger siblings and be more able to accept responsibility than their later-born siblings (Ansbacher & Ansbacher, 1956). Firstborns tend to choose careers that involve a high degree of responsibility and are relatively conformist (such as doctor or lawyer), perhaps reflecting their dislike for disruption of the status quo (Adler, 1969).

According to Adler, the middle child is in a favorable position because he or she is unlikely to be pampered. Furthermore, the presence of an older sibling acts as an impetus to excel. In Adler's view, middle children tend to be highly competitive, socially adept, and able to assert themselves to overcome feelings of inferiority.

Although youngest children escape the pain of being "dethroned" by newly arriving siblings, they are in the unfortunate position of being pampered by both parents and older siblings, thus compounding their feelings of inadequacy. Whereas the presence of multiple older siblings may produce a high degree of ambition and a tendency to choose unique paths, pampering may deprive the youngest child of opportunities to set goals and strive for their achievement. Adler considered last-born children to be the second highest risk group for inferiority complexes, but added that the stimulation provided by older siblings may, in some instances, inspire last-borns to excel.

Only-children are in the unique position of never being dethroned and may continue to be pampered by their parents. The result, in Adler's view, is that only-children sometimes overestimate their own importance and may have difficulties interacting with peers (Adler, 1958).

Contemporary Research on Adler's Theory   The importance of birth order in Adler's theory of personality development stimulated much research. Is birth order as important to career choice or to the development of achievement motivation as Adler predicted? Perhaps, but not necessarily for the reasons that Adler suggested. It is well established that firstborns, for instance, rather than appearing to suffer from debilitating inferiority complexes, are more likely than their siblings to achieve eminence in their professional lives, are more likely to seek higher education (Schachter, 1963), and tend to score higher on numerous standardized tests than their later-born siblings (Eysenck & Cookson, 1969). There is evidence, however, that firstborns are more obedient and willing to accept positions of responsibility in social situations than later-borns (Sutton-Smith & Rosenberg, 1970). Hilton (1967) noted that mothers demanded more of their firstborns, were more likely to withhold affection if they did not succeed on tasks, and yet were extremely warm and affectionate toward them when they did perform well. You may recognize, in this pattern, the key elements of the authoritative parenting style discussed earlier. Birth order appears to have a bidirectional effect: Both parent and child behaviors are modified by the birth of a sibling, and those changes are assimilated into the developing personality.

The situation with later-borns is significantly more complex. Perhaps the second-born is also the first girl in the family, or the youngest child happens to be the youngest of 12 rather than the youngest of 3. Does a general model of first-, middle-, and later-born effects account adequately for such differences in family composition? What is the influence of socioeconomic status differences between families? Cultural differences? Attempts have been made to address these questions (for examples, see Sutton-Smith & Rosenberg, 1970; Zajonc & Markus, 1975). Despite these factors, birth order differences in people's ability to get along with others tend to persist: Youngest children are perceived as more affable than either middle children or firstborns. And although firstborns appear to initiate social interactions with greater frequency than their siblings, their attempts are not as successful as those of either middle or youngest children (Miller & Maruyama, 1976).

Interest in birth order research has been renewed by Sulloway's (1996) finding that firstborns tend to support the status quo and later-borns tend to rebel against it. Sulloway's approach to examining interactions between birth order and other factors, such as gender, temperament, and family structure, is likely to stimulate a new wave of research on this topic. Many psychologists and psychiatrists, such as James (2002), continue to believe that the family dynamics experienced during early childhood become the major influence on adult personality and social behavior. Others, however, strongly criticize Sulloway's theory of birth order and argue that peer group interactions during later childhood and adolescence are far more influential than early family dynamics (Harris, 1998).

Sullivan's Interpersonal Approach—Peer Influences

Intrapsychic phenomena (Freud), attachment histories (Bowlby and others), parenting styles (Rogers), and birth order (Adler) each contribute in complex ways to the developing personality. Sullivan (1953), however, was among the first theorists to emphasize the critical role of peers in the definition and development of a unique personality. In Sullivan's view, friendships formed in the preadolescent phase, particularly the development of a close same-sex friendship (or "chumship"), provide a new opportunity to amend and adjust maladaptive personality features developed in the context of early family interactions. Sullivan describes the chumship as a forum for the "clearing of warps" resulting from the unique treatment of the child in his or her early environment. In the context of a secure relationship, chums provide important feedback about the appropriateness and desirability of each other's actions and developing belief systems. The sharing of ideas, values, and opinions characteristic of a chumship acts as a mirror for adjusting and smoothing out the rough edges of one's personality. For example, children who were adored by their parents may develop a heightened sense of their own importance, which may be less favorably received in the peer group. In the context of a trusting friendship such information can be shared and adjustments made without the threat of abandonment. A chumship provides the individuals involved with the opportunity to note similarities and differences and make adjustments in their developing view of themselves and their place in the world.

The emergence of a chumship in preadolescence is made possible, in part, by increased cognitive capacities of the child (Piaget, 1960). Whereas toddler and early childhood interactions tend to be centered around object play, shared interests, and "propinquity" (geographical convenience), friendships in preadolescence and adolescence increasingly involve intimacy, self-disclosure, mutual trust, and loyalty (Bigelow, 1977; Brenner & Mueller,1982; Savin-Williams & Berndt, 1990; Youniss & Smollar, 1985). Although some of the interchanges between chums remain at a relatively concrete level (such as the exchange of opinion about appearances), the creative work of the chumship lies in each individual's capacity to take the perspective of the other and to make observations and assertions from the vantage point of sensing how it will be received by the other. This capacity for multiple perspective-taking is both a cognitive accomplishment and an outgrowth of emotional development (the capacity for empathy). However, the individual's ability and willingness to adjust behaviors and beliefs as a response to mutual exchanges in a trusting relationship are largely the products of an emotional investment in the peer. Sullivan observes that a chumship differs from other friendships in intensity and level of commitment. In chumships, the individuals care as much or more for the welfare of the other as they do for themselves. Thus, emotional investment and mutual support are the core features enabling genuine personality transformation in the context of a preadolescent chumship.

The Sociocultural Approach of Horney

As we have seen, sociocultural and biosocial theories present a complex and multifaceted view of human motivation and personality development. In some instances, sociocultural perspectives have enhanced previous theoretical perspectives. Karen Horney (1885—1952), for example, influenced Rogers's view of conflict within the self. Like other neo-Freudians, (e.g., Bowlby), Horney emphasized the importance of human relationships in personality development. In contrast to Freud, who believed that human disturbance is born of the conflict between environmental factors and repressed instinctual impulses, Horney believed that inner conflicts arose from contradictory needs. For example, an individual may experience a conflict between needs for camaraderie and equally compelling needs for privacy. The ability to negotiate disparate demands within the self stands as a hallmark of healthy adaptation in Horney's theory.

Horney (1945) identified three trends basic to all individuals: the tendency to (1) move toward others, (2) move away from others, or (3) move against others. Although present in everyone, these trends are essentially mutually exclusive, requiring the individual to negotiate competing urges within the self. In healthy individuals the tendency to move away, toward, or against others is largely dependent on the context. Thus, while it may be appropriate to move toward others in a new work environment, a normally functioning person has the flexibility to move away from or against an assailant on the street. In the neurotic personality, one trend has emerged as dominant, and all interpersonal interactions are approached from that perspective.

Most of us have experienced individuals who might be called extreme in their tendency to move against others. Often regarded as troublemakers or bullies by teachers and peers, or as hostile or volatile by employers, the extreme "moving against" person has a Machiavellian worldview, grounded in the need for control and a tendency to exploit others for self-serving ends. Conversely, an extreme "moving toward others" is often viewed as overly solicitous, compliant, and malleable in interpersonal interactions. Needs for love, approval, and affection are so pervasive among the extreme "moving toward" individual that all other urges are subjugated. Finally, individuals with extreme tendencies to "move away from others" are frequently identified as shy or withdrawn. The tendency toward isolation and detachment in the "moving away from others" person is a source of both discomfort and solace to the individual who feels that it is perhaps best to fend for oneself, since others cannot be relied upon to provide security. Each of these extreme stances, in Horney's view, is the result of differences in the child's early experience of security and safety in interpersonal relationships.

Contemporary Research on Horney's Theory   In a series of studies designed to examine the stability and consequences of extreme tendencies to move against others or move away from others, Caspi, Elder, and Bem (1987, 1988) suggested that two parallel processes conspire to increase the stability of these personality characteristics. The first, *cumulative continuity*, involves a self-selection process. For example, in the case of "moving against the world,"

> the boy whose ill-temper leads him to drop out of school thereby limits his future career opportunities and selects himself into frustrating life circumstances that further evoke a pattern of striking out against the world. It is the progressive accumulation of their own consequences [which produces] cumulative continuity. (Caspi et al., 1988, p. 824)

The second, *interactional continuity*, involves the individual's expectations about interpersonal interactions. In a kind of self-fulfilling prophecy, the individual who expects to be treated with hostility may act in ways that evoke aggressive or hostile reactions in others.

Caspi, Elder, and Bem (1987) examined archival data from the Berkeley Guidance Study to identify children (8 to 10 years old) with explosive behavior patterns (moving against the world). During the 1960s, two follow-up interviews were conducted. Individuals with childhood histories of aggression (in their 30s and 40s at follow-up) continued to exhibit aggressive behavior styles in adulthood and were more likely to be divorced than their even-tempered peers. Men with histories of aggressive behavior experienced a progressive deterioration of economic status, with work lives reflecting erratic employment. Women with explosive histories were likely to marry men from lower socioeconomic groups, tended to be ill-tempered in their interactions with their children, and often transmitted their explosive style to the next generation—their children (Caspi & Elder, 1988).

In a similar study, Caspi, Elder, and Bem (1988) identified individuals with childhood histories of shyness (moving away from others). In adulthood, the consequences of shy behavior were most striking in males. Men with childhood histories of shyness delayed marriage and parenthood, had greater levels of marital disruption, and took a longer time establishing stable careers than their non-shy peers.

For women reaching midlife in the 1960s, shyness did not affect the timing of marriage and childbirth. However, women identified as shy in childhood were more likely to conform to traditional marriage and childbirth patterns. Given that these data were collected in the 1940s, most of the women studied did not establish stable careers outside the home (outgoing women averaged nine years in the labor force, compared to six years for shy women) and the range of occupational status was slim. Shy women were more likely than non-shys to have no work history or to cease outside employment upon marriage or childbirth and not reenter the labor force.

Caspi and his colleagues suggest that childhood shyness expresses itself in later life situations that require taking the initiative (such as in negotiating career steps, and proposing marriage). As the definitions of sex roles in society have broadened, the demands upon women to take the initiative, particularly in career settings, have increased. In a study of contemporary college women, Kelly (1988) noted that shyness acted as a restraining barrier to women's career and educational aspirations. This more recent data on career patterns among shy women closely mirrors findings observed in men's career aspirations in the 1950s. Thus the long-term consequences of shyness are determined, in part, by the expectations of the individual's cohort and society (Cheek & Krasnoperova, 1999; Kerr, Lambert, & Bem, 1996).

The development and stability of personality characteristics such as shyness and aggression are determined by a diverse constellation of factors. Culturally prescribed sex roles, the accumulation of consequences of the individual's behavior (cumulative continuity), and the expectations that individuals carry into their interactions with other people (interactional continuity) together influence the life course of personality characteristics.

FUTURE DIRECTIONS: TOWARD A TRANSACTIONAL THEORY OF PERSONALITY DEVELOPMENT

If we look back at Table 5.1, we can see that contemporary work in personality psychology has gone beyond the simple either-or assumptions underlying the psychoanalytic, behaviorist, and humanistic approaches to personality development. Rather than arguments about good versus bad human nature, inner versus outer causes of behavior, or free will versus determinism, we need a new model that accounts for the complex developmental transactions between the person and the social environment. This model must explain how the biological building blocks of the individual become transformed through encounters with parents, siblings, peers, and the broader culture into the dynamic structures of adult personality (see Table 5.6). Although no one has yet constructed

Table 5.6 | Elements of the Personality Equation for Adult Personality Tendencies

---

Adult personality tendencies (APT) are the outgrowth of complex developmental transactions among a number of elements that mutually influence each other during childhood and adolescence:

$$APT = T \times M \times F \times C \times U \times SA$$

T = Temperament, which includes genetics and constitutional, biological factors;

M = Motives, which includes needs and goals;

F = Family, which includes family dynamics and the unique way each child experiences them;

C = Culture, which includes broad national culture and subcultures (ethnicity, religion, class, kinship, gender; peer groups);

U = Unconscious, which includes traces of early personal experiences, family and cultural values, and collective or sociobiological aspects of being a member of the human species;

SA = Self-Awareness, which includes conscious self-concept and thoughts and feelings about the 5 preceding elements (T, M, F, C, and U) that open the possibility of choice and future change in developing one's creative self.

The system of Adult Personality Tendencies made up of these elements contributes to our understanding of each individual, along with consideration of her or his social roles and relationships. Psychologists say that Behavior is a Function of complex interactions between a Person and a Situation, often written as $B = f(P \times S)$. Adult Personality Tendencies are a key part of the "P" or Person part of this behavioral equation, and personality also influences how different individuals will subjectively perceive and uniquely interpret the objectively same Situation.

---

such a comprehensive theory, promising new developments in that direction include Robert Hogan's socioanalytic theory of personality (Hogan & Smither, 2001, chap. 12) and Albert Bandura's (2001) social cognitive theory. The contemporary research in areas such as gender roles, self-concept, motives, emotions, and culture, described in the following chapters, informs you about the current status of the major elements of the personality equation.

SUMMARY

This chapter examines four major theoretical approaches to the study of personality development: psychoanalytic, behavioral, humanistic, and sociocultural or biosocial. The psychoanalytic tradition began with Freud, and his theory continues to influence personality psychologists. Current research on attachment patterns in personality development represent a revision in the Freudian view of the primacy of the id instincts (sex and aggression) in personality formation. Ego psychologists and neoanalytic researchers such as Bowlby (1969) and Ainsworth, Blehar, Waters, and Wall (1978) have included the need for "felt security" among the constellation of factors that motivate human behavior. The infant's feeling of security, arising out of early interactions with the primary caregiver, contributes to the development of an internal working model of attachment that serves as a template or guide for action in subsequent relationships.

Longitudinal research through the first six years of life suggests that such internal working models may persist at least through the early primary grades. Related research involving late adolescents and adults suggests that secure, anxious/resistant, and avoidant attachment patterns continue to be represented in roughly the same proportions as were found in toddler groups. Furthermore, adults' descriptions of their own attachment to their parents tended to coincide with their attachment behavior toward their infants in the strange situation.

Although these findings suggest that attachment patterns may persist over the life course, further longitudinal work is needed to assess whether attachment patterns change markedly as a result of diverse life experiences. Recent critiques of attachment theory have suggested that the influence of attachment with primary caregivers on later attachment styles may weaken over time, and that attachment styles may be more related to temperament differences than was previously recognized.

Behaviorism represents a radical departure from intrapsychic and ego psychological perspectives on personality development. Behaviorists view the external environment as the major determinant of personality and social behavior. Personality is shaped as a consequence of the selective reinforcement of behavior and through vicarious reinforcement (observing reinforcement of models). Current cognitive social learning theorists (Bandura and Mischel) emphasize the roles of perceived self-efficacy (what the person thinks he or she can do) and self-efficacy expectancies (one's anticipation of success or failure) in determining behavior.

Humanistic psychology adopts an optimistic attitude toward personality development. Rogers asserted that unconditional positive regard in parent-child interactions promotes the development of a "fully functioning person"—one whose innate potential has been realized. Recent research suggests that a lack of unconditional positive regard from parents (conditional support) may contribute to feelings of hopelessness, which, in turn, lead to "false self" behavior—behaving "like a phony" or "putting on an act" rather than expressing how one really thinks and feels. Contemporary research on parenting styles and fostering creativity suggests that an authoritative child-rearing style characterized by warmth, discipline, clear parent-child communications, and clear demands for the child's maturity fosters confidence, exploration, and creative potential in the growing child.

Biosocial theorists stress the importance of social relationships with parents, siblings, and peers and the contributions of the social context to personality development. Adlerian theory suggests that individuals are aware of their relative helplessness and dependency in infancy and strive to overcome the feelings (striving for superiority). Healthy social interest channels these strivings in directions that serve the society as well as the individual. Birth order contributes to individual differences in personality, influencing the level of "pampering" the child experiences, and subsequently determining whether the child develops an inferiority complex.

Sullivan stressed the role of chumships during later childhood in "clearing the warps" of early childhood experiences. Horney posited three neurotic interpersonal styles that result from the failure to provide the infant with safety and satisfaction of needs: moving toward (excessive compliance), moving away (withdrawal), and moving against (hostility). Hostile/explosive and withdrawn styles tend to persist across the life course, influencing marital and employment patterns (Caspi, Elder, & Bem, 1987, 1988). Hostile patterns show continuity across generations as well (Caspi & Elder, 1988).

Current research and theory reflect the growing sophistication of personality psychologists in dealing with the complex interactions among biological, intrapsychic, interpersonal, and sociocultural factors as they contribute to personality development.

DISCUSSION QUESTIONS

1. Freud's influence appears in words now incorporated into our everyday language. For example, we often speak of someone who is "egotistical." How does Freud's definition of "ego" differ from, and how is it similar to, our everyday use of the word?

2. How might the three main styles of attachment fit in with Bandura's model of perceived self-efficacy? Do you think that the three attachment styles can be ranked from one that has the most self-efficacy to one that has the least self-efficacy?

3. Imagine that you are a parent and your 15-year-old son or daughter wants to go to the beach for the weekend with older peers. There will be no adult supervision. According to research on Rogers's concept of unconditional positive regard and Baumrind's three parenting styles, what approach should you take with your teenager in responding to this request? Why?

4. In what ways are birth-order theory and horoscopes similar? How easy or difficult is it to design convincing research studies about the influences of birth order on personality development and adult social behavior?

5. How would each of Horney's three interpersonal styles (moving toward, away from, or against others) affect a youngster's ability to form chumships? What impact might this have on the development of his or her adult personality?

6. In what ways does the personality "equation" for adult personality tendencies in Table 5.6 help you to answer the question that began this chapter: How did you become the person you are today?

SUGGESTED READINGS

Bandura, A. (2001). Social cognitive theory: An agentic perspective. *Annual Review of Psychology*, 52, 1–26. A new version of cognitive social learning theory that goes far beyond behaviorism by incorporating the development of intentionality and self-reflectiveness and proposing a model of biosocial coevolution.

Feeney, J., & Noller, P. (1996). *Adult attachment*. Thousand Oaks, CA: Sage. An excellent summary of previous research on attachment and a description of the application of the attachment model to adulthood.

Harter, S. (2002). Authenticity. In C. R. Snyder & S. J. Lopez (Eds.), *Handbook of positive psychology* (pp. 382–394). New York: Oxford University Press. Reviews research and theory on developmental factors in childhood and adolescence that foster true-self versus false-self behavior.

Hogan, R., & Smither, R. (2001). *Personality: Theories and applications.* Boulder, CO: Westview. An excellent book-length treatment of the theories of personality development and dynamics that were presented in this chapter.

Horney, K. (1945). *Our inner conflicts.* New York: Norton. A theoretical overview of the development of neurotic interpersonal styles.

SUGGESTED WEB SITES

http://www.freud.org.uk/

Web site of the Freud Museum in London that presents excellent coverage of the contributions of Sigmund and Anna Freud to the development of psychoanalysis.

http://www.personalityresearch.org/attachment.html

Descriptions of infant and adult attachment styles and summaries of new research, including interesting references to attachment research with monkeys, dogs, and other animals.

http://www.emory.edu/EDUCATION/mfp/bandurabio.html

An interesting, illustrated biography of Albert Bandura that describes his 50 years of contributions to the psychology of personality development and provides links to his latest work on cognitive social learning theory.

http://library.thinkquest.org/C004361/index1.html

An educational web site that presents information about personality development and personality theorists in a lively, attractive format.

INFOTRAC COLLEGE EDITION SEARCH TOPICS

Psychoanalysis	Learning theory	Biosocial theory
Attachment theory	Humanistic psychology	Sociocultural theory

REFERENCES

Adler, A. (1958). *What life should mean to you.* New York: Capricorn Books.

Adler, A. (1969). *The science of living.* New York: Anchor Books.

Ainsworth, M. D., Blehar, M. C., Waters, E., & Wall, S. (1978). *Patterns of attachment.* Hillsdale, NJ: Erlbaum.

Ainsworth, M. D. S., Bell, S. M., & Stayton, D. J. (1974). Infant-mother attachment and social development: Socialization as a product of reciprocal responsiveness to signals. In M. P. M. Richards (Ed.), *The integration of the child into a social world* (pp. 99–135). London: Cambridge University Press.

Ansbacher, H. L., & Ansbacher, R. R. (Eds.). (1956). *The individual psychology of Alfred Adler.* New York: Basic Books.

Arend, R., Gove, F. L., & Sroufe, L. A. (1979). Continuity of individual adaptation from infancy to kindergarten: A predictive study of ego-resiliency and curiosity in preschoolers. *Child Development, 50,* 950–959.

Bandura, A. (1965). Influence of models' reinforcement contingencies on the acquisition of imitative responses. *Journal of Personality and Social Psychology, 1,* 589–595.

Bandura, A. (1997). *Self-efficacy: The exercise of control.* New York: W. H. Freeman.

Bandura, A. (2001). Social cognitive theory: An agentic perspective. *Annual Review of Psychology, 52,* 1–26.

Baumrind, D. (1967). Child care practices anteceding three patterns of preschool behavior. *Genetic Psychology Monographs, 75,* 43–88.

Bigelow, B. J. (1977). Children's friendship expectations: A cognitive-developmental study. *Child Development, 48*, 246–253.

Block, J., & Block, J. (1980). The role of ego-development and ego-resiliency in the organization of behavior. In W. A. Collins (Ed.), *The Minnesota symposia on child psychology: Vol. 13. Development of cognition, affect, and social relations* (pp. 39–101). Hillsdale, NJ: Erlbaum.

Bowlby, J. (1969). *Attachment and loss. Vol. 1: Attachment* (2nd ed.). New York: Basic Books.

Bowlby, J. (1988). *A secure base: Parent-child attachment and healthy human development*. New York: Basic Books.

Brennan, K. A., Clark, C. L., & Shaver, P. R. (1998). Self-report measurement of adult romantic attachment: An integrative overview. In J. A. Simpson & W. S. Rholes (Eds.), *Attachment theory and close relationships* (pp. 46–76). New York: Guilford.

Brenner, J., & Mueller, E. (1982). Shared meaning in boy toddlers' peer relations. *Child Development, 53*, 380–391.

Campos, J. J., Barrett, K. C., Lamb, M. E., Goldsmith, H. H., & Stenberg, C. (1983). Socio-emotional development. In M. M. Haith & J. J. Campos (Eds.), *Handbook of child psychology. Vol 2: Infancy and psychobiology* (pp. 783–915). New York: Wiley.

Caspi, A., & Elder, G. H., Jr. (1988). Emergent family patterns: The intergenerational construction of problem behaviour and relationships. In R. A. Hinde & J. Stevenson-Hinde (Eds.), *Relationships within families: Mutual influences* (pp. 218–240). New York: Oxford University Press.

Caspi, A., Elder, G. H., Jr., & Bem., D. J. (1987). Moving against the world: Life-course patterns of explosive children. *Developmental Psychology, 23*, 308–313.

Caspi, A., Elder, G. H., Jr., & Bem, D. J. (1988). Moving away from the world: Life-course patterns of shy children. *Developmental Psychology, 24*, 824–431.

Cassidy, J. (1988). Child-mother attachment and the self in six-year-olds. *Child Development, 59*, 121–134.

Cheek, J. M., & Krasnoperova, E. N. (1999). Varieties of shyness in adolescence and adulthood. In L. A. Schmidt & J. Schulkin (Eds.), *Extreme fear, shyness, and social phobia: Origins, biological mechanisms, and clinical outcomes* (pp. 224–250). New York: Oxford University Press.

Erickson, M. F., Sroufe, L. A., & Egelund, B. (1985). The relationship between quality of attachment and behavior problems in preschool in a high-risk sample. *Monographs of the Society for Research in Child Development, 50*(1–2). Serial No. 209.

Erikson, E. (1963). *Childhood and society*. New York: Norton.

Eysenck, H. J., & Cookson, D. (1969). Personality in primary school children: 3. Family background. *British Journal of Educational Psychology, 40*, 117–131.

Finnegan, R., & Perry, D. (1993, March). *Preadolescents' self-reported attachments to their mothers and their social behavior with peers*. Paper presented at the biennial meetings of the Society for Research in Child Development, New Orleans.

Fox, N. (1995). Of the way we were: Adult memories about attachment experiences and their role in determining infant-parent relationships: A commentary on van Ijzendoorn (1995). *Psychological Bulletin, 117*, 404–410.

Freud, A. (1958). *The ego and the mechanism of defense*. New York: International Universities Press.

Freud, S. (1933). The dissection of the psychical personality. *New introductory lectures on psychoanalysis*. New York: Norton.

George, C., Kaplan, N., & Main, M. (1984). *The Berkeley Adult Attachment Interview*. Unpublished protocol, Department of Psychology, University of California, Berkeley.

Harlow, H. F. (1958). The nature of love. *American Psychologist, 13*, 673–685.

Harrington, D., Block, J., & Block, J. (1987). Testing aspects of Carl Rogers' theory of creative environments: Child-rearing antecedents of creative potential in young adolescents. *Journal of Personality and Social Psychology, 52*, 851–856.

Harris, J. R. (1998). *The nurture assumption: Why children turn out the way they do*. New York: Free Press.

Harter, S. (2002). Authenticity. In C. R. Snyder & S. J. Lopez (Eds.), *Handbook of positive psychology* (pp. 382–394). New York: Oxford University Press.

Harter, S., Marold, D. B., & Whitesell, N. R. (1992). Model of psychosocial risk factors leading to suicidal ideation in young adolescents. *Development and Psychopathology, 4*, 167–188.

Harter, S., Marold, D. B., Whitesell, N. R., & Cobbs, G. (1996). A model of the effects of perceived parent and peer support on adolescent false self behavior. *Child Development, 67,* 360–374.

Harter, S., Waters, P. L., & Whitesell, N. R. (1997). Lack of voice as a manifestation of false self behavior among adolescents: The school setting as a stage upon which the drama of authenticity is enacted. *Educational Psychologist, 32,* 153–173.

Harter, S., Waters, P. L., Whitesell, N. R., & Kastelic, D. (1998). Level of voice among female and male high school students: Relational context, support, and gender orientation. *Developmental Psychology, 34,* 892–901.

Hazan, C., & Shaver, P. (1987). Romantic love conceptualized as an attachment process. *Journal of Personality and Social Psychology, 52,* 511–524.

Hilton, I. (1967). Differences in the behavior of mothers toward first and later born children. *Journal of Personality and Social Psychology, 7,* 282–290.

Hogan, R., & Smither, R. (2001). *Personality: Theories and applications.* Boulder, CO: Westview.

Horney, K. (1945). *Our inner conflicts.* New York: Norton.

Horney, K. (1967). *Feminine psychology.* New York: Norton.

James, O. (2002). *They f*** you up: How to survive family life.* London: Bloomsbury.

Kelly, K. L. (1988). *Shyness and educational and vocational development at Wellesley College.* Unpublished B.A. honors thesis, Wellesley College, Wellesley, MA.

Kerr, M., Lambert, W. W., & Bem, D. J. (1996). Life course sequelae of childhood shyness in Sweden: Comparisons with the United States. *Developmental Psychology, 32,* 1100–1105.

Kline, P. (1984). *Psychology and Freudian theory.* London: Methuen.

Kobak, R. (1985). *Attitudes towards attachment relations and social competence among first year college students.* Unpublished doctoral dissertation, University of Virginia, Charlottesville.

Kobak, R., & Cole, H. (1994). Attachment and meta-monitoring: Implications for adolescent autonomy and psychopathology. In D. Cicchetti & S. Toth (Eds.), *Rochester symposium on developmental psychopathology. Vol. 5: Disorders and dysfunctions of the self* (pp. 267–297). Rochester, NY: University of Rochester Press.

Kobak, R., Cole, H., Ferenz-Gillies, R., Fleming, W., & Gamble, W. (1993). Attachment and emotion regulation during mother-teen problem solving: A control theory analysis. *Child Development, 64,* 231–245.

Kobak, R., & Sceery, A. (1988). Attachment in late adolescence: Working models, affect regulation, and representations of self and others. *Child Development, 59,* 135–146.

Main, M., & Cassidy, J. (1988). Categories of responses to reunion with the parent at age 6: Predictable from infant attachment classifications and stable over a 1-month period. *Developmental Psychology, 24,* 415–426.

Main, M., Kaplan, N., & Cassidy, J. (1985). Security in infancy, childhood, and adulthood: A move to the level of representation. *Monographs of the Society for Research in Child Development, 50* (1 & 2, Serial no. 209), 66–104.

Miller, J. B. (1976). *Toward a new psychology of women.* Boston: Beacon Press.

Miller, N., & Maruyama, G. (1976). Ordinal position and peer popularity. *Journal of Personality and Social Psychology, 33,* 123–131.

Mischel, W. (1984). Convergences and challenges in the search for consistency. *American Psychologist, 39,* 351–364.

Parke, R. D., & Devr, J. L. (1972). Schedule of punishment and inhibition of aggression in children. *Developmental Psychology, 7,* 266–269.

Piaget, J. (1960). *The child's conception of the world.* London: Routledge.

Quartz, S. R., & Sejnowski, T. J. (2002). *Liars, lovers, and heroes: What the new brain science reveals about how we become who we are.* New York: William Morrow.

Renken, B. Egelund, B., Marvinney, D., Mangelsdorf, S., & Sroufe, L. A. (1989). Early childhood antecedents of aggression and passive withdrawal in early elementary school. *Journal of Personality, 57,* 257–282.

Rogers, C. (1951). *Client-centered therapy: Its current practice, implications and theory.* Boston: Houghton Mifflin.

Rogers, C. (1961). *On becoming a person.* Boston: Houghton Mifflin.

Rutter, M. (1979). Maternal deprivation, 1972–1978: New findings, new concepts, new approaches. *Child Development, 50,* 283–305.

Savin-Williams, R., & Berndt, T. (1990). Friendship and peer relations. In S. Feldman & G. Elliott (Eds.), *At the threshold: The developing adolescent* (pp. 277–307). Cambridge, MA: Harvard University Press.

Schachter, S. (1963). Birth order, eminence, and higher education. *American Sociological Review, 28,* 757–767.

Skinner, B. F. (1953). *Science and human behavior.* New York: Macmillan.

Spitz, R. A. (1945). Hospitalism: An inquiry into the genesis of psychiatric conditions in early childhood. In A. Freud (Ed.), *The psychoanalytic study of the child* (Vol.1, pp. 53–74). New York: International Universities Press.

Sroufe, L. A. (1983). Infant-caregiver attachment and adaptation in the preschool: The roots of competence and maladaptation. In M. Perlmutter (Ed.), The *Minnesota symposia on child psychology: Vol. 16. Development and policy concerning children with special needs* (pp. 41–83). Hillsdale, NJ: Erlbaum.

Sroufe, L. A., Schork, E., Motti, F., Lawroski, N., & LaFreniere, P. (1984). The role of affect in social competence. In C. E. Izard, J. Kagan, & R. B. Zajonc (Eds.), *Emotions, cognition and behavior* (pp. 289–319). Cambridge: Cambridge University Press.

Sullivan, H. S. (1953). *The interpersonal theory of psychiatry.* New York: Norton.

Sulloway, F. J. (1996). *Born to rebel: Birth order, family dynamics, and creative lives.* New York: Pantheon.

Sutton-Smith, B., & Rosenberg, B. G. (1970). *The sibling.* New York: Holt, Rinehart & Winston.

Van Ijzendoorn, M. H. (1995). Adult attachment representations, parental responsiveness, and infant attachment: A meta-analysis on the predictive validity of the adult attachment interview. *Psychological Bulletin, 117,* 387–403.

Waters, E. Wippman, J., & Sroufe, L. A. (1979). Attachment, positive affect, and competence in the peer group: Two studies in construct validation. *Child Development, 50,* 821–829.

Watson, J. B. (1928). *Psychological care of infant and child.* New York: Norton.

Watson, J. B. (1930). *Behaviorism* (rev. ed.). New York: Norton.

Winnicott, D. W. (1960). The theory of the parent-infant relationship. *International Journal of Psychoanalysis, 41,* 585–595.

Youniss, J., & Smollar, J. (1985). *Adolescent relations with mothers, fathers, and friends* (pp. 125–139). Chicago: University of Chicago Press.

Zajonc, R. B., & Markus, G. B. (1975). Birth order and intellectual development. *Psychological Review, 82,* 74–88.

6 | Motives

BARBARA A. WOIKE

DAN P. MCADAMS

What do people really want? This is a central question in personality psychology. When we perceive ourselves and others, we notice that our lives seem generally organized and directed as if they are being guided by something. Although some of our behavior may seem random or erratic, much of it does in fact appear as though we want something. Indeed, we seem to devote a good deal of time in striving toward desired ends. Our actions are guided by personal goals, desires, plans, wishes, concerns, and expectations. Whatever it is that we want appears to energize and direct our behavior across situations and over time. In simple and general terms, motives can be defined as recurrent "wants" that get us moving in certain directions in our lives. These wants set behavior into motion, channel behavior into particular directions, make for the persistence of behavior in the face of obstacles, and stop and start behavior over time. So what is it that we want?

THREE TRADITIONS IN THE STUDY OF HUMAN MOTIVATION

Western scholars have taken different approaches to answering the question of what people want. Maddi (1996) has suggested that motivational approaches to personality may be organized according to three basic assumptions. First, and perhaps most appealing, some theorists have taken the view that our behavior is driven by the desire to fulfill our greatest potential for happiness and mastery. Second, many influential theorists have taken a more pessimistic view by arguing that humans are in conflict and that the main thing that they are trying to do is to satisfy their opposing needs as best they can. A third view is that we are striving to maintain a sense of consistency in our lives and that our behavior is governed largely by what we have learned in the past and our expectations for the future. We may think of these three approaches as the models of fulfillment, conflict, and maintenance. People want to fulfill their potential. People want to reduce conflict. People want to maintain consistency.

Fulfillment Theories: Reaching One's Potential

Most of us would like to think that we are striving for what is best. We are free to make choices that allow us to fulfill our deepest desires, hopes, and wishes. At the root of this assumption is often the belief that we can rationally evaluate our lives and our daily situations in order to make well-informed decisions about our behavior. We often believe that reason drives our behavior and guides our lives. Our belief is grounded in the general realization that human beings have been specially endowed with abilities for abstract thinking and rational decision making that sharply differentiate us from the rest of the animal kingdom.

Over two thousand years ago, the Greek philosopher Plato (427?–347? B.C.) recognized the human person's privileged place in the world as one of being capable of reason. In *The Republic*, Plato presented one of the first motivational theories on record. Human behavior is energized and directed, he argued, by three essential motives, each corresponding to a distinct portion of the mind. These are (1) the appetites, which are basic bodily needs and wants; (2) courage and fortitude, which motivate people, especially soldiers, to do heroic acts; and (3) reason, which motivates some people to strive for "the Good." By contemplating the nature of reality in an abstract and purely rational manner, some human beings (especially those designated to be the leaders, or "philosopher kings," in a utopian republic) may come to understand what is true, good, and harmonious. Reason is the great guiding light of human behavior, the motivational beacon of the virtuous life.

Centuries after Plato, European poets and philosophers of the Enlightenment, such as Alexander Pope (1688–1744) and Jean Jacques Rousseau (1712–1778), celebrated the enlightened status of human beings as potentially rational and peace-loving creatures. In Pope's view, human behavior is driven by self-love but guided by reason. Therefore although selfish wants may energize us to act, rational thought tempers our selfishness and provides good direction for behavior. According to Rousseau, human beings are born into a natural state of goodness and perfection. Society, however, is capable of perverting human goodness and substituting destructive motives for benevolent, reasonable ones. Rousseau believed that only by ignoring societal trappings and returning to nature could human beings fully realize their own goodness.

The Platonic and Enlightenment views of human motivation have made their way into the 20th century in the forms of influential humanistic theories that portray human beings as motivated to realize, actualize, and perfect the self (Maslow, 1968; Rogers, 1951). Maslow proposed that human needs emerge from the organismic level. The arrangement of these needs is depicted in a pyramid-shaped hierarchy featuring five clusters that range from relatively potent survival needs to relatively weak growth needs. The first set of motives contains those physiological needs necessary for bodily homeostasis, quiescence, and survival. All the other needs in the hierarchy (safety and security, love and belongingness, esteem, and self-actualization) rest upon this foundation. The hierarchical presentation conveys three fundamental themes about the nature of human needs (Maslow, 1943). First, needs arrange themselves in the hierarchy according to potency or strength. Hence the lower needs at the broad base of the hierarchy have a stronger influence on behavior and emerge sooner in the developmental sequences. An infant's physiological needs for food, shelter, warmth, and basic care must be met before the emergence of the needs for safety and security and so on. The lower needs represent survival or deficiency needs, which have a great deal of control over both human and non-human functioning. If these needs are gratified in humans, growth needs begin to emerge that are more idiosyncratic than the lower level deficiency needs and involve choice and free will. The pinnacle of human growth potential in Maslow's view is self-actualization. Although the idea of this level of human potential is a positive one, it is difficult to achieve. Maslow estimated that less than 1% of the population ever reached self-actualization.

Recently, the positive psychology movement (Seligman, 2002; Seligman, & Csikzentmihalyi, 2000) has begun to revitalize the notion of human potential but without the exclusivity of self-actualization. Positive psychology aims to study three areas of human functioning that have been neglected in modern psychology, namely, positive emotions; positive traits, including strengths, virtues and abilities; and the environments that support positive emotions and traits. By shifting the focus from pathology and mental illness to understanding the positive aspects of human psychological functioning, including our motivations for happiness, well-being, and growth, researchers are attempting to discover the roots of human happiness. Research shows that most people are happy and that qualities contributing to happiness, such as optimism, resiliency, and confidence, can be cultivated through self-awareness and positive intention (Diener, Suh, Lucas, & Smith, 1999; Seligman, 2002).

Another contemporary formulation whose roots may be traced to the tradition of the fulfillment model is self-determination theory (Deci & Ryan, 1991; Ryan, 1995). According to this theory, human beings are endowed with natural motivations to encounter, master, and synthesize new challenges that will promote their self-development. People seek opportunities to engage in intrinsically enjoyable and meaningful tasks and optimal challenges, even when they are not given outside rewards for doing so. Such intrinsically motivated behaviors are experienced "with a full sense of choice, with the experience of doing what one wants, and without the feeling of coercion or compulsion" (Deci & Ryan, 1991, p. 253). A large body of research demonstrates how pervasive intrinsically motivated behavior can be, especially when social environments provide the resources that enable people to experience autonomy, competence, and a sense of belonging—the three environmental "nutrients" that nourish self-determination and a sense of psychological integration (Kasser & Ryan, 1996; Ryan, 1995).

Conflict Theories: Striving to Reduce Opposition

In contrast to fulfillment approaches, conflict theories are rooted in the assumption that humans are in constant struggle between their instinctual wishes or the demands of the environment. People find themselves in two basic types of conflict. First, there may be opposition between one's inner desires and those of one's social group or environment. For instance, an individual may have a strong desire to be powerful or successful, but the social environment demands that the person place the group's needs first and thereby show cooperation and work toward valued group goals. Or, there may be a conflict between opposing needs within the individual. One may have a strong desire to be autonomous and free, but at the same time feel an equally strong need for close relationships and a sense of belonging to a group.

The theory of the evolution of the species introduced by Darwin in the 19th century suggested that human beings are in a constant struggle for survival against a harsh environment. The needs to survive and to reproduce are the basic motivating forces in human experience, as they are for all other animals. Over thousands of years, humans have struggled to achieve these basic needs in the face of threatening environments containing limited resources and among other threatening and competing individuals. This process of natural selection has favored the basic human traits that promote survival and procreation. The most adaptive human wants are those that have maximized the individual's "fitness" in the environment over thousands of years (Wilson, 1978). Humans have evolved to live in small social groups as a way to maximize their resources. Therefore, the most basic psychological motives may be those that enable the individual to prosper in group living. So not only do people need to be motivated to compete for resources but they also need to cooperate and to help others. Or, as Hogan (1987) argues, humans are fundamentally motivated to "get along" and "get ahead."

Contemporary approaches to evolutionary psychology emphasize the many different ways in which human beings strive to get along and get ahead. Natural selection would appear to have endowed human beings with a relatively large number of domain-specific mechanisms for solving adaptive problems (Buss, 1991; Tooby & Cosmides, 1990). In other words, the environment has honed certain motives in human beings. In solving the evolutionary problem of "successful intrasexual competition," for example, the individual must engage in particular behaviors that enable him (by displaying resources, attaining status) or her (by displaying beauty, showing care) to win out over others and gain access to desirable members of the opposite sex, so that sexual reproduction can occur (Buss, 1991). To solve the evolutionary problem of "coalition building and maintenance," by contrast, the individual may need to engage in a very different set of behaviors (such as cultivating long-term friendships, displaying integrity) aimed at cooperating with others in order to build coalitions that compete successfully with rival groups. To solve the evolutionary problem of "parental care and socialization," the individual would need to engage in a different set of motivated behaviors (for example, forming attachments to the young, providing guidance and instruction). Each of the many different evolutionary challenges facing humans, therefore, provides its own unique motivational agenda, specifying particular tactics, strategies, and goals (Buss, 1991).

While these tactics, strategies, and goals may be refined by rational thought and planning, evolutionarily adaptive goal-directed behavior does not always require the assistance of reason or even consciousness in order to be effective. Indeed, we may assume that long before the advent of reason, that is, before the human brain evolved to the point that it was capable of rational thought, our ancestors were motivated to engage in the behaviors that met the evolutionary challenges facing them (Pinker, 2002; Wright, 1994).

In the 20th century, the most influential spokesperson for the conflict view of human motivation was undoubtedly Sigmund Freud (1900/1953, 1930/1961). According to Freud's psychoanalytic view, all behavior is determined or motivated by forces over which we have little control. These forces are in constant opposition with one another, and this is why people suffer from persistent anxiety. The forces and conflicts that determine our behavior are unconscious, so we cannot know what we want because we are not consciously aware of what we want. If we were to know, however, we would shudder in disbelief and repugnance because our behavior is primarily driven by raw unconscious instincts of sex and aggression. All other expressions of human living, such as art, altruism, love, science, are considered substitutions for and defenses against these primal, selfish desires.

Like evolutionary psychology, the psychoanalytic view emphasizes the struggle between our instinctual wants and the forces of the environment that act to thwart and ultimately reshape their expression. Thus these unconscious urgings are able to operate in surprisingly flexible and adaptive ways, as recent writings on human instinct and evolution have convincingly shown (Pinker, 2002). If these instinctual promptings were not so flexible and efficient, human beings would not be here today to display them!

Consistency Theories: Striving for Prediction and Control

Conflict theories assume that struggle between the individual and instinctual wishes or the environment is continuous, unavoidable, and though controllable, not eradicable. Consistency approaches, on the other hand, are based on the idea that inconsistency is avoidable and much more context specific than conflicts (Maddi, 1996). The hallmark of consistency theories is their emphasis on the formative influence of feedback from the external world on the individual. When we approach interaction with the world, we usually do so with some expectations based on past experiences. So life may be understood as the extended attempt to maintain consistency with our learned expectations. Consistency theories encompass learning perspectives in which the individual's expectations are shaped by the environment, as well as cognitive perspectives that portray individuals as problem solvers seeking to reduce inconsistencies in their thoughts, feelings, and behavior.

In the famous terms of John Locke (1632–1704), the human mind at birth is a tabula rasa, or "blank slate." Over time and with experience in the world, the person comes to receive the particular contents of human life, essentially learning from society what he or she should or should not want. That is, a person's expectations are shaped by the environment. If the environment is beneficent and predictable, the individual learns to be motivated to act in ways commensurate with society's expectations and values. An unpredictable or chaotic environment breeds conflict and dissonance, as well as uncertainty in how to engage with the environment. We are, therefore, a product of the contingencies or lack thereof that we experience in our environment.

The most influential spokesperson for the learning approach in 20th century psychology has been B. F. Skinner (1971). Skinner's brand of operant behaviorism looks for the motivators of human behavior in the environment rather than the person. According to this view, psychologists should not make inferences about the internal wants, needs, desires, and expectations of the person because these internal phenomena cannot be observed directly or measured precisely. Instead, the psychologist must examine carefully the particular environments within which behavior is displayed in order to understand how the environment rewards or reinforces certain behaviors and punishes or fails to reinforce others. Thus, human behavior is considered malleable as is the environment in which it is exhibited. This learning perspective has influenced contemporary research on human motivation that emphasizes how learning shapes goals, plans, and motives.

Social learning theories share behaviorism's emphasis on observation, the environment, and learning, but they tend to adopt broader and more eclectic viewpoints that incorporate the cognitive dimensions of human motivation. These theories emphasize that most human learning occurs in a social context as people learn to anticipate what others will do and then act on those anticipations. Based on the social learning approach, Mischel (1973,1979) has put forth a list of five cognitive social learning variables that need to be considered when one attempts to predict what a person will do in a given situation: (1) competencies refer to what a person knows and can do; (2) encoding strategies deal with the manner in which one interprets information; (3) expectancies refer to a person's confidence that he or she will be able to perform a specific behavior in a particular situation, and the outcome and meaning of the behavior; (4) subjective values refer to what a person likes, dislikes, and fears with respect to specific outcomes of behavior; and (5) self-regulatory systems and plans deal with the ways one regulates and guides his or her own behavior through self-imposed goals and standards .

Mischel's theory is one example of social learning approaches that are mainly concerned with predicting what a person will do in a particular situation. In contrast, Bandura's (1971, 1977) highly influential theory of social observational learning emphasizes the acquisition of behavior. Bandura argues that learning often occurs outside the bounds of direct reinforcement. Human beings learn a great deal simply by watching other people, reading about what people do, and generally observing the world. There are four steps in this process: (1) the person must attend to a model of behavior; (2) the person must encode, retain, and make sense of the observed behavior; (3) the person must have a capacity to reproduce the observed behavior; and (4) the person must in some way want to imitate the behavior. Thus, motivation plays a key role in whether observed behavior is actually reproduced by the individual who observes it.

Many cognitive theories of motivation emphasize how humans seek predictive power (Epstein, 1973; Kelly, 1955) and consistency (Festinger, 1957; Swann, 1983) in their understanding of self and world. Kelly's (1955) personal construct theory suggests that people are engaged in a continual attempt to predict and control their experiences. In doing so, they approach the task of living as scientists testing out their hypotheses. The first step of scientific inquiry is the classification of experience. Science begins when the observer seeks to make initial sense of the world by imposing some kind of organization upon it. What psychologist William James (1892/1963) called the "blooming, buzzing confusion" of subjective human experience must be ordered, classified, and divided into categories if the scientist is to know anything at all. From these initial classifications are built synthesizing theories, from which subsequent hypotheses are drawn and tested out in the world. Kelly postulated that each of us has a limited number of bipolar constructs (smart/unintelligent; friendly/unfriendly) that we use to understand and test hypotheses about the world. We seek experiences that match our personal constructions and may alter our behavior to be consistent with these constructions of ourselves and others.

Theories of cognitive dissonance (e.g., Aronson, 1969; Festinger, 1957) focus on the motivational implications of attitude-behavior contradictions. The basic assumption is that people find the experience of dissonance psychologically aversive and are therefore motivated to reduce it by striving to maintain consistency in their thoughts, beliefs, attitudes, opinions, values, and behaviors. Common dissonance-arousing situations include making a choice; having insufficient justification for one's thoughts, feelings, or actions; needing to justify one's effort toward a goal; and integrating new information into one's belief system (Festinger, 1957). These situations can lead people into self-observation in which they become aware that they believe one thing but actually do the opposite. For instance, an individual may hold pro-environmental beliefs such as these: Clean water, clean air, energy conservation, and nature preservation are good, and polluting air, water, or land is irresponsible and immoral. The environmentalist's beliefs are consistent. But this same person drives a car to work every day, and thus contributes to the pollution of the environment. If the environmentalist becomes aware of this contradiction between attitude and behavior, he or she will experience dissonance, or an uncomfortable affective state sometimes labeled guilt. There are four main ways to reduce dissonance and restore harmony. The person can remove the dissonant belief or behavior (e.g., stop driving the car to work or deny it contributes to pollution), reduce the importance of the dissonant belief or behavior (e.g., rationalize that one car contributes only a small amount to overall pollution), add a new consonant belief or behavior, (e.g., riding a bicycle whenever possible), or increase the importance of the consonant belief (e.g., riding a bike more often than driving a car). The awareness of inconsistencies between one's thoughts and behaviors can be a powerful motivator for change (Aronson, 1999).

In sum, ancient and modern theories of human motivation can be grouped into the three perspectives of fulfillment, conflict, and consistency (Maddi, 1996). The dialectic of body versus mind cuts across all three models. Most contemporary views of motivation emphasize both the way in which motivation springs from the exigencies of the body and how it is guided by high-order thinking processes at the same time.

BODY VERSUS MIND IN HUMAN MOTIVATION

Scientific research into human motivation has tended to proceed according to two different classes of metaphors (Weiner, 1992). The first class emphasizes the biological or bodily aspects of human existence and implicitly compares human beings to various kinds of machines. Such mechanistic metaphors provide conceptual space for an understanding of the person as an intricate biological mechanism that obeys the laws of biochemistry and physiology. Like other members of the animal kingdom, humans must meet the incessant demands of thirst and hunger, and they are completely beholden to the vagaries of pain, sickness, disease, and bodily breakdown. By contrast, a second class of metaphors emphasizes that relative to all other organisms, human beings are endowed with incomparable powers of the mind. These powers enable individuals to reflect on their biological condition, to ponder their own mortality and imagine alternatives to it, to be conscious of their own predicament, and to think about virtually anything at all. Rather than a mere machine, the human being is almost godlike (Weiner, 1992). This second class of metaphors, then, focuses on the cognitive or mindful aspects of human existence through rational idealizations that predominate in Western culture. A comprehensive approach to the question of what people really want requires a consideration of both body and mind.

Body: Drive, Reward, Emotion

Hull (1943) formulated a comprehensive and influential theory of motivation and behavior that centered on the concept of generalized drive. According to Hull, drive refers to the sum total of the forces within the organism arising from sexual desires, fear, hunger, thirst, and other basic biologically linked needs. Though various kinds of needs may contribute to an organism's current drive state, there is only one kind of drive, and it functions as a general energizer for behavior. An animal or human being in a strong drive state will act in a vigorous fashion to reduce the drive and thereby relieve the tension of the drive. The reduction of tension through behavior is rewarding, and as a result the behavior that successfully reduces the tension of strong drive is reinforced. The greater the drive reduction, the greater is the reinforcement. Therefore, responses that reduce high levels of drive should be learned more quickly and emitted more intensely than responses that reduce moderate to low levels of drive. Exactly what the organism will do to reduce drive, however, is not directly determined by drive. Rather, the direction of behavior is determined by other factors, most notably the habits or behavioral patterns that the organism has learned in the past under similar stimulus conditions. Hull referred to this factor as habit strength. In general, a behavioral response was considered to be a product of both drive (the energizer) and habit strength (the director).

Although Hull derived his theory of drive and habit strength from animal studies, other researchers applied the theory directly to humans. For instance, Spence (1958) proposed that every person is characterized by a particular level of emotionality that contributes directly to drive level. Taylor (1953) designed the Manifest Anxiety Scale (MAS) to assess individual differences in chronic anxiety, which was thought to be a major source of emotionality. Research employing the MAS has shown that anxious persons, who are presumably in a higher drive state, perform better on simple tasks than do less anxious individuals but do more poorly on difficult tasks, especially when the performance situation involves high levels of stress (Spence, Farber, & McFann, 1956; Spielberger & Smith, 1966). Thus, the presumed energizing effect of high levels of drive, as operationalized on the MAS, promotes simple performance but interferes with performance on more complex, stressful tasks.

Another application of drive theory to human behavior is research on social facilitation. A person's performance is often enhanced or facilitated by the mere presence of others, although sometimes the presence of others can have the opposite effect. Zajonc (1965) provided a Hullian explanation for social facilitation, arguing that the presence of others increases a person's drive level, which in turn energizes dominant or readily available responses. Numerous studies have shown that the mere presence of others facilitates performance of well-learned responses but slows the learning of new ones. For instance, Hunt and Hillery (1973) showed that people were more effective during early attempts to solve a maze-learning task while working alone than when accompanied by others. Once the maze had become familiar through practice, however, the presence of others led to better performance than that shown by individuals working alone.

Why would social facilitation increase drive? Zajonc (1980) offered three possible explanations: (1) The presence of others may create uncertainty about how others will behave, (2) other people might distract the individual, and (3) others may be seen as potential judges or evaluators of one's actions. In other words, drive may be increased by greater levels of uncertainty, distraction, or concern about social evaluation.

Over the past 35 years, there has been a steady decline in the status of the concept of biologically based drive to explain human motivation. Today, many psychologists find the concept of a generalized and nonspecific drive that energizes all behavior to be untenable. Instead, there are numerous empirical studies suggesting that (1) behaviors are often motivated by particular rather than general forces, (2) reinforcement for behavior often does not produce a reduction in drive, and (3) many behaviors appear to occur in the absence of reinforcement (drive reducing or otherwise). Moreover, organisms may seek arousal rather than seek to reduce it (Weiner, 1992; White, 1959). Reinforcement appears to be much more complex than originally supposed, and behavior appears to be motivated by more specific processes than a generalized energizer. With respect to the issue of reinforcement, studies of electrical stimulation of animal brains reveal discrete "reward centers" that appear to have nothing to do with drive (Olds, 1977). Mild electrical stimulation of these cortical areas, located mostly in the brain's limbic system, is highly reinforcing, motivating rats and other animals studied to engage in a wide range of behaviors to obtain the stimulation.

In the past 20 years, researchers have learned a great deal about the biology of reward and reinforcement. Research on animal learning and physiology has identified a behavioral activation system (BAS) that appears to have evolved to motivate forward movement and search behavior as a means of acquiring rewards (Depue, Luciana, Arbisi, Collins, & Leon, 1994). This brain system is thought to initiate or increase an organism's movement toward goals that are likely to be reinforcing and to be closely tied to impulsive behavior. The BAS is also thought to be responsible for positive feelings, such as happiness in humans (Gray, 1990). Key to the workings of the BAS is the neurotransmitter dopamine. Animal research suggests that BAS processes are strongly associated with the activity of dopamine pathways arising from particular cell groups in the midbrain. Thus, dopamine activity in particular parts of the brain may promote approach behavior and be implicated in the subjective reward experiences. Within the human population, significant individual differences may be observed in a general motivational-emotional disposition toward positive affectivity, and these differences can be readily identified through self-reported trait questionnaires (Tellegen, 1985). Persons who score high on measures of positive affectivity tend to be impulsive and sociable, to experience high levels of stimulation and reward compared to individuals low in positive affectivity. A number of researchers now believe that these individual differences in reward-seeking in humans are linked in complex ways to the activity of dopaminergic brain systems that comprise the BAS.

Studies of the brain systems implicated in reward offer a biological perspective on a proposition about motivation that is at least 2,000 years old: that organisms seek to maximize pleasure and minimize pain. An interesting twist on this idea has been proposed by Solomon (1980) in his opponent-process theory of motivation. According to Solomon, the brains of all mammals are organized to oppose or suppress certain types of emotional arousal. A highly positive or negative emotional process (Process A) automatically sets into motion an opposite emotional process (Process B). With repeated experiences, the intensity of Process A dissipates, but Process B continues to build up. For example, a skydiver is likely to experience tremendous anxiety before his or her first jump. The anxiety dissipates rapidly just after the jump, however, and is followed by a rush of positive affect that, over time slowly dissipates until the person is back to a steadier emotional state. According to Solomon, the anxiety (Process A) automatically sets into operation the euphoria (Process B), which overwhelms Process A and becomes the dominant emotional experience following the jump. With successive jumps, Process A is likely to lessen in magnitude, but Process B continues to build up. Therefore, successive jumps are preceded by less and less anxiety but followed by greater and greater levels of positive affect. In this way, the parachutist may get "hooked on" skydiving over time. Similarly, a positive Process A can be opposed by a negative Process B, as in the case of drug addiction. For the novice drug user, the initial ingestion of a drug produces a highly pleasurable response that is followed by a relatively mild negative reaction once the Process A has worn off. Repeated use of the drug may bring with it less and less positive pleasurable response, which may lead the drug user to take greater dosages to achieve the desired high; the negative reactions of Process B continue to build up. Over time, then, the motivation for drug usage may become less a matter of seeking the positive results of Process A and more a matter of avoiding the distressing effects of Process B. Pleasure-seeking behavior is thus transformed, over time, into behavior motivated by the desperate avoidance of pain.

Research strongly suggests that the experience of pleasure or reward is almost always associated with the release of dopamine in certain parts of the midbrain and forebrain. For example, enjoying food depends on dopamine activity. Hungry rats that are given food have increased release of dopamine in the midbrain's nucleus accumbens, and the greater the hunger, the greater the release of dopamine (Rolls, Burton, & Mora, 1980). Food tastes better when you are hungry and water is more rewarding when you are thirsty because there is greater release of dopamine under deprived than nondeprived conditions. Dopamine is also involved in learned rewards, such as receiving social reinforcement, monetary rewards, and the like. Drugs that block the release of dopamine appear to suppress the rewarding qualities of most activities.

The mesolimbic dopamine system is the major brain system involved in positive reinforcement from drug use, including alcohol, nicotine, and cocaine.

Ingestion of these drugs increases dopamine release or prevents normal termination of its neural signal. Most researchers have concluded that the release of dopamine is a necessary condition for the reinforcement and dependency associated with drugs (Koob, 1999). Other biological systems that play a major role in motivation include the hypothalamus and the brain's prefrontal cortex. The hypothalamus regulates physiological responses to stimuli and organizes behaviors that maintain homeostasis with respect to hunger, thirst, and sex. The frontal lobes, especially the prefrontal cortex, are important for integrating information from the senses, memory systems, and reward systems via their connections to the thalamus and limbic centers. The prefrontal cortex is also involved in formulating goals, plans, and strategies. Damage to the prefrontal cortex is associated with difficulty in making plans and executing behaviors that are necessary for achieving goals. Patients with prefrontal damage often show normal levels of intelligence but they seem unable to translate their cognitive activities into motivated behavioral sequences. Although they may be able to formulate nascent plans, they often cannot follow through on them. Scientists believe that people with prefrontal damage have difficulty focusing on motivated tasks because they are unable to ignore other distracting stimuli in their environment (Knight & Grabowecky, 1995).

Mind: Expectancies, Attributions, Conscious Goals

Even during the heyday of Hull's influence, drive theory was pitted against a competing cognitive approach to motivation termed expectancy-value theory. Drawing on the early work of Tolman (1932) and Lewin (1936), this general approach contends that the basis for motivation is anticipation of the outcome of behavior when those consequences have value for the person. The expectancy of being rewarded (or punished) for a particular response provides the individual with an incentive for behavior. Maximum incentive occurs when the individual is given the opportunity to perform behavior for which he or she strongly expects (high expectancy) to receive highly valued rewards (high value) (Rotter, 1954).

The expectancy-value approach suggests that cognition, such as expectancies about reward, is more important than biological drives in the motivation of behavior. Whereas Hull argued that reinforcement always involves the reduction of drive, expectancy-value theory holds that reinforcement shapes behavior by creating expectancies of additional reinforcements that have some value to the person. According to this view, the student who studies hard for an exam is motivated by the cognitive expectation of reinforcement for performance (a high grade) rather than by reduction of drive. In this example, the drive approach might focus instead on the reduction of anxiety (an aversive high-drive state) that studying for the test would bring.

Along with the rise of a great many cognitive approaches to psychology since the late 1950s, expectancy-value theory paved the way for modern approaches to human motivation emphasizing conscious thought and cognition. Notably, Higgins (1997) has introduced the concept of regulatory focus as a cognitive factor that underlines approach and avoidance behavior as well as expectancy-value relations. According to this theory, different orientations toward desired end-states are learned through developmental experiences. In a nurturing environment, people learn to anticipate the presence or absence of positive outcomes and develop a promotion focus concerned with advancement, growth, and accomplishment. In a punitive environment, people become oriented to the presence or absence of negative outcomes (e.g., punishment) and develop a prevention focus that emphasizes protection, safety, and responsibility. Thus, people's motivations toward the same desired end-state may be rooted in either trying to bring about positive outcomes (e.g., doing well on an exam, making lots of friends) or avoiding negative outcomes (e.g., not doing poorly on an exam, avoiding loneliness by making friends).

Many recent theories suggest that human behavior is primarily energized and directed by a wide array of cognitive factors. These factors may be categorized into three distinct yet overlapping groups. The first class of cognitive variables that motivate behavior consists of those pertaining to the self-concept. The self-concept is made up of self-schemas that are cognitive "generalizations about the self derived from repeated categorizations and evaluations of behavior by oneself and by others" (Markus & Sentis, 1982, p. 45). People tend to act in accord with their consciously constructed self-schemas (Markus, 1977) or personified images of self (McAdams, 1985a). Thus, a person who consciously views himself or herself as a kind and nurturing parent is likely to engage in behaviors that are consistent with this image. A hard-nosed drill sergeant will consciously cultivate a very different image of self. In both cases, a self-schema serves to energize and direct certain forms of behavior. People seem to want to act in ways that are consistent with their own views of themselves. Possible selves are a person's representations of what he or she might become, might like to become, or might fear to become. Such representations of what the self might be have great motivational power, according to Markus and Nurius (1986), for they are "the cognitive components of hopes, fears, goals, and threats, and they give the specific self relevant form, meaning, organization, and direction to these dynamics" (p. 954).

Goals and plans are a second group of cognitive factors that motivate behavior. Plans have been studied as hierarchical arrangements of goals that specify sequences of behavior that are appropriate in particular situations. In this way, plans guide behavior by providing a blueprint for action (Miller, Galanter, & Pribaum, 1960; Pervin, 1983). Current concerns (Klinger, 1977), personal projects (Palys & Little, 1983), and personal strivings (Emmons, 1986) are specific types of personal goals that an individual is currently working on and therefore influence the individual's choices of action. An impressive example of a research program pertaining to specific goals and plans is the research on personal strivings (Emmons, 1992). To assess personal strivings, Emmons asks the person to list the "characteristic, recurring goals that the person is trying to accomplish" (Emmons, 1992, p. 292). Descriptions of strivings often reflect more general motivational goals concerning power, achievement, intimacy, and self-maintenance (Emmons & McAdams, 1991). In addition, strivings provide a sensitive reading of the extent to which a person experiences motivational conflict and ambivalence. For example, a young woman's striving to "improve my relationship with my mother" may conflict with her strong striving to "gain independence." Emmons (1986) administered various striving measures to undergraduate students who then reported their daily moods and thoughts for three weeks. Positive emotional experiences during that period were associated with reports of strivings that were highly valued and for which the person had experienced success in the past. Negative emotional experiences were associated with striving ambivalence and with greater levels of conflict between different strivings.

In a similar study, Emmons and King (1988) found that conflict and ambivalence in strivings were associated with higher levels of negative affect, depression, neuroticism, and psychosomatic complaints and with a greater number of illnesses and visits to the campus health center. In examining the connections between strivings and behavior, the researchers also found that when people reported conflicting strivings they often were unable to act upon those strivings but instead spent an inordinate amount of time thinking about the conflict itself. Finally, Sheldon and Emmons (1995) found that people who are able to link their personal strivings together into more abstract and integrated life goals tend to feel more successful in their strivings than persons whose different strivings show less integration. In sum, it would appear that people experience clarity and satisfaction in their lives when their behavior is energized and directed by manageable daily goals that tend not to conflict with each other but rather to complement each other in working toward larger life aims.

Finally, there are cognitive-motivational concepts that serve to organize people's lifetime scripts, expectations, and ambitions. A life task is a problem that an individual is motivated to solve—one to which he or she devotes considerable energy or time and sees as organizing daily activity during a particular life period or life transition (Cantor & Zirkel, 1990). Life tasks may arise from developmental demands—challenges and opportunities that need to be confronted at particular stages in life (Erikson, 1963). For instance, a recent college graduate may see her main task as that of "becoming established in a line of work" or "beginning a family," whereas a college freshman may be most concerned with the task of "adjusting to leaving home" and "finding an academic major."

In Tomkins's (1987) script theory of personality, the person is viewed as a playwright who fashions a self-defining drama by linking affectively charged scenes together into life scripts through a process termed psychological magnification. Two important scripts are found in the life stories of many people. Commitment scripts involve clear ideal scenes and the striving to overcome obstacles, as when one endures hardship to achieve success. Nuclear scripts involve ambivalent and confusing scenes and the repetition of sequences in which good things turn bad, as when success is followed by unhappiness. People are often motivated to repeat the sequences and dynamics of their most salient personal scripts over the course of their lives.

McAdams (1985a) has offered the concept of the imago as a personified and idealized image of the self that functions as a "main character" in a person's "life story." Imagoes are stock characters such as the "caregiver," "the clown," "the warrior," that people adopt or develop as parts of themselves. Specific motivations energize and direct behavior through these imagoes that serve as grounding aspects of an individual's life story or script. Thus, three groups of cognitive factors—self-schemas, goals and plans, and lifetime scripts—play a significant role in energizing and directing human behavior.

Another class of cognitive variables assumed to exert some motivational influence on human behavior is attributions. Attributions are the causal explanations that people formulate for the behavior of others and for their own behavior. Attribution theorists have delineated a number of rules that people implicitly follow in assigning causes to behavior (Kelley, 1973). In general, attribution theory focuses more on the explanations that people give for motivation—what energizes and directs certain behaviors—than on motivation per se. However, explanations may themselves have motivational power. Attributions, once made, appear to influence subsequent behavior of the person who made them. In an extensive research program, Weiner (1992) has shown how individuals' attributions about their own successes and failures have powerful emotional consequences, which eventually influence how they approach and avoid achievement goals in the future. There are three main dimensions on which people make attributions: (1) The cause can be attributable to an internal characteristic of the person, or to external, situational factors; (2) the cause may be stable and unchangeable, or unstable and changeable with circumstances; and (3) the cause may be general and global, or specific to the circumstances.

A well-known research program on learned helplessness has shown that people who perennially explain negative events in their lives in terms of internal, stable, and global attributions (e.g., "Bad things happen to me because I am generally dumb, and I have always been dumb") tend to manifest depressive symptoms, such as sad affect and low activity (Abramson, Seligman, & Teasdale, 1978; Peterson & Seligman, 1984). According to the attribution theory of depression, these cognitive explanations are part of a vicious cycle that precedes depressive affect and motivates self-defeating behaviors, thereby maintaining depression.

Building on research in attribution theory, Dweck (2000; Dweck & Leggett, 1988) has identified two different coping styles in achievement situations. Students who believe their intellectual ability is a fixed, unchangeable quality tend to develop a "helpless" pattern in challenging academic situations. Because they believe that their performance is diagnostic of their innate ability, they experience failure as evidence for their lack of ability and do not perceive any avenues for improvement. By contrast, students who believe their intelligence can be cultivated over time display a "mastery-oriented" coping pattern. They focus on the goal of learning, rather than just looking smart, and interpret failures as challenges to expend more effort or to try a new approach.

In sum, biological approaches to human motivation have tended to emphasize the workings of generalized drive, reward or activation centers in the brain, and pre-rational emotional processes. By contrast, cognitive approaches focus on the expectations, attributions, and conscious goals and plans that people formulate to make sense of their past behavior and to orient them to the future. Moving now from general processes to individual differences, people appear to vary considerably in the extent to which they make sense of their past behavior and orient themselves to the future with respect to three social goals. These goals concern achieving success, attaining power, and experiencing closeness with other human beings.

INDIVIDUAL DIFFERENCES IN THREE SOCIAL MOTIVES

One of the most fruitful approaches to research on human motives and personality has focused on three recurrent social needs that energize and direct behavior: achievement, power, and intimacy. Pioneered by Murray (1938) and McClelland (1961), this approach seeks to assess individual differences in social motives by analyzing imaginative stories and fantasies that people tell for key motivational themes. Social motives are defined as encompassing strong affective associations characterized by anticipatory goal reactions and based on past associations of certain cues with pleasure or pain.

The Murray-McClelland approach borrows liberally from a number of different theoretical trends already mentioned. It shares with fulfillment models the idea that individuals have the basic motivation to engage in intrinsically enjoyable tasks and challenges that provide a sense of personal satisfaction. Recently, Koestner and McClelland (1990) integrated research on achievement motivation with self-determination theory, showing that people seek out optimal challenges that promote their self-development.

The social motive approach also shares Freud's view, articulated within the conflict perspective, that human beings do not consciously know their motives for doing things. So, rather than asking people about their motives directly, this approach employs indirect methods of interpreting fantasies and imaginative narratives that are assumed to reveal less than fully conscious wants and needs, or what McClelland termed implicit motives (McClelland, Koestner, & Weinberger, 1989) to reflect their hypothetical relationship to different levels of consciousness. These may be contrasted with self-attributed motives that represent an individual's conscious, readily articulated concerns that are measured directly with self-report questionnaires (e.g., "Do you like hard work?" "Are social events important to you?").

Moreover, the Murray-McClelland approach shares a certain affinity with contemporary evolutionary understandings of human motivation in suggesting that achievement, power, and intimacy motivation may ultimately be derived from basic natural incentives that have proven adaptive for the species over the course of human evolution (McClelland, 1985). Finally, the Murray-McClelland approach may also be seen as a consistency model, in that mild discrepancies between one's expectations and the environment are believed to be more motivating than stimuli that are too familiar or too novel. In addition, the social motive approach emphasizes the cognitive dimensions of human motives, seen first in Atkinson's (1957) expectancy-value approach to achievement motivations and risk-taking behavior.

Murray (1938) and his colleagues invented a number of different methods for measuring aspects of personality, like human motives, that do not appear to be fully conscious and amenable to self-report. The best known is the Thematic Apperception Test (TAT). In the TAT, the individual is presented with a series of ambiguous pictures of social situations and asked to compose a story about each picture. The assumption is that the individual will "project" his or her own needs, conflicts, and wishes onto the ambiguous picture. The ambiguous picture is merely a cue designed to put into motion the process of constructing an imaginative narrative response (Lindzey, 1959). In Murray's view, these stories reveal partially hidden themes of the personality, especially those concerning basic needs, conflicts, and complexes. In a standardized research setting, the individual is given about five minutes to write one story in response to each of five or six TAT pictures. Therefore, the entire procedure requires about half an hour to complete. Each story is an imaginative narrative that tells what is going on in the picture now, what led up to the current situation, what may happen in the future, and what the characters in the story are feeling, thinking, and wanting. The researcher then scores the stories according to objective coding manuals developed for each of the three social motives. A sample of the general procedure is provided in Activity Box 6.1.

Wanting to Do Better: The Achievement Motive

From an early age, most of us delight in "doing well." We strive to engage our environments in a competent, independent, and efficient manner, to be successful in our explorations and manipulations of the world. The developmental origins of a concern for successful performance may be traced back to the earliest months of life, at which time the infant experiences the basic emotions of interest and surprise (Izard, 1978). In the first months of life, infants find modest variety and discrepancy in their environment to be especially interesting, and they will spend more time focusing their attention on these mild variations from expectancy than on stimuli that are too familiar or too novel. The adaptive function of such interest is "to focus and maintain attention and to motivate exploratory activity" (Izard, 1978, p. 397). Later, as they become able to walk and talk, babies explore their environments in more active ways, seeking out events that will elicit interest and surprise as they function with greater and greater levels of autonomy (Erikson, 1963). With respect to cognitive development, toddlers come to understand and appreciate the existence of primitive standards for "good" performance (Kagan, 1984). On a simple but compelling level, they realize that "things work in a certain way." They seek to find out what these ways are and to master them.

According to some psychologists, early experiences of interest and subsequent exploration signal a biologically rooted and evolutionarily adaptive human tendency toward engaging the world as a curious and innovative achiever (McClelland, 1985). Although all human beings may be endowed with this tendency, marked individual differences in this expression can be observed. Therefore, although virtually all adults want to do well in some sense and in some areas of their lives, some people have a stronger and more pervasive desire for achievement. The achievement motive is a recurrent preference or readiness for experiences of doing better and being successful, and it is assumed to energize and direct behavior in certain situations that provide incentives for achievement-oriented behavior. People composing TAT stories in which characters repeatedly strive for successful performance score relatively high in achievement motivation.

A substantial empirical literature suggests that people who score high on TAT achievement motivation behave in different ways from people who score low. For instance, people high in achievement motivation tend to prefer and show high performance in tasks of moderate challenge that provide immediate feedback concerning success and failure; they tend to be persistent and highly efficient in many kinds of performance, sometimes cutting corners or even cheating in order to maximize productivity; they tend to exhibit high self-control and future time-perspective; and they tend to be restless, innovative, and drawn toward change and movement (McClelland, 1985; Spangler, 1992; Winter & Carlson, 1988).

One of the most interesting lines of research on achievement motivation concerns how people who differ on this motive pursue careers and adapt to work settings. For many students, personal involvement in a career begins in college, where they take courses that are specially designed to prepare them for a certain career path. Research has shown that being high in achievement motivation, assessed on the TAT, does not necessarily guarantee high grades in college courses (Entwisle, 1972). However, when the courses are perceived as directly relevant to their future careers, students high in achievement motivation earn higher grades than students who are low in achievement motivation. Furthermore, students high in achievement motivation appear to have more realistic career aspirations. Mahone (1960) found that students high in achievement motivation had more realistic vocational choices when their intelligence test scores, grade point averages, and major fields were taken into account, than those low in achievement motivation. Therefore students high in achievement motivation appear to better understand their own assets and liabilities with respect to future careers and chose career paths that match their abilities and opportunities. In keeping with other research on achievement motivation, these students adopt a level-headed and pragmatic strategy in making career choices, settling on a path that is likely to offer moderate challenge and risk. Baruch (1967) and Stewart (1975) found that college women who scored high in achievement motivation tended to pursue more challenging careers than did college women scoring low on the motive. Moreover, Bloom (1971) showed that adolescent girls aiming to combine career and family were higher in achievement motivation than girls who did not plan to pursue a career.

When they graduate from college and, in some cases, professional schools, how do people high in achievement motivation fashion and adapt to careers? In a nationwide survey of adults, U.S. men high in achievement motivation reported more job satisfaction, evaluated their jobs as more interesting, and preferred work to leisure to a greater extent than did men low in achievement motivation (Veroff, 1982). The same relations were not found for American women. However, in a later study, Jenkins (1987) reported that college women's level of achievement motivation predicted their work values, job perceptions, and sources of satisfaction at age 32 but only if they were career-oriented.

Activity Box 6.1   Scoring Stories for Power and Intimacy Motives

To see how psychologists assess individual differences in the power motive and the intimacy motive, take ten minutes to do the following exercise. You need two sheets of paper and a pencil. The task is to write a story in response to each of the two pictures.

Look at the first picture briefly and then close the book. Take five minutes to write a short imaginative story. The story should say a little bit about what is going on in the picture now, what led up to this situation, and what may happen in the future. The story should also say something about what the characters are thinking and feeling. You should know that this is not a "test" in the sense that there are "right' and "wrong" stories. Any story you write is fine. The important thing is to relax and be creative. Use the picture as a stimulus to get your imagination going. After five minutes, look at the second picture and repeat the procedure.

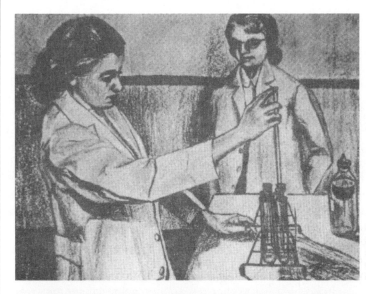

Source: Veroff, J., Atkinson, J. W., Feld, S. C., & Gurin, G. (1960). The use of thematic apperception to assess motivation in a nationwide interview study. *Psychological Monographs, 74*(12), Whole number 499.

Activity Box 6.1 *(continued)*

You are now ready to interpret the stories in terms of power and intimacy motivation. Detailed scoring manuals for both of these motives have been developed. Typically, a scorer would be trained with the detailed manuals, going through over 200 practice stories in order to learn each system. This procedure would require about seven to nine hours of work. Here, we will simply take a brief look at a few of the scoring categories that are used. The exercise is intended only to give you a feel for the general procedure; it is not a valid measure of your power and intimacy motivation.

For each of the two motives, the scorer looks for certain themes or categories in the stories. Take a look now at your first story, in response to the picture of the two women in the laboratory. You may have power themes in this story. Let us consider four possible themes. For each you may check to see whether the theme is present or absent in the story. If it is present, give yourself 1 point for power; if it is absent, you give yourself 0 points for power. With respect to these four themes, the maximum score you could get in a story would be 4 (all four themes are present); the minimum would be 0.

Power theme 1: General power category. A character in the story desires to have impact or make an impression on others. This may be accomplished through strong, forceful actions (like aggression), giving unsolicited help, or trying to control, persuade, or impress. *Examples:* "The woman on the left is trying to sabotage her colleague's experiment"; "She convinced her friend that she was right."

Power theme 2: Increased prestige. The setting of the story or a character is described in ways that increase prestige or position. *Example:* "She was a world-famous scientist."

Power theme 3: Lower prestige. The setting of the story or a character is described in ways that decrease prestige or position. *Example.* "The scoundrel was up to no good."

Power theme 4: Effect. A power action produces a major, striking effect. *Example:* "The world was shocked by her bold words and brazen acts."

Now let us look at your second story, in response to the picture of two people sitting on a bench. You may have intimacy themes in this one. We will look at four of those themes. The scoring procedure is the same: You receive 1 point if the theme is present or 0 points if it is absent.

Intimacy theme 1: Positive affect. A relationship among characters in the story promotes positive feelings, such as joy, excitement, love, liking, or happiness. *Examples.* "She believes that she is in love with this man"; "Two good friends enjoy their day off."

Intimacy theme 2: Dialogue. Characters in the story communicate with each other in a reciprocal and noninstrumental fashion. *Example.* "They talked all afternoon about anything that came to their minds."

Intimacy theme 3: Commitment or concern. A character commits himself or herself to another or expresses humanitarian concern, as in helping another. *Example.* "Don had pity on the old woman and spent the next hour trying to cheer her up."

Intimacy theme 4: Surrender of control. Characters in the story find themselves in a relationship that they cannot control; they give up any attempts to control and let events transpire spontaneously. *Example.* "She could not help herself; the sympathy she felt for him made her stay and talk to him, even though she knew better."

Source: Based on Winter (1973) and McAdams (1980).

A longitudinal study of both men and women showed that high achievement motivation at age 31 was associated with relatively high income ten years later (McClelland & Franz, 1992). With respect to career choice, young American men high in achievement motivation tend to be drawn to careers in business that manifest patterns of personal interests and values similar to those expressed by stockbrokers, real estate salesmen, advertising managers, merchandise buyers, and factory managers (McClelland, 1961). McClelland argued that business is a good match for the achievement motive because business requires that people take moderate risks, assume personal responsibility for their own performance, pay close attention to feedback in terms of costs and profits, and find new or innovative ways to make products, provide serves, and market what they offer to consumers.

Wanting to Have Impact: The Power Motive

Achievement and power can be very different experiences. Achievement involves doing better or performing well against an external or internal standard, whereas power involves influencing others, having impact, and feeling strong. McClelland (1985) speculated that the developmental origins of power motivations may reside in early emotional experiences of anger and excitement. Babies begin to express anger between 4 and 6 months of age (Izard, 1978). Though infants show wide individual differences in the intensity and range of anger responses, they are most likely to show anger when confronted with frustrations, restraints, and barriers. Anger likely serves an adaptive function. According to Izard (1978), "anger increases the infant's opportunities to sense self-as-causal-agent and hence to experience self as separate, distinct, and capable," and it contributes "to self-development through increasing the infant's sense of self-control and self-determination in the face of frustrating and distasteful situations" (p. 399). While anger, therefore, may intensify the infant's efforts to have a "big impact" on the environment, producing such impacts may be intrinsically satisfying, eliciting positive emotions such as excitement in infants, children, and adults (McClelland, 1985; White, 1959). In general, "having an impact" may be viewed as an evolutionarily adaptive, natural incentive in human life, manifested in such widely varied behavior patterns as aggressive play, fighting, dominance, leadership, debate, and so on.

The power motive is a recurrent preference or readiness for experiences of having an impact and feeling strong, and like the achievement motive, it is assumed to energize and direct behavior in situations that provide power incentives. A large number of studies have employed the TAT scoring system for assessing individual differences in power motivation developed by Winter (1973). In these studies, power motivation has been positively associated with (1) holding elected offices, (2) acting forcefully in small groups, (3) accumulating prestigious possessions, (4) taking risks to gain public visibility, (5) getting into arguments, (6) choosing occupations in which one strongly directs the behavior of others (such as executive, teacher, psychologist), (7) creating a life story for oneself emphasizing agentic themes of mastery and control and magnifying emotional experiences centered on anger and excitement, and, among men only, (8) exhibiting impulsive and aggressive behavior (Jenkins, 1994; McAdams, 1985b; Winter, 1973; Woike, 1994a).

A number of studies have shown that people who perennially adopt strong leadership roles and/or rise to positions of high influence tend to score relatively high on power motivation (McAdams, Rothman, & Lichter, 1982; Winter, 1973, 1988). In laboratory studies that have looked closely at how the person with high power motivation actually exerts impact in a leadership role, groups with a leader high in power motivation tended to present fewer proposals for consideration, to discuss fewer alternative plans, and to show less moral concern about their activities than did groups with a leader low in power (Fodor & Smith, 1982). The researchers interpreted these findings to mean that leaders high in power motivation encourage "groupthink"—a form of hasty decision making characterized by diffusion of responsibility, failure to consider long-term ramifications, and the domination by a single strong leader whose opinion generally goes unchallenged. In support of this interpretation, high power-motivated supervisors, as compared to low power-motivated supervisors, are more likely to (1) respond favorably to workers who curry favor and act ingratiating, (2) perceive themselves as exerting considerable over their group, and (3) view subordinates as relatively unimportant and ineffectual. Noting that college men high in power motivation tend to prefer friends who are not particularly popular or well known, Winter (1973) explains that such friends are attractive because they pose little threat to the power-motivated person's prestige.

What about the personal lives of people high in power motivation? On this topic, intriguing sex differences have been found. Men and women do not differ in overall levels of power motivation. However, high power motivation seems to be related to different patterns of love relationships for men and women. In the case of men, high power motivation has been associated with greater dissatisfaction in marriage and dating relationships, less stability in dating, more sexual partners over time, and higher levels of divorce (McAdams, 1984). For women, however, none of these negative outcomes have been observed as a function of power motivation. Rather, one study suggests that power motivation in women is positively associated with marital satisfaction (Veroff, 1982). Further, well-educated women high in power motivation tend to marry successful men (Winter, McClelland, & Stewart, 1981). Winter (1988) speculates that because women tend to be socialized to accept roles of caregiving in which they are responsible for other people, a woman with high power motivation is likely to express the motive in more benevolent ways than a man high in power motivation—ways that may promote rather than undermine intimate relationships.

Moving from love to health, some research suggests that power motivation may be implicated in a complex pattern of factors predicting susceptibility to sickness and disease (Jemmott, 1987). Some evidence suggests that people high in power motivation are predisposed to heightened activation of the sympathetic nervous system when faced with obstacles to, or frustrations in, the experience of feeling strong and having impact (Fodor, 1984, 1985). Because of this heightened activity, over time a strong power motive may increase a person's vulnerability to illness if the person's need for power is inhibited, challenged, or blocked (McClelland, 1979). Supporting this claim, research has shown individuals with (1) relatively high power motivation, (2) low-intimacy motivation, (3) high self-control (sometimes called "activity inhibition," suggesting a tendency to "block" or "inhibit" one's own expression of power), and (4) a high number of power stresses (such as problems with an employer, substantial academic disappointment) reported more physical illnesses over time than did other individuals with fewer of these traits. Thus, the highly controlled and highly power-oriented person may "bottle up" frustrations in such a way as to tax severely his or her internal physiological equilibrium. The result may be a greater number of colds, bouts of flu, and other physical maladies, especially during times of excessive power stress.

Wanting to Be Close: The Intimacy Motive

While our desires for achievement and power may motivate us to assert ourselves in effective and influential ways and to control, even master, our environments, our longings for close and warm relationships with other human beings pull us in a different direction, that is, toward the private life of intimate interpersonal communion (Bakan, 1966), where we are able to experience what Baumeister and Leary (1995) describe as the general "need to belong." The developmental origins of a general motive toward experiencing warm, close, and supportive relationships with intimate others may reside in the joyful face-to-face play of 3- to 5-month-old babies and their caregivers (Stern, 1985) and the subsequent bond of love formed between infant and caregiver in the second half of the first year of life, termed attachment (Bowlby, 1969). The dominant, biologically grounded emotion of secure attachment is joy—an emotion first experienced around the age of 2 months and demonstrated in an infant's initial smiling responses to faces, voices, and other social stimuli and familiar events (Sroufe & Waters, 1976). The emotions of fear and sadness, which tend to appear toward the end of the first year in response to strangers and separation, are also complexly related to attachment. So by the end of the first year of life, the infant knows the experiences of joyful communion with, fear of separation from, and sadness after the temporary loss of such primary caregivers as mothers, father, and babysitter.

Bowlby (1969) has outlined how the caregiver-infant bond is likely to have proven adaptive in the evolution of human beings, serving as a flexible but instinctually based behavioral system that assured mother-infant proximity and protection from predators in the dangerous ancestral environment. Others have suggested that a resultant need for close, warm, and supportive relationships with others may be considered an evolutionarily adaptive feature of human nature (Hogan, 1987). Human beings have evolved as hunters and gatherers traditionally living in small groups, and such a fundamental human need is likely to have promoted cooperation and other key features of group living. Yet, striking individual differences in a general need for intimacy and belonging may be observed, and these are readily assessed via the TAT.

The intimacy motive is a recurrent preference or readiness for experiences of warm, close, and communicative interaction with others. The person high in intimacy motivation desires intimacy in daily life to a greater degree than a person low in intimacy motivation. Empirical research shows that people high in intimacy motivation (1) spend more time, over the course of a normal day, thinking about relationships with others; (2) engage in a greater number of friendly conversations and write more personal letters; (3) report more positive emotion in the presence of other people; (4) laugh, smile, and make more eye contact when conversing with others; and (5) construct life stories for themselves that emphasize themes of love and friendship and magnify emotional experiences involving joy (McAdams, 1982, 1985b, 1989; McAdams & Constantian, 1983; McAdams, Jackson, & Kirshnit, 1984; Woike, 1994a). However, the person high in intimacy motivation is not necessarily more outgoing, sociable, or extraverted. Instead, he or she is likely to prefer close one-on-one exchanges to more boisterous group activities. When confronted with a large social group, he or she is likely to promote group harmony and cohesiveness, viewing group activities as opportunities for everybody to get involved rather than for one or two people to dominate the action (McAdams & Powers, 1981). Perhaps partly for this reason, people high in intimacy motivation are rated by their friends and acquaintances as especially "sincere," "natural," "loving," "not dominant," and "not self-centered" (McAdams, 1980). In a series of studies investigating relations between both intimacy and power motivation on the one hand and patterns of friendships on the other, McAdams (1984) found that students high in intimacy motivation tended to have more one-on-one interactions with a single friend whereas students high on power motivation preferred more large-group interactions. In general, intimacy motivation is associated with a communal friendship style that places prime importance on being together and sharing confidences with others; power motivation is associated with an agentic style of friendship that emphasizes doing things and helping others.

Studies have examined the relations between intimacy motivation and overall psychological well-being. McAdams and Vaillant (1982) found that high-intimacy motivation at age 30 among males significantly predicted overall psychosocial adjustment 17 years later, when men were in their mid-40s. Those men high in intimacy motivation in early adulthood reported greater marital satisfaction, job satisfaction, and even a marginally higher income at midlife compared to men low in intimacy motivation. In another study, medical students high in intimacy motivation (and low in power motivation) showed the highest levels of well-being while in medical school (Zeldow, Daugherty, & McAdams, 1988). From a large nationwide sample, McAdams and Bryant (1987) found that high-intimacy motivation among women was associated with greater overall happiness and life satisfaction with life roles (such as worker, mother, wife) than appeared among women with low-intimacy motivation. Among men, intimacy motivation predicted less strain in life and less uncertainty. Thus, though intimacy motivation appears to bring certain benefits for both men and women, the benefits do not seem to be exactly the same for both sexes. High-intimacy women are relatively happy and satisfied when compared with low-intimacy women. By contrast, high-intimacy men are not necessarily happier and more satisfied, but they do report less strain in life and less uncertainty than low-intimacy men.

Finally, research has shown that women tend to score higher in intimacy motivation than men (McAdams, Lester, Brand, McNamara, & Lensky, 1988), a difference that shows up as early as fourth grade (McAdams & Losoff, 1984). The difference is small but relatively consistent, and it is in keeping with the generally accepted view in American society that women tend to be more concerned with the vicissitudes of interpersonal relationships than are men.

Three Social Motives and Autobiographical Memory

Until recently, research on achievement, power, and intimacy motivation has focused almost exclusively on the behavioral correlates of the motives. Researchers have now begun to shift their attention to possible cognitive correlates of the motives by considering how social motives influence our perception and understanding of the events in our own lives. Autobiographical memory is a discrete memory system that pertains to the encoding, organization, storage, and retrieval of personal life events (Robinson, 1986). It is not possible for people to remember all the events in their lives. Therefore, understanding a person's social motives may provide a way to understand why people remember some events but forget others. Indeed, researchers have found that when individuals are asked to describe significant and/or emotionally involving life experiences, those with strong achievement or power motives are consistently more likely to recall experiences about achievement, dominance, self-mastery, or losing face, whereas individuals with strong intimacy motives are more likely to recall experiences pertaining to love, friendship, or social rejection (McAdams, 1982, 1984, 1985b; McAdams, Hoffman, Mansfield, & Day, 1996; Woike 1994a, 1994b; Woike, Gershkovich, Piorkowski, & Polo, 1999). For instance, McAdams (1982) collected open-ended recollections of autobiographical memories from two samples. The memories were coded for power themes (e.g., personal power, increased fame or recognition) and for intimacy themes (e.g., love and friendship, reciprocal communication or sharing). A positive correlation was found between people's power motivation scores and the power themes found in narratives of "peak" experiences and emotionally satisfying experiences. Likewise, there was a positive relationship between intimacy scores and intimacy themes in the descriptions of peak and satisfying experiences. However, there were no significant relationships between motive scores and less personally meaningful or affectively neutral experiences.

In another study, Woike, Gershkovich, Piorkowski, and Polo (1999) asked people to recall events in which they felt three positive emotions (happiness, pride, and relief) and three negative emotions (anger, sadness, and fear). They recalled experiences with motive-congruent themes for the happy and angry memory. Individuals high in achievement and/or power motivation recalled experiences of success and recognition for the happy memory and experiences of loss of face through betrayal for the angry memory. Individuals high in intimacy motivation, on the other hand, recalled experiences of love and friendship for the happy memory and experiences of betrayal through a violation of trust for the angry memory. Most people, regardless of their motivation, recalled an agentlike event (e.g., scholastic achievement) for the pride memory and recalled a communal experience (e.g., loss of a loved one) for the sad memory. The content of the relief and fear memories was mixed, some not pertaining to agency and communion at all. For instance, many of the fear memories were about personal safety. The findings are in line with McClelland's assertion that implicit motives are related to specific, affective states, not affective states in general (Zurbriggen & Sturman, 2002).

Thus, there is a good deal of research showing that these three social motives influence which experiences are remembered in an individual's life. On another level, these motives also appear to play a role in memory organization. The achievement motive and the power motive reflect a desire for distinction as in being more successful or more influential over others. The experience of intimacy, on the other hand, has to do with being close and connected to others. By extension, Woike (1994b) reasoned that achievement and power motivation may be related to perceiving differences, distinctions, and contrasts whereas intimacy motivation may be related to perceiving experiences in terms of similarities, links, and inter-relationships. These different ways of organizing experience may help individuals to feel different from others or feel connected to others. For instance, those concerned with reaching a standard of excellence may engage in making many distinctions and comparisons between themselves and others, or between their own and others' abilities, or against external standards and demands. An individual may achieve greater impact and control by imposing restrictions on information presented to others and by being alert to the restrictions and conditions imposed on incoming information. On the other hand, perceiving oneself, others, and events as integrated may allow communal people to satisfy their needs for greater connection with others. Perceiving similarities, understanding common interests, and seeing how people and events influence each other provide ways for communal people to meet their needs for belonging and connection with others.

Analyses of people's written recall of significant life experiences in several studies have shown support for this idea (Woike, 1994b; Woike, et al., 1999; Woike & Polo, 2001). Power-motivated individuals tend to perceive their experiences through distinctions and differences; for instance, they make comparisons between themselves and others on abilities, characteristics, and preferences. Intimacy-motivated people, on the other hand, tend to emphasize the similarities and links in their experiences with others; they view themselves as the same as other people on a number of dimensions. Woike, Lavezzary, and Barsky (2001) found that people high in achievement and power were more accurate in their recall and recognition of phrases about differences as opposed to similarities in stories (e.g., Sarah was a better player than Ana). People high in intimacy were more accurate in recalling and recognizing similarity phrases (e.g., Sarah and Ana had sports in common). This suggests that social motives influence not only what types of memories are recalled but also the way they are organized in memory. Individuals concerned with achievement and power focus on differences and those concerned with intimacy focus on similarities.

Comparing Implicit and Self-Reported Motives

A long-standing controversy in the motivational literature has centered on the well-documented fact that TAT scores on achievement, power, and intimacy motivation do not correlate highly with scores on self-report questionnaires designed to measure achievement, as well as dominance and affiliation, which correspond to power and intimacy, respectively. McClelland, Koestner, and Weinberger (1989) argued that the two different measurement strategies actually measure two very different kinds of motivation. The TAT assesses implicit motives that are hypothesized to energize and direct motive-related behavior in situations that provide intrinsic incentives whereas self-report questionnaires assess self-attributed motivation, which is hypothesized to energize and direct achievement-related behavior in situations that provide social or extrinsic incentives. For instance, the person high in TAT achievement seeks opportunities to do well because the spontaneous activity of doing well is affectively satisfying, connecting to primary emotional experiences of interest and surprise. The person scoring high in self-attributed achievement motivation, by contrast, performs well in highly structured social situations in which he or she is expected to perform well, behaving in accord with a conscious, cognitively elaborated self-image of a high-achieving person. Supporting this view, numerous studies suggest that implicit motivation predicts long-term trends in spontaneous activity whereas self-attributed motivation predicts immediate responses in structured situations.

Implicit and self-reported motives are assessed through different cognitive procedures (telling a story versus answering highly structured self-report questions) and are believed to operate at different levels of consciousness. How might these motives differ in their relationship to autobiographical memory? To compare the influence of implicit and self-reported motives on memory, Woike (1995) asked participants to complete implicit and self-reported measures of achievement and intimacy motives and record their most memorable experiences (MMEs) each day for two months. The content of the MMEs was analyzed for affective and routine daily experiences that corresponded to the achievement (or task) and intimacy (or social) domains. People who had a stronger implicit motive for achievement recalled more emotional experiences about achievement, such as feeling satisfied to have done well on a test. On the other hand, people who had a stronger implicit motive for intimacy recalled more emotional experiences about interpersonal relationships such as feeling good after talking with one's best friend. By contrast, the stronger an individual's self-reported motive, the more routine experiences he or she recalled. More self-reported achievement motivation was related to the recall of more experiences about routine achievement tasks, such as writing a term paper; and more self-reported intimacy related to the recall of more experiences about routine social activities, such as meeting friends. The findings suggest that the two different motivational systems are related to the encoding of different experiences. It appears that the motive type (achievement or intimacy) is related to what is remembered—that is, whether one remembers task-related or social experiences—and the level of motivation (implicit or self-report) is related to whether the experience is remembered as an emotional or a routine event.

SUMMARY

The study of human motivation centers on the recurrent wants and needs that energize and direct human behavior and thereby provide people's lives with organization, direction, and purpose. Western scholars have traditionally viewed human motivation from three perspectives, suggesting that (1) human beings are motivated by reason to attain their greatest potential; (2) human beings are motivated by conflicts both internal and environmental that are part of the human condition; or (3) human beings are motivated to reduce discrepancies among their learned expectations, behavior, and feedback from the environment. Among contemporary views of human motivation, those focusing on the biological bases of behavior have emphasized generalized drive, the physiology of reward, and instinctually grounded emotions. Contemporary cognitive approaches to motivation, by contrast, have emphasized the energizing and directing influences of such factors as expectancies, cognitive plans, schemas, scripts, conscious strivings, and attributions.

A research tradition pioneered by Murray and McClelland integrates various strands of historical and contemporary approaches to motivation, including both biological and cognitive concepts. This approach focuses on three important social motives: achievement, power, and intimacy. Individual differences in these motives are assessed through content analysis of imaginative stories written in response to pictures of the Thematic Apperception Test. A large body of research has demonstrated significant relations between these three motives, on the one hand, and features of social behavior, career striving, personal relationships, autobiographical memory, psychological adjustment, and health, on the other.

DISCUSSION QUESTIONS

1. Think about what the typical college student wants. Which of the three motivational perspectives best explains his or her motivations?
2. What is your definition of a fully satisfied person? Is it possible to achieve? If so, how can it be maintained over time?
3. Evolutionary theory provides an explanation for some observed gender differences in mating strategies. What alternative explanations can be developed emphasizing learning theories from the consistency perspective? Can these different explanations be reconciled?
4. Can people be high in both power and intimacy motivation? What problems and possibilities might such a motivational profile provide?

5. Consider applying thematic scoring systems for power and intimacy to materials such as the content of movies, literary works, or even conversations. Would such an analysis be useful in understanding an individual's motivations?

SUGGESTED READINGS

Cantor, N., & Zirkel, S. (1990). Personality, cognition, and purposeful behavior. In L. Pervin (Ed.), *Handbook of personality and theory and research* (pp. 135–164). New York: Guilford. This comprehensive chapter reviews many current cognitive approaches to studying human motivation, including those focusing on life tasks, personal strivings, personal objects, current concerns, and other goal concepts.

Dweck, C. S. (2000). *Self-theories: Their role in motivation, personality, and development.* Philadelphia, PA: Psychology Press. Drawing on self theories, this book presents recent research on adaptive and maladaptive cognitive-motivational patterns including their origins and consequences.

Freud, S. (1900/1953). *The interpretation of dreams.* London: Hogarth. One of the classics of 20th-century psychology, Freud's book provides an overview of much of his early theorizing and focuses on how the psychologist may discern motivational themes in dreams.

McAdams, D. P. (1985). *Power, intimacy, and the life story: Personological inquiries into identity.* New York: Guilford Press. Drawing on research into power and intimacy motivation, this book applies motivational theory to the study of the storied self and human identity.

McClelland, D. C. (1961). *The achieving society.* New York: Free Press. This is McClelland's best-known work, in which he analyzes the economic rise and fall of entire civilizations in terms of collective achievement motivation, as assessed through content analysis of popular literature, folk tales, and children's readers.

Weiner, B. (1992). *Human motivation: Metaphors, theories, and research.* Newbury Park, CA: Sage. This authoritative text provides a thorough overview of the drive and expectancy-value theories of motivation that dominated American psychology in the middle years of the 20th century and describes a great deal of recent research and theorizing on human motivation from the standpoint of attribution theory.

SUGGESTED WEB SITE

http://www.letus.org/foley/index.htm

This web site features research conducted at Northwestern University under the direction of Professor Dan P. McAdams, Director of the Foley Center for the Study of Lives. Funded by the Foley Family Foundation, the Foley Center is dedicated to the empirical study of personality and social development in the adult years, with an emphasis on prosocial features of development such as generativity, wisdom, leadership, and citizenship. A major research emphasis for the center is the thematic analysis of adults' life narratives, focusing on the motivational themes of power and intimacy, and the emotional themes of redemption and contamination.

INFOTRAC COLLEGE EDITION SEARCH TOPICS

Personality	Implicit motives	Body versus mind
Motivation	Goals	

REFERENCES

Abramson, L. Y., Seligman, M. E. P., & Teasdale, J. D. (1978). Learned helplessness in humans: Critique and reformulation. *Journal of Abnormal Psychology, 87*, 49–74.

Aronson, E. (1969). The theory of cognitive dissonance: A current perspective. In L. Berkowitz (Ed.), *Advances in experimental social psychology* (Vol. 4, pp. 1–34). New York: Academic Press.

Atkinson, J. W. (1957). Motivational determinants of risk-taking behavior. *Psychological Review, 64*, 359–372.

Aronson, E. (1999). Dissonance, hypocrisy, and the self-concept. In E. Harmon-Jones & J. Mills (Eds.), *Cognitive dissonance: Progress on a pivotal theory in social psychology* (pp. 103–126). Washington, DC: American Psychological Association.

Bakan, D. (1966). *The duality of human existence: Isolation and communion in Western man.* Boston, MA: Beacon Press.

Bandura, A. (1971). *Social learning theory.* Morristown, NJ: General Learning Press.

Bandura, A. (1977). *Social learning theory* (2nd ed.). Englewood Cliffs, NJ: Prentice-Hall.

Baruch, R. (1967). The achievement motive in women: Implications for career development. *Journal of Personality and Social Psychology, 5*, 260–267.

Baumeister, R. F., & Leary, M. R. (1995). The need to belong: Desire for interpersonal attachments as a fundamental human motivation. *Psychological Bulletin, 117*, 497–529.

Bloom, A. R. (1971). *Achievement motivation and occupational choice: A study of adolescent girls.* Unpublished doctoral dissertation, Bryn Mawr College, Bryn Mawr, PA.

Bowlby, J. (1969). *Attachment.* New York: Basic Books.

Buss, D. M. (1991). Evolutionary personality psychology. In M. R. Rosenzwig & L. W. Porter (Eds.), *Annual review of psychology* (pp. 459–491). Palo Alto, CA: Annual Reviews.

Cantor, N., & Zirkel, S. (1990). Personality, cognitive, and purposive behavior. In L. Pervin (Ed.), *Handbook of personality theory and research* (pp. 135–164). New York: Guilford.

Deci, E. L., & Ryan, R. M. (1991). A motivational approach to self: Integration in personality. In R.

Dienstbier & R. M. Ryan (Eds.), *Nebraska symposium on motivation: 1990* (pp. 237–288). Lincoln: University of Nebraska Press.

Depue, R. A., Luciana, M., Arbisi, P., Collins, P., & Leon, A. (1994). Dopamine and the structure of personality: Relation of agonist-induced dopamine activity to positive emotionality. *Journal of Personality and Social Psychology, 67*, 485–498.

Diener, E., Suh, E., Lucas, R., & Smith, H. (1999). Subjective well-being: Three decades of progress. *Psychological Bulletin, 125*, 276–302.

Dweck, C. S. (2000). *Self-theories: Their role in motivation, personality, and development.* Philadelphia, PA: Psychology Press.

Dweck, C. S., & Leggett, E. L. (1988). A social-cognitive approach to motivation and personality. *Psychological Review, 95*, 256–273.

Emmons, R. A. (1986). Personal strivings: An approach to personality and subjective well-being. *Journal of Personality and Social Psychology, 51*, 1058–1068.

Emmons, R. A. (1992). Abstract versus concrete goals: Personal striving level, physical illness, and psychological well-being. *Journal of Personality and Social Psychology, 62*, 292–300.

Emmons, R. A., & King, L. A. (1988). Conflict among personal strivings: Immediate and long-term implications for psychological and physical well-being. *Journal of Personality and Social Psychology, 54*, 1041–1048.

Emmons, R. A., & McAdams, D. P. (1991). Personal strivings and motive dispositions: Exploring the links. *Personality and Social Psychology Bulletin, 17*, 648–654.

Entwisle, D. R. (1972). To dispel fantasies about fantasy-based measures of achievement motivation. *Psychological Bulletin, 77*, 377–391.

Epstein, S. (1973). The self-concept revisited: Or a theory of a theory. *American Psychologist, 28*, 404–416.

Erikson, E. H. (1963). *Childhood and society* (2nd ed.). New York: Norton.

Festinger, L. (1957). *A theory of cognitive dissonance.* Stanford, CA: Stanford University Press.

Fodor, E. M. (1984). The power motive and reactivity to power stresses. *Journal of Personality and Social Psychology, 47*, 853–859.

Fodor, E. M. (1985). The power motive, group conflict, and physiological arousal. *Journal of*

Personality and Social Psychology, 49, 1408–1415.

Fodor, E. M., & Smith, T. (1982). The power motive as an influence on group decision making. *Journal of Personality and Social Psychology, 42,* 178–185.

Freud, S. (1900/1953). *The interpretation of dreams.* In J. Strachey (Ed.), *The standard edition of the complete psychological works of Sigmund Freud. Vols. 4 and 5.* London: Hogarth. Freud, S. (1930/1961). *Civilization and its discontents.* In J. Strachey (Ed.), *The standard edition of the complete psychological works of Sigmund Freud. Vol. 21.* London: Hogarth.

Gray, J. A. (1990). Brain systems that mediate both emotion and cognition. *Cognition and Emotion, 4,* 269–288.

Higgins, E. T. (1997). Beyond pleasure and pain. *American Psychologist, 52,* 1280–1300.

Hogan, R. (1987). Personality psychology: Back to basics. In J. Aronoff, A. I. Rabin, & R. A. Zucker (Eds.), *The emergence of personality* (pp. 79–104). New York: Springer.

Hull, C. L. (1943). *Principles of behavior: An introduction to behavior theory.* New York: Appleton-Century-Crofts.

Hunt, P. J., & Hillery, J. M. (1973). Social facilitation in a coaction setting: An examination of the effects over learning trials. *Journal of Experimental Social Psychology, 9,* 563–571.

Izard, C. E. (1978). On the ontogenesis of emotion and emotion-cognition relationships in infancy. In M. Lewis & L. A. Rosenblum (Eds.), *The development of affect* (pp. 389–413). New York: Plenum.

James, W. (1892/1963). *Psychology.* Greenwich, CT: Fawcett.

Jemmot, J. B. (1987). Social motives and susceptibility to disease: Stalking individual differences in health risks. *Journal of Personality, 55,* 267–298.

Jenkins, S. R. (1987). Need for achievement and women's careers over fourteen years: Evidence for occupational structure effects. *Journal of Personality and Social Psychology, 53,* 922—932.

Jenkins, S. R. (1994). Need for power and women's careers over fourteen years: Structural power, job satisfaction, and motive change. *Journal of Personality and Social Psychology, 66,* 155–165.

Kagan, J. (1984). *The nature of the child.* New York: Basic Books.

Kasser, T., & Ryan, R. M. (1996). Further examining the American dream: Differential correlates of intrinsic and extrinsic goals. *Personality and Social Psychology Bulletin, 22,* 280–287.

Kelley, H. H. (1973). The process of casual attribution. *American Psychologist, 28,* 107–128.

Kelly, G. (1955). *The psychology of personal constructs.* New York: Norton.

Klinger, E. (1977). *Meaning and void: Inner experience and the incentives in people's lives.* Minneapolis: University of Minnesota Press.

Knight, R. T., & Grabowecky, M. (1995). Escape from linear time: Prefrontal cortex and conscious experience. In M. S. Gazzaniga (Ed.), *The cognitive neurosciences* (pp. 1357–1371). Cambridge, MA: MIT Press.

Koestner, R., & McClelland, D. C. (1990). Perspectives on competence motivation. In L. Pervin (Ed.), *Handbook of personality theory and research* (pp. 527–548). New York: Guilford.

Koob, G. F. (1999). Drug reward and addiction. In M. J. Zigmond, F. E. Bloom, S. C. Landis, J. L. Roberts, & L. R. Squire (Eds.), *Fundamentals of neuroscience* (pp. 1261–1279). San Diego, CA: Academic Press.

Lewin, K. (1936). *Principles of topological psychology.* New York: McGraw-Hill.

Lindzey, G. (1959). Thematic Apperception Test: Interpretative assumptions and related empirical evidence. *Psychological Bulletin, 56,* 158–168.

Maddi, S. R. (1996). *Personality theories: A comparative analysis* (6th ed.). Prospect Heights, IL: Waveland Press.

Mahone, C. H. (1960). Fear of failure and unrealistic vocational aspiration. *Journal of Abnormal and Social Psychology, 60,* 253–261.

Markus, H. (1977). Self-schemata and the processing of information about the self. *Journal of Personality and Social Psychology, 35,* 63–78.

Markus, H., & Nurius, P. (1986). Possible selves. *American Psychologist, 41,* 954–969.

Markus, H., & Sentis, K. (1982). The self in social information processing. In J. Suls (Ed.), *Psychological perspectives on the self* (Vol. 1, pp. 41–70). Hillsdale, NJ: Erlbaum.

Maslow, A. H. (1943). A theory of human motivation. *Psychological Review, 50,* 370–396.

Maslow, A. H. (1968). *Toward a psychology of being.* New York: Van Nostrand Reinhold.

McAdams, D. P. (1980). A thematic coding system for the intimacy motive. *Journal of Research in Personality, 14,* 413–432.

McAdams, D. P. (1982). Experiences of intimacy and power: Relationships between social motives and autobiographical memory. *Journal of Personality and Social Psychology, 42,* 292–302.

McAdams, D. P. (1984). Human motives and personal relationships. In V. J. Derlega (Ed.), *Communication, intimacy, and close relationships* (pp. 41–70). New York: Academic Press.

McAdams, D. P. (1985a). The "imago": A key narrative component of identity. In P. Shaver (Ed.), *Review of personality and social psychology* (Vol. 6, pp. 115–141). Beverly Hills, CA: Sage.

McAdams, D. P. (1985b). *Power, intimacy, and the life story: Personological inquiries into identity.* New York: Guilford.

McAdams, D. P. (1989). *Intimacy: The need to be close.* New York: Doubleday.

McAdams, D. P., & Bryant, F. B. (1987). Intimacy motivation and subjective mental health in a nationwide sample. *Journal of Personality, 55,* 395–413.

McAdams, D. P., & Constantian, C. A. (1983). Intimacy and affiliation motives in daily living: An experience-sampling analysis. *Journal of Personality and Social Psychology, 45,* 851–861.

McAdams, D. P., Hoffman, B. J., Mansfield, E. D., & Day, R. (1996). Themes of agency and communion in significant autobiographical scenes. *Journal of Personality, 64,* 339–377.

McAdams, D. P., Jackson, R. J., & Kirshnit, C. (1984). Looking, laughing, and smiling in dyads as a function of intimacy motivation and reciprocity. *Journal of Personality, 52,* 261–273.

McAdams, D. P., Lester, R., Brand, P., McNamara, W., & Lensky, D. B. (1988). Sex and the TAT: Are women more intimate than men? Do men fear intimacy? *Journal of Personality Assessment, 52,* 397–409.

McAdams, D. P., & Losoff, M. (1984). Friendship motivation in fourth- and sixth-graders: A thematic analysis. *Journal of Social and Personal Relationships, 1,* 11–27.

McAdams, D. P., & Powers, J. (1981). Themes of intimacy in behavior and thought. *Journal of Personality and Social Psychology, 40,* 573–584.

McAdams, D. P., Rothman, S., & Lichter, S. R. (1982). Motivational profiles: A study of former political radicals and politically moderate adults. *Personality and Social Psychology Bulletin, 8,* 593–603.

McAdams, D. P., & Vaillant, G. E. (1982). Intimacy motivation and psychosocial adjustment: A longitudinal study. *Journal of Personality Assessment, 46,* 586–593.

McClelland, D. C. (1961). *The achieving society.* New York: Free Press.

McClelland, D. C. (1979). Inhibited power motivation and high blood pressure in men. *Journal of Abnormal Psychology, 88,* 182–190.

McClelland, D. C. (1985). *Human motivation.* Glenview, IL: Scott Foresman.

McClelland, D. C., & Franz, C. (1992). Motivational and other sources of work accomplishments in mid-life: A longitudinal study. *Journal of Personality, 60,* 679–707.

McClelland, D. C., Koestner, R., & Weinberger, J. (1989). How do self-attributed and implicit motives differ? *Psychological Review, 96,* 690–702.

Miller, G. A., Galanter, E., & Pribram, K. H. (1960). *Plans and the structure of behavior.* New York: Holt, Rinehart & Winston.

Mischel, W. (1973). Toward a cognitive social learning reconceptualization of personality. *Psychological Review, 80,* 252–283.

Mischel, W. (1979). On the interface of cognition and personality: Beyond the person-situation debate. *American Psychologist, 34,* 740–754.

Murray, H. A. (1938). *Explorations in personality.* New York: Oxford University Press.

Olds, J. (1977). *Drives and reinforcements: Behavioral studies of hypothalamic functions.* New York: Raven.

Palys, T. S., & Little, B. R. (1983). Perceived life satisfaction and the organization of personal project systems. *Journal of Personality and Social Psychology, 44,* 1221–1230.

Pervin, L. A. (1983). The stasis and flow of behavior: Toward a theory of goals. In M. M. Page (Ed.), *Nebraska symposium on motivation: 1982* (pp. 1–53). Lincoln: University of Nebraska Press.

Peterson, C., & Seligman, M. E. P. (1984). Causal explanations as a risk factor for depression: Theory and evidence. *Psychological Review, 91,* 347–374.

Pinker, S. (2002). *The blank slate: The modern denial of human nature.* New York: Viking Press.

Robinson, J. A. (1986). Autobiographical memory: A historical prologue. In D. C. Rubin (Ed.), *Autobiographical memory* (pp. 19–24). Cambridge, England: Cambridge University Press.

Rogers, C. R. (1951). *Client-centered therapy.* Boston, MA: Houghton Mifflin.

Rolls, E. T., Burton, M. J., & Mora, F. (1980). Neurophysiological analysis of brain-stimulation reward in the monkey. *Brain Research, 194,* 339–357.

Rotter, J. B. (1954). *Social learning theory and clinical psychology.* Englewood Cliffs, NJ: Prentice Hall.

Ryan, R. M. (1995). Psychological needs and the facilitation of integrative processes. *Journal of Personality, 63,* 397–427.

Seligman, M. E. P. (2002). *Authentic happiness.* New York: Free Press.

Seligman, M. E. P., & Csikzentmihalyi, M. (2000). Positive psychology: An introduction. *American Psychologist, 55,* 5–14.

Sheldon, K. M., & Emmons, R. A. (1995). Comparing differentiation and integration within goal systems. *Personality and Individual Differences, 18,* 39–45.

Skinner, B. F. (1971). *Beyond freedom and dignity.* New York: Knopf.

Solomon, R. L. (1980). The opponent-process theory of acquired motivation: The costs of pleasure and the benefits of pain. *American Psychologist, 35,* 691–712.

Spangler, W. D. (1992). Validity of questionnaire and TAT measures of need for achievement: Two meta-analyses. *Psychological Bulletin, 112,* 140–154.

Spence, K. W. (1958). A theory of emotionality based drive (D) and its relation to performance in simple learning situations. *American Psychologist, 13,* 131–141.

Spence, K. W., Farber, I. E., & McFann, H. H. (1956). The relation of anxiety (drive) level of performance in competitional and noncompetitional paired-associates learning. *Journal of Experimental Psychology, 52,* 296–305.

Spielberger, C. D., & Smith, L. H. (1966). Anxiety (drive), stress, and serial-position effects in serial-verbal learning. *Journal of Experimental Psychology, 72,* 589–595.

Sroufe, L. A., & Waters, E. (1976). The ontogenesis of smiling and laughter. *Psychological Review, 83,* 173–187.

Stern, D. N. (1985). *The interpersonal world of the infant.* New York: Basic Books.

Stewart, A. J. (1975). *Longitudinal prediction from personality to life outcomes among college-educated women.* Unpublished doctoral dissertation, Harvard University, Cambridge, MA.

Swann, W. B., Jr. (1983). Self-verification: Bringing social reality into harmony with the self. In J. Suls & A. G. Greenwald (Eds.), *Psychological perspectives on the self* (Vol. 2, pp. 33–66). Hillsdale, NJ: Erlbaum.

Taylor, J. A. (1953). A personality scale of manifest anxiety. *Journal of Abnormal and Social Psychology, 8,* 285–290.

Tellegen, A. (1985). Structure of mood and personality and their relevance to assessing anxiety with an emphasis on self-report. In A. H. Turna & J. D. Masser (Eds.), *Anxiety and the anxiety disorders* (pp. 681–716). Hillsdale, NJ: Erlbaum.

Tolman, E. C. (1932). *Purposive behavior in animals and men.* New York: Appleton-Century.

Tomkins, S. S. (1987). Script theory. In J. Arnoff, A. I. Rabin, & R. A. Zucker (Eds.), *The emergence of personality* (pp. 147–216). New York: Springer.

Tooby, J., & Cosmides, L. (1990). On the universality of human nature and the uniqueness of the individual: The role of genetics and adaptation. *Journal of Personality, 58,* 17–67.

Veroff, J. (1982). Assertive motivations: Achievement versus power. In A. J. Stewart (Ed.), *Motivation and society* (pp. 99–132). San Francisco, CA: Jossey-Bass.

Weiner, B. (1992). *Human motivation: Metaphors, theory, and research.* Newbury Park, CA: Sage.

White, R. W. (1959) Motivation reconsidered: The concept of competence. *Psychological Review, 66,* 297–333.

Wilson, E. O. (1978). *On human nature.* Cambridge, MA: Harvard University Press.

Winter, D. G. (1973). *The power motive.* New York: Free Press.

Winter, D. G. (1988). The power motive in women and men. *Journal of Personality and Social Psychology, 54,* 510–519.

Winter, D. G., & Carlson, L. (1988). Using motive scores in the psychobiographical study of the individual: The case of Richard Nixon. *Journal of Personality, 56,* 75–103.

Winter, D. G., McClelland, D. C., & Stewart, A. J. (1981). *A new case for the liberal arts: Assessing institutional goals and student development.* San Francisco, CA: Jossey-Bass.

Woike, B. A. (1994a). Vivid recollection as a technique to arouse implicit motive-related affect. *Motivation and Emotion, 18,* 335–349.

Woike, B. A. (1994a). The use of differentiation and

integration processes: Empirical studies of "separate" and "connected" ways of thinking. *Journal of Personality and Social Psychology, 67,* 142–150.

Woike, B. A. (1995). Most memorable experiences: Evidence for a link between implicit and explicit motives and social cognitive processes in everyday life. *Journal of Personality and Social Psychology, 68,* 1081–1091.

Woike, B. A., Gershkovich, I., Piorkowski, R., & Polo, M. (1999). The role of personality motives in the content and structure of autobiographical memories. *Journal of Personality and Social Psychology, 76,* 600–612.

Woike, B. A., Lavezzary, E., & Barsky, J. (2001). The influence of implicit motives on memory processes. *Journal of Personality and Social Psychology, 81,* 935–945.

Woike, B. A., & Polo, M. (2001). Motive-related memories: Content, structure, and affect. *Journal of Personality, 69,* 391–415.

Wright, R. (1994). *The moral animal.* New York: Pantheon.

Zajonc, R. B. (1965) Social facilitation. *Science, 149,* 269–274.

Zajonc, R. B. (1980). Comprescence. In P. B. Paulus (Ed.), *The psychology of group process* (pp. 35–60). Hillsdale, NJ: Erlbaum.

Zeldow, P. B., Daugherty, S. R., & McAdams, D. P. (1988). Intimacy, power, and psychological well-being in medical students. *Journal of Nervous and Mental Disease, 176,* 182–187.

Zurbriggen, E. L., & Sturman, T. S. (2002). Linking motives and emotions: A test of McClelland's hypothesis. *Personality and Social Psychology Bulletin, 28,* 521–535.

Topics in Personality Research

7 | Personality Structure

ROBERT R. MCCRAE

A structure is an organization of elements, and the phrase *personality structure* has been given two very different meanings in the history of psychology. The older and perhaps more obvious one is the organization of components in an individual's psyche. Freud's model of id, ego, and superego is surely the most famous of these, although many more have been offered. Personality structure in this sense—*intrapsychic personality structure*—is concerned with identifying aspects of the mind and how they interact and give rise to behavior and experience.

In personality research, however, *personality structure* usually refers to the organization of traits in a population. This is a more abstract and impersonal concept, especially because it is usually expressed in the language of factor analysis. The mathematics of factor analysis is fairly complicated, but the basic ideas are not difficult, and the results are generally consistent with common sense. If I tell you that someone is generous, do you think she is more likely to be courteous or rude? If you guessed "courteous," it is because you already understand a great deal about personality trait structure.

CONCEPTUALIZING INTRAPSYCHIC PERSONALITY STRUCTURE

It is relatively easy to understand the structure of the human body because it can be dissected, showing exactly what organs are found where. Understanding physiology—the dynamic operation of the organs—is more difficult, but it is greatly simplified by knowledge of anatomy. Studying the structure and functioning of personality is far more challenging because personality is an abstract, intangible construct. Instead of seeing what the structure is directly, we are obliged to invent models of what it might be like. We must infer the structure from evidence of its operation—as if we observed people breathing in and breathing out and had to infer the existence of lungs.

Personality theorists like Freud, Jung, and Rogers made their mark because they were willing to make such inferences, and did so persuasively. From what we know today, none of the classic theories is adequate. For example, as we will see, interactions of children with their parents are far less important for personality trait development than classic theories suggest (McCrae & Costa, 1994). Adequate accounts of intrapsychic personality structure need to be based on a better understanding of the origin, development, and expression of personality, one based on contemporary personality research.

Although the goal of personality theory is chiefly to explain how each individual functions, the best way to understand the individual is sometimes through studies of groups. Suppose, for example, that we are interested in the relation between parent-child relations and adult personality traits. If we have only a single individual to study, we cannot make any causal inferences. We may learn that Mr. Smith's father was a strict disciplinarian, and that Mr. Smith is now prone to anxiety, but we cannot know whether the discipline *caused* the anxiety. Even if Mr. Smith himself believes this is the case and can offer a likely scenario ("My father used to punish me for the smallest offense, and I got more and more afraid of him, and eventually began to fear everything and everyone"), it isn't necessarily true. Perhaps Mr. Smith was simply born high in anxiety, and blaming his father is only a rationalization. People have only one childhood, so we cannot assign them to different conditions and see how they turn out. Because it is unethical and infeasible to manipulate parental child-rearing practices, the only way we can make causal inferences in a case like this is through a "natural experiment," in which we examine differences between groups of adults who did and did not have strict discipline in childhood. If the rate of anxiety were substantially higher among those who did, then we would have a basis for claiming that harsh discipline may be a contributing cause to later anxiety. Indirectly, we would also have learned something about intrapsychic personality structure, because if this causal interpretation were correct (which, incidentally, it probably isn't), we would know there must be some part of personality that retains the imprint of earlier events and can translate them into personality traits many years later. Studying individual differences can tell us a great deal about the structure and operation of personality in the individual.

PERSONALITY TRAITS AND THEIR STRUCTURE

Individuals differ in many respects: in past experiences, in intellectual gifts, in political opinions, in job performance. Personality psychologists are chiefly interested in individual differences in personality traits, which can be defined as "*dimensions of individual differences in tendencies to show consistent patterns of thoughts, feelings, and actions*" (McCrae & Costa, 2003, p. 25). Informally, traits are familiar as adjectives, such as *nervous, enthusiastic, original, altruistic*, and *careful*. The formal definition spells out some of the characteristics of traits:

- They are dimensions of individual differences; people can score low, high, or average on them; most people fall in the middle, forming a bell-shaped curve.
- They are tendencies, not determinants. Behavior is usually shaped mostly by the requirements of the circumstances: Even the most talkative extravert does not chatter loudly during moments of silent prayer. However, across a range of circumstances, extraverts are more likely than introverts to talk.
- They are recognized by consistent patterns, which means that they do not change from day to day. In fact, trait levels are usually stable over periods of many years.
- They are expressed pervasively, in thoughts, feelings, and actions. In this respect, traits are to be distinguished from habits like chewing gum, which are relatively thoughtless behavior patterns.

There are literally thousands of adjectives in the English language that describe traits, and trait lexicons are found in every human language. In addition to these lay conceptions of traits, there are hundreds of scientific trait constructs (like ego strength and locus of control) that have been proposed by personality theorists and researchers. It has long been obvious to personality psychologists that some kind of organization of this mass of constructs is necessary. Otherwise, researchers would accumulate bits of knowledge on scattered traits but never be able to combine them into meaningful generalizations or conduct systematic research. If, for example, you wanted to know what happens to personality traits as people age (McCrae & Costa, 2003), you would be faced with the task of selecting some subset of traits to study, with no guarantee that you had included the most important traits or those most affected by aging.

There are many synonyms among trait descriptive adjectives. *Careful, cautious*, and *thoughtful* all express a similar conception of people who consider the consequences before acting and avoid unnecessary risk. It would be possible to do a rational classification of the thousands of adjectives on this basis, but there are distinct limitations to that process. Should *conservative* be added to the cluster of Caution adjectives, or does it belong with *traditional* and *dogmatic*? Different judges would probably come up with very different classification systems, and it is by no means clear how we would choose among them. We could convene a panel of experts and adopt their recommendations, as psychiatrists have done in compiling the official list of mental disorders, the *DSM-IV* (American Psychiatric Association, 1994). Almost any system would be better than nothing. But personality psychologists would prefer an empirically based classification.

The Search for Structure

The first step in the process of discovering the structure of personality is the hardest, one that preoccupied psychologists for decades. What variables should be assessed? Measuring all known traits is not feasible even today, and in the days before computers, only a very small number of variables could be handled. How could anyone be sure that he or she had chosen the right ones? What turned out to be the most useful approach was based on the *lexical hypothesis*, which states that all important traits must have been encoded in the natural language. In daily life you need to be able to warn your friends that someone you just met is untrustworthy and deceitful, and you want to be able to sort your neighbors into those who are lazy and those who are ambitious. That is why we have words like *deceitful* and *ambitious*. Over the centuries, any socially important trait ought (according to the lexical hypothesis) to have been named. Consequently, you can find an exhaustive listing of personality traits by consulting an unabridged dictionary. Allport and Odbert (1936) did just that, identifying a pool of trait adjectives and setting a precedent for research that has now gone on around the world (De Raad & Perugini, 2002).

If the lexical hypothesis is correct (and it is, roughly), then it solves the problem of completeness: If we measure every trait listed in the dictionary, we will not overlook anything of importance. But we have already noted that there are simply too many trait terms in the dictionary, and many of them, like *davered, halituous*, and *raptril* (Norman, 1967) are unfamiliar to most English speakers. Most researchers have therefore proceeded by narrowing the list to familiar terms and combining synonyms (Cattell, 1946), or by sampling terms at random (Tellegen, Grove, & Waller, 1991). The result is likely to be a set of 20 to 100 variables.

The next step in an empirical classification system is to find some way to quantify the relatedness of pairs of traits. Are two words exact synonyms, or near synonyms, or antonyms? In place of rational judgments, psychologists rely on correlations. That is, they measure the two variables (see Chapters 1 and 2) in a sample of people and assess the degree to which high scores on one variable go with high scores on the other, and low scores with low scores—the extent to which they covary. The result is expressed as a correlation coefficient, ranging from –1.0 (perfect inverse association) to +1.0 (perfect covariation). Note that this measure tells us how much traits tend to go together in the people in a given sample. The relation is empirical, not semantic. For example, *gloomy* and *cheerful* are semantic antonyms, but they are not inversely related traits. It is possible to be both a gloomy and a cheerful person (though usually not at the same time). Note also that the correlations are based on the sample one happens to study, and there is no guarantee that the same correlations would be found in different samples. Do traits covary the same way in children and adults? Men and women? Americans and Moroccans? These are important questions that have been extensively addressed by researchers.

Once one has a correlation matrix indicating the association of each trait with every other trait, one can begin to look for patterns. For example, the traits *careful* and *cautious* may have a strong positive correlation, whereas *reckless* has large negative correlations with both of them. This could justify identifying them as a cluster of related traits. But as Briggs noted in Chapter 2, examining correlations between pairs of variables becomes increasingly difficult as the number of traits increases. In the 1930s, J. P. Guilford began the tradition of studying the structure of personality variables using factor analysis (Guilford & Guilford, 1934). Factor analysis is a statistical technique that condenses a set of variables into a smaller set of factors. For example, one might find a Caution factor defined by *careful, cautious*, and (low*) reckless*.

Factors are also called dimensions, because they are conceptually and mathematically similar to the dimensions of space. Just as any point on Earth can be specified by its latitude, longitude, and altitude, so any trait can be located in factor space. For example, assertiveness is high on an Extraversion dimension, but rather low on an Agreeableness dimension. Variables that define the same factor tend to show high correlations among themselves, and relatively low correlations with other variables. Factor structure is thus a convenient, quantitative way of representing personality trait structure.

There are many possible ways to describe data using factor analysis. The factors, for example, may be independent, at 90-degree angles to each other, or they can be oblique (at other angles); they can be rotated in various ways, just as a physical object can be turned and observed from different angles. Most important, the number of factors can vary from one to as many as there are variables. Normally one wants a much smaller set of factors than there are variables in order to have a parsimonious model, but the exact number can still vary considerably. Eysenck (Eysenck & Eysenck, 1975) thought there were two or three basic factors; Cattell (Cattell, Eber, & Tatsuoka, 1970) thought there were 16. Naturally, these two models described very different structures, about which personality psychologists argued for decades.

In 1961, two Air Force psychologists collected several different data sets and showed that five very similar factors could be found in each (Tupes & Christal, 1961/1992). Because the traits they factored were distilled from lexical studies, they had reason to believe that their model was comprehensive. Conceptually, the factors made sense as very broad descriptions of individual differences in personality. But for various reasons, including perhaps the fact that Tupes and Christal were outside the academic mainstream, their Five-Factor Model (FFM) had little impact until it was rediscovered around 1980 (Digman & Takemoto-Chock, 1981; Goldberg, 1981). Since that time, however, it has become increasingly accepted as our best guess about how personality traits are structured.

Traits of the Five-Factor Model

Before reading further, please complete the task described in Activity Box 7.1.

Activity Box 7.1   **An Intuitive Factor Analysis**

People often use trait adjectives to describe themselves and their acquaintances, and some traits seem to go together. For example, people who are strong are usually also healthy, and people who are rich are often famous. Below you will find 30 adjectives listed in alphabetical order. Please read through all the words at least twice, and then sort them into five groups of related traits, each with six words. Write down the five groups of traits. Try to form groups such that people who have one of the traits in the group are also likely to have the other traits.

When you have finished sorting the terms, try to define what it is they have in common. Is there a single name for the full set of traits? For each group, what is the difference between people who have a lot of these characteristics and people who have very little?

Active	Generous	Self-pitying
Anxious	Imaginative	Sympathetic
Appreciative	Insightful	Talkative
Artistic	Kind	Tense
Assertive	Organized	Thorough
Curious	Original	Touchy
Efficient	Outgoing	Trusting
Energetic	Planful	Unstable
Enthusiastic	Reliable	Wide interests
Forgiving	Responsible	Worrying

The sorting task in Activity Box 7.1 asked if you could reconstruct the FFM intuitively, on the basis of your knowledge of the meaning of words and your experience with people in the world. The correct answers are the following: 1. *anxious, self-pitying, tense, touchy, unstable,* and *worrying;* 2. *active, assertive, energetic, enthusiastic, outgoing,* and *talkative;* 3. *artistic, curious, imaginative, insightful, original,* and *wide interests;* 4. *appreciative, forgiving, generous, kind, sympathetic,* and *trusting;* and 5. *efficient, organized, planful, reliable, responsible,* and *thorough.* You probably did well on this task. We gave it to 76 Introductory Psychology students at the University of California, Riverside, who said they were not familiar with the FFM, and on each factor, over 70% of them classified at least five of the six items correctly (Sneed, McCrae, & Funder, 1998). These answers are "correct" in the sense that numerous studies have shown that these traits do in fact cluster this way when trait assessments are factored.

The fact that students' guesses about personality structure closely resemble the empirically derived structure is remarkable. On the one hand, it means that knowledge about personality structure is already coded in our heads—a fact that was discovered when researchers factored ratings of strangers and found a good approximation to the FFM (Passini & Norman, 1966). In part, this reflects the nature of language: Any competent English speaker knows that *generous* and *kind* are related words. In part, it reflects our common experience dealing with people. *Responsible* and *organized* are not semantic synonyms, but most of us know that people who are responsible are usually well organized. The convergence of empirical evidence of structure with lexical and intuitive ideas about structure means that the FFM is easy to understand. More profoundly, it means that human beings are, in a sense, rational; they accurately perceive and understand themselves and their fellows. This is one of the ways in which contemporary personality theory differs most radically from psychoanalysis, where the irrational unconscious is considered the ultimate determinant of behavior.

On the other hand, the ease with which laypersons can sort adjectives into the five factors seems to be an embarrassment to personality psychologists who had to labor for decades in order to grasp personality structure. The difference, of course, is that your task was much simpler than theirs. You were given 30 terms, each a good marker of one and only one factor, and you knew that you had to sort them into five groups of six. Personality psychologists started with many more terms, some of which were rather poor markers of any factor, or good markers of more than one, and they did not know how many clusters they should be looking for. There is another difference as well: All your terms defined the same pole of the factor. Where would you have put the trait *relaxed*? It belongs in the first cluster, but at the low end—it is the opposite of *anxious.* Many scientific problems seem easy to solve in hindsight, but they required hard work and ingenuity at the outset.

Interpreting the Factors

The second task in Action Box 7.1 was to interpret the factors by giving them a label or a definition and by conceptualizing both high and low poles of each factor. In psychological research, factor interpretation is a two-stage process. First, researchers examine the variables that define a factor and try to identify the underlying construct that accounts for it. Second, they validate this interpretation by showing that the factor actually works as it should if it measures this construct. Suppose, for example, that in an analysis of self-report data you found a factor defined by *great, impressive,* and *superior*. On its face, this factor seems to measure eminence, and you might expect Nobel laureates to score high on it. But instead, you might find that high scorers are not really superior; they are merely conceited. Empirical findings would fail to validate your first interpretation, and you might decide this is better interpreted as a narcissism factor. (That interpretation might be checked by correlating factor scores with an established Narcissism scale.)

In the case of the FFM, rational interpretations turn out to be pretty good guides to the meaning of the factors. Hundreds of studies have yielded results that are consistent with the interpretation of these five factors as Neuroticism (N), Extraversion (E), Openness to Experience (O), Agreeableness (A), and Conscientiousness (C). Each of the factors is very broad and very basic, and no single term is really adequate to characterize it. Some researchers call Neuroticism by its opposite pole, Emotional Stability. Extraversion is also known as Surgency, Openness as Intellect, and Agreeableness as Friendly Compliance. Conscientiousness is closely related to a factor called Constraint. Table 7.1 offers some descriptions of the characteristics measured by the five factors.

Many different instruments have been developed to assess the FFM (De Raad & Perugini, 2002), but the most widely used and researched is the Revised NEO Personality Inventory or NEO-PI-R (Costa & McCrae, 1992a). The NEO-PI-R is a questionnaire with 240 items that are grouped into 30 eight-item facet scales to measure specific aspects of each of the five factors. Table 7.2 reports an example of a factor analysis of the 30 facets. On the left the 30 facet scales are

Table 7.1 | Brief Descriptions of the Five Factors

Factor	The Factor Assesses . . .
Neuroticism	Adjustment vs. emotional instability. Identifies individuals prone to psychological distress, unrealistic ideas, excessive cravings or urges, and maladaptive coping responses.
Extraversion	Quantity and intensity of interpersonal interaction; activity level; need for stimulation; and capacity for joy.
Openness	Proactive seeking and appreciation of experience for its own sake; toleration for and exploration of the unfamiliar.
Agreeableness	The quality of one's interpersonal orientation along a continuum from compassion to antagonism in thoughts, feelings, and attitudes.
Conscientiousness	The individual's degree of organization, persistence, and motivation in goal-directed behavior. Contrasts dependable, fastidious people with those who are lackadaisical and sloppy.

Source: Adapted from Costa and McCrae (1985). Reproduced by special permission of the Publisher, Psychological Assessment Resources, Inc., 16204 North Florida Avenue, Lutz, Florida 33549, from the NEO Personality Inventory–Revised, by Paul Costa, and Robert McCrae, Copyright 1978, 1985, 1989, 1992 by PAR, Inc. Further reproduction is prohibited without permission of PAR, Inc.

Table 7.2 | Factor Structure of the Revised NEO Personality Inventory

NEO-PI-R Facet	Factor				
	N	E	O	A	C
N1: Anxiety	**.80**	−.18	−.07	.04	−.20
N2: Angry Hostility	**.65**	−.15	−.07	**−.47**	−.17
N3: Depression	**.80**	−.22	−.08	−.01	−.19
N4: Self-Consciousness	**.77**	−.15	−.15	.06	−.14
N5: Impulsiveness	**.55**	.33	.17	−.28	−.37
N6: Vulnerability	**.61**	−.27	−.13	.06	**−.52**
E1: Warmth	−.24	**.67**	.26	.33	.17
E2: Gregariousness	−.36	**.66**	−.01	−.08	−.13
E3: Assertiveness	−.37	.38	.19	−.38	.31
E4: Activity	−.18	**.48**	.05	−.19	**.45**
E5: Excitement-Seeking	−.09	**.70**	.07	−.18	−.10
E6: Positive Emotions	−.14	**.74**	.24	−.08	.19
O1: Fantasy	.25	.25	**.65**	−.19	−.18
O2: Aesthetics	.10	.18	**.68**	.19	.14
O3: Feelings	.38	**.44**	**.61**	.13	.11
O4: Actions	−.35	.13	**.49**	−.06	−.12
O5: Ideas	−.08	.07	**.73**	.01	.26
O6: Values	−.11	.09	**.60**	.14	−.20
A1: Trust	−.25	.36	.03	**.60**	−.11
A2: Straightforwardness	.01	−.10	−.11	**.68**	.19
A3: Altruism	.03	.30	.23	**.58**	.37
A4: Compliance	−.25	−.05	.05	**.76**	.13
A5: Modesty	.14	−.19	−.20	**.58**	.06
A6: Tender-Mindedness	.07	.17	.14	**.65**	.17
C1: Competence	−.37	.20	.18	.05	**.69**
C2: Order	−.05	−.01	−.05	.19	**.79**
C3: Dutifulness	−.11	.03	−.17	.34	**.75**
C4: Achievement Striving	−.22	.37	.11	−.04	**.73**
C5: Self-Discipline	−.34	−.07	.05	.19	**.77**
C6: Deliberation	−.33	−.17	−.11	.18	**.68**

Note: N = 373. N = Neuroticism, E = Extraversion, O = Openness to Experience, A = Agreeableness, C = Conscientiousness. Factor loadings greater than .40 in absolute magnitude are given in boldface. This is a Procrustes rotation of data from Szirmak and Nagy (2002), in which factors have been maximally aligned to the American target.

listed. N1 through N6 are facets chiefly related to Neuroticism; E1 to E6 are Extraversion facets. The names of the O facets are a bit cryptic; they refer to the aspect of experience to which people may be open or closed, and are usually read as "Openness to Fantasy," "Openness to Aesthetics," and so on.

The five columns of numbers in Table 7.2 are the loadings of the facets on each of the five factors. Factor loadings can be interpreted as correlation coefficients. The loadings for A1: Trust, for example, say that it is strongly related to A (.60), but it is also positively related to E (.36) and negatively related to N (–.25). Trusting people are highly agreeable, and they tend to be sociable and not neurotic.

With the exception of E3: Assertiveness, all the facet scales in this analysis have their largest loading on the factor they are supposed to define. Assertiveness has nearly equal loadings on three different factors, but they are all reasonable: Assertive people are well-adjusted extraverts who can also be a bit domineering and disagreeable. The pattern of factor loadings seen here is very similar to that in the "official," normative sample of 1,000 adult men and women (Costa & McCrae, 1992a). Factor similarity can be quantified by a congruence coefficient, where identical factor loadings yield a coefficient of 1.0. For the five factors in this table, congruence coefficients range from .95 to .98. Thus, we can conclude that the factor structure of the NEO-PI-R has been replicated in this new sample and that the structure of personality traits is very similar in the two samples.

One way to understand the factors is by considering the component traits: Individuals high in Neuroticism are often anxious, they get angry easily, they are prone to feelings of sadness and dejection, they are uncomfortable around others, they have difficulty controlling their impulses, and they are particularly vulnerable to stress. But the facet scale labels identify only the high pole of each trait, and the constructs cannot be understood without also considering the low pole. For example, people who score low on E1: Warmth are not hostile toward others; they are merely indifferent. Similarly, low scorers on E6: Positive Emotions are not depressed; they simply lack enthusiasm. One way trait research refines common sense is by showing that semantic opposites are not necessarily psychological opposites.

Implications for Intrapsychic Structure

What does the discovery of a replicable factor structure in different groups tell us about the individual? First, it means that we can make educated guesses about the level of some traits in a person if we know the level of other traits. If Mr. Jones is high in Achievement Striving, then he is probably going to be high in Order and Dutifulness, because these three traits define the same factor. However, from our knowledge of his Achievement Striving level, we have no idea how modest Mr. Jones is. Achievement Striving and Modesty define different factors and are statistically independent.

Factor analyses like those in Table 7.2 also tell us something about the intrapsychic structure of personality. When variables covary across a sample of people, it is because they share some common cause, which might be physiological or psychological. For example, we might hypothesize that there is a neurotransmitter X that tends to make people sociable and also tends to make them active and cheerful. Then people with chronically high levels of X would be extraverts. At present we have no evidence of such a neurotransmitter X, but some mechanism like it must exist to account for the Extraversion factor. Evidence for the FFM tells us that there are at least five such mechanisms in intrapsychic structure that express themselves in a variety of observable personality traits.

EMPIRICAL FINDINGS ABOUT THE FIVE FACTORS

If all we knew about personality traits was that they formed five clusters, we would not be able to make much sense of intrapsychic structure. But fortunately, we now know much more. The availability of a comprehensive taxonomy of personality traits has stimulated a great deal of research over the past 20 years and has led to a number of key findings. A brief review of these is the next step in explaining personality structure.

Universality

Replication is the hallmark of science. A scientist may claim to be able to produce cold fusion, but unless others can replicate the work, it is not accepted as a scientific fact. In the natural sciences, replication may sometimes require duplication of findings to many decimal places; in psychology, where assessment is less refined and the basic constructs are more abstract, it is usually considered sufficient if the same general pattern of results is found.

Replication studies answer two questions. First, they seek to determine whether the original results were a fluke or whether they are a meaningful description of reality. In Table 7.2, N2: Angry Hostility has a substantial negative loading on A, suggesting that angry people are disagreeable. That makes sense, but is it just a coincidence in these data? In the normative sample the loading of Angry Hostility on A is -.48, almost identical to the value found in Table 7.2. It is extremely unlikely that such similar values would be found by chance.

Replication studies are also useful in assessing the generalizability of findings. We might find that the structure of personality varied across different age groups or different sexes or cultures. This question has now been addressed in dozens of studies, and the results are clear: At least from age 12 on, the structure of personality is the same in all age groups, and the structure in men is virtually identical to that in women (McCrae & Costa, 2003).

What about cross-culturally? Many social scientists assume that culture has profound effects on personality and would be surprised to find the same structure—or even the same traits—in different cultures. In commenting on translations of the NEO-PI-R into other languages, Juni (1996) expressed this view forcefully:

Different cultures and different languages should give rise to other models that have little chance of being five in number nor of having any of the factors that resemble those derived from the linguistic/social network of middle-class Americans. (p. 864)

But in fact, within a year from the publication of those comments, McCrae and Costa (1997) showed that nearly identical NEO-PI-R structures could be found in Portuguese, German, Israeli, Chinese, Korean, and Japanese samples. Although the FFM was originally identified through studies of English language trait terms, the basic constructs appear to apply equally well to those who speak other languages. This fact is even more impressive when the range of languages is considered. English is closely related to German, so perhaps it is not surprising that similar factor structures are found in both these languages. Both of them also share Indo-European roots with Portuguese. But Hebrew is a Hamito-Semitic language, Chinese is Sino-Tibetan, Korean is Altaic, and Japanese is unrelated to any known language, yet they, too, show the expected FFM structure (see also Chapter 15 by Church & Ortiz).

The data in Table 7.2 are from yet another language family: Uralic. These languages originated in the northern Ural Mountains, which separate Europe from Asia, and they spread as far west as Finland and Hungary. The data in Table 7.2 are from a sample of 373 men and women aged 17 to 58 who completed a Hungarian translation of the NEO-PI-R. Nor is this an isolated example. By now the NEO-PI-R has been translated into over 40 languages, and the structure has been replicated more or less exactly in every case in which it has been studied (Rolland, 2002). The five intrapsychic mechanisms that give rise to personality traits in Americans appear to be a part of human nature.

Sources of Structure

How does personality trait structure arise? Why, for example, are dutiful people likely to also be deliberate and disciplined, defining a Conscientiousness factor? One obvious hypothesis is that some people are dutiful, deliberate, and self-disciplined because their parents cherished these values and instilled them in their children through example, instruction, and correction. Other people are lax, impulsive, and weak-willed because their parents did not care enough to raise them properly, or perhaps because they thought it was more important that their children be happy and spontaneous than highly conscientious.

But that hypothesis is challenged by behavior genetic studies. In Chapter 3, Rowe and van den Oord discussed the heritability of traits. There is now considerable evidence that all five trait factors—and all 30 facets assessed by the NEO-PI-R—are substantially influenced by genes (Jang, McCrae, Angleitner, Riemann, & Livesley, 1998). Rowe and van den Oord also reported a well-established but counterintuitive fact: Environmental influences shared by children in the same family apparently have little or no effect on adult personality. Adopted siblings do not resemble each other as adults, and resemblances among biological siblings can be explained entirely by the genes they share.

It is certainly the case that parents, for good or ill, have a tremendous influence on their children's behavior. But behavior genetics studies suggest that parents have very little lasting impact on their children's personality traits. Despite some instances of favoritism or a double standard with regard to boys and girls, in general parents treat all their children similarly. They provide the same role models, cook the same food, and transmit the same religious beliefs to all their sons and daughters. In a study of child-rearing practices (McCrae & Costa, 1988) we asked adults to recall how they had been treated as children. Scores were given for how loving versus rejecting, casual versus demanding, and attentive mother and father were. Some of the participants were siblings, so we were able to compare their assessments about how their parents had acted. We found strong agreement, with correlations ranging from .26 to .67. These data confirm that parents generally treat their children similarly. But Rowe and van den Oord showed that children's similar environments have no influence on their adult personality. Thus, whether parents are loving or rejecting, demanding or casual does not seem to affect the development of personality traits.

Our study provided a more direct test of that hypothesis: We correlated recalled parent-child relation scores with measures of the FFM in the adult children (McCrae & Costa, 1988). The median absolute correlation was a meager .11. The strongest and most consistent correlation (about .30) was between recalled parental rejection and current Neuroticism. That might mean that parental rejection accounts for about 10% of adult levels of Neuroticism. But it might only mean that adults who are prone to anxiety and depression are more likely to accuse their parents of having been rejecting, even if they weren't. Under any interpretation, parental influences appear to be much less important than classic theories of personality development hypothesized.

If parental influences do not account for the covariation of dutifulness, deliberation, and self-discipline, what does? One study suggested that the answer is genetics (McCrae, Jang, Livesley, Riemann, & Angleitner, 2001). In the usual behavior genetics study, we analyze the correlation of Trait A across pairs of twins. If a trait is heritable, monozygotic (identical) twins should have similar scores on measures of the trait; the more similar, the stronger the genetic influence. In genetic covariance analyses, we analyze the correlations among different traits. If Trait A is correlated with Trait B across pairs of monozygotic twins, it indicates that some of the same genes that influence Trait A influence Trait B. It is possible to look at the correlations among all 30 NEO-PI-R facet scales this way, and to factor the resulting correlation matrix. What emerges is the familiar FFM. Personality trait structure can be attributed almost entirely to genetic influences.

Trait Development

Personality traits show predictable developmental curves. Between adolescence and middle adulthood, Neuroticism, Extraversion, and Openness decline, whereas Agreeableness and Conscientiousness increase. Adults are less emotional and flexible, but more nurturing and responsible than college students. The differences are rather small in magnitude, but they are consistent for men and women, and they are replicable across many different cultures (McCrae et al., 1999). That cross-cultural invariance is rather surprising, because different countries have had very different recent histories, and one might have guessed that these events would have shaped personality differently. The Chinese who lived through the tumultuous Cultural Revolution show the same generational differences as Americans who lived through the same period in comparative tranquility (Yang et al., 1998).

Why is personality development so consistent? Why doesn't Neuroticism increase in some cultures and decrease in others? There are three possibilities. First, it could be that trait development is shaped by historical forces shared by everyone in the world. Personality may be influenced by events in childhood that persist throughout life. These are known as *cohort effects*, because they influence everyone who shares the same birth cohort. For example, adolescents all over the world have grown up watching television, whereas their grandparents did not. That might perhaps explain why young people everywhere are more neurotic and disagreeable than their elders. Again, greater educational opportunities among younger cohorts worldwide may account for their higher levels of Openness to Experience.

A second possibility is that personality traits change in response to social requirements that are very similar in all societies. In particular, the transition to adulthood almost invariably brings new responsibilities for work and raising a family. Societies everywhere may encourage responsibility and nurturance as people age because these qualities are needed everywhere.

There is, however, a third possibility. Perhaps these changes are simply programmed into human development. People everywhere show many of the same signs of biological aging: menopause, wrinkles, and memory loss are common to older adults around the world. Perhaps declines in Extraversion and Openness are governed by the same kind of biological clock. One can even imagine an evolutionary explanation for the changes: Extraversion and Openness may be highly adaptive when seeking a mate and finding a way in the world, but Agreeableness and Conscientiousness may become more important once one has a growing family. Genes that turn these traits off and on may have been preferentially selected over eons of human evolution.

The Stability of Individual Differences

It is part of the definition of traits that they are relatively enduring. A characteristic that changed from week to week would not be considered a trait. But that does not mean that traits cannot change over periods of many years. Indeed, the developmental curves we have just examined prove that traits are not immutable. But aside from general trends common to everyone, individuals may show idiosyncratic changes in personality traits.

It is possible to estimate developmental curves from cross-sectional data (in which a sample of people of different ages are assessed at the same time), but in order to examine stability or change in the individual, it is necessary to conduct longitudinal studies. In these, a sample of individuals is assessed at Time 1 and then reassessed with the same measures at Times 2, 3, and so on. We would not expect identical scores even over an interval of a few weeks,

because personality measures are imperfect. Test-retest reliability (the correlation of scores on two occasions over a relatively brief time interval) is usually
in the range of .70 to .90 for personality scales. Over a period of years or
decades, the retest correlations must be smaller than this because they include
both unreliability and true change.

Longitudinal studies are difficult and, by definition, time-consuming, and
relatively few have been conducted. Several were begun in the 1960s and began
to yield results in the 1970s (Block, 1977; Costa & McCrae, 1978; Costa, Mc-
Crae, & Arenberg, 1980). Different researchers used different instruments and
different samples, but all came to the same conclusion: Individual differences in
personality traits are extremely stable in adults, with retest correlations in the
.60 to .80 range over periods of up to 30 years. Subsequent research has confirmed this finding for all five factors and for men and women (McCrae &
Costa, 2003), but has also shown that personality is more fluid in younger
adults and adolescents (Roberts & DelVecchio, 2000).

These findings do not mean that personality cannot change, but they do
imply that for most people, traits do not change much. The most extraverted
member of a college class is likely to be among the most extraverted at the 50th
class reunion—although everyone there may be a bit less extraverted than they
were in college. Well-adjusted midlifers are not likely to become anxious and
depressed senior citizens (although, unfortunately, anxious and depressed
midlifers are likely to remain that way).

When these results were first published, they astounded even their authors.
No one expected such high levels of stability because life experience varies so
much. A few people have stable marriages and remain in the same job for a
lifetime, but even they see their children grow up and move out, encounter
health problems, and live through different political administrations. In 20th-
century America divorce and remarriage are common, most people change jobs
several times, and the typical family moves its residence every few years. People read books, watch television, make new friends. Most people undergo some
kind of traumatic experience—an automobile accident, criminal assault, bank-
ruptcy, the death of a relative, a natural disaster or an act of war. Yet the net result of all these life experiences on personality traits is apparently—nothing!

There have been some direct tests of this hypothesis. In one, Costa, Metter,
and McCrae (1994) examined medical records of individuals whose personality had been assessed twice over a six-year interval. Some people remained free
of major diseases whereas others developed serious medical conditions, such as
cancer, diabetes, or a heart attack. At the time of retest, of course, all these individuals had recovered sufficiently to remain in the study. But was there any
impact of disease on personality? The retest correlations for Neuroticism, Extraversion, Openness, Agreeableness, and Conscientiousness were .80, .81, .82,
.58, and .77 for those who showed no decline in health; they were .84, .84, .84,
.60, and .70 for those who did decline. These near-identical results suggest that
physical health has no lasting impact on personality traits. Costa, Herbst, Mc-
Crae, and Siegler (2000) reached a similar conclusion with regard to a long list
of life events, although there was some evidence that marriage and divorce had
a small effect.

A CONTEMPORARY VIEW OF INTRAPSYCHIC STRUCTURE

We have now examined some of the major findings with regard to the functioning of personality traits, and we are in a position to formulate a model of intrapsychic structure. Watching people breathe in and out, we can make some guesses about the anatomy of lungs, even if we have never dissected a cadaver. In the same way, we can make inferences about how personality must be structured in people in order to account for the observed facts. Here is what we need to explain:

- Traits covary to define five factors, and the same traits and factors are found everywhere: in men and women, adolescents and adults, people from cultures around the world.
- The reason these five factors appear is genetic: Traits that define the same factor appear to share some genetic influences (although traits also have their own unique genetic components).
- On average, traits increase or decrease over time in regular patterns. At any one time, cross-sectional age differences are similar around the world.
- Individual differences in traits are extremely stable over long periods of adulthood, even though people have vastly different life experiences.

In addition, we need to take into account all the obvious evidence of change and difference. People in Zimbabwe act very differently from people in Malaysia; men and women express their feelings differently; the life of every individual is marked by learning new skills and habits. People make and lose friends, acquire tastes for new foods, change their attitudes toward handguns or affirmative action. All these things are surely related to personality, but how can we reconcile these undeniable differences and changes with the uniformity and stability that we find in studies of personality traits?

A Five-Factor Theory

One effort to make sense of these findings and observations is called Five-Factor Theory or FFT (McCrae & Costa, 1999). It is not so much a theory of the factors themselves as it is an account of how people operate that is consistent with research findings on the FFM. FFT says that personality is a system, with input and output and a defined internal structure. A fairly elaborate depiction of the system is given in Figure 7.1. A simpler version, highlighting the key concepts, is given in Table 7.3.

Components of the System   The ellipses in Figure 7.1 are the peripheral components of the system, the points of contact with the rest of the world. On the right are *Biological Bases*, including principally the brain, whose structure and function are determined largely by genes but also by accidents of development, diseases, and pharmacological interventions. On the left are *Environmental Influences*, opportunities and limitations presented by the situation at each moment in time. At the broadest scale, Environmental Influences arise in the context of a particular culture and history. These two inputs are familiar as nature

Figure 7.1 | A representation of the personality system, with categories of variables, specific examples, and arrows indicating causal pathways.

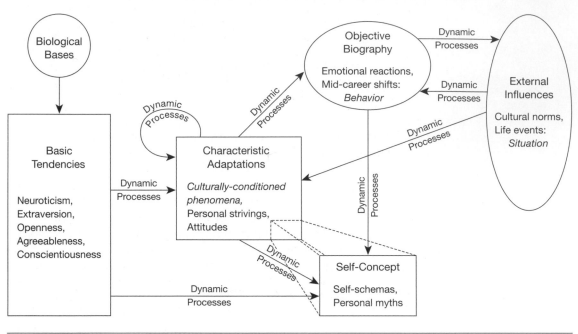

Source: Adapted from McCrae and Costa (1999).

and nurture. On the top of the figure is an ellipse representing the *Objective Biography*. It is the output of the personality system and consists of the cumulative record of everything the individual does, thinks, or feels. Many psychologists believe that this is what personality psychology is supposed to explain.

The heart of FFT is contained in the two rectangles labeled *Basic Tendencies* and *Characteristic Adaptations*. Basic Tendencies are the abstract potentials and dispositions of the individual. They include a wide range of contents, from the ability to use language to sexual orientation (assuming that it is innate, not chosen). Most important, it includes personality traits. Neuroticism,

Table 7.3 | Key Concepts in Five-Factor Theory

- Abstract Basic Tendencies, including personality traits, are distinguished from concrete Characteristic Adaptations
- Behavior results from the interaction of Characteristic Adaptations with External Influences
- Characteristic Adaptations develop from the interaction of Basic Tendencies and External Influences
- Basic Tendencies and their development over time are determined solely by Biological Bases

Extraversion, Openness to Experience, Agreeableness, and Conscientiousness, and all the traits that define them, are regarded by FFT as Basic Tendencies.

Characteristic Adaptations, by contrast, are not traits, but represent a wide variety of psychological features, including skills, habits, beliefs, plans, goals, and the intrapsychic aspects of roles and relationships. One very important subset of Characteristic Adaptations consists of the *Self-Concept*: beliefs, feelings, and stories about the self. The Self-Concept is given a separate box because it is of such interest to psychologists, but conceptually it is a part of Characteristic Adaptations.

Operation of the System   FFT says that these components interact in defined ways, as indicated in the figure by arrows. Various *Dynamic Processes* (like learning and planning) make things happen, but—according to FFT—only certain pathways are followed. To begin at the end, the Objective Biography is determined by the interaction of External Influences and Characteristic Adaptations. Suppose, for example, you receive an invitation to a wedding. That is an External Influence, but how you respond depends on your Characteristic Adaptations. You must be able to read the invitation (a skill), then decide if you want to go (a preference) or are obliged to go (a relationship). You will have to consider whether you will be free to go (by consulting your plans and schedules) and can afford to go (by consulting your financial self-concept). If you decide to go, you will have to follow a host of cultural conventions you have learned about what to wear, whether to bring a gift, and how to behave before, during, and after the ceremony. These elaborate sorts of interactions occur a thousand times a day.

Notice that in this account there was no mention of personality traits. According to FFT, traits do not have a direct influence on behavior or experience; their influence is always mediated by Characteristic Adaptations. For example, if you are an introvert, your self-concept will contain the information that you find social gatherings tedious, and perhaps you will have developed a long list of excuses that help you decline social invitations. The operation of introversion on invitation-rejecting behavior is mediated by self-knowledge and social skills, which are Characteristic Adaptations.

Characteristic Adaptations themselves result from the interaction of External Influences with Basic Tendencies (or previously developed Characteristic Adaptations). Perhaps the clearest example of this is the acquisition of language. No dog will ever learn a human language, but any healthy human infant can; the capacity for language is a Basic Tendency universal in the human species. But which language a child learns to speak depends entirely on External Influences, on where he or she grows up. Speaking Urdu is a Characteristic Adaptation of a human being raised in Pakistan.

In the same way, personality traits interact with life experiences to help shape the ongoing psychology of the individual. For example, people who are high in Neuroticism are prone to worry. But whether they worry about sorcery or eternal damnation or job layoffs is a matter of the cultural and historical circumstances they find themselves in. Again, people high in Openness may be naturally inquisitive, but they will be very limited in what they can learn if they are not taught to read and given other educational opportunities. Characteristic Adaptations are *characteristic* because they reflect the individual's dispositions; they are *adaptations* because they develop in response to the specific demands and opportunities of the environment.

Parents and parenting have a tremendous influence on Characteristic Adaptations. Food preferences, religious beliefs, languages spoken, and styles of dress are all affected by the examples and teachings of one's parents. The relationship one has with one's parents may last a lifetime, and it is likely to be an important determinant of one's life structure—for example, it may form the basis for financial support for young families, or for years of caregiving to aging parents. Parents and parenting surely matter—though not in shaping personality traits.

In fact, the most controversial feature of FFT is the assertion that Basic Tendencies themselves are rooted only in Biological Bases. Most theories of personality assume that traits are shaped by the environment or by some combination of environment and temperament. Why not add an arrow from External Influences to Basic Tendencies? There are two reasons. First, scientific theories should be as simple as possible because if they are simple and correct, they will be very powerful, making straightforward predictions. If they are simple and incorrect, we should find that out very soon. At this stage in the development of FFT, we have opted for a simple model, but of course, when the data convince us that this model is inadequate, we will add other arrows. We have already conceded that the environment can influence traits by influencing biology (McCrae & Costa, 2003). For example, administering psychoactive drugs has at least a temporary effect on traits.

The second reason for claiming that traits are determined only by biology is that it seems to account for most of the empirical findings. If External Influences affected traits, one would expect (as Juni, 1996, did) that trait structure would be different in different cultures—but it isn't. If External Influences affected traits, one would expect that nations' different histories would lead to different cohort effects and thus to distinct patterns of age differences—but they don't. If External Influences affected traits, one would expect that life events and experiences would change traits in unique ways, reshaping personality dramatically over the course of years. But most people seem impervious to such influences, showing great stability in the full range of traits over decades of adult life.

There is strong evidence from studies of twins and adopted siblings that genes account for a substantial portion of the variation in trait levels, and that experiences common to all the children in a family have little or no influence (see Chapter 3). But that leaves a considerable amount of variance unaccounted for. Some researchers have attempted to trace the influence of experiences unique to each child, but so far that effort has had little success. FFT suggests that we should consider nongenetic aspects of biological bases. To take a dramatic example, Alzheimer's disease has a devastating effect on the brain, and it also has a pronounced effect on personality, with increases in Vulnerability and marked declines in Conscientiousness reported by caregiver raters of Alzheimer's patients (Siegler et al., 1991).

FFT appears to account for the basic empirical findings about the origins and operation of traits. By distinguishing between Basic Tendencies and Characteristic Adaptations, it can account for the reasons that people both change and stay the same: Their Characteristic Adaptations change, whereas their Basic Tendencies do not (or at least, not in response to life experience). The universality of the FFM is understood as a reflection of the fact that all human beings share a common genome. The puzzling finding of behavior geneticists, that the shared environment has no effect on personality, is not so puzzling if we recognize that traits are shaped solely by biology.

Evaluating Five-Factor Theory

Is FFT a good account of the intrapsychic structure of personality? There are three issues that need to be addressed to answer that question: Its palatability, its empirical support, and its conceptual adequacy as a model of intrapsychic structure.

Many people simply don't like the large role FFT assigns to genes. Consider the finding that Japanese samples tend to score higher on measures of Neuroticism than do Danish samples (McCrae, 2002). According to FFT, that might mean that the Japanese are genetically more inclined to experience anxiety and depression than are Danes. Most social scientists are uncomfortable imputing genetically determined characteristics to groups, because such characterizations may be used to justify discrimination. If a theory is liable to be abused, then its advocates have to be particularly careful to discuss the implications and limitations of their work. In this case, it must be noted that the differences between Japanese and Danes might have nothing to do with genes: They might instead be due to sampling error, or to inequivalence in the translations of the NEO-PI-R, or to cultural differences in response style or self-presentational strategy. And generalizations about groups should not be applied indiscriminately to individuals: Some Danes are surely higher in Neuroticism than most Japanese.

However, once these ethical requirements are met, recall that the comfort level of social scientists says nothing about the scientific merit of FFT. What we like and what is true are not necessarily the same. But is FFT true? Or, more realistically, is it a reasonable approximation of the truth? The basic ideas in FFT were developed to account for findings from longitudinal studies in the United States (Costa & McCrae, 1992b), so it is not surprising that FFT can account for the stability of personality. But the same ideas can be used to understand the results from cross-cultural studies conducted years later. All the cross-cultural results can therefore be considered tests of FFT, and they show striking support for it.

But no one would claim that the theory has been adequately tested so far, and some pieces of evidence seem inconsistent. For example, McCrae, Yik, Trapnell, Bond, and Paulhus (1998) compared scores from ethnic Hong Kong Chinese living in Canada. Some had been born in Canada, some had moved there recently. If personality scores are solely a matter of biology, then the experience of growing up in Canada shouldn't have had any impact, and the two groups should have been comparable. For some traits they were, but on others there were significant differences. It appeared that enculturation in Canada led to higher levels of Openness and Agreeableness. If such findings are replicated, and if alternative explanations can be ruled out, they would require a revision of FFT, adding an arrow from certain kinds of External Influences to Basic Tendencies.

Beyond such empirical tests, there is one last way in which FFT must be judged. Perhaps it does what it sets out to do—explain the operation of personality traits in the light of research findings on the FFM—but does it adequately explain intrapsychic structure? Many psychologists would probably say *no*. The theory is certainly underdeveloped. The Dynamic Processes that activate the model (such as social comparison and attitude formation) have been extensively studied, especially by social psychologists, but FFT does not even bother to enumerate them. Although there is a well-established taxonomy of personality traits, there is no taxonomy of Characteristic Adaptations. Personality psychology, and FFT, would benefit from such a systematic treatment of both Dynamic Processes and Characteristic Adaptations.

But details aside, is FFT a good sketch of the personality system? It might be argued that the theory assigns far too much importance to traits. For example, a search of the PsycINFO database showed 16,575 articles for which *trait* was a keyword, but 202,681—twelve times as many—that mentioned *self*. Psychologists as a whole seem to think the self is a more important aspect of personality than traits, and yet the self-concept is relegated to a fairly minor corner of FFT. Maybe a better account of intrapsychic structure would draw its major distinctions between self-concept and self-esteem, or focus on ideal or possible selves (see Baumeister's Chapter 9). Of course, it would be possible to incorporate such distinctions into FFT, but rather awkwardly. Some system other than that shown in Figure 7.1 might accommodate the important aspects of personality more easily and fruitfully.

We cannot say at this point whether FFT is a very good beginning or a primitive guess that will soon be superseded and forgotten. We can say with some assurance that it is a better map of intrapsychic structure than those provided by the classic personality theories of Freud, Jung, Rogers, and their peers (Mendelsohn, 1993). It is better because it has built on their insights, corrected by decades of rigorous research. A good model of the structure of traits—the Five-Factor Model—has allowed us to learn systematically about the operation of traits, and from these results we can make inferences about the intrapsychic structure of personality. Five-Factor Theory is one such set of inferences, and it offers one view of the structure of personality.

SUMMARY

Personality structure can refer either to the organization of elements in an individual's mind that accounts for behavior and experience, or to the patterns of covariation of personality traits in a group of people. The Five-Factor Model has been shown to provide an account of personality trait structure that is generalizable across age, gender, and culture. Research on the traits of the Five-

Factor Model has shown that trait structure is primarily rooted in genetics, that traits show a regular developmental pattern, and that individual differences are very stable in adulthood. Five-Factor Theory offers an explanation for these findings in terms of a hypothesized intrapsychic structure: Personality is a system containing Characteristic Adaptations, which are acquired and may be changed, and Basic Tendencies—including personality traits—that are innate and resist change. Five-Factor Theory may not be the optimal representation of intrapsychic structure, but it does provide one model that is consistent with a large body of empirical findings.

DISCUSSION QUESTIONS

1. The Five-Factor Model claims to be comprehensive and thus relevant to most aspects of personality. Pick another chapter in this book and examine its central constructs. To which, if any, of the five factors are they related? Are they better considered Basic Tendencies or Characteristic Adaptations?
2. How might the id, ego, and superego (see Chapter 5) be reconceptualized in terms of Five-Factor Theory?
3. What if there really are genetic differences between ethnic groups that lead to differences in the mean levels of personality traits? How would this affect intercultural understanding? What problems could it lead to, and how should they be addressed?
4. As you look back over your life, do your traits appear to be stable or changing? If there are changes, to what do you attribute them? Did some event trigger them, or did you simply change as you grew older? Does your personal experience square with empirical findings?
5. This chapter does not discuss gender differences in personality traits. On the basis of Five-Factor Theory, what predictions would you make about gender differences in American samples? In other cultures? See Costa, Terracciano, and McCrae (2001) for some data on this question.
6. How many Dynamic Processes can you list? Can you organize them as you did the traits in Activity Box 7.1? Compare your organization to that of one of your classmates. Is there any consensus?

SUGGESTED READINGS

Block, J. (1995). A contrarian view of the five-factor approach to personality description. *Psychological Bulletin, 117,* 187–215. This most-cited critique of the Five-Factor Model provides a different perspective on trait structure. See also the accompanying responses.

McAdams, D. P. (1996). Personality, modernity, and the storied self: A contemporary framework for studying persons. *Psychological Inquiry, 7,* 295–321. McAdams offers a different but related view of intrapsychic structure in terms of three levels of personality.

McCrae, R. R., & Costa, P. T., Jr. (1987). Validation of the Five-Factor Model of personality across instruments and observers. *Journal of Personality and Social Psychology, 52,* 81–90. Early evidence on the comprehensiveness of the Five-Factor Model.

McCrae, R. R., & Costa, P. T., Jr. (1996). Toward a new generation of personality theories: Theoretical contexts for the Five-Factor Model. In J. S. Wiggins

(Ed.), *The Five-Factor Model of personality: Theoretical perspectives* (pp. 51–87). New York: Guilford. The first formal statement of Five-Factor Theory.

McCrae, R. R., & Costa, P. T., Jr. (2003). *Personality in adulthood: A Five-Factor Theory perspective* (2nd ed.). New York: Guilford. This volume summarizes evidence on personality stability and change after adolescence.

Tupes, E. C., & Christal, R. E. (1992). Recurrent personality factors based on trait ratings. *Journal of Personality, 60,* 225–251. (Original work published 1961). This classic reanalysis of eight studies is widely considered to constitute the "discovery" of the Five-Factor Model.

SUGGESTED WEB SITES

http://www.wwu.edu/~culture
This Web site is a set of readings in cross-cultural psychology that includes, but goes far beyond, personality traits and culture.

http://www.personality-project.org/personality.html
This Web site was organized by William Revelle as a resource in personality psychology.

http://lpcwww.grc.nia.nih.gov/www-psc-rrm.html
This Web site provides McCrae's complete bibliography.

INFOTRAC COLLEGE EDITION SEARCH TOPICS

Traits	Five-Factor Model	Basic tendencies
Factor analysis	Personality system	Characteristic adaptations

REFERENCES

Allport, G. W., & Odbert, H. S. (1936). Trait names: A psycho-lexical study. *Psychological Monographs, 47,* (1 Whole No. 211).

American Psychiatric Association. (1994). *Diagnostic and statistical manual of mental disorders* (4th ed.). Washington, DC: Author.

Block, J. (1977). Advancing the psychology of personality: Paradigmatic shift or improving the quality of research? In D. Magnusson & N. S. Endler (Eds.), *Personality at the cross-roads: Current issues in interactional psychology* (pp. 37–64). Hillsdale, NJ: Erlbaum.

Cattell, R. B. (1946). *The description and measurement of personality.* Yonkers, NY: World Book.

Cattell, R. B., Eber, H. W., & Tatsuoka, M. M. (1970). *The handbook for the Sixteen Personality Factor Questionnaire.* Champaign, IL: Institute for Personality and Ability Testing.

Costa, P. T., Jr., Herbst, J. H., McCrae, R. R., & Siegler, I. C. (2000). Personality at midlife: Stability, intrinsic maturation, and response to life events. *Assessment, 7,* 365–378.

Costa, P. T., Jr., & McCrae, R. R. (1978). Objective personality assessment. In M. Storandt, I. C. Siegler, & M. F. Elias (Eds.), *The clinical psychology of aging* (pp. 119–143). New York: Plenum Press.

Costa, P. T., Jr., & McCrae, R. R. (1992a). *Revised NEO Personality Inventory (NEO-PI-R) and NEO Five-Factor Inventory (NEO-FFI) professional manual.* Odessa, FL: Psychological Assessment Resources.

Costa, P. T., Jr., & McCrae, R. R. (1992b, August). "Set like plaster"? Evidence for the stability of adult personality. In J. Weinberger (Chair), *Personality in the life course.* Symposium presented at the American Psychological Association Convention, Washington, DC.

Costa, P. T., Jr., McCrae, R. R., & Arenberg, D. (1980). Enduring dispositions in adult males *Journal of Personality and Social Psychology, 38,* 793–800.

Costa, P. T., Jr., Metter, E. J., & McCrae, R. R. (1994). Personality stability and its contribution to successful aging. *Journal of Geriatric Psychiatry, 27,* 41–59.

Costa, P. T., Jr., Terracciano, A., & McCrae, R. R. (2001). Gender differences in personality traits across cultures: Robust and surprising findings. *Journal of Personality and Social Psychology, 81,* 322–331.

De Raad, B., & Perugini, M. (Eds.). (2002). *Big Five assessment.* Gottingen, Germany: Hogrefe & Huber. Digman, J. M., & Takemoto-Chock, N. K. (1981). Factors in the natural language of personality: Re-analysis, comparison, and interpretation of six major studies. *Multivariate Behavioral Research, 16,* 149–170.

Eysenck, H. J., & Eysenck, S. B. G. (1975). *Manual of the Eysenck Personality Questionnaire.* San Diego: EdITS.

Goldberg, L. R. (1981). Language and individual differences: The search for universals in personality lexicons. In L. Wheeler (Ed.), *Review of personality and social psychology* (Vol. 2, pp. 141–165). Beverly Hills, CA: Sage.

Guilford, J. P., & Guilford, R. B. (1934). An analysis of the factors in a typical test of introversion-extroversion. *Journal of Abnormal and Social Psychology, 28,* 377–399.

Jang, K. L., McCrae, R. R., Angleitner, A., Riemann, R., & Livesley, W. J. (1998). Heritability of facet-level traits in a cross-cultural twin sample: Support for a hierarchical model of personality. *Journal of Personality and Social Psychology, 74,* 1556–1565.

Juni, S. (1996). Review of the Revised NEO Personality Inventory. In J. C. Conoley & J. C. Impara (Eds.), *12th Mental Measurements Yearbook* (pp. 863–868). Lincoln: University of Nebraska Press.

McCrae, R. R. (2002). NEO-PI-R data from 36 cultures: Further intercultural comparisons. In R. R. McCrae & J. Allik (Eds.), *The Five-Factor Model of personality across cultures* (pp. 105–125). New York: Kluwer Academic/Plenum. McCrae, R. R., & Costa, P. T., Jr. (1994). The paradox of parental influence: Understanding retrospective studies of parent-child relations and adult personality. In C. Perris, W. A. Arrindell, & M. Eisemann (Eds.), *Parenting and psychopathology* (pp. 107–125). New York: Wiley.

McCrae, R. R., & Costa, P. T., Jr. (1997). Personality trait structure as a human universal. *American Psychologist, 52,* 509–516.

McCrae, R. R., & Costa, P. T., Jr. (1999). A Five-Factor Theory of personality. In L. A. Pervin &

O. P. John (Eds.), *Handbook of personality: Theory and research* (2nd ed., pp. 139–153). New York: Guilford.

McCrae, R. R., & Costa, P. T., Jr. (2003). *Personality in adulthood: A Five-Factor Theory perspective* (2nd ed.). New York: Guilford.

McCrae, R. R., & Costa, P. T., Jr. (1988). Recalled parent-child relations and adult personality *Journal of Personality, 56,* 417–434.

McCrae, R. R., Costa, P. T., Jr., Lima, M. P., Simões, A., Ostendorf, F., Angleitner, A., Marušić, I., Bratko, D., Caprara, G. V., Barbaranelli, C., Chae, J.-H., & Piedmont, R. L. (1999). Age differences in personality across the adult life span: Parallels in five cultures. *Developmental Psychology, 35,* 466–477.

McCrae, R. R., Jang, K. L., Livesley, W. J., Riemann, R., & Angleitner, A. (2001). Sources of structure: Genetic, environmental, and artifactual influences on the covariation of personality traits. *Journal of Personality, 69,* 511–535.

McCrae, R. R., Yik, M. S. M., Trapnell, P. D., Bond, M. H., & Paulhus, D. L. (1998). Interpreting personality profiles across cultures: Bilingual, acculturation, and peer rating studies of Chinese undergraduates. *Journal of Personality and Social Psychology, 74,* 1041–1055.

Mendelsohn, G. A. (1993). It's time to put theories of personality in their place, or, Allport and Stagner got it right, why can't we? In K. H. Craik, R. Hogan, & R. N. Wolfe (Eds.), *Fifty years of personality psychology* (pp. 103–115). New York: Plenum.

Norman, W. T. (1967). *2800 Personality trait descriptors: Normative operating characteristics for a university population.* Ann Arbor: University of Michigan.

Passini, F. T., & Norman, W. T. (1966). A universal conception of personality structure? *Journal of Personality and Social Psychology, 4,* 44–49.

Roberts, B. W., & DelVecchio, W. F. (2000). The rank-order consistency of personality traits from childhood to old age: A quantitative review of longitudinal studies. *Psychological Bulletin, 126,* 3–25.

Rolland, J.-P. (2002). Cross-cultural generalizability of the Five-Factor Model of personality. In R. R. McCrae & J. Allik (Eds.), *The Five-Factor Model of personality across cultures* (pp. 7–28). New York: Kluwer Academic/Plenum. Siegler, I. C., Welsh, K. A., Dawson, D. V., Fillenbaum, G. G., Earl, N. L., Kaplan, E. B., & Clark, C. M.

(1991). Ratings of personality change in patients being evaluated for memory disorders. *Alzheimer Disease and Associated Disorders, 5,* 240–250.

Sneed, C. D., McCrae, R. R., & Funder, D. C. (1998). Lay conceptions of the Five-Factor Model and its indicators. *Personality and Social Psychology Bulletin, 24,* 115–126.

Tellegen, A., Grove, W. M., & Waller, N. G. (1991). *Inventory of Personal Characteristics #7 (IPC7).* Unpublished materials, University of Minnesota.

Tupes, E. C., & Christal, R. E. (1992). Recurrent personality factors based on trait ratings. *Journal of Personality, 60,* 225–251. (Original work published 1961)

Yang, J., McCrae, R. R., & Costa, P. T., Jr. (1998). Adult age differences in personality traits in the United States and the People's Republic of China. *Journal of Gerontology: Psychological Sciences, 53B,* P375–P383.

The Psychological Unconscious | 8

MICHAEL NASH

A BRIEF BACKGROUND

From the dawn of the Age of Reason, when 17th- and 18th-century figures like Voltaire and Benjamin Franklin argued against received truth and superstition, championing instead rational inquiry, people in Western civilization began to think of human nature as reasoned, lawful, and ultimately accessible to science. In some sense Europe seized on the notion that humans are the masters of their own destiny. Suddenly, after centuries, men and women were beginning to construe their thoughts and actions as *not* predetermined by celestial will and political potentate. They believed the key to our individual and collective destiny is our ability to reason things through for ourselves, consciously reflecting on all the factors, and then making a decision (a decision to be a republican or a democrat, to be a dentist or a construction worker, to go to war, to sue for peace). Of course this entire approach is predicated on the assumption that we indeed are conscious of (notice, remember, comprehend) all the reasons we might behave or feel one way or another. This assumption was broadly accepted by the founders of the Age of Reason. Clearly, invisible influences on human behavior were "out" and visible (knowable) forces were "in." It was immensely gratifying to believe that the decisions we make (spouse, vocation, favored music, parenthood), emotions we experience (sadness, elation, anger), and the motives we embrace (altruism, vengeance, generosity) are the logical consequences of factors that are accessible (conscious), understandable, and therefore controllable.

But as far back as the 18th-century philosopher Leibnitz and the 19th-century psychophysicist Helmholtz, the scientific community began to suspect that there might be a fly somewhere in this ointment of optimistic rationalism: Scientists began to suspect that we do not, and indeed cannot, notice, comprehend, and remember all the influential aspects of our experience, all the factors that influence, and determine, our thoughts, actions, and emotions. In a word they began to think about the "invisible" again, not devils, imps, and spirits this time, but things emerging from an annoyingly more abstract abode: the unconscious.

It is Freud who is usually given the credit for the elaboration of "the unconscious," and it follows that when people think of the unconscious they think of the *psychoanalytic unconscious* (Freud, 1900/1953). This is unnecessary on two counts: First, Freud was not the first, nor was he the only theorist postulating the influence of unconscious processes at the end of the 19th century (note Pierre Janet in France, and Morton Prince in America; see Ellenberger, 1970, for a thorough treatment of this topic). Second, contemporary advances in cognitive science have enabled us to define and empirically examine the possibility of unconscious influence in human experience without needing to address the elaborate, and sometimes quite speculative, metapsychological "baggage" that accompanies psychoanalysis. It is in fact the intention of this chapter to disengage the review of unconscious processes from psychoanalytic theory. I am broadly psychoanalytically oriented; and I am convinced that some (not all) of the operations of the unconscious do in fact conform to ideas formulated by contemporary psychoanalytic theory (Westen, 1998). Thus I in no way wish to simply dismiss psychoanalytic formulations of how unconscious processes work. But it is certainly possible for us to examine *if* unconscious influences are important without assessing the merits of any particular theory about *how* they work, including that of psychoanalysis. Accordingly, in this chapter I defer on the question of *how*, so that we may focus on the more fundamental and still controversial question of *if*.

ORGANIZING OUR IDEAS ABOUT THE UNCONSCIOUS

It is my intent to proceed with consideration of the unconscious in a very pragmatic fashion: sidestepping the sometimes tempting (but all-too-often entrapping) theoretical contentions of one school or another, employing instead what I believe is a pragmatic organizational approach to the problem. I will then sample the scientific literature to date, avoiding arcane jargon when possible. Finally, I will present a series of related studies on hypnotic age regression we carried out in our laboratory to show how a topic gets studied in this controversial area of personality functioning. First we have the task of defining the question, operationalizing our terms, and organizing our approach.

The Question

Put simply: Are there important influences on human thought and action that are products of a psychological unconscious?

Defining the Psychological Unconscious

For the purposes of this chapter I use a conventionally accepted definition derived from Kihlstrom (1987): The psychological unconscious refers to the idea that mental structures—cognitions, emotions, and motives—operating outside phenomenal awareness, can nevertheless influence ongoing experience, thought, and action.

What We Are Not Talking About

First, it is patently true that a host of physiological processes operate outside of our awareness and have an important impact on our experience and behavior: for example, pupillary dilation, operation of the adrenal cortex, brain stem activity, broad sensory accommodation to external stimulation. This is not what we mean by *psychological unconscious*. Second, much of human maturation proceeds without our awareness, and is influential. Just as surely, we remember little or nothing about the first two years of our life yet those events are immensely formative. But these are biological and historical *events*, not mental structures. Our definition of the psychological unconscious requires a *mental structure* (e.g., a memory, perception, fantasy) that impacts the individual. Developmental or historical events themselves do not qualify. If, on the other hand, it can be shown that the adult possesses an archaic, vestigial mental structure for being "2 years old" that operates outside of awareness (as postulated by Freud), then this does fall within our purview. Similarly, if an adult retains a memory for an incident when 2 years old, and this memory is influential and somehow resides outside of awareness, then (again) we must examine the evidence. But in both cases it is the influence of the contemporary mental structure, not the biological or historical event per se that is relevant to the concept of the psychological unconscious.

A PRAGMATIC APPROACH TO THE QUESTION

One of the most articulate theorists/researchers on the topic of the unconscious is Kenneth Bowers. I have adapted and expanded upon Bowers's (1984) two-factor model of the unconscious to organize material presented in this chapter. Generally speaking, Bowers contends that there are two factors to consider when we examine the unconscious: attention and comprehension. I review "what kind of case can be made" for four types of unconscious influence:

The Unconscious as the Unnoticed

Can a stimulus or experience be processed in such a way that it influences thoughts or actions, yet be unconscious by virtue of its being unnoticed?

Example: A subject cannot tell whether cards that are very briefly flashed are blank or have symbols. A few minutes later he is given a large group of symbols on one sheet (some of which had been flashed earlier and some of which had not been). He is asked to point-out which symbols are most aesthetically appealing. The subject unwittingly selects the ones that were flashed to him earlier. His choices were in fact influenced by the symbols which he had earlier perceived in some way, but not noticed. (Zajonc, 1980)

The Unconscious as the Noticed, but Uncomprehended

Can a noticed stimulus or experience be processed in such a way that it influences thoughts or actions, yet be unconscious by virtue of its being unappreciated as influential?

Example: When asked to choose the highest quality nylon stocking from a choice of five pairs lined up in a row, mall shoppers had sometimes very strong convictions for their choice. Subjects all gave various reasons for their choice (softer, lighter, finer weave). What they did not know was that all five pairs were identical. The strongest determinant of choice was in fact position: People tended to chose the pair farthest to the right. When asked, they would acknowledge that the stocking they chose was indeed farthest to the right, but they always (and sometimes quite firmly) denied that position had anything to do with it. Clearly subject choice was influenced by position. Further, subjects did perceive and notice the position, but failed to appreciate its influence on them. (Nisbett & Wilson, 1977)

The Unconscious as Retained, but Unavailable, Memory of Actual Event

Can a past event be coded or stored in memory in such a way that it influences thought and action, yet for an extended time remains unavailable to conscious awareness?

Example: A 10-year-old boy is sexually molested by a group of older boys. As an adult psychotherapy patient he has no memory of this incident. Nevertheless, he sometimes dreams of scenes suggestive of such an event and has some sexual difficulties. Eventually he begins to remember more detail, and confirms from others that the molestation did indeed occur. Thus we can say (1) the abuse was not recalled for a time; (2) it nevertheless influenced thought and emotion (dreams, sexual difficulties); and (3) a reasonably accurate memory eventually emerged (confirming the presence of a mental structure. (Nash, 1994)

The Unconscious as Personal Fiction That "Feels Like" Memory of Actual Event

Can noticed stimuli and experiences be encoded and stored in such a way that they elicit "memories" of events that in fact never occurred; and the source of the false memory is unappreciated?

Example: An adult research subject begins to remember in great detail that once, as a small child, he was frightened and lost in a shopping mall. This was not true at all and was in fact a product of a subtle collaboration and interview technique involving the experimenter and a sibling. Though the subject certainly perceived and noticed the discussions with the experimenter and sibling, he was unwittingly influenced by the procedure in such a way that he first came to believe and then broadly elaborated upon an event that never happened. (Loftus, 1993)

THE UNCONSCIOUS AS THE UNNOTICED

Can we be exposed to information in the environment that we do not notice (consciously attend) but that has an important impact upon our behavior, feelings, and thoughts? The answer championed by the 17th- and 18th-century scions of rationality and reason is clearly "no." Indeed, some contemporary psychologists contend that stimuli cannot be processed for meaning unless they have been consciously attended to (Ericsson & Simon, 1984). But many cognitive scientists now view conscious awareness as something that happens quite late in the perception-processing-response sequence (Bowers, 1984; Ceci, Loftus, Leichtman, & Bruck, 1994; Greenwald, Draine, & Abrams, 1996; Merikle, Smilek, & Eastwood, 2001; Neisser & Harsch, 1992; Schacter, 1995). In other words, perception is not the same thing as noticing. "Perception" involves the initial registration and processing of information; "noticing" involves actually being aware of the perceived information. Noticing can (but does not always) happen after perceiving. In fact, many theorists contend that consciousness of a stimulus (noticing something) happens well after perception, and that a person can be influenced by a stimulus even though it is never noticed at all (consciously represented). In some ways this idea seems counterintuitive. Can we really be influenced by something we do not even notice? Why on earth would theorists come to believe such a thing? Because I cannot do justice to the immense store of evidence on this topic, I will limit myself to describing some interesting research traditions that speak to the question of perceiving without noticing.

"Blind Sight": Organic and Histrionic

What would happen if you were to place a blind patient (due to brain damage) in a chair, and present a series of 30 cards, one at a time, on a table in front of her? On 15 cards is a triangle; on the other 15 is a circle. You present to the blind patient each card (one at a time), and ask her to "look" at it carefully. You ask her whether the card has a triangle on it, or a circle. Well first, you note that the patient states emphatically: "Don't you understand, I'm blind. I can't SEE the cards." But you gently ask her to go ahead and just give you the best guess she can. If someone were securely blindfolded and administered this test, you would expect to get a 50% hit rate by chance (50% of the cards correctly identified). So how would you expect this blind patient to do: Would you expect a chance hit rate of 50%, or something else?

Well, under some circumstances, with a specific type of brain damage in Area 17 of the visual cortex, we find that blind patients perform well above chance on such discrimination tasks, even though they report that they saw (noticed) absolutely nothing at all (Weiskrantz, Warrington, Sanders, & Marshall, 1974; Wust, Kasten, & Sabel, 2002). But because of the brain damage and the above-chance response rate, we can be certain of three things: (1) These patients are blind in every sense of the word. They do not "notice" any visual cue; (2) nevertheless, somehow the information from the cards (triangle or circle) is processed (perceived); (3) even though the information is not noticed, it affects behavior (successful discrimination). We can infer from this that one part of the brain might be dedicated to registration of visual information and another devoted to awareness of visual information. With the above patients, it may be the "higher" cortical function of awareness that is compromised (therefore they are blind). But registration of the stimulus itself proceeds unimpeded because this part of the process is governed by lower visual brain centers. The take-home message here is that perceiving and noticing may be different *structurally*. That is, they take place in different parts of the brain.

But there is an interesting variant of "blind sight" that is more subtle, functional, and complex. This involves hysterical blindness or psychogenic blindness. Here there is no detectable brain damage or neural lesions associated with the blindness. Rather, there typically is a history of trauma and emotional difficulties that seem to express themselves in an inability to see. These gross types of conversion disorders are rare but not unheard of in contemporary psychiatry (Wynick, Hobson, & Jones, 1997). When these hysterically blind patients are exposed to the types of discrimination tasks described above, they also typically score at nonchance levels. But the direction of the nonchance responding seems dependent on what the experimenter communicated to the patient about the procedures (Sackeim, Nordlie, & Gur, 1979). If the experimenter simply indulgently expressed a wish for the patient to "just do the best you can," hysterically blind patients often performed at above-chance levels on these discrimination tasks, even though they report not seeing anything. If, on the other hand, the patient was sternly told that the experimenter suspected that the patient was able to see, and that the procedure was a kind of lie detector test, the patient typically performed significantly BELOW chance levels (e.g., got significantly fewer "hits" than would be expected by chance), even though he or she reported not seeing anything. Similar results are obtained with normal subjects who are given suggestions for hypnotic blindness.

Whether hysterically blind patients or hypnotically blind subjects score above or below chance, it is clear that the information is being processed, albeit outside of awareness. Again, as was the case with organically blind individuals (visual cortex area 17), psychogenically blind individuals process and respond to the social demands of the situation, even though they report no visual stimulation whatsoever.

Preferring Things That We Never Noticed

For almost 30 years it has been well documented that "familiarity does *not* breed contempt," at least within the cloistered confines of the psychological laboratory (Zajonc, 1980). When people are exposed to a host of novel stimuli (music, drawings, photographs, nonsense words, flavors), they will later prefer those previously experienced stimuli over other completely novel stimuli. In general, we prefer music that we've heard before, drawings that we have seen before, flavors we have tasted before, and even nonsense words we have encountered before. In short, all things being equal we prefer what we know (Peretz, Gaudreau, & Bonnell, 1998). This seems to be the way it works with nonhuman animals as well (e.g., Brown, 2002; Seppa, Laurila, Peuhkuri, Piironen, & Lower, 2001). But all the human research was carried out with the initial exposure long enough (say, 10 seconds) that the stimuli were fully noticed by the subject. That is, the stimuli (the music, the words, the drawings) were presented to the subject in a manner that insured they would be perceived, noticed, and remembered.

What would happen if the kinds of visual stimuli used in the above research (nonsense words, drawings, photographs) were instead presented in short 1 millisecond bursts, so as to render the stimuli undetectable to the subject? That way the subject would have no idea what, if any, stimulus was presented. The exposure would simply be experienced as a flash of light, with no content. Would we still get the same subjects later picking (preferring) these stimuli from a larger list, even though they in no way recognized them as familiar? The answer is "Yes" (Zajonc, 1980). People prefer nonsense words, drawings, and photos they were briefly exposed to but could not possibly have noticed, experienced, or remembered. Here again, a large body of studies leads us to believe that information that is not noticed can nonetheless affect how we subsequently think, feel, and act. Indeed there is good reason to believe that humans may be even more emotionally responsive to material presented suboptimally (that they are less conscious of) than they are to material presented optimally (Murphy & Zajonc, 1993; Rotteveel, de-Groot, Geutskens, & Phaf, 2001).

Responding Emotionally to Something Unnoticed

A research tradition stemming originally from psychoanalytic theory also has important implications for our discussion of the unconscious as the unnoticed. Lloyd Silverman and his colleagues at New York University (Silverman, 1976) proposed that when certain pre-potently emotional and positive messages are presented to subjects or patients subliminally (i.e., in extremely brief visual flashes of approximately 4 milliseconds, which subjects report they cannot detect), these messages "bypass" the ego's defenses and produce emotional reactions that are usually quite positive and facilitative of adaptive behavior (see Hardaway, 1990, for a thorough review of this work; also see Weinberger, Kelner, & McClelland, 1997; but see also Fudin, 2001). The phrase typically flashed is "*Mommy and I are one.*" A control group is usually exposed to the neutral phrase: "*People are walking.*" The idea here is that the "*Mommy and I are one*" message may trigger associations to archaic and powerful representations of reunion and succor that are hardwired in the human species.

What is particularly impressive about this methodology is that it is double blind: Neither the researcher nor the subject is aware of the stimulus that is being used on any specific occasion. These procedures have been used with clinical and nonclinical groups, with samples including undergraduates, schizophrenics, depressives, alcoholics, phobics, and eating disordered individuals. While the results have been by no means consistent, and the debate continues to be heated, a meta-analysis of 64 methodologically sound studies (Hardaway, 1990) revealed that there is a small, but significant effect of subliminal exposure such that the "*Mommy and I are one*" groups demonstrate behaviors and attitudes consistent with a positive emotional state. Further, there is some "softer" evidence that the effect of this message is greatly *lessened* if it is presented for a long-enough period of time (e.g., 10 seconds) that the subject both perceives and notices what the message actually is. Apparently noticing the message actually reduces its influence.

The idea that perceived, but unnoticed, information can affect mental function is now not so hotly contested. The general acceptance of the importance of preconsciously processed information (information that is registered without reaching awareness) can be traced to how cognitive scientists have conducted research over the past 20 years: First they successfully disengaged the concept of a cognitive unconscious from some of its more arcane Freudian connections (Bowers, 1984). They did this by proceeding in a more inductive fashion, research observation by research observation, rather than by proceeding deductively by explicitly testing Freud's hypotheses. Second, cognitive scientists conducted careful, sometimes brilliant, programmatic research that netted a great deal of respect within the general scientific community (see, for instance, John Kilhstrom's [1987] review article "The Cognitive Unconscious," published in the influential journal *Science)*.

THE UNCONSCIOUS AS THE NOTICED, BUT UNCOMPREHENDED

Up to this point we have sampled some evidence suggesting that we can indeed be influenced by stimuli that we cannot, or do not, notice. But simply equating the unconscious with what is "unnoticed but influential" is logically over-restrictive. There is the possibility that we might selectively attend to an event (notice it), be powerfully influenced by it, yet remain oblivious to its effect on our thoughts, attitudes, feelings, and actions. Even if we notice it, if we do not *comprehend* the effect of a stimulus feature or event, we have been unconsciously influenced by it.

Nisbett and Wilson (1977) presented a comprehensive, empirically based argument that humans simply have little or no direct access to their own higher-order cognitive processes. That is, people know what they do, what they feel, and what they think, but they do not really know why or how they "got there." Surely people offer articulate, believed-in explanations for almost everything: why they feel attracted to a lover, why they hired a certain individual, how they solved a problem, or why they behaved in one way or another. But Nisbett and Wilson argue that these explanations are almost always off the mark. Typically people fail to notice what is in fact influential.

Nisbett and Wilson (1977) begin with a description of a fascinating study on insight. Maier (1931) hung two cords from his laboratory ceiling. The room was a jumble of tools, clamps, and poles. The subject was asked to solve a problem: He or she must find a way to tie the two cords together. The problem was that the cords were placed far enough apart that the subject could not hold on to one cord and reach the other without letting go the first cord. While the subject puzzled over the task, Maier wandered around the room aimlessly for several minutes. There were three ways to solve the problem, but Maier was interested in one particular solution: The subject could tie pliers to one cord and begin to swing it widely; meanwhile he or she could run to the second cord bringing it as close as possible to the first (swinging) cord; then he or she could catch the swinging first cord and tie the two together. About 40% of the subjects eventually solved the problem within 10 minutes. But for those who did not, Maier casually, but cunningly wandered over to one of the cords, "happening" to set the cord in motion. He found that within 45 seconds the subject invariably solved the problem. Yet when these subjects were later asked how they arrived at the solution, most offered no reference to the clue: "It just dawned on me"; "It was the only thing left," and so on. Further probing by Maier after free recall was relatively futile: Subjects apparently had no recognition or appreciation that the clue helped them solve the problem.

There is much of the anecdote in Maier's report. But as Nisbett and Wilson (1977) point out, the research literature is replete with subjects who are influenced by events and stimulus features they notice but do not appreciate as relevant to their response. Earlier in this chapter I briefly described the nylon stocking experiment (Nisbett & Wilson, 1977) in which subjects were powerfully influenced by the position of the stockings (farthest to the right), yet remained adamant that this played no role in their decision as to which stocking was of highest quality. But there are many more such studies across a broad range of social influence factors illustrating that we are unaware of much of what goes on in our minds. Or as Pascal put it: The heart has reasons which reason does not know. For instance:

1. French students rate capital W, the least common letter in French, as their least favorite. These subjects dismiss the idea that it is lack of familiarity that causes disliking (Nuttin, 1987).
2. We prefer mirror image pictures of ourselves over real-image pictures of ourselves apparently because that is what we most often see when we gaze into the mirror (Mita, Dermer, & Knight, 1977).
3. Even when we systematically chart our moods along with daily events we have little or no insight into what situations were actually related to our moods (Stone, Hedges, Neale, & Satin, 1985).
4. Subjects who were about to be exposed to increasing levels of electrical shock were first given a placebo pill and told that it causes heart palpitations and breathing irregularities (some usual effects of being shocked). These subjects endured four times more electric shock than control subjects who were not given such a placebo, presumably because they could blame the symptoms on the pill and not the shock. Yet when questioned about why they endured so much more shock than average, they did not mention the pill at all. When directly informed of the study's results, the subjects politely assured the researchers that while this might be true for some subjects, it was not true for them (Nisbett & Wilson, 1977).
5. People are less likely to help a distressed person as the number of witnesses or bystanders increases (Latané & Darley, 1970). Yet when subjects in these experiments are explicitly asked whether they believe that the number of bystanders influenced their behavior, they uniformly deny this possibility.

Although his comment seems to violate the cherished, commonsense idea about our capacity for self-knowledge, Winston Churchill was quite probably right when he surmised that man will occasionally stumble over the truth, but most of the time he will pick himself up and continue on. Though we often mumble quite impressive explanations as to how we came to be on the ground, and why we got up, the fact is that we may have little special knowledge of either. Readers may want to try the exercise in Activity Box 8.1. The activity illustrates how someone may cause an event but not understand how their actions make it occur.

THE UNCONSCIOUS AS RETAINED, BUT UNAVAILABLE, MEMORY OF ACTUAL EVENT

So far we have examined the evidence for the unconscious as unnoticed, and the unconscious as the noticed, but not appreciated. Now we consider the unconscious as something akin to "the repressed." First, let me be clear about what we are *not* addressing in this section. We are *not* asking: Can an *event* (an early trauma, a neglectful or loving early environment) be influential even though it is not remembered? The answer to this question is an unimpeachable "of course." For instance, it is almost certain that the first three years of our

Activity Box 8.1	**Chevreul's Pendulum**

On an 8 1/2 by 11 inch paper draw the largest circle you can (say, 4" radius). Draw two perpendicular straight lines through the center of the circle. Now you have a circle with four equal parts. Next have some kind of pendulum by your side. It could be something as simple as a string tied to a small, but heavy metal bolt, a watch bob with a long chain, or a crystal pendant of some kind. The string or chain should be 15 to 18 inches long. Have a friend sit in a chair beside you. Place in her lap the paper with one of the axes pointed directly at her belly button. The other axis will of course be perpendicular. Now, have your friend hold the pendulum in front of her so the heavy end of the pendulum is just an inch or so above the center of the circle. Next, you set the pendulum swinging on the vertical axis (the axis that points toward the subject). Right after you do this, instruct the subject in the following way:

> Now I would like you to concentrate really hard on the idea that this pendulum will begin to swing along the other axis (sideways). Think really really hard about this. Keep your eyes focused on the end of the pendulum and concentrate on the pendulum swinging sideways . . . swinging sideways, concentrate really hard on it swinging sideways.

In a few moments what you will almost inevitably find is that the pendulum does in fact begin to swing sideways to some extent. Your friend will note this, but will probably be completely unaware of the reason for it.

What *is* the reason? Is the "mental energy" of your friend's thoughts forcing the pendulum to swing sideways? Well, in a way, yes. The physical properties of the pendulum are such that it exaggerates the very very small muscle movements which your friend is making without knowing it. The visual result (a sideways swing) is much more noticeable than the tiny movements that produce them. Your friend is actually causing the sideways swing by making these little muscle movements in her fingers and hand. But she does not know it. Typically it is difficult to convince the subject that she is indeed physically making the pendulum swing sideways, or that she is making any tiny movements at all.

This phenomenon is called the Chevreul's Pendulum Illusion and has been studied extensively (e.g., Easton & Shor, 1976). Almost everyone experiences it, unless he or she is consciously trying to oppose it. As such, it is not considered to be a hypnotic phenomenon. Thus the subject is aware of your directions to think of the pendulum swinging sideways, but is not aware of how the sideways swinging happens.

lives are immensely formative; yet, as adults, we remember almost nothing of them. It is a bitter pill to swallow, but it is probably true that because of how the brain functions and matures, no adult memory exists for most of the really influential early events (before age 2 or 3) that shaped who we are as people; and some of the adult memories we do have about our childhood may be quite trivial (Howe & Courage, 1993, 1997; Simcock, & Hayne, 2002).

Notes on the Nature of Memory

Instead, what we are asking is: Can a memory be stored and influential, yet unnoticed (not retrievable)? Before we throw ourselves into this question, we need to be aware of two misconceptions about memory that can obstruct our understanding of unconscious processes. First, memory is not immaculate. Everything that happens to us is not literally "stored somewhere" in the brain as it happened, as though our brain was some type of carbon-based videotape or compact disk. Our memory does not work like a soap opera flashback. What occurs to us over the years is imperfectly encoded and stored in a fashion that conforms to our ways of seeing the world and ourselves (Schacter, 1995). As these ways of seeing the world change for one reason or another (e.g., maturation, psychotherapy, brainwashing, new information, religious conversion, being a parent, loss of a loved one), the memories change.

Second, memory is not one "thing." Though much of the time we experience memory as a unitary process, we are fairly sure now that there are different kinds of memory that are "housed" or processed in different parts of the brain. For our purposes the distinction between explicit and implicit memory is exceedingly important and is discussed below. But we must be mindful that even though it seems like a cakewalk for us in our day-to-day lives, the process of memory is complex and multiphasic (not unitary). I will now very briefly describe two ways in which memories might be nonconscious but still have obvious effects on behavior.

When We Implicitly "Know," but Explicitly "Don't Know"

People suffering from a neurological condition, Korsakoff's syndrome, which is often associated with chronic alcoholism, have a peculiar pattern of memory dysfunction: That is, when asked what they were doing just a few moments ago, they will have no idea whatsoever. They have no ability to recall any episode that has happened to them no matter how recent (Kihlstrom, 1987). In other words they have no explicit memory for any episodes or events that happen to them. Nevertheless, they are perfectly capable of learning new factual information, motor skills, and vocabulary skills. If a Korsakoff patient walks over to the office calendar to find out the date of the office picnic, when she returns to her own office she will have no memory whatsoever of having walked to the office calendar (no explicit memory for the event). Yet if asked when the office picnic is, she knows (displays implicit memory). When asked how she knows, she draws a blank. This is sometimes called source amnesia. She does not know how or where she acquired the information. Clearly this is an example of some type of memory trace being influential, even though there is no appreciation for how the information was acquired.

The distinction between explicit and implicit memory has been demonstrated with nonpatients as well. For instance, dichotic listening is a procedure in which a subject is given two different messages, one in each ear, and is instructed to attend to and "shadow" only one. When, for instance, subjects listen to and immediately repeat word-for-word a speech heard over one side of their headset, it has been shown that they never remember different information presented on the other side of the headset. Subjects seem "too busy" shadowing the speech to attend to the other headset speaker (Bryden & MacRae, 1989; MacKay, 1973; Voyer & Flight, 2000). However, even though the subjects do not explicitly remember the information on the unattended side (subjects cannot remember what words were presented), the information has an effect on how these same subjects interpreted words and sentences presented to them later (implicit memory).

In sum, memory is not just a unitary, single-stage process. Explicit memory and implicit memory are distinct, and it appears that we can have access to the latter without access to the former. Our moods, thoughts, and actions may be influenced by new information we have no memory of acquiring. At these times, we may find ourselves acting upon, knowing, or thinking about information we cannot remember encountering.

Repression as Freud Would Have It

Thus far we have illustrated how memory of an event can be stored in such a way that it is inaccessible (no explicit memory), but influential (implicit memory). When this occurs, the context in which the information was learned, the actual initial encounter with the information, is not retrievable ever. In these cases implicit never becomes explicit. Psychoanalytic concepts of the unconscious go much further than this: Psychoanalytic theory contends that memories that are fully encoded, stored, and influential can nonetheless be held outside of awareness *and that under certain circumstances these memories are fully retrievable.*

The quintessential illustration of repression is still posthypnotic amnesia. In fact, it was by observing hypnotic patients in a 19th-century French medical facility that eventually led Freud to hypothesize the concept of repression. Consider this typical experimental scenario: A very good hypnotic subject is hypnotized and given a number of suggestions to which he responds splendidly. Sometime during the procedure he is told (correctly) that Bob Hope's father was a fireman. Near the end of the procedure the experimenter suggests that after hypnosis is terminated the subject will be wide awake, but will remember *nothing* of what happened during hypnosis until the experimenter gives him a signal. Further, the subject is told that after hypnosis is over, whenever the experimenter says the word "three" the subject will switch chairs, but not know why. Hypnosis is then terminated and the subject is asked what happened: He can remember nothing. He is offered money to remember anything about what happened during hypnosis—still nothing. The experimenter casually says "three" during the interaction . . . the subject gets up and moves to another chair. When asked why, the subject says, "I don't really know." When pressed, he says: "Well, it just looked more comfortable." He is asked several obscure questions, one of which is about the occupation of Bob Hope's father. He says "fireman." He does not know where that knowledge comes from. Then, with a pre-arranged signal, the experimenter lifts the amnesia and asks, "Now what do you remember about the hypnosis." The subject gives a full accounting of all the suggestions including the posthypnotic suggestion for switching chairs.

This is the type of demonstration that impressed Freud so much. And it is the type of scenario that has been examined in many research studies (for a review, see Pettinati, 1988; also see Barnier, 2002). Now on the surface of it, this example looks like another case of source amnesia: The subject initially does not remember how or when he acquired the signal to switch chairs or the oc-cupation of Bob Hope's father, but he both performs and answers correctly. But there is an exceedingly important difference here: The amnesia is reversible. Un-like Korsakoff patients who never remember what they have forgotten, unlike the dichotic listening subjects who simply have no way of accessing what they heard in the unattended ear, our hypnotic subject remembered everything quite clearly once the suggestion to remember was given. This is important because it documents that a fully intact (implicit and explicit) memory of the events dur-ing hypnosis was present, yet inaccessible immediately after hypnosis.

This is the prototype that Freud applied to his concept of repression. In fact, as Kihlstrom (in press) points out: "Posthypnotic amnesia is the only memory disorder studied under laboratory conditions where implicit memories can be restored to explicit recollection." For Freud, the person outside hypno-sis is motivated to repress a certain memory not because of an outside influence (the hypnotist's suggestion in hypnosis), but because the memory is somehow horribly threatening. For Freud, repression was a type of motivated forgetting, but a forgetting that could be undone.

Other than in the hypnosis laboratory, what is the research evidence that this particular type of repression occurs? The answer is that the scientific com-munity is nowhere near agreement. Two influential articles reviewed nearly the same research literature and came to astonishingly opposite conclusions on whether repression exists or not (Erdelyi, 1985; Holmes, 1990). The atmos-phere is so thick with controversy that even the following anemic synthesis I offer here would probably draw withering fire from both camps:

> Under certain circumstances, events that might otherwise be accurately represented in memory may nonetheless fail to reach awareness because they are associated with feelings of threat or fear. These events might later be remembered in weakened form. But, there is precious little evidence for the idea that people can experience a com-plete, decades-long amnesia for some particular event (e.g., childhood sexual trauma), then later in life suddenly remember it in exquisite and accurate detail.

I feel this to be a reasonable, but admittedly "middle of the road" position. It is flanked by two admirably well-entrenched camps: people who feel repres-sion simply never happens (see Loftus, 1993) and people who feel that it is ubiquitous (Herman, 1992).

THE UNCONSCIOUS AS PERSONAL FICTION THAT "FEELS LIKE" MEMORY OF ACTUAL EVENT

The Fallibility of Memory

Can noticed stimuli and experiences be encoded and stored in such a way that they elicit "memories" of events that in fact never occurred; and the interper-sonal/social factors that create these memory errors are unappreciated by the subject? If cultural and psychological factors can create the need to forget (re-press) memories of events that occurred, why then can these same factors not operate in such a way as to create memories of events that never happened?

The conceptual sword surely cuts both ways. Consider this actual case from Garry and Loftus (1994, pp. 363–364):

> A woman and her daughter were bound, raped, and sodomized at gun point in their home. The next day the woman's boyfriend insisted that the rapist must be somebody she knew. "You've seen him in the neighborhood, you've seen him somewhere before . . . at the grocery store, or at church. . . at a party somewhere . . ." Suddenly at the word "party" the woman "saw" the face of a man Clarence Von Williams (the husband of a co-worker). In short, though there was no collaborating evidence, Mr. Von Williams was convicted of aggravated rape and sentenced to 50 years in prison. Two months later a 32-year-old man was arrested and confessed to 70 crimes in seven states, one of which was the Von Williams case. Mr. Von Williams was immediately released. When the woman viewed the taped confession, she refused to believe it, insisting that Von Williams was the rapist, even though the videotaped confessions disclosed details that only the rapist could have known. The woman remained unimpressed.

Similarly, consider the media attention devoted to satanic ritual abuse, UFO abductions, and past life regressions. People who report these types of phenomena are for the most part well-intentioned people who genuinely believe they have undergone these experiences. Ganaway (1991) reports that up to 50% of hospitalized patients with multiple personality disorder (people who experience themselves as having more than one personality) report satanic ritualistic abuse involving heinous, even cannibalistic crimes carried out by an organized network of secret covens. These fantastic accounts, although compellingly rendered, have never been confirmed by law enforcement authorities. Much of the same can be said for UFO abduction stories (Newman, 1997) and reports of having lived a past-life (Spanos, Burgess, & Burgess, 1994). What is fascinating about all these stories is that they are by and large not hoaxes but are intensely believed-in fantasies that people experience as vivid memory.

How on earth can people be so absolutely certain they have experienced something when indeed they have not? First, it is wrapped up in the nature of memory itself. Memory is not emblazoned on the brain at the time of the event, never to be changed. Rather, memory is constantly shifting, changing, and expanding according to new information. Second, there is the problem of source amnesia. Under certain situations humans may have little ability to distinguish the actual episode (explicit context) in which they acquired the "memory": Was it an actual event? Was it a daydream? Was it a bit of misinformation embedded in a question asked by the investigator? Was it a wish?

A fine theory you say, but can it be demonstrated in the laboratory. The answer is yes. A growing number of studies appear to document that false memories can, and do, occur under laboratory and field conditions (Loftus, 1994, 1997).

Embedding Inaccurate Information in Memories

It is patently clear now that an eyewitness's memory can be changed via subtle misinformation embedded in the investigator's questioning. Subjects who were asked how fast the cars were going when they "smashed into each other" reported more broken glass at the scene then those asked the same question using the words "hit" or "collide." There was no glass in actuality. If the investigator asks a question about the speed of the car as it passed a fictional barn, subjects later confidently report having seen a barn (Garry & Loftus, 1994).

Creating Complete Memories for Events That Never Happened

From the laboratory we have Loftus and Pickrell's (1995) report of experimentally implanting memories of childhood trauma that in fact never occurred. Loftus asked several subjects to write down daily what they could remember of four incidents that purportedly happened in their childhood; three of the events actually did happen, and one false event was supplied by a family member. Each day the subjects wrote what they could remember. If they could remember nothing, they were instructed to report this. In all cases the false memory was of being lost in a shopping center at a very young age, then finally being rescued. Subjects ranging in age from 8 to 42 years of age came to believe quite adamantly that the false memory was true, supplying sometimes vivid detail as to the smells, colors, and emotions of the event.

Ceci, Loftus, Leichtman, and Bruck (1994) found that by asking leading questions it was possible to mislead preschoolers into believing they had experienced things that in fact never happened.

In summing up this sampler of research on the unconscious I would like to share a quote by Kenneth Bowers: "Our days of labor and expectant waiting are occasionally interrupted by our reveries, our contemplations, and our dreams, and it is perhaps the surfacing of this unconscious, night side of thinking that permits some of our best ideas to see the light of day" (Bowers, 1984, p. 264).

SUMMARY OF UNCONSCIOUS INFLUENCE

While many questions about the unconscious await answer, we now do know more about how we are affected by events outside our awareness:

We are unconsciously influenced by the unnoticed. We somehow are influenced by events we perceive, but do not (or cannot) notice.

We are unconsciously influenced by the noticed, but unappreciated. We may notice events that indeed affect us, but sometimes we utterly fail to *comprehend* that they are having a powerful effect on us.

We are unconsciously influenced by "irretrievable" memories. We sometimes can operate on the basis of information that seems to be stored in our brain, but we can see no explicit connection to how or when it was learned.

We can unwittingly come to "believe our own propaganda" about the past. Our memories are not written in stone but instead are quite malleable. We can be unwittingly influenced so that memories change or are entirely fabricated via suggestion, fancy, imagination, and wish. We have little or no capacity to know whether this has happened, or to "correct" it when it has.

ON EXHUMING UNCONSCIOUS MEMORIES: WHAT, IF ANYTHING, IS REGRESSED ABOUT HYPNOTIC AGE REGRESSION?

I will now share a series of studies on hypnotic age regression to illustrate the pitfalls of research in the field of memory and repression. As a first step though, it is necessary to delineate how hypnosis and hypnotizability are measured.

Hypnotic scales are administered to individual subjects and involve rigorously standardized hypnotic induction procedures (a set of instructions administered by the hypnotist that invites the subject to become hypnotized and typically includes suggestions for relaxation and for full experience of suggestions during the session). Typically the induction is followed by a series of 12 suggestions to which the subject either responds behaviorally or not. If the subject responds behaviorally to the suggestion, he or she passes that item. If he or she does not respond to the suggestion, he or she fails that item. The subject's score is the total number of items (or suggestions) passed. Thus scores on these tests can range from 0 (no items passed) to 12 (all items passed) with individuals scoring on the lower end of the spectrum being less "hypnotizable," and those at the upper end being more hypnotizable. Hypnotizability is roughly normally distributed. More people score in the midrange (5–7) than in the low (0–4) or high (8–12) ranges. Most people (95%) can experience hypnosis to some extent. Hypnotizability is a very stable trait with test-retest reliabilities quite similar to those for intelligence even when the second test is 30 years after the first (Piccione, Hilgard, & Zimbardo, 1989).

In hypnotic age regression, a hypnotized person is typically given suggestions to relive an event that occurred at an earlier age and to "be and feel like" a child of that age. In the case of a highly hypnotizable adult given suggestions to regress to childhood, the changes in behavior and demeanor are often dramatic (e.g., childlike language, tears, infantile behavior, vivid details of surroundings, compelling emotion, regressed drawings). The subject herself sometimes becomes so startled by the vivid experience she experiences herself as "reliving," and not just remembering, the past during hypnosis. Several years ago my laboratory carried out a series of studies on this topic that successfully validated what we thought was a novel new twist on the genuineness of these regressions. But as is all too often the case in such matters, our "clever" ideas were eventually turned upside down and inside out by new data.

The question at issue was this: Does hypnotic age regression enable subjects to exhibit developmentally previous (i.e., genuinely childlike) modes of mental functioning? If it does, and hypnotically regressed adults can behave and think more like actual children than can unhypnotized adults, we have some reasonably solid evidence for a psychoanalytic notion of the unconscious as repository of "repressed" but ultimately accessible memory. It is an important and exciting possibility. Indeed, when one reviews the 80-year research history on this topic, one discovers claims that hypnotically age regressed adults resemble children in that their EEG patterns mimic those of childhood; their eye movements are childlike; they display the Babinski response; their IQ test responses are age appropriate, their vocabulary is childlike; they respond to Piagetian cognitive tasks as children do; they respond to perceptual illusions as children do; they respond to a host of projective and objective personality tests like children; and they write and spell like children. Unfortunately, most of this literature is methodologically flawed (Nash, 1987). When we critically examine only the methodologically sound studies we generally find the behavior of age regressed adults is not really similar to that of actual children. And on the rare occasion when it is, motivated, nonhypnotized subjects can do just as well. Generally the performance of hypnotically age regressed subjects is no more genuine than that of any adult trying to "act" childlike. Nor does memory for details of the past seem any sharper.

But we were nonetheless impressed with two aspects of hypnotic age regression: its marked emotional intensity, and its helpfulness with patients in psychotherapy. It occurred to us that we might still rescue the "genuine regression" idea. We noted that almost all the previous research was carried out in the emotionally sterile confines of a laboratory. Could it be that the flesh and blood of hypnotic age regression might express itself most clearly under conditions of heightened emotion? If extremely emotional material (more typical of actual clinical situations) were meaningfully presented to hypnotically age regressed subjects, they might display a more complete reinstatement of childlike emotional processes than would nonhypnotized control subjects. Thus, we embarked on a psychoanalytically informed empirical test of this idea. It was to lead us places we did not intend to go.

Study 1: Operationalizing Our Ideas and Testing Them

Our initial, and most important, decision was how to define a childlike emotional response: We had to pick something fairly subtle so that adult controls might be fooled (Nash, Johnson, & Tipton, 1979). We settled on the concept of the transitional object as delineated by D. W. Winnicott (1953). In short, infants of both sexes become attached to some external plaything—for example, a teddy bear, blanket, furry animal, soft or hard toy. The first "not me" possession is transitional in two ways: First, the teddy bear or blanket is symbolic, representing the love and security of the mother. Second, the transitional object involves a mix of primitive ways of relating to the self and others such that it pulls for profound affect (typically 3-year-olds love their object fiercely). What makes this psychoanalytic construct of the transitional object so useful is that it has been studied empirically. We actually know something about how real children use these objects. So we know that 59% of children in Western cultures have these objects. Further we know (Gaddini & Gaddini, 1970; Rudhe & Ekecrantz, 1974) the following characteristics of transitional objects for 3-year-olds:

1. *Spontaneously desired.* They become absolutely necessary at bedtime or at times of loneliness, depression, or threat. Sixty percent of children have a transitional object, and they are spontaneously requested at times of stress.
2. *Specific.* Seventy-eight percent of small children who have a transitional object display rigid and vigorous adherence to one, and only one, such object. They will accept no substitutes.

3. *Emotionally intense.* The transitional object is affectionately cuddled as well as excitedly loved, sometimes until quite tattered.

Our idea for a research project began to take form. What would happen if we screened for, and selected, outstandingly responsive hypnotic subjects and exposed each subject individually to the following procedure: hypnotize and hypnotically age regress subjects to the age of 3? The wording of the hypnotic age regression suggestion would be this:

> In a moment I am going to count backward from (your present age) to 3. As I do, you will go backward in time. When I reach the count of "three" you will be 3 years old. You will continue to hear me and do what I tell you to do, but you will otherwise be and feel as you did when you were 3 years old. You will be 3 years old. But no matter what you experience you will continue to hear my voice even if you do not recognize me. . . . [As the experimenter counts back he intersperses the numbers with comments.] You are getting smaller and smaller, younger and younger, once more a little boy/girl.

We would then suggest that Mommy was out of sight and further suggest fear of being alone; and then ask open questions: "What is happening? What else is happening? What are you touching?" Would the subject *spontaneously* mention or request a transitional object? Would the object be *specific*, or would more than one object be requested? Would independent judges rate the response to be emotionally intense? If adult hypnotic subjects really responded to these situations like actual 3-year-olds, 59% of them should display a transitional object spontaneously, about 78% of these objects should be specific, and the response to the object should be quite emotional.

But the informed skeptic might well say: "Even if you get the results you think you will, with hypnotized subjects acting like children, that does not necessarily mean that the hypnotized subjects did anything special. After all, there is no need to theorize about the unconscious if normal unhypnotized people can guess what the experimenter wants and successfully mimic 3-year-old behavior relying only on their own conscious understanding of how children behave at that age." This is a very good point. Thus is born the control group, or more precisely, the quasi-control group.

For our study we chose a design that would enable us to assess the possibility that the childlike behavior of our hypnotic subjects had little to do with hypnosis and everything to do with an attempt to please the experimenter and conform to the role of a good hypnotic subject. Our control group consisted of special subjects (simulators) whom we had earlier found to be unable to enter hypnosis in any substantial way. Just before the experimental situation the project director told all these subjects that in a few minutes they would be working with a hypnotist. Each subject was to FAKE being a good hypnotic subject. No coaching was given. The simulating subjects were told that success was related to intelligent use of situational cues. And they were told that the hypnotist did not know who were real hypnotic subjects and who were faking, but if the experimenter detected someone faking, he would stop the experiment immediately. It was in fact true that the experimenter/hypnotist did not know who was real and who was faking (it is essentially impossible for even the most experienced hypnotists to tell the difference anyway). But it was *not* true that the experimenter would stop the procedure. Subjects were then led to the experimental room and were treated precisely as were the real hypnotic subjects.

There is a two-step logic to this design: First, if meaningful hypnotic age regression involves a reinstatement of genuinely childlike affective processes, then the behavior of real hypnotic subjects should closely correspond to that of actual children (their transitional objects should be spontaneous, specific, and emotionally intense). Second, before we can confidently attribute any childlike response of our hypnotic subjects to a reinstatement of unconscious modes of relating, we must eliminate the possibility that these responses could be the product of conscious role-playing. We can be reasonably sure that play acting is not a major factor if the simulators do a miserable job mimicking the behavior of the real hypnotized subjects (and by extension, that of children).

We hypothesized that hypnotized subjects and actual children would look much the same across spontaneity, specificity, and intensity; and that simulators would perform quite differently from both the real hypnotized subjects and children on these same measures. We carefully scripted all these procedures and completed the study.

The experimenter considered an object to be a spontaneous transitional object if the subject mentioned its presence or desired presence in two of three stress situations. A spontaneous response was scored as 1, and a nonspontaneous response was scored as 0. For the specificity measure, the number of objects named in response to the question "Would you like anything else?" was recorded. A negative response (specific) was scored as 1, a positive response of any number was scored as 0. Four intensity ratings were obtained for each subject. The hypnotist/experimenter evaluated the intensity manifested in the subject's response to the last three questions on a scale from 1 to 5. The hypnotist/experimenter also gave a subjective intensity rating from 1 to 5, low to high, based on general affect and nonverbal behaviors. By testing some subjects preexperimentally, interrater reliability was found to be acceptable on these ratings. All four intensity measures were summed across questions to give each subject an intensity score with a possible range of 4 to 20.

Figure 8.1 summarizes the results. Eleven of 16 hypnotized subjects spontaneously produced transitional objects under stress (69%). Just four of the 15 simulators were spontaneous under the same conditions (27%). Approximately 60% of children are reported to require transitional objects during stressful times. Similarly, 75% of hypnotized subjects requested just one object (i.e., were specific), compared to 41% for simulators. Again, the norm for children is approximately 78%. Finally the experimenter (blind to whether subjects were hypnotized or simulators) rated emotional intensity on a scale from 4 to 20. Hypnotized subjects' emotional intensity was significantly higher ($M = 13.50$), compared to the emotional intensity of simulators ($M = 7.53$), $p < .05$. As Figure 8.1 demonstrates, across spontaneity and specificity measures hypnotized adults and actual children looked similar in their response to transitional objects. That similarity could not be mimicked by simulators exposed to exactly the same procedures. Not only were simulators significantly different from hypnotized subjects; they were also significantly

Figure 8.1 | Performance of children, hypnotized subjects, and simulators on the spontaneity and specificity measure.

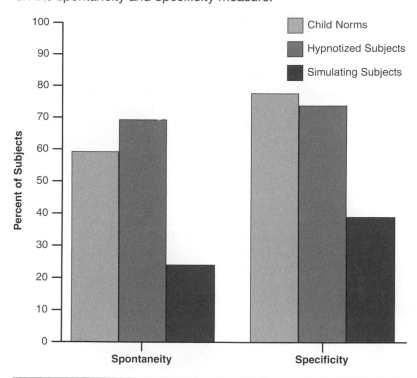

different from children. We boldly interpreted these findings to mean that there was a more complete reinstatement of a past (otherwise unconscious) emotional state for subjects experiencing meaningful hypnotic age regression.

Study 2: Replicating and Extending Our Findings

We were encouraged, but still puzzled. Our positive findings concerning genuine regression seemed to run counter to the bulk of empirical work, which suggested that hypnotic age regression was nothing more than good acting. Further, most empirical studies suggest that after the age of 10, people's earliest recollections do not date back before the age of 3 or 4 (Howe & Courage, 1993, 1997). Our results seem to fly in the face of these findings. We were on record saying that the procedure had elicited personalized, strong feelings. Maybe this accounted for our unusual findings. Or maybe it was because the measures taken during the procedure focused on emotion (rather than thinking). In a follow-up study (Nash, Lynn, Stanley, Frauman, & Rhue, 1985) we decided to examine the first possibility. In our first study we scared, and in some cases terrified, our hypnotically regressed subjects by suggesting that "Mommy" was inexplicably "gone." In a sense we induced separation anxiety. What would happen if our hypnotic subjects were not overwrought, if they were regressed to age 3 but given suggestions for Mommy to be right there with them (in sight), in several different contexts. Would we lose our effects because the experimental situation was no longer "electric" with emotions?

The answer is "no." The hypnotic subjects ($n = 16$) in our second study were indeed quite calm. And they were understandably disinclined to spontaneously ask for a transitional object under such serene conditions (why ask for a Mommy-substitute when you have the real thing right there?). But when a transitional object was explicitly suggested, the hypnotic subjects were specific in their selection (one and only one object), and they were rated as being more emotionally attached to the object than the simulators. Simulators ($n = 15$) were unerringly miserable in their rendition of what a real hypnotic subject would do (or a child for that matter). They tended to ask for multiple objects, and they were not particularly attached to them. With the exception of the spontaneity variable, the pattern of results of Study 2 conformed to that of Study 1. All of this seemed to suggest that it was not WHAT we did with our Study 1 subjects (render them emotionally overwrought) that accounted for our results, but rather it was WHERE we looked for the regressed effect: in the realm of emotional functioning. Study 2 subjects could be perfectly calm but elicit the same accurate childlike responses.

Study 3: The Wake-Up Call

When we submitted our manuscripts to professional journals, it became clear to us that we were meeting with unusually stiff resistance. In retrospect, between the time that Study 1 and Study 2 were conducted, the American Medical Association and the Society for Clinical and Experimental Hypnosis had both issued stern public statements about the inadvisability of using hypnosis for law enforcement purposes: Their point was that hypnosis does not really "refresh" memory, and it actually causes problems with overconfidence once the hypnosis is ended. Our studies were running against this current in some respects. Reviewers pressed us on two points:

First, we had acknowledged in Study 2 that the differences between hypnotized subjects and simulators in regard to transitional objects could conceivably be due not to the presence/absence of hypnosis, but to differential history with transitional objects. That is, simulators were all low hypnotizables; hypnotic subjects were all high hypnotizables. Maybe people who are low hypnotizables, as children, just have less experience with transitional objects. Thus they would be at a loss to know how to respond appropriately. This seemed a "stretch" to us, but maybe worth a look. Second, those who bemoaned the fallibility of memory during forensic hypnosis did not "like" our results. They tended to harp on the first point and slyly hint (correctly) that we really did not know for sure whether the transitional objects mentioned during hypnosis were in fact real or imagined.

We were skeptical about these objections and somewhat inclined to dismiss them, when we realized that we might be able to actually test their validity. By a stroke of good luck, we had retained the campus addresses of subjects in the second study, both hypnotic subjects and simulators. Put simply, we called their moms (Nash, Drake, Wiley, & Khalsa, 1986). Several months after the experimental procedure we conducted (with subjects' permission) telephone interviews with the mothers of 24 of the original 30 subjects (mothers of 14 in the hypnotized group, and 10 in the control group). These interviews covered such developmental topics as birth order, methods of discipline, behavioral problems, toilet training, and imaginary playmates. Embedded in this interview was an item that described the concept of transitional objects and asked mothers to identify what, if any, were used by the subject in question. The interviews with mothers were conducted by research assistants who were not aware of experimental group membership, nor were they informed of the specific nature of the investigation.

An independent panel of raters judged the matches between transitional objects reported by the subject and those reported by the mother. Raters also judged whether objects reported in the hypnotic recollection condition matched objects reported in the posthypnotic recollection condition. A match was scored between two reports if all three judges agreed that the object referred to in both reports was indeed the same object. If there was any disagreement, the two reports were assumed not to be a match. The interrater reliability for this task was excellent, with only one disagreement on one comparison. To calculate the number of hits in each group, a hit was defined as occurring when any one of the transitional objects (or report of no transitional object) described by the subject was judged to match any one of the transitional objects (or report of no transitional object) described by the mother.

The results are summarized in Figure 8.2. First, by their mothers' accounts, 64% of hypnotized subjects and 50% of control subjects had had a transitional object when a child. This difference is not significant and is consistent with the research showing that 59% of children in Western cultures have a transitional object. These results support the findings of an earlier unpublished study that found no relationship between hypnotizability and history of transitional objects among 750 subjects (Nash, 1982).

But Figure 8.2 illustrates a vexing pattern of results concerning the accuracy of hypnotic subject report. During the hypnotic age regression procedure all 14 hypnotic subjects reported having at least one transitional object, but only three of these (21%) were confirmed by the mother. Among the controls (i.e., the simulators asked about transitional objects after the experiment was over, post-simulation), seven of them either reported a transitional object that matched one reported by the mother (three subjects) or agreed with the mother that there was no transitional object (four subjects), for a 70% accuracy. We subjected these data to a number of statistical analyses and in all cases the difference in accuracy was significant. During hypnosis, hypnotized subjects had significantly fewer "hits" with mothers than did simulators during the post-simulation interview. Even after hypnosis was terminated, subjects in the hypnotized group still had significantly fewer "hits" than did those who had been in the simulating group. In addition, the ratio of number of responses matching parent report to total number of responses given by the subject was calculated for hypnotic recollection and controls (people who had been simulating). The mean accuracy ratios were .178 and .633 for hypnotic

Figure 8.2   Percentage of "hits" between subject and parent description of transitional objects for hypnosis and control subjects.

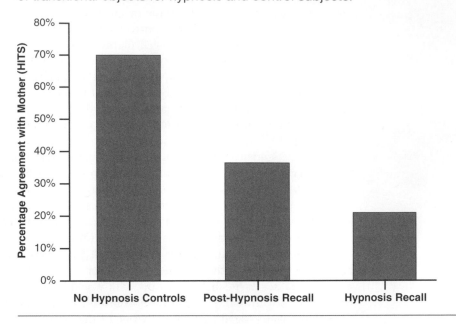

and post-simulation conditions, respectively. This difference was significant, with a greater accuracy ratio evident in the post-simulation condition.

Clearly, hypnotic subjects were enthusiastically productive. They reported a lot of transitional objects during the age regression procedure (15 of them). But this productivity was at the cost of accuracy (they were wrong almost 80% of the time). Further (we might say "worse yet"), upon post-experimental questioning, subjects who had been hypnotized went right on believing that they had had these transitional objects. In fact, during the post-experimental questioning they reported seven more transitional objects that they had not reported during hypnosis. Their post-hypnosis accuracy was 36%. The point here is that hypnotic subjects do not just believe what they report only when they are in hypnosis; they believe it afterward as well.

Maybe hypnotized subjects were just extraordinarily accurate about their transitional objects, and it was their *mothers* who were wrong. This was in fact a point never raised by the reviewers, but we did consider it. There are several good reasons to reject this position. First, the mothers of hypnotic subjects were just about on the mark when 64% of them reported that their child had had a transitional object (remember, 59% is the norm); second, our suggested regressed age (3) was right on the upper edge of childhood amnesia. Given this apparently biologically based barrier to recall it seems unlikely that an adult (even when hypnotized) would accurately remember anything earlier than age 3 or 4. The task for mothers was much simpler. They were asked as adults to remember something (i.e., their child's transitional object) that occurred *while* they themselves were adults. Third, because transitional objects are by definition ever-present companions that operate as mother-substitutes, one might reasonably expect that mothers' repeated exposure to these objects night after night, over many months and even years, would be sufficient opportunity for memory encoding Fourth, if mothers were so extraordinarily inaccurate as to be wrong about their child's transitional object (79% of the time among our hypnotized group), how would one explain that the mothers of our controls agreed with their children 70% of the time?

Why then would hypnotized subjects be so inaccurate about their transitional objects? It is a fact that under certain circumstances all of us unwittingly confabulate (fill in the gaps of our memory, Schacter, 1995). Over the past ten years it is now abundantly clear that hypnosis is a condition which, for highly hypnotizable individuals, appears to exaggerate this tendency. Further, hypnotic subjects emerge from hypnosis more confident about the validity of these confabulations than would be the case if they had never been hypnotized (Kihlstrom & Barnhardt, 1993; McConkey, 1992).

In sum, the results of Study 3 led us to agree with our critics: To the extent that a psychoanalytic conception of the "unconscious mind" implies a memory bank of detailed, pristine representations of the past, our research is not supportive. The especially distorted recall of hypnotic subjects concerning their transitional objects contradicts our contentions in Studies 1 and 2. As so often is the case in science, our data led us to a paradox: There was a genuine, age-appropriate emotional response to objects that were nonetheless inaccurately remembered or entirely made up.

How do we solve or understand this? How can something be emotionally true, completely believed in, and yet patently fictional? It is important to keep in mind that this is an ancient paradox encountered by tribal shamans, mythographers, playwrights, and thoughtful psychotherapists among others. Most psychotherapists acknowledge that the emotional tone and expressive style connected to a conflicted and believed-in "memory" of an event can be of immense help and validity in psychotherapy, even when the event has in fact never happened. Early on, Freud stopped assuming that everything his patients "remembered" about past traumas was literally true. But he adamantly maintained that the emotional tone and expressive style connected to a conflicted (and believed-in) "memory" can be of immense clinical import and validity, even when the memory is inaccurate.

It could be that hypnosis (and by extension psychotherapy) enhances access to important emotional material, but this in no way implies an accurate reliving of a specific event. The emotion is in some sense "true," but the content (e.g., the story, the details, the event) may not be. Maybe it is not "finding out the truth," or plumbing the unconscious depths for hidden events that sets us free from distress, whether in the mall reflecting on how we sorted out the quality of nylon stocking (while being pressed by a vaguely sneering experimenter), or in the therapist's office earnestly reflecting on where we "went wrong" in our life. Instead, maybe it is the telling of a compelling story about ourselves, our world, and our feelings that heals and reassures us. We are undoubtedly moved by unconscious influences, not the least of which is the deeply rooted compulsion to create and explain ourselves.

SUMMARY

The chapter begins by offering a model (first articulated by Ken Bowers) for organizing and understanding possible avenues for unconscious influence. This model focuses on *the unconscious as unnoticed* (Can a stimulus or experience be processed in such a way that it influences thoughts or actions, yet be unconscious by virtue of its being unnoticed?), *the unconscious as the noticed, but uncomprehended* (Can a noticed stimulus or experience be processed in such a way that it influences thoughts or actions, yet be unconscious by virtue of its being unappreciated as influential?), *the unconscious as a retained, but unavailable, memory of an actual event* (Can a past event be coded or stored in memory in such a way that it influences thought and action, but remains unavailable to conscious awareness?) and *the unconscious as personal fiction that "feels like" a memory of an actual event* (Can noticed stimuli and experiences be encoded and stored in such a way that they elicit "memories" of events that in fact never occurred, and the source of the false memory is unappreciated?).

The chapter then samples the research literature as it relates to each of these constructions of unconscious influence. Investigations on subliminal perception, social influence, human judgment, intuition, creativity, hypnosis, learning, and neuropathology are woven into the fabric of this treatment. While psychoanalytic notions of the unconscious are in no way dismissed, the broader perspective of cognitive science is embraced. Finally, programmatic research on hypnotic age regression as it relates to unconscious processes is presented to further illustrate the logic and challenge of such work. This line of research revealed that it is probably not accurate to think of the "unconscious mind" as a memory bank of detailed, uncontaminated representations of the past.

DISCUSSION QUESTIONS

1. Can you remember an event that happened before you were 2 years old? Are you sure it is a memory of the event itself? Or is it something you pieced together from other sources (e.g., hearing people recount the event; seeing photographs)?
2. Have you ever been absolutely certain that you witnessed an event, and later you found out the event never happened, or that you could not have witnessed it?
3. Have you ever been absolutely certain that you did *not* witness an event, and later found out that you did?
4. Have you ever used a Ouija board? How do you think it works?
5. Do you think people can influence your feelings and ideas without your being aware of it? If so, give an example.

SUGGESTED READINGS

Ellenberger, H. F. (1970). *The discovery of the unconscious: The history and evolution of dynamic psychiatry*. New York: Basic Books. This book is *the* classic, comprehensive, and scholarly treatment of Freud, and all that went before.

Bowers, K. (1976). *Hypnosis for the seriously curious*. New York: Norton. Still the most accessible, lucid description of how hypnosis fits into our understanding of how the human mind works.

Loftus, E. F. (1993). The reality of repressed memories. *American Psychologist, 48*, 518–537. Forget the title: The author critiques the research and then explains why she believes the concept of repression is bankrupt and misleading.

Loftus, F., & Pickrell, J. (1995). The formation of false memories. *Psychiatric Annals, 25, 720–725.*

Nash, M. R. (2001). The truth and hype of hypnosis. *Scientific American, 285*, 46–55. A brief and pithy primer on what hypnosis is, and what it isn't.

Nisbett, R. E., & Ross, L. (1980). *Human inference: Strategies and shortcomings of social judgment*. Englewood Cliffs, NJ: Prentice-Hall. Read this book if you want to understand how little we really know about why we do what we do in life.

Schacter, D. (Ed.). (1995). *Memory distortion: How minds, brains, and societies reconstruct the past*. Cambridge, MA: Harvard University Press. This edited book brings together some fine papers by neurologists, psychologists, and other cognitive scientists who present their views and findings on how memory becomes distorted.

SUGGESTED WEB SITES

http://sunsite.utk.edu/IJCEH/

The web site of the *International Journal of Clinical and Experimental Hypnosis* informs the reader of what hypnosis is, and what it is not.

http://ist-socrates.berkeley.edu/~psy001/jk/ psych1mem5.html

A concise overview of the psychological unconscious.

http://www.institute-shot.com/hypnosis_theories_ &_explanations.htm

The web site of the Institute for the Study of Healthcare Organizations & Transactions offers information on the history, theory, and applications of hypnosis.

INFOTRAC COLLEGE EDITION SEARCH TOPICS

Unconscious	Hypnosis	Freud
Memory	Repression	False memory

REFERENCES

Barnier, A. J. (2002). Posthypnotic amnesia for autobiographical episodes: A laboratory model of functional amnesia? *Psychological Science, 13,* 232–237.

Bowers, K. S. (1984). On being unconsciously influenced and informed. In K. S. Bowers & D. Meichenbaum (Eds.), *The unconscious reconsidered* (pp. 227–272). New York: Wiley.

Brown, C. (2002). Do female rainbowfish (Melanotaenia spp.) prefer to shoal with familiar individuals under predation pressure? *Journal of Ethology, 20*, 89–94.

Bryden, M. P., & MacRae, L. (1989). Dichotic laterality effects obtained with emotional words. *Neuropsychiatry, Neuropsychology and Behavioral Neurology, 3*, 171–176.

Ceci, S. J., Loftus, E. F., Leichtman, M. D., & Bruck, M. (1994). The possible role of source misattributions in the creation of false beliefs among preschoolers. *International Journal of Clinical and Experimental Hypnosis, 42*, 304–320.

Easton, R. D., & Shor, R. E. (1976). Information processing analysis of the Chevreul Pendulum illusion. *Journal of Experimental Psychology: Human Perception and Performance, 1,* 231–236.

Ellenberger, H. F. (1970). *The discovery of the unconscious: The history and evolution of dynamic psychiatry.* New York: Basic Books.

Erdelyi, M. H. (1985). *Psychoanalysis: Freud's cognitive psychology.* New York: Freeman.

Ericsson, K. A., & Simon, H. A. (1984). *Protocol analysis: Verbal reports as data.* Cambridge, MA: MIT Press.

Freud, S. (1900/1953). The interpretation of dreams. In J. Strachey (Ed. and Trans.), *The standard edition of the complete psychological works of Sigmund Freud* (Vol. 4, pp. 1–338; Vol. 5, pp. 339–621). London: Hogarth Press. (Original work published 1900)

Fudin, R. (2001). Problems in Silverman's work indicate the need for a new approach to research on subliminal psychodynamic activation. *Perceptual and Motor Skills, 92,* 611–622.

Gaddini, R., & Gaddini, E. (1970). Transitional objects and the process of individuation. *Journal of the American Academy of Child Psychiatry, 9,* 479–486.

Ganaway, G. K. (1991, August). *Alternative hypothesis regarding satanic ritual abuse memories.* Paper presented at the 99th annual convention of the American Psychological Association, San Francisco.

Garry, M., & Loftus, E. F. (1994). Pseudomemories without hypnosis. *International Journal of Clinical and Experimental Hypnosis, 42,* 363–378.

Greenwald, A. G., Draine, S. C., & Abrams, R. L. (1996). Three cognitive markers of unconscious semantic activation. *Science, 273,* 1699–1702.

Hardaway, R. A. (1990). Subliminally activated symbiotic fantasies: Facts and artifacts. *Psychological Bulletin, 107,* 177–195.

Herman, J. (1992). *Trauma and recovery.* New York: Simon & Schuster.

Holmes, D. (1990). The evidence for repression: An examination of sixty years of research. In J. L. Singer (Ed.), *Repression and dissociation: Implications for personality, theory, psychopathology, and health* (pp. 85–102). Chicago: University of Chicago Press.

Howe, M. L., & Courage, M. L. (1993). On resolving the enigma of infantile amnesia. *Psychological Bulletin, 113,* 305–326.

Howe, M. L., & Courage, M. L. (1997). The emergence and early development of autobiographical memory. *Psychological Review, 104,* 499–523.

Kihlstrom, J. F. (1987). The cognitive unconscious. *Science, 237,* 1445–1452.

Kihlstrom, J. F., & Barnhardt, T. M. (1993). The self-regulation of memory for better and for worse, with and without hypnosis. In D. M. Wegner & J. W. Pennebaker (Eds.), *Handbook of mental control* (pp. 88–125) Englewood Cliffs, NJ: Prentice-Hall.

Latané, B., & Darley, J. M. (1970). *The unresponsive bystander: Why doesn't he help?* New York: Appleton-Century Crofts.

Loftus, E. F. (1993). The reality of repressed memories. *American Psychologist, 48,* 518–537.

Loftus, E. F. (1997). Creating false memories. *Scientific American, 277,* 70–75.

MacKay, D. (1973). Aspects of the theory of comprehension, memory, and attention. *Quarterly Journal of Experimental Psychology, 25,* 22–40.

Maier, N. R. F. (1931). Reasoning in humans: II. The solution of a problem and its appearance in consciousness. *Journal of Comparative Psychology, 12,* 181–194.

McConkey, K. M. (1992). The effects of hypnotic procedures on remembering: The experimental findings and their implications for forensic hypnosis. In E. Fromm & M. R. Nash (Eds.), *Contemporary hypnosis research* (pp. 405–426). New York: Guilford.

Merikle, P. M., Smilek, D., & Eastwood, J. D. (2001) Perception without awareness: Perspectives from cognitive psychology. *Cognition, 79,* 115–134.

Mita, T. H., Dermer, M., & Knight, J. (1977). Reversed facial images and the mere-exposure hypothesis. *Journal of Personality and Social Psychology, 35,* 597–601.

Murphy, S. T., & Zajonc, R. B. (1993). Affect, cognition, and awareness: Affective priming with optimal and suboptimal stimulus exposure. *Journal of Personality and Social Psychology, 64,* 723–739.

Nash, M. R. (1982). *Hypnotizability and the report of having had transitional objects.* Unpublished manuscript. Ohio University, Athens, Ohio.

Nash, M. R. (1987). What, if anything, is regressed about hypnotic age regression? A review of the empirical literature. *Psychological Bulletin, 102,* 42–52.

Nash, M. R. (1994). Memory distortion and sexual trauma: The problem of false negatives and false positives. *International Journal of Clinical and Experimental Hypnosis, 42,* 346–362.

Nash, M. R., Drake, S. D., Wiley, S., & Khalsa, S. (1986). The accuracy of recall by hypnotically age regressed subjects. *Journal of Abnormal Psychology, 95,* 298–300.

Nash, M. R., Johnson, L. S., & Tipton, R. (1979). Hypnotic age regression and the occurrence of transitional object relationships. *Journal of Abnormal Psychology, 88,* 547–555.

Nash, M. R., Lynn, S. J., Stanley S., Frauman, D., & Rhue, J. (1985). Hypnotic age regression and the importance of assessing interpersonally relevant affect. *International Journal of Clinical and Experimental Hypnosis, 23,* 224–235.

Neisser, U., & Harsch, N. (1992). Phantom flash-bulbs: False recollections of hearing the news about Challenger. In E. Winograd & U. Neisser (Eds.), *Affect and accuracy in recall: Studies of "flashbulb" memories* (pp. 9–31). New York: Cambridge University Press.

Newman, L. S. (1997). Intergalactic hostages: People who report abduction by UFOs. *Journal of Social and Clinical Psychology, 16,* 151–177.

Nisbett, R. E., & Wilson, T. D. (1977). Telling more than we can know: Verbal reports on mental processes. *Psychological Review, 84,* 231–259.

Nuttin, J. M. (1987). Affective consequences of mere ownership: The name letter effect in twelve European languages. *European Journal of Social Psychology, 17,* 318–402.

Peretz, I., Gaudreau, D., & Bonnel, A. M. (1998). Exposure effects on music preference and recognition. *Memory and Cognition, 26,* 884–902.

Pettinati, H. (1988). *Hypnosis and memory.* New York: Guilford.

Piccione, C., Hilgard, E. R., & Zimbardo, P. G. (1989). On the degree of stability of measured hypnotizability over a 25-year period. *Journal of Personality and Social Psychology, 56,* 289–295.

Rotteveel, M., de-Groot, P., Geutskens, A., & Phaf, R. H. (2001). Stronger suboptimal than optimal affective priming? *Emotion, 1,* 348–368.

Rudhe, L., & Ekecrantz, L. (1974). Transitional phenomena. *Acta Psychiatrica Scandinavica, 50,* 381–400.

Sackheim, H. A., Nordlie, J. W., & Gur, R. C. (1979). A model of hysterical and hypnotic blindness: Cognition, motivation and awareness. *Journal of Abnormal Psychology, 88,* 474–489.

Schacter, D. (1995). *Memory distortion: How minds, brains, and societies reconstruct the past.* Cambridge, MA: Harvard University Press.

Seppa, T., Laurila, A., Peuhkuri, N., Piironen, J., & Lower, N. (2001). Early familiarity has fitness consequences for Arctic char (*Salvelinus alpinus*) juveniles. *Canadian Journal of Fisheries and Aquatic Sciences, 58,* 1380–1385.

Simcock, G., & Hayne, H. (2002). Breaking the barrier? Children fail to translate their preverbal memories into language. *Psychological Science, 13,* 225–231.

Silverman, L. H. (1976). Psychoanalytic theory: The reports of my death are greatly exaggerated. *American Psychologist, 31,* 621–637.

Spanos, N. P., Burgess, C. A., & Burgess, M. F. (1994). Past-life identities, UFO abductions, the satanic ritual abuse—the social construction of memories. *International Journal of Clinical and Experimental Hypnosis, 42,* 433–446.

Stone, A. A., Hedges, S. M., Neale, J. M., & Satin, M. S. (1985). Prospective and cross-sectional mood reports offer no evidence of a "blue Monday" phenomenon. *Journal of Personality and Social Psychology, 49,* 129–134.

Voyer, D., & Flight, J. (2000). Reliability of a dichotic consonant-vowel pairs task using an ABX procedure. *Brain and Cognition, 43,* 417–421.

Weinberger, J., Kelner, S., & McClelland, D. (1997). The effects of subliminal symbiotic stimulation on free-response and self-report mood. *Journal of Nervous and Mental Disease, 185,* 599–605.

Weiskrantz, L., Warrington, E. K., Sanders, M. D., & Marshall, J. (1974). Visual capacity in the hemianopic field following a restricted occipital ablation. *Brain, 97,* 709–729.

Westen, D. (1998). The scientific legacy of Sigmund Freud: Toward a psychodynamically informed psychological science. *Psychological Bulletin, 124,* 333–371.

Winnicott, D. W. (1953). Transitional objects and transitional phenomena: A study of the first not-me possession. *International Journal of Psychoanalysis, 34,* 89–97.

Wust, S., Kasten, E., & Sabel, B. A. (2002). Blindsight after optic nerve injury indicates functionality of spared fibers. *Journal of Cognitive Neuroscience, 14,* 243–253.

Wynick, S., Hobson, R. P., & Jones R. B. (1997). Psychogenic disorders of vision in childhood ("visual conversion reactions"): Perspectives from adolescence: A research note. *Journal of Child Psychology and Psychiatry and Allied Disciplines, 38,* 375–379.

Zajonc, R. B. (1980). Feeling and thinking: Preferences need no inferences. *American Psychologist, 35,* 151–175.

9 | Self-Concept, Self-Esteem, and Identity

ROY F. BAUMEISTER

CHAPTER OUTLINE

BACKGROUND

What is the self? When asked that question, small children answer by indicating their bodies. Self starts with body, in the sense that people first develop a notion of self that is based on the physical self. Older children and adults, however, have notions of selfhood that go far beyond the physical self. These notions include social identity, reputation, personal values, and other factors. They think of the self as something that exists "inside," that is, somewhere not visible to physical inspection and something separate from the palpable, physical body.

If you are asked to identify yourself, you might respond in quite different ways depending on what you were doing and who was asking. Feelings about the self may also change from time to time. There is probably a stable core to the self, but different parts or versions of the self are apparent in different circumstances. Moreover, selves do change over time in fundamental ways, so even the most stable core of the self may not be fixed and constant. You can see why it has proven difficult for psychology to come up with firm answers about the nature of the self, for the self includes stability and change, visible manifestations and inner phenomena, ideas and feelings, and other complexities.

In this chapter we will be concerned with one large region of the self—namely, self-concept and identity. Self-concept and identity refer to ideas about the self, to definitions placed on the self. This part of the self is constructed out of *meaning*. Unlike the body, which is made out of biochemical substances, the self-concept is made of meaning, which is a symbolic, social, linguistic phenomenon. Without symbols or language, there would be no self-concepts. Another way of putting this is that the self-concept is a network of interrelated ideas.

Definitions

Self is perhaps the broadest term. It has been used in many different ways, referring to many parts of a whole set of experiences and thoughts. Sometimes it is used to refer to the whole set. Some related terms are *ego, identity, self-concept, self-schema*. Because the term *self* has many meanings, different theorists have used it in different ways, and this varying usage generates some confusion. It's not always safe to assume that what one writer means by "self" is the same as what another writer means by it.

In this chapter, we will use "self" pretty much the same way the word is used in ordinary language. Your self is the totality of you, including your body, your sense of identity, your reputation (how others know you), and so on. It encompasses both the physical self and the self that is constructed out of meaning.

Self-Concept: Your Idea(s) About Yourself. The self-concept is the individual's beliefs about himself or herself, including the person's attributes and who and what the self is. The self-concept includes many things that might not be part of one's identity. For example, a person's self-concept might include many personality attributes, such as being friendly or talkative.

Self-Esteem: How You Evaluate Yourself.   An important part of the self-concept is self-esteem. A self-concept is not merely an abstract summary or notion of the self, but it is full of evaluations, that is, of perceptions of the self as good, bad, or mediocre. Self-esteem refers to the person's broadest self-evaluation. Of course, people also have levels of specific self-esteem for specific domains. Someone may regard herself, for example, as an excellent tennis player, a mediocre student, and a poor cook.

Identity: Who You Are.   Identity is a definition placed on the self. Your sense of identity refers to your knowledge of who you are. Identity always answers the question, "Who are you?" Self-concept, in contrast, may contain answers to other questions like "What kind of person are you?" and "How good are you?"

Identity may contain material that is not part of the self-concept, because identity is not fully contained inside the person's own mind. To use an extreme example, newborn babies do not have self-concepts, but they do have identities: They belong to a certain family, they soon have a name, and so on.

The concept of identity rests on two notions, sameness (continuity) and difference. Identity means being the same person you were yesterday or ten years ago; it also means being different from someone else. The task of eyewitness identification is to decide which person in the police lineup is the person who committed some crime. This means identifying someone as being the same person who performed some other deed and differentiating that person from other, innocent people. Likewise, a campus identification card links your identity across time (you have the same card for a period of time) and differentiates you from other people (for example, you are permitted to use campus facilities that others may not use).

SELF-CONCEPT

This section will cover current knowledge about the self-concept, except self-esteem, which is covered in the next section. Self-esteem is the aspect of self that has received the greatest amount of research attention as well as interest from the mass media and popular culture. It is, however, only one part of the self-concept, and so we begin with the broader issues of self-concept and self-knowledge.

Formation of the Self-Concept

Although psychology still has much to learn about how self-concepts form and develop, there is reasonable amount of information available. Psychologists have recently devised several very clever strategies to study self-concepts in very young children.

The first step in forming a self-concept is learning to distinguish between one's own body and the rest of the world. The infant learns that some things are always there, whereas others come and go. The bed, like Daddy, is only present at certain times, but one's own hands and feet are always there. Gradually the infant learns the boundaries of its own body. For a long time, self is equated with body.

How early does sense of self start? There is no way to be certain, but the signs suggest that it starts very early in life. By the time an infant is 3 months old, it likes to look at itself in the mirror, presumably because it can see that its own body movements "magically" produce movements in the image (Lewis & Brooks-Gunn, 1979). Recognizing oneself on the basis of facial features— such as recognizing a photograph rather than a moving image in a mirror— happens during the second year of life.

During this second year of life, children begin to understand that they need to conform to external standards and rules, and they begin to evaluate their own actions against external standards (Kagan, 1981). This is a big step in the growth of self-awareness. Children learn to evaluate their actions as good or bad, and they develop some concept of *mastery,* as in knowing how to do things. Obviously, at this age, there are many things one cannot do, but the child's mastery of simple skills brings him or her pleasure and satisfaction. One sign of this is that children will smile when they successfully accomplish something (Kagan, 1981). This suggests a feeling of self as capable of performing up to certain external standards.

The proper beginnings of a self-concept seem to occur around 15 months of age. At this point, children are able to identify themselves (and others) on the basis of gender and age (Damon & Hart, 1982; Lewis & Brooks-Gunn, 1979). Of course, they do not understand numerical age this early, but merely the difference between children and adults. Thus, age and gender seem to be the first ingredients of the self-concept. Familiarity is also important, implying that children's self-concepts also soon incorporate some sense of belonging to a certain family group.

During the second year of life, the child's self-concept begins to include active skills. Perhaps the first such skill to have a major impact on self-concept is the ability to walk (Erikson, 1968; Mahler, Pine, & Bergman, 1975). From ages 3 to 5, self-concepts of children seem to emphasize skills and abilities. The self is understood in terms of what it can and cannot do (Keller, Ford, & Meacham, 1978). The child's concept of self revolves around whether she can brush her teeth, tie her shoes, ride a tricycle or bicycle, tell time, and so on.

From ages 6 to 12, children's sense of competency and control normally tends to increase in a steady fashion (e.g., Brim, 1976; Erikson, 1968). Children begin to see their competencies in more complex ways than simply what they can versus cannot do. In particular, they begin to compare their competencies against those of others and to measure them by hierarchies of standards. To the young child, the issue is simply whether one can ride a bike or not. The older child is concerned with riding a bike faster, farther, or better than other children (Damon & Hart, 1982).

Another development of the period from age 6 to age 12 is the beginning of a conception of self as something inner or hidden. If you ask a young child about the self, the child will point to the body, for the young child has no other way of thinking about the self. Older children begin to develop notions of a more psychological self, including thoughts, feelings, and intentions, that go beyond the mere physical self (Mohr, 1978). The idea of an inner self is difficult for children at first, and they tend to accept whatever their parents (or other authority figures) tell them. Indeed, 11-year-old children, when asked "Who knows best what kind of person you really are, deep down inside, your mother or father or yourself?" tend to say that the mother or father knows the child better than the child knows himself or herself (Rosenberg, 1979). The idea of knowing one's own self better than anyone else—the principle of *privileged access* to one's inner self—does not become firm until adolescence.

The self-concept undergoes further refinements during the teen years. Increases in mental abilities greatly improve children's capacity to consider themselves from other, outside perspectives. In particular, teenagers are much better than younger children at imagining how they appear to someone else. As a result, self-consciousness increases greatly around age 12 or 13 (Simmons, Rosenberg, & Rosenberg, 1973; Tice, Buder, & Baumeister, 1985). Moral issues and dilemmas become important, and adolescents seek to ground their self-concept in a firm set of values, often in the form of universal or abstract principles. The self-concept comes to include ideological beliefs such as religious, political, and philosophical views (Montemayor & Eisen, 1977). Many people undergo identity crises at this age (Erikson, 1968). We shall return to the nature of identity crises at the end of this chapter.

Pursuit of Self-Knowledge

Undoubtedly people are very interested in finding out about themselves. From reading horoscopes to comparing oneself with others to buying self-help books to enrolling in psychology courses, much human behavior is marked by the quest for information about the self. The self-concept is largely the result of this process.

There seem to be three main motives that shape the quest for self-knowledge. The first is the desire to gain accurate information about oneself (Trope, 1983, 1986). The second is to gain some confirmation of what one already knows and believes about oneself (Swann, 1985, 1987). The third is to learn positive, favorable things about oneself. These have been called the self-assessment, self-verification, and self-enhancement motives, respectively. They do not always concur in what sort of information people want to hear.

How do the three motives compare? From the standpoint of practical, adaptive benefits, one could make clear predictions. The self-assessment motive should be the strongest, because accurate information about the self is the most useful. The self-verification motive should be next, because maintaining a stable understanding of self and world (even if occasionally inaccurate) is useful too. The self-enhancement motive should be weakest, because hearing favorable things about oneself creates pleasant emotional states but when these are not accurate they should have little or no practical value. If you are trying to decide what courses to take or what romantic partner to pursue, it is useful to know (accurately) how your own abilities and sex appeal stack up. Having an unrealistically positive view could lead you into wasting time and effort, not to mention failure or heartbreak. Hence, it seems logical that people should be most eager to get accurate information about themselves.

Research, however, has concluded that the opposite ranking is closer to the truth (Sedikides, 1993). The self-enhancement motive appears to be the strongest of the three, with the preference for consistency a distant second and the interest in simply accurate information about the self a very distant third. The quest for self-knowledge is thus dominated by the emotionally potent (but informationally dubious) preference to find out positive, flattering things about oneself. There is however some evidence that even though people may prefer highly favorable feedback about themselves, their sober cognitive responses may be skeptical, and so the cognitive (as opposed to emotional) responses to self-knowledge are influenced by the self-verification and self-assessment motives. Still, the immediate and emotional reaction strongly favors positivity.

A broad review of the research literature has concluded that self-knowledge is typically subject to three main patterns of distortion (Taylor & Brown, 1988). First, people overestimate their good qualities. They believe themselves to be somewhat smarter, more attractive, more socially adept, and otherwise more likable and competent than they really are. Second, they overestimate their degree of control over their lives. They believe that they can accomplish the things they want to and that their successes and failures in life will depend mainly on their own actions and choices instead of on external forces and fate or luck. Third, they are unrealistically optimistic. People overestimate the likelihood that good things will happen to them (such as a major promotion, becoming wealthy, or having a gifted child) and underestimate the likelihood that bad things will happen (such as being seriously injured in an accident, or having a retarded child, or being fired from a job).

In short, the average person regards himself or herself as being above average. This is true in terms of one's worth as a person, one's control over life, and one's prospects of having life turn out well. Although these illusions and distortions may depart from the truth, they do seem to help people feel good, bounce back from misfortune, and have confidence to tackle ambitious projects. Indeed, research suggests that people who show all these biases are in general an exceptionally happy group of people (Campbell, 1981). Meanwhile, depressed people seem to lack these biases and see the world in a much more accurate, unbiased, even-handed fashion (Alloy & Abramson, 1979; Taylor & Brown, 1988), which is a rather sad advertisement for being in touch with reality!

Spontaneous Self-Concept

Is the self-concept stable, or does it change and fluctuate from day to day? Many people think it fluctuates, but most researchers have found self-concepts to be quite stable. Attempts to raise or lower self-esteem often have weak or negligible effects.

One reason for this discrepancy between popular wisdom and research beliefs is that the self-concept is very large and complex, and although the entire structure of self-concept may remain rather stable, the parts of it that come to mind immediately may fluctuate. On the surface, self-concepts may seem to change from day to day, even from hour to hour, as different features of the self come to the forefront of one's mind. The concept of self is not really changing; rather, different parts of it are coming to light.

What is changing, then, is that part of the self-concept that happens to be present on one's mind at a given moment. This is sometimes called the "spontaneous self-concept" or the "phenomenal self." There is indeed evidence that the spontaneous self-concept changes, even though self-esteem and the deeper aspects of the self-concept appear to be quite resistant to change. The immediate social context brings out different features of the self, causing the spontaneous self-concept to change.

Changes in the spontaneous self-concept have been shown in a series of clever studies by McGuire and his colleagues (McGuire & McGuire, 1982; McGuire, McGuire, Child, & Fujioka, 1978). They reasoned that people will become aware of their attributes that make them stand out in a given situation. For example, being an American may not come to mind readily when you think about yourself here in America, because everyone else is an American too. But if you travel alone overseas, you may often be quite conscious of being an American, because it sets you apart from most of the people you encounter.

The researchers tested this idea by asking schoolchildren to describe themselves in writing. The children were tested in groups, and the researchers made sure that each group was composed of either all boys except for one girl, or of all girls except for one boy. The child who was the only one present of his or her sex was much more likely to mention that fact in describing himself or herself. In other words, a girl was much more likely to mention being a girl as part of her self-concept if she were the lone girl in a group of boys than if she were in a group of girls. Likewise, boys were more conscious of being boys when they were alone in a group of girls. Thus, the spontaneous self-concept changed in response to the social context.

It is important to remember that these changes occurred only on the surface of the self-concept, that is, only at the level of what features of the self are on one's mind at a given time. McGuire and his colleagues were certainly not claiming that a boy in a group of boys ceases to consider himself a boy. If you asked him whether he is a boy, he would certainly say yes. But if nobody asks him, he is not likely to be paying much attention to the fact that he is a boy. Being surrounded by girls, however, will make him very aware of being a boy. The immediate social context brings out certain features of the self and makes others seem temporarily unimportant, minor, or irrelevant.

In short, not all of one's self-concept is present in one's mind at any given moment. Indeed, some researchers have suggested that the self-concept is like a large, complex set of files, and current events cause people to pull out one drawer or another of these files. People may "scan" their files in different ways depending on the immediate context and recent experiences.

Self-Schemas

Another important approach to self-knowledge rejects the notion that each person has one single, integrated self-concept. Rather, it may be that people have a loose collection of specific ideas about themselves. For example, someone may regard herself as intelligent, friendly, lazy, talkative, helpful, dependent, sympathetic, and sensitive. Perhaps the important thing is not how all these traits fit together to compose a single "self-concept" with a given level of global self-esteem. The important thing may be the individual pieces: being intelligent, friendly, and so forth. In this view, each trait or attribute about oneself is a "self-schema." A self-schema is thus a concept of some particular attribute of the self. Instead of one large self-concept, this approach emphasizes many small concepts of parts and features of the self (Markus, 1977).

One important feature of the self-schema approach is that it makes changes in self-concept easier to understand. The person may feel that he or she remains pretty much the same across time, although specific schemas about the self may change. Another important implication of the self-schema approach is that on some dimensions, many people simply don't have self-schemas. Thus, for example, some people may think of themselves as talkative, others may think of themselves as quiet and reticent, but many other people may not think of themselves as characteristically being either one. It is not that they regard themselves as somewhat or moderately talkative; rather, they may think that in some circumstances they are extremely talkative, while in other situations they are extremely shy and quiet. Or perhaps they have simply never thought about themselves in terms of talkativeness or quietness.

Thus, not all self-concepts are made out of the same ingredients. Dimensions or traits that may be extremely important to some self-concepts may simply be irrelevant to others. Each individual self-concept is made up of several self-schemas on certain dimensions, but other dimensions are left out.

Culture and Interdependence

Do people in different cultures hold systematically different self-concepts? Intuition says that they must, but researchers were slow to establish any clear evidence of cultural variations. Recent work, however, has identified one important dimension on which self-concepts vary across major cultural boundaries.

The dimension runs from independence to interdependence (Markus & Kitayama, 1991; also see chapter 15 in this book). To have an independent self-construal (self-construal is any kind of self-schema or specific view of self) is to focus on the things that make oneself stand out as different and special. In particular, you might focus on your unique traits and accomplishments. In contrast, an interdependent self-construal downplays these unique aspects of the self and instead emphasizes the self as part of a network of social relationships. If two people were both asked to describe what is important about themselves, the interdependent person would start by listing family and other groups to which he or she belongs, thus expressing the view that the self is important only as a part of these groups and relationships. In contrast, the independent person would answer the same question by listing what he or she has achieved and what traits set the person apart from others, often while downplaying any connections to others.

Independent self-construals are predominant in Western culture—Europe and North America. Interdependent self-construals are more common in Asian cultures. Asian cultural traditions are sometimes described as collectivist, which means that they see the value of the individual mainly in being part of the group. Collectivist views also held sway in the West, but starting around the Renaissance (in the 15th century) Europeans began to place more emphasis on the individual, and the United States was founded with an explicit commitment to individualism. As a result of this heritage, Europeans and North Americans are unusually prone to focus their self-concepts on what is unique or special about themselves.

Self-Concept Change

People have the impression that they frequently change their opinions of themselves, but in fact researchers have tended to find the opposite: Self-concepts are remarkably durable and stable. People avoid, ignore, or discount events that can change their self-opinions. It appears that changing the self-concept is often a last resort. Indeed, psychotherapists know very well how difficult it is to induce change in the self-concept, even when the client wants to change.

Still, it is important to know how self-concepts can change. One method was identified in early research studies, based on a theory of *biased scanning*. According to the biased scanning theory, people can be induced to think about themselves in new, different ways. People all have a great deal of widely assorted information about themselves, and the trick is to get them to scan it in a one-sided (biased) fashion so they only attend to part of it. In these studies, researchers asked people to recall incidents in which they acted in an extraverted, outgoing fashion—or, alternatively, in an introverted, socially withdrawn fashion. By remembering only such incidents, people came to think of themselves in that way, and their subsequent views of themselves (and their corresponding actions, such as whether they would strike up a conversation with a stranger) followed suit (Fazio, Effrein, & Fallender, 1981; Jones, Rhodewalt, Berglas, & Skelton, 1981).

More recent work has indicated that social interactions play a crucial role in these self-concept changes. Tice (1992) asked some people to answer biased questions about introverted versus extraverted behavior either in a face-to-face interview with another person, or in an anonymous session with only a tape recorder. The mental scanning should have been the same, but self-concept change occurred only in the face-to-face interview. Tice concluded that biased scanning only changes the self-concept if other people are involved to lend social reality to the interaction. Schlenker, Dlugolecki, and Doherty (1994) confirmed her findings and even challenged the biased scanning view. They conducted an experiment in which people presented themselves one way in social interaction but then the researchers privately conducted biased scanning for the opposite view of self. The self-concept change followed the way they had presented themselves to others rather than the private memory scan. For example, many people are far from certain how creative they are. You can probably think of several events from your life that suggest you are a creative person, if you specifically search your memory for them. On the other hand, if you were to make the opposite search to find evidence that you are not particularly creative, you can probably find some of that too. Neither of these private exercises is likely to have a major impact on your self-concept. But if you were to try hard to convince somebody else of either of those positions—either that you're very creative, or not very creative—that exercise would end up affecting how you think about yourself. Getting other people to see you in a certain way ends up having a bigger impact on your self-concept than simply ruminating privately about it.

At present, then, there is some question as to how important the role of biased memory scanning is, but it does not seem able to induce self-concept change by itself. Undoubtedly there is some role for processes such as memory shifts. Still, the interpersonal dimension seems to be strong and decisive. To change the self, it is helpful and powerful to change the way one is perceived by other people, and these socially reflected views of self can then be internalized (see also Wicklund & Gollwitzer, 1982). Moreover, when people do try to change, other people's input and perceptions seem to make a big difference (Heatherton & Nichols, 1994). If you tell everyone that you want to quit smoking or lose weight or take up a new hobby, you are more likely to follow through and succeed than if you keep your plans for change to yourself.

SELF-ESTEEM

Of all the aspects of the self-concept, one of the most important is self-esteem. When researchers set out to study the self-concept, they usually end up studying self-esteem. This is because people instantly recognize the importance of self-esteem. When self-esteem goes up, they often feel happy, whereas events that lower self-esteem generally make people feel terrible. Another reason people study self-esteem is that it is easy and convenient to measure.

There is no single measure of self-esteem that is used by everyone. Rather, there are many such measures, partly because the topic is quite important and partly because researchers criticize one another's ways of measuring it. As already noted, one approach was to look for discrepancies between the real self and the ideal self. Another way is to ask a series of simple questions about global self-regard (e.g., Rosenberg, 1965). The most common approach is to ask a series of questions about different attributes and add them up. The problem is that such a measure might not lend the right importance to the various attributes or dimensions. Most of the common self-esteem measures tend to emphasize social self-esteem, for example. To get an understanding of this approach, please consult the Activity Box 9.1, "Measuring Self-Esteem."

The results of these self-esteem measures yield a continuum of scores. Although everyone speaks of high and low self-esteem as if these were distinct types, they are not types in the sense of distinct clusters of scores. Rather, there is a continuum and people may range anywhere along it. Dividing the scores into high and low self-esteem groups is done for the sake of conceptual convenience (i.e., it makes results easier to talk about). Sometimes researchers divide their scores into two groups for analyzing their data—that is, to compare the typical behaviors of highversus low self-esteem groups. There are some minor statistical problems with that approach (e.g., it ignores the fact that the highest score in the low-esteem group is probably closer to the lowest score in

Activity Box 9.1   Measuring Your Self-Esteem

Most measures of self-esteem rely on asking the person to rate himself or herself on various dimensions. Here are some sample items that are similar to those used on actual scales. Try to rate yourself on each one. Give yourself a numerical rating from 0 to 6 on each scale, such that 0 = Very Often, or Very Much, and 6 = Almost Never, or Not at All.

_____   1. How often do you feel superior to most other people?
_____   2. How often do you think that one day you will accomplish great things?
_____   3. Do you worry about making a good impression on other people?
_____   4. Do you frequently fear that other people will dislike you or think badly of you?
_____   5. When you complete an assignment or test, do you usually have the feeling that you did a poor or inadequate job?
_____   6. Do you consider yourself more physically attractive than the average person you know?
_____   7. How often do you do things that seem clumsy or uncoordinated?

Self-esteem is then scored by computing a total based on the number of points per item. For questions #3, 4, 5, and 7, your rating (0 to 6) is your score. The other three items (#1, 2, and 6) are *reverse scored;* that is, you compute your score by subtracting your rating from 6. For example, if you responded to question #2 by rating yourself 4, your score would be 6 – 4 = 2.

These questions refer to various areas or facets of self-esteem. Questions 1 and 2 refer to "global self-esteem"—that is, the person's overall appraisal of self. Questions 3 and 4 measure social self-esteem, that is, feelings of confidence and inhibition about getting along with other people. Question 5 refers to school (intellectual) abilities (confidence in your ability to do good work). Questions 6 and 7 refer to body image; #6 is concerned with attractiveness and #7 is concerned with physical skills and ability.

Most self-esteem scales use more items than these (see Fleming & Courtney, 1984, for a good example of a complete scale), so you should not place much trust in the reliability of your total score from these few items. Still, you can get a rough idea of how self-esteem is measured by considering these items and similar ones.

the high-esteem group than to the lowest score in the low-esteem group), but these can safely be overlooked in making rough comparisons.

The goal of understanding and measuring self-esteem is further complicated by new distinctions that researchers are starting to make. In recent years, there has been an upsurge of interest in a trait called narcissism, which can be understood as an obnoxious kind of high self-esteem (Emmons, 1984; Morf & Rhodewalt, 2001). The term *narcissism* is derived from a Greek myth, in which Narcissus was a young man who fell in love with his own reflected image, and narcissism is therefore used to refer to excessive or absurd self-love. Narcissistic individuals hold high opinions of themselves and want other people to regard them favorably also—or else! If you let a narcissist know that you do not admire him or her, you may become the target of his or her anger and venom.

Self-Esteem and Self-Concept

Self-esteem is essentially the evaluative dimension of the self-concept. Any piece of information about the self may be incorporated into the self-concept. It only affects self-esteem once it takes on a value judgment: Is it good or bad? High self-esteem denotes thinking well of oneself. This may include a healthy self-confidence and proper appreciation of one's genuine accomplishments and abilities. It may also exaggerate or distort the truth wildly. High self-esteem can mean being conceited, egotistical, arrogant, and narcissistic. The common thread is thinking well of oneself—regardless of whether this is justified.

In theory, low self-esteem is the opposite of high self-esteem, and so it should mean having a negative, unflattering view of self. In practice, however, relatively few people are firmly convinced that they are bad people. Most researchers define "low self-esteem" as anyone who scores in the bottom half or bottom third of a sample of scores on a self-esteem scale. An examination of these scores shows that usually they are in the middle range of *possible* scores, because almost no one scores at the low end (Baumeister, Tice, & Hutton, 1989). In other words, in response to self-esteem scale questions such as "Do you often feel inferior to most other people?" a high self-esteem person will answer "Never" but a typical low self-esteem person will say "Sometimes" rather than "Frequently." In fact, hardly anyone says "Frequently" in answer to such questions.

Thus, low self-esteem is the absence of positives more than the presence of negative beliefs about the self (Baumeister, 1993). People with high self-esteem hold firm, highly favorable beliefs about themselves. People with low self-esteem lack those beliefs, but they generally do not hold firm *unfavorable* beliefs about themselves.

A powerful and influential line of research on the self-conceptions that accompany different levels of self-esteem was conducted by Campbell (1990; Campbell & Lavallee, 1993). The broad conclusion is that low self-esteem is marked by *self-concept confusion*. That is, people with high self-esteem have clear, consistent, and definite ideas about themselves, whereas people with low self-esteem do not. When people with low self-esteem answer questions about themselves, they differ from people with high self-esteem in several key ways. They tend to give uncertain answers or say they do not know. They give contradictory or inconsistent answers to similar questions. They give different answers to the same questions on different occasions. All of these suggest that low self-esteem is marked by a lack of firm self-knowledge. Once again, then, low self-esteem is not a matter of being convinced that you are bad. More commonly, it is simply the lack of firm conviction that you are good.

Self-esteem and narcissism are not quite the same thing. Most narcissists have high self-esteem, but many people with high self-esteem are not narcissists. A person with high self-esteem might be a conceited, obnoxious fool or a person with a reasonable appreciation of his or her genuine talents and achievements. Some people with high self-esteem simply accept themselves and do not worry about what others think. In contrast, narcissists tend to feel superior to others and to want very badly to have other people confirm this view.

Roots of Self-Esteem

The roots of self-esteem were the target of many years of research by Coopersmith (1967). He concluded that three factors contributed to high self-esteem among children. The first was *unconditional positive regard*, which means that parents (or others) should convey to the child the message that the child was loved no matter what. Many parents give the impression that they love the child only when the child behaves well. For building a strong, healthy self-concept, however, the foundation is apparently the sense that one is loved and valued regardless of how one is behaving.

The second factor identified by Coopersmith was the existence of clear and strong standards. That is, parents can build self-esteem by setting forth firm, definite criteria as to how the child should behave and expecting the child to live up to them. These include rules and limits on what the child is allowed to do. The modern self-esteem movement's message has been misinterpreted by many modern parents to believe that in order to build self-esteem they should approve of the child's behavior regardless of whether it is good. However, Coopersmith found that children ended up with higher self-esteem if they knew definitely what was expected of them and if these expectations were clear and consistent.

The third ingredient was that parents should give the child freedom, latitude, and respect for behavior that lies within the limits. In particular, it is important that the parents show some positive approval when the child does live up to expectations. Some parents make rules and set expectations but only show any feelings when the child falls short. It is better for self-esteem, apparently, if the parent *also* expresses pride and other positive feelings when the child succeeds.

One might think that the first and second features contradict each other: The first says to love the child no matter what, whereas the second says to set firm rules and punish the child when the child performs badly. The resolution of this seeming contradiction is that it is fine, even desirable, to disapprove of specific behaviors, but one should continue to feel and show love for the child. When the child disobeys, or fails to complete chores, or does badly in school, the ideal parental message will be, "I love you, but I hate what you are doing." Parents who can effectively combine steady love with firm rules (and consistent punishments) while they give the child freedom and approval for behavior that satisfies these rules will likely raise the child with the strongest, healthiest self-esteem.

Self-esteem may begin to take shape in childhood, but it can continue to change and develop throughout life. Recent work has begun to show the life course of self-esteem (Robins, Trzesniewski, Tracy, Gosling, & Potter, 2002). Self-esteem is relatively high during childhood, and in fact, many children hold very positive, confident, unrealistic views about themselves. During adolescence, self-esteem is often somewhat lower. Adolescents worry about how others view them and about learning how to get others to like them. After adolescence, self-esteem rises slowly into middle adulthood, and its peak is found in late midlife. Perhaps surprisingly, on average self-esteem is highest among people in their early 60s. Then it drops again (sharply) as people reach their 70s and 80s, probably due to multiple factors, including physical impairments, loss of occupational roles and death of spouse, and gradual decline in one's physical and mental powers.

Is High Self-Esteem a Good Thing?

Interest in self-esteem has extended beyond the research community to society at large. California created a state task force to develop ideas for raising the self-esteem of all residents, in the belief that self-esteem would serve as a "social vaccine" to combat a broad array of personal and social problems, including drug abuse, teen pregnancy, crime, school failure, debt, and mental illness (California Task Force, 1990). Many school systems now devote considerable time and effort to boosting self-esteem, even devoting class time to it rather than to academic topics.

Although beliefs remain strong in the positive value of self-esteem, the research evidence does not justify them. Even while the California Task Force was touting the benefits of self-esteem, a group of researchers they commissioned to study those benefits were publishing a contrary conclusion: "The news most consistently reported, however, is that the associations between self-esteem and its expected consequences are mixed, insignificant, or absent" (Mecca, Smelser, & Vasconcellos, 1989, p. 15). Raising self-esteem does not appear to be an effective way to prevent teen pregnancy, drug abuse, school failure, or the like.

There are two crucial questions. First, are people with high self-esteem better off in important ways than people with low self-esteem? Second, does high self-esteem actually cause people to be better off? Hundreds of research studies have tried to answer those questions. Recently some researchers have begun wading through the hundreds of published reports to come up with broad, general conclusions (see Baumeister, Campbell, Krueger, & Vohs, 2003; Emler, 2001).

The answer to the first question appears to be a qualified yes. To the second question, the answer is mostly no.

People with high self-esteem seem to enjoy being able to feel good about themselves. They consistently rate themselves as doing well on many measures. They rate themselves as being smarter, more popular, more physically handsome or beautiful, better able to get along with others, healthier, happier, and better adjusted than other people. Unfortunately, these patterns tell more about how people with high self-esteem flatter themselves than about objective reality. When researchers get objective measures, most of these advantages of high self-esteem disappear. Thus, people with high self-esteem rate themselves as more intelligent than people with low self-esteem, but actual IQ tests show no difference (Gabriel, Critelli, & Ee, 1994). Likewise, they rate themselves as better looking than people with low self-esteem, but when judges rate photographs for facial beauty, people with high self-esteem are not any more attractive than those with low (Diener, Wolsic, & Fujita, 1995; Gabriel et al., 1994).

There are many reasons to expect that high self-esteem will lead people to do better in school, and studies have tried to show that self-esteem leads to better grades or other signs of intellectual achievement. It doesn't. Doing well in school may lead to a slight rise in self-esteem, and certain factors like having a good family background or having high intelligence can lead to both success in school and high self-esteem, but self-esteem has not been found to have any causal impact on school performance (Bachman & O'Malley, 1977, 1986; Maruyama, Rubin, & Kingsbury, 1981; Pottebaum, Keith, & Ehly, 1986; Rosenberg, Schooler, & Schoenbach, 1989).

Likewise, many psychologists have long advocated the view that "in order to love others, you must first love yourself," but careful studies have failed to show that high self-esteem leads to better interpersonal relationships or greater popularity. Laboratory studies have tested the effects of self-esteem by having people meet and get acquainted and then afterward rate their impressions of each other. People with high self-esteem often think they made a great impression (and better than the impression that people with low self-esteem think they made), but their interaction partners give them about the same rating that they do people with low self-esteem (Brockner & Lloyd, 1986; Campbell & Fehr, 1990). If anything, people sometimes end up liking the person with low self-esteem better than the one with high self-esteem, especially if the low-esteem person has been criticized or offended. People with high self-esteem tend to respond to criticism or other threats to esteem by becoming huffy or obnoxious, and so they make a bad impression on others (Heatherton & Vohs, 2000).

The link to violence may even be the opposite of what the self-esteem movement assumed. A large-scale review of the research literature by Baumeister, Smart, and Boden (1996) found that the evidence massively contradicted the theory that low self-esteem causes violence. In general, violence seems to occur primarily among people who hold very favorable, even inflated views of themselves—and who then encounter someone who questions or challenges their high self-esteem. From gang members who shoot someone who "disses" (i.e., shows disrespect to) them, to adults who beat their spouses and lovers to prove that they should be the boss in the family, to playground bullies who victimize other children to prove their own superiority, to tyrannical governments headed by megalomaniacal dictators, to nations who make war to avenge threats to their honor, to ethnic groups who oppress or attack others based on flimsy notions of racial pride, the same pattern was found over and over: Threatened egotism is the decisive cause of violence and aggression. Not all high self-esteem causes aggression, but when self-esteem consists of inflated, exaggerated, or narcissistic notions of personal superiority, the results can be dangerous. In controlled laboratory studies, people with high self-esteem are found among both the aggressive and nonaggressive individuals—while the most aggressive people were prone to narcissism, which is a rather nasty and obnoxious form of high self-esteem (Bushman & Baumeister, 1998).

Are there any benefits to high self-esteem? Two main benefits were identified after a long search by Baumeister et al. (2003; see also Emler, 2001). The first is that high self-esteem supports initiative. People with high self-esteem are more willing to approach strangers to strike up a conversation, more likely to speak up in a group (especially when they do not agree with what the group is doing), more able to resist other people's attempts to tell them what to do, and better able to persist in the face of failure. People with high self-esteem are more likely than others to be bullies—but they are also more likely to be the one who stands up to the bully and protects the victim. Probably the difference in initiative has to do with simple confidence: High self-esteem fosters a confidence that one's own judgment is sound and one's actions will lead to good outcomes. Meanwhile people with low self-esteem may suffer from self-doubts and therefore be reluctant to take independent action.

The second benefit of high self-esteem is that it appears to consist of a stock of good feelings. In a sense, high self-esteem is an emotional resource that people can draw upon. People with high self-esteem are happier than others, better able to recover from trauma or cope with stress, and less vulnerable to mood swings in response to external events. Common sense tells us that it simply feels good to think well of yourself, and in this respect common sense appears to be quite right.

Thus, researchers are slowly moving toward a more balanced view of self-esteem that acknowledges both its advantages and its disadvantages, as well as recognizing that its causal impact on important social and personal problems may be far weaker than previously hoped. Low self-esteem is linked to social anxiety and shyness, which can impair people's chances of making friends and getting along with others (Leary & Kowalski, 1995; Schlenker & Leary, 1982)—but people with inflated (high) self-esteem tend to irritate others and turn them off, and in the long run these self-centered, conceited individuals show poor social skills and psychological maladjustment (Colvin, Block, & Funder, 1995). Low self-esteem is associated with some patterns of self-defeating behavior, such as giving up too easily—but high self-esteem is associated with other patterns, such as overconfidence (Heatherton & Ambady, 1993). When things are going well, people with high self-esteem manage themselves better than those with low, such as by making appropriate commitments and selecting optimal performance goals—but in response to an ego threat, people with high self-esteem often become irrational and set unrealistic, macho goals for themselves, leading to costly failures (Baumeister, Heatherton, & Tice, 1993; McFarlin & Blascovich, 1981).

Much of the downside of high self-esteem seems to involve overestimating oneself, as in being conceited or narcissistic. The present state of the evidence does not indicate that there is anything wrong with having an accurate appreciation of one's good points and strengths, particularly if this is tempered with some interpersonal humility and with an accurate recognition of one's faults and weaknesses. Some experts conclude from this that there are right and wrong (or "true" and "false") kinds of high self-esteem. To make such a distinction, however, is already to shift the focus away from self-esteem per se (in the sense of thinking well of oneself) and on to the issue of how good a person one can manage to be.

To understand this, suppose there were an effective way to sort "true" from "false" versions of high self-esteem. For example, a team of researchers might identify all the students who think they are smart and then give them an IQ test to see which ones are really smart. The ones who are smart and know it have "true" high self-esteem, and the ones who overestimate their intelligence have "false" high self-esteem. Suppose, then, that the researchers found that "true" high self-esteem was associated with success in school, whereas "false" high self-esteem tended to backfire (a likely outcome). Would this show that some forms of self-esteem are better than others? On the contrary, it seems to show that self-esteem is irrelevant. Remember, the students with "true" self-esteem are by definition smarter than those with false high self-esteem, and so it is no surprise that they do better in school. Both groups think they're equally smart—which suggests that the mere fact of thinking oneself smart is irrelevant. What matters is the underlying reality of actually being smart.

In other words, it is perhaps the underlying reality rather than the perception that matters most. Self-esteem is merely the perception, not the reality. When perception does matter, the best state may well be close to accurate—neither overestimating nor underestimating oneself. Those who underestimate their intelligence may avoid challenges or give up too easily. Those who overestimate their intelligence may get in over their heads or may not bother to work hard enough. Either distortion can interfere with learning.

Achieving a balanced, accurate appraisal of oneself is unfortunately quite difficult. In the meantime, the world might be a better place if more people would forget about trying to boost their self-esteem and concentrate instead on trying to be a better person. Focusing on self-esteem, after all, is merely a matter of trying to *think* that you're a better person.

Why Care About Self-Esteem?

People everywhere care about self-esteem. Anything that gives a boost in self-esteem is almost universally welcome, and by the same token hardly anyone enjoys events that constitute a blow or loss to their self-esteem. Yet as we have seen, self-esteem does not lead to many palpable, direct material benefits. Self-esteem does not make people richer, smarter, better liked, or more successful. In a few small ways, people with high self-esteem do better than others; in a few other ways they do worse—and the overall effect is quite small. Why are people so concerned with something that seems to mean so little?

The emotional implications of self-esteem contain a partial answer, but only a partial one. People do feel better when their self-esteem is high or rising, and they feel bad when self-esteem is low or dropping, and so it is only natural that they should become concerned about self-esteem. Yet this answer is hardly satisfactory because it raises the next question of why emotions should be so strongly tied to something that has little practical value. We have emotions for good reasons: They help us adapt to the world and pass on our genes to the next generation. Fear makes us avoid danger. Love makes us stay with desirable partners, especially when we may reproduce. Anger helps us assert our rights and tackle obstacles. But why should self-esteem be linked to emotions?

At present, several possible answers have been suggested, but none is fully satisfactory. One answer is that people are driven by fear of death, and self-esteem helps comfort them in the face of human mortality (Becker, 1973; Greenberg, Pyszczynski, & Solomon; 1986; Pyszczynski, Greenberg, & Solomon, 1997). Critics of this view point out that self-esteem does not seem to correlate with death anxiety and that high self-esteem would seemingly make death seem worse, not better (because the value of one's own life is higher). In support of this view, however, researchers have shown that high self-esteem seems to hold back anxiety in response to cues designed to evoke thoughts of death and pain (Greenberg, Solomon, et al., 1992).

Another view is that self-esteem is sought because it is a valuable aid in coping with stress, trauma, and misfortunes (Steele, 1988). Self-esteem may be of little value under normal circumstances, but in response to adversity people need self-esteem to keep their spirits up and to keep striving for positive outcomes. Self-esteem is thus a valuable resource. This theory does correspond well with the actual, limited benefits of self-esteem, especially the emotional benefits and the improved capacity to persist in the face of failure, but it is not clear that people want self-esteem merely in order to have a resource in case they encounter misfortune. Even when times are good, people seem to want self-esteem. Moreover, this theory still does not explain why it is that people should find that self-esteem helps them cope with failure or misfortune.

A third view is that self-esteem is a *sociometer*, that is, an internal measure of how well one is connected to other human beings (Leary, Tambor, Terdal, & Downs, 1995). There is a large amount of evidence that forming good social relations and getting along with others is conducive to health, happiness, and well-being, as well as the evolutionary goal of survival and reproduction, and it is fair to say that human beings are partly driven by a fundamental and powerful *need to belong* (Baumeister & Leary, 1995). Self-esteem may be fairly unimportant in terms of its direct consequences, but it could be very important as an inner meter that keeps track of this all-important project of forming and maintaining social bonds. (By analogy, the gas gauge in the car has no direct importance for helping the car run, but it is very important as a measure of something crucial, namely how much fuel the car has.) To support this theory, Leary and his colleagues (1995) showed that self-esteem rises based on events that are linked to social inclusion—such as being accepted by others, proving one's competence, being found attractive, and so forth. Meanwhile, events that can lead to social rejection also tend to lower self-esteem. Moreover, we have already seen that self-esteem is strongly (inversely) correlated with social anxiety, which means that low self-esteem is often linked to a fear of social rejection.

The sociometer theory is a novel solution to the question of why self-esteem matters. It leaves several issues unresolved, however. Can people have high self-esteem even if they do not have strong social connections and relationships? And how can some people have low self-esteem even when they seem to be well connected to family and friends? Still, it is probably no mere coincidence that the main criteria on which self-esteem is based—being likable, attractive, and competent—are the same criteria that groups use to include versus exclude individuals.

Social Motives

What do people with low self-esteem want? This question has led various theorists to pose a wide assortment of answers. Some have asserted that people with low self-esteem desire to fail or suffer. Some have proposed that they want to confirm their bad opinions of themselves. Some have proposed that they want to gain esteem at all costs. Others have proposed that their motivations are largely the same as those of people with high self-esteem.

After many years of research, some answers have finally emerged. The notion that people with low self-esteem desire to fail or suffer in order to prove how bad they are has not been confirmed. People with low self-esteem want to succeed as much as people with high self-esteem; they are simply less confident that they will be able to do so (McFarlin & Blascovich, 1981).

The broadest motivational pattern associated with low self-esteem seems to be one of self-protection (Baumeister, Tice, & Hutton, 1989). That is, people with low self-esteem worry about failure, rejection, humiliation, and other unpleasant outcomes, and they seem to go through life watching out for such dangers and trying to minimize them. People with high self-esteem, in contrast, seem to spend much less time worrying about failure or protecting themselves from it. They do hate to fail, but in general they do not expect it to happen, and so self-protection is not an overriding concern.

To put this in broader perspective, it is helpful to realize that nearly everyone wants to do well—to succeed at work, to make friends, to have good intimate relationships, and so forth. As part of that, nearly everyone wants to be well regarded by others and to be able to respect himself or herself too. This motive to think well of oneself can be subdivided into two motives: *self-enhancement*, which is the desire to gain esteem, and *self-protection*, which is the desire to avoid losing esteem. Often the self-enhancement motive and the self-protection motive operate together, in tandem, as when someone tries to make the best possible score on an examination.

Other times, however, the two motives are opposed. For example, calling someone up to ask for a date pits the two motives against each other. If the other person accepts the invitation, you may feel a gain in esteem; but if the other person rejects you, you may lose esteem. Asking someone out is therefore risky from an esteem point of view. If the self-enhancement motive predominates and you are mainly concerned with the opportunity to gain esteem, then you may well take the chance. But if the self-protection motive predominates, you would not make the call, to prevent the possibility of being rejected. Similar arguments apply in many other situations, such as accepting a challenge or undertaking a public performance when there are significant opportunities for both gaining and losing esteem.

In general, people with high self-esteem are oriented toward self-enhancement. They are looking for ways to gain esteem and to do even better than they have done so far. They do not expect to fail or be rejected and so they do not worry about it much. In contrast, people with low self-esteem give priority to self-protection. They might be happy to gain esteem, but gaining esteem does not dominate their outlook on life. Instead, they look for ways to avoid or minimize possible failures, rejections, and setbacks.

Plasticity

People with low self-esteem tend to be more malleable and gullible than people with high self-esteem (Brockner 1984). This is a common pattern across many spheres of behavior. People with low self-esteem are more likely to change their attitudes when someone tries to persuade them (e.g., Janis, 1954). They may yield or conform to group influence more than others, and they are more willing to take advice. Their behavior changes more from one situation to another.

The malleability may well be connected with the broad patterns we have already identified. First, because people with low self-esteem lack firm, consistent self-concepts, it is harder for them than for other people to resist situational influences and follow their own inner promptings. Second, because they are oriented toward self-protection, they may find it safer to go along with the group and do what they are told rather than strike out on their own. Third, because high self-esteem is linked to greater initiative, people who have it may be more willing to resist someone else's influence or pressure. It may take confidence to reject someone's advice and do what you think best, because if you end up being proven wrong, the other person can say "I told you so." With high self-esteem, a person will tend to think that he or she will not be proven wrong, so the person does not worry about that possibility.

Emotion and Coping

High self-esteem does not contribute to a great many advantages or successes in life, but it does undoubtedly make one feel better. As a result, some of the most important differences between high and low self-esteem involve emotion.

One difference is simply in the overall positivity of emotion. People with low self-esteem are more likely to suffer unpleasant emotional states. As we have already seen, low self-esteem correlates strongly with anxiety and depression, which are two of the most common and serious patterns of emotional distress. In a recent study in which people kept diaries of their emotions, people with low self-esteem showed more negative emotions of all sorts (Campbell, Chew, & Scratchley, 1991). They had more bad moods and fewer good moods.

Beyond the simple issue of good versus bad emotions, however, there is another emotional difference. People with low self-esteem have higher emotional *lability* than people with high self-esteem (Campbell et al., 1991; Campbell & Lavallee, 1993). That is, their emotions fluctuate more widely from one day to the next or one hour to the next. High self-esteem apparently helps keep one on an even keel, whereas low self-esteem can have one riding an emotional roller coaster.

Probably the emotional lability of low self-esteem is linked to the plasticity of low self-esteem. After all, it is hard not to respond to the immediate event or situation if you are having a strong emotional reaction to it. The self-concept confusion may also be connected. If your ideas about yourself are not firmly fixed, then each event can have a bigger impact on the way you think and feel about yourself, which in turn will set off stronger emotional reactions.

Self-esteem can thus be understood as an emotional resource, and this may explain the difference in resiliency in the face of stress, trauma, and setbacks. People with high self-esteem seem to have a stock of positive feelings, possibly associated with all the positive beliefs they hold about themselves, and so when something goes wrong they can draw on these beliefs and feelings to help themselves shrug off the misfortune, feel better, and maybe try again (Steele, 1988).

In contrast, people with low self-esteem have a much smaller stock of positive beliefs and feelings, and so they may feel overwhelmed or devastated when something goes wrong.

Prejudice

On the surface, it seems that people with low self-esteem are more prejudiced than people with high self-esteem. Several studies have shown, for example, that people with low self-esteem give more negative ratings to minority group members and other stereotyped groups. But one must recall that low self-esteem means giving *oneself* a negative rating. To examine prejudice, one must ask: Do people with low self-esteem rate others worse than themselves?

The answer appears to be no. People with low self-esteem rate themselves, members of their own group, and members of other groups all about the same (Crocker & Schwartz, 1985). All of these ratings tend to be somewhat negative relative to the ratings given by people with high self-esteem. But the negativity does not reflect any selective prejudice, for it applies to everyone. People with low self-esteem are apparently more critical of everyone—including minority groups and themselves. When one looks at the difference between how one rates oneself and how one rates members of outgroups, it is people with high self-esteem who emerge as more prejudiced (Crocker & Schwartz, 1985; Crocker et al., 1987). A meta-analysis (i.e., a statistical technique that combines the results of many different studies, thereby furnishing especially conclusive findings) recently confirmed that prejudice and discrimination are higher among people who have high self-esteem. They rate the groups to which they belong more favorably than outgroups, and they tend to give preferential treatment to members of their own groups. People with low self-esteem tend to treat ingroups and outgroups about the same (Aberson et al., 2000).

Maintaining Self-Esteem

How do people keep their self-esteem up? And why do some people seem unable to form a favorable view of themselves? In principle, one way to achieve high self-esteem would be to succeed at everything. As long as work and social life go well, there is not much danger to one's self-esteem. Unfortunately, life does not usually cooperate, and nearly everyone experiences periodic setbacks, failures, rejections, interpersonal conflicts, and other events that strike painful blows to one's sense of self-worth.

Most studies have not found that people with high self-esteem are really more talented, intelligent, likable, attractive, or otherwise superior. Indeed, the more common finding among laboratory researchers is that the actual performance of people with high self-esteem is, on average, no different from that of people with low self-esteem. People with high self-esteem do *believe* they are better: They rate their performance better, they consider themselves more beautiful or handsome, and so forth, compared with people who have low self-esteem. But the difference seems to be mainly one of perception. As we have already noted, studies that ask unbiased judges to rate people's attractiveness conclude that people with high and low self-esteem are about equally attractive—but studies that ask people to rate their own physical appearance find that people with high, compared to low, self-esteem consistently rate themselves as being more attractive (e.g., Harter, 1993).

Success in life depends on more than ability, however. Two people may have precisely the same amount of talent, but one may succeed better than the other by virtue of choosing more appropriate undertakings. (For example, two equally smart and equally knowledgeable people may get different grades depending on which courses they take.) Remember, people with high self-esteem seem to have superior knowledge about themselves (Campbell, 1990), and this knowledge can prove very useful in selecting the optimal courses, jobs, challenges, projects, and dating partners. Experiments have indeed shown that people with high self-esteem are better at choosing the right level of challenge for themselves to ensure maximum success (as long as they are not distracted by an ego threat; Baumeister, Heatherton, & Tice, 1993). This kind of advantage may be what helps people with high self-esteem to perform a little better in school (and elsewhere) without actually being any smarter (Felson, 1993; Hattie & Hansford, 1982).

Thus, it is plausible that some people can sustain higher self-esteem than others by achieving more successes, even without any superior gifts. Undoubtedly, however, the other route to maintaining high self-esteem involves various styles of thinking that boost one's self-appraisal. Many of these techniques involve self-deception, to the extent that people fool themselves in systematic ways to maintain comfortable, flattering illusions about how great they are. A famous article by Anthony Greenwald (1980) compared the self to a totalitarian regime in the way it rewrites history to make itself look good. Researchers have identified several esteem-boosting and self-deception techniques, described in the following paragraphs (from Baumeister, 1998).

First, people systematically take credit for success but deny blame for failure. This *self-serving bias* has been widely documented in many contexts and studies (Zuckerman, 1979). When something important happens, people are quick to judge whether they are responsible, and they make those judgments in a one-sided fashion. People with high self-esteem are especially prone to show this pattern of grabbing the credit but denying the blame (e.g., Fitch, 1970).

Second, people happily and uncritically accept information that makes them look good, but when someone criticizes them they often stop to find faults or flaws in the critic's reasons. For example, when people take a test and are then asked whether the test was valid, their answers depend heavily on how well they are told they performed (Pyszczynski, Greenberg, & Holt, 1985; Wyer & Frey, 1983; see also Kunda, 1990). As many instructors know, students who do well think the test was fair and objective, whereas those who do badly are more likely to believe that the test was biased or inappropriate. A variation on this is that people dismiss criticism as motivated by prejudice or personal animosity, and so their self-esteem is unaffected even when someone tells them that they have done badly or have undesirable traits (Crocker & Major, 1989; Crocker, Voelkl, Testa, & Major, 1991).

Third, people shift the amount of attention they pay when they receive feedback about their abilities or performances (Baumeister & Cairns, 1992). When people receive positive, flattering feedback, they often linger over it, study it carefully, and let its full implications sink in. In contrast, when they hear criticism of unfavorable remarks, they tend to skip over them or pay much less attention.

Fourth, people show biased memory. They recall their successes and good points better than their failures and bad points (Crary, 1966; Kuiper & Derry, 1982; Mischel, Ebbesen, & Zeiss, 1976).

Fifth, they have ways of sorting through their memory to prove to themselves that they fit whatever pattern is desirable. Thus, when people are led to believe that being an introvert leads to success, they recall more of their own actions as introverted, and they are quicker to come up with introverted memories, than when they are told that extraversion is associated with success (Sanitioso, Kunda, & Fong, 1990).

Sixth, they compare themselves selectively against targets that make them feel good. In particular, they engage in downward comparison, which means that they identify people who are doing worse than themselves to use as a baseline for evaluating themselves (Wills, 1981). People like to have some contact with people who are less intelligent, less attractive, or fatter than they are because seeing such individuals makes them feel good about themselves.

Seventh, people distort their perceptions of others so as to furnish a rosy view of their own traits and opinions. With opinions and beliefs, people exhibit a *false consensus effect*, which means that they overestimate the proportion of people who would agree with them—and which encourages them to think they must be right: "I must be correct, because everybody agrees with me." In contrast, with abilities, people show a *false uniqueness effect*, which means that they underestimate the proportion of others who are similar. This helps people feel that their abilities are special because they think hardly anyone could perform as well as they do. The combination of false uniqueness and false consensus effects has been especially linked to high self-esteem, and indeed it seems well designed to give people a comfortable sense of personal superiority (Campbell, 1986; Marks, 1984; Suls & Wan, 1987).

These patterns are fairly common and widespread. This is not to say that everyone always uses them, but most people do show some of them. More to the point, people with high self-esteem use them more than others. We noted earlier that self-esteem seems to be somewhat inflated across the U.S. population today, and these techniques indicate how people give their self-esteem an extra boost, perhaps beyond what is warranted. These are the means, in other words, by which the average person convinces himself (or herself) that he is above average.

IDENTITY

We turn now to consider identity. Although the terms *identity* and *self-concept* have some things in common, they are different. A self-concept exists only in one person's mind, whereas identity is essentially social. That is, identity rests on a definition of the self that is shared by the person, other people, and society at large.

Structure and Functions of Identity

Identity, as we said earlier, is a definition of the self. It is actually a composite definition made up of several partial definitions. The components of identity are these partial definitions. Any answer to the question "Who are you?" is an identity component, for to answer that question is to give a partial definition of oneself. Examples of identity components include being an employee of a certain company, a lawyer, a student, someone's nephew, a member of the swim team, and so on.

If identity is a definition, then there have to be certain criteria used for defining it. There are two major *defining criteria* of identity—namely, continuity and differentiation. *Continuity* means sameness over time. Part of having an identity is being the same person today as yesterday, last week, and last year. People do change in various ways, but they retain some continuity of identity, as signified by having the same name and other things. *Differentiation* refers to the things that distinguish someone from other people. Being identified with a certain family or organization, for example, marks one off as distinct from nonmembers.

Anything that furnishes continuity and differentiation thus helps to define identity. A strong sense of identity arises from having many sources of continuity and differentiation. A stable home, strong family ties, a secure job, an established reputation, and such things make identity secure, and someone with all those things is not likely to have identity problems. One reason for the increased concern over identity in modern life is that many things that once provided continuity and differentiation no longer do so (Baumeister, 1986). For example, in previous centuries many people would live their entire lives in the same locale, even having the same neighbors and friends, but now people are much more mobile, so home and friendship networks are no longer the sources of stability that they once were.

The makeup of each individual identity is different, but there are certain broad common features. Identity seems to include at least three major types of things. First, it includes one's interpersonal self: how others know you, your interpersonal style, your reputation, and so forth. Second, it includes some concept of potentiality, that is, of what you may become. Third, it includes some general values, principles, and priorities.

Identity Crises

The notion of an "identity crisis" appears to be a modern phenomenon. People in the Middle Ages, for example, do not seem to have had identity crises or anything resembling them. Likewise, there is not much evidence of identity crises in cultures very different from our own. Probably identity crises are fostered by some of the unique features of modern Western cultures (see Baumeister, 1986, 1987).

The term *identity crisis* was coined by Erik Erikson in the 1940s. It was quickly adopted and used by many people, which suggests that it named an experience that was already common and widespread. Erikson thought that nearly everyone has an identity crisis during adolescence, although in many cases this could be an unconscious crisis so the person would be unaware of it. Erikson believed that the identity crisis resulted from the need to separate oneself emotionally from one's parents (cf. Blos, 1962) and to make basic decisions about one's values, goals, and ambitions in life.

In the 1960s, psychologists started to do research on identity crises. They soon abandoned Erikson's original theory that everyone goes through an identity crisis. Instead, they began to think that some people go through life without ever having such a crisis, although many others have important crises. Researchers became interested in comparing people who had identity crises against people who did not have them.

James Marcia (1966, 1967) developed a typology of people based on identity crises. Four types of people were distinguished, based on two dimensions: (1) Has the person ever had an active period of identity crisis? (2) Does the person have a stable identity based on firm commitments? Here are the four types:

Identity Achieved: Crisis plus Commitment   People who have had an identity crisis and resolved it are classified as identity-achieved. They are typically regarded as being mature, capable individuals, whose identity is solidly based on the outcome of a personal struggle.

Moratorium: Crisis but no Commitment   When there is evidence of an identity crisis but firm commitments are lacking, the individual is classified as having "moratorium" status. In most cases, this means that the identity crisis is currently in progress. These people are thus currently, actively struggling to form an identity. They are often thoughtful individuals, open to experimenting with new ideas and lifestyles. They sometimes seem to change their personalities and styles from day to day. Part of this process of change results from their efforts to try out different ways of being in order to see how these feel and what reactions they get. The term *moratorium* comes from Erikson's term *psychosocial moratorium*, which he used to refer to the modern status of adolescence in which the individual is psychologically grown up in many respects but is not well integrated into society. Rather, the person is left for several years (as in college) with minimal social obligations and commitments so as to be free to try out different ways of forming an identity.

Foreclosure: Commitment Without Crisis   When the person has a stable, committed identity but there is no sign of having had a period of crisis, he or she is classified as foreclosure status. In most cases, these are people who have remained close to how their parents brought them up, perhaps with minor modifications (usually ones that the parents would approve). Children are almost all classified as having "foreclosed identities" until an identity crisis starts, and if no crisis ever happens the person simply remains in the foreclosed status.

Foreclosure status is a complex one. On the surface, these people tend to seem unusually mature, often having adult values, plans, and opinions while still in their teens. But this is partly an illusion, for these signs of maturity are simply accepted from the parents rather than acquired personally. Upon closer inspection, many people with foreclosed identities turn out to be rigid and inflexible, defensive, even insecure. They are often the exact opposite of the "moratorium" status individuals who are open to trying out new things; foreclosures tend to be uninterested in new ideas or experimental lifestyles. The rigidity of the foreclosed individual may cause problems when the person comes under stress or tries to form intimate relationships.

Other work soon showed, however, that foreclosure status is a reasonably healthy one for females (e.g., Damon, 1983; Waterman, 1982). Apparently, females can grow up to be normal and capable without an identity crisis. In our culture, maturity may require the male to reject parental teachings and find his or her own identity, but a female may do just fine to remain close to the values and goals her parents taught her. Given the rapid recent changes in the feminine sex role and woman's places in society, these results are likely to change from one generation to the next. For the present, though, it is important to remember that most of the disadvantages of the foreclosure status have mainly been documented among males.

Identity Diffusion: Neither Crisis nor Commitment   The last category refers to people who have neither had an identity crisis not remained foreclosed in the commitments they were brought up with. These "identity diffuse" people lack a stable, committed identity, but they do not seem to mind this, and they are not engaged in any struggle to form one. Identity diffusion can border on psychopathology. This may be because the mentally ill do not tend to have and resolve identity crises and are most comfortable with a vague, uncommitted position in society. At best, individuals with diffuse identities tend to be "perpetual teenagers," people who seem to thrive on the uncommitted lifestyle of adolescence and who may seek to prolong it long after others have formed adult identities. They may shun long-term relationships that might lead to marriage, and they postpone career choices and other decisions that solidify the adult identity.

Perhaps surprising, most of the research suggests that identity crises are good for you, even though they may be unpleasant. Research shows that people who experience identity crises—especially people who successfully resolve them and reach identity-achieved status—are superior to others on many things, including academic performance at college, motivation and ambition, ability to adapt and perform under stress, and ability to form mature, intimate relationships (Bernard, 1981; Bourne, 1978). Many of the studies providing this evidence used males only, so it is less clear whether identity crises are good for females. There is some suggestion that women with foreclosed identities are just as capable and mature as those with achieved identities, although identity-diffuse females are worse off (e.g., Marcia & Scheidel, 1983). There is almost nothing to suggest that identity crises have negative effects on males or females. The best conclusion at present, then, is that identity crises are beneficial for males and either beneficial or neutral for females.

What is an identity crisis like, and how does it happen? When researchers attempted to answer this question, they came to the conclusion that all identity crises are not the same. There appear to be at least two major types of identity crises, which follow quite different patterns and processes. These two types of identity crisis may be called *identity deficit* and *identity conflict* (Baumeister, Shapiro, & Tice, 1985; Baumeister, 1986). Let's take a look at these two types of identity crisis.

Identity deficit is just what it sounds like, that is, the person does not have "enough" identity to deal with life and make major decisions. This type of identity crisis may be caused by reaching a point in life where major decisions need to be made, but the person does not have a satisfactory inner basis for making them. Adolescence is a prime example, for in our culture adolescents need to make the choices that will shape their adult identities—especially choosing a career and a spouse—but such decisions are enormously difficult because one lacks information and there are many possible options. As a result, the person often feels a need to look inside himself or herself to find the basis for making these decisions. Sometimes a person will "look inside" and immediately feel a strong preference for one course of action, but in many other cases there is nothing inside to make the choice. That is called an identity deficit.

Identity deficits arise when people reject some beliefs or values or ambitions that they have been taught or have long held. Adolescents, for example, are often in the process of rejecting many things their parents taught them. Evidence suggests that adolescent identity crises may be more common in males than females, probably because males tend to make more drastic breaks with their parents than females do (e.g., Blos, 1962). There is also evidence that adolescents are more likely to have an identity crisis if they attend college than if they go right to work out of high school (Morash, 1980), because college presents individuals with many new ideas and opinions that encourage them to question parental teachings.

The individual who rejects many of his or her beliefs, values, and goals thus creates an inner vacuum that constitutes the identity deficit. This inner vacuum often causes an active search for new views to replace the discarded ones. People having identity deficit crises are often very interesting people, for they are busily exploring and trying out many new ideas and new ways of relating to others. They are also more vulnerable to influence than other people are, probably because the inner vacuum makes them receptive to new views. Recruiters for religious cults, for example, may often have their best success with people in the midst of identity deficit crises.

The emotional side of an identity deficit may seem like a roller-coaster ride from despair to euphoria and back again, in rapid succession. People having such crises may feel depressed and bewildered at times, and the lack of certainty about where their lives are going may seem alternately like an exhilarating breadth of opportunity and freedom, and a dispiriting, confusing meaninglessness.

Not everyone has an identity crisis at adolescence, of course, and not everyone who does have one manages to resolve it. But for those who do, the resolution of an identity deficit seems to be a two-step process. First, the person resolves the fundamental issues of value and meaning. That is, he or she decides on basic, abstract principles, such as what is important in life. The second step is to translate these abstract values and convictions into concrete, realistic ambitions. For example, someone may first struggle to reach the decision that what he wants out of life is to help others and to earn a comfortable salary; in the second stage, these general values are elaborated into a specific desire, such as becoming a physician or psychotherapist. Once this is done, the identity crisis is ended, and the person begins to work toward fulfilling these goals.

Identity crises are most common at adolescence, but there may be a second set of them at midlife (Levinson, 1978). Some evidence indicates that many men grow dissatisfied with their lives around the age of 40. They often feel that things have not turned out the way they had envisioned them. They come to realize that the goals that have guided them ever since adolescence are either not going to be reached—or, if they do reach them, this will not bring satisfaction and fulfillment. As a result, many men begin to discard, downplay, or reject these goals, and an identity deficit is the result. Males with midlife crises show many of the same signs and symptoms of adolescent identity crises. They may detach themselves from their family, experiment with new opinions and lifestyles, rethink their career ambitions or even change careers, and so forth. Most often, they change their priorities among career, family, religion, and other involvements, such as by deciding to work less hard and spend more time with their wives and children. Although this initial research has used only male subjects, there may well be comparable patterns for women.

If identity deficit means having too little identity to make vital life decisions, identity *conflict* is the opposite problem. An identity conflict is an inconsistency or incompatibility between two parts of the self. In most cases, these parts of the self were not initially in conflict, but circumstances brought them into conflict (such as by forcing a decision that affects both parts). Identity conflict means that the person has several identity components that disagree about the best decision to make. For example, a working mother who is offered a promotion that would entail increased responsibility and travel may be torn between her work identity (which tells her to accept the promotion) and her identity as a mother (which may tell her not to take time away from her family). This form of identity crisis also occurs among immigrants, who want to remain loyal to their old culture while embracing the new one. It can also occur in marriages between people who come from strong but different religious backgrounds, especially if there is pressure to convert. Loyalty to spouse may then conflict with maintaining one's most deeply held beliefs. It may well also arise among students who are the first in their family to attend college: They may be proud and highly motivated to get an education beyond what their parents and relatives received, yet they may also find that the education moves them away from their heritage and causes them to question the values that linked them to their families.

We saw earlier that identity deficits can be an emotional roller coaster, with both exhilarating and depressing phases. Identity conflicts do not appear to have these fluctuations, for there is little that is positive or pleasant about identity conflict. People having such crises tend to suffer, to feel that they are being "traitors" who are "betraying" some important part of themselves and others as well. They do not tend to show the openness to new ideas or the exploration and experimentation typical of identity deficits. Also, unlike the effect of identity deficits, there is nothing to suggest that identity conflicts are good for you.

Resolving an identity conflict is a difficult matter. Sometimes people simply have to renounce some important part of themselves. In other cases, there are various compromise solutions. The person may choose one of the conflicting parts of identity but find some way of retaining something of the "loser" of this inner struggle. Some people compartmentalize—that is, try to keep two rigidly separate spheres of their lives, to prevent the two parts of their identity from coming into open conflict.

Identity crises, whether deficit or conflict, are difficult periods in life. They involve changing the self to adapt to new circumstances. Although they may be depressing and even painful, most people apparently come through them quite well in the end. In many cases, the person is better off for having had the crisis.

SUMMARY

The self is a large, complex structure. Self-concept refers to how the person thinks of himself or herself, that is, the person's own beliefs and ideas about this self. Self-esteem refers to the evaluative dimension of the self-concept—that is, how good a person one is. Identity refers to definitions of the self that are created jointly by the individual, relatives and acquaintances, and society.

Children's self-concepts begin with awareness of their bodies and with knowing that they are male or female children belonging to a particular family. Around age 2, self-concept begins to be heavily based on knowledge of what the child can and cannot do. The emphasis on competency and control grows steadily through the later phase of childhood and increasingly involves comparing one's own abilities against those of other children. Older children also gradually begin to develop a notion of the self as something inner, including thoughts and feelings.

The quest for self-knowledge is dominated by three main motives: the desire to learn accurate information about oneself, the desire to confirm what one already knows about oneself, and the desire to hear favorable, flattering things about oneself. The first (self-assessment) of these motive is seemingly the most adaptive, because it should yield the most useful information. Nonetheless, the last (self-enhancement) motive seems to be the most powerful.

Self-knowledge does not seem to be all integrated into a single, unified structure. Rather, people have a great deal of knowledge and information about the self that is only loosely interrelated. At various times, different aspects of self-knowledge take center stage in awareness, often in response to the immediate situation or context, so people may regard themselves differently in different situations. Rather than speaking of a single self-concept, it seems more appropriate to speak of a collection of self-schemas. These include ideas about what sort of person one is, as well as ideas about how one might possibly become or would want to avoid being.

Once people form ideas about themselves, these are often strongly resistant to change. Self-concept change can occur, however, especially when people internalize their own actions or new ways of looking at themselves. The social network of interpersonal interactions seems to play a strong role in facilitating versus preventing change in the self-concept.

Self-esteem is a very important and influential aspect of the self-concept. Most people think well of themselves and desire to increase their esteem (self-enhancement) and desire to avoid loss of esteem (self-protection). In general, people with high self-esteem are oriented toward self-enhancement, whereas those with low self-esteem lean toward self-protection. Low self-esteem is associated with greater vulnerability or susceptibility to influence, confusion in self-knowledge, unpleasant and fluctuating emotional states, greater difficulty in bouncing back after adversity, and less prejudice toward members of other groups. High self-esteem appears to have the benefits of bringing a stock of good feelings that can be a valuable resource (such as in times of stress) and supporting greater initiative by the person.

Self-esteem does not seem to be as valuable or beneficial as is widely supposed, and indeed high self-esteem (such as in a conceited person) can have significant drawbacks and dangers. Nonetheless, people have a strong desire to maintain self-esteem and think well of themselves. There are competing theories about why people are so concerned with self-esteem, including the view that it helps them cope with misfortune, that it shields them from fear of death, or that it keeps track of their social standing with regard to getting along with other people. People pursue and protect their self-esteem with a broad variety of strategies, many of which involve stretching or distorting the truth so as to make themselves look and feel better.

Three main patterns of parenting seem to be associated with strong, high self-esteem in children. These include showing unconditional love for the child, setting firm rules and expectations, and giving the child approval and freedom when the child's behavior stays within the prescribed limits.

Identity consists of a set of partial definitions of the self, each of which is one answer to the question "Who are you?" Identity is defined according to continuity across time and differentiation from others. It has three functional aspects: an interpersonal aspect (social roles and reputation), a potentiality aspect, and a values aspect.

Not everyone has identity crises, but many people do. The two main types of crisis include identity deficit, in which an inner vacuum is created when the person rejects some important parts of the self, and identity conflict, in which two or more parts of the self disagree about the best course of action. Identity deficits occur most commonly at adolescence and midlife; they appear to have beneficial effects on males, and perhaps for females as well. Identity conflicts can occur at any point in life. They are difficult to resolve and seem to have little positive value for the individual.

DISCUSSION QUESTIONS

1. When people tell you about themselves, how much can you believe them? What factors might prevent them from giving accurate answers?
2. Should American schools try to increase self-esteem among pupils?
3. Is self-esteem as important in other cultures as it is in modern North America?
4. Do you think an identity crisis is a beneficial experience for most people? What people might benefit most and least from it?

5. Do you think people are born with a certain level of self-esteem, or is self-esteem entirely the result of experiences?
6. Why do you think people are so interested in learning about themselves—yet so willing to hear biased or distorted or unreliable information (such as in horoscopes)?

SUGGESTED READINGS

Baumeister, R. F. (1998). The self. In D. T. Gilbert, S. T. Fiske, & G. Lindzey (Eds.), *Handbook of social psychology* (4th ed., pp. 680–740). New York: McGraw-Hill. This is a thorough coverage of what personality and social psychologists have learned about the self.

Emler, N. (2001). *Self-esteem: The costs and consequences of low self-worth*. York, England: York Publishing Services. A recent and easy-to-read summary of research on self-esteem, presenting a balanced view of what high self-esteem does and does not contribute to desirable outcomes.

Erikson, E. (1968). *Identity: Youth and crisis*. New York: Norton. This is one of the classic works on identity, in which Erikson explains his seminal theory of identity based on clinical observations.

Kagan, J. (1981) *The second year: The emergence of self-awareness*. Cambridge, MA: Harvard University Press. An eminent child psychologist describes in a vivid and entertaining manner how children learn to know themselves.

Taylor, S. E., & Brown, J. D. (1988). Illusion and well-being: A social psychological perspective on mental health. *Psychological Bulletin, 103,* 193–210. One of the most heavily cited articles on the self of all time, this review of multiple studies shows how self-concepts are systematically distorted—and argues that such distortions are not only normal but even healthy and desirable.

SUGGESTED WEB SITES

http://www.psych.neu.edu/ISSI/

This is the official site of the International Society for Self and Identity, which as the title indicates is an international organization of experts and researchers on the topic. The site reports the doings of the organization and useful new information in the study of self and identity.

http://www.tandf.co.uk/journals/pp/ selfandidentity.html

This web site is devoted to the scientific journal *Self and Identity*, which publishes cutting-edge new research on those topics. Log on to learn the latest findings by leaders in the field.

INFOTRAC COLLEGE EDITION SEARCH TOPICS

Self-concept
Self-knowledge

Self-esteem
Identity

Identity crisis

REFERENCES

Aberson, C. L., Healy, M., & Romero, V. (2000). In-group bias and self-esteem: A meta-analysis. *Personality and Social Psychology Review, 4,* 157–173.

Alloy, L. B., & Abramson, L. Y. (1979). Judgment of contingency in depressed and nondepressed students: Sadder but wiser? *Journal of Experimental Psychology: General, 108,* 441–485.

Bachman, J. G., & O'Malley, P. M. (1977). Self-esteem in young men: A longitudinal analysis of the impact of educational and occupational attainment. *Journal of Personality and Social Psychology, 35*, 365–380.

Bachman, J. G., & O'Malley, P. M. (1986). Self-concepts, self-esteem, and educational experiences: The frog pond revisited (again). *Journal of Personality and Social Psychology, 50*, 35–46.

Baumeister, R. F. (1986). *Identity: Cultural change and the struggle for self*. New York: Oxford University Press.

Baumeister, R. F. (1987). How the self became a problem: A psychological review of historical research. *Journal of Personality and Social Psychology, 52*, 163–176.

Baumeister, R. F. (1993). Understanding the inner nature of low self-esteem: Uncertain, fragile, protective, and conflicted. In R. Baumeister (Ed.), *Self-esteem: The puzzle of low self-regard* (pp. 201–218). New York: Plenum.

Baumeister, R. F. (1998). The self. In D. T. Gilbert, S. T. Fiske, & G. Lindzey (Eds.), *Handbook of social psychology* (4th ed., pp. 680–740). New York: McGraw-Hill.

Baumeister, R. F., & Cairns, K. J. (1992). Repression and self-presentation: When audiences interfere with self-deceptive strategies. *Journal of Personality and Social Psychology, 62*, 851–862.

Baumeister, R. F., Campbell, J. D., & Krueger, J. I., & Vohs, K. D. (2003). Does high self-esteem cause better performance interpersonal success, happiness, or healthier lifestyles? *Psychological Science in the Public Interest, 4*, 1–44.

Baumeister, R. F., Heatherton, T. F., & Tice, D. M. (1993). When ego threats lead to self-regulation failure: Negative consequences of high self-esteem. *Journal of Personality and Social Psychology, 64*, 141–156.

Baumeister, R. F., & Leary, M. R. (1995). The need to belong: Desire for interpersonal attachments as a fundamental human motivation. *Psychological Bulletin, 117*, 497–529.

Baumeister, R. F., Shapiro, J. J., & Tice, D. M. (1985). Two kinds of identity crisis. *Journal of Personality, 53*, 407–424.

Baumeister, R. F., Smart, L., & Boden, J. M. (1996). Relation of threatened egotism to violence and aggression: The dark side of high self-esteem. *Psychological Review, 103*, 5–33.

Baumeister, R. F., Tice, D. M., & Hutton, D. G. (1989). Self-presentational motivations and personality differences in self-esteem. *Journal of Personality, 57*, 547–579.

Becker, E. (1973). *The denial of death*. New York: Free Press.

Bernard, H. S. (1981). Identity formation during late adolescence: A review of some empirical findings. *Adolescence, 16*, 349–357.

Blos, P. (1962) *On adolescence*. New York: Free Press.

Bourne, E. (1978). The state of research on ego identity: A review and appraisal. Part II. *Journal of Youth and Adolescence, 7*, 371–392.

Brim, O. G. (1976) Life-span development of the theory of oneself: Implications for child development. In H. Reese (Ed.), *Advances in child development and behavior* (Vol. 2, pp. 241–251). New York: Academic Press.

Brockner, J. (1984). Low self-esteem and behavioral plasticity: Some implications for personality and social psychology. In L. Wheeler (Ed.), *Review of personality and social psychology* (Vol. 4, pp. 237–271). Beverly Hills, CA: Sage.

Brockner, J., & Lloyd, K. (1986). Self-esteem and likability: Separating fact from fantasy. *Journal of Research in Personality, 20*, 496–508.

Bushman, B. J., & Baumeister, R. F. (1998). Threatened egotism, narcissism, self-esteem, and direct and displaced aggression: Does self-love or self-hate lead to violence? *Journal of Personality and Social Psychology, 75*, 219–229.

California Task Force to Promote Self-Esteem and Personal and Social Responsibility. (1990). *Toward a state of self-esteem*. Sacramento: California State Department of Education.

Campbell, J. D., & Fehr, B .A. (1990). Self-esteem and perceptions of conveyed impressions: Is negative affectivity associated with greater realism? *Journal of Personality and Social Psychology, 58*, 122–133.

Campbell, A. (1981). *The sense of well-being in America*. New York: McGraw-Hill.

Campbell, J. D. (1986). Similarity and uniqueness: The effects of attribute type, relevance, and individual differences in self-esteem and depression. *Journal of Personality and Social Psychology, 50*, 281–294.

Campbell, J. D. (1990). Self-esteem and clarity of the self-concept. *Journal of Personality and Social Psychology, 59*, 538–549.

Campbell, J. D., Chew, B., & Scratchley, L. S. (1991). Cognitive and emotional reactions to daily events: The effects of self-esteem and self-complexity. *Journal of Personality, 59,* 473–505.

Campbell, J. D., & Lavallee, L.F. (1993). Who am I? The role of self-concept confusion in understanding the behavior of people with low self-esteem. In R. Baumeister (Ed.), *Self-esteem: The puzzle of low self-regard* (pp. 3–20). New York: Plenum.

Colvin, C. R., Block, J., & Funder, D. C. (1995). Overly positive evaluations and personality: Negative implications for mental health. *Journal of Personality and Social Psychology, 68,* 1152–1162.

Coopersmith, S. (1967). *The antecedents of self-esteem.* San Francisco, CA: Freeman.

Crary, W. G. (1966). Reactions to incongruent self-experiences. *Journal of Consulting Psychology, 30,* 246–252.

Crocker, J., & Major, B. (1989). Social stigma and self-esteem: The self-protective properties of stigma. *Psychological Review, 96,* 608–630.

Crocker, J., & Schwartz, I. (1985). Prejudice and in-group favoritism in a minimal intergroup situation: Effects of self-esteem. *Personality and Social Psychology Bulletin, 11,* 379–386.

Crocker, J., Thompson, L. L., McGraw, K. M., & Ingerman, C. (1987). Downward comparison, prejudice, and evaluations of others: Effects of self-esteem and threat. *Journal of Personality and Social Psychology, 52,* 907–916.

Crocker, J., Voelkl, K., Testa, M., & Major, B. (1991). Social stigma: The affective consequences of attributional ambiguity. *Journal of Personality and Social Psychology, 60,* 218–228.

Damon, W. (1983) *Social and personality development.* New York: Norton.

Damon, W., & Hart, D. (1982) The development of self-understanding from infancy through adolescence. *Child Development, 53,* 841–864.

Diener, E., Wolsic, B., & Fujita, F. (1995). Physical attractiveness and subjective well-being. *Journal of Personality and Social Psychology, 69,* 120–129.

Emler, N. (2001). *Self-esteem: The costs and causes of low self-worth.* York, England: York Publishing Services.

Emmons, R. A. (1984).Factor analysis and construct validity of the Narcissistic Personality Inventory. *Journal of Personality Assessment, 48,* 291–300.

Erikson, E. H. (1968) *Identity: Youth and crisis.* New York: Norton.

Fazio, R. H., Effrein, E. A., & Falender, V. J. (1981). Self-perceptions following social interactions. *Journal of Personality and Social Psychology, 41,* 232–242.

Felson, R. B. (1993). The (somewhat) social self: How others affect self-appraisals. In J. Suls (Ed.), *Psychological perspectives on the self* (Vol. 4, pp. 1–26). Hillsdale, NJ: Erlbaum.

Fitch, G. (1970). Effects of self-esteem, perceived performance, and choice on causal attributions. *Journal of Personality and Social Psychology, 16,* 311–315.

Fleming, J. S., & Courtney, B. E. (1984). The dimensionality of self-esteem: II. Hierarchical facet model for revised measurement scales. *Journal of Personality and Social Psychology, 46,* 404–421.

Gabriel, M. T., Critelli, J. W., & Ee, J. S. (1994). Narcissistic illusions in self-evaluations of intelligence and attractiveness. *Journal of Personality, 62,* 143–155.

Greenberg, J., Pyszczynski, T., & Solomon, S. (1986). The causes and consequences of self-esteem: A terror management theory. In R. Baumeister (Ed.), *Public self and private self.* New York: Springer-Verlag.

Greenberg, J., Solomon, S., Pyszczynski, T., Rosenblatt, A., Burling, J., Lyon, D., Simon, L., & Pinel, E. (1992). Why do people need self-esteem? Converging evidence that self-esteem serves an anxiety-buffering function. *Journal of Personality and Social Psychology, 63,* 913–922.

Greenwald, A. G. (1980). The totalitarian ego: Fabrication and revision of personal history. *American Psychologist, 35,* 603–613.

Harter, S. (1993). Causes and consequences of low self-esteem in children and adolescents. In R. Baumeister (Ed.), *Self-esteem: The puzzle of low self-regard* (pp. 87–116). New York: Plenum.

Hattie, J. A., & Hansford, B. C. (1982). Self measures and achievement: Comparing a traditional review of literature with meta-analysis. *Australian Journal of Education, 26,* 71–75.

Heatherton, T. F., & Ambady, N. (1993). Self-esteem, self-prediction, and living up to commitments. In R. Baumeister (Ed.), *Self-esteem: The puzzle of low self-regard* (pp. 131–145). New York: Plenum.

Heatherton, T. F., & Nichols, P. A. (1994). Personal accounts of successful versus failed attempts at life change. *Personality and Social Psychology Bulletin, 20,* 664–6756.

Heatherton, T. F., & Vohs, K. D. (2000). Interpersonal evaluations following threats to self: Role of self-esteem. *Journal of Personality and Social Psychology, 78,* 725–736.

Janis, I. L. (1954). Personality correlates of susceptibility to persuasion. *Journal of Personality, 22,* 504–518.

Jones, E. E., Rhodewalt, F., Berglas, S. C., & Skelton, A. (1981). Effects of strategic self-presentation on subsequent self-esteem. *Journal of Personality and Social Psychology, 41,* 407–421.

Kagan, J. (1981). *The second year: The emergence of self-awareness.* Cambridge, MA: Harvard University Press.

Keller, A., Ford, L. H., & Meacham, J. A. (1978). Dimensions of self-concept in preschool children. *Developmental Psychology, 14,* 483–489.

Kuiper, N. A., & Derry, P. A. (1982). Depressed and nondepressed content self-reference in mild depression. *Journal of Personality, 50,* 67–79.

Kunda, Z. (1990). The case for motivated reasoning. *Psychological Bulletin, 108,* 480–498.

Leary, M. R., & Kowalski, R. (1995). *Social anxiety.* New York: Guilford.

Leary, M. R., Tambor, E. S., Terdal, S. K., & Downs, D. L. (1995). Self-esteem as an interpersonal monitor: The sociometer hypothesis. *Journal of Personality and Social Psychology, 68,* 518–530.

Levinson, D. J. (1978). *The seasons of a man's life.* New York: Ballantine.

Lewis, M., & Brooks-Gunn, J. (1979). *Social cognition and the acquisition of self.* New York: Plenum.

Mahler, M. S., Pine, F., & Bergman, A. (1975). *The psychological birth of the human infant: Symbiosis and individuation.* New York: Basic Books.

Marcia, J. E. (1966). Development and validation of ego-identity status. *Journal of Personality and Social Psychology, 3,* 551–558.

Marcia, J. E. (1967) Ego identity status: Relationship to change in self-esteem, "general maladjustment," and authoritarianism. *Journal of Personality, 35,* 118–133.

Marcia, J. E., & Scheidel, D. G. (1983). *Ego identity, intimacy, sex role orientation, and gender.* Presented at the annual meeting of the Eastern Psychological Association, Philadelphia, PA.

Marks, G. (1984). Thinking one's abilities are unique and one's opinions are common. *Personality and Social Psychology Bulletin, 10,* 203–208.

Markus, H. (1977). Self-schemata and processing information about the self. *Journal of Personality and Social Psychology, 35,* 63–78.

Markus, H. R., & Kitayama, S. (1991). Culture and the self: Implications for cognition, emotion, and motivation. *Psychological Review, 98,* 224–253.

Maruyama, G., Rubin, R. A., & Kingsbury, G. G. (1981). Self-esteem and educational achievement: Independent constructs with a common cause? *Journal of Personality and Social Psychology, 40,* 962–975.

McFarlin, D. B., & Blascovich, J. (1981). Effects of self-esteem and performance feedback on future affective preferences and cognitive expectations. *Journal of Personality and Social Psychology, 40,* 521–531.

McGuire, W. J., & McGuire, C. V. (1982). Significant others in self space: Sex differences and developmental trends in social self. In J. Suls (Ed.), *Psychological perspectives on the self* (pp. 73–120). Hillsdale, NJ: Erlbaum.

McGuire, W. J., McGuire, C. V., Child, P., & Fujioka, T. (1978). Salience of ethnicity in the spontaneous self-concept as a function of one's ethnic distinctiveness in the social environment. *Journal of Personality and Social Psychology, 36,* 511–520.

Mecca, A. M., Smelser, N. J., & Vasconcellos, J. (Eds.). (1989). *The social importance of self-esteem.* Berkeley, CA: University of California Press.

Mischel, W., Ebbesen, E. B., & Zeiss, A. R. (1976). Determinants of selective memory about the self. *Journal of Consulting and Clinical Psychology, 44,* 92–103.

Mohr, D. M. (1978). Development of attributes of personal identity. *Developmental Psychology, 14,* 427–428.

Montemayor, R., & Eisen, M. (1977). The development of self-conceptions from childhood to adolescence. *Developmental Psychology, 13,* 314–319.

Morash, M. A. (1980). Working class membership and the adolescent identity crisis. *Adolescence, 15,* 313–320.

Morf, C. C., & Rhodewalt, F. (2001). Unraveling the paradoxes of narcissism: A dynamic self-regulatory processing model. *Psychological Inquiry, 12,* 177–196.

Pottebaum, S. M., Keith, T. Z., & Ehly, S. W. (1986). Is there a causal relation between self-concept and academic achievement? *Journal of Educational Research, 79,* 140–144.

Pyszczynski, T., Greenberg, J., & Holt, K. (1985). Maintaining consistency between self-serving beliefs and available data: A bias in information processing. *Personality and Social Psychology Bulletin, 11,* 179–190.

Pyszczynski, T., Greenberg, J., & Solomon, S. (1997). Why do we need what we need? A terror management perspective on the roots of human social motivation. *Psychological Inquiry, 8,* 1–20.

Robins, R. W., Trzesniewski, K. H., Tracy, J. L., Gosling, S. D., & Potter, J. (2002) Global self-esteem across the life span. *Psychology and Aging, 17,* 423–434.

Rosenberg, M. (1965). *Society and the adolescent self-image.* Princeton, NJ: Princeton University Press.

Rosenberg, M. (1979). *Conceiving the self.* New York: Basic Books.

Rosenberg, M., Schooler, C., & Schoenbach, C. (1989). Self-esteem and adolescent problems: Modeling reciprocal effects. *American Sociological Review, 54,* 1004–1018.

Sanitioso, R., Kunda, Z., & Fong, G. T. (1990). Motivated recruitment of autobiographical memory. *Journal of Personality and Social Psychology, 59,* 229–241.

Schlenker, B. R., Dlugolecki, D. W., & Doherty, K. (1994). The impact of self-presentations on self-appraisals and behavior: The roles of commitment and biased scanning. *Personality and Social Psychology Bulletin, 20,* 20–33.

Schlenker, B. R., & Leary, M. R. (1982). Social anxiety and self-presentation: A conceptualization and model. *Psychological Bulletin, 92,* 641–669.

Sedikides, C. (1993). Assessment, enhancement, and verification determinants of the selfevaluation process. *Journal of Personality and Social Psychology, 65,* 317–338.

Simmons, R., Rosenberg, F., & Rosenberg, M. (1973). Disturbances in the self-image at adolescence. *American Sociological Review, 38,* 553–568.

Steele, C. M. (1988). The psychology of self-affirmation: Sustaining the integrity of the self. In L. Berkowitz (Ed.), *Advances in experimental social psychology* (Vol. 21, pp. 261–302). New York: Academic Press.

Suls, J., & Wan, C. K. (1987). In search of the false uniqueness phenomenon: Fear and estimates of social consensus. *Journal of Personality and Social Psychology, 52,* 211–217.

Swann, W. B. (1985). The self as architect of social reality. In B. R. Schlenker (Ed.), *The self and social life* (pp. 100–125). New York: McGraw-Hill.

Swann, W. B. (1987). Identity negotiation: Where two roads meet. *Journal of Personality and Social Psychology, 53,* 1038–1051.

Taylor, S. E., & Brown, J. D. (1988). Illusion and well-being: A social psychological perspective on mental health. *Psychological Bulletin, 103,* 193–210.

Tice, D. M. (1992). Self-presentation and self-concept change: The looking glass self as magnifying glass. *Journal of Personality and Social Psychology, 63,* 435–451.

Tice, D. M., Buder, J., & Baumeister, R. F. (1985). Development of self-consciousness: At what age does audience pressure disrupt performance? *Adolescence, 20,* 301–305.

Trope, Y. (1983). Self-assessment in achievement behavior. In J. Suls & A. Greenwald (Eds.), *Psychological perspectives on the self* (Vol. 2, pp. 93–121). Hillsdale, NJ: Erlbaum.

Trope, Y. (1986). Self-enhancement and self-assessment in achievement behavior. In R. Sorrentino & E. T. Higgins (Eds.), *Handbook of motivation and cognition* (Vol. 2, pp. 350–378). New York: Guilford.

Waterman, A. S. (1982). Identity development from adolescence to adulthood: An extension of theory and a review of research. *Developmental Psychology,18,* 341–358.

Wicklund, R. A., & Gollwitzer, P. M. (1982). *Symbolic self-completion.* Hillsdale, NJ: Erlbaum.

Wills, T. A. (1981). Downward comparison principles in social psychology. *Psychological Bulletin, 90,* 245–271.

Wyer, R. S., & Frey, D. (1983). The effects of feedback about self and others on the recall and judgments of feedback-relevant information. *Journal of Experimental Social Psychology, 19,* 540–559.

Zuckerman, M. (1979). Attribution of success and failure revisited, or: The motivational bias is alive and well in attribution theory. *Journal of Personality, 47,* 245–287.

Self-Awareness and Self-Consciousness | 10

STEPHEN L. FRANZOI

MARK H. DAVIS

How attentive are you to your emotions during the day? That is, if asked to describe your feelings, how sure would you be about your answers? How well do you know your own motives? Do you ever do things and yet find yourself later unable to figure out why? Likewise, how well do you know other people's impressions of you? For example, what sort of opinion do you think your friends have about your level of intelligence? How affectionate and caring would your sister or brother say you are?

The common feature of these questions is your self-knowledge, which can be attained only through self-awareness, a psychological state in which you take yourself as an object of attention. To have a self-concept, you must be able to engage in self-awareness. The purpose of this chapter is to consider some of the ways social and personality psychologists have studied self-awareness, the origin of the fundamental ideas, and the theories that currently shape scientific research. As we proceed, we will see that some of the questions about self-awareness with which psychology is wrestling today are very similar to questions that have been around for centuries (Bermúdez, 1998; Natsoulas, 1998). Our continuing interest in these issues is a testimony to their importance and fascination to us.

In introducing this topic, we need to make an important distinction that will help us understand how self-awareness has been studied. This is the distinction between private self-awareness and public self-awareness. Private self-awareness refers to a psychological state in which we are aware of those aspects of ourselves that are hidden from public view—our thoughts, feelings, attitudes, wishes, dreams, and fantasies. When we become aware of internal emotional and physiological states such as happiness and hunger, when we think about our innermost fears and hopes, when we try to figure out why in the world we behave the way we do, we are in a state of private self-awareness. In contrast, public self-awareness is a psychological state in which we are aware of those aspects of ourselves that are observable by other people—our physical appearance, public words and actions, and expressions of emotions. When we think about how we look to others, when we examine ourselves in a full-length mirror at the clothing store, when we rehearse our end of a phone call before dialing the number, we are in a state of public self-awareness.

This differentiation between public and private self-awareness is a very fundamental one. In fact, some have suggested that the private-public distinction may be an example of a more general and very fundamental concept in social and personality psychology, what has been termed the *inner-outer metaphor* (Hogan & Cheek, 1983). This metaphor manifests itself in many ways. For example, Jung's (1921) theory of personality emphasizes the concept of introversion-extraversion—the idea that people differ in terms of whether they characteristically turn psychic energy inward toward the inner world, or outward toward the external world. Similarly, such personality traits as field-dependence-independence (Witkin, Lewis, Hertzman, Machover, Meissner, & Wapner, 1954), locus of control (Rotter, 1966), and self-monitoring (Snyder, 1974) echo this distinction between attention to and knowledge of internal matters and attention to and knowledge of external forces. We believe that this inner-outer theme persists in psychology because it is so useful in making sense of our personalities. Later in the chapter we will examine some of the findings that illustrate this usefulness.

Although widespread today, this distinction between private and public aspects of self may be a relatively recent development in human history. For example, Roy Baumeister (1986) argues that in earlier times (such as in medieval Europe), public and private aspects of the self were viewed as equivalent. The widespread expectation that private aspects of the self will often be separate and distinct from public behavior and appearances gradually evolved over the past few centuries (Harbus, 2002). In the 21st century, this distinction between the private self and the public self is firmly embedded within the socialization practices of most modern cultures. With this understanding, let us turn our attention to a separate consideration of some modern concepts related to private and public self-awareness.

CONCEPTS RELATED TO PRIVATE SELF-AWARENESS

Many modern theorists have contributed to our knowledge about the private self, but perhaps the single strongest contribution came from Sigmund Freud. His emphasis on the unseen, internal, private world of the mind profoundly shaped later attempts to understand the self (Freud, 1950/1895). In particular, Freud (1926) stressed the difficulty people have in understanding their true motives and desires. According to Freud, because many of our impulses and motives are too threatening for us to acknowledge consciously, they are relegated to the unconscious.

This emphasis on the unconscious raises interesting questions regarding our ability to be aware of our private selves. For example, if our true motives and desires are largely concealed, how accurate is our self-understanding? Freud believed that because of the pervasive nature of unconscious motivation, self-understanding is always necessarily inaccurate. A related matter is the issue of self-deception. In Freud's view, a primary reason that people have inaccurate self-views is that they deliberately, although unconsciously, deceive themselves about their true feelings, desires, and wishes. Freud (1917) catalogued a long list of techniques, called defense mechanisms that we employ to conceal unpleasant and threatening information from ourselves.

The issues of accuracy and self-deception have stimulated contemporary research in an effort to discover whether Freud's ideas are tenable. As one example, Gur and Sackheim (1979) attempted to demonstrate self-deception through an intriguing experiment. First, they defined self-deception as consisting of three elements: (a) the individual simultaneously holds two contradictory beliefs; (b) the individual is not aware of holding one of these beliefs; and (c) the reason the person is not aware of one of the beliefs is that he or she is motivated not to know it (i.e., it is more pleasant not to be aware). In pursuing evidence for the existence of self-deception, Gur and Sackheim presented research participants with audio recordings of different voices, including the participants' own voices. The key result was that the participants' physiological responses (a measure of arousal) were much stronger when they heard their own voices than when they heard someone else's, even when they did not con-sciously recognize the voice as their own. That is, at the very same time that participants were saying "No, that isn't my voice," measures of their physical arousal indicated self-recognition. Gur and Sackheim interpreted this as evi-dence of self-deception—evidence that people at times are not consciously aware of private information that they possess. This and other research (Ayduk, Mischel, & Downey, 2002; Greenwald & Farnham, 2000) suggests that pri-vate self-awareness may also exist below the threshold of consciousness.

CONCEPTS RELATED TO PUBLIC SELF-AWARENESS

Although Freud's work on the private, hidden aspects of personality consider-ably influenced modern views about private self-awareness, it has had much less impact on conceptions of public self-awareness. Instead, the ideas that have shaped modern views of public self-awareness have largely come from other sources, including the psychologist William James (1890) and the sociologist George Herbert Mead (1934). The ideas generated by these and other social scientists revolve around the common theme that in addition to any awareness people may or may not have about their inner selves, they are acutely aware of their outer selves. In particular, they are attentive to how their appearance and behavior are seen and judged by others, and this awareness significantly shapes their future actions.

Sociologist Charles Cooley (1902) used the term *looking-glass self* to de-scribe the way we form our own self-images by seeing how others react to us. Just as we use a mirror to understand what our outward appearance is like, we use other people as mirrors to understand what kind of people we are. Does everyone laugh at our jokes? Then we must have a pretty good sense of humor. Do friends frequently tell us what a good and attentive listener we are? We must therefore be warm and sympathetic. According to this view, later devel-oped into a sociological theory known as symbolic interactionism (Blumer, 1969), our self-concept is directly shaped by the ways in which others respond to us in everyday interaction.

One modern outgrowth of this perspective on the self has been the devel-opment of the impression management viewpoint in social psychology, which focuses on the innumerable ways that we try to influence the way others per-ceive and judge us (Leary, 1996; Schlenker, 1980). This approach takes the basic symbolic interactionist idea that we are strongly affected by others' judg-ments of us and extends the concept to a consideration of what that must mean for our behavior. What it seems to mean, according to the evidence, is that we constantly strive to influence how others judge our attitudes, personalities, be-haviors, families, possessions, appearance, and values.

Over the past 30 years social psychologists have catalogued a number of different strategies people use for this purpose, the most important of which may be ingratiation. In using ingratiation, self-presenters attempt to flatter their audience by saying positive things about them (Gordon, 1996; Jones, 1990). Other common techniques come into play when we find ourselves in danger of being viewed negatively by others. In such situations, we may offer excuses, which are attempts to convince an audience that we are not responsible for some event that threatens our public self-image (Weiner, Amirkhan, Folkes, & Verette, 1987). For example, someone's image as a good student can be threatened by failing miserably on an exam on which others performed well. An excuse that explains the failure on an external and uncontrollable event ("I had to take care of my sick grandmother and, thus, had no time to study") may successfully preserve one's public self-presentation.

In 1974, psychologist Mark Snyder took a different and quite fascinating approach to impression management. Previously, the assumption had been that everyone engaged in self-presentation techniques. Snyder's view was that although everyone at times uses these techniques, some people use them much more frequently and successfully than others. That is, there may be individual differences in the tendency to engage in impression management. The term Snyder used to describe this characteristic tendency or skill is *self-monitoring* (Snyder, 1974, 1987).

A considerable amount of research supports Snyder's personality concept. High self-monitoring persons are especially attuned to social cues concerning appropriate behavior in a given situation (Gangestad & Snyder, 2000; John et al., 1996; Koestner, Bernieri, & Zuckerman, 1992). They are skilled impression managers who try to behave in a way that projects an appropriate self-image, even if some degree of deception is required (Chen, Shecter, & Chaiken, 1996; Leck & Simpson, 1999). For example, when trying to initiate a dating relationship, high self-monitoring men and women behave in a chameleon-like fashion, strategically and often deceptively changing their self-presentations in an attempt to appear more desirable (Leck & Simpson, 1999; Rowatt, Cunningham, & Druen, 1998). On the other hand, low self-monitors are less attentive to situational cues, and their behavior is guided more by inner attitudes and beliefs. As a result, their behavior is more consistent across situations. They are also less interested than those high in self-monitoring in projecting a positive self-image that others will respect (Gonnerman, Parker, Lavine, & Huff, 2000).

CURRENT SELF-AWARENESS AND SELF-CONSCIOUSNESS THEORIES

The remainder of this chapter focuses in more detail on a specific line of research that deals specifically with the causes and consequences of paying attention to private and public aspects of the self. Several different terms are used in describing the variables and processes central to this line of work, and we will identify them as we proceed. We begin with one of the most important distinctions, namely, the difference between self-awareness and self-consciousness.

Self-Awareness Versus Self-Consciousness

As previously defined, the term *self-awareness* refers to the actual psychological state of being attentive to oneself. Our earlier distinction between private self-awareness and public self-awareness remains in effect.

Regarding self-consciousness, it is a personality trait that refers to a relatively permanent tendency on the part of the individual to spend more or less time in the state of self-awareness. Again, the private-public distinction is relevant. Private self-consciousness is the dispositional tendency to engage in private self-awareness, whereas public self-consciousness is the dispositional tendency to engage in public self-awareness. Although it may be confusing at first, the research literature makes clear distinctions between states and traits, and uses the awareness/consciousness terminology to reflect this distinction. Before discussing the actual theories of self-awareness and self-consciousness, however, let us examine the assessment device used to measure the personality traits of private and public self-consciousness.

The Self-Consciousness Scale

In the early 1970s, Allan Fenigstein, Michael Scheier, and Arnold Buss developed an individual difference measure to assess the dispositional tendency to engage in self-awareness. Using a statistical procedure called factor analysis, they constructed a list of 23 items, which were separated into three factors or scales. These scales, known collectively as the Self-Consciousness Scale (SCS), appear in Activity Box 10.1.

Fenigstein and his colleagues named the first scale, which consists of 10 items, Private Self-Consciousness, because a person who agrees with these items would be one who habitually looks inside the self, fantasizes, and examines moods, motives, and mental processes. The second scale, containing 7 items, was named Public Self-Consciousness. People who agree with these items would be habitually aware of and concerned about their appearance, social behavior, and the general impression they make on others. Public self-consciousness generally correlates in the low .30s with private self-consciousness, but the two kinds of self-consciousness have different relationships with other traits (see Buss, 2001 for a review). Finally, the third scale consists of 6 items and was named Social Anxiety. Social anxiety is considered a possible by-product of high public self-consciousness; a person who agrees with these items would generally be shy, easily embarrassed, and anxious in social situations.

A number of studies have not only confirmed the factor structure of the SCS (Britt, 1992; Nystedt & Ljungberg, 2002) but have also found it to be a stable and valid measure of these three personality traits (Carver & Glass, 1976; Chang, Hau, & Guo, 2001; Davis & Franzoi, 1991; Fenigstein, 1979; Hass, 1984). The scale has been translated into a number of foreign languages (Alanazi, 2001; Hamid, Lai, & Cheng, 2001; Merz, 1984; Shek, 1994; Sugawara, 1984; Vleeming & Engelse, 1981), and today it is used by personality researchers throughout the world to investigate a wide variety of issues. Michael Scheier and Charles Carver also introduced a revised version of the scale (Scheier & Carver, 1985) designed for use with noncollege populations, but the original scale remains the most popular version.

ACTIVITY BOX 10.1   **What Are Your Levels of Private and Public Self-Consciousness?**

The personality traits of private and public self-consciousness are measured by items on the Self-Consciousness Scale (SCS; Fenigstein, Scheier, & Buss, 1975). To take the SCS, read each item below and then indicate how well each statement describes you using the following scale:

0 = extremely uncharacteristic (not at all like me)

1 = uncharacteristic (somewhat unlike me)

2 = neither characteristic nor uncharacteristic

3 = characteristic (somewhat like me)

4 = extremely characteristic (very much like me)

1. I'm always trying to figure myself out.
2. I'm concerned about my style of doing things.
3. Generally, I'm not very aware of myself.*
4. I reflect about myself a lot.
5. I'm concerned about the way I present myself.
6. I'm often the subject of my own fantasies.
7. I never scrutinize myself.*
8. I'm self-conscious about the way I look.
9. I'm generally attentive to my inner feelings.
10. I usually worry about making a good impression.
11. I'm constantly examining my motives.
12. One of the last things I do before I leave my house is look in the mirror.
13. I sometimes have the feeling that I'm off somewhere watching myself.
14. I'm concerned about what other people think of me.
15. I'm alert to changes in my mood.
16. I'm usually aware of my appearance.
17. I'm aware of the way my mind works when I work through a problem.

DIRECTIONS FOR SCORING

Several of the SCS items are reverse-scored; that is, for these items a lower rating actually indicates a higher level of self-consciousness. Before summing the items, recode those with an asterisk ("*") so that 0 = 4, 1 = 3, 3 = 1, and 4 = 0.

Private self-consciousness. To calculate your private self-consciousness score, add up your responses to the following items: 1, 3*, 4, 6, 7*, 9, 11, 13, 15, and 17.

Public self-consciousness. To calculate your public self-consciousness score, add up your responses to the following items: 2, 5, 8, 10, 12, 14, and 16.

When Fenigstein, Scheier, and Buss developed the SCS in 1975, the mean college score for college students on private self-consciousness was about 26, whereas the average score of public self-consciousness was about 19. The higher your score is above one of these values, the more of this type of self-consciousness you probably possess. The lower your score is below one of these values, the less of this type of self-consciousness you probably possess. Of course, you should remember that any individual person's scores on these two scales are far from perfect as indicators of that person's "true" self-consciousness levels. This questionnaire is included here to give you a sense of how this construct is usually measured by researchers and not to provide a reliable measure of your own personality.

One final comment about the scale is in order. Although all investigators who study the personality traits of private and public self-consciousness use the SCS to measure these traits, they do not all share the same assumptions about those traits. Thus, as you will discover shortly, different theories offer different interpretations of what the scores on this measure represent. In fact, the first theory we will discuss has little if any use at all for the SCS!

Duval and Wicklund's Approach: Objective Self-Awareness

Prior to the development of the Self-Consciousness Scale, and before there was any interest in self-consciousness as a trait, Shelley Duval and Robert Wicklund wrote a book entitled *A Theory of Objective Self-Awareness* (1972). This book outlined a theory that triggered much of the recent interest in the issues of self-awareness and self-consciousness. Although Wicklund has been more active than Duval in promoting and defending this theory over the past 30 years, Duval recently proposed a revision of the original theory that places more emphasis on the nature and operation of the standards we attend to in the self-aware state (Duval, Silvia, & Lalwani, 2001). Despite the possibility that this revision may one day supplant the original theory, in this section we will focus our discussion on the hypotheses and findings derived from the original theory.

Objective self-awareness (OSA) theory takes as its starting point the assumption that a person's conscious attention can be focused in only one of two directions: either internally toward the self or externally toward the environment. When attention is turned toward the self, an important sequence of events is set in motion. Duval and Wicklund maintain that self-focused attention leads us almost invariably to a critical self-evaluation, judging ourselves as soon as our attention becomes self-focused. What we focus on is whatever dimension of the self is most important or salient to us at the time. Thus, if you become self-aware while taking the SAT exams, the most salient self-aspect may well be your intelligence. If you become self-aware while getting ready for a big date, you may focus instead on your physical attractiveness.

Once attention is focused on some salient aspect of self, the theory makes an important assumption. It assumes that there is a difference between our real self on that dimension (i.e., how intelligent or physically attractive we perceive ourselves to be) and our ideal self (how intelligent or physically attractive we desire to be). In fact, Duval and Wicklund propose that we almost always fall short of our ideal self, and thus self-focused attention makes us uncomfortably aware of our shortcomings. This uncomfortable feeling is aversive and we are motivated to somehow reduce the negative feeling. For this reason, OSA theory is referred to as a motivational theory.

According to the theory, there are two basic ways that we can reduce this unpleasant motivational state. One way is to escape the self-aware state itself; after all, if focusing attention on the self causes this negative feeling in the first place, then focusing attention back on the environment should stop it. The other way to reduce the unpleasant state is to somehow reduce the discrepancy between the real and ideal selves. Of course, at times it will be difficult to change the real self and bring it closer to the ideal.

Before discussing some evidence regarding OSA theory, we must mention one more issue. Focusing attention on the self is what initiates the self-evaluative process. Yet what induces self-awareness in the first place? Unlike other theories we will discuss shortly, Duval and Wicklund's theory does not assume that people are chronic self-focusers, nor does it assume that they are chronic non-self-focusers. The theory simply does not discuss the possibility of individual differences in self-awareness. Instead, it focuses on how situational cues manipulate the direction of consciousness. Specifically, Duval and Wicklund believe that there are certain stimuli in the environment that have the effect of making us aware of ourselves as objects in the world. For example, seeing a photo of ourselves tends to focus our attention inward rather than outward toward the environment; it makes us see ourselves in the way that others do. Hearing our own voice on a recording has the same effect. However, a mirror may most directly induce self-awareness, because when we see ourselves in a mirror our attention is literally turned back on us by the reflective properties of the mirror. It is not surprising, then, that many of the experiments designed to test this theory used mirrors to create self-focused attention among participants.

Research has provided considerable support for various aspects of OSA theory. For example, Duval, Wicklund, and Fine (1972) tested the notion that people seek to escape self-focused attention when the discrepancy between the real and ideal selves is negative. Student participants were given false information about their levels of creativity and intelligence supposedly on the basis of personality questionnaires they had filled out at the beginning of the semester. Half of the students were told that they had done quite well on the tests, scoring in the upper 10% of their class; for these students, their real selves were quite successful. The other half of the participants were told that they had not done so well on the tests, scoring in the lower 10% of the class; thus, these students were led to believe that their real selves were not very successful. Remember, of course, that this information was false, but the participants did not know it at the time.

The participants were next led to a separate room, ostensibly for a second and unrelated experiment. For half of them, the room contained a mirror that faced them and a television camera that pointed toward them. For the other participants, the mirror was turned around so that its nonreflecting side was facing the students, and the television camera was also pointed away from them. Thus, half of the participants should be engaging in self-focused attention (due to the mirror and camera), and the other half should not. The participants were then told to wait there for the second experimenter, but that if he did not show up in 5 minutes, to go look for him in another room. The dependent measure in the experiment was simply how long students were willing to wait in the room.

The theory would predict that one group should be especially likely to leave the room quickly. Those students who believed that they had done poorly on the personality tests (high discrepancy between real and ideal selves) and who were facing a mirror and television camera (self-focused attention) should be feeling the most discomfort because they were being made aware of their shortcomings. The other three groups were either not focusing attention on the self or had less real-ideal discrepancy, and thus, they should not be very motivated to escape the room. Results supported these predictions.

Carver (1975) tested the second prediction of the theory: that people who focus attention on the self will try to bring the real self into line with the ideal self. After pretesting students early in the semester concerning whether they thought the use of strong punishment in teaching is justified, Carver selected a group of students with strong pro-punishment attitudes and a group with strong anti-punishment attitudes. Later in the semester, these students played the role of "teacher" in an experiment in which they also had the power to use what they thought were real electric shocks on another student (the "learner") to improve his learning.

For half the students, there was a mirror in front of them as they delivered the shocks; for the other half there was no mirror. According to the theory, those in the mirror condition should experience self-focused attention and thus, should be aware of the discrepancy between the ideal self (the attitudes they expressed earlier in the semester) and the real self (what kind of shocks they actually delivered). In order to minimize the real-ideal discrepancy, these students should strive to act in accordance with their attitudes and thus should make the real self conform to the ideal self. Those who were not facing a mirror should not be self-aware and thus should feel less pressure to match behavior to attitudes. This is exactly the pattern that was found. Participants with "pro-shock" attitudes who were facing a mirror administered the most intense shocks, whereas those with "anti-shock" attitudes facing a mirror administered the weakest shocks. This general pattern has been found repeatedly with a variety of other attitudes and behaviors (see Buss, 2001).

All told, considerable evidence supports this theory, especially for situations in which there is a clear comparison standard. However, there have been empirical criticisms, one of which has been a challenge to Duval and Wicklund's contention that self-awareness inevitably leads to the experience of negative affect (Carver & Scheier, 1978; Franzoi & Brewer, 1984; Hull & Levy, 1979; Steenbarger & Aderman, 1979). In an attempt to resolve this controversy, Fejfar and Hoyle (2000) conducted a meta-analysis of 79 studies that had examined the relationship between private self-awareness and negative affect, and their findings revealed a small overall effect ($r = .20$). Thus, consistent with objective self-awareness theory, it does appear that negative affect is somewhat more likely when one is in the privately self-aware state. However, in line with critics' contentions, these findings suggest that self-awareness does not inevitably induce negative affect. Additional research suggests that aversive reactions to self-awareness are most likely following failure on a task or when one is negatively evaluated (Arndt, Greenberg, Simon, Pyszczynski, & Solomon, 1998; Green & Sedikides, 1999). We shall return to this point later on, in our discussion of Charles Carver and Michael Scheier's self-regulation model.

Buss's Approach: Self-Consciousness Theory

In the mid-1970s, as research spurred by objective self-awareness theory began to accumulate, Arnold Buss was developing his own theoretical viewpoint regarding self-awareness and self-consciousness. Although there is some similarity between Buss's approach and Duval and Wicklund's, Buss's theory in many ways is quite different. One important difference is the strong emphasis Buss places on distinguishing between private self-awareness or self-consciousness and public self-awareness or self-consciousness, a distinction that Duval and Wicklund ignore. Another difference is that Buss's theory essentially makes no use of the concept of an ideal self, or behavioral standard, which is the centerpiece of Duval and Wicklund's approach. Instead, Buss conceptualized the processes of private and public self-awareness in a way that pays little attention to such ideals. Because the foundation of Buss's self-consciousness theory is the distinction between private and public self-aspects, let us consider each of these in turn.

Private Self-Aspects   Buss holds that when attention is focused on private aspects of the self, two processes result: intensification of affect and clarification of knowledge. Intensification of affect means that any positive or negative feelings present during private self-awareness are intensified. To illustrate this process, consider your feelings of anger after being insulted. In this negatively charged affective event, focusing attention on the private self serves to intensify your feelings of anger. Similarly, your feelings of happiness after doing well on an exam are affectively charged (positively) and will be intensified by private self-awareness. In contrast, your memory of what your elementary school looked like is probably an affectively neutral event because it does not produce any emotional reaction. As a result, there can be no intensification of affect regarding that memory.

However, the second consequence of private self-awareness does apply to neutral private events. Clarification of knowledge means that in the private self-aware state all private events, whether affectively charged or not, become clearer and more distinct. In effect, Buss claims that paying attention to the private self leads us to have clearer and more accurate knowledge about it. Private self-awareness will therefore make us more clearly aware of an aching muscle, will let us more accurately know our attitudes, and will bring our memories or fantasies more sharply into focus.

What would cause someone to focus attention on private self-aspects? Buss argued that keeping a diary is one activity that should focus attention on the private self, because it forces us to think about our feelings, motives, and reasons for acting—all things that are private. In addition, Buss held that a certain type of mirror will also induce private self-awareness: a small mirror of the type found on bathroom cabinets, one that provides an image of the head and shoulders. Small mirrors, but not large ones, are said to produce this private self-focus because the image they provide us with is so familiar. After literally thousands of exposures to our images in bathroom mirrors, these reflections eventually tell us nothing especially new about how we look to others. As a result, the ability of small mirrors to make us publicly self-aware is usually quite weak. Instead, small mirrors direct our attention back toward ourselves and eventually produce in us an attention to our private, unseen aspects. Larger mirrors provide us with less familiar images of ourselves and have a different effect that we shall examine shortly.

Finally, Buss made quite explicit the difference between self-awareness and self-consciousness. When some stimulus in the environment, like a diary or a mirror, focuses our attention on the private self, that focus is only temporary. In addition to this transient state of private self-awareness, people differ in their tendency to engage in private self-awareness, which we previously identified as the personality trait of private self-consciousness. However, the effect

Table 10.1 | Inducers and Effects of Private and Public Self-Awareness

Private Self-Awareness

Inducers ⇒	Focus ⇒	Effects
Being asked about your current mood	Mood	Intensification of affect
Hunger or pain signals	Body processes	Clearer self-knowledge
Small mirror	Emotions	
Keeping a diary	Motives	Adherence to personal standards
Private self-consciousness	Personal standards	

Public Self-Awareness

Inducers ⇒	Focus ⇒	Effects
Being watched(or ignored) by others	Unspecified public self-aspects	Evaluation apprehension Temporary loss of self-esteem
Cameras, tape recorders, large mirrors	Physical appearance, voice	Adherence to social standards

Source: Based on *Self-Consciousness and Social Anxiety,* by A. H. Buss, 1980, San Francisco: W. H. Freeman; *Psychological Dimensions of the Self,* by A. H. Buss, 2001, Thousand Oaks, CA: Sage.

of engaging in private self-awareness, whether caused by dispositions or inducers, is the same: It leads to intensification of affect and clarification of knowledge. Table 10.1 presents an outline of the basic elements in Buss's view of private self-awareness.

What evidence is there for Buss's theory concerning attention to private self-aspects? One body of evidence supports his prediction that private self-awareness leads to intensification of affect. Numerous studies have found that people who score high on the private self-consciousness scale attend to private self-aspects. Additional research indicates that high private self-conscious (PRSC) persons react more intensely to stimuli that produce an affective response. For example, Scheier and Carver (1977) exposed college men to enjoyable slides (photographs of beautiful nude women) and unpleasant slides (such as photographs of dead bodies). High-PRSC men rated the enjoyable slides more positively and the unpleasant slides more negatively than did low-PRSC men. Thus, the feelings produced by the slides, both positive and negative, were intensified by a disposition to focus on the private self. In that same investigation, viewing the slides in front of a small mirror led to a similar intensification of affect, just as Buss's theory would predict.

More recent studies largely support the intensification hypothesis. For example, in one study (Lyubomirsky, Caldwell, & Nolen-Hoeksema, 1998), mildly depressed and nondepressed participants were instructed either to think about their current level of energy, their feelings, their character, and why they turned out the way they had (self-focused condition), or to think about clouds in the sky, what a well-known painting looked like, and the look of a shiny trumpet (distraction condition). Results indicated that although the self-focus/distraction manipulations had no effect on the nondepressed individuals, the depressed individuals in the self-focus condition reported being more depressed than those in the distraction condition. In other words, inducing self-awareness led to intensification only when there was an emotion to intensify. There is also evidence to support the prediction that private self-awareness leads to clearer and more distinct self-knowledge (Kemmelmeier, 2001; Macrae, Bodenhausen, & Milne, 1998). For example, research indicates that the self-reports of high-PRSC individuals are more accurate than the self-reports of low private PRSC persons (Hjelle & Bernard, 1994; Nasby, 1989). Although reliability of self-reports does not necessarily indicate their validity, researchers have found that self-reports of high-PRSC individuals are indeed more valid than those of their less self-conscious counterparts. In one such study, Scheier, Buss, and Buss (1978) asked high- and low-PRSC college students a number of questions concerning how frequently they had aggressive thoughts or engaged in aggressive behavior. Several weeks later they took part in an experiment in which they were given the opportunity to deliver (so they thought) painful electric shocks to another student. The intensity of the shocks administered by the students was the primary dependent variable.

From the standpoint of Buss's theory, what should be the pattern of results? High-PRSC persons should have had clearer self-knowledge and thus have reported more accurately about their aggressive tendencies earlier in the semester. Consequently, when they later had a chance to display their aggressive tendencies through actual behavior, that behavior should have corresponded closely to their earlier self-reports. In contrast, low-PRSC individuals should have been less accurate in their early self-descriptions and thus should have later acted in ways that might not have corresponded very closely to their relatively inaccurate self-reports. This is exactly what the researchers found. Thus, it appears that people high in private self-consciousness do possess clearer and more accurate self-knowledge. Very similar findings were also reported when the initial questionnaire was completed with the participant either in front of a small mirror or without the mirror; correlations between self-reports and behavior were much higher when those self-reports were made in front of a mirror, apparently because of the person's greater private self-awareness during the self-report (Pryor, Gibbons, Wicklund, Fazio, & Hood, 1977, Experiment 1).

Public Self-Aspects   According to Buss, the effects of being publicly self-aware depend on the particular inducer that leads to that awareness. What things can make us aware of our public selves? First, according to Buss, it is other people who make us publicly self-aware, particularly groups of people, and especially strangers. Thus, to find a group of strangers staring at us is a very powerful inducer of public self-attention and leads us to question whether our appearance and behavior are appropriate. It is also possible, as Buss notes, for a lack of attention from others to induce public self-awareness. If your friends suddenly ignore your presence, this will trigger an intense awareness of your public self.

Another kind of inducer of public self-awareness that has similar effects is a recording device such as a still camera, tape recorder, or video camera. Such devices in effect are mechanical substitutes for live audiences and thus make us aware of ourselves in the same way that live audiences do. What both of these classes of inducers have in common is that in each one the individual is being observed, either by a live audience or by a mechanical substitute. As a result, both of these classes of inducers will have similar effects on the individual.

There is, however, another class of inducers that provide actual perceptual feedback to targets. Unlike cameras or audiences, that simply make us aware that we are being observed, this kind of inducer presents us with information about how we are actually perceived by others. Examples would be photographs or videotapes, audiotapes of our voices, or the sight of ourselves in three-piece, full-length mirrors like those found in clothing stores. In each case, we are faced with an image of ourselves to which we are not accustomed, and this makes us publicly self-aware. Large mirrors are said to make us publicly rather than privately self-aware, then, because the image they provide is novel and unusual.

According to this theory, public self-awareness leads to different effects, depending on whether it is induced by observation from others or from perceptual feedback. Buss describes the effects of being observed as uneasiness and discomfort; when other people (or mechanical substitutes) are watching us, we become uncomfortably aware of ourselves. According to Buss, we learn through painful experience that scrutiny from others (such as teachers, parents, and peers) usually means that we are doing something unusual or wrong. Thus, when we become aware that others are observing us, our immediate reaction is to become vaguely uncomfortable and wonder what aspect of our appearance is causing this unwanted attention.

The effect of perceptual feedback is slightly different. When we suddenly come across a photograph or recording of ourselves or see ourselves in a full-length clothing mirror, we see aspects of ourselves in a way that is novel and unexpected. Quite literally, we become self-aware about some specific feature of our public image that the perceptual feedback presents to us. For example, people are typically surprised when they hear a recording of their voices because the sound is so different from what they are used to hearing. Seeing ourselves in a full-length mirror also presents us with a view that we rarely see, although other people see that view all the time. Thus, we suddenly become aware of an aspect of ourselves (voice, hair, weight) in the way that other people are aware of it. Buss also assumes that this new awareness is almost always less than flattering; voices sound tinny, figures look less attractive, hairlines recede alarmingly. As a result of perceptual feedback, then, we become aware of a discrepancy between our imagined public self and the actual public self; this awareness will lead to a temporary loss of self-esteem. Table 10.1 illustrates in outline form Buss's theory regarding public self-awareness.

Just as Buss made a distinction between the state of private self-awareness and the trait of private self-consciousness, he makes a similar distinction with regard to the public self. As previously noted, the dispositional tendency to engage in public self-awareness is referred to as public self-consciousness. Buss also points out that most of the time even those high in public self-consciousness (PUSC) will not focus attention on the public self without some kind of inducer. What distinguishes high-PUSC people from low-PUSC people is their reaction to inducers; high PUSCs react more strongly to an audience, whereas low PUSCs are much less likely to become self-aware in such situations.

Over the past 30 years, a number of studies have examined Buss's predictions concerning the effects of situationally induced and habitual attention to public self-awareness (Bushman, 1993; Chang, Hau, & Guo, 2001; Culos-Reed, Brawley, Martin, & Leary, 2002; Fenigstein & Abrams, 1993; Ryckman et al., 1991). Allan Fenigstein (1979), for example, directly compared the reactions of high- and low-PUSC individuals in a social situation. In that experiment, three college women waited in a room for an experiment to begin. Unbeknown to the third woman, the other two were confederates of Fenigstein. In the control condition, these two confederates acted in a normal and friendly manner, while in the "shunning condition" they deliberately shunned the real participant by ignoring her and speaking only to each other. If she spoke to them directly, they responded as briefly as possible and seemed quite uninterested in what she said.

What effect should this have on the targeted participant? According to Buss, this obvious lack of attention from others should produce public self-awareness, similar to the confederates' openly staring at her. Thus, the woman in the "shunning" condition should be uncomfortable. However, a high-PUSC individual should be especially uneasy because of her greater sensitivity to inducers such as audiences. To measure this discomfort, Fenigstein separated the three women and told them that in the experiment itself they would have a choice of continuing with the same two women they had shared the waiting room with or continuing with a new pair of participants. Fenigstein found that for the high-PUSC women, shunning made a big difference. If they were not shunned, 75% chose to keep the original partners, but if they had been shunned, only 15% did so. In contrast, shunning had little impact on the low-PUSC women: 50% of the shunned women chose to stay with the same two women, as did 70% of the non-shunned women. Thus, high PUSCs showed the predicted strong reaction to an inducer of public self-awareness.

Much of the research dealing with public self-consciousness has also simultaneously investigated private self-consciousness (Carver & Humphries, 1981; Carver & Scheier, 1981). This is because in many situations private and public self-awareness should lead to different, and sometimes opposite, behaviors. In particular, private self-attention should lead us to act in keeping with our private beliefs whereas public self-attention should lead us to act in ways that we think others approve, regardless of our private beliefs. According to this logic, people who are high in private self-consciousness and low in public self-consciousness should most likely act in accord with their attitudes, because they know their attitudes better (clarification) and they are relatively unconcerned about others' scrutiny. The other combinations of private and public self-consciousness should show much less consistency between private attitudes and public behavior. Low-PRSC individuals would not have the clear knowledge of their attitudes necessary to act consistently with them, whereas a high-PRSC person who is also high in public self-consciousness would have the necessary knowledge but might not act consistently because of a concern about the judgment of others.

In a direct test of this idea, Michael Scheier (1980) first measured students' private attitudes toward the use of physical punishment as a learning technique. Several months later some of these same people came to the laboratory in groups of two, three, or four. They were told that they would be writing an essay on the use of punishment in child rearing and that they would later publicly discuss their views with the other group members. Independent raters later evaluated the essays as to how favorable they were toward the use of punishment. How consistent were the students' previous privately expressed attitudes with their later public expressions? As expected, those high in private and low in public self-consciousness showed a very strong correlation ($r = .64$) between their initial attitudes and later essay, whereas those with any other combination of private and public self-consciousness showed almost no correlation. Thus, it appears that even when people have an accurate self-knowledge resulting from high private self-focus, being simultaneously high in public self-consciousness can lead to behavior that does not reflect that self-knowledge, because the concern over evaluation by others is too strong.

Carver and Scheier's Approach: A Control Theory Model

The final approach to the issue of self-consciousness and self-awareness that we will discuss is Charles Carver and Michael Scheier's self-regulation, or control theory model (Carver, 1979; Carver & Scheier, 1981, 1986, 1998). In this theory, they assume that human behavior is regulated in a system of feedback control. Perhaps the easiest way to explain this feedback control theory is to start with the concept of a TOTE unit (Miller, Galanter, & Pribram, 1960). TOTE is an acronym that stands for Test-Operate-Test-Exit, which are the steps taken during the execution of a TOTE unit. Figure 10.1 displays the processes making up a TOTE unit.

In essence, a TOTE unit is a sequence of activities that serve to control some behavior. The first step in the sequence is the test phase, which is a comparison between an existing state and some predetermined standard. If this comparison reveals that there is a discrepancy between one's present state and the standard, then the next phase in the process, the operate phase, is initiated. Generally speaking, the operate phase has the effect of altering the existing state in some fashion. Once this has been completed, the test phase is initiated again, and a comparison of the present state and standard again determines whether a discrepancy exists. The test and operate phases alternate until there is no difference between the present state and standard. At this point a new phase—exit—is initiated, which ends the sequence.

A very simple example of a TOTE unit would be the room thermostat connected to an air conditioner. A thermostat measures the temperature of the air in the room (the existing state) and compares it to the temperature that has been preset (the predetermined standard). This is the test phase. If there is a difference between the two, then a signal is sent to the air conditioner, which be-

Figure 10.1   The TOTE model.

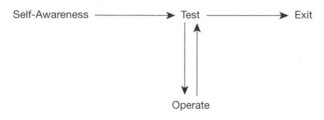

gins cooling the air (the operate phase). Eventually there is another test, and if the temperature in the room is now the same as the preset value, the air conditioner is turned off (exit). On the human level, a TOTE unit example might involve a student trying to achieve a better grade in her psychology course. The test phase would involve the student comparing her current grade in the course to the ultimate grade she desires at the end of the semester. If her current grade is lower than her desired grade, she increases her study efforts (the operate phase). Her next exam in the course is quite literally the next "test" phase in the TOTE unit. If her current grade in the course is now the same as her sought-after grade, she ends the test-operate sequence and exits (at least temporarily) from this self-regulatory process.

As this example suggests, Carver and Scheier believe that people continually set personal goals and standards, which they then use as reference points for their behavior. When people compare their actual behavior to these standards and goals (test) and when discrepancies exist, they attempt to change their actions to bring themselves in line with the standards (operate). Where does self-awareness fit into this scheme? According to the theory, the comparison or test phase results from a focusing of attention on the self. Greater self-directed attention leads to "more frequent comparisons, or a more thorough comparison, between present behavior and the standard" (Carver & Scheier, 1981, p. 144). This greater degree of comparison results in a greater tendency to alter behavior so that it matches the standard. Thus, focusing attention on the self should lead ultimately to greater attempts to act in accordance with our standards of behavior (Carver & Scheier, 1990). However, if repeated attempts to match the relevant standard or attain the desired goal prove unsuccessful, Carver and Scheier contend that people will interrupt their current action and reassess the likelihood of being able to complete the intended behavior successfully. People whose confidence level is still sufficiently high will continue in their efforts, while those whose confidence has lagged will withdraw from the activity (see Carver & Scheier, 1993).

You may be wondering at this point what the difference is between this theory and Duval and Wicklund's theory. After all, OSA theory also proposes that self-awareness leads to an attempt to bring an existing state (the real self) into line with a predetermined standard (the ideal self). Aren't both theories saying the same thing? To a large degree they are. However, one key difference is their explanation of why a discrepancy between existing state and standard leads to behavior change. Duval and Wicklund claim that the discrepancy leads to an unpleasant motivational state, and that in order to eliminate this unpleasant feeling we strive to reduce the discrepancies. Thus, their theory is a motivational theory. Carver and Scheier claim that such discrepancies do not necessarily lead to an unpleasant motivational state. That is, simply being aware that there is a discrepancy between one's ideal and real selves does not mean that a person will necessarily experience any negative feelings. As a result, there is no pressure to get rid of those feelings by reducing the real–ideal discrepancy. Instead, Carver and Scheier believe that the shifting of behavior to bring it into line with standards occurs almost automatically. As they describe it, the shift is simply "a natural consequence of the engagement of a discrepancy-reducing feedback loop" (i.e., a TOTE unit). Thus, they do not believe that behavior is produced by a desire to reduce unpleasant motivational states, and thus, control theory is not a motivational theory in the manner of objective self-awareness theory.

At one level, of course, this difference between the two theories doesn't matter. The motivational and nonmotivational approaches still generally make the same predictions about how people will act; they only differ as to exactly why. In fact, the vast majority of the research that supports the Duval and Wicklund approach also supports the Carver and Scheier approach because both approaches make the same predictions so much of the time. Carver and Scheier do believe, however, that some research indicates that their approach is superior. Specifically, they point to the prediction of objective self-awareness theory that becoming self-aware almost always leads to negative affect because of the real–ideal self discrepancy. As noted earlier, research indicates that the state of self-awareness does not always produce unpleasant feelings. Carver and Scheier contend that there is only one kind of situation in which self-awareness will lead to negative affect—when the discrepancy between the existing state and the standard cannot be reduced. That is, only when we become aware of a shortcoming that cannot be overcome will unpleasant feelings result. People facing such a situation might also be especially likely to seek escape from self-awareness more quickly.

Two other differences between these theories may be more important than the question of motivation. First, while Duval and Wicklund's theory does not deal with the question of individual differences, Carver and Scheier explicitly acknowledge that not only can stimuli in the environment serve to focus attention on the self but that some people are simply more likely to do so spontaneously. Thus, unlike Duval and Wicklund—but similar to Buss—Carver and Scheier are concerned not only with the state of self-awareness but also with the trait of self-consciousness. Carver and Scheier believe that the process resulting from both the state and trait is the same: attention to the self, whether resulting from dispositions or cues, instigates the comparison process of the TOTE unit, which in turn produces behavioral change. In fact, Carver and Scheier have frequently carried out their experiments twice—once manipulating self-attention with a mirror and the second time measuring dispositional private self-awareness with the SCS—and they have consistently found identical patterns of results with each approach (Carver & Scheier, 1978; Scheier, 1976; Scheier & Carver, 1977, 1980; Scheier, Carver, & Gibbons, 1979).

The other difference between the two approaches is that Carver and Scheier, unlike Duval and Wicklund (but again like Buss), clearly distinguish between private and public self-awareness as well as between private and public self-consciousness. For Carver and Scheier, the difference between private and public self-awareness is simple but important. Being privately self-aware produces a comparison between an existing state and a private standard (e.g., one's own values), whereas being publicly self-aware produces a comparison between an existing state and a public standard (e.g., one's belief about what other people value). In either case, however, this comparison leads to a behavior shift designed to bring the existing state into line with the standard. It should be clear by now that Carver and Scheier's theory is similar to Duval and Wicklund's approach in some ways, but similar to Buss's approach in others. Like Buss, Carver and Scheier emphasize the public-private distinction and the difference between the state of self-awareness and the trait of self-consciousness, both of which Duval and Wicklund essentially ignore. Like them, however, Carver and Scheier emphasize the comparison of an existing state to a predetermined standard as the chief mechanism for governing behavior, a position with which Buss takes issue. In a way, then, and this is an oversimplification, Carver and Scheier have provided a new way of understanding self-attention processes that is a synthesis and extension of the other two approaches.

Self-Awareness: Beneficial or Detrimental?

One issue that has received considerable attention from self-awareness theorists and researchers in recent years concerns the possible costs and benefits of self-focus. That is, researchers have asked whether it is better or worse for one's overall physical and mental health to be habitually self-attentive. Because the majority of studies investigating the advantages and disadvantages of self-attention have focused on private self-awareness and self-consciousness (rather than public), we will restrict our discussion to the private realm.

One set of studies indicates that greater self-attentiveness can benefit intimate relationships. In both adolescent and young adult samples, Franzoi and Davis found that those high in private self-consciousness were more likely to reveal private self-aspects to their friends and romantic partners, and this self-disclosure in turn reduced loneliness and increased relationship satisfaction (Davis & Franzoi, 1986; Franzoi & Davis, 1985; Franzoi, Davis, & Young, 1985). These findings suggest that habitual self-attention can facilitate an intimate social sharing that strengthens close relationships.

In addition to these findings, other studies suggest that attentiveness to inner states may help ward off stress-induced illnesses. Specifically, Suls and his colleagues (Mullen & Suls, 1982; Suls & Fletcher, 1985) found that the health of people high in private self-consciousness was unaffected by the incidence of undesirable and uncontrollable events in their lives, but low self-conscious persons became more susceptible to illness as these events accumulated. One explanation for this finding is that people who regularly pay attention to their physiological states (an aspect of the private self) are more likely to become aware of early warning signs of illness-inducing stress, and thus are more likely to take precautionary steps to avoid the onset of illness.

Although these studies suggest that private self-awareness is related to specific health-promoting behaviors, other studies indicate that it can also be a contributing factor to such dysfunctional behavior as anxiety, alcohol abuse, and depression (Bartholow, Sher, & Strathman, 2000; Hull, Young, & Jouriles, 1986; Ingram, 1990; Schwarzer & Wicklund, 1991). In particular, the connection between private self-awareness and depression has received considerable attention in recent years.

Why would we expect heightened self-focus to be associated with depression? One reason is derived directly from Buss's theoretical position that greater attention to private self-aspects should intensify whatever emotional response is present, including negative affective states such as depression. Thus, dispositional private self-consciousness or situationally induced private self-awareness might increase depressive affect among those who are already depressed, and in fact evidence in support of this proposition has been found. Individuals who were already depressed reported even greater levels of depression following the induction of self-focused attention (Gibbons et al., 1985). Moreover, depressed individuals who were induced to focus attention externally demonstrated the opposite effect and reported lower levels of pessimism (Pyszczynski, Holt, & Greenberg, 1987) and depressed mood (Nix, Watson, Pyszczynski, & Greenberg, 1995).

Another possibility, one that is compatible with the Carver and Scheier perspective, is that heightened self-attention makes one more aware of the discrepancy existing between personal standards/goals and actual accomplishments. As a result, this discrepancy should be a more powerful determinant of depression for people who are self-focused than for those who are not. Hull, Reilly, and Ennis (1991) offer some support for this possibility. These investigators studied college students and measured the degree to which the students believed that they were "living up" to what they felt a college student should be. As they expected, these researchers found that failing to live up to the student role was more strongly linked to depressive affect for students who were higher in private self-consciousness and thus more sensitive to the discrepancy.

Finally, Pyszczynski and Greenberg's (1987, 1992) self-regulatory perseveration theory of depression suggests an even more complex connection between self-focused attention and depression. In a nutshell, this theory argues that after some serious loss, individuals frequently enter a self-regulatory cycle (i.e, a TOTE unit) in which self-focused attention is increased. Under certain circumstances, they are unable to exit this cycle, and an inescapable depressive state is created. How does this occur? Pyszczynski and Greenberg argue that when the object of one's loss is both irreplaceable and of great personal importance, then no ready solution to the problem is available. As a result, the discrepancy between the desired state (having the lost object back) and the actual state (irretrievable loss) cannot be reduced. This produces a state of depression, which increases self-focus, which increases depression, and so forth. Thus, self-focus in this theory can be thought of as both resulting from depression as well as contributing to it. In Pyszczynski and Greenberg's view, then, self-awareness per se does not lead to dysfunctional depressive behavior. Under certain circumstances, however, in which one cannot meet personal standards, habitual self-awareness can be associated with increased risk for dysfunctional behavior due to depressive self-focus.

Taking all of these studies into account, it appears safe to conclude that there are both benefits and drawbacks to self-focused attention. For people high in private self-consciousness, there is not only a greater likelihood of understanding themselves better and sharing this knowledge with loved ones, but there is a possibility that their greater self-attentiveness provides them with a better early warning system for physical illness. On the other hand, self-attentiveness can also make people more susceptible to negative emotional states such as depression because of a greater focus on negative outcomes and a susceptibility to entering destructive self-regulatory cycles.

Concluding Remarks

We end our discussion with two conclusions. First, regardless of the specific theoretical mechanism said to produce it, attention to private aspects of the self clearly has the effect of making people act in ways that are consistent with their attitudes, beliefs, and values, whereas attention to public self-aspects results in a tendency for people to behave in ways consistent with social standards or the behavior of relevant reference groups. These findings should not be underemphasized. One of the most durable controversies in social and personality psychology has concerned the degree to which internal factors, like attitudes, versus external factors, like reference groups, actually guide overt behavior (Abelson, 1972; LaPiere, 1934; Wicker, 1969). That the two different kinds of self-focused attention produce different responses to social pressure is a notable accomplishment.

A second conclusion concerns one possible direction for future research. An issue that has not yet been adequately investigated is how individual differences in private and public self-consciousness develop. As we have seen, the effects of such individual differences are sometimes powerful and have been clearly documented. An important task, then, is to account for the development of those individual tendencies in the first place. Buss (1980, 2001) has speculated that children who are socially isolated may be more likely to develop a tendency toward private self-consciousness, partially as a compensation for the lack of social activity. He also suggests that children who experience chronic health problems may learn to pay extra attention to internal bodily states and thus develop a permanent tendency toward private self-scrutiny. He further hypothesizes that children with an artistic or "open" personality style might develop the sort of internal focus typical of high private self-consciousness. Regarding public self-consciousness, Buss (2001) speculates that the children of parents who set strict rules of appearance and deportment are likely to become high in public self-consciousness, whereas parents who are casual about appearance and demeanor are likely to raise children with low public self-consciousness. In addition, children who receive a great deal of public attention because they are members of a conspicuous family or because they themselves possess an unusual trait that invites public scrutiny are likely to become high in public self-consciousness.

To our knowledge, only a few studies have investigated these hypotheses. In one study, Klonsky, Dutton, and Liebel (1990) surveyed college students who differed in their levels of private and public self-consciousness, asking them questions about their childhood and adolescence. The researchers found a weak tendency for men (but not women) high in private self-consciousness to report more health problems during their childhood. In contrast, high private self-conscious women did not report health problems, but did report being overprotected by their mothers when young. For both women and men, public self-consciousness was associated with greater parental authority, discipline, and demands for achievement during childhood and adolescence. In another study, Morin (2000) found that among men (but not women) a history of frequent exposure to the attention of large audiences was significantly but weakly correlated with high public self-consciousness. Together, these findings suggest three possible conclusions: (1) the development of private self-consciousness may be related to childhood health problems and an overprotective parental style that causes children to be relatively socially isolated from their peers, (2) the development of public self-consciousness may be associated with unusually high levels of public scrutiny and strongly discipline-oriented parents who stress high achievement in their children, and (3) private and public self-consciousness may develop differently for women and men.

SUMMARY

In this chapter we present three current theories that deal with the issues of self-awareness and self-consciousness. Shelley Duval and Robert Wicklund's theory of objective self-awareness was the first of these modern theories. According to this theory, when something in the environment (like a mirror) directs our attention back toward ourselves, it makes us aware of the discrepancy that typically exists between our actual behavior and the idealized standards of behavior that we possess. Becoming aware of our shortcomings then produces an unpleasant affective state, which leads either to attempted escape from the self-focused attention or to efforts directed toward a reduction of the real–ideal discrepancy. One common outcome of self-awareness, then, is said to be a closer correspondence between one's actual behavior and one's behavioral standards.

A second modern view of self-awareness comes from Arnold Buss. Buss essentially discards the notion of ideal behavioral standards and instead makes the claim that self-focused attention simply brings people to know themselves better as a result of the increased attention to their private aspects. Thus, individuals with greater self-awareness may behave in ways more consistent with their internal attitudes, but for reasons different from those proposed by Duval and Wicklund. Importantly, too, Buss distinguishes between attention to private aspects of self and public aspects of self and claims that different kinds of behavior will follow from these different types of self-awareness. In addition, and unlike Duval and Wicklund, Buss acknowledges that individuals may differ among themselves in terms of their ongoing dispositional tendency to be self-aware.

The third modern approach is in some ways a hybrid of the two foregoing views. Charles Carver and Michael Scheier propose a cybernetic model of self-attention, which holds that behavior is regulated by a set of internal processes that compare current behavior with a preset behavioral standard and then strive to minimize any discrepancies. Although this view clearly has some similarities to Duval and Wicklund's approach, it differs from that theory in its rejection of unpleasant affect as the motivator of behavior change. In addition, Carver and Scheier's view is similar to Buss's with regard to its emphasis on distinguishing between public and private self-attention and in its differentiation between the state and trait of self-focused attention.

Over the past 30 years, research interest in self-awareness and self-consciousness has grown at a phenomenal pace. One of the reasons for this interest should be obvious: self-awareness and self-consciousness have proven to have considerable impact on important human behaviors. The evidence reported here illustrates just how successful these concepts have been, and in psychology as in any other field, interest follows success. However, it seems to us that this area has attracted intense attention for another reason as well: people—psychologists included—are simply intrigued by questions of self-knowledge. How much do we know about ourselves? How accurate is that knowledge? What do we do with such knowledge? Recent theories dealing with these issues are exciting at least in part because they offer us new ways to satisfy an age-old curiosity. Perhaps it should not surprise us, therefore, to find that these fresh perspectives on fundamental questions are as attractive as they are. Happily, if the evidence thus far is any indication, the attention given to these approaches has not been misplaced, and all indications are that these lines of research will remain vital and productive for years to come.

DISCUSSION QUESTIONS

1. What are some of the similarities and differences between objective self-awareness theory and control theory?
2. How might high versus low private self-conscious persons respond differently to various psychological therapies that either promote or do not promote "insight" in solving psychological problems?
3. Based on research suggesting that public self-awareness increases adherence to social standards, how might you use this knowledge in designing ad campaigns to reduce binge drinking of alcohol on college campuses?
4. What might be some potential mental health benefits and deficits for people who are high or low on private self-consciousness?

SUGGESTED READINGS

Buss, A. H. (2001). *Psychological dimensions of the self*. Thousand Oaks, CA: Sage. A highly readable analysis of contemporary theory and research on the self.

Carver, C. S., & Scheier, M. F. (1998). *On the self-regulation of behavior*. New York: Cambridge University Press. An update of the authors' original control theory in which they propose that human beings are complex goal-directed systems that self-regulate their actions with respect to those goals.

Duval, T. S., Silvia, P., & Lalwani, N. (2001). *Self-awareness and causal attribution: A dual systems theory*. Boston: Kluwer Academic. An update of objective self-awareness theory that outlines how self-awareness affects thought, feeling, and action.

Leary, M. (1996). *Self-presentation: Impression management and interpersonal behavior*. Boulder, CO: Westview Press. A thorough and engaging overview of contemporary theory and research on the topic of self-presentation, written for a student audience.

Wicklund, R. A., & Eckert, M. (1992). *The self-knower: A hero under control*. New York: Plenum. A thought-provoking critique of what the authors label the "self-knowledge movement," as well as a review of existing knowledge about self-awareness research, written for a student audience.

SUGGESTED WEB SITES

http://www.conscioiusness.arizona.edu/
Center for Consciousness Studies

This web site at the University of Arizona offers on-line articles, as well as information on conferences, bibliographical references, and related web sites.

http://www.psych.new.edu/ISSI/
International Society for Self & Identity

This is the official web site for the International Society for Self & Identity, which is an association of social and behavioral scientists who are dedicated to studying the self.

http://www2.canisius.edu/~gallaghr/pi.html
Research Sources on Concepts of Person and Self

This web site contains numerous references to both philosophical and psychological articles and books related to the self, including self-consciousness.

INFOTRAC COLLEGE EDITION SEARCH TOPICS

Self-awareness	Private self	Self-regulation
Self-consciousness	Public self	

REFERENCES

Abelson, R.P. (1972). Are attitudes necessary? In B. T. King & E. McGinnies (Eds.), *Attitudes, conflict, and social change*. New York: Academic Press.

Alanazi, F. M. (2001). The revised self-consciousness scale: An assessment of factor structure, reliability, and gender differences in Saudi Arabia. *Social Behavior and Personality, 29*, 763–776.

Arndt, J., Greenberg, J., Simon, L., Pyszczynski, T., & Solomon, S. (1998). Terror management and self-awareness: Evidence that mortality salience provokes avoidance of the self-focused state. *Personality and Social Pscyhology Bulletin, 24*, 1216–1227.

Ayduk, O., Mischel, W., & Downey, G. (2002). Attentional mechanisms linking rejection to hostile reactivity: The role of "hot" versus "cool" focus. *Psychological Science, 13*, 443–448.

Bartholow, B. D., Sher, K. J., & Strathman, A. (2000). Moderation of the expectancy-alcohol use relation by private self-consciousness: Data from a longitudinal study. *Personality and Social Psychology Bulletin, 26*, 1409–1420.

Baumeister, R. F. (1986). *Identity: Cultural change and the struggle for self*. New York: Oxford University Press.

Bermúdez, J. L. (1998). *The paradox of self-consciousness*. Cambridge, MA: MIT Press.

Blumer, H. (1969). *Symbolic interactionism: Perspective and method*. Englewood Cliffs, NJ: Prentice-Hall.

Britt, T.W. (1992). The self-consciousness scale: On the stability of the three-factor structure. *Personality and Social Psychology Bulletin, 18*, 748–755.

Bushman, B.J. (1993). What's in a name? The moderating role of public self-consciousness on the relation between brand label and brand preference. *Journal of Applied Psychology, 78,* 857–861.

Buss, A. H. (1980). *Self-consciousness and social anxiety*. San Francisco: W. H. Freeman.

Buss, A. H. (2001). *Psychological dimensions of the self*. Thousand Oaks, CA: Sage.

Carver, C. S. (1975). Physical aggression as a function of objective self-awareness and attitudes toward punishment. *Journal of Experimental Social Psychology, 11,* 510–519.

Carver, C. S. (1979). A cybernetic model of self-attention processes. *Journal of Personality and Social Psychology, 37,* 1251–1281.

Carver, C. S., & Glass, D. C. (1976). The self-consciousness scale: A discriminant validity study. *Journal of Personality Assessment, 40,* 169–172.

Carver, C. S., & Humphries, C. (1981). Havana daydreaming: A study of self-consciousness and the negative reference group among Cuban Americans. *Journal of Personality and Social Psychology, 40,* 545–552.

Carver, C. S., & Scheier, M. F. (1978). Self-focusing effects of dispositional self-consciousness, mirror presence, and audience presence. *Journal of Personality and Social Psychology, 36,* 324–332.

Carver, C. S., & Scheier, M. F. (1981). *Attention and self-regulation: A control-theory approach to human behavior*. New York: Springer-Verlag.

Carver, C. S., & Scheier, M. F. (1986). Functional and dysfunctional responses to anxiety: The interaction between expectancies and self-focused attention. In R. Schwarzer (Ed.), *Self-related cognitions in anxiety and motivation* (pp. 111–141). Hillsdale, NJ: Erlbaum.

Carver, C. S., & Scheier, M. F. (1990). Principles of self-regulation: Action and emotion. In E. T. Higgins & R. M. Sorrentino (Eds.), *Handbook of motivation and cognition: Foundations of social behavior* (Vol. 2, pp. 3–52). New York: Guilford.

Carver, C. S., & Scheier, M. F. (1993). Vigilant and avoidant coping in two patient samples. In H. W. Krohne (Ed.), *Attention and avoidance: Strategies in coping with aversiveness* (pp. 295–319). Seattle, WA: Hogrefe & Huber.

Carver, C. S., & Scheier, M. F. (1998). *On the self-regulation of behavior*. Cambridge, UK: Cambridge University Press.

Chang, L., Hau, K. T., & Guo, A. M. (2001). The effect of self-consciousness on the expression of gender views. *Journal of Applied Social Psychology, 31,* 340–351.

Chen, S., Shecter, D., & Chaiken, S. (1996). Getting at the truth or getting along: Accuracy versus impression-motivated heuristic and systematic processing. *Journal of Personality and Social Psychology, 71,* 262–275.

Cooley, C. H. (1902). *Human nature and the social order*. New York: Scribner's.

Culos-Reed, S. N., Brawley, L. R., Martin, K. A., & Leary, M. R. (2002). Self-presentation concerns and health behaviors among cosmetic surgery patients. *Journal of Applied Social Psychology, 32,* 560–569.

Davis, M. H., & Franzoi, S. L. (1986). Adolescent loneliness, self-disclosure, and private self-consciousness: A longitudinal investigation. *Journal of Personality and Social Psychology, 51,* 595–608.

Davis, M. H., & Franzoi, S. L. (1991). Stability and change in adolescent self-consciousness and empathy. *Journal of Research in Personality, 25,* 70–87.

Duval, T. S., Silvia, P., & Lalwani, N. (2001). *Self-awareness and causal attribution: A dual systems theory*. Boston: Kluwer Academic. Duval, S., & Wicklund, R. A. (1972). *A theory of objective self-awareness*. New York: Academic Press.

Duval, S., Wicklund, R. A., & Fine, R. L. (1972). Avoidance of objective self-awareness under conditions of high and low intra-self discrepancy. In S. Duval & R. A. Wicklund, *A theory of objective self-awareness* (pp. 16–21). New York: Academic Press.

Fejfar, M. C., & Hoyle, R. H. (2000). Effect of private self-awareness on negative affect and self-referent attribution: A quantitative review. *Personality and Social Psychology Review, 4,* 132–142.

Fenigstein, A. (1979). Self-consciousness, self-attention, and social interaction. *Journal of Personality and Social Psychology, 37,* 75–86.

Fenigstein, A., & Abrams, D. (1993). Self-attention and the egocentric assumption of shared perspectives. *Journal of Experimental Social Psychology, 29,* 287–303.

Fenigstein, A., Scheier, M. F., & Buss, A. H. (1975). Public and private self-consciousness: Assessment and theory. *Journal of Consulting and Clinical Psychology, 43,* 522–527.

Franzoi, S. L., & Brewer, L. C. (1984). The experience of self-awareness and its relation to level of self-consciousness: An experiential sampling study. *Journal of Research in Personality, 18,* 522–540.

Franzoi, S. L., & Davis, M. H. (1985). Adolescent self-disclosure and loneliness: Private self-consciousness and parental influences. *Journal of Personality and Social Psychology, 48,* 768–780.

Franzoi, S. L., Davis, M. H., & Young, R. D. (1985). The effects of private self-consciousness and perspective taking on satisfaction in close relationships. *Journal of Personality and Social Psychology, 48,* 1584–1594.

Freud, S. (1959). Introductory lectures on psychoanalysis. Part III. General theory of the neurosis. In J. Strachey (Ed. & Trans.), *The standard edition of the complete psychological works of Sigmund Freud* (Vol. 16, pp. 243–496). London: Hogarth Press. (Original work published 1917)

Freud, S. (1959). Inhibitions, symptoms, and anxiety. In J. Strachey (Ed. & Trans.), *The standard edition of the complete psychological works of Sigmund Freud* (Vol. 20, pp. 87–174). London: Hogarth Press. (Original work published 1926)

Freud, S. (1966). Project for a scientific psychology. In J. Strachey (Ed. & Trans.), *The standard edition of the complete psychological works of Sigmund Freud* (Vol. 1, pp. 282–398). London: Hogarth Press. (Original work published 1895)

Gangestad, S. W., & Snyder, M. (2000). Self-monitoring: Appraisal and reappraisal. *Psychological Bulletin, 126,* 530–555.

Gibbons, F. X., Smith, T. W., Ingram, R. E., Pearce, K., Brehm, S. S., & Schroeder, D. (1985). Self-awareness and self-confrontation: Effects of self-focused attention on members of a clinical population. *Journal of Personality and Social Psychology, 48,* 662–675.

Gonnerman, M. E., Jr., Parker, C. P., Lavine, H., & Huff, J. (2000). The relationship between self-discrepancies and affective states: The moderating roles of self-monitoring and standpoints on the self. *Personality and Social Psychology Bulletin, 26,* 810–819.

Gordon, R. A. (1996). Impact of ingratiation on judgments and evaluations: A meta-analytic investigation. *Journal of Personality and Social Psychology, 71,* 54–70.

Green, J. D., & Sedikides, C. (1999). Affect and self-focused attention revisited: The role of affect orientation. *Personality and Social Pscyhology Bulletin, 25,* 104–119.

Greenwald, A. G., & Farnham, S. D. (2000). Using the Implicit Association Test to measure self-esteem and self-concept. *Journal of Personality and Social Psychology, 79,* 1022–1038.

Gur, R. C., & Sackheim, H. A. (1979). Self-deception: A concept in search of a phenomenon. *Journal of Personality and Social Psychology, 37,* 147–169.

Hamid, P. N., Lai, J. C. L., & Cheng, S.-T. (2001). Response bias and public and private self-consciousness in Chinese. *Social Behavior & Personality, 29,* 733–742.

Harbus, A. (2002). The medieval concept of the self in Anglo-Saxon England. *Self and Identity, 1,* 77–97.

Hass, R. G. (1984). Perspective taking and self-awareness: Drawing an E on your forehead. *Journal of Personality and Social Psychology, 46,* 788–798.

Hjelle, L. A., & Bernard, M. (1994). Private self-consciousness and the retest reliability of self-reports. *Journal of Research in Personality, 28,* 52–67.

Hogan, R., & Cheek, J. (1983). Identity, authenticity, and maturity. In T. R. Sarbin, & K. E. Scheibe (Eds.), *Studies in Social Identity* (pp. 339–357). New York: Praeger.

Hull, J. G., & Levy, A. S. (1979). The organization functions of the self: An alternative to the Duval and Wicklund model of self-awareness. *Journal of Personality and Social Psychology, 37,* 756–768.

Hull, J. G., Reilly, N. P., & Ennis, L. C. (1991). Self-consciousness, role discrepancy, and depressive affect. In R. Schwarzer & R. Wicklund (Eds.), *Anxiety and self-focused attention* (pp. 27–40). London: Harwood Academic.

Hull, J. G., Young, R. D., & Jouriles, E. (1986). Applications of the self-awareness model of alcohol consumption: Predicting patterns of use and abuse. *Journal of Personality and Social Psychology, 51,* 790–796.

Ingram, R. E. (1990). Self-focused attention in clinical disorders: Reviews and a conceptual model. *Psychological Bulletin, 107,* 156–176.

James, W. (1890). *The principles of psychology.* New York: Holt, Rinehart & Winston.

John, O. P., Cheek, J. M., & Klohnen, E. C. (1996). On the nature of self-monitoring: Construct explication with Q-sort ratings. *Journal of Personality and Social Psychology, 71,* 763–776.

Jones, E. E. (1990). *Interpersonal perception.* New York: W. H. Freeman.

Jung, C. G. (1921). *Psychological types.* New York: Harcourt, Brace.

Kemmelmeier, M. (2001). Private self-consciousness as a moderator of the relationship between value orientations and attitudes. *Journal of Social Psychology, 141,* 61–74.

Koestner, R., Bernieri, F., & Zuckerman, M. (1992). Self-regulation and consistency between attitudes, traits, and behaviors. *Personality and Social Psychology Bulletin, 18,* 52–59.

Klonsky, B. G., Dutton, D. L., & Liebel, C. N. (1990). Developmental antecedents of private self-consciousness, public self-consciousness, and social anxiety. *Genetic, Social, and General Psychology Monographs, 116,* 273–297.

LaPiere, R. T. (1934). Attitudes versus actions. *Social Forces, 13,* 230–237.

Leary, M. R. (1996). *Self-presentation: Impression management and interpersonal behavior.* Boulder, CO: Westview.

Leck, K., & Simpson, J. (1999). Feigning romantic interest: The role of self-monitoring. *Journal of Research in Personality, 33,* 69–91.

Lyubomirsky, S., Caldwell, N. D., & Nolen-Hoeksema, S. (1998). Effects of ruminative and distracting responses to depressed mood on retrieval of autobiographical memories. *Journal of Personality and Social Psychology, 75,* 166–177.

Macrae, C. N., Bodenhausen, G. V., & Milne, A. B. (1998). Saying no to unwanted thoughts: Self-focus and the regulation of mental life. *Journal of Personality and Social Psychology, 74,* 578–589.

Mead, G. H. (1934). *Mind, self, and society.* Chicago: University of Chicago Press.

Merz, J. (1984). The self-consciousness scale of Fenigstein, Scheier, and Buss: Empirical results. *Psychologische Beitrage, 26,* 239–249.

Miller, G. A., Galanter, E., & Pribram, K. H. (1960). *Plans and the structure of behavior.* New York: Holt, Rinehart & Winston.

Morin, A. (2000). History of exposure to audiences as a developmental antecedent of public self-consciousness. *Current Research in Social Psychology, 5*(3), 33–46.

Mullen, B., & Suls, J. (1982). Know thyself: Stressful life change and the amelioratve effect of private self-consciousness. *Journal of Experimental Social Psychology, 18,* 43–55.

Nasby, W. (1989). Private self-consciousness, self-awareness, and the reliability of self-reports. *Journal of Personality and Social Psychology, 56,* 950-957.

Natsoulas, T. (1998). Consciousness and self-awareness. In M. Ferrari & R. J. Sternberg (Eds.), *Self-awareness: It's nature and development* (pp. 12–33). New York: Guilford.

Nix, G., Watson, C., Pyszczynski, T., & Greenberg, J. (1995). Reducing depressive affect through external focus of attention. *Journal of Social and Clinical Psychology, 14,* 36–52.

Nystedt, L., & Ljungberg, A. (2002). Facets of private and public self-consciousness: Construct and discriminant validity. *European Journal of Personality, 16,* 143–159.

Pryor, J. B., Gibbons, F. X., Wicklund, R. A., Fazio, R. H., & Hood, R. (1977). Self-focused attention and self-report validity. *Journal of Personality, 45,* 514–527.

Pyszczynski, T., & Greenberg, J. (1987). Self-regulatory perseveration and the depressive self-focusig style: A self-awareness theory of reactive depression. *Psychological Bulletin, 102,* 1–17.

Pyszczynski, T., & Greenberg, J. (1992). *Hanging on and letting go: Understanding the onset, maintenance, and remission of depression.* New York: Springer-Verlag.

Pyszczynski, T., Holt, K., & Greenberg, J. (1987). Depression, self-focused attention and expectancies for future positive and negative events for self and others. *Journal of Personality and Social Psychology, 52,* 994–1001.

Rotter, J. B. (1966). Generalized expectancies for internal versus external control of reinforcement. *Psychological Monographs, 80,* 1–28.

Rowatt, W. C., Cunningham, M. R., & Druen, P. B. (1998). Deception to get a date. *Personality and Social Psychology Bulletin, 24,* 1228–1242.

Ryckman, R. M., Robbins, M. A., Thornton, B., Kaczor, L. M., Gayton, S. L., & Anderson, C. V. (1991). Public self-consciousness and physique stereotyping. *Personality and Social Psychology Bulletin, 17,* 400–405.

Scheier, M. F. (1976). Self-awareness, self-consciousness, and angry aggression. *Journal of Personality, 44,* 627–644.

Scheier, M. F. (1980). Effects of public and private self-consciousness on the public expression of personal beliefs. *Journal of Personality and Social Psychology, 39,* 514–521.

Scheier, M. F., Buss, A. H., & Buss, D. M. (1978). Self-consciousness, self-report of aggressiveness, and aggression. *Journal of Research in Personality, 12*, 133–140.

Scheier, M. F., & Carver, C. S. (1977). Self-focused attention and the experience of emotion: Attraction, repulsion, elation, and depression. *Journal of Personality and Social Psychology, 35*, 625–636.

Scheier, M. F., & Carver, C. S. (1980). Private and public self-attention, resistance to change, and dissonance reduction. *Journal of Personality and Social Psychology, 39*, 390–405.

Scheier, M. F., & Carver, C. S. (1985). The self-consciousness scale: A revised version for use with general populations. *Journal of Applied Social Psychology, 15*, 687–699.

Scheier, M. F., Carver, C. S., & Gibbons, F. X. (1979). Self-directed attention, awareness of bodily states, and suggestibility. *Journal of Personality and Social Psychology, 37*, 1576–1588.

Schlenker, B. R. (1980). *Impression management: The self-concept, social identity, and interpersonal relations.* Monterey, CA: Brooks/Cole.

Schwarzer, R., & Wicklund, R. A. (Eds). (1991). *Anxiety and self-focused attention.* London: Harwood Academic.

Shek, D. T. L. (1994). Assessment of private and public self-consciousness: A Chinese replication. *Journal of Clinical Psychology, 50*, 341–348.

Snyder, M. (1974). Self-monitoring of expressive behavior. *Journal of Personality and Social Psychology, 30*, 526–537.

Snyder, M. (1987). *Public appearances/Private realities: The psychology of self-monitoring.* New York: W. H. Freeman.

Steenbarger, B. N., & Aderman, D. (1979). Objective self-awareness as a non-aversive state: Effect of anticipating discrepancy reduction. *Journal of Personality, 47*, 330–339.

Sugawara, K. (1984). An attempting to construct the self-consciousness scale for Japanese. *Japanese Journal of Psychology, 55*, 184–188.

Suls, J., & Fletcher, B. (1985). Self-attention, life stress, and illness: A prospective study. *Psychosomatic Medicine, 47*, 469–481.

Vleeming, R. G., & Engelse, J. A. (1981). Assessment of private and public self-consciousness: A Dutch replication. *Journal of Personality Assessment, 45*, 385–389.

Weiner, B., Amirkhan, J., Folkes, V. S., & Verette, J. A. (1987). An attributional analysis of excuse-giving: Studies of a naive theory of emotion. *Journal of Personality and Social Psychology, 52*, 316–324.

Wicker, A. W. (1969). Attitudes vs. actions: The relationship of verbal and overt behavioral responses to attitude objects. *Journal of Social Issues, 25*, 41–78.

Witkin, H. A., Lewis, H. B., Hertzman, M., Machover, K., Meissner, P. B., & Wapner, S. (1954). *Personality through perception.* New York: Harper.

Personality and Control

JERRY M. BURGER

| 11

CHAPTER OUTLINE

Lord, give me
The strength to change the things that I can,
The patience to accept the things that I can not,
And the wisdom to know the difference.

I have seen various forms of this quote, also known as the Serenity Prayer, attributed to an old Jewish prayer, an old Dutch saying, an old German saying, Thomas Jefferson, Abraham Lincoln, Mark Twain, and Reinhold Niebuhr. The widespread credit for this sentiment suggests that it captures more than a touch of truth and wisdom for many people. There are some things in life that we can and probably should do something about. Exercising control over the events in our lives allows us to meet our needs, avoid experiences we dislike, and feel like capable and competent individuals. However, there also are limitations on what and how much we can control. Although we all recognize the obvious limitations—for example, we cannot flap our arms and fly—there is a large gray area of events over which we may or may not have some influence. As the saying suggests, having the wisdom to know when we can make a difference and when we should accept things as they are would seem to be one of the keys to happiness.

It should not be surprising, therefore, that most major personality theorists have in one way or another wrestled with the question of how much control people have over their environment and how this affects behavior. Debates among personality theorists have often centered around the question of control. For example, B. F. Skinner (1971) argued that people incorrectly attribute their behavior to their own free choices. He urged people to acknowledge that our behavior is largely controlled by the environment and to abandon the illusion of personal control that most of us now maintain. On the other hand, Carl Rogers (1961) emphasized free choice in his theory of personality. He encouraged people to recognize the extent to which they are personally responsible for what happens to them and to stop attributing their actions to forces outside their control.

Other personality psychologists have described an innate human desire to exercise personal control. For example, Robert White (1959) and Richard deCharms (1968) have identified a need to control the events in one's life as a primary human motive. Still other theorists have focused on how the perception of personal control influences personality development and behavior. For example, Alfred Adler centered his theory of personality around the notion of *striving for superiority* (Ansbacher & Ansbacher, 1956). He argued that some people are highly motivated to overcome feelings of inferiority. These people are driven to conquer life's obstacles and reach high levels of achievement. Adler identified other people who incorrectly accept their inferiority. These people are overwhelmed by a perceived inability to control their fate.

The concept of personal control also has been embraced by a large number of personality researchers. The bulk of this research has been concerned with responses to *perceived* rather than actual control. That is, how much people can actually influence events is not as important as the amount of control they believe they have. If you perceive no ability to control the grade you received in a particular class, then you probably will do nothing to improve that grade.

However, if you believe the grade you receive is largely up to you, most likely you will study hard, attend classes, and so on. But notice that whether you actually *can* control your grade is relatively unimportant in determining your behavior. Of course, how people react when they find their perceptions of control are in error is an interesting issue. We will examine the research on this question later in the chapter.

We'll begin our exploration of control and personality by examining the various reactions people have to perceived personal control. Next, we'll look at two relevant individual difference variables. These are *locus of control*, the extent to which we typically see ourselves in control of what happens to us, and *desire for control*, the extent to which we generally are motivated to control the events in our lives. Where people fall on each of these personality dimensions can have an impact on a large number of behaviors.

THE IMPACT OF PERCEIVED PERSONAL CONTROL

Is perceived personal control good or bad? Is it better to feel you can influence the events in your life or to accept that most of what happens is out of your control? Should we encourage students, patients, older citizens, and others to seek control, or should these people let more capable others take charge? Most of the theories of personality mentioned earlier seem to assume that the more control a person has, the better off that person is. However, a great deal of research suggests that the answer to these questions is not so simple. Believing you have control over important aspects of your life clearly has benefits. But personal control can be a two-edged sword. Sometimes we are better off letting someone else control the situation.

Positive Aspects of Perceived Control

A strong case can be made that feeling in control of events is tantamount to good personal adjustment and mental health. As evidence for this conclusion, we can point to a large number of studies that find adverse reactions when people are deprived of control over important events. Much of the early research demonstrating these effects was designed to test the theory of *learned helplessness* (Seligman, 1975). According to the original version of the theory, learned helplessness begins when we perceive an inability to control some important aspect of our lives. For example, you may conclude that nothing you do is going to help you to get into medical school. In fact, this might be a reasonable conclusion. If you cannot change the outcome, it would be a waste of time, energy, and emotion for you to pursue an unattainable goal. However, people sometimes incorrectly generalize their perception of no control in one situation to other situations over which they might exercise some control. Thus, after a string of rejection letters, the frustrated pre-med student might also decide that he or she is unable to do well at any type of job, unable to make friends, or incapable of succeeding at other personal challenges. In essence, the person has *learned* (incorrectly) that he or she is *helpless* to do anything about the problems and opportunities that life throws his or her way. The result is a decline in motivation and productivity. If nothing is done to break this thinking, the person may become a candidate for depression.

Learned helplessness has been demonstrated in a large number of laboratory investigations (Peterson & Seligman, 1984). The standard procedure presents study participants with several trials of an aversive stimulus, such as blasts of irritating noise (Hiroto & Seligman, 1975). Some participants can do something to stop (control) the noise, such as solving a simple word puzzle. Others can do nothing to stop the noise. Following their exposure to controllable or uncontrollable noise, participants typically are given a different type of task to work on, and perhaps a measure of depression. People subjected to the uncontrollable aversive noise often inappropriately generalize their perception of no control to this second task. They perform more poorly than participants in the controllable-noise condition and report higher levels of depression.

More recent work has expanded the basic learned helplessness model (Gillham, Shatte, Reivich, & Seligman, 2001; Seligman, 1991). Some of this research examines the explanations people give for why they cannot control a given situation. For example, if you attribute your inability to get a good grade in a math class to your general lack of intelligence, you will have a very different reaction than if you decide the particular teacher is unfair or that you simply can't do math at 8:00 in the morning. According to the theory, people are more likely to develop learned helplessness when they attribute their lack of control to internal, stable, and global factors (Abramson, Seligman, & Teasdale, 1978). That is, you are most likely to experience learned helplessness and depression when you attribute the lack of control to something about yourself that lasts a long time and affects many aspects of your life. Other research finds that some people are more likely to make these depression-prone attributions than others (Gillham et al., 2001). Researchers refer to these differences in how we explain events as *explanatory style*.

An excellent example of how findings from laboratory experiments on learned helplessness can be applied to real-world issues is found in a study conducted among residents of an old-age home (Langer & Rodin, 1976). Residents on one floor of a retirement home were instructed to take more control of their own lives. They were encouraged to recognize the influence they could have over the course of daily events at the home. Activities on the floor were arranged to emphasize the role of residents' personal responsibility. Another floor of the home served as a comparison group. These residents were given no control-enhancing instructions and no increased opportunities for control. The investigators found that the residents who were given increased personal control became more active, better adjusted, and healthier than the group not given this perception. A follow-up investigation at the same residence found that the positive effects of the control-enhancing instructions could still be seen 18 months later (Rodin & Langer, 1977).

Negative Aspects of Perceived Control

Does this mean that the more control we have in our lives the better? Not always. Although perceiving oneself as in control usually is beneficial, there are some important exceptions (Burger, 1989; Shapiro, Schwartz, & Astin, 1996;

Thompson, Cheek, & Graham, 1988). At least three features of perceived personal control may make it less than desirable for some people some times. First, when we are given control over a situation, it also means that we typically are held more responsible for outcomes. This increase in responsibility can lead to an increase in concern for what others will think of us and a subsequent increase in anxiety. For example, a businesswoman who is promoted to a position of increased power may enjoy her ability to control the direction the company takes. But the woman also will be held responsible in the event of a poor company performance. Consequently, increased control can carry with it increased pressure and anxiety.

This phenomenon was demonstrated in a laboratory experiment in which participants were told they would be tested on one of three tasks (Burger, Brown, & Allen, 1983). Some participants were allowed to select which task they wanted to try. In addition to the general benefits that come with feeling in control, the choice seemingly allowed participants to select the task they would do best on, and thereby make them feel better about their chances of performing well. However, these participants reported *higher* levels of anxiety just before working on the task than participants not given this choice. Apparently the increased control also led to an increase in the participants' concern for how they would be evaluated. In support of this interpretation, when a new experimenter unaware of the participants' choice was used to administer the task (thereby reducing the participants' concern for what the experimenter would think of them), no increase in anxiety was found. Other studies find that people sometimes are so concerned about their public image in case of failure that they deliberately reduce the amount of control they have over the outcome of a task (Arkin & Baumgardner, 1985). Research participants in these situations sometimes listen to distracting music or take performance-inhibiting drugs. This behavior creates an increased likelihood of failure, but it allows participants to take less responsibility for the outcome. Researchers refer to this phenomenon as *self-handicapping*.

A second consequence of personal control is an increase in predictability. When we control an event, we also usually know what will happen and when it will happen. Although generally people prefer predictable events to unpredictable ones (Kelly, 1955), research in this area is quite mixed (Miller, 1981; Thompson, 1981). Knowing when something will happen may be desirable, but sometimes people prefer to not know. For example, in one study participants who watched a clock count down the seconds to the moment they would receive an electric shock experienced more anxiety than participants who did not know when the shock was coming (Monat, Averill, & Lazarus, 1972). This may be why most people prefer to have someone else take a blood sample from them rather than having to prick their own finger (Burger, McWard, & LaTorre, 1989).

Third, sometimes being in control increases rather than decreases the chances of experiencing something aversive. There are many situations that are likely to turn out worse if I am given control instead of someone who might be more competent. This is why people typically give some control of their health care to a doctor they trust, and why people who have been drinking (hopefully) allow someone else to drive them home from a party. In an empirical demonstration of this effect, participants in one study were given the choice of performing a reaction-time task themselves or of turning control of the task over to a partner (Miller, 1980). Although most people preferred to keep control when they thought they were good at the task, most participants relinquished control to their partner when they were led to believe the other person would do a better job and thereby avoid an electric shock for both of them. In another study, physicians either allowed patients with end-stage renal disease to administer their own treatment or left the treatment in the hands of the medical staff (Eitel, Hatchett, Friend, Griffin, & Wadhwa, 1995). The self-administration patients showed lower levels of depression when they felt they were capable of performing the task. However, when patients experienced more severe and less controllable symptoms, those given responsibility for their own treatment reported higher levels of depression than those attended to by the staff.

Finding Control in Uncontrollable Situations

Despite these exceptions, most people prefer control over the events in their lives. Moreover, a good deal of research suggests that people who see themselves in control typically are happier and more successful than those who do not (Taylor, 1989). Unfortunately, life does not always cooperate with our desires. Sometimes we encounter situations and events that we simply have little control over. This lack of control may be particularly notable when we face serious health conditions. Although there are many actions people can take to reduce their chance of contracting a life-threatening illness such as cancer or AIDS, once diagnosed the patient's ability to control the course of the disease faces realistic limitations. How do people respond to such situations?

One way to cope with these events is to employ what some researchers refer to as *secondary control* (Rothbaum, Weisz, & Snyder, 1982). That is, people sometimes retain a sense of control or mastery by accepting the situation, trusting in fate or God, or simply interpreting events in a positive way. Another strategy people use when faced with an uncontrollable situation is to focus on the things they *can* do something about (Taylor, 1983). That is, beyond following medical advice, a patient usually has little control over whether a disease will be cured or whether the condition will return. However, in most cases the patient can exercise some control over how he or she deals with physical limitations resulting from the disease, his or her relationships with others, and so on. Exercising control over these aspects of one's life can provide a sense of mastery and avoid learned helplessness-type reactions.

The effectiveness of this strategy was demonstrated in a study with women who had been diagnosed with breast cancer (Thompson, Sobolew-Shubin, Galbraith, Schwankovsky, & Cruzen, 1993). Women who believed they could control the consequences associated with their disease (secondary control), such as their emotional reaction and daily physical symptoms, rather than believing they could control the course of the disease itself (primary control), showed the highest levels of emotional adjustment to their condition. Similar reactions have been found in studies with HIV-positive men (Thompson, Collins, Newcomb,

& Hunt, 1996; Thompson, Nanni, & Levine, 1994). The men obviously could not make their disease go away. But those who retained a sense of control over other features of their daily life, such as day-to-day activities and the quality of their relationships, were less depressed than those who did not.

In sum, a slightly exaggerated sense of one's ability to control events probably is beneficial (Taylor, 1989). However, there are limits to the advantages of unrealistic beliefs in control (Thompson, 1993; Zuckerman, Knee, Kieffer, Rawsthorne, & Bruce, 1996). Believing in the impossible (e.g., that an amputated limb will return) is unlikely to prove effective in the long run. But recognizing the extent to which recovery and adjustment from medical procedures is under one's control most likely will be helpful. In other words, it's probably best to change the things we can and to accept the things we cannot. As the saying goes, the key may be the wisdom to know the difference.

Self-Efficacy

Although there are exceptions, the message to this point appears to be that control is a good thing. But who's to say what is controllable? For example, consider the man encouraged by his doctor to start exercising daily. The man joins a health club, and each morning the first week he rises early and puts in 30 minutes on the treadmill before work. By the second week, the man makes it to the club only every other day, and by the end of the month he stops going altogether. When his doctor asks about daily exercise, the patient explains, "I just *can't* do it."

In this example, are the health benefits of exercise outside the patient's control? On the one hand, the man says he *can't* do the exercise, suggesting the desired outcome is uncontrollable. On the other hand, the doctor may explain that the decision to exercise is up to the patient, indicating that the health benefits are something the man *can* control. The difference between these two perspectives illustrates the distinction Albert Bandura (1977, 1997) draws between outcome expectations and efficacy expectations. *Outcome expectations* refer to the extent to which people believe that their actions will lead to certain outcomes. In the exercise example, the patient probably would acknowledge that he *could* improve his health by exercising every day. That's his outcome expectation. *Efficacy expectations* reflect the extent to which people believe they are capable of bringing about a particular outcome. Although the man admits that exercise will result in better health, he also holds the efficacy expectation that he is not capable of reaching this goal. As this example illustrates, it is the efficacy expectation that determines the behavior. Whether the health benefits are controllable in theory does not really matter.

According to Bandura, people obtain a sense of *self-efficacy* when they believe they are capable of controlling outcomes. Self-efficacy has been found to play a key role in many therapy situations (Bandura, Adams, & Beyer, 1977; Bandura, Pastorelli, Babaranelli, & Caprara, 1999; Bauer & Bonanno, 2001; Williams, 1995). Clients are not likely to overcome a fear of snakes or stop smoking if they don't believe they are capable of making the necessary changes. Thus, successful therapy often involves changing the clients' efficacy expectations. But how can this be done? Bandura argues that efficacy expectations come from four sources. In order of their effectiveness, these four are enactive mastery experiences, vicarious experiences, verbal persuasion, and physiological and affective states.

Enactive mastery experiences are successful past attempts to reach the outcome. A woman who gets butterflies just before speaking in front of a large audience can overcome her anxiety by reminding herself of past speeches she has given to similar groups without incident. When working with clients, therapists can use a procedure known as *guided mastery* (Bandura, 1997) to achieve this effect. Therapists using guided mastery break the treatment into small steps that can be easily accomplished. For example, a man with a fear of enclosed spaces might be assisted in walking quickly through a small, enclosed space. After success at this small step, the client may be asked to spend 10 seconds in an enclosed space. With each step the client is saying to himself, "You see, you can do this." If successful, the client eventually changes his efficacy expectation from *I can't* to *I can*.

Efficacy expectations also can be changed by watching other people—that is, through *vicarious experiences*. When a man who wants to lose weight sees other members of his weight-loss group reach their goals, he may conclude, "If they can do it, so can I." Although less effective, efficacy expectations also can be changed through *verbal persuasion*. A woman who is afraid to fly might be convinced to board a plane when her friends tell her "you can do it." However, the new efficacy expectation probably will be retained only if she has a successful experience on the flight. Finally, awareness of *physiological and affective states* can affect efficacy expectations. A man who notices his heart racing just before a scheduled job interview may conclude that he is incapable of going through with the interview. However, if the man notices how calm he feels prior to the interview, he may decide that he is more confident than he realized.

INDIVIDUAL DIFFERENCES IN PERCEIVED CONTROL: LOCUS OF CONTROL

Is getting a good job up to you, or is it the result of luck or knowing the right person? Can you make friends if you want to, or do you have to be in the right circumstances? When your car breaks down, is there something you could have done to prevent it, or are such problems inevitable? Because the answers are not clear, people respond to these questions differently. Some people tend to say that getting a job, making friends, and keeping their car running are all for the most part up to them. But others will tell you that these things are largely out of their control. These different perceptions reflect a personality variable researchers call *locus of control*.

The notion of individual differences in perceived personal control evolved from Julian Rotter's (1954) social learning theory of personality. Rotter (1966) proposed that people differ in the extent to which they typically expect to control a given situation. At one end of the locus of control dimension we find people who believe that almost everything that happens to them is under their control. They take credit for their successes, blame for their failures, and believe there are actions they can take to overcome obstacles and prevent future problems from developing. Rotter called these people *internals*. At the other extreme we find people who believe that most of what happens to them is caused by forces outside of their control. These individuals attribute successes and failures to such things as luck or the actions of powerful forces (e.g., "administrators" or "the system"). People who generally hold this orientation are called *externals*.

Of course, most of us fall somewhere between these two extremes. Like other individual difference variables, locus of control should be thought of as a continuum of points along a dimension ranging from extreme internals at one end to extreme externals at the other. Rotter (1966) developed a self-report personality inventory to measure individual differences in locus of control. Externals taking this inventory tend to agree with statements such as "Many of the unhappy things in people's lives are partly due to bad luck," whereas internals tend to agree with statements such as "People's misfortunes result from the mistakes they make."

Since Rotter introduced the locus of control concept, hundreds if not thousands of studies have been conducted comparing internals and externals on nearly every relevant behavior and personality dimension imaginable (Lefcourt, 1992). In fact, it is difficult to think of many situations for which the question of personal control is not an important one. How much effort I put into almost any situation probably is a reflection of how much control I believe I have. To illustrate the importance of this personality variable, we'll look briefly at research that ties locus of control to academic achievement, health behavior, and depression.

Who do you suppose is more likely to do well in school, an internal or an external? Imagine an internal college student and an external student enrolled in a class that is reputed to be difficult and taught by a professor who is known to be a tough grader. The internal probably approaches the class with the idea that with enough effort it is possible to beat the odds and get a good grade. The external, on the other hand, is more likely to conclude that there is no way to do well in this class no matter how hard he or she studies. Given the different approaches to the class, it's not hard to imagine that the internal will study more, do better on the tests, and get the higher grade. In fact, this is what researchers typically find (Findley & Cooper, 1983; Kalechstein & Nowicki, 1997). Although there are exceptions, researchers find a fairly consistent relationship between an internal locus of control and higher academic achievement in all grade levels. Similar differences between internals and externals are found when researchers look at achievement in the business world (Judge & Bono, 2001).

Internals and externals also may approach health care differently (Strickland, 1989; Wallston, 1993). Most of the research in this area looks specifically at beliefs about control over health rather than at locus of control generally. Researchers find that people who believe they have a lot of control over their health report fewer health problems than those who hold a more external set of beliefs (Johansson et al., 2001; Marshall, 1991; Simoni & Ng, 2002). Why might this be so? In truth, good health habits—exercise, good nutrition, following doctors' orders—contribute to a person's overall health. People with an internal locus of control are likely to recognize their role in staying healthy and take steps to maintain their health (Steptoe & Wardle, 2001). On the other hand, people with an external orientation are less likely to see that their actions affect their health and thus are less likely to engage in good health habits. Other studies find that internals reap these health benefits only when they also have a strong interest in maintaining their health (Wallston, 1993). That is, locus of control will affect health only when a person desires good health *and* believes he or she can do something about it.

Finally, many researchers find that locus of control is related to depression (Benassi, Sweeney, & Dufour, 1988). Although there obviously are exceptions, on average internals tend to be less prone to depression than externals. This finding is consistent with the laboratory research on learned helplessness presented earlier. Like the laboratory participants who felt they could control the aversive noise, internals tend to believe that they can do something to control the difficulties they encounter in life. On the other hand, externals are more likely to believe that there is little they can do to resolve a problem or to make a bad situation better. Like the laboratory participants who could not control the aversive noise, these people may be susceptible to depression.

INDIVIDUAL DIFFERENCES IN MOTIVATION FOR CONTROL: DESIRE FOR CONTROL

Although personal control has its good and bad side, there is general agreement among researchers that all people are motivated to exercise at least some control over the events in their lives and the environment in which they live. However, if you were to spend even a little time watching people interact in a group or go about their daily tasks, you would quickly see that the desire to exercise control is not the same for all people. Some people dominate the groups they join; others are content to let the leaders make decisions. Some people work harder when faced with a challenging task; others are quick to admit they can't or don't want to expend the effort. Consistent with these observations, researchers find there are relatively stable individual differences in the extent to which people prefer to see themselves in control (Burger, 1992a). That is, some people have a strong need to control what happens to them, and other people do not. Like other personality trait variables, this individual difference is assumed to be relatively stable over time and across different situations.

Before reading further, you may want to complete the personality inventory found in Activity Box 11.1. This is the Desirability of Control Scale developed by Burger and Cooper (1979). The scale identifies the extent to which people typically are high or low in their motivation for control. People who score high on the scale are described as "decisive, assertive, and active. They generally seek to influence others when such influence is advantageous" (p. 383). People high in desire for control prefer to make their own decisions and often become leaders in group situations. In contrast, those who score low

Activity Box 11.1   The Desirability of Control Scale

You can take the following test to get an idea of your own level of desire for control. Using a seven-point scale, indicate the extent to which each of the following statements applies to you. That is, if the statement always applies to you, place a 7 in the appropriate space. If the statement doesn't apply to you at all, answer 1. Use the numbers 2 through 6 to indicate degrees of partial agreement.

1. I prefer a job where I have a lot of control over what I do and when I do it.
2. I enjoy political participation because I want to have as much of a say in running government as possible.
3. I try to avoid situations where someone else tells me what to do.
4. I would prefer to be a leader than a follower.
5. I enjoy being able to influence the actions of others.
6. I am careful to check everything on an automobile before I leave for a long trip.
7. Others usually know what is best for me.
8. I enjoy making my own decisions.
9. I enjoy having control over my own destiny.
10. I would rather someone else take over the leadership role when I'm involved in a group project.
11. I consider myself to be generally more capable of handling situations than others are.
12. I'd rather run my own business and make my own mistakes than listen to someone else's orders.
13. I like to get a good idea of what a job is all about before I begin.
14. When I see a problem, I prefer to do something about it rather than sit by and let it continue.
15. When it comes to orders, I would rather give them than receive them.
16. I wish I could push many of life's daily decisions off on someone else.
17. When driving, I try to avoid putting myself in a situation where I could be hurt by someone else's mistake.
18. I prefer to avoid situations where someone else has to tell me what I should be doing.
19. There are many situations in which I would prefer only one choice rather than having to make a decision.
20. I like to wait and see if someone else is going to solve a problem so that I don't have to be bothered with it.

To determine your score, reverse the values you gave items 7, 10, 16, 19, and 20 (i.e., 1 = 7, 2 = 6, 3 = 5, 4 = 4, 5 = 3, 6 = 2, 7 = 1). Then, add the 20 values together. The higher the score, the higher your desire for control. You can compare your score with those of other college students who have taken this test by looking at Table 11.1.

Table 11.1 | Norms for Desirability of Control

	Mean	Standard Deviation
Men	102.7	11.31
Women	97.3	11.64
Combined	99.1	11.80

Source: From "The Desirability of Control," by J. M. Burger and H. M. Cooper, *Motivation and Emotion, 3*, Table 1, pp. 384–385. Copyright © 1979 Kluwer Academic/Plenum Publishers. Reprinted with permission. These norms should be used for comparison and descriptive purposes only. It would be inappropriate to diagnose oneself as, for example, prone to depression, with this information alone.

are described as "generally nonassertive, passive and indecisive. These people are less likely to attempt to influence others and may prefer that many of their daily decisions be made by others" (p. 383). Scores on the scale have been found to be only slightly related to scores on measures of locus of control (Burger, 1992a). Thus, knowing how much you typically want to control events does not tell us much about whether you tend see yourself in control.

The Desirability of Control Scale is designed to measure *general* differences in desire for control. That is, researchers assume that people who want a lot of control over what happens to them at work also will display this desire in their relationships, on the tennis court, in the doctor's office, and so on. As illustrated in the research examples that follow, this assumption has been supported in studies that find desire for control is related to behaviors in a wide variety of areas. Of course, you might not have a higher desire for control in one area of life than in another. Indeed, researchers have developed scales to measure desire for control in specific domains. For example, one team of investigators has examined desire for control over dental procedures (Law, Logan, & Baron, 1994). These researchers find people who desire a lot of control over dental procedures but believe they have little control are the most likely to experience pain and distress when visiting a dentist. Other investigators have developed a scale to measure desire for control in the workplace (Greenberger, Strasser, & Lee, 1988). Workers scoring high on this scale are more likely to seek out information about the job, develop networks with colleagues, and negotiate changes in their job descriptions than those scoring low on the scale (Ashford & Black, 1996).

Since it was first published in 1979, well over a hundred studies have been conducted with the Desirability of Control Scale. As with locus of control, reviewing all of this research is not possible here. Instead, research examining the role of desire for control in four general areas will be presented. A large number of studies find that individual differences in desire for control relate to social behavior, achievement, well-being, and information processing.

Social Behavior

People are by nature social creatures. We spend a large part of each day in the presence of others and most people belong to a number of formal or informal groups and organizations. Moreover, very few aspects of our lives are as important to us as our relationships with friends and loved ones. Thus, it may be no surprise to find that exercising control over social interactions is important for people with a high desire for control. Research finds that individual differences in desire for control show up in our social interactions in at least two areas: efforts to influence others and interpersonal interaction style.

Compared to people with a low desire for control, people with a high desire for control use more direct and indirect tactics to change the behavior of the people around them (Caldwell & Burger, 1997). For example, high desire for control people might argue persuasively for their position or offer to do something nice in return for people who will shift to their position on an issue.

These people also are more likely than lows to seek out a position of power and influence. One study found that college students with a high desire for control were more likely to take on leadership roles in campus clubs and organizations (Burger, 1992a). Similarly, high desire for control citizens are more likely to get involved with political and social activities (Zimmerman, 1990; Zimmerman & Rappaport, 1988). These activities provide avenues for influencing public policies, thus enabling people to exercise control over important community events. Differences between high and low desire for control people also surface when we look at how they react to other people's efforts to influence them. People with a high desire for control prefer to make up their own minds about issues. High desire for control people are more resistant to peer pressure than lows when hearing the evaluations of others in a group and when told that most people agree with an advocated position (Burger, 1987a).

If high desire for control people prefer to exercise control and influence others in group and community settings, do they take this same approach in their daily interpersonal encounters? Not necessarily. Researchers find at least two strategies employed by people with a high desire for control when interacting with others. One strategy is to take direct action to control the flow of the interaction. There are several things a person with a high desire for control can do to influence a conversation. Researchers find that high desire for control people interacting with strangers often speak louder, interrupt more often, and speak more rapidly than lows (Burger, 1990; Dembroski, MacDougall, & Musante, 1984). Controlling a social interaction sometimes means deciding when it will end. We are especially likely to see this when each person in an argument wants to get "the last word." To test this notion, participants in one study were asked to describe their longest conversation each day for an entire week (Burger, 1990). The high desire for control participants were more likely than lows to report that they were the one who decided when the conversation would end.

Thus, one strategy employed by people with a high desire for control is to actively attempt to control the flow and outcome of the interaction. However, at times these people pursue just the opposite strategy. That is, social interactions also can be threatening to one's sense of control. A high desire for control person is especially concerned about being manipulated, embarrassed, or emotionally vulnerable during a social encounter. Like a crafty poker player, these people prefer to find out what others are thinking rather than tip their hand too soon. Consistent with this description, high desire for control people in one study were less likely than lows to reveal intimate information about themselves to a stranger (Burger, 1990).

The findings from these studies suggest that high desire for control people will speak up and dominate a conversation when they believe these tactics will provide a sense of control, but other times they will allow people to talk about themselves first when this strategy seems more likely to meet their needs. Interestingly, high desire for control people tend to have fewer close friends than lows (Burger, 1992a). However, they also tend to prefer fewer friends, and thus are less likely than lows to experience feelings of loneliness (Solano, 1987).

Achievement

How would you expect high desire for control people to react when they encounter a difficult problem at work or in school? Some people in this situation give up, admit the problem is too difficult, or perhaps ask someone else for help. But a person with a high desire for control is not likely to do any of these things. To these people, a difficult task is a challenge, maybe even a threat to their ability to control the situation. Moreover, challenging tasks provide them an opportunity to demonstrate their personal competence and mastery over the environment. Thus, by working harder and overcoming obstacles, high desire for control people can reaffirm that they are capable of exercising a great deal of control over the events in their lives. Given this approach to difficult tasks, we should not be surprised to find that people with a high desire for control generally achieve more than lows. High desire for control college students typically get higher grades (Burger, 1992b), and high desire for control workers report higher levels of success at various jobs (Reed, 1989).

Additional research has identified four reasons why high desire for control people typically do better at achievement tasks (Burger, 1985, 1987b). First, people with a high desire for control may have higher and more realistic aspiration levels than lows. Not only do high desire for control people predict they will do better and choose to work on harder tasks in laboratory studies, but they also are better able to adjust their predictions in a realistic manner when they find their initial estimates are too high. High desire for control students approach their classes in a similar manner (Burger, 1992b). Second, people with a high desire for control work harder when faced with a challenging task, whereas low desire for control people show little increased motivation when the task becomes more difficult. Third, high desire for control people are more persistent when they encounter a problem they cannot solve right away. Finally, desire for control level is related to the explanations people give for their successes and failures. High desire for control people tend to explain their performances in ways that help them maintain a sense of control. They are likely to attribute their successes to their own efforts and abilities, but attribute their failures to causes that don't imply a future lack of control. Thus, winning a tennis game might be attributed to superior ability, whereas losing the game might be attributed to some lucky breaks for the opponent.

Why are high desire for control people so motivated to achieve? Do they want the rewards that come with accomplishments, or is it the sense of satisfaction that comes from demonstrating their own mastery over challenges? Some research suggests not only that the latter is the case, but that one way to undermine a high desire for control person's motivation to achieve is to emphasize the external rewards. A large number of studies demonstrate that rewarding people for something they already enjoy doing often reduces the person's motivation to perform the task when not rewarded (Deci, Koestner, & Ryan, 1999). Presumably the person's perception about why he or she engages in the activity has been changed from one of personal choice to external control. Although all people may be susceptible to this effect, those with a high desire for control have been found to be especially likely to lose interest in an activity when extrinsic rewards are offered (Thompson, Chaiken, &

Hazlewood, 1993). Because these people are highly motivated to see themselves as masters of their own choices, they are especially sensitive to information suggesting otherwise.

Well-Being

Who do you suppose is happier—high or low desire for control people? I find most people guess high desire for control predicts happiness and fewer psychological problems. Indeed, as discussed earlier in this chapter, theorists often identify perceived control and a striving for mastery as both a cause and consequence of good mental health. However, researchers find the relation between desire for control and well-being is more complicated than this.

Psychologists who study well-being typically examine a wide variety of indicators of happiness and distress. These include measures of anxiety, depression, stress, self-acceptance, personal growth, and the like. In general, when investigators correlate these kinds of measures with desire for control, they find moderate but significant correlations (Aspinwall & Taylor, 1992; Cooper, Okamura, & McNeil, 1995; DeNeve & Cooper, 1998). Higher desire for control scores are associated with a stronger sense of well-being and with lower levels of distress. Moreover, researchers consistently find a positive correlation between desire for control and measures of self-esteem (Burger, 1995).

Thus, it would seem that a high desire for control contributes to well-being or is symptomatic of people who have achieved a positive sense of themselves and satisfaction with their lives. However, a closer look suggests this is not always the case. For example, several studies find that high desire for control people are *more* likely than lows to respond to certain situations with negative emotions (Braith, McCullough, & Bush, 1988; Burger, Oakman, & Bullard, 1983; Lawler, Schmied, Armstead, & Lacy, 1990). Moreover, under certain circumstances high desire for control people are more likely than lows to experience depression (Burger, 1984; Burger & Arkin, 1980). Finally, a high desire for control has sometimes been associated with certain negative psychological experiences, such as growing up in a home where one or more parent abused alcohol (Burger, 1995).

How do we reconcile these seemingly inconsistent research findings? Investigators have identified at least two explanations for the exceptions to the rule. First, high desire for control people are more likely than lows to react to situations that threaten their sense of control. This is why researchers sometimes find higher levels of anxiety in high desire for control individuals. However, this increased anxiety appears to be relatively short-lived. This is because high desire for control people tend to use more effective coping strategies than lows (Burger, 1992a). As a rule, highs are more likely to take stressful situations into their own hands (Burger et al., 1989). Thus, although people with a high desire for control may react strongly when faced with potential stressors, their ability to deal with these stressors helps them maintain their high level of well-being.

A second explanation has to do with the causes of depression. People with a high desire for control are most prone to depression when they encounter events they are unable to change. Because exercising control is important to them, high desire for control people are more aware of their lack of control in certain situations than are lows, and this awareness sometimes triggers depression (Burger, 1993). However, this does not mean high desire for control people generally are more depressed than lows. Correlations between desire for control scores and scores on depression inventories typically are near zero (Burger, 1984). This low correlation may be because in addition to being more aware of what they are unable to control, high desire for control people also are more aware of what they *can* control. By attending to events over which they can exercise control, high desire for control people may avoid learned helplessness and extended depression when encountering the inevitable uncontrollable event (Burger, 1993).

Information Processing

One key to controlling an event is knowing *why* things happen. For example, we are better able to influence the people we work with if we know why our colleagues act the way they do. Similarly, you probably will be in a better position to overcome a health problem if you know why you developed that problem. One might conclude from this observation that most of us are constantly examining situations to figure out what causes what. However, this is simply not the case. Researchers find instead that most of us are cognitively lazy. That is, rather than expend a great deal of effort contemplating the many possible causes behind a given behavior or outcome, we are content to rely on general rules of thumb. If I see someone acting rudely, it's easier to say he or she is a grouch than to explore the dozens of other possible explanations for the inconsiderate behavior.

However, it also is the case that the more we rely on unexamined explanations, the more often we'll be incorrect and the less likely we are to control the situation. If knowing the causes of events is a key to controlling events, then it follows that high desire for control people would be highly motivated to find out why things happen. Consistent with this reasoning, researchers find that people with a high desire for control also tend to have a high need to evaluate (Jarvis & Petty, 1996) and a high need for cognition (Thompson et al., 1993). That is, these individuals tend to analyze and think about situations and events more than most of us. Moreover, laboratory studies find that high desire for control people are more likely than lows to pay attention to information that will help them understand the causes of another person's behavior and are more likely to think about and come up with more complex explanations for their own behavior (Burger & Hemans, 1988; Keinan & Sivan, 2001).

But does this increased cognitive activity mean that high desire for control people are more accurate than lows in their appraisals of how things are? Not necessarily. A high desire for control may make people more vulnerable to what has been called the *illusion of control* (Thompson, Armstrong, & Thomas, 1998). The illusion of control is demonstrated when people believe they have some control over the outcome of events that a rational observer would easily recognize as chance-determined, such as when tossing a coin or throwing dice. This illusion is likely to develop when chance-determined events are made to resemble skill-determined events (Langer, 1975). For example, people allowed to throw the dice themselves often feel more control over the outcome of the throw than those who simply watch. Although the dice thrower cannot possibly influence the outcome of the toss, somehow having the dice in one's hand creates the illusion of control.

Several studies find that people with a high desire for control often are more susceptible to the illusion of control than are lows (Burger, 1986; Burger & Schnerring, 1982; Sprott, Brumbaugh, & Miyazaki, 2001). For example, high desire for control participants in one study placed higher bets on a dice-tossing game when they knew what the winning number was and could throw the dice themselves (Burger & Cooper, 1979). Other studies find that high desire for control people are more likely than lows to fall for the illusion of control when playing with familiar rather than unfamiliar cards, and when they are led to believe that they have guessed correctly during the initial trials in a "heads or tails" coin-toss game (Burger, 1986). In the latter example, high desire for control college students who had an early string of luck guessing heads or tails actually predicted that on average they could guess the outcome of future coin tosses nearly 60% of the time. Investigators also find that people with a high desire for control are more likely than lows to engage in superstitious behavior, presumably to aid them in controlling outcomes (Keinan, 2002).

These research findings suggest an intriguing possibility. If high desire for control people are susceptible to the illusion of control, they may also be more susceptible than most people to problem gambling. Consistent with this notion, some research has found that desire for control is related to *how* people gamble. For example, problem gamblers with a high desire for control are more likely to bet on events that contain an element of control, such as poker and horse racing, than games that are entirely chance-determined (Burger & Smith, 1985). Similarly, high desire for control lottery players are more likely than lows to select their own numbers rather than accept a machine-generated random selection of numbers, and bingo players with a high desire for control are more likely than lows to use good luck charms and rely on other superstitions (Burger, 1991).

Although desire for control affects how people gamble, researchers have had a more difficult time determining the connection between desire for control and *how much* people gamble. In some gambling settings, a high desire for control seems to predict higher bets and more frequent gambling. But in other situations, a high desire for control is associated with lower bets and less frequent gambling. How can we reconcile all these findings? One explanation relates back to the way desire for control affects information processing (Burger, 1993). That is, people with a high desire for control tend to interpret situations by attending to control-relevant information. If the readily available cues in a situation indicate that outcomes are controllable, high desire for control people will attend to those cues and base their actions on them. However, if the cues indicate little control is available, high desire for control people will respond to that information as well. Thus, it may be that some gambling situations appear more controllable than others, and that high desire for control people respond accordingly.

SUMMARY

Researchers have identified a number of benefits that come from perceiving that we are in control of the events in our lives. People who find they are unable to control important events may suffer from learned helplessness and depression. However, researchers also have found some important exceptions to this rule. Sometimes people experience increased anxiety when given control over a situation or choose to relinquish control to a more competent person. People who find they cannot directly control important outcomes sometimes rely on secondary control, such as focusing their attention on what they can control. Researchers and therapists often find it useful to distinguish between what people can control and what people believe they are capable of achieving.

Self-efficacy theory draws a distinction between outcome expectations and efficacy expectations. The former are beliefs about whether actions can lead to outcomes, whereas the latter refer to what people believe they are capable of accomplishing. Albert Bandura argues that therapy clients are not likely to change during treatment unless they possess appropriate efficacy expectations. Efficacy expectations come from many sources, but most noteworthy are those from successful performances of the desired behavior.

People differ in the extent to which they typically believe they can control events. This individual difference is known as locus of control. People identified as internals on this personality dimension are more likely to see events as controllable than are those identified as externals. Internals and externals have been found to differ in many ways. Three examples of these differences are found in research on academic achievement, health behavior, and depression.

Researchers also find that people differ in the extent to which they typically want to control the events in their lives. Psychologists refer to this individual difference as desire for control. People with a high desire for control often attempt to influence others, but sometimes they retain a sense of control by not revealing information about themselves. High desire for control people typically achieve more than lows. These people have higher aspirations, try harder on difficult tasks, are more persistent when faced with a challenge, and explain outcomes in a way that maintains the perception that they are in control. A high desire for control also has been associated with psychological well-being, but there are some important exceptions to this pattern. Finally, people with a high desire for control more actively try to explain the causes of behavior than do lows. Although this difference in information processing is related to how high and low desire for control people gamble, it does not easily predict how much people will gamble.

DISCUSSION QUESTIONS

1. When do people find increases in perceived control undesirable? Give an example for each of the three negative aspects of perceived control described in the chapter.
2. What role do efficacy expectations play in psychotherapy? How might a therapist alter the efficacy expectations of a client who suffers from a fear of heights?

3. How do individual differences in locus of control affect performance in school and one's health?
4. How are individual differences in desire for control related to happiness and well-being?
5. What is the illusion of control, and how have researchers tied illusion of control and desire for control to gambling behavior?

SUGGESTED READINGS

Burger, J. M. (1992). *Desire for control: Personality, social and clinical perspectives.* New York: Plenum. A review of research on individual differences in desire for control. The book includes results from many unpublished studies and a discussion of concepts in personality psychology related to control motivation.

Shapiro, D. H., Schwartz, C. E., & Astin, J. A. (1996). Controlling ourselves, controlling our world: Psychology's role in understanding positive and negative consequences of seeking and gaining control. *American Psychologist, 51,* 1213–1230. A review of studies identifying some of the positive and negative outcomes of perceived personal control and a discussion of how this distinction can be used by psychotherapists.

Skinner, E. A. (1995). *Perceived control, motivation, and coping.* Thousand Oaks, CA: Sage. Ellen Skinner discusses the causes and consequences of perceived control. Topics include changes in perceived control over the life span and some of the positive and negative effects of increased control.

Thompson, S. C., Armstrong, W., & Thomas, C. (1998). Illusions of control, underestimations, and accuracy: A control heuristic explanation. *Psychological Bulletin, 123,* 143–161. A review of research on the illusion of control. The authors identify five conditions that influence judgments of personal control over chance-determined outcomes and describe the psychological processes behind these judgments.

SUGGESTED WEB SITES

http://www.uiowa.edu/~grpproc/crisp/crisp.5.15.htm

An essay from the journal *Current Research in Social Psychology* examining the usability and validity of the Desirability of Control Scale.

http://www.guardian.co.uk/print/0,3858,4566078-103425,00.html

This article from the *Guardian* newspaper in the UK examines the role of control in the likelihood that someone will be superstitious.

INFOTRAC COLLEGE EDITION SEARCH TOPICS

Personal control
Self-efficacy

Locus of control
Desire for control

REFERENCES

Abramson, L. Y., Seligman, M. E. P., & Teasdale, J. D. (1978). Learned helplessness in humans: Critique and reformulation. *Journal of Abnormal Psychology, 87,* 49–74.

Ansbacher, H. L., & Ansbacher, R. R. (Eds.). (1956). *The individual psychology of Alfred Adler.* New York: Basic Books.

Arkin, R. M., & Baumgardner, A. H. (1985). Self-handicapping. In J. H. Harvey & G. Weary (Eds.). *Attribution: Basic issues and applications* (pp. 169–202). San Diego, CA: Academic Press.

Ashford, S. J., & Black, J. S. (1996). Proactivity during organizational entry: The role of desire for control. *Journal of Applied Psychology, 81,* 199–214.

Aspinwall, L. G., & Taylor, S. E. (1992). Modeling cognitive adaptation: A longitudinal investigation of the impact of individual differences and coping on college adjustment and performance. *Journal of Personality and Social Psychology, 63,* 898–1003.

Bandura, A. (1977). Self-efficacy: Toward a unifying theory of behavioral change. *Psychological Review, 84,* 191–215.

Bandura, A. (1997). *Self-efficacy: The exercise of control.* New York: Freeman.

Bandura, A., Adams, N. E., & Beyer, J. (1977). Cognitive processes mediating behavioral change. *Journal of Personality and Social Psychology, 35,* 125–139.

Bandura, A., Pastorelli, C., Barbaranelli, C., & Caprara, G. V. (1999). Self-efficacy pathways to childhood depression. *Journal of Personality and Social Psychology, 76,* 258–269.

Bauer, J. J., & Bonanno, G. A. (2001). I can, I do, I am: The narrative differentiation of self-efficacy and other self-evaluations while adapting to bereavement. *Journal of Research in Personality, 35,* 424–448.

Benassi, V. A., Sweeney, P. D., & Dufour, C. L. (1988). Is there a relationship between locus of control orientation and depression? *Journal of Abnormal Psychology, 97,* 357–367.

Braith, J. A., McCullough, J. P., & Bush, J. P. (1988). Relaxation-induced anxiety in a subclinical sample of chronically anxious subjects. *Journal of Behavior Therapy and Experimental Psychiatry, 19,* 193–198.

Burger, J. M. (1984). Desire for control, locus of control, and proneness to depression. *Journal of Personality, 52,* 71–89.

Burger, J. M. (1985). Desire for control and achievement-related behaviors. *Journal of Personality and Social Psychology, 48,* 1520–1533.

Burger, J. M. (1986). Desire for control and the illusion of control: The effects of familiarity and sequence of outcomes. *Journal of Research in Personality, 20,* 66–76.

Burger, J. M. (1987a). Desire for control and conformity to a perceived norm. *Journal of Personality and Social Psychology, 53,* 355–360.

Burger, J. M. (1987b). The effects of desire for control on attributions and task performance. *Basic and Applied Social Psychology, 8,* 309–320.

Burger, J. M. (1989). Negative reactions to increases in perceived personal control. *Journal of Personality and Social Psychology, 56,* 246–256.

Burger, J. M. (1990). Desire for control and interpersonal interaction style. *Journal of Research in Personality, 24,* 32–44.

Burger, J. M. (1991). The effects of desire for control in situations with chance-determined outcomes: Gambling behavior in lotto and bingo players. *Journal of Research in Personality, 25,* 196–204.

Burger, J. M. (1992a). *Desire for control: Personality, social and clinical perspectives.* New York: Plenum.

Burger, J. M. (1992b). Desire for control and academic performance. *Canadian Journal of Behavioural Science, 24,* 147–155.

Burger, J. M. (1993). Individual differences in control motivation and social information processing. In G. Weary, F. Gleicher, & K. L. Marsh (Eds.), *Control motivation and social cognition* (pp. 203–219). New York: Springer-Verlag.

Burger, J. M. (1995). Need for control and self-esteem: Two routes to a high desire for control. In M. H. Kernis (Ed.), *Efficacy, agency, and self-esteem* (pp. 217–233). New York: Plenum.

Burger, J. M., & Arkin, R. M. (1980). Prediction, control and learned helplessness. *Journal of Personality and Social Psychology, 38,* 482–491.

Burger, J. M., Brown, R., & Allen, C. K. (1983). Negative reactions to personal control. *Journal of Social and Clinical Psychology, 1,* 322–342.

Burger, J. M., & Cooper, H. M. (1979). The desirability of control. *Motivation and Emotion, 3,* 381–393.

Burger, J. M., & Hemans, L. T. (1988). Desire for control and the use of attribution processes. *Journal of Personality, 56,* 531–546.

Burger, J. M., McWard, J., & LaTorre, D. (1989). Boundaries of self-control: Relinquishing control over aversive events. *Journal of Social and Clinical Psychology, 8,* 209–221.

Burger, J. M., Oakman, J. A., & Bullard, N. G. (1983). Desire for control and the perception of crowding. *Personality and Social Psychology Bulletin, 9,* 475–479.

Burger, J. M., & Schnerring, D. A. (1982). The effects of desire for control and extrinsic rewards on the illusion of control and gambling. *Motivation and Emotion, 6,* 329–335.

Burger, J. M., & Smith, N. G. (1985). Desire for control and gambling behavior among problem gamblers. *Personality and Social Psychology Bulletin, 11*, 145–152.

Caldwell, D. C., & Burger, J. M. (1997). Personality and social influence strategies in the workplace. *Personality and Social Psychology Bulletin, 23*, 1003–1012.

Cooper, H., Okamura, L., & McNeil, P. (1995). Situation and personality correlates of psychological well-being: Social activity and personal control. *Journal of Research in Personality, 29*, 395–417.

deCharms, R. (1968). *Personal causation*. New York: Academic Press.

Deci, E. L., Koestner, R., & Ryan, R. M. (1999). A meta-analytic review of experiments examining the effects of extrinsic rewards on intrinsic motivation. *Psychological Bulletin, 125*, 627–668.

Dembroski, T. M., MacDougall, J. M., & Musante, L. (1984). Desirability of control versus locus of control: Relationship to paralinguistics in the Type A interview. *Health Psychology, 3*, 15–26.

DeNeve, K. M., & Cooper, H. M. (1998). The happy personality: A meta-analysis of 137 personality traits and subjective well-being. *Psychological Bulletin, 124*, 197–229.

Eitel, P., Hatchett, L., Friend, R., Griffin, K. W., & Wadhwa, N. K. (1995). Burden of self-care in seriously ill patients: Impact on adjustment. *Health Psychology, 14*, 457–463.

Findley, M. J., & Cooper, H. M. (1983). Locus of control and academic achievement: A literature review. *Journal of Personality and Social Psychology, 44*, 419–427.

Gillham, J. E., Shatte, A. J., Reivich, K. J., & Seligman, M. E. P. (2001). Optimism, pessimism, and explanatory style. In E. C. Chang (Ed.), *Optimism and pessimism: Implications for theory, research, and practice* (pp. 53–75). Washington, DC: American Psychological Association.

Greenberger, D. B., Strasser, S., & Lee, S. (1988). Personal control as a mediator between perceptions of supervisory behaviors and employee reactions. *Academy of Management Journal, 31*, 405–417.

Hiroto, D. S., & Seligman, M. E. P. (1975). Generality of learned helplessness in humans. *Journal of Personality and Social Psychology, 31*, 311–327.

Jarvis, W. B. G., & Petty, R. E. (1996). The need to evaluate. *Journal of Personality and Social Psychology, 70*, 172–194.

Johansson, B., Grant, J. D., Plomin, R., Pedersen, N. L., Ahern, F., Berg, S. et al. (2001). Health locus of control in late life: A study of genetic and environmental influences in twins aged 80 years and older. *Health Psychology, 20*, 33–40.

Judge, T. A., & Bono, J. E. (2001). Relationship of core self-evaluations traits—self-esteem, generalized self-efficacy, locus of control, and emotional stability—with job satisfaction and job performance: A meta-analysis. *Journal of Applied Psychology, 86*, 80–92.

Kalechstein, A. D., & Nowicki, S. (1997). A meta-analytic examination of the relationship between control expectancies and academic achievement: An 11-year follow-up to Findley and Cooper. *Genetic, Social and General Psychology Monographs, 123*, 27–56.

Keinan, G. (2002). The effects of stress and desire for control on superstitious behavior. *Personality and Social Psychology Bulletin, 28*, 102–108.

Keinan, G., & Sivan, D. (2001). The effects of stress and desire for control on the formation of causal attributions. *Journal of Research in Personality, 35*, 127–137.

Kelly, G. A. (1955). *The psychology of personal constructs*. New York: Norton.

Langer, E. J. (1975). The illusion of control. *Journal of Personality and Social Psychology, 32*, 311–328.

Langer, E. J., & Rodin, J. (1976). The effects of choice and enhanced personal responsibility for the aged: A field experiment in an institutional setting. *Journal of Personality and Social Psychology, 34*, 191–198.

Law, A., Logan, H., & Baron, R. S. (1994). Desire for control, felt control, and stress inoculation training during dental treatment. *Journal of Personality and Social Psychology, 67*, 926–936.

Lawler, K. A., Schmied, L. A., Armstead, C. A., & Lacy, J. E. (1990). Type A behavior, desire for control, and cardiovascular reactivity in young adult women. *Journal of Social Behavior and Personality, 5*, 135–158.

Lefcourt, H. M. (1992). Durability and impact of the locus of control construct. *Psychological Bulletin, 112*, 411–414.

Marshall, G. N. (1991). A multidimensional analysis of internal health locus of control beliefs: Separating the wheat from the chaff? *Journal of Personality and Social Psychology, 61*, 483–491.

Miller, S. M. (1980). Why having control reduces stress: If I can stop the roller coaster, I don't want to get off. In J. Garber & M. E. P. Seligman (Eds.), *Human helplessness: Theory and applications* (pp. 71–95). New York: Academic Press.

Miller, S. M. (1981). Predictability and human stress: Toward a clarification of evidence and theory. In L. Berkowitz (Ed.), *Advances in experimental social psychology* (Vol. 14, pp. 203–256). New York: Academic Press.

Monat, A., Averill, J. R., & Lazarus, R. S. (1972). Anticipatory stress and coping reactions under various conditions of uncertainty. *Journal of Personality and Social Psychology, 24,* 237–253.

Peterson, C., & Seligman, M. E. P. (1984). Causal explanations as a risk factor for depression: Theory and evidence. *Psychological Review, 91,* 347–374.

Reed, T. F. (1989). Do union organizers matter? Individual differences, campaign practices, and representation election outcomes. *Industrial and Labor Relations Review, 43,* 103–119.

Rodin, J., & Langer, E. J. (1977). Long-term effects of control-relevant intervention with the institutionalized aged. *Journal of Personality and Social Psychology, 35,* 897–902.

Rogers, C. R. (1961). *On becoming a person: A therapist's view of psychotherapy.* Boston: Houghton-Mifflin.

Rothbaum, F., Weisz, J. R., & Snyder, S. S. (1982). Changing the world and changing the self: A two-process model of perceived control. *Journal of Personality and Social Psychology, 42,* 5–37.

Rotter, J. B. (1954). *Social learning and clinical psychology.* Englewood Cliffs, NJ: Prentice-Hall.

Rotter, J. B. (1966). Generalized expectancies for internal versus external control of reinforcement. *Psychological Monographs, 80,* (1, Whole No. 609).

Seligman, M. E. P. (1975). *Helplessness: On depression, development and death.* San Francisco: Freeman.

Seligman, M. E. P. (1991). *Learned optimism.* New York: Random House.

Shapiro, D. H., Schwartz, C. E., & Astin, J. A. (1996). Controlling ourselves, controlling our world: Psychology's role in understanding positive and negative consequences of seeking and gaining control. *American Psychologist, 51,* 1213–1230.

Simoni, J. M., & Ng, M. T. (2002). Abuse, health locus of control, and perceived health among HIV-positive women. *Health Psychology, 21,* 89–93.

Skinner, B. F. (1971). *Beyond freedom and dignity.* New York: Bantam.

Solano, C. H. (1987). Loneliness and perceptions of control: General traits versus specific attributions. *Journal of Social Behavior and Personality, 2,* 210–214.

Sprott, D. E., Brumbaugh, A. M., & Miyazaki, A. D. (2001). Motivation and ability as predictors of play behavior in state-sponsored lotteries: An empirical assessment of psychological control. *Psychology and Marketing, 18,* 973–983.

Steptoe, A., & Wardle, J. (2001). Locus of control and health behaviour revisited: A multivariate analysis of young adults from 18 countries. *British Journal of Psychology, 92,* 659–672.

Strickland, B. R. (1989). Internal-external control expectancies: From contingency to creativity. *American Psychologist, 44,* 1–12.

Taylor, S. E. (1983). Adjustment to threatening events: A theory of cognitive adaptation. *American Psychologist, 38,* 1161–1173.

Taylor, S. E. (1989). *Positive illusions: Creative self-deception and the healthy mind.* NewYork: Basic Books.

Thompson, E. P., Chaiken, S., & Hazlewood, J. D. (1993). Need for cognition and desire for control as moderators of extrinsic reward effects: A person X situation approach to the study of intrinsic motivation. *Journal of Personality and Social Psychology, 64,* 987–999.

Thompson, S. C. (1981). Will it hurt less if I can control it? A complex answer to a simple question. *Psychological Bulletin, 90,* 89–101.

Thompson, S. C. (1993). Naturally occurring perceptions of control: A model of bounded flexibility. In G. Weary, F. Gleicher, & K. L. Marsh (Eds.), *Control motivation and social cognition* (pp. 74–93). New York: Springer-Verlag.

Thompson, S. C., Armstrong, W., & Thomas, C. (1998). Illusions of control, underestimations, and accuracy: A control heuristic explanation. *Psychological Bulletin, 123,* 143–161.

Thompson, S. C., Cheek, P., & Graham, M. (1988). The other side of perceived control: Disadvantages and negative effects. In S. Oskamp & S. Spacapan (Eds.), *The social psychology of health* (pp. 69–93). Beverly Hills, CA: Sage.

Thompson, S. C., Collins, M. A., Newcomb, M. D., & Hunt, W. (1996). On fighting versus accepting stressful circumstances: Primary and secondary control among HIV-positive men in prison.

Journal of Personality and Social Psychology, 70, 1307–1317.

Thompson, S. C., Nanni, C., & Levine, A. (1994). Primary versus secondary and central versus consequence-related control in HIV-positive men. *Journal of Personality and Social Psychology, 67,* 540–547.

Thompson, S. C., Sobolew-Shubin, A., Galbraith, M. E., Schwankovsky, L., & Cruzen, D. (1993). Maintaining perceptions of control: Finding perceived control in low-control circumstances. *Journal of Personality and Social Psychology, 64,* 293–304.

Wallston, K. A. (1993). Hocus-pocus, the focus isn't strictly on locus: Rotter's social learning theory modified for health. *Cognitive Therapy and Research, 16,* 183–199.

White, R. (1959). Motivation reconsidered: The concept of competence. *Psychological Review, 66,* 297–330.

Williams, S. L. (1995). Self-efficacy and anxiety and phobic disorders. In J. E. Maddux (Ed.), *Self-efficacy, adaptation, and adjustment: Theory, research, and application* (pp. 69–108). New York: Plenum.

Zimmerman, M. A. (1990). Toward a theory of learned hopefulness: A structural model analysis of participation and empowerment. *Journal of Research in Personality, 24,* 71–86.

Zimmerman, M. A., & Rappaport, J. (1988). Citizen participation, perceived control and psychological empowerment. *American Journal of Community Psychology, 16,* 725–750.

Zuckerman, M., Knee, C. R., Kieffer, S. C., Rawsthorne, L., & Bruce, L. M. (1996). Beliefs in realistic and unrealistic control: Assessment and implications. *Journal of Personality, 64,* 435–464.

12 | **Sex and Gender**

RICHARD A. LIPPA

CHAPTER OUTLINE

Before you read this chapter, take a minute or two and write down on a piece of paper three ways in which you are masculine and three ways in which you are feminine. Finished? Which list was harder for you to complete? What kinds of masculine and feminine characteristics did you use to describe yourself? Were they personality traits (e.g., assertive, passive, aggressive, tender-hearted), physical traits (muscular, curvy, hairy, strong, weak), sexual traits (high sex drive, coy, heterosexual, gay), interests (like to watch football, like to crochet), college majors (physics major, theater arts major), occupations (engineer, nurse), nonverbal behaviors (have a high-pitched voice, use forceful gestures), grooming (wear dresses, wear jewelry, have tattoos), social roles (son, daughter, boyfriend, girlfriend) . . . or what?

It probably wasn't hard for you to list at least a few masculine and feminine traits that you possess, and it may seem obvious to you that people do in fact vary in how masculine or feminine they are. So it may come as a surprise for you to learn that personality psychologists have argued for decades about the nature of masculinity and femininity, and in recent years, some personality theorists have even concluded that these traits don't really exist, but are rather "in the eyes of the beholder" (Bem, 1987; Spence & Buckner, 1995).

STUDYING SEX, GENDER, AND PERSONALITY

To understand the controversy that swirls around research on sex, gender, and personality, it helps first to consider briefly the study of sex and gender more broadly, and to define several important terms.

Basic Terms and Concepts

The word *sex* refers to the biological categories of male and female. Human males are individuals with XY chromosomes and male genitals, and human females are individuals with XX chromosomes and female genitals. Although a small percentage of people (termed intersex individuals) are ambiguous in regard to some components of their biological sex, the huge majority of people can be unambiguously classified as male or female (Fausto-Sterling, 2000).

The word *gender* is used to refer to all those aspects of maleness and femaleness that, in humans, are socially determined and culturally learned. Thus, the differing hair length and dress of many men and women are a matter of gender, whereas the differing genitals of men and women are a matter of biological sex. There is still considerable debate about the extent to which various psychological sex differences (e.g., differences in physical aggressiveness, visual-spatial abilities, and sexual behaviors and attitudes) are influenced by biological versus social factors, and thus the distinction between sex and gender is not clear for many behaviors and psychological traits (see Lippa, 2002b; Walsh, 1997).

This chapter will use the term *sex differences* to refer to differences between biological males and females. Use of this term is not meant to imply anything about the causes of such differences, which may be biological, social, or both. It's important to note that even when men and women show *on average* differences, there is often considerable overlap in the distributions of men and women on various traits. Height provides an obvious example. Although men are, on average, taller than women, there are many tall women and many short men. A central question to be addressed by this chapter is this: Are there sex differences in human personality?

The term *gender role* refers to a society's norms and expectations about the behavior of men and women (and boys and girls). Gender roles are both descriptive and prescriptive (Eagly, 1987); they comprise societies' beliefs about the behavior of males and females (e.g., "Women are better than men at taking care of babies and small children"), and they inform males and females about how society expects them to behave ("Women *ought* to take care of babies and small children"). Gender roles influence many aspects of human life, including dress styles, nonverbal mannerisms, abilities, interests, educational pursuits, occupations, and family activities and responsibilities.

The term *gender stereotype* refers to beliefs shared by people in a given society about the characteristics of males and females (e.g., "men are more aggressive than women," "women are more emotional than men"). Researchers today tend to view stereotypes as probabilistic rather than black-and-white beliefs (e.g., Deaux & Lewis, 1984). For example, many people believe that men are more likely to be violent than women, but no one believes that all men are violent or that all women are nonviolent. The term *stereotype* should not be taken to imply that all beliefs about men and women are "in our heads" and therefore false. Certainly, some gender stereotypes may be false, and some may be exaggerations of real differences between the sexes. However, recent research suggests that our beliefs about men and women tend to be reasonably accurate (Eagly & Diekman, 1997; Hall & Carter, 1999). Such accuracy makes sense when you consider that most of us have had lots of experience with boys and girls and with men and women over the course of our lives, and thus our beliefs about males and females often reflect our observations of their actual behaviors.

Approaches to the Study of Sex and Gender: Essentialism Versus Social Constructionism

The study of sex and gender is sometimes a contest between two contrasting points of view: essentialism and social constructionism (see Fausto-Sterling, 1992; Lippa, 2002b; Unger, 2001). Essentialists believe that there are some real sex differences in people's psychological traits and behaviors. They also believe that masculinity and femininity are real traits that vary among men and among women—traits that can be measured with psychological tests. In contrast, social constructionists believe that gender is not a real "thing" that exists inside of people. Rather, they view gender as created by social beliefs (e.g., stereotypes about the two sexes), social structure (e.g., patriarchy, which gives more power to men than to women), and social interaction. Essentialists tend to be sympathetic to the notion that there may be biological factors (such as differences in brain structures and hormone levels) that contribute to sex differences in behavior and to individual differences in masculinity and femininity. In contrast, social constructionists tend to reject biological explanations and focus instead on cultural factors, social learning, and social beliefs as explanations for why men and women behave as they do.

Social constructionists often assert that we "do gender." By this they mean that our behavior as men and women and as masculine and feminine individuals is a kind of "performance" that we put on in some settings but not in others, with some people but not with others. For example, a woman may act in a soft and "feminine" fashion when on a date, but may be tough and "masculine" when working as a high-powered corporate manager. Similarly, a teenage boy may be "macho" with his tough male friends, but gentle with his grandmother. Social constructionists propose that gender is socially defined and socially enforced, and that masculinity and femininity are social concepts or "constructs" that may readily change and even disappear if society changes (e.g., if parents rear boys and girls the same, if schools teach boys and girls equally, if gender stereotypes are abolished, if patriarchal social structures are demolished, and if society provides equal opportunities for men and women).

Essentialists counter that there are some real inborn differences between men and women, difference that are not just the result of socialization. Furthermore, essentialists argue that variations in individuals' masculinity and femininity are not simply a matter of socialization and social settings. Rather, masculinity and femininity are real, core traits that are molded, in part, by genetic and biological influences (for a broader discussion of the nature and nurture of gender, see Lippa, 2002b).

TWO BASIC QUESTIONS ABOUT SEX, GENDER, AND PERSONALITY

This chapter will pose two basic questions about sex, gender, and personality: (1) Do men and women (and boys and girls) differ in their personalities? (2) Are there meaningful individual differences (i.e., variations) in masculinity and femininity within each sex?

Each of these questions suggests many additional questions. For example, if men and women do in fact differ in personality, what causes these differences? Do sex differences in personality result from genetic differences, hormonal factors, parental rearing, peer influences, social roles, gender stereotypes, or what? Similarly, if men vary in their masculinity and if women vary in their femininity, what causes these variations? Do variations in masculinity and femininity result from genetic and hormonal variations, from the varying parental, peer, teacher, and societal influences that affect each individual, or from a complex mixture of biological and social factors?

Research psychologists must pose another basic question about masculinity and femininity: What is the best way to conceptualize and measure these traits? (See chapter 2 for a discussion of personality measurement.) And social constructionists pose perhaps the most basic question of all about masculinity and femininity: Do these traits really exist, or are they merely social "fictions" and cultural inventions?

The two primary questions mentioned before—are there sex differences in personality, and are there meaningful variations in masculinity and femininity within each sex?—are closely interlinked. The reason for this is that sex differences in personality (e.g., "men are more aggressive than women," "women are more tender-minded and compassionate than men") have often been used in past research to define variations in masculinity and femininity within each sex (e.g., a man who is nonaggressive and tender-minded is feminine, whereas a woman who is aggressive, tough-minded, and noncompassionate is masculine).

QUESTION 1: ARE THERE SEX DIFFERENCES IN PERSONALITY?

As you know from other chapters in this book, there are many approaches to the study of personality, and many of these approaches have been applied to the study of sex, gender, and personality. Trait theories (see chapter 7) argue that human personality is best conceptualized in terms of stable internal factors (such as extroversion, neuroticism, and conscientiousness), which lead people to behave in consistent ways over time and across situations. Social learning theories argue that variations in individuals' behavior (e.g., moral behavior; see chapter 14) result from the myriad learning processes that mold individuals' behavior—processes such as classical conditioning, operant conditioning, modeling, and imitation. Freudian theories propose that early sexual attractions and emotional attachments to parents influence individuals' later behavior as men and women. Contemporary research on gender and personality has tended to focus most of its attention on trait theories and on social learning theories (which include cognitive theories that focus on men's and women's gender-related beliefs and self-concepts). In keeping with this emphasis, this chapter will focus mostly on these two broad approaches.

Sex Difference in Big Five Traits

Because trait research has measured personality in standardized ways (see chapters 2 and 7), it has provided abundant data that can be used to study sex differences in personality. In recent years, many personality psychologists have reached a consensus that at the broadest level of analysis there are five global personality traits that provide a fairly comprehensive description of human personality (see chapter 7). These traits (called, appropriately enough, the "Big Five") are extraversion, agreeableness, conscientiousness, neuroticism, and openness to experience. One way to study sex differences in personality, then, is to study whether men and women differ on the Big Five personality traits.

Yale psychologist Alan Feingold (1994) summarized evidence on sex differences in Big Five traits (using a technique called meta-analysis, which is a statistical method for combining the results from many different studies). Feingold found that men and women differed most strongly on certain aspects of extraversion and agreeableness. Specifically, men are more assertive than women (assertiveness is a component of extraversion) and that women are more tender-minded and nurturant than men (tender-mindedness is a component of agreeableness). These differences were, respectively, moderate and large in magnitude (based on conventional statistical measures of the size of the difference between two groups; see Lippa, 2002b, for details).

There was a smaller, but still statistically significant, sex difference in neuroticism, with women higher (i.e., more anxious, tense, and nervous) than men. There was little difference in men's and women's mean levels of conscientiousness and openness to experience. Self-esteem, which can be viewed as a facet of neuroticism (low self-esteem is related to high neuroticism), showed a small sex difference, with men having higher self-esteem than women, on average. A more recent meta-analysis also found a small sex difference in self-esteem and found in addition that this difference is greatest during adolescence (Kling, Hyde, Showers, & Buswell, 1999).

Costa, Terracciano, and McCrae (2001) recently analyzed sex differences in Big Five personality traits in over 23,000 people from 26 cultures. Women consistently scored higher than men on many facets of neuroticism and agreeableness. Men scored higher than women on assertiveness and excitement seeking (extraversion facets), competence (a facet of conscientiousness), and fantasy and openness to ideas (facets of openness). Costa and his colleagues found that sex differences in personality tended to be stronger in economically advanced countries with liberal gender ideologies (e.g., the United States and European countries) than in less economically advanced countries with more traditional gender roles (Asian, African, and Latin American countries). We'll return to these unexpected findings later, when we consider possible causes of sex differences in personality.

Sex Differences in Risk Taking and Sensation Seeking

There are some aspects of personality that are not directly (or sometimes even indirectly) captured by the Big Five model of personality. Risk taking is one. A recent study compiled evidence from 150 laboratory and questionnaire studies of risk taking in men and women (Byrnes, Miller, & Schafer, 1999), and it found a small to moderate sex difference, with men showing a higher tendency to take risks than women. Sex differences in risk taking were larger for some kinds of behaviors than others. For example, men were particularly more likely than women to take risks when exposing themselves to danger (e.g., electric shocks) in experiments, when taking intellectual risks, and in games of physical skill.

Sensation seeking refers to an individual's tendency to seek out arousing, novel, and thrilling settings (Zuckerman, 1994). People who like to skydive, bungie cord jump, and downhill ski tend to be high on sensation seeking, for example. Sensation seeking may be related to risk taking, particularly when risks involve action-packed, arousing, and sometimes dangerous activities (such as bobsled racing or being a jet fighter pilot). Research consistently shows that men score higher than women on measures of sensation seeking (Zuckerman, Buchsbaum, & Murphy, 1980; Zuckerman & Kuhlman, 2000), and these differences are small to moderate in magnitude.

Sex Differences in Aggressiveness

Meta-analyses of the results of laboratory studies on aggression (which have generally been conducted on college men and women) show small to moderate sex differences in laboratory aggression (e.g., delivering shocks to an obnoxious confederate), with men more aggressive than women (Bettancourt & Miller, 1996; Eagly & Steffen, 1986; Hyde, 1986). Sex differences in aggression tend to be larger in children than in adults (Hyde, 1986), perhaps because children have not learned as well as adults to inhibit their aggressiveness. Self-report personality scales of physical aggressiveness tend to show larger sex differences than laboratory studies do (Buss & Perry, 1992; Lippa, 1995), and of course, social statistics that assess real-life kinds of aggressiveness (such as violent crimes, assaults, murder, and participation in warfare) generally show much higher rates of male aggressiveness (Daly & Wilson, 1988; Kenrick, 1987).

Sex Differences in Authoritarianism and Social Dominance Orientation

Two personality traits—authoritarianism and social dominance orientation—have been studied in relation to prejudice. Authoritarianism (see chapter 3) refers to the degree to which people defer to authority, accept conventional and conservative social rules and norms (e.g., religious beliefs, political ideas), and show hostility to "outsiders" who break social norms (Adorno, Frenkel-Brunswick, Levinson, & Sanford, 1950; Altemeyer, 1998). Social dominance orientation refers to the degree to which people believe that some social groups are better than others. People who are high on social dominance orientation tend to view the social world in terms of hierarchy (i.e., whether people are "higher up" or "lower down" on the social ladder), and they tend to view inequality as a natural and expected part of society (Pratto, Sidanius, Stallworth, & Malle, 1994).

Recent research shows that men and women do not differ much in their levels of authoritarianism, but men consistently show higher levels of social dominance orientation than women do (Altemeyer, 1998; Lippa, 1995; Lippa & Arad, 1999; Sidanius, Pratto, & Bobo, 1994). As a result, men tend to be somewhat more prejudiced than women—for example, in their attitudes toward women's rights, gays and lesbians, and racial inequality.

Sex Differences in Interests and Vocational Preferences

People's personalities can partly be described in terms of their interests and vocational choices. The vocational psychologist John Holland (1992) developed an influential model of interests that proposes six main kinds of occupations: realistic, investigative, artistic, social, enterprising, and conventional (see Figure 12.1). Realistic occupations (e.g., carpenter, farmer, electrician) involve working with tools, machines, and equipment. Investigative occupations (e.g., biologist, chemist, research psychologist) entail scientific thought and research. Artistic occupations (writer, painter) involve the production of artistic products. Social occupations (counselor, teacher, social worker) entail managing, teaching, or guiding other people. Enterprising occupations (salesperson, stockbroker) involve working with others in business organizations, often with the goal of making profits. And finally, conventional occupations (accountant, clerk, bookkeeper) entail keeping records, processing data, and conducting routine sorts of office work. It's important to note that Holland's six occupational

Figure 12.1 | Holland's six occupational types and ideas-data and people-things dimensions.

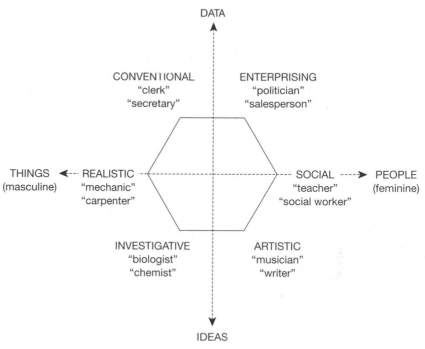

types don't simply classify occupations. They also describe individual differences in personality, for people vary in how much they like or dislike each of the six kinds of occupations.

Do men and women differ in their interest in the six kinds of occupations? Compilation of data from over 14,000 participants from six separate studies showed that men prefer realistic occupations much more strongly than women do (Lippa, 2001a). In contrast, women prefer social and artistic occupations more than men do—a moderate difference in each case. Men are somewhat more interested than women in investigative occupations, women are somewhat more interested than men in enterprising occupations, and there is virtually no difference in men's and women's level of interest in conventional occupations.

The Strong Interest Inventory, a much-used test of vocational interests, has "basic interest" scales as well as scales for the six Holland occupational types (Hansen & Campbell, 1985). A recent study of over 900 men and women ranging in age from 16 to 65 found that women scored much higher than men on interest scales for domestic activities and office practices, whereas men scored much higher than women on interest scales for adventure, mechanical activities, athletics, and military activities (Kaufman & McLean, 1998). People who score high on the adventure scale "are willing to take risks, act on the spur of the moment, be spontaneous, and perhaps act recklessly" (Kaufman &

MacLean, 1998, p. 290). Thus the large sex difference on the adventure scale is consistent with sex differences in sensation seeking discussed earlier.

Factor analytic and multidimensional scaling analyses of people's vocational interests have shown that there are two fundamental dimensions that underlie Holland's six occupational types: the People-Things dimension and the Ideas-Data dimension (Prediger, 1982; Rounds, 1995; see Figure 12.1). The People-Things dimension assesses the degree to which individuals like occupations that deal with people versus occupations that deal with inanimate things. The Ideas-Data dimension assesses the degree to which individuals like occupations that deal with creative and abstract thought versus occupations that deal with concrete data and record keeping. Men and women show quite large differences on the People-Things dimension, with women tending to be more people-oriented and men more thing-oriented (Lippa, 1998b). In contrast, there is virtually no sex difference on the Ideas-Data dimension. The People-Things dimension is largely unrelated to the Big Five personality traits, and thus the sizeable sex differences observed in people-orientation versus thing-orientation are independent of sex differences in Big Five traits and subtraits such as assertiveness and nurturance (Lippa, 1998b). Interestingly, sex differences in people-orientation versus thing-orientation are present quite early in life (Goodenough, 1957).

Sex Differences in Sexual Traits

Freudians have long viewed sexual development and sexual dispositions as important components of personality, and in recent years trait psychologists have begun to investigate more thoroughly links between personality traits and sexual behaviors (Hendrick & Hendrick, 1999). Are there sex differences in people's sexual traits, attitudes, and behaviors?

The answer for many sexual traits is yes. On average, men hold more positive attitudes toward casual sex than women do, and this difference is quite large (Oliver & Hyde, 1993). Men tend to report higher levels of most sorts of sexual activities than women do, and this difference is particularly large for self-reported masturbation (Oliver & Hyde, 1993). Roy Baumeister, Kathleen Catanese, and Kathleen Vohs (2001) recently compiled evidence showing that in comparison to women, men desire sex more, fantasize about sex more, desire more variety in sexual acts and partners, and are more willing to take risks for sex. In contrast, women are more willing than men to forgo sex. Based on this evidence, Baumeister and his colleagues concluded that men, on average, have higher sex drives than women do.

Men and women may also differ on the degree to which their sexual behavior is influenced by social rules and situational pressures. Roy Baumeister (2000) summarized evidence showing that women's sexual behavior is more flexible, varied, and responsive to social norms, whereas men's sexual behavior is more rigid, urgent, and unresponsive to social pressures. For example, individual women vary more over the course of their lives than do men in whether they have sexual relations with men, women, or with both sexes. Women are likely to have larger variations than men, over the course of their lives, in sexual activity levels, and women's sexual behaviors vary with social influences and pressures (e.g., education levels, religious beliefs) more than men's sexual behaviors do.

Finally, it's worth noting an obvious but very large sex difference: On average, men are much more sexually attracted to women than women are, and on average, women are much more sexually attracted to men than men are (Lippa, 2002a). Despite the huge sex differences on attraction to men and attraction to women, some men are sexually attracted to other men and some women are sexually attracted to other women, and individual differences in the degree to which people are attracted to one sex or the other may be related to variations in masculinity and femininity (more on this later).

Sex Differences in Mental Illness

Personality is related to abnormal as well as to normal traits and behaviors. Indeed, according to one recent view, some kinds of mental illness represent maladaptive extremes of normal trait dimensions (Costa & McCrae, 1992; see chapter 18 in this volume). For example, depression and anxiety disorders are linked to the Big Five trait of neuroticism, with people high on neuroticism more likely to suffer from depression and anxiety disorders. If men and women differ on certain personality traits (such as neuroticism), then this could lead to sex differences in the rates of some kinds of mental disorders.

Hartung and Widiger (1998) recently summarized evidence on sex differences in various mental disorders. They found that males are much more likely than females to suffer from autism and attention deficit disorders. Conversely, females are much more likely than males to suffer from various kinds of mood disorders (e.g., depression) and eating disorders. Men suffer from substance abuse disorders more than women do, and they are also more likely than women to experience sexual and gender identity disorders. Personality disorders that show a "male tilt" include schizotypal disorders (characterized by strange thought processes), antisocial disorders (characterized by a lack of conscience and unethical, manipulative behaviors), and narcissistic disorders (characterized by self-aggrandizement and self-centeredness). Personality disorders that show a "female tilt" include borderline and histrionic disorders (characterized by poor relations with others, overly dramatic behavior, identity confusion, and self-destructive behaviors). In self-report questionnaires of interpersonal problems, men tend to report more than women do that they are overly autocratic, vindictive, and socially avoidant, whereas women tend to report more than men do that they are subassertive, exploitable, and overly dependent and merged with others (Lippa, 1995).

In many ways, sex differences in mental illness and interpersonal problems are consistent with other sex differences in personality. For example, men's greater assertiveness, aggressiveness, and risk taking and men's lower agreeableness may, in their most extreme forms, show themselves as antisocial and narcissistic personality disorders. Women's greater neuroticism and agreeableness and their lower assertiveness may, in their most extreme forms, show themselves as mood disorders and interpersonal problems with assertion and dependency. Males' much greater thing-orientation may show itself, in extreme form, in higher male rates of autism (Baron-Cohen, 2000). And higher male levels of risk taking and sensation seeking may be linked to higher male levels of substance abuse.

Why Are There Sex Differences in Personality?

Explanations for sex differences in personality fall into two broad categories: (1) biological theories and (2) socialization and social learning theories. Biological theories include evolutionary theory (which considers more distal causes over long time spans) and hormonal theories (which consider more proximal causes over the course of individual development). Social theories include social learning theory, social role theory, and theories about the self-fulfilling nature of stereotypes. Let's briefly describe each of these theories.

Darwin's theory of evolution argues that natural selection determines which traits get passed from generation to generation and which traits are established within species and sometimes, within sexes. In most species, males produce abundant, small, traveling gametes (sperm), and they invest less than females in offspring. In contrast, females produce fewer, larger, stationary gametes (eggs), and they invest more in offspring. In mammals, maternal investment in offspring is especially high because mammalian mothers carry fetuses inside their bodies, contribute valuable nutrients to the developing fetus, and then nurse, rear, and protect their offspring for an extended time after birth.

Evolutionary theory argues that because of their different reproductive natures, males and females have evolved somewhat different traits and behaviors. These differences are most clearly seen in the realm of sexuality. Men presumably have evolved to be more interested in short-term mating with multiple partners, whereas women have evolved to be more interested in committed relationships with males who possess good resources (see Buss, 1999). Evolutionary theories also suggest that men have evolved to have more urgent sexual impulses, whereas women have evolved to better control their sexual impulses and to use sex as a resource to offer males in exchange for other goods (food, security, protection of offspring).

Evolutionary theory may help also to explain sex differences in personality traits that are not directly related to sexuality. For example, greater male aggressiveness may result from sexual selection, which occurs when traits evolve that help animals compete with same-sex members of their species and attract opposite-sex members. Greater male risk taking and sensation seeking can be seen as sexually selected traits that help males establish dominance over other males and attract mates. Similarly, greater female tender-mindedness, nurturance, and people-orientation can be seen as evolved traits that foster child rearing.

The effects of biological evolution are mediated by physiological mechanisms within individual organisms. For example, males and females have evolved to have somewhat different bodily characteristics (e.g., height, musculature, body fat distribution, genitals), and these physical differences are caused by differences in sex hormone levels at various stages of development. Sex differences in personality, like sex differences in bodily traits, may result from sex differences in hormone levels, both prenatally and in adulthood (Collaer & Hines, 1995).

Testosterone (an androgen, or male hormone) has been most studied in relation to human behavior (see Dabbs, 2000, for a review). In both men and women, variations in individuals' testosterone levels are related to levels of dominance, risk taking, sensation seeking, aggressiveness, criminality, and sexual activity. Most research on testosterone has studied how variations in testosterone levels *within each sex* are related to behavior, and thus this research does not directly address the question of whether sex differences in testosterone produce sex differences in personality. Still, it is worth noting that men's average testosterone levels are eight or more times the level of women's, and many of the behaviors and traits that are linked to testosterone within the sexes are also behaviors and traits that show on-average differences between the sexes.

In contrast to evolutionary and hormonal theories, socialization and social learning theories argue that sex differences in personality result from learning processes, such as classical conditioning, operant conditioning, and modeling (Bussey & Bandura, 1999). For example, boys in most cultures are trained to be more independent, whereas girls are trained to be more nurturant and domestic (Barry, Bacon, & Child, 1957). Parents treat boys and girls somewhat differently and encourage sex-typed behaviors in their sons and daughters (Lytton & Romney, 1991). The different toys that parents give to their sons and daughters provides an obvious example of how parents sometimes treat boys and girls differently. However, it is also possible that boys and girls *prefer* to play with different toys and that adults simply accommodate these different preferences.

In modern industrial society, the mass media play an important role in teaching gender roles and gender stereotypes. The media often portray the two sexes quite differently, and boys and girls learn different "gender lessons" from the media (Furnham & Mak, 1999; Signorielli, 1993). In sum, according to the socialization and social learning view, boys and girls are differentially rewarded and punished for a host of behaviors (e.g., aggressiveness, nurturance, doll play, truck play, wearing dresses), and they imitate different models. Modern social learning theories also propose that self-labeling serves to heighten sex differences in personality. For example, when children are old enough to label accurately whether they are boys and girls, they are then motivated to behave in ways consistent with their sex, and they are more likely to imitate same-sex models (Martin, 2000).

Alice Eagly's social role theory provides a social psychological account of how sex differences in personality emerge. This theory argues that sex differences result not just from the different learning histories and role models of males and females, but also from the different roles imposed on men and women by society (Eagly, 1987; Eagly, Wood, & Diekman, 2000). According to Eagly, traditional gender roles have enforced three fundamental differences between men and women: (1) Men are more responsible for income-producing work and women for the care of children and the home. (2) Men work more in some kinds of occupations (e.g., truck driver, engineer) and women in others (stenographer, librarian). (3) men tend to occupy higher-status roles in society (e.g., executive, doctor, professor), whereas women tend to occupy lower-status roles (secretary, nurse, kindergarten teacher).

Social role theory proposes that sex differences in personality result from these sex differences in prescribed social roles, not from innate differences between men and women. For example, men's greater participation in the rough-and-tumble world of work encourages competitiveness, assertiveness, and instrumental traits, whereas women's greater participation in child rearing and domestic activities encourages cooperativeness, nurturance, and expressive traits. High-status roles and occupations (e.g., political leader, corporate executive) encourage instrumental traits (independence, risk taking), whereas low-status roles and occupations encourage more passive traits (dependence, deference). Jean Twenge (2001) recently compiled evidence showing that women's mean levels of assertiveness rose and fell with women's status from 1931 to 1993, and these findings are consistent with social role theory's contention that gender roles can influence women's mean trait levels and, by implication, sex differences in personality.

A number of social psychology theories have focused on the power of gender stereotypes to mold people's behavior and produce sex differences in behavior. For example, social psychologists have long argued that stereotypes can become self-fulfilling prophecies—that they lead people to behave in ways that confirm the stereotypes (Merton, 1948; Snyder, 1981). Most measures of personality traits use self-report scales (i.e., people are asked to rate their own traits and behaviors in response to questionnaire questions), and the use of self-reports raises an important methodological question: Do gender stereotypes influence and bias the way people rate their personalities on personality scales and inventories?

As described earlier, Costa, Terracciano, and McCrae (2001) found that sex differences in self-report trait scales are larger in industrialized countries with liberal gender ideologies than in less-developed countries with more traditional gender ideologies. These results seem to run counter to social role theory, which predicts that weaker gender roles should lead to weaker sex differences. Costa, Terracciano, and McCrae suggested that in countries with strong, traditional gender roles (e.g., countries that don't offer many educational or work opportunities to women), men and women attribute their differing behaviors to their societies' obviously powerful gender roles. However, in countries with weaker gender roles, which don't so obviously constrain their behavior, men and women attribute their differing behaviors more to internal factors (e.g., personality traits). If this attributional explanation is correct, then future research will need to study sex differences in personality using methods other than just self-report scales.

QUESTION 2: ARE THERE MEANINGFUL INDIVIDUAL DIFFERENCES IN MASCULINITY AND FEMININITY WITHIN EACH SEX?

As noted before, the study of masculinity and femininity is intimately tied to the study of sex differences in personality, for individual differences in masculinity and femininity have often been defined in terms of sex differences. This was certainly true of the very first masculinity-femininity tests.

The Bipolar Approach to Masculinity-Femininity

Stanford University psychologist Lewis Terman developed the first masculinity-femininity (M-F) test in the 1920s, and in 1936, Terman and his colleague Catherine Cox Miles described much of their early research on M-F in a classic book entitled, *Sex and Personality*. A noted intelligence researcher, Terman saw an analogy between M-F and intelligence; he believed both were cohesive traits that could be assessed with properly designed tests.

Terman and Miles made an important assumption about M-F—that masculinity and femininity make up opposite sides of a single trait dimension—and this assumption would influence theory and research on M-F throughout much of the 20th century. Stated more concretely, Terman and Miles believed that the more masculine an individual is, the less feminine he or she is; and vice versa. Terman and Miles developed a long, 456-item test (called the Attitude Interest Analysis Survey) to measure M-F. Items were selected that distinguished between men and women (or boys and girls) in large normative samples. The Terman and Miles test contained quite varied content, including questions about general knowledge, emotional reactions, occupational preferences, interests, and word associations.

To illustrate how the Terman and Miles test worked, consider the following two M-F items: "Would you like or dislike being an auto racer?" and "Would you like or dislike being a librarian?" These items were considered M-F items because previous research had shown that, on average, men expressed more interest than women did in being an auto racer, and on average, women expressed more interest than men did in being a librarian. For every masculine response a person gave to an M-F item, Terman and Miles added a point to the person's M-F score, and for every feminine response, they subtracted a point. Thus, an individual's M-F score could range from negative (feminine) to positive (masculine).

Many personality and interest inventories developed in the mid-20th century included M-F scales based on Terman and Miles's bipolar (i.e., either-or) approach. Among the best-known M-F scales were those of the Guilford-Zimmerman Temperament Inventory (Gilford & Zimmerman, 1956), the California Psychological Inventory (Gough, 1957), the Strong Vocational Interest Blank (Campbell, 1971; Strong, 1936, 1943), and the Minnesota Multiphasic Personality Inventory (MMPI; Hathaway & McKinley, 1951). The MMPI was (and still is) the most widely used personality inventory in the study of mental illness, and the developers of the MMPF M-F scale (called the Mf scale) used a somewhat unusual strategy in generating their M-F items. Rather than selecting questions that distinguished men from women, they initially used items that distinguished gay men from heterosexual men (Hathaway, 1956).

What was the portrait of masculinity and femininity that emerged from the M-F scales of the mid-20th century? The Guilford-Zimmerman M-F scale characterized masculinity in terms of low emotional expressiveness, male-typical occupational interests, and emotional traits such as fearlessness and lack of empathy. The California Psychological Inventory M-F scale (which was keyed so that higher scores were more feminine) described feminine individuals as being socially sensitive and perceptive, compassionate, interested in female-typical activities and occupations, and not very interested in politics and social action. The MMPI Mf scale (which, keep in mind, was more focused on psychopathology than the other scales were) portrayed feminine individuals as being passive, narcissistic, and socially reticent, and as having stereotypical feminine interests and showing "heterosexual discomfort" (at least, for males) (Green, 1991). Overall, there seemed to be several broad themes that ran through the various M-F scales of the mid-20th century: male- and female-typical interests, gender-related emotional traits, sensitivity and supportiveness, assertiveness, risk taking and coarseness, and (particularly, in the MMPI) behaviors and feelings related to sexual orientation.

Did the early M-F tests show validity—that is, did they predict socially significant behaviors and outcomes? Terman and Miles's (1936) early research found that M-F scores were somewhat linked to age—for example, men tended to score highest on masculinity in their late teens and early 20s. Perhaps not surprisingly, Terman and Miles found that people's M-F scores were related to their interests and educational choices. Masculine men tended to be more interested in science, technical subjects, and mechanical things, whereas feminine men tended to be more interested in the humanities, cultural subjects, and the arts. In women, masculinity was associated with greater educational accomplishments and more intellectual interests, and in this sense, one could argue that masculinity was "good" for women.

Many studies suggested that femininity in boys and masculinity in girls was associated with higher creativity, educational success, and giftedness (Maccoby, 1966), and recent research has tended to replicate these results (Lippa, 1998a; Lubinski & Humphreys, 1990). These findings are interesting because they suggest that in terms of academic and intellectual accomplishment, it may not be good for boys to be too masculine or for girls to be too feminine. Other research using M-F scales showed that highly masculine boys were overly impulsive and aggressive, whereas highly feminine girls were overly meek and inhibited (Maccoby, 1966). Among girls and women, high femininity was often associated with poor self-esteem, low confidence, and anxiety—traits indicating social and psychological maladjustment (Constantino & Heilbrun, 1964; Gall, 1969; Harford, Willis, & Deabler, 1967; Webb, 1963). Overall, these early findings hinted that extremely feminine females and extremely masculine males did not show optimal psychological adjustment or intellectual achievement.

Many studies investigated whether M-F was related to sexual orientation (see Pillard, 1991). Terman and Miles (1936) found a strong difference between the M-F scores of gay and heterosexual men. However, Terman and Miles's subject population would today be considered quite biased and suspect—for example, many of the gay men studied by Terman and Miles were from prison populations. Terman and Miles's research reflected social prejudices of its day, which viewed homosexuality to be a kind of mental illness. (Since the early 1970s, both the American Psychological Association and the American Psychiatric Association have concluded that homosexuality is *not* a mental illness.)

The Two-Dimensional Approach: Instrumentality and Expressiveness

In the late 1960s and early 1970s the modern women's movement blossomed, and this "second wave" of 20th-century feminism led psychologists to change their views of masculinity and femininity. Growing discontent with M-F tests in the Terman and Miles tradition crystallized in a 1973 *Psychological Bulletin* article by Vassar College psychologist Ann Constantinople. According to Constantinople, existing M-F scales contained a meaningless hodgepodge of items, with the result that masculinity and femininity seemed "to be among the muddiest concepts in the psychologist's vocabulary" (p. 390). The reason for the hodgepodge, Constantinople contended, was that items had been selected based on one criterion only—that they discriminate men from women.

Constantinople noted that factor analytic studies showed M-F scales to be multifactorial, and this implied that individual M-F scales measured many unrelated dimensions (such as male- and female-typical interests, anxiety, self-confidence, assertiveness, vulgarity) rather than a single, cohesive M-F dimension. Many of the M-F scales developed in the mid-20th century did not correlate strongly with one another, and Constantinople concluded from this that these scales did not measure a single, cohesive trait. Furthermore, research evidence showed that people's M-F scores varied systematically with demographic factors such as age, education levels, and social class. This suggested to Constantinople that M-F scales were measuring social stereotypes and social roles rather than personality traits (for additional criticism of traditional M-F scales see Lewin, 1984a, 1984b; Spence & Sawin, 1985).

Drawing on Constantinople's critique, researchers in the early 1970s came up with new conceptions and new measures of masculinity and femininity. At Stanford University, feminist psychologist Sandra Bem developed the Bem Sex-Role Inventory (BSRI), a personality test that assessed masculinity and femininity as two separate dimensions (Bem, 1974, 1981a). At about the same time, University of Texas at Austin researchers Janet Spence, Bob Helmreich, and Joy Stapp developed a similar test, the Personal Attributes Inventory (PAQ), which also assessed masculinity and femininity as two dimensions (Spence, Helmreich, & Stapp, 1974; Spence & Helmreich, 1978). Both the BSRI and the PAQ conceptualized masculinity in terms of instrumental, agentic personality traits (such as *assertiveness, independence, forcefulness*, and *self-confidence*), and femininity in terms of expressive, communal personality traits (such as *warmth, sympathy, compassion*, and *concern for others' feelings*).

There are several points to note about the scales of the BSRI and PAQ. First, they focused on gender-related *personality traits* and excluded other kinds of content that was common in earlier M-F scales (such as male- and female-typical occupational preferences, interests, and sexual attractions and orientations). Second, the items of the BSRI and PAQ scales were selected because they were *stereotypically* true of men and women. In contrast, earlier M-F scales selected items that showed *actual* sex differences in item response. Finally, the masculinity and femininity scales of the BSRI and PAQ overlap substantially with the Big Five personality traits. Specifically, masculinity (i.e., instrumentality, agency) scales correlate strongly with facets of extraversion

Figure 12.2 | The two-dimensional conception: Masculinity as instrumentality and femininity as expressiveness.

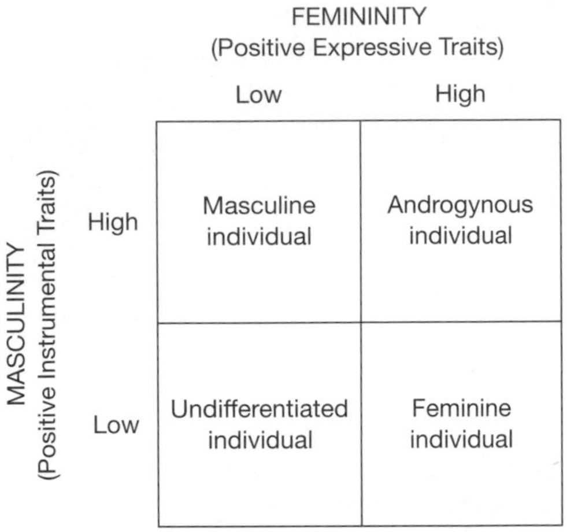

FEMININITY
(Positive Expressive Traits)

	Low	High
High	Masculine individual	Androgynous individual
Low	Undifferentiated individual	Feminine individual

MASCULINITY
(Positive Instrumental Traits)

and neuroticism. And femininity (i.e., expressiveness, communality) scales correlate strongly with facets of agreeableness and conscientiousness (Lippa, 1991, 1995). This overlap was not known when the BSRI and PAQ scales were first developed, because the Big Five model had not yet emerged as the dominant taxonomy of personality traits.

What was gained by conceptualizing masculinity and femininity as two separate dimensions? Sandra Bem (1974, 1975) argued that the two-dimensional conception of masculinity and femininity provided a liberating alternative to earlier bipolar conceptions of M-F. According to one commonly used classification system, individuals could be either low or high (below or above the median value in a population) on masculinity; and similarly, they could be either low or high on femininity. This yielded four categories of people: low M-high F (traditionally feminine) individuals, high M-low F (traditionally masculine) individuals, low M-low F (undifferentiated) individuals, and high M-high F (androgynous—i.e., possessing both male and female characteristics) individuals (see Figure 12.2). According to many researchers, these classifications assessed individuals' "sex-role identities" and "gender-role orientations."

Bem (1975; Bem & Lenney, 1976) proposed that psychological androgyny constituted a new standard of mental health and gender role flexibility: The androgynous person could be both assertive and tactful, both competitive and sensitive, both a leader and a nurturer—depending on what the situation called for. In contrast, the traditionally masculine person (who was often male) might show desirable masculine traits (e.g., independence, sticking to one's guns in the face of pressure), but he would often fail to show desirable feminine traits (warmth, concern for others). Conversely, the traditionally feminine person (who was often female) might show desirable feminine traits (e.g., compassion, sensitivity), but she would often fail to show positive masculine traits (assertiveness, leadership ability). The undifferentiated person, who reported being low on both positive masculine and feminine traits, could be viewed as a low-self-esteem person who didn't acknowledge possessing positive traits, regardless of whether they were masculine or feminine.

Spurred by Bem's hypothesis that androgyny defined a new standard of mental health, many researchers studied the relationship between masculinity, femininity, and various measures of psychological adjustment and maladjustment (e.g., measures of self-esteem, depression, anxiety, coping strategies, marital happiness). In general, studies found that masculinity was related to adjustment measures more strongly than femininity was, with high masculinity associated with better adjustment (Bassoff & Glass, 1982; Whitley, 1983, 1984). Thus, because of their higher masculinity (i.e., instrumentality) scores, masculine and androgynous individuals tended to score higher on self-esteem scales and lower on anxiety and depression scales than feminine and undifferentiated individuals did. However, these findings did not support the notion that androgyny (the *combination* of high masculinity and high femininity) was uniquely related to optimal adjustment.

Other studies showed that femininity (expressiveness, nurturance) was related to certain kinds of positive outcomes. For example, people who are high on femininity tend to be good friends and marriage partners (Antill, 1983; Kurdek & Schmitt, 1986; Langis, Sabourin, Lussier, & Mathieu, 1994) and show greater empathy in personal relationships (Spence & Helmreich, 1978). These findings indicate that because of their higher femininity (i.e., expressiveness) scores, feminine and androgynous people tend to be more successful in personal relationships than masculine and undifferentiated people are. But once again, these findings did not support the notion that androgyny (the *combination* of high masculinity and high femininity) was uniquely related to optimal adjustment.

Janet Spence and Bob Helmreich (1980), two of the developers of the PAQ, came to believe, by the early 1980s, that "masculinity" and "femininity" scales had been mislabeled. They argued that these scales were in fact instrumentality and expressiveness scales. By the 1980s, many studies had shown that the masculinity scales of the PAQ and BSRI predicted instrumental behaviors fairly well (i.e., behaviors such as assertiveness and resistance to conformity in the face of group pressures) and that the femininity scales of the PAQ and BSRI predicted nurturant behaviors fairly well (behaviors such as comforting a peer in need of support) (Taylor & Hall, 1982). However, this would be expected simply based on the content of these scales, not because the scales were assessing "masculinity," "femininity," or "gender-role orientations."

Sandra Bem too revised her notion of masculinity, femininity, and androgyny. By the 1980s, she concluded that the masculinity and femininity scales of tests like the BSRI and PAQ had repeated a mistake made by the older M-F scales: They inappropriately reified (i.e., made real) masculinity and femininity. Bem argued that masculinity, femininity, and M-F scales were all guilty of conceptualizing masculinity and femininity as fixed, inner traits of the individual rather than as cultural constructs. In her gender schema theory, Bem (1981b, 1985, 1993) shifted her focus from individuals' traits to individuals' thought processes. According to this theory, some people (termed gender schematic individuals) strongly view the world in terms of "male" and "female," "masculine" and "feminine." In contrast, gender aschematic individuals do not conceptualize the social world so strongly in terms of gender—they do not judge others or monitor their own behaviors so much in terms of maleness or femaleness, masculinity or femininity.

Thus, Bem came to see traditionally masculine men and traditionally feminine women as gender schematic individuals, and she came to see androgynous men and women as gender aschematic individuals. Presumably, socialization determined whether a person grew up to be gender schematic or gender aschematic. A person who grew up in a family or in a culture in which all activities and behavior were classified by gender (e.g., boys tend sheep, girls grind grain; boys go to school, girls take care of the home) would be more likely to become a gender schematic individual. In contrast, a person who grew up in a family or in a culture that didn't classify activities and behavior by gender (boys and girls engage in the same tasks and activities) was more likely to become a gender aschematic individual.

In developing gender schema theory, Bem moved to a strongly social constructionist view of masculinity and femininity: Masculinity and femininity are *not* fixed traits of the individual, according to this view. Rather, they are cultural constructs and social conventions, whereby an arbitrary collection of traits and behaviors are labeled as "masculine" or "feminine." By 1987, Bem had concluded that "masculinity and femininity do not exist 'out there' in the world of objective realities. . . . [they] exist only in the mind of the perceiver" (p. 309).

Assessing Masculinity-Femininity in Terms of Gender-Related Interests

Although the two-dimensional approach to masculinity and femininity was beginning to show its age by the late 1980s (e.g., see Huston, 1983), it nonetheless represented an advance over the bipolar approach to M-F in one important sense: The two-dimensional approach "purified" the content of masculinity and femininity measures. Specifically, the two-dimensional approach defined masculinity in terms of instrumental, agentic traits and femininity in terms of expressive, communal traits. As a result, the masculinity and femininity scales of the BSRI and the PAQ did not contain the wildly heterogeneous content of earlier M-F scales.

But in retrospect, the exclusive focus on gender-stereotypic personality traits may have, in some ways, thrown the baby out with the bathwater. Clearly, there were many commonsense components of masculinity and femininity that were not assessed by instrumentality and expressiveness scales. This was demonstrated by studies that asked people to describe their everyday, commonsense notions of masculinity, femininity, and gender (e.g., Deaux & Lewis, 1983, 1984; Helgeson, 1994; Myers & Gonda, 1982). Laypeople report that masculinity and femininity have many components, including physical traits (muscular, soft, curvy), personality traits other than instrumentality and expressiveness (fragile, macho, tough), biological characteristics (bears children, high testosterone), sexuality (gay, heterosexual, high sex drive), interests (hunting, flower arranging, cars, fashion), occupations (truck driver, secretary, engineer, nurse), and social roles (mother, big brother). (It might be interesting for you, at this point, to go back and look at the list of masculine and feminine characteristics you used to describe yourself at the start of this chapter.)

Which components of masculinity and femininity do you think should be central in research psychologists' definitions of masculinity and femininity? One promising candidate, I believe, is gender-related interests (e.g., hobbies, everyday activities, occupational preferences). Gender-related interest items were commonly included in traditional M-F scales. Indeed, the M-F scales that were common in older versions of vocational interest tests focused almost exclusively on gender-related interests (e.g., see Strong, 1943). Two empirical findings support the notion that gender-related interests are an important part of M-F: (1) Gender-related interests emerge very early in life, well before boys and girls can accurately label their own or others' sex (Huston, 1983; Ruble & Martin, 1998), and (2) sex-typical and sex-atypical childhood interests are strongly related to adult sexual orientation (Bailey & Zucker, 1995).

Over the past 15 years, I have used male-typical and female-typical interests to assess individual differences in M-F. My way of measuring M-F is termed *gender diagnosticity*, which refers to the probability that an individual is classified as male or female based on his or her pattern of gender-related interests. The computation of gender diagnosticity scores makes use of advanced statistical techniques (for details, see Lippa & Connally, 1990; Lippa, 2002a, chapter 2). However, you can gain a commonsense view of how gender diagnosticity measures work by completing the simplified scale presented in Activity Box 12.1.

The key point for you to understand about gender diagnosticity measures is that they assess M-F in terms of people's gender-related interests—that is, in terms of their gender-related occupational preferences, their hobby preferences, and their degree of participation in gender-related activities. Unlike traditional M-F scales, the gender diagnosticity approach allows for the possibility that masculine and feminine interests are, to some extent, socially constructed and culturally variable. This is because gender diagnosticity scores are always computed based on "local" standards of masculinity and femininity—the degree to which interests are male-typical or female-typical in a given group of men and women. To illustrate: If you filled in the scale in Activity Box 12.1, how might we decide if your responses are "masculine" or "feminine"? According to the gender diagnosticity approach, this can only be answered by comparing your pattern of responses to those of a particular group of men and women. The Activity Box compares your responses to a group of California college men and women.

A number of studies have shown that measures of gender-related interests are quite reliable, and this reliability is present within the sexes as well as in mixed-sex groups (Lippa & Connally, 1990; Lippa, 1991, 1995). Furthermore, measures of gender-related interests are largely uncorrelated with Big Five traits and with instrumentality and expressiveness (Lippa, 1991, 1995). Thus, measures of gender-related interests seem to capture a gender-related personality di-

Activity Box 12.1   A Short M-F Scale Based on Gender-Related Occupational Preferences and Their Relation to Gender Diagnosticity

Please rate how much you are interested in the following occupations. Do not worry about whether you are educated or trained for the occupations, how much you will get ahead, or whether you will make a lot of money. Make your ratings just based on how much you would like to do that job. Use the following scale when making your ratings:

1	2	3	4	5
Strongly Dislike	Slightly Dislike	Neutral or Indifferent	Slightly Like	Strongly Like

1.____Auto mechanic

2.____Beauty consultant

3.____Auto salesperson

4.____Costume designer

5.____Building contractor

6.____Dance teacher

7.____Carpenter

8.____Grade school teacher

9.____Computer programmer

10.____Fashion model

11.____Electrical engineer

12.____Florist

13.____Inventor

14.____Interior decorator

15.____Mechanical engineer

16.____Nurse

17.____Professional athlete

18.____Social worker

To score this scale, add your ratings for all the odd-numbered occupations and subtract your ratings for all the even-numbered occupations to form a single M-F score. Higher scores are more masculine (i.e., male-typical), and lower scores are more feminine (female-typical).

When this scale was given to 986 California college students (654 women and 332 men), the median score for women was −13 (i.e., half the women scored lower and half scored higher than this value), and the median score for men was 5 (half the men scored lower and half scored higher than this value). Figure 12.3 shows the distributions of M-F scores for men and women, which, as you can see, did not overlap much.

More advanced statistical methods were used to compute gender diagnosticity (GD) scores for these same college men and women, based on their responses to a larger set of occupational preference items. As the text notes, gender diagnosticity refers to the probability that an individual is male or female, based on his or her occupational preference ratings. M-F scores computed from the short M-F scale correlated .95 with men's gender diagnosticity scores and .95 with women's gender diagnosticity scores, and this in-

dicates that the M-F scale presented here is an extremely good proxy for a formally computed gender diagnosticity measure. Figure 12.4 shows the GD scores that correspond to various scores on the short M-F scale, again for the sample of 986 California college students. For example, a student who scored −3 on the short M-F scale had a GD score of about .5. This means that this student had an equal probability of being male or female—that is, this person's occupational preferences were neither male- nor female-typical. In contrast, a student who scored −20 on the short M-F scale had a GD score of .24, which means the probability was low that this person was a male (or equivalently, the probability was high that this person was female). Finally, a student who scored 20 on the short M-F scale had a GD score of .82, which means the probability was high that this person was male (and low that this person was female). By comparing your M-F

Figure 12.3   Distributions of M-F scores for 654 college women and 332 college men.

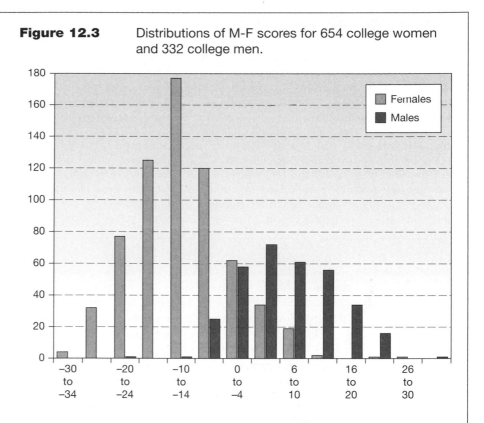

Figure 12.4   Gender diagnosticity scores that correspond to M-F scores for 986 California college students.

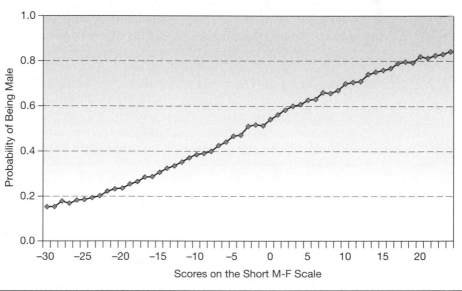

(continued)

Activity Box 12.1 *(continued)*

score with the data presented in Figures 12.3 and 12.4, you can gain a sense of how feminine or masculine your occupational preferences are, *compared to a particular sample of California college men and women.*

The text describes some traits and outcomes that are associated with M-F as measured by scales like the one presented here. These include self-ascribed masculinity and femininity, masculinity and femininity as judged by outside observers, men's prejudice, sexual orientation, mortality risk, and people-orientation versus thing-orientation. Whatever your M-F score, you should note that there are no "good" or "bad" scores. Some men and women score low on this M-F scale (i.e., in a more feminine direction), and some men and women score high (in a more masculine direction). There are pluses and minuses to being either masculine or feminine. The goal of research on masculinity and femininity is not to make value judgments about individuals who score any particular way on M-F scales. Rather, it is to understand the many fascinating ways in which people vary on masculinity and femininity.

---

mension that is not assessed by Big Five, instrumentality, or expressiveness scales. In fact, this dimension proves to be closely linked to the People-Things dimension of occupational preferences (Lippa, 1998b; see Figure 12.1).

Do gender-related interest measures show validity—that is, do they predict the kind of criteria that you would expect a good M-F scale to predict? Perhaps the most obvious criteria to be predicted by M-F scales are people's self-ascribed masculinity and femininity. For example, rate now (on a seven-point scale that ranges from "1—not at all" to "7—extremely") how masculine and feminine you are. These ratings reflect what I call your self-ascribed masculinity and femininity—your conscious sense of how masculine or feminine you are. In a number of studies, I asked college men and women to complete instrumentality scales, expressiveness scales, scales of gender-related interests, and scales of self-ascribed masculinity and femininity. In general, I found that gender-related interests better predicted students' self-ascribed masculinity and femininity than instrumentality and expressiveness scales did (Lippa, 1991).

In other studies, I asked outside observers to rate people's masculinity and femininity, and then I studied whether these outside observers' ratings correlated more strongly with targets' self-reported instrumentality, expressiveness, or gender-related interest scores (Lippa, 1997, 1998a). In general, observers' ratings of college students' masculinity and femininity correlated more strongly with the students' gender-related interest scores than with their instrumentality or expressiveness scores.

As you already know, much past research has examined the relationship between masculinity and femininity measures and adjustment (e.g., self-esteem, depression, anxiety, interpersonal problems). In one study, I compared the power of instrumentality, expressiveness, and gender-related interest scales to predict various kinds of adjustment (such as depression, anxiety, self-esteem, prejudice, and interpersonal problems such as overbearingness, vindictiveness, intrusiveness, subassertiveness, and letting others take advantage of you) (Lippa, 1995). The results showed that instrumentality, expressiveness, and gender-related interest scales predicted different kinds of adjustment. High instrumentality was associated with being nonanxious and nondepressed, and with having good self-esteem (positive traits), but also with being vindictive, domineering, and intrusive (negative traits). High expressiveness was associated with interpersonal niceness (a positive trait), but also with being overly nurturant and exploitable (negative traits). Among men but among not women, masculine interests were associated with social dominance, authoritarianism, prejudice toward gays and lesbians, and negative attitudes toward women's rights.

Over the past century, much research has examined whether masculinity and femininity are related to sexual orientation. In a series of studies, I administered instrumentality, expressiveness, and gender-related interest scales to large numbers of gay men, heterosexual men, lesbian women, and heterosexual women (Lippa, 2000, 2002b). In general, scales of gender-related interests showed much larger links to sexual orientation than did instrumentality and expressiveness scales. Specifically, gay men tend to have more female-typical and less male-typical interests, on average, than heterosexual men do, and lesbian women tend to have more male-typical and less female-typical interests, on average, than heterosexual women do.

In another recent study, I compared masculinity and femininity measures in transsexual and non-transsexual individuals (Lippa, 2001b). It seemed a reasonable prediction that male-to-female transsexuals (individuals who are genetically male, but who wish to live as females and, sometimes, to be surgically reassigned to be females) should be more feminine than the average man is. And similarly, it seemed a reasonable prediction that female-to-male transsexuals should be more masculine than the average woman is. The results of my study showed that gender-related interests distinguished between transsexual and non-transsexual individuals much more strongly than instrumentality and expressiveness did. Thus, a number of recent studies show that gender-related interest measures outperform instrumentality and expressiveness scales in predicting various criteria that we might reasonably expect to be related to masculinity and femininity.

In a recent study with colleagues Howard Friedman and Leslie Martin, I found that gender-related interests predict another socially significant criterion—namely, mortality rates (Lippa, Friedman, & Martin, 2000). Using data from Lewis Terman's "gifted children" study, we analyzed occupational preference data collected more than 60 years ago to predict the probability the men and women would die at various ages. The results showed that people who were more masculine (as assessed by gender-related occupational preferences) were more likely to die at any given age, and this finding held for both men and women. Furthermore, the link between masculine interests and mortality remained even when Big Five traits (and by implication, instrumentality and expressiveness) were statistically controlled for. We're not yet sure what caused the masculinity-mortality link, but several possibilities are that masculine individuals engage in riskier hobbies and occupations, have more dangerous habits (e.g., smoking, drinking), and have poorer social support. (For more complete summaries of recent research on M-F measures based on gender-related interest, see Lippa, 2001a and 2002a.)

Three general conclusions can be drawn from recent research on masculinity and femininity: (1) Individual differences in masculinity and femininity can be measured in meaningful ways, and the measures that are most commonly used today assess instrumentality, expressiveness, and gender-related interests. (2) Measures of masculinity and femininity predict a number of socially significant criteria, including psychological adjustment, intellectual choices and achievements, prejudice, sexual orientation, and health and mortality. (3) For a number of criteria (e.g., self-ascribed masculinity and femininity, masculinity and femininity as rated by outside observers, sexual orientation, transsexual versus non-transsexual status, prejudice and authoritarianism, and mortality) gender-related interests do a better job of predicting criteria than instrumentality and expressiveness scales do. On the other hand, instrumentality and expressiveness scales best predict behaviors that are directly related to their content—for example, instrumentality scales predict assertiveness and independence, and expressiveness scales predict nurturance and success in close relationships.

What Causes Individual Differences in Instrumentality, Expressiveness, and Gender-Related Interests?

Explanations for variations in masculinity and femininity fall into two main categories: (1) biological theories and (2) socialization and social learning theories. Evolutionary theory has tended to focus more on sex differences in behavior than on individual differences within the sexes. Nonetheless, evolutionary theory offers some possible explanations for within-sex variations in masculinity and femininity. For example, variations in masculinity and femininity within each sex may represent adaptations to specialized "niches" in the mating game (e.g., Miller, 2000). For example, some men may attract mates by being sexy, virile, and dominant (i.e., masculine), whereas others may attract mates by being trustworthy, committed, kind, and people-oriented (i.e., more feminine).

Another evolutionary view of individual differences in masculinity and femininity is that they reflect "random noise" in evolutionary processes (Markow, 1994; Moller & Swaddle, 1998; Tooby & Cosmides, 1990). Presumably, male-typical and female-typical traits are produced by genes and by hormonal processes that are guided by genes. However, individuals' genes vary because of mutations (changes that result from copying errors and from environmental damage). Furthermore, the action of genes and hormonal processes can be "jiggled" by numerous environmental factors (variations in nutrition, stress levels, exposure to infectious diseases, etc.), and these factors can result in individual differences in how male-typical or female-typical (i.e., how masculine or feminine) any given individual is.

Hormonal theories propose that variations in hormone levels, both prenatally and postnatally, can lead to variations both in sex-linked brain structures and in behaviors related to masculinity and femininity (e.g., see Lippa, 2003). As noted earlier, variations in testosterone levels are associated with variations in behaviors that are linked to masculinity, such as dominance, aggressiveness, risk taking, and sexual activity levels. Furthermore, people who are exposed to atypical levels of sex hormones, due to genetic disorders or medical treatments, often show gender-atypical behaviors (Collaer & Hines, 1995). For example, girls with congenital adrenal hyperplasia (a genetic disorder that leads to high androgen levels because of malfunctioning adrenal glands) show more male-typical play, interests, and sexual attractions than nonaffected girls do (Berenbaum, 2002).

Behavior genetic studies show that masculinity and femininity, like most other personality traits, show substantial heritability (Lippa & Hershberger, 1999; Loehlin, 1992; Mitchell, Baker, & Jacklin, 1989; Rowe, 1982; see chapter 3). For example, studies that compare trait similarity in identical and fraternal twins show that a substantial proportion of the variation in people's masculinity and femininity (as assessed by instrumentality, expressiveness, and gender-related interest scales) is due to genetic variation (Lippa & Hershberger, 1999). Most of the remaining variation within each sex (the environmental component) is due to nonshared environmental factors (which tend to make siblings different) rather than to shared environmental factors (which tend to make siblings similar).

In contrast to biological theories, socialization and social learning theories propose that variations in masculinity and femininity result from variations in parental rearing, teacher influences, peer influences, and the gender stereotypes we learn from our culture. Many socialization studies have found correlations between parents' gender-related behaviors and attitudes and those of their children (Huston, 1983; Ruble & Martin, 1998). Socialization theorists interpret these results to mean that parents influence their children's masculinity and femininity. However, genetic and biological theorists respond that parents and children also show similarities in their masculinity and femininity because of their shared genes.

Gender schema theory argues that people's self-concepts and the degree to which they categorize the world by gender is a cause of variations in masculinity and femininity (Bem, 1981b, 1985; Martin, 2000). Gender-schematic people are hypothesized to strongly conceptualize the world in terms of male and female, masculine and feminine. As a result, gender schematic people monitor their own behavior on masculinity and femininity and strive to behave in sex-typed ways. In contrast, gender-aschematic people don't strongly conceptualize the world in terms of gender, and as a result, their behavior is more flexible and less sex-typed. One weakness of gender schema theory is that studies have not generally supported the proposition that people possess cohesive and consistent gender schemas (Ruble & Stangor, 1986). Furthermore, studies have not demonstrated strong relationships between people's gender schemas and their gender-related behaviors (Martin, Ruble, & Szkrybalo, 2002).

Social role theory can help explain variations in masculinity and femininity in terms of societies' gender roles. Presumably, in societies with strong and rigid gender roles (boys go to school, but girls do not; men work, but women stay at home), men and women should show large differences in their behavior but little variation in masculinity and femininity within each sex. However, in societies with weaker and more flexible gender roles (men can be truck drivers or kindergarten teachers; women can be secretaries or senators), there should be weaker sex differences in behavior, but more variations in masculinity and femininity within each sex. A promising direction for future research, then, will be to study whether the strength of gender roles, across cultures, is related both to the size of sex differences in personality and to the amount of variation observed in measures of masculinity and femininity within each sex.

SUMMARY

This chapter posed two basic questions about sex, gender, and personality: (1) Are there sex differences in human personality, and (2) are there meaningful individual differences in masculinity and femininity within each sex? Essentialists are more likely to answer "yes" and social constructionists are more likely to answer "no" to each of these questions. In theorizing about sex differences and variations in masculinity and femininity, essentialists tend to be more sympathetic to biological explanations and social constructionists tend to be more sympathetic to cultural, socialization, social role, and social learning explanations.

Men and women show a number of on-average differences in personality. In terms of Big Five traits, men tend to be higher than women on some facets of extraversion (e.g., assertiveness), whereas women tend to be higher than men on many facets of agreeableness and neuroticism. On average, men are higher than women are on risk taking, sensation seeking, aggressiveness, and social dominance orientation. Men and women show a number of strong differences in their sexual traits and behaviors. There are systematic differences in men's and women's occupational preferences and interests, with men tending to be more thing-oriented and women more people-oriented. Finally, men and women show a number of differences in various kinds of mental illnesses, and some of these differences are likely related to other sex differences in personality. Both biological (evolutionary, hormonal) and social (social learning, social role) theories have been used to explain sex differences in personality.

Psychologists have measured masculinity and femininity in several different ways. Early research conceptualized masculinity-femininity (M-F) as a single, bipolar trait. Early M-F scales were composed of items that discriminated males from females; however, they suffered from heterogeneous content. Beginning in the early 1970s, masculinity and femininity were conceptualized as two separate trait dimensions, with masculinity defined in terms of instrumental personality traits and femininity in terms of expressive traits. Instrumentality is related to behaviors such as independence in the face of social pressure, and expressiveness is related to warmth and success in close relationships; however, these traits probably do not broadly assess "masculinity," "femininity," or "gender-role orientations." Recent research has returned to a bipolar conception of M-F, this time focusing on male-typical and female-typical interests. Research shows that individuals' gender-related interests are related to their self-ascribed masculinity and femininity, others' perceptions of their masculinity and femininity, gender-related prejudice, sexual orientation, transsexual versus non-transsexual status, and mortality.

Both biological (evolutionary, hormonal, genetic) theories and social (socialization, social learning, social role, gender schema) theories have attempted to explain why people vary in masculinity and femininity. A major task for future research will be to better integrate these biological and social perspectives.

DISCUSSION QUESTIONS

1. What is the difference between *sex* and *gender*? Can you list research strategies for determining how much a given sex difference (e.g., in physical aggressiveness) is due to biology and how much it's due to social and cultural factors?

2. Describe the differing viewpoints of essentialists and social constructionists. Is one of these approaches more "scientific" than the other? Do essentialism and social constructionism suggest different research strategies for studying gender?

3. Discuss some of the sex differences in personality described in this chapter. What do you think their causes are? Do you think some of these sex differences have changed in recent years? How early do you think these sex differences appear in individuals' lives? Are sex differences in personality consistent or variable across cultures? Do other species sometimes show sex differences similar to the ones described in this chapter? Do the answers to these questions have implications for how you might explain sex differences in personality?

4. Discuss some men you know who are "masculine" or "feminine." Similarly, discuss some women you know who are "masculine" or "feminine." What characteristics of these individuals led you to label them as "masculine" or "feminine"? How well do your commonsense conceptions of masculinity and femininity correspond with the ways personality psychologists have measured these traits?

5. Is it "good" or "bad" for a man to be masculine? . . . or to be feminine? Similarly, is it "good" or "bad" for a woman to be masculine? . . . or to be feminine? Can these questions be answered objectively, based on scientific research, or do answers to these questions always involve "value judgments"? Why do you think so many people in our society worry about whether individual men and women are "masculine" or "feminine"?

6. As this chapter describes, recent research has found that sexual orientation is related to some measures of masculinity and femininity. Do you think gay men and heterosexual men have different personalities, on average? Similarly, do you think lesbian women and heterosexual women have different personalities, on average? If so, what differences do you perceive, and what do you think causes these differences? Can you think of both biological and social theories that might explain homosexual-heterosexual differences in personality? How much do you think people's images of the personalities of homosexual and heterosexual people reflect social stereotypes, and how much do you think they reflect real traits?

SUGGESTED READINGS

Bem, S. L. (1993). *The lenses of gender: Transforming the debate on sexual inequality*. New Haven: Yale University Press. Bem discusses her research on the two-dimensional approach to masculinity and femininity and gender schema theory. Bem also discusses broader social and legal issues regarding how society tends to classify people too much based on sex and gender, masculinity and femininity.

Eagly, A. H. (1995). The science and politics of comparing women and men. *American Psychologist, 50*, 145–158. Eagly is a major proponent of social role theory and has conducted many meta-analytic reviews of sex differences in various domains. Given that this chapter summarizes sex differences in personality, Eagly's article offers further commentary on the promise and pitfalls of studying sex differences.

Lippa, R. A. (2001). On deconstructing and reconstructing masculinity-femininity. *Journal of Research in Personality, 35*, 168–207. This scholarly review summarizes past research on masculinity and femininity and argues that there are three, largely independent dimensions that contemporary researchers should focus on when assessing masculinity and

femininity: instrumentality, expressiveness, and gender-related interests.

Lippa, R. A. (2002). *Gender, nature, and nurture*. Mahwah, NJ: Lawrence Erlbaum. This book summarizes the nature-nurture debate, as applied to gender. Chapter 2 provides an accessible summary of research and theory on masculinity and femininity. The book also summarizes research on sex differences and various theories of gender.

Spence, J. T., & Helmreich, R. L. (1978). *Masculinity and femininity: Their psychological dimensions, correlates, and antecedents*. Austin: University of Texas Press. In this book, Spence and Helmreich summarize much of their early research on the two-dimensional approach to masculinity and femininity.

Terman, L. M., & Miles, C. C. (1936). *Sex and personality: Studies in masculinity and femininity*. New York: McGraw-Hill. Whether you love it or hate it, this is the book that started modern research on masculinity and femininity. Almost 70 years after its publication, this book is still cited—an indication of its lasting influence.

SUGGESTED WEB SITES

http://bms.brown.edu/faculty/f/afs/afs.html

Home page of Anne Fausto-Sterling, Professor of Biology and Women's Studies at Brown University. Anne Fausto-Sterling is a leading proponent of social constructionist views of sex and gender and is author of the books *Myths of Gender: Biological Theories About Men and Women*, and *Sexing the Body: Gender Politics and the Construction of Sexuality*. Dr. Fausto-Sterling's web site provides additional information about the social construction of gender and social factors that influence scientific research on gender.

http://psych.fullerton.edu/rlippa/

Home page of the author of this chapter, Richard Lippa, Professor of Psychology at California State University, Fullerton. My web site provides additional information about my research on masculinity and femininity. In addition, it gives you the opportu-

nity to participate in some online surveys and studies that are related to masculinity and femininity.

http://www.pbs.org/wgbh/nova/gender/

Web page for the excellent PBS "Nova" documentary, "Sex: Unknown." This fascinating program describes the famous "John/Joan" case, in which one of two identical twin baby boys lost his penis as a result of a botched circumcision procedure. Following the advice of doctors, the boy's parents agreed for him to be surgically reassigned as a girl and to then rear him as a girl. Unfortunately, this reassignment did not "take," and today, as an adult, this sex-reassigned individual has resumed a male identity. The PBS site provides information about intersex individuals and about the social constructionist view of gender. It also presents a fascinating animated portrayal of how sex develops over the course of human fetal development.

INFOTRAC COLLEGE EDITION SEARCH TOPICS

Sex	Gender diagnosticity	Femininity
Gender	Sex differences	Masculinity-femininity
Gender schemas	Masculinity	

REFERENCES

Adorno, T. W., Frenkel-Brunswik, E., Levinson, D. J., & Sanford, R. N. (1950). *The authoritarian personality*. New York: Harper Row.

Altemeyer, B. (1998). The other "authoritarian personality." In M. P. Zanna (Ed.), *Advances in experimental social psychology* (Vol. 30, pp. 47–92). San Diego: Academic Press.

Antill, J. T. (1983). Sex role complementarity versus similarity in married couples. *Journal of Personality and Social Psychology, 45*, 145–155.

Bailey, J. M., & Zucker, K. J. (1995). Childhood sex-typed behavior and sexual orientation: A conceptual analysis and quantitative review. *Developmental Psychology, 31*, 43–55.

Baron-Cohen, S. (2000). The cognitive neuroscience of autism: Evolutionary approaches. In M. S. Gazzaniga (Ed.). (2000). *The new cognitive neurosciences* (2nd ed.). Cambridge, MA: MIT Press.

Barry, H., Bacon, M. K., & Child, I. L. (1957). A cross-cultural survey of same sex differences in socialization. *Journal of Abnormal and Social Psychology, 55*, 327–332.

Bassoff, E. S., & Glass, G. V. (1982). The relationship between sex roles and mental health: A meta-analysis of twenty-six studies. *Counseling Psychologist, 10*, 105–112.

Baumeister, R. F. (2000). Gender differences in erotic plasticity: The female sex drive as socially flexible and responsive. *Psychological Bulletin, 126*, 347–374.

Baumeister, R. F., Cantanese, K. R., & Vohs, K. D. (2001). Is there a gender difference in strength of sex drive? Theoretical views, conceptual distinctions, and a review of relevant evidence. *Personality and Social Psychology Review, 5*, 242–273.

Bem, S. L. (1974). The measurement of psychological androgyny. *Journal of Consulting and Clinical Psychology, 42*, 165–172.

Bem, S. L. (1975). Sex role adaptability: One consequence of psychological androgyny. *Journal of Consulting and Clinical Psychology, 42*, 155–162.

Bem, S. L. (1981a). *Bem Sex-Role Inventory professional manual*. Palo Alto, CA: Consulting Psychologists Press.

Bem, S. L. (1981b). Gender schema theory: A cognitive account of sex typing. *Psychological Review, 88*, 354–364.

Bem, S. L. (1985). Androgyny and gender schema theory: A conceptual and empirical integration. In T. B. Sonderegger (Ed.), *Psychology and gender: Nebraska Symposium on Motivation, 1984* (pp. 179–226). Lincoln: University of Nebraska Press.

Bem, S. L. (1987). Masculinity and femininity exist only in the mind of the perceiver. In J. M. Reinisch, L. A. Rosenblum, & S. A. Sanders, (Eds.), *Masculinity/femininity: Basic perspectives* (pp. 304–311). New York: Oxford University Press.

Bem, S. L. (1993). *The lenses of gender: Transforming the debate on sexual inequality*. New Haven: Yale University Press.

Bem, S. L., & Lenney, E. (1976). Sex typing and the avoidance of cross-sex behavior. *Journal of Personality and Social Psychology, 33*, 48–54.

Berenbaum, S. A. (2002). Prenatal androgens and sexual differentiation of behavior. In E. A. Eugster & O. H. Pescovitz (Eds.), *Developmental endocrinology: From research to clinical practice* (pp. 293–311). Totowa, NJ: Humana Press.

Bettencourt, B. A., & Miller, N. (1996). Gender differences in aggression as a function of provocation: A meta-analysis. *Psychological Bulletin: 119*, 422–447.

Buss, A. H., & Perry, M. (1992). The aggression questionnaire. *Journal of Personality and Social Psychology, 62*, 452–459.

Buss, D. M. (1999). *Evolutionary psychology: The new science of the mind*. Boston: Allyn and Bacon.

Bussey, K., & Bandura, A. (1999). Social cognitive theory of gender development and differentiation. *Psychological Review, 106*, 676–713.

Byrnes, J. P., Miller, D. C., & Schafer, W. D. (1999). Gender differences in risk taking: A meta-analysis. *Psychological Bulletin, 125,* 367–383.

Campbell, D. P. (1971). *Handbook for the Strong Vocational Interest Blank.* Stanford, CA: Stanford University Press.

Collaer, M. L., & Hines, M. (1995). Human behavior sex differences: A role for gonadal hormones during early developments? *Psychological Bulletin, 118,* 55–107.

Constantino, F., & Heilbrun, A. B. (1964). Anxiety correlates of sex-role identity in college students. *Psychological Reports, 14,* 729–730.

Constantinople, A. (1973). Masculinity-femininity: An exception to a famous dictum. *Psychological Bulletin, 80,* 389–407.

Costa, P. T., Jr., & McCrae, R. R. (1992). The five-factor model of personality and its relevance to personality disorders. *Journal of Personality Disorders, 6,* 343–359.

Costa, P. T., Jr., Terracciano, A., & McCrae, R. R. (2001). Gender differences in personality across cultures: Robust and surprising results. *Journal of Personality and Social Psychology, 81,* 322–331.

Dabbs, J. M. (2000). *Heroes, rogues, and lovers: Testosterone and behavior.* New York: McGraw-Hill.

Daly, M., & Wilson, M. (1983). *Sex, evolution, and behavior* (2nd ed.). Boston: Willard Grant Press.

Deaux, K., & Lewis, L. L. (1983). Components of gender stereotypes. *Psychological Documents, 13,* 25.

Deaux, K., & Lewis, L. L. (1984). Structure of gender stereotypes: Interrelationships among components and gender label. *Journal of Personality and Social Psychology, 46,* 991–1004.

Eagly, A. H. (1987). *Sex differences in social behavior: A social-role interpretation.* Hillsdale, NJ: Erlbaum.

Eagly, A. H., & Diekman, A. B. (1997). The accuracy of gender stereotypes: A dilemma for feminism. *Revue Internationale de Psychologie/*International Review of Social Psychology, *10,* 11–30.

Eagly, A. H., & Steffen, V. J. (1986). Gender and aggressive behavior: A meta-analytic review of the social psychological literature. *Psychological Bulletin, 100,* 309–330.

Eagly, A. H., Wood, W., & Diekman, A. B. (2000). Social role theory of sex differences and similarities: A current appraisal. In T. Eckes & H. M Trautner (Eds.), *The developmental social psychology of gender* (pp. 123–174). Mahwah, NJ: Erlbaum.

Fausto-Sterling, A. (1992). *Myths of gender* (2nd ed.). New York: Basic Books.

Fausto-Sterling, A. (2000). *Sexing the body: Gender politics and the construction of sexuality.* New York: Basic Books.

Feingold, A. (1994). Gender differences in personality: A meta-analysis. *Psychological Bulletin, 116,* 429–456.

Furnham, A., & Mak, T. (1999). Sex-role stereotyping in television commercials: A review and comparison of fourteen studies done on five continents over 25 years. *Sex Roles, 41,* 413–437.

Gall, M. D. (1969). The relationship between masculinity-femininity and manifest anxiety. *Journal of Clinical Psychology, 25,* 294–295.

Goodenough, E. W. (1957). Interest in persons as an aspect of sex difference in the early years. *Genetic Psychology Monographs, 55,* 287–323.

Gough, H. G. (1957). *Manual for the California Psychological Inventory.* Palo Alto: Consulting Psychologists Press.

Greene, R. L. (1991). MMPI-2/MMPI: An interpretive manual. Boston: Allyn and Bacon

Guilford, J. P., & Zimmerman, W. S. (1956). Fourteen dimensions of temperament. *Psychological Monographs, 70,* 11–24.

Hall, J. A., & Carter, J. D. (1999). Gender-stereotype accuracy as an individual difference. *Journal of Personality and Social Psychology, 77,* 350–359.

Hansen, J. C., & Campbell, D. P. (1985). *Manual for the SVIB-SCII* (4th ed.) Stanford, CA: Stanford University Press (Distributed by Consulting Psychologists Press).

Harford, T. C., Willis, C. H., & Deabler, H. L. (1967). Personality correlates of masculinity-femininity. *Psychological Reports, 21,* 881–884.

Hartung, C. M., & Widiger, T. A. (1998). Gender differences in the diagnosis of mental disorders: Conclusions and controversies of the *DSM-IV. Psychological Bulletin, 123,* 260–278.

Hathaway, S. R. (1956). Scales 5 (Masculinity-Femininity), 6 (Paranoia), and 8 (Schizophrenia). In G. S. Welsh & W. G. Dahlstrom (Eds.), *Basic readings on the MMPI in psychology and medicine* (pp. 104–111). Minneapolis: University of Minnesota Press.

Hathaway, S. R., & McKinley, J. C. (1951). *MMPI manual*. New York: Psychological Corporation.

Helgeson, V. S. (1994). Prototypes and dimensions of masculinity and femininity. *Sex Roles, 31,* 653–682.

Hendrick, S. S., & Hendrick, C. (1999). Personality and human sexuality. In V. J. Derlega, B. A. Winstead, & W. H. Jones (Eds.), *Personality: Contemporary theory and research* (2nd ed., pp. 432–457). Belmont, CA: Wadsworth.

Holland, J. L. (1992). *Making vocational choices* (2nd ed.). Odessa, FL: Psychological Assessment Resources.

Huston, A. C. (1983). Sex-typing. In P. H. Mussen (Ed.), *Handbook of child psychology: Socialization, personality, and social development* (Vol. 4, pp. 388–467). New York: John Wiley.

Hyde, J. S. (1986). Gender differences in aggression. In J. S. Hyde & M. C. Lynn (Eds.), *The psychology of gender: Advances through meta-analysis.* Baltimore, MD: Johns Hopkins University Press.

Kaufman, A.S., & McLean, J. E. (1998). An investigation into the relationship between interests and intelligence. *Journal of Clinical Psychology, 54,* 279–295.

Kenrick, D. T. (1987). Gender, genes, and the social environment: A biosocial interactionist perspective. In P. Shaver & C. Hendrick (Eds.), *Sex and Gender: Review of personality and social psychology* (Vol. 7, pp. 14–43). Newbury Park, CA: Sage.

Kling, K. C., Hyde J. S., Showers, C. J., & Buswell, B. N. (1999). Gender differences in self-esteem: A meta-analysis. *Psychological Bulletin, 125,* 470–500.

Kurdek, L. A., & Schmitt, J. P. (1986). Interaction of sex role self-concept with relationship quality and relationship beliefs in married, heterosexual cohabiting, gay, and lesbian couples. *Journal of Personality and Social Psychology, 51,* 365–370.

Langis, J., Sabourin, S., Lussier, Y., & Mathieu, M. (1994). Masculinity, femininity, and marital adjustment. *Journal of Personality, 62,* 393–414.

Lewin, M. (1984a). "Rather worse than folly?" Psychology measures femininity and masculinity, 1: From Terman and Miles to the Guilfords. In M. Lewin (Ed.), *In the shadow of the past: Psychology portrays the sexes* (pp. 152–178). New York: Columbia University Press.

Lewin, M. (1984b). "Rather worse than folly?" Psychology measures femininity and masculinity, 2: From "13 gay men" to the instrumental-expressive distinction. In M. Lewin (Ed.), *In the shadow of the past: Psychology portrays the sexes* (pp. 179–204). New York: Columbia University Press.

Lippa, R. (1991). Some psychometric characteristics of gender diagnosticity measures: Reliability, validity, consistency across domains and relationship to the Big Five. *Journal of Personality and Social Psychology, 61,* 1000–1011.

Lippa, R. (1995). Gender-related individual differences and psychological adjustment in terms of the Big Five and circumplex models. *Journal of Personality and Social Psychology, 69,* 1184–1202.

Lippa, R. (1997). The display of masculinity, femininity, and gender diagnosticity in self-descriptive photo essays. *Journal of Personality, 65,* 137–169.

Lippa, R. (1998a). The nonverbal judgment and display of extraversion, masculinity, femininity, and gender diagnosticity: A lens model analysis. *Journal of Research in Personality, 32,* 80–107.

Lippa, R. (1998b). Gender-related individual difference and the structure of vocational interests: The importance of the "People-Things" dimension. *Journal of Personality and Social Psychology, 74,* 996–1009.

Lippa, R. A. (2000). Gender-related traits in gay men, lesbian women, and heterosexual men and women: The virtual identity of homosexual-heterosexual diagnosticity and gender diagnosticity. *Journal of Personality, 68,* 899–926.

Lippa, R. A. (2001a). On deconstructing and reconstructing masculinity-femininity. *Journal of Research in Personality, 35,* 168–207.

Lippa, R. A. (2001b). Gender-related traits in transsexuals and nontranssexuals. *Archives of Sexual Behavior, 30,* 603–614.

Lippa, R. A. (2002a). *Gender, nature, and nurture.* Mahwah, NJ: Erlbaum.

Lippa, R. A. (2002b). Gender-related traits of heterosexual and homosexual men and women. *Archives of Sexual Behavior, 31,* 77–92.

Lippa, R. A. (2003). Are 2D:4D finger-length ratios related to sexual orientation? Yes for men, no for women. *Journal of Personality and Social Psychology, 85,* 179–188.

Lippa, R., & Arad, S. (1999). Gender, personality, and prejudice: The display of authoritarianism and social dominance in interviews with college men and women. *Journal of Research in Personality, 33,* 463–493.

Lippa, R., & Connelly, S. C. (1990). Gender diagnosticity: A new Bayesian approach to gender-related individual differences. *Journal of Personality and Social Psychology, 59,* 1051–1065.

Lippa, R., & Hershberger, S. (1999). Genetic and environmental influences on individual differences in masculinity, femininity, and gender diagnosticity: Analyzing data from a classic twin study. *Journal of Personality, 67,* 27–55.

Lippa, R. A., Martin, L. R., & Friedman, H. S. (2000). Gender-related individual differences and mortality in the Terman longitudinal study: Is masculinity hazardous to your health? *Personality and Social Psychology Bulletin, 26,* 1560–1570.

Loehlin, J. C. (1992). *Genes and environment in personality development.* Newbury Park, CA: Sage.

Lubinski, D., & Humphreys, L. G. (1990). A broadly based analysis of mathematical giftedness. *Intelligence, 14,* 327–355.

Lytton, H., & Romney, D. M. (1991). Parents' differential socialization of boys and girls: A meta-analysis. *Psychological Bulletin, 109,* 267–296.

Maccoby, E. E. (1966). Sex differences in intellectual functioning. In E. E. Maccoby (Ed.), *The development of sex differences* (pp. 25–55). Stanford, CA: Stanford University Press.

Markow, T. A. (1994). *Developmental instability, its origins and evolutionary implications.* Boston: Kluwer Academic.

Martin, C. L. (2000). Cognitive theories of gender development. In T. Eckes & Hanns Trautner (Eds.), *The developmental social psychology of gender* (pp. 91–121). Mahwah, NJ: Erlbaum.

Martin, C. L., Ruble, D. N., & Szkrybalo, J. (2002). Cognitive theories of early gender development. *Psychological Bulletin, 128,* 903–933.

Merton, R. D. (1948). The self-fulfilling prophecy. *Antioch Review, 8,* 193–210.

Miller, E. M. (2000). Homosexuality, birth order, and evolution: Toward an equilibrium reproductive economics of homosexuality. *Archives of Sexual Behavior, 29,* 1–34.

Mitchell, J. E., Baker, L. A., & Jacklin, C. N. (1989). Masculinity and femininity in twin children: Genetic and environmental factors. *Child Development, 60,* 1475–1485.

Moller, A. P., & Swaddle, J. P. (1998). *Asymmetry, developmental stability and evolution.* New York: Oxford University Press.

Myers, A. M., & Gonda, G. (1982). Utility of the masculinity-femininity construct: Comparison of traditional and androgyny approaches. *Journal of Personality and Social Psychology, 43,* 514–522.

Oliver, M. B., & Hyde, J. S. (1993). Gender differences in sexuality: A meta-analysis. *Psychological Bulletin, 114,* 29–51.

Pillard, R. C. (1991). Masculinity and femininity in homosexuality: "Inversion" revisited. In J. C. Gonsiorek & J. D. Weinrich (Eds.), *Homosexuality: Research implications for public policy* (pp. 32–43). Newbury Park, CA: Sage.

Pratto, F., Sidanius, J., Stallworth, L., & Malle, B. (1994). Social dominance orientation: A personality variable predicting social and political attitudes. *Journal of Personality and Social Psychology, 72,* 37–53.

Prediger, D. J. (1982). Dimensions underlying Holland's hexagon: Missing link between interests and occupations? *Journal of Vocational Behavior, 21,* 259–287.

Rounds, J. (1995). Vocational interests: Evaluating structural hypotheses. In D. Lubinski & R. V. Dawis (Eds.), *Assessing individual differences in human behavior: New concepts, methods, and findings* (pp. 177–232). Palo Alto, CA: Davies-Black.

Rowe, D. C. (1982). Sources of variability in sex-linked personality attributes. *Developmental Psychology, 18,* 431–434.

Ruble, D. N., & Martin, C. L. (1998). Gender development. In W. Damon & N. Eisenberg (Eds.), *Handbook of child psychology* (5th ed., Vol 3): *Social, emotional, and personality development* (pp. 993–1016). New York: John Wiley. Ruble, D. N., & Stangor, C. (1986). Stalking the elusive gender schema: Insights from developmental and social-psychological analyses of gender schemas. *Social Cognition, 4,* 227–261.

Sidanius, J., Pratto, F., & Bobo, L. (1994). Social dominance orientation and the political psychology of gender: A case of invariance? *Journal of Personality and Social Psychology, 67,* 998–1011.

Signorielli, N. (1993). Television, the portrayal of women, and children's attitudes. In G. L. Berry & J. K. Samen (Eds.), *Children and television: Images in a changing sociocultural worlds* (pp. 229–242). Newbury Park, CA: Sage.

Snyder, M. (1981). On the self-perpetuating nature of social stereotypes. In D. L. Hamilton (Ed.),

Cognitive processes in stereotyping and inter-group behavior (pp. 183–212). Hillsdale, NJ: Erlbaum.

Spence, J. T., & Buckner, C. (1995). Masculinity and femininity: Defining the undefinable. In P. J. Kalbfleisch & M. J. Cody, (Eds.), *Gender, power, and communication in human relationships* (pp. 105–138). Hillsdale, NJ: Erlbaum.

Spence, J. T., & Helmreich, R. L. (1978). *Masculinity and femininity: Their psychological dimensions, correlates, and antecedents.* Austin: University of Texas Press.

Spence, J. T., & Helmreich, R. L. (1980). Masculine instrumentality and feminine expressiveness: Their relationships with sex role attitudes and behaviors. *Psychology of Women Quarterly, 5,* 147–163.

Spence, J. T., Helmreich, R. L., & Stapp, J. (1974). The Personal Attributes Questionnaire: A measure of sex role stereotypes and masculinity-femininity. *JSAS, Catalog of Selected Documents in Psychology, 4,* 43–44 (MS. No. 617).

Spence, J. T., & Sawin, L. L. (1985). Images of masculinity and femininity: A reconceptualization. In V. E. O'Leary, R. K. Unger, & B. S. Wallston (Eds.), *Women, gender, and social psychology* (pp. 35–66). Hillsdale, NJ: Erlbaum.

Strong, E. K., Jr. (1943). *Vocational interests of men and women.* Stanford, CA: Stanford University Press.

Strong, E. K., Jr., (1936). Interests of men and women. *Journal of Social Psychology, 9,* 49–67.

Taylor, M. C., & Hall, J. A. (1982). Psychological androgyny: Theories, methods, and conclusions. *Psychological Bulletin, 92,* 347–366.

Terman, L. M., & Miles, C. C. (1936). *Sex and personality: Studies in masculinity and femininity.* New York: McGraw-Hill.

Tooby, J., & Cosmides, L. (1990). On the universality of human nature and the uniqueness of the individual: The role of genetics and adaptation. *Journal of Personality, 58,* 17–67.

Twenge, J. M. (2001). Changes in women's assertiveness in response to status and role: A cross-temporal meta-analysis. *Journal of Personality and Social Psychology, 81,* 133–145.

Unger, R. K. (Ed.) (2001). *Handbook of the psychology of women and gender.* New York: Wiley.

Walsh, M. R. (1997). *Men, women, and gender: Ongoing debates.* New Haven: Yale University Press.

Webb, A. P. (1963). Sex-role preferences and adjustment in early adolescents. *Child Development, 34,* 609–618.

Whitley, B. E., Jr. (1983). Sex-role orientation and self-esteem: A critical meta-analytic review. *Journal of Personality and Social Psychology, 44,* 765–785.

Whitley, B. E., Jr. (1984). Sex-role orientation and psychological well-being: Two meta-analyses. *Sex Roles, 12,* 207–225.

Zuckerman, M. (1994). *Behavioral expressions and biosocial bases of sensation seeking.* Cambridge: Cambridge University Press.

Zuckerman, M., Buchsbaum, M. S., & Murphy, D. L. (1980). Sensation seeking and its biological correlates. *Psychological Bulletin, 88,* 187–214.

Zuckerman, M., & Kuhlman, M. D. (2000). Personality and risk-taking: Common biosocial factors. *Journal of Personality, 68,* 999–1029.

13 | Emotions

ROWLAND S. MILLER

Emotional experiences pervade our lives. Some of them demonstrate what it means to be human because they require advanced cognitive skills that occur only in humans and other primates (Miller, 1996). Other emotions reflect our animal heritage, occurring in us much like they do in cats and dogs. The study of emotions thus ranges from the most basic mechanisms of the brain to the most elaborate capacities of humankind.

Furthermore, emotional experiences emerge from the interactive influences of both nature and nurture. They are shaped both by the individual genetic predispositions with which each of us is born, and by the idiosyncratic experiences we encounter thereafter. For this reason, they are a principal focus of inquiry for personality studies, including both those that examine the characteristics all people share and those that scrutinize the styles that distinguish one individual from another.

More important, emotional experiences play key roles in the fundamental dimensions that make up human personality. The most basic differences among people involve variation in the amount and manner of their positive moods and emotions—their optimism, enthusiasm, and joy—and their negative emotions—their anxiety, sadness, and fear (Yik & Russell, 2001). Moreover, the defining characteristics that distinguish different types of abnormal behavior are often emotional in nature. Personality disorders usually involve excessive or inappropriate emotions, and other common problems such as anxiety disorders and affective disorders (such as depression or bipolar disorder) *are* emotional problems, by definition.

Emotion is thus a central topic in personality, and the study of emotion involves several different areas of psychology. As a result, this chapter will refer you to several concepts and ideas discussed in other chapters. However, before we can appreciate the integrative nature of emotion research, we need to specify what we mean by "emotion." What are emotions?

THE NATURE OF EMOTION

Most people use the terms *mood* and *emotion* interchangeably, but psychologists ordinarily differentiate the two. Moods are feeling states that last for hours or days (Ekman, 1994); they may linger as after-effects of earlier emotional reactions (for instance, a period of irritability may follow an episode of anger), but they often seem to have no obvious source (Frijda, 1994). Because of their duration, moods can color a person's outlook for extended periods, and at any given time, people's current moods substantially influence how they feel about themselves (Forgas & Vargas, 2000) and the decisions they make (Isen, 2000).

In contrast, emotions are brief sequences of sensation and behavior that result from specific events. They occur quickly and—to a greater extent than moods—involve physiological changes and distinctive expressive and behavioral responses (Davidson, 1994b; Ekman, 1992). All of these components help distinguish different emotions.

For instance, the circumstances that cause joy are obviously different from the events that engender sadness. A first step in the experience of an emotion is one's realization that significant, personally meaningful events are taking place; one's *appraisal*, or interpretation, of those events sets one's subsequent responses in motion (Roseman & Smith, 2001). Our appraisals of events largely determine the emotions that result; a surprising knock on our door late at night may engender a variety of reactions—for instance, either fear or delight—that depend on our snap judgments of who is likely to be at the door. Involuntary *physical changes* then occur; some emotions feel different from others in part because they are accompanied by somewhat different autonomic (Levenson, 1992) and neurological (Davidson, 2001) responses. Thereafter, the rush of subjective *feeling* that embodies emotion is often accompanied by particular facial *expressions* (Keltner & Ekman, 2000) and nonverbal behavior (Keltner, 1995) that help identify the emotion and communicate to others what one is feeling. Finally, emotions tend to arouse specific motives (Roseman, Wiest, & Swartz, 1994) so that one's subsequent *actions* are likely to vary from emotion to emotion (Frijda & Mesquita, 1998). People behave very differently when they are angry from the way they do when they are sad. Altogether, emotions are brief episodes that influence both our feelings and our behavior, often in consequential ways.

Personality researchers have discovered important patterns in the way individuals experience both emotions and moods over time, and individual differences in emotional experience are key ingredients of human personality. However, researchers have found that *universal* elements of emotional experience are also part of who and what we are. Indeed, emotions seem to operate similarly in all normal members of our species.

THE UNIVERSALITY OF EMOTION

Human cultures can differ in the meaning they attach to specific emotions (Shweder & Haidt, 2000), the exact events that elicit them (Mesquita & Ellsworth, 2001), and the norms that regulate them (Scherer & Wallbott, 1994). This isn't surprising; cultures can vary considerably in the types of behavior they encourage in certain situations, and (as we'll see) emotional behavior *is* shaped by teaching and training. There may even be regional differences within the same broad culture. For instance, people from the southern United States are much more likely than "Yankees" from the north to get angry if they are crudely insulted by a stranger (Cohen, Nisbett, Bowdle, & Schwarz, 1996). The northerners usually don't attach much importance to such insults, but southerners consider them personal attacks on their honor and dignity that have to be redressed. Nisbett and Cohen (1996) suggested that these different appraisals emerge from the different historic lifestyles and traditions of the two regions and generally underlie the higher rates of angry violence in the American South. So, cultures do differ, and emotional experiences are influenced by the predominant norms of a particular culture.

On the other hand, when an emotion does occur, the feelings and physiological changes people experience, and the nonverbal expressions they display, are remarkably similar around the world (Scherer & Wallbott, 1994). Moreover, despite the influence of idiosyncratic cultural norms, the general types of events that elicit a given emotion and the changes in motivation and behavior that accompany the emotion are much the same from culture to culture (Shaver, Wu, & Schwartz, 1992). These fundamental similarities suggest that several basic emotional experiences are universal human events, occurring naturally in all people (Ekman, 1999). Cultural influences can modify superficial aspects of such basic emotions, but the core experiences are thought to be the same in everyone.

The best-studied examples of this conclusion are the reliable facial expressions that accompany key emotions. Across cultures, people tend to display the same expressions when they experience a given emotion; for instance, people everywhere pull up the corners of their mouths and crinkle the skin alongside their eyes when they are genuinely happy (Keltner & Ekman, 2000). As a result, people everywhere can tell whether a stranger appears to be cheerful (and can then act accordingly). In a famous demonstration of this point, Ekman, Sorenson, and Friesen (1969) found that members of an isolated tribe in New Guinea who had had almost no contact with Western civilization were nevertheless able to identify the facial expressions of North Americans with good accuracy. Although cultures do have various norms, or "display rules," that influence expressive behavior (Mesquita, 2001), humans seem to be equipped with innate, universal facial expressions that can be clear signals of what a person is feeling (Keltner & Ekman, 2000).

Emotional experiences appear to be one way in which all people are elementally alike. Emotions appear to be characteristic of our species and presumably exist because eons of evolution gradually bred them into us. Why did this occur? There is no certain answer to this question, but emotion researchers generally agree that emotions are commonplace because they fulfill important functions in our everyday lives.

THE EVOLUTION OF EMOTION

Scientists usually accept two central assumptions when they consider complex behaviors such as emotions. First, they presume that nature is parsimonious: It favors simple systems over those that are unnecessarily complex. As a result, the reasoning goes, emotions must be useful in some way or they would never have developed. Thus, "the reason the primary, prototypic emotions developed in the first place, were shaped and reshaped over the millennia, and continued to survive, was because they were adaptive" (Hatfield & Rapson, 1990, p. 129). Being "adaptive" means that emotions conferred advantages that improved a person's chances of living long enough to reproduce; it does not mean that the emotions themselves were pleasant experiences.

Second, scientists assume that the usefulness and value of biological adaptations can vary as environments and cultures change, and cultures change faster than genes do. Because evolution is such a gradual, protracted process, our species still displays the characteristics that helped our distant ancestors survive (Cosmides & Tooby, 2000). In a sense, "all people are living fossils" (Buss, 1990, p. 282) with features that reflect the survival pressures of long, long ago. We behave now in ways that used to be effective and that reflect the ways humans used to live, and such actions may not necessarily be advantageous today.

Using this framework, theorists typically assume that emotions are evolutionary adaptations that help us cope with important situations like those that were repeatedly faced by our forebears (Keltner & Haidt, 2001). In this light, emotions are thought to be inborn systems for reacting quickly and reflexively to "fundamental life-tasks" (Ekman, 1992) that were key elements of survival for early humans. In short, "for recurring problems like escaping from predators, responding to strangers, meeting aggressive threats, caring for infants, falling in love, and so on, we are equipped with genetically based mechanisms that provide outline scripts for behavior that has been successful in the past" (Oatley & Jenkins, 1996, p. 82).

There may be two general ways in which emotions have been useful. First, they prepare us for *action*, focusing our attention and mobilizing our resources to deal with various threats (Oatley, 1992). Fear, for instance, prepares us to flee physical danger (Ellsworth & Smith, 1988), and the faster and more automatic an appropriate fear response is, the more helpful it is in keeping us safe. Second, emotions provide dependable *signals* to others about what we are feeling: "They communicate information from one animal to another about what is likely to happen and thereby affect the chances of survival" (Plutchik, 1980, p. 5). This social function of emotions may have been especially important to early humans, who probably lived as hunter-gatherers in small groups; those whose faces provided reliable signals of their emotions may have been more likely to be accepted by the group than were those whose intentions were typically more mysterious (Keltner & Haidt, 2001).

In fact, remembering that emotions have both personal *and* interpersonal effects provides potential explanations for phenomena that would otherwise be rather puzzling. Consider facial blushing, the visible reddening of the face and neck that often accompanies embarrassment. When people blush, the small veins in their skin dilate, allowing more blood near the surface of the skin and causing the reddish hue of the blush. The remarkable thing is that those veins are the only ones in the body that respond that way; elsewhere, peripheral veins constrict when the sympathetic nervous system is aroused, forcing more blood to the major muscles to prepare the body for action (Cutlip & Leary, 1993). Why do the facial veins behave differently from the other veins in our bodies? One possibility is that blushing evolved to provide a *reliable signal* of whether a person was upset or chagrined by his or her misbehavior. Blushing occurs only when people are consciously concerned about others' opinions of them (Miller, 1996), so it may act as an authentic nonverbal *apology* for undesirable conduct (Castelfranchi & Poggi, 1990). A blush shows that someone is genuinely abashed; such a person probably regrets recent events, and can be counted on to (try to) do better next time. In contrast, someone who breaks social norms without blushing may be ruthless and remorseless and is more worrisome. In our distant past, people who blushed may have had a handy means of overcoming minor social sins that made them more desirable group members than were those who were less able to communicate chagrin. Because of this effect, and perhaps for no other reason, blushing may have gradually become a routine human emotional response.

This analysis of blushing is speculative, but it fits everything we know about this exceptional behavior (Miller, 2001), and it's a good example of an evolutionary perspective on emotions. The most important point here for understanding human personality is that the design for our emotions may be woven into our basic animal nature with a blueprint that is shared by everyone. So, one major component of our emotional lives is their universality: People everywhere seem to experience similar emotions for similar reasons and in similar ways.

We should remember, however, that we still react with emotions that are products of the distant past, and reactions that were profitable long ago may not be as advantageous today (Buss, 2000). The quick anger that may have aided prehistoric survival by scaring off competitors for a source of food may be quite *mal*adaptive and dangerous in an environment in which adolescents carry guns to school. Evolution continues, and our emotions may be gradually changing; perhaps in several thousand generations our species will be better equipped emotionally to handle new technologies that produce modern frustrations such as "road rage." For now, it may help to understand our shared emotional human nature and keep trying to do the best we can.

INDIVIDUALITY IN EMOTIONAL EXPERIENCE

Of course, we are all individuals, too. We may share fundamental emotional capacities and predispositions, but the joint influences of nature and nurture make each of us a unique being as well (Tooby & Cosmides, 1990). Let's return for a moment to the example of blushing. All normal people can blush (Leary, Britt, Cutlip, & Templeton, 1992), but some of us are clearly more prone to blushing than others. People who are especially susceptible to embarrassment—who are said to be high in the trait of *embarrassability*—blush both more often and in a wider variety of situations than less embarrassable people do (Leary & Meadows, 1991). Some people are even plagued with chronic blushing and find themselves turning red in ordinary situations several times a day (Edelmann, 2001). Thus, humans are normally capable of blushing, but there are meaningful differences among individuals in the likelihood that a given event will elicit a blush.

Studies of emotional experience often find such patterns. Emotions seem to operate similarly in all normal people, but there are important differences among people in their susceptibility to certain emotions, the intensity of the emotions that result, and the skill with which people are able to regulate them. Moreover, in many cases, these emotional differences appear to be stable *traits* that can reliably distinguish individuals over time. In fact, one set of studies that tracked people for 30 years, from childhood into middle age, found impressive continuity in their emotional styles and the types of adult lives that resulted from them (Caspi, Elder, & Bem, 1987, 1988; Caspi, Elder, & Herbener, 1990). For instance, boys who were ill-tempered and touchy grew up to hold low-status jobs and to have trouble staying married. Boys who were shy took longer to get jobs and to get married after they became adults. Similar continuities have been observed in other studies (for instance, Caspi, 2000), and in general, children's emotional traits predict their adult styles quite well.

Other studies have found that the emotional experiences of elderly people are similar to those of younger adults. The good news is that older people seem to experience just as much joy and delight but fewer and shorter nega-tive emotions than younger people do (Charles, Reynolds, & Gatz, 2001), so our emotional styles may slowly change some over time. Nevertheless, differ-ences in emotional reactivity that distinguish us from others appear to last our entire lives (Caspi, 2000). Understanding these intriguing and influential indi-vidual differences in emotional behavior has been a major focus of personal-ity studies, and one important line of research has examined the development of such individuality. From whence might different styles of emotional expe-rience come?

INDIVIDUAL ORIGINS OF EMOTIONAL EXPERIENCE

Like many other human characteristics, emotional traits are produced by sev-eral interdependent influences that can be roughly grouped into those that are inborn (representing "nature") and those that emerge from learning and expe-rience (or "nurture"). As you might expect, given the evolutionary origins and biological basis of emotions, some emotional predispositions are inherited from our parents. On the other hand, the physical and social environments we en-counter—including, in particular, our interactions with the adults who parent us—play important roles in shaping our emotional experiences, too. In this sec-tion of the chapter, we'll examine four major influences on our emotions that illustrate how they spring from both genetic and experiential sources.

Brain Activity

Each of us is born with specific structures in our brains that appear to be espe-cially equipped to regulate emotion. For instance, we all have an amygdala, an almond-shaped structure in the limbic system of the brain that helps control the circuits that allow us to feel fear (LeDoux & Phelps, 2000). Clearly, normal brains are capable of producing this and many other emotions.

However, different levels of activity in certain areas of the brain may make particular emotions relatively more or less likely. The two different sides of the front of our brains seem to specialize in regulating either negative emotions such as sadness, fear, disgust, or anger (that's the job of the right side) or posi-tive emotions such as happiness and amusement (the left side's function) (see Davidson, 2001, and chapter 4 of this text). There is stronger activity in the right side than in the left when negative, distressing emotions occur, and the left is more active when positive, pleasurable emotions arise.

Furthermore, one region is more active than the other much of the time in some people, predisposing them to that set of emotions (again, see chapter 4). When these different levels of activation of the anterior regions of the brain are stable over time, they cause reliable differences in individuals' susceptibilities to positive or negative emotion (Davidson, Jackson, & Kalin, 2000). People whose right brains are especially active tend to be notably shy or fearful and ex-perience stronger emotion in response to negative events; on the other hand, people whose left brains are more active respond more intensely to positive events and tend to be enthusiastic and cheerful (Davidson et al., 2000).

When it occurs, such asymmetry in activation is present early in life and appears to be inborn (Davidson, 2001). However, even this basic mechanism can be affected by experience. Drugs can have temporary effects, so that, for instance, antidepressants may alleviate gloominess by increasing activity in the left side of the brain (Depue, 1995), and injury can cause lasting changes, so that damage to the left anterior brain can produce enduring apathy and depression (Gainotti, 1972). It is even possible that there is a critical period for brain development when our experiences can have lasting effect on our neurotransmitter levels—resulting in anterior asymmetry—after we're born (Davidson, 1994a). Brain activity seems to underlie important individual differences in emotional experience, and although we may be born with a certain pattern of such activity, it can be modified by events later in life.

Temperament

Brain activity is one of the factors underlying a person's *temperament*, the stable pattern of emotional reactions to events that appears early in life (Bates, 2000). A child's temperament predisposes him or her to react to a given situation in a particular way (Rothbart, Ahadi, & Evans, 2000), so that when they meet strangers, some children respond with cheerful interest whereas others react with timidity and fear. The precise nature of such "emotional individuality" (Goldsmith & Harman, 1994) is still a matter of debate, but most researchers consider temperament to have at least three components (Rothbart & Bates, 1998). The first of these is positive emotionality, or *approach*, which describes a person's normal level of enthusiasm, sociability, and happiness. People high in approach tendencies actively engage the environment, seeking rewards with cheerful optimism and energy, and they tend to be extraverted (Rothbart et al., 2000). The second component of temperament is negative emotionality, or *anxiety*, which describes a person's irritability and fearfulness. People high in anxiousness tend to nervously withdraw from the environment in an effort to avoid punishment, and they tend to be shy and inhibited and high in neuroticism (Kagan, 2001). The final ingredient of temperament is self-regulation, or *control*. People high in constraint are conscientious and temperate, whereas those low in constraint are impulsive and impetuous (Jensen-Campbell et al., 2002).

These three components combine to produce recognizably different emotional styles in children. For instance, when they encounter unfamiliar situations, some children react sociably and fearlessly; they are high in approach and low in anxiety and are often said to have "easy temperaments" (Chess & Thomas, 1990). In contrast, other children react cautiously and are more inhibited; some of them have moderate levels of approach and anxiety and are just "slow-to-warm-up," but others, who are high in anxiety and low in approach, have frequent negative moods and have "difficult temperaments" (Chess & Thomas, 1990).

Notably, we are born with some of these emotional tendencies. Studies comparing identical twins to fraternal twins and ordinary siblings demonstrate that each of the three components of temperament has a genetic basis (Saudino, McGuire, Reiss, Hetherington, & Plomin, 1995; Zawadzki,

Strelau, Oniszcenko, Riemann, & Angleitner, 2001). Very young children are naturally blessed (or burdened) with different levels of positive and negative emotionality. Some infants are genuinely bubbly, merry, happy children, whereas others are chronically sour and crabby.

Moreover, to varying degrees, these tendencies persist throughout one's life. Temperament is fairly stable during childhood and adolescence, so that "difficult" children tend to be moody, impulsive teenagers (Caspi, Henry, McGee, Moffitt, & Silva, 1995), whereas "easy" children tend to become happy and well-adjusted adolescents (Stams, Juffer, & van Ijzendoorn, 2002). One study tracked 1,037 toddlers in New Zealand for 15 years and found notable continuity in temperament over that time (Caspi & Silva, 1995). In particular, individual proclivities toward positive emotions and negative emotions are reliable emotional traits that are quite stable over time (Watson & Clark, 1994).

On the other hand, like brain activity, temperament can be affected by the experiences we encounter after our births (Calkins & Fox, 1994). The interactions of a child with his or her parents are especially important (Clark, Kochanska, & Ready, 2000; Gallagher, 2002). Of all the dimensions of temperament, negative emotionality—or "anxiety"—is the most stable, changing the least during childhood and adolescence (Plomin et al., 1993). However, even anxiety can be greatly affected by the style of parenting a child encounters. If parents respond to their children with generally positive mood and interest despite the child's fussiness and anxiety, negative emotionality may decline significantly over the first year of life (Belsky, Fish, & Isabella, 1991).

In general, a person's temperament may be more or less variable over time depending on how well it fits the situations the person encounters. There is a *"good fit"* between a person's emotional style and his or her environment when the person is able to meet the demands of the situation and master its challenges without undue stress (Chess & Thomas, 1990, 1991). There is *"poor fit"* when coping is difficult. Negative emotion and maladaptive development often emerge from a poor fit, so such circumstances usually make people unhappy (working against "easy" temperaments) or keep them that way (perpetuating "difficult" temperaments). Good fits encourage positive emotion and self-esteem and so reinforce "easy" temperaments while they gradually change "difficult" ones.

When children first go to school, for instance, those high in approach tendencies will be likely to adapt quickly to the novel situation, participating actively and making new friends; their temperament fits the situation well. The first day of school is more daunting for children who are low in approach; if they have "difficult" temperaments, they may respond with temper tantrums that elicit disapproval from others and make their problems worse. This would obviously be a poor fit between the person and the situation. However, if a patient teacher allows such children to stay on the sidelines and adjust at a leisurely pace, there is a better fit between the child and that situation, and even unsociable children may have little trouble getting used to school (Chess & Thomas, 1991).

In such a manner, our inborn emotional predispositions interact with the situations we encounter to shape our emotions over time (Rothbart et al., 2000). Another important influence on emotional life that illustrates this process is the type of attachment a child shares with his or her parents.

Attachment Style

Children develop different types of emotional bonds to those who care for them (see chapter 5 by Waters and Cheek). This fact is pertinent here because attachment styles take the form of disparate, relatively stable patterns of emotionality that influence love relationships, reactions to stress or loss, and other emotional dilemmas in one's life (Cassidy & Shaver, 1999). As adults, for instance, avoidant people suffer less heartache after the end of romantic love affairs than secure and anxious-ambivalent people do (Simpson, 1990); they are also less prone to jealousy (Guerrero, 1998). Different attachment styles create different emotional trajectories for a developing child (Magai & McFadden, 1995).

Attachment is influenced by temperament, so that "difficult" children are less likely than "easy" children to be securely attached to their caregivers (Fox & Calkins, 1993). In fact, it is possible to predict toddlers' attachment styles at 14 months of age from simple measurements of their temperament when they are only two days old! When researchers assessed newborn infants' reactions to having their pacifiers plucked from their mouths, they found that the greater the babies' distress, the less likely they were to be securely attached to their mothers a year later (Calkins & Fox, 1992).

However, attachment is also obviously affected by the interactions of and the relationship shared by children and their parents (Conger, Cui, Bryant, & Elder, 2000). Children who are securely attached enjoy smooth, pleasurable interactions with their mothers (Isabella, 1998), who attend and respond to all of their children's emotions instead of ignoring some of them as the mothers of insecure children do (Goldberg, MacKay-Soroka, & Rochester, 1994). Indeed, mothers who enjoy intimacy and who are content with closeness tend to have children who share that style; secure mothers tend to have secure children, whereas insecure mothers have insecure children. Because of this, it is possible to predict with 75% accuracy what attachment style a child will have by assessing the mother's style before her baby is even born (Fonagy, Steele, & Steele, 1991)!

One intriguing investigation was even able to manipulate attachment style by giving mothers either a cloth baby carrier that would keep their newborns close to their chests or a plastic seat that would keep their babies at a distance. Thirteen months later, toddlers who had been carried in the cloth contraptions were more likely to be securely attached than were infants who had been placed in the seats (Anisfeld, Casper, Nozyce, & Cunningham, 1990).

Thus, nurture unquestionably influences attachment style, but nature does, too. Some children are easier to parent than others and some parents are more attentive than others, and these influences seem to act in concert to shape a child's affectional life: "Attachment and temperament exert reciprocal influences on one another. Each provides an important context for the development of the other" (Goldsmith & Harman, 1994, p. 54).

Socialization

Emotional experience can also be substantially affected by influences that have little to do with who we are but much to do with what we have been taught. As we grow, we gradually learn the predominant norms and values of the surrounding culture. This process of *socialization* teaches us how normal people behave, and it affects our emotions, too. We learn where and when we are likely to experience particular emotions, and we learn what emotions other people expect from us and how they are likely to react. Modeling and imitation, rewards and punishments, and straightforward teaching all gradually shape our emotional lives (Saarni, 2000).

Parents are influential here, of course. The more often parents talk about emotions with their children, the better able the children are to recognize diverse feelings in others later on (Dunn, Brown, & Beardsall, 1991). In addition, parents are likely to communicate their own views and preferences concerning emotions to their children, often through explicit coaching and training. For instance, parents who explicitly teach their children how to deal with sadness and anger are likely to have healthy, well-behaved children years later (Hooven, Gottman, & Katz, 1995).

Not all socialization is explicit, however. Even without wishing to, parents may respond more reliably to some emotions than to others (Goldberg, MacKay-Soroka, & Rochester, 1994), and they may provide unintended examples of emotional responding for their children to imitate. Over time, for instance, babies' emotional expressions become increasingly similar to those of their mothers (Malatesta & Haviland, 1982). If a mother frequently displays happiness, her infant does, too; if she often looks angry, however, her infant will as well.

Studies of socialization remind us that although emotions spring from biological imperatives, they are shaped by teaching and training. As Kemper (1990, p. 16) asserted, "emotions are not irrevocable, biologically-guided, natural phenomena that just happen to people. Rather, they are amenable to social direction, enhancement, and suppression." Many emotional traits may be inborn, but others may simply be learned.

INDIVIDUAL DIFFERENCES IN EMOTIONAL EXPERIENCE

The diverse influences of brain activity, temperament, attachment style, and socialization combine to make each of us a unique individual. As a result, we may all experience the same emotions, but we may also differ in our abilities to recognize and regulate our feelings, in the strength of our emotions, and in our tendencies to experience some emotions more readily than others. In this section, we'll examine these and other ways in which individuals differ in emotional experience.

Affect Intensity

People who are high in "affect intensity" experience emotions that are stronger and more variable than those felt by other people (Larsen, Diener, & Emmons, 1986). (The term *affect* is used in psychology as a synonym for "feeling" or "emotion.") People with low affect intensity typically experience mild emotions that fluctuate only gradually. Such people describe themselves as "calm and cool" and disagree with statements such as "I get overly enthusiastic" or "The sight of someone who is hurt badly affects me strongly" (Larsen et al., p. 814). In contrast, those with high affect intensity agree with such statements and experience stronger, more forceful emotions that change relatively quickly. Their "highs" are higher and their "lows" are lower, and they switch from one to the other more readily as well.

All of us have strong emotions now and then, but high affect intensity individuals typically feel stronger emotions in response to the same events that elicit lesser reactions from others (Larsen et al., 1986). This means that their joys are more intense, but their fears are more powerful, too, and they tend to experience more physical complaints, such as headaches, than do those with less potent emotions. To some extent, high intensity people "are paying a somatic and psychological price for their regular experience of strong positive and strong negative emotions" (Larsen & Diener, 1987, p. 21).

For better or worse, women tend to be higher in affect intensity than men (Diener, Sandvik, & Larsen, 1985), experiencing stronger and more volatile emotions their whole lives (Brody & Hall, 2000). On the one hand, we shouldn't make too much of this, because both women and men may be either high or low in affect intensity. We shouldn't think of women as generally high and men as generally low, because that simply isn't true. On the other hand, across the enormous range of human individuality, the sexes differ on the whole in the strength of their emotions.

It's interesting to wonder why, but there may be several factors contributing to a sex difference like this (see chapter 12 by Lippa). For instance, to the extent that we *expect* women to be more emotional than men, we may often *encourage* them to be, socializing girls to be more emotional than boys (Brody, 2000). In any case, for whatever reasons, by the time they are adults, women both report stronger emotions and have stronger physiological responses to emotional events than men do (Alexander & Wood, 2000).

Emotional Intelligence

The strength of one's emotions may be less important than the skill with which one manages them. Some people are adept at handling their emotions; they know what they and others are feeling, and they are able to use their emotions to guide effective behavior. Other people, by contrast, seem emotionally inept; they are blind to others' feelings, or they are impulsive and rash, acting more out of passion than out of good sense. Evidently, people differ in *emotional intelligence*, the set of skills that allow them to manage emotion most effectively (Salovey, Woolery, & Mayer, 2001). At least three types of abilities appear to be involved: "the accurate appraisal and expression of emotion in oneself and others, the effective regulation of emotion in self and others, and the use of feelings to motivate, plan, and achieve in one's life" (Salovey, Hsee, & Mayer, 1993, p. 258). Several personality traits influence these abilities.

Accurate Appraisal and Expression   Given the same event, people may differ in their judgments of what happened, how they feel about it, and what they communicate to others. Personality influences operate at each of these steps, and notable individual differences exist.

For instance, people tend to adopt stable habits of *explanatory style*, characteristic ways of explaining why things happen the way they do (Buchanan & Seligman, 1995). Different explanatory styles can cause dissimilar appraisals of the same event, resulting in different emotions. If you blame yourself for being stupid after a poor exam grade, for example, you're likely to feel much more distress than you would if you assumed that you were merely unlucky or that the test was unfair. Diverting the blame for a poor performance to influences that don't reflect on you can help protect you from depression and despair. However, the most adaptive explanation may be to admit that you didn't study hard enough; there's nothing you can do about stupidity or bad luck, but studying is controllable and offers some hope that you'll do better on the next test. In this way, a person's immediate emotion and optimism for the future emerge from his or her appraisals of events (Metalsky, Joiner, Hardin, & Abramson, 1993). People with high emotional intelligence are routinely optimistic rather than pessimistic (Goleman, 1995), and they tend to use adaptive explanatory styles (Gohm & Clore, 2002).

Once an emotion occurs, emotionally savvy people will recognize it correctly, too. People differ in the empathy with which they detect and decode others' emotions (Riggio, 1986), and they also differ in the nature of the emotional displays they send to others. People high in dispositional expressiveness spontaneously adopt facial expressions that are more vivid, more frequent, and longer lasting than those used by people who are low in expressiveness (Kring, Smith, & Neale, 1994). These talents of reading and communicating emotional expressions are valuable in our dealings with others, but they are especially beneficial in close relationships, where partners often need to know what their lovers are feeling; in fact, empathy and expressiveness are both correlated with marital satisfaction (Noller, 1980).

Effective Regulation of Emotion   The ability to manage and direct one's emotions so that they serve one's ends is one of the most important components of emotional intelligence (Salovey et al., 2001). Emotion regulation can involve changing the focus of one's attention ("I tried not to think about it"), reconceptualizing events ("He wasn't really hurt; those were just special effects"), setting reasonable goals ("I don't think I'll try that"), devising clever strategies ("Let's leave the big present for last"), and controlling one's behavior ("Take long, slow, deep breaths, and relax"). At bottom, however, it usually involves efforts to (1) maintain moods and emotions that facilitate one's goals, and (2) minimize or prevent emotions that interfere with one's ends (Bonanno, 2001). People who are skilled at emotion regulation can delay gratification, control their impulses, and persist in the face of frustration.

One ingenious test of emotion regulation was devised by Walter Mischel (1974), who gave 4-year-olds the choice of either an immediate small reward or a delayed, larger reward. Mischel showed children a small candy bar and told them that if they waited to eat it until he returned from an errand, he would give them a larger candy bar as a reward; if they couldn't wait, they'd only get the small treat, but they could have it without delay. The children were then left alone with the enticing candy for 15 long minutes. Remarkably, most of them were able to refrain from gobbling it down; they looked away, distracted themselves, and controlled themselves to obtain the bigger payoff. However, a third of the children could not wait and grabbed the candy quickly. What makes these results compelling is that years later, when the same children were teenagers, those who had resisted temptation as preschoolers were clearly more socially competent; they were doing better in school, enjoyed closer friendships with others, and had better control of their negative emotions (Shoda, Mischel, & Peake, 1990).

In general, it seems that people who are able to understand and regulate their emotions have a tremendous advantage over people who are prisoners of their passions (Salovey et al., 2001; Goleman, 1995). This is especially true when we inspect the difficulties of those whose emotions are out of control.

Emotions and Psychopathology

Disorders of personality are discussed in chapter 18, so I will not say much about disturbed personalities here. Nevertheless, a proper appreciation of the role of emotion in human affairs prompts me to remind you of a point made in passing at the beginning of this chapter: Abnormal or poorly regulated emotions play important roles in most mental disorders and are a defining feature of many (Kring, 2001). Dysfunction can occur either when normal emotions are too strong or when they are too weak (Magai & McFadden, 1995). Too much sadness precipitates depression, uncontrolled fear causes panic disorders, and too much embarrassment becomes social phobia (Clark, Watson, & Mineka, 1994; Miller, 2001). On the other hand, too little fear breeds antisocial personality disorders (Patrick, 1994), and insufficient emotion characterizes schizophrenia. Most human maladjustments involve disruptions in emotional experience, and with some disorders, inappropriate emotion is the primary complaint.

Unwanted emotion may spring from all of the influences we have described thus far, but sometimes the sources are more specific. I have investigated the origins of embarrassability, and would like to tell you about them.

PERSONALITY IN ACTION: THE CASE OF EMBARRASSABILITY

I became interested in people's susceptibility to embarrassment when I had a striking experience that left me both puzzled and intrigued. I was alone, watching a movie on a small TV, when I found myself cringing at the situation on screen. In *Save the Tiger*, Jack Lemmon played a clothing manufacturer who has a psychotic breakdown in front of a large audience; he starts hallucinating and ruins a vitally important speech on which the future of his business depends. (Lemmon won the 1973 Oscar for Best Actor for his performance.) It was tough for me to watch. I felt very uneasy. It was embarrassing to watch someone— even a fictitious character—in such a humiliating public debacle. I realized I had felt that way once before, when I witnessed the grim spectacle of a comedian who had completely failed to make anyone laugh. Was this something unique about me, I puzzled, or were other people affected in similar ways?

Witnessing Others' Predicaments

Was *empathic embarrassment* possible, I wondered? Could people be embarrassed by simply watching other people endure embarrassing predicaments? No conclusive answer existed; at that time, embarrassment was generally considered to be an emotion people felt only after their own pratfalls and errors. I thought empathic embarrassment did exist, however, and so I tried to create it in the lab.

Pairs of college students, either two men or two women, participated in my procedure (Miller, 1987). By the flip of a coin, one became the actor, the other an observer; the actor was then asked to perform a series of either embarrassing or innocuous tasks while the observer watched from an adjacent room. The observers were given one of two sets of instructions. In one case, they were asked to try to imagine what the actor was feeling; in the other case, they were asked to simply watch the actor's behavior carefully, noting "hand gestures" and other actions. The luck of the draw determined what happened next; actors in an embarrassing condition pulled a sheet of instructions from an envelope that asked them to (1) sing "The Star- Spangled Banner"; (2) laugh for 30 seconds as if they had just heard a joke; (3) dance to recorded music for 60 seconds; and (4) imitate a 5-year-old throwing a temper tantrum at bedtime. These were grueling tasks that were much more difficult than the innocuous tasks, which involved merely listening to the music and writing out the words to "The Star-Spangled Banner" among other duties.

I knew the embarrassing tasks would embarrass the actors (see Apsler, 1975); the point of the study was to see how the observers would react to the things they saw. While they were watching, electrodes attached to a hand and arm assessed the small changes in the conductivity of the observers' skin; this was a measure of their general emotional arousal. Then, after the actors' performances, the observers reported what they had been thinking and feeling.

Several emotions were common in the observers who watched the embarrassing tasks. They were surprised, amused, and sympathetic, but they said they were embarrassed, too. Moreover, the physical measures of their arousal were more closely related to these reports of embarrassment than to any other emotion. It did appear that they had been embarrassed by simply witnessing someone else's public predicament.

However, not everyone responded the same way. People who had been asked to visualize the actors' feelings reported stronger empathic embarrassment than did those who watched with more detachment. In addition, there were meaningful individual differences in this subtle phenomenon. Before the tasks, I had given the actors and observers a personality inventory created by Andre Modigliani (1968) that assessed susceptibility to embarrassment; this Embarrassability Scale, which is reprinted in Activity Box 13.1, asks respondents what they would feel in 26 potentially embarrassing situations. Modigliani found that high scorers were more embarrassed than low scorers by awkward situations.

I found the same thing. The Embarrassability Scale accurately predicted how embarrassed both the actors and the observers would be by my procedure.

Activity Box 13.1   Assess Your Own Embarrassability–The Embarrassability Scale

These questions ask whether certain social situations would cause you embarrassment. Read each item, and try to imagine as vividly as possible that each of these events is happening to you. If they have occurred to you in the past, think back to how you felt at the time. Then, rate how embarrassed you would feel if the event were actually happening to you by using the scale below to describe your reaction:

1 = I would not feel the least embarrassed: not awkward or uncomfortable at all.
2 = I would feel slightly embarrassed.
3 = I would feel fairly embarrassed: somewhat self-conscious and rather awkward and uncomfortable.
4 = I would feel quite embarrassed.
5 = I would feel strongly embarrassed: extremely self-conscious, awkward, and uncomfortable.

_____ 1. Suppose you were just beginning a talk in front of a class.
_____ 2. Suppose you slipped and fell on a patch of ice in a public place, dropping a bag of groceries.
_____ 3. Suppose you were a dinner guest, and the guest seated next to you spilled his plate on his lap while trying to cut his meat.
_____ 4. Suppose someone stopped you on the street by asking you something, and he turned out to be quite drunk and incoherent.
_____ 5. Suppose a group of friends were singing "Happy Birthday" to you.
_____ 6. Suppose you discovered you were the only person at a particular social occasion without a coat and tie (or dress).
_____ 7. Suppose you were watching an amateur show and one of the performers was trying to do a comedy act but was unable to make anyone laugh.
_____ 8. Suppose you were calling up a person you had just met for the first time in order to ask him or her for a date.
_____ 9. Suppose you were muttering aloud to yourself in an apparently empty room and discovered that someone else was present.
_____ 10. Suppose you walked into a bathroom at someone else's house and discovered it was occupied by a member of the opposite sex.
_____ 11. Suppose you were watching a play from the audience when it suddenly became clear that one of the actors had forgotten her lines, causing the play to come to a standstill.
_____ 12. Suppose you were unable to stop coughing while listening to a lecture.
_____ 13. Suppose you were being lavishly complimented on your pleasant personality by your companion on your first date.
_____ 14. Suppose you were in a class and you noticed that the teacher had completely neglected to zip his fly.
_____ 15. Suppose you entered an apparently empty classroom, turned on the lights, and surprised a couple necking.
_____ 16. Suppose you were talking to a stranger who stuttered badly due to a speech impediment.
_____ 17. Suppose your mother had come to visit you and was accompanying you to all your classes.

(continued)

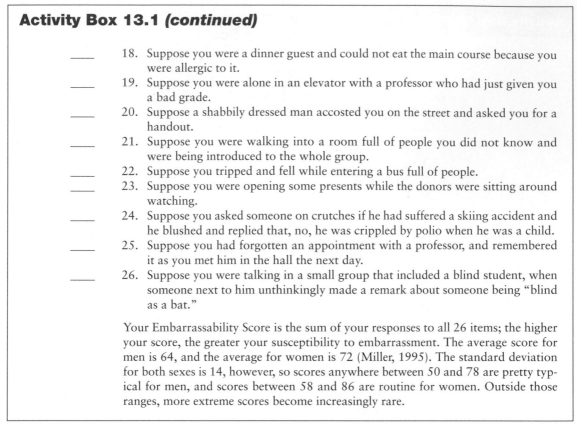

Activity Box 13.1 (continued)

_____   18. Suppose you were a dinner guest and could not eat the main course because you were allergic to it.

_____   19. Suppose you were alone in an elevator with a professor who had just given you a bad grade.

_____   20. Suppose a shabbily dressed man accosted you on the street and asked you for a handout.

_____   21. Suppose you were walking into a room full of people you did not know and were being introduced to the whole group.

_____   22. Suppose you tripped and fell while entering a bus full of people.

_____   23. Suppose you were opening some presents while the donors were sitting around watching.

_____   24. Suppose you asked someone on crutches if he had suffered a skiing accident and he blushed and replied that, no, he was crippled by polio when he was a child.

_____   25. Suppose you had forgotten an appointment with a professor, and remembered it as you met him in the hall the next day.

_____   26. Suppose you were talking in a small group that included a blind student, when someone next to him unthinkingly made a remark about someone being "blind as a bat."

Your Embarrassability Score is the sum of your responses to all 26 items; the higher your score, the greater your susceptibility to embarrassment. The average score for men is 64, and the average for women is 72 (Miller, 1995). The standard deviation for both sexes is 14, however, so scores anywhere between 50 and 78 are pretty typical for men, and scores between 58 and 86 are routine for women. Outside those ranges, more extreme scores become increasingly rare.

Note. The Embarrassability Scale was copyrighted 1968 by Andre Modigliani, and is adapted and used with his permission.

High scorers suffered more intense embarrassment whether they were performing the tasks or simply watching someone else perform them. Individuals obviously differed in the extent of their embarrassed emotion in response to a difficult social situation.

Tracking Ordinary Embarrassments

I think I showed that empathic embarrassment was possible, but I had to admit that it was a mild form of embarrassment that was probably rather rare. To assess its frequency and to examine other kinds of real-life embarrassment, I conducted two survey studies that targeted naturally occurring embarrassments (see Miller, 1996). In the first of these, I asked 350 people from New York, North Carolina, and Texas to complete the Embarrassability Scale and then tell me about the last time they were embarrassed. In the second study, I invited people to keep "embarrassment diaries" for a month or more, providing weekly reports of the embarrassments they encountered. In both studies, individual differences in embarrassability were apparent. Highly embarrassable people experienced more intense embarrassment when unwanted predicaments occurred. They did not suffer different kinds of embarrassment than anyone else—that is, they blundered into the same types of predicaments as those who were less embarrassable—but they reacted more strongly and became embarrassed more often. They blushed more readily, too (Leary & Meadows, 1991).

Thus, in carefully controlled laboratory procedures and in ordinary, natural surroundings, the trait of embarrassability predicted the intensity of individuals' responses to embarrassing predicaments. I thought that a closer look at the components of embarrassability might illuminate the nature of embarrassment itself, and so I examined embarrassability in more detail.

The Nature of Embarrassability

There are several feasible reasons for why we often react to unwanted social predicaments with emotional chagrin and abashment (see Miller, 1996). One possibility is that awkward situations dash our expectations and rob us of our poise, leaving us at sea for what to do and say next. This uncertainty may be very uncomfortable and may be the major reason we experience the unpleasant arousal we call embarrassment. Alternatively, a more important influence may be our concern for what others are thinking of us; regardless of whether we know what to do, we may dread embarrassing situations because we fear that they make us look bad to others (Miller, 1996). Certainly, both awkward uncertainty and worry about others' judgments typically occur when embarrassment strikes (Parrott & Smith, 1991). However, I thought it likely that one of these influences was more potent than the other, and I believed that the trait of embarrassability might show which one it was.

If awkward uncertainty is the primary cause of embarrassment, I reasoned, then a person's social skills should influence his or her embarrassability. People who are clumsy or inept should be particularly prone to embarrassment because they are (1) clueless more often and (2) less able to gracefully repair awkward situations once they occur. On the other hand, if worry over others' judgments is the wellspring of embarrassment, a person's embarrassability should be more closely related to his or her fear of negative evaluation, or chronic dread of disapproval from others. To distinguish these possibilities, I asked 310 people to complete the Embarrassability Scale, a social skill inventory, and various measures assessing fear of negative evaluation and need for approval (Miller, 1995).

A clear picture emerged. Highly embarrassable people tended to be preoccupied with what others were thinking of them. Worse, they tended to fear that others were disapproving of them. They paid close attention to social norms and held themselves to rather strict, unforgiving codes of propriety and manners and thus were more rattled when minor mistakes occurred. They were less skilled at small talk and other social graces but did not lack social skills on the whole. In general, embarrassability had less to do with social skills than it did with nervous concern about doing the right thing and being accepted by others. I concluded that whatever their social skills, "if people were heedless of others' opinions, they would not be very embarrassable" (Miller, 1995, p. 326).

Why should an unpleasant emotion hinge like this on our worries about what others are thinking of us? The answer may lie in our ancient prehistory. As we noted with blushing, early humans who had an embarrassment warning system that alerted them to their social transgressions may have had an adaptive emotional mechanism that promoted their survival. Because embarrassment is aversive, they may have been less likely to misbehave and incur others' wrath; moreover, after accidental malfeasance, their displays of embarrassment may have reassured their audiences and reduced their chances of being abandoned by others.

This would make moderate levels of embarrassability a good thing (Miller, 2001). On the other hand, excessive sensitivity to others' evaluations might be needless and painful, causing useless worry and inhibiting one's normal behavior (Miller, 2001). With embarrassability, as with other emotional traits, too much of a good thing may be maladaptive.

EMOTIONS IN PERSONALITY

Finally, let me remind you again of the central role that emotional traits play in human personality. Some of the most fundamental distinctions researchers make among humans simply distinguish different styles of emotional life. The different emotional temperaments that emerge in children predict well what their adult personalities will be (Angleitner & Ostendorf, 1994). In particular, the two key traits of positive emotionality and negative emotionality closely overlap the fundamental personality dimensions of Extraversion and Neuroticism, respectively (Clark & Watson, 1999). In many respects, the most important human traits, the variables that have dominated the study of personality in recent years, describe stable differences in emotional experience.

SUMMARY

Emotions play key roles in personality, underlying vital differences in individual experience. Variations in emotional style emerge from some of the most fundamental influences on personality, including those that are genetic and inborn and those that result from teaching, training, and other experiences.

Different patterns of brain activity seem to produce disparate emotional tendencies. Pleasant, happy emotions are readily produced in those whose left frontal lobe is more active than the right, whereas sad and fearful emotions are especially accessible when the right brain is more active. For this and other reasons, people are born with styles of temperament that predispose them to particular happy, sour, or wary patterns of emotion. The way children interact with their parents shapes their emotional habits, too, however, and socialization can make certain emotions more or less likely.

As a result of these influences, reliable differences exist among people in the usual intensity of their emotions and in the manner in which they attend to, express, and regulate their emotional experiences. These latter traits contribute to emotional intelligence, the global skill with which people are able to manage their emotions to behave effectively and accomplish their goals.

Underlying this individuality are universal characteristics of emotional experience that seem to be shared by all people. The commonality of such experiences reflects the common evolutionary pressures that all humans have faced; many theorists believe that emotions have their present form because of past eons of natural selection.

Embarrassability is a good example of an emotional trait. It varies substantially from person to person but is present in all normal people, perhaps because it is useful (even if it is unpleasant). Either too little or too much embarrassability may be disadvantageous, but such differences among people are key elements of their personalities, illustrating the centrality of emotion to the understanding of personality.

DISCUSSION QUESTIONS

1. Abnormalities in personality often occur when normal processes are absent or exaggerated. How does that apply to emotions?
2. Evolutionary psychologists assume that emotions are inborn components of human nature because they operate similarly in all people all around the world. What else could explain the lack of cultural differences in emotional experience?
3. Why do emotions exist?
4. Both nature and nurture influence our emotions. Which is the more important influence on emotional experience?
5. How might differences in temperament affect people's lives?
6. What levels of affect intensity and emotional intelligence would you prefer in a spouse?
7. Embarrassment is an unpleasant experience, but we would probably be much worse off without it. Why?

SUGGESTED READINGS

Ekman, P., & Davidson, R. J. (Eds.). (1994). *The nature of emotion: Fundamental questions*. New York: Oxford University Press. In this remarkable volume, eminent emotion researchers debate the nature, functions, physiology, and operation of emotion. Various views are represented, and there is no better introduction to the consensus and controversy that shape emotion research.

Goleman, D. (1995). *Emotional intelligence*. New York: Bantam Books. This popular book surveys the practical value of emotional competence in everyday life. It is based on solid science but is written for a general audience.

Lewis, M., & Haviland-Lewis, J. M. (Eds.). (2000). *Handbook of emotions* (2nd edition). New York:

Guilford Press. This is a key reference for advanced study in the field. It contains 43 chapters that address the biology, psychology, and sociology of emotional experience.

Mayne, T. J., & Bonanno, G. A. (Eds.). (2001). *Emotions: Current issues and future directions*. New York: Guilford Press. This is a collection of chapters that describe biological and cultural influences on emotional experience and survey the role of emotions in psychopathology and health.

Miller, R. S. (1996). *Embarrassment: Poise and peril in everyday life*. New York: Guilford Press. Complete coverage of an influential, uniquely human social emotion. Contains a full chapter on individual differences in embarrassability.

SUGGESTED WEB SITES

http://www.nimh.nih.gov/publicat/feel.cfm
A page from the National Institute of Mental Health on Imaging Emotion in the Brain.

http://emotions.psychologie.uni-sb.de/kultur/anleiten.htm
This page invites you to participate in a cross-cultural study of the recognition of facial expressions. Test yourself against the rest of the world!

http://www.apa.org/pubinfo/anger.html
Advice on "Controlling Anger—Before It Controls You" from the American Psychological Association.

http://www.utne.com/interact/test_iq.html
This page links to ten questions that allow you to test your emotional intelligence.

INFOTRAC COLLEGE EDITION SEARCH TOPICS

Emotion
Temperament
Attachment style

Socialization
Affect intensity

Emotional intelligence
Embarassability

REFERENCES

Alexander, M. G., & Wood, W. (2000). Women, men, and positive emotions: A social role interpretation. In A. H. Fischer (Ed.), *Gender and emotion: Social psychological perspectives* (pp. 189–210). Cambridge, UK: Cambridge University Press.

Angleitner, A., & Ostendorf, F. (1994). Temperament and the Big Five factors of personality. In C. F. Halverson, Jr., G. A. Kohnstamm, & R. P. Martin (Eds.), *The developing structure of temperament and personality from infancy to adulthood* (pp. 69–90). Hillsdale, NJ: Erlbaum.

Anisfeld, E., Casper, V., Nozyce, M., & Cunningham, N. (1990). Does infant carrying promote attachment? An experimental study of the effects of increased physical contact on the development of attachment. *Child Development, 61,* 1617–1627.

Apsler, R. (1975). Effects of embarrassment on behavior toward others. *Journal of Personality and Social Psychology, 32,* 145–153.

Bates, J. E. (2000). Temperament as an emotion construct: Theoretical and practical issues. In M. Lewis & J. M. Haviland-Jones (Eds.), *Handbook of emotions* (2nd ed., pp. 382–396). New York: Guilford Press.

Belsky, J., Fish, M., & Isabella, R. (1991). Continuity and discontinuity in infant negative and positive emotionality: Family antecedents and attachment consequences. *Developmental Psychology, 27,* 421–431.

Bonanno, G. A. (2001). Emotion self-regulation. In T. J. Mayne & G. A. Bonanno (Eds.), *Emotions: Current issues and future directions* (pp. 251–285). New York: Guilford Press.

Brody, L. R. (2000). The socialization of gender differences in emotional expression: Display rules, infant temperament, and differentiation. In A. H. Fischer (Ed.), *Gender and emotion: Social psychological perspectives* (pp. 24–47). Cambridge, UK: Cambridge University Press.

Brody, L. R., & Hall, J. A. (2000). Gender, emotion, and expression. In M. Lewis & J. M. Haviland-Jones (Eds.), *Handbook of emotions* (2nd ed., pp. 338–349). New York: Guilford Press.

Buchanan, G. M., & Seligman, M. E. P. (Eds.). (1995). *Explanatory style.* Hillsdale, NJ: Erlbaum.

Buss, D. M. (1990). Evolutionary social psychology: Prospects and pitfalls. *Motivation and Emotion, 14,* 265–286.

Buss, D. M. (2000). *The dangerous passion: Why jealousy is as necessary as love and sex.* New York: Free Press.

Calkins, S. D., & Fox, N. A. (1992). The relations among infant temperament, security of attachment, and behavioral inhibition at twenty-four months. *Child Development, 63,* 1456–1472.

Calkins, S. D., & Fox, N. A. (1994). Individual differences in the biological aspects of temperament. In J. E. Bates & T. D. Wachs (Eds.), *Temperament: *Individual differences at the interface of biology and behavior* (pp. 199–217). Washington, DC: American Psychological Association.

Caspi, A. (2000). The child is father of the man: Personality continuities from childhood to adulthood. *Journal of Personality and Social Psychology, 78,* 158–172.

Caspi, A., Elder, G. H., & Bem, D. J. (1987). Moving against the world: Life course patterns of explosive children. *Developmental Psychology, 23,* 308–313.

Caspi, A., Elder, G. H., & Bem, D. J. (1988). Moving away from the world: Life course patterns of shy children. *Developmental Psychology, 24,* 824–831.

Caspi, A., Elder, G. H., & Herbener, E. S. (1990). Childhood personality and the prediction of life-course patterns. In L. N. Robins & M. Rutter (Eds.), *Straight and devious pathways from childhood to adulthood* (pp. 13–35). Cambridge, UK: Cambridge University Press.

Caspi, A., Henry, B., McGee, R. O., Moffitt, T. E., & Silva, P. A. (1995). Temperamental origins of child and adolescent behavior problems: From age three to fifteen. *Child Development, 66,* 55–68.

Caspi, A., & Silva, P. A. (1995). Temperamental qualities at age three predict personality traits in young adulthood: Longitudinal evidence from a birth cohort. *Child Development, 66,* 486–498.

Cassidy, J., & Shaver, P. R. (Eds.). (1999). *Handbook of attachment: Theory, research and clinical applications.* New York: Guilford Press.

Castelfranchi, C., & Poggi, I. (1990). Blushing as a discourse: Was Darwin wrong? In W. R. Crozier (Ed.), *Shyness and embarrassment: Perspectives from social psychology* (pp. 230–251). Cambridge, UK: Cambridge University Press.

Charles, S. T., Reynolds, C. A., & Gatz, M. (2001). Age-related differences and change in positive and negative affect over 23 years. *Journal of Personality and Social Psychology, 80,* 136–151.

Chess, S., & Thomas, A. (1990). Continuities and discontinuities in temperament. In L. N. Robins & M. Rutter (Eds.), *Straight and devious pathways from childhood to adulthood* (pp. 205–220). Cambridge, UK: Cambridge University Press.

Chess, S., & Thomas, A. (1991). Temperament and the concept of goodness of fit. In J. Strelau & A. Angleitner (Eds.), *Explorations in temperament:*

International perspectives on theory and measurement (pp. 15–28). New York: Plenum Press.

Clark, L. A., Kochanska, G., & Ready, R. (2000). Mothers' personality and its interaction with child temperament as predictors of parenting behavior. *Journal of Personality and Social Psychology, 79,* 274–285.

Clark, L. A., & Watson, D. (1999). Temperament: A new paradigm for trait psychology. In L. A. Pervin & O. P. John (Eds.), *Handbook of personality: Theory and research* (2nd ed., pp. 399–423). New York: Guilford Press.

Clark, L. A., Watson, D., & Mineka, S. (1994). Temperament, personality, and the mood and anxiety disorders. *Journal of Abnormal Psychology, 103,* 103–116.

Cohen, D., Nisbett, R. E., Bowdle, B. F., & Schwarz, N. (1996). Insult, aggression, and the southern culture of honor: An "experimental ethnography." *Journal of Personality and Social Psychology, 70,* 945–960.

Conger, R. D., Cui, M., Bryant, C. M., & Elder, G. H., Jr. (2000). Competence in early adult romantic relationships: A developmental perspective on family influences. *Journal of Personality and Social Psychology, 79,* 224–237.

Cosmides, L., & Tooby, J. (2000). Evolutionary psychology and the emotions. In M. Lewis & J. M. Haviland-Jones (Eds.), *Handbook of emotions* (2nd ed., pp. 91–115). New York: Guilford Press.

Cutlip, W. D., II, & Leary, M. R. (1993). Anatomic and physiological bases of social blushing: Speculations from neurology and psychology. *Behavioural Neurology, 6,* 181–185.

Davidson, R. J. (1994a). Asymmetric brain function, affective style, and psychopathology: The role of early experience and plasticity. *Development and Psychopathology, 6,* 741–758.

Davidson, R. J. (1994b). On emotion, mood, and related affective constructs. In P. Ekman & R. J. Davidson (Eds.), *The nature of emotion: Fundamental questions* (pp. 51–55). New York: Oxford University Press.

Davidson, R. J. (2001). Toward a biology of personality and emotion. In A. R. Damasio, A. Harrington, J. Kagan, B. S. McEwen, H. Moss, & R. Shaikh (Eds.), *Unity of knowledge: The convergence of natural and human science. Annals of the New York Academy of Sciences* (Vol. 935, pp. 191–207). New York: New York Academy of Sciences.

Davidson, R. J., Jackson, D. C., & Kalin, N. H. (2000). Emotion, plasticity, context, and regulation: Perspectives from affective neuroscience. *Psychological Bulletin, 126,* 890–909.

Diener, E., Sandvik, E., & Larsen, R. J. (1985). Age and sex effects for emotional intensity. *Developmental Psychology, 21,* 542–546.

Depue, R. A. (1995). Neurobiological factors in personality and depression. *European Journal of Personality, 9,* 413–439.

Dunn, J., Brown, J., & Beardsall, L. (1991). Family talk about feeling states and children's later understanding of others' emotions. *Developmental Psychology, 27,* 448–455.

Edelmann, R. J. (2001). Blushing. In W. R. Crozier & L. E. Alden (Eds.), *International handbook of social anxiety: Concepts, research and interventions relating to the self and shyness* (pp. 301–323). Chichester, UK: Wiley.

Ekman, P. (1992). An argument for basic emotions. *Cognition and Emotion, 6,* 169–200.

Ekman, P. (1994). Moods, emotions, and traits. In P. Ekman & R. J. Davidson (Eds.), *The nature of emotion: Fundamental questions* (pp. 56–58). New York: Oxford University Press.

Ekman, P. (1999). Basic emotions. In T. Dalgleish & M. J. Power (Eds.), *Handbook of cognition and emotion* (pp. 45–60). Chichester, UK: Wiley.

Ekman, P., Sorenson, E. R., & Friesen, W. V. (1969). Pan-cultural elements in the facial displays of emotion. *Science, 221,* 1208–1210.

Ellsworth, P. C., & Smith, C. A. (1988). From appraisal to emotion: Differences among unpleasant feelings. *Motivation and Emotion, 12,* 271–302.

Fonagy, P., Steele, H., & Steele, M. (1991). Maternal representations of attachment during pregnancy predict the organization of infant-mother attachment at one year of age. *Child Development, 62,* 891–905.

Forgas, J. P., & Vargas, P. T. (2000). The effects of mood on social judgment and reasoning. In M. Lewis & J. M. Haviland-Lewis (Eds.), *Handbook of emotions* (2nd ed., pp. 350–367). New York: Guilford Press.

Fox, N. A., & Calkins, S. D. (1993). Pathways to aggression and social withdrawal: Interactions among temperament, attachment, and regulation. In K. H. Rubin & J. B. Asendorpf (Eds.), *Social withdrawal, inhibition, and shyness in childhood* (pp. 81–100). Hillsdale, NJ: Erlbaum.

Frijda, N. H. (1994). Varieties of affect: Emotions and episodes, moods, and sentiments. In P. Ekman & R. J. Davidson (Eds.), *The nature of emotion: Fundamental questions* (pp. 59–67). New York: Oxford University Press.

Frijda, N. H., & Mesquita, B. (1998). The analysis of emotions: Dimensions of variation. In M. F. Mascolo & S. Griffin (Eds.), *What develops in emotional development?* (pp. 273–295). New York: Plenum Press.

Gainotti, G. (1972). Emotional behavior and hemispheric side of lesion. *Cortex, 8,* 41–55.

Gallagher, K. C. (2002). Does child temperament moderate the influence of parenting on adjustment? *Developmental Review, 22,* 623–643.

Gohm, C. L., & Clore, G. L. (2002). Four latent traits of emotional experience and their involvement in well-being, coping, and attributional style. *Cognition and Emotion, 16,* 495–518.

Goldberg, S., MacKay-Soroka, S., & Rochester, M. (1994). Affect, attachment, and material responsiveness. *Infant Behavior and Development, 17,* 335–339.

Goldsmith, H. H., & Harman, C. (1994). Temperament and attachment; individuals and relationships. *Current Directions in Psychological Science, 3,* 53–57.

Goleman, D. (1995). *Emotional intelligence.* New York: Bantam Books.

Guerrero, L. K. (1998). Attachment style differences in the experience and expression of romantic jealousy. *Personal Relationships, 5,* 273–291.

Hatfield, E., & Rapson, R. L. (1990). Passionate love in intimate relationships. In B. Moore & A. Isen (Eds.), *Affect and social behavior* (pp. 126–151). Cambridge, UK: Cambridge University Press.

Hooven, C., Gottman, J. M., & Katz, L. F. (1995). Parental meta-emotion structure predicts family and child outcomes. *Cognition and Emotion, 9,* 229–264.

Isen, A. M. (2000). Positive affect and decision making. In M. Lewis & J. M. Haviland-Lewis (Eds.), *Handbook of emotions* (2nd ed., pp. 417–435). New York: Guilford Press.

Isabella, R. A. (1998). Origins of attachment: The role of context, duration, frequency of observation, and infant age in measuring maternal behavior. *Journal of Social and Personal Relationships, 15,* 538–554.

Jensen-Campbell, L. A., Rosseli, M., Workman, K. A., Santisi, M., Rios, J. D., & Bojan, D. (2002). Agreeableness, conscientiousness, and effortful control processes. *Journal of Research in Personality, 36,* 476–789.

Kagan, J. (2001). Temperamental contributions to affective and behavioral profiles in childhood. In S. G. Hofmann & P. M. DiBartolo (Eds.), *From social anxiety to social phobia: Multiple perspectives* (pp. 216–234). Boston: Allyn and Bacon.

Keltner, D. (1995). Signs of appeasement: Evidence for the distinct displays of embarrassment, amusement, and shame. *Journal of Personality and Social Psychology, 68,* 441–454.

Keltner, D., & Ekman, P. (2000). Facial expression of emotion. In M. Lewis & J. M. Haviland-Lewis (Eds.), *Handbook of emotions* (2nd ed., pp. 236–249). New York: Guilford Press.

Keltner, D., & Haidt, J. (2001). Social functions of emotions. In T. J. Mayne & G. A. Bonanno (Eds.), *Emotions: Current issues and future directions* (pp. 192–213). New York: Guilford Press.

Kemper, T. D. (1990). Themes and variations in the sociology of emotions. In T. D. Kemper (Ed.), *Research agendas in the sociology of emotion* (pp. 3–23). Albany: State University of New York Press.

Kring, A. M. (2001). Emotion and psychopathology. In T. J. Mayne & G. A. Bonanno (Eds.), *Emotions: Current issues and future directions* (pp. 337–360). New York: Guilford Press.

Kring, A. M., Smith, D. A., & Neale, J. M. (1994). Individual differences in dispositional expressiveness: Development and validation of the Emotional Expressivity Scale. *Journal of Personality and Social Psychology, 66,* 934–949.

Larsen, R. J., & Diener, E. (1987). Affect intensity as an individual difference characteristic: A review. *Journal of Research in Personality, 21,* 1–39.

Larsen, R. J., Diener, E., & Emmons, R. A. (1986). Affect intensity and reactions to daily life events. *Journal of Personality and Social Psychology, 51,* 803–814.

Leary, M. R., Britt, T. W., Cutlip, W. D., II, & Templeton, J. L. (1992). Social blushing. *Psychological Bulletin, 112,* 446–460.

Leary, M. R., & Meadows, S. (1991). Predictors, elicitors, and concomitants of social blushing. *Journal of Personality and Social Psychology, 60,* 254–262.

LeDoux, J. E., & Phelps, E. A. (2000). Emotional networks in the brain. In M. Lewis & J. M. Haviland-Lewis (Eds.), *Handbook of emotions* (2nd ed., pp. 157–172). New York: Guilford Press.

Levenson, R. W. (1992). Autonomic nervous system differences among emotions. *Psychological Science, 3,* 23–27.

Magai, C., & McFadden, S. H. (1995). *The role of emotions in social and personality development: History, theory, and research.* New York: Plenum.

Malatesta, C. Z., & Haviland, J. M. (1982). Learning display rules: The socialization of emotion expression in infancy. *Child Development, 53,* 991–1003.

Mesquita, B. (2001). Culture and emotion: Different approaches to the question. In T. J. Mayne & G. A. Bonanno (Eds.), *Emotions: Current issues and future directions* (pp. 214–250). New York: Guilford Press.

Mesquita, B., & Ellsworth, P. C. (2001). The role of culture in appraisal. In K. R. Scherer, A. Schorr, & T. Johnstone (Eds.), *Appraisal processes in emotion: Theory, methods, research* (pp. 233–248). New York: Oxford University Press.

Metalsky, G. I., Joiner, T. E., Hardin, T. S., & Abramson, L. Y. (1993). Depressive reactions to failure in a naturalistic setting: A test of the hopelessness and self-esteem theories of depression. *Journal of Abnormal Psychology, 102,* 101–109.

Miller, R. S. (1987). Empathic embarrassment: Situational and personal determinants of reactions to the embarrassment of another. *Journal of Personality and Social Psychology, 53,* 1061–1069.

Miller, R. S. (1995). On the nature of embarrassability: Shyness, social evaluation, and social skill. *Journal of Personality, 63,* 315–339.

Miller, R. S. (1996). *Embarrassment: Poise and peril in everyday life.* New York: Guilford Press.

Miller, R. S. (2001). Embarrassment and social phobia: Distant cousins or close kin? In S. G. Hofmann & P. M. DiBartolo (Eds.), *From social anxiety to social phobia: Multiple perspectives* (pp. 65–85). Boston: Allyn and Bacon.

Mischel, W. (1974). Processes in delay of gratification. In L. Berkowitz (Ed.), *Advances in experimental social psychology* (Vol. 7, pp. 249–292). New York: Academic Press.

Modigliani, A. (1968). Embarrassment and embarrassability. *Sociometry, 31,* 313–326.

Nisbett, R. E., & Cohen, D. (1996). *Culture of honor: The psychology of violence in the South*. Boulder, CO: Westview Press.

Noller, P. (1980). Misunderstandings in marital communication: A study of couples' nonverbal communication. *Journal of Personality and Social Psychology, 39,* 1135–1148.

Oatley, K. (1992). *Best laid schemes: The psychology of emotions*. Cambridge, UK: Cambridge University Press.

Oatley, K., & Jenkins, J. M. (1996). *Understanding emotions*. Cambridge, MA: Blackwell.

Parrott, W. G., & Smith, S. F. (1991). Embarrassment: Actual vs. typical cases, classical vs. prototypical representations. *Cognition and Emotion, 5,* 467–488.

Patrick, C. J. (1994). Emotion and psychopathy: Startling new insights. *Psychophysiology, 31,* 319–330.

Plomin, R., Emde, R. N., Braungart, J. M., Campos, J., Corley, R., Fulker, D. W. et al. (1993). Genetic change and continuity from fourteen to twenty months: The MacArthur Longitudinal Twin Study. *Child Development, 64,* 1354–1376.

Plutchik, R. (1980). *Emotion: A psychoevolutionary synthesis*. New York: Harper & Row.

Riggio, R. E. (1986). Assessment of basic social skills. *Journal of Personality and Social Psychology, 51,* 649–660.

Roseman, I. J., & Smith, C. A. (2001). Appraisal theory: Overview, assumptions, varieties, controversies. In K. R. Scherer, A. Schorr, & T. Johnstone (Eds.), *Appraisal processes in emotion: Theory, methods, research* (pp. 3–19). New York: Oxford University Press.

Roseman, I. J., Wiest, C., & Swartz, T. S. (1994). Phenomenology, behaviors, and goals differentiate discrete emotions. *Journal of Personality and Social Psychology, 67,* 206–221.

Rothbart, M. K., Ahadi, S. A., & Evans, D. E. (2000). Temperament and personality: Origins and outcomes. *Journal of Personality and Social Psychology, 78,* 122–135.

Rothbart, M. K., & Bates, J. E. (1998). Temperament. In W. Damon & N. Eisenberg (Eds.), *Handbook of child psychology* (5th ed., Vol. 5, pp. 105–176). New York: Wiley.

Saarni, C. (2000). The social context of emotional development. In M. Lewis & J. M. Haviland-Lewis (Eds.), *Handbook of emotions* (2nd ed., pp. 306–322). New York: Guilford Press.

Salovey, P., Hsee, C. K., & Mayer, J. D. (1993). Emotional intelligence and the self-regulation of affect. In D. M. Wegner & J. W. Pennebaker (Eds.), *Handbook of mental control* (pp. 258–277). Englewood Cliffs, NJ: Prentice Hall.

Salovey, P., Woolery, A., & Mayer, J. D. (2001). Emotional intelligence: Conceptualization and measurement. In G. J. O. Fletcher & M. S. Clark (Eds.), *Blackwell handbook of social psychology: Interpersonal processes* (pp. 279–307). Malden, MA: Blackwell.

Saudino, K. J., McGuire, S., Reiss, D., Hetherington, E. M., & Plomin, R. (1995). Parent ratings of EAS temperaments in twins, full siblings, half siblings, and step siblings. *Journal of Personality and Social Psychology, 68,* 723–733.

Scherer, K. R., & Wallbott, H. G. (1994). Evidence for universality and cultural variation of differential emotion response patterning. *Journal of Personality and Social Psychology, 66,* 310–328.

Shaver, P. R., Wu, S., & Schwartz, J. C. (1992). Cross-cultural similarities and differences in emotion and its representation. In M. Clark (Ed.), *Emotion* (pp. 175–212). Newbury Park, CA: Sage.

Shoda, Y., Mischel, W., & Peake, P. K. (1990). Predicting adolescent cognitive and self-regulatory competencies from preschool delay of gratification: Identifying diagnostic conditions. *Developmental Psychology, 26,* 978–986.

Shweder, R. A., & Haidt, J. (2000). The cultural psychology of the emotions: Ancient and new. In M. Lewis & J. M. Haviland-Lewis (Eds.), *Handbook of emotions* (2nd ed., pp. 397–414). New York: Guilford Press.

Simpson. J. A. (1990). Influence of attachment styles on romantic relationships. *Journal of Personality and Social Psychology, 59,* 971–980.

Stams, G. J. J. M., Juffer, F., & van Ijzendoorn, M. H. (2002). Maternal sensitivity, infant attachment, and temperament in early childhood predict adjustment in middle childhood: The case of adopted children and their biologically unrelated parents. *Developmental Psychology, 38,* 806–821.

Tooby, J., & Cosmides, L. (1990). On the universality of human nature and the uniqueness of the individual: The role of genetics and adaptation. *Journal of Personality, 58,* 17–67.

Watson, D., & Clark, L. A. (1994). Emotions, moods, traits, and temperaments: Conceptual distinctions and empirical findings. In P. Ekman & R. J. Davidson (Eds.), *The nature of emotion: Fundamental questions* (pp. 89–93). New York: Oxford University Press.

Yik, M. S. M., & Russell, J. A. (2001). Predicting the Big Two of Affect from the Big Five of per-sonality. *Journal of Research in Personality, 35,* 247–277.

Zawadzki, B., Strelau, J., Oniszcenko, W., Riemann, R., & Angleitner, A. (2001). Genetic and environ-mental influences on temperament. *European Psychologist, 6,* 272–286.

14 | Moral Character

NICHOLAS EMLER

CHAPTER OUTLINE

MORAL CHARACTER: THE FALL AND RISE OF A CONCEPT

One fundamental problem we all face in our relations with others is figuring out who we should get into bed with, both figuratively and literally. We need to form relationships with other people to achieve almost everything that may matter to us, whether raising a family, doing well in our jobs, pursuing a career in politics, or running a business. But which others? Common sense suggests we should try to avoid entanglements of any kind—whether business, romantic, recreational or political—with anyone who is morally suspect, which is to say anyone who might cheat, betray, exploit, or harm us. In consequence, it is wise to enquire about the moral character of potential partners in business, marriage, and other relationships, before commitments are made and costs are incurred. We are sometimes aware of being subject to this kind of scrutiny ourselves. Banks may ask us to give character witnesses; we may ask our teachers to provide us with character references to support the job applications we make; landlords and rental agencies may have asked our references for judgments on our reliability, honesty, and lack of criminal convictions before they will allow us to rent their property. Behind such inquiries—both those we make of others and those they make of us—lies the assumption that people do have moral qualities—virtues and vices—about which such inquiries can sensibly be made.

The people who make these inquiries, no less than the people who provide character references or indeed those about whom they are provided, might be somewhat surprised to learn that some psychologists have regarded these kinds of exercises as a complete waste of time. The use of character assessments in making decisions about employment, loans, or rentals is inappropriate, according to this view, but not because referees have conflicting interests and cannot be relied upon to give candid evaluations. Nor is the objection that it is inappropriate only because people cannot make these kinds of judgments very reliably. These would be reasonable objections to the practice if true and they may indeed be justified. But those psychologists came up with an altogether more serious difficulty: the concept of moral character has no foundation in fact. This concept implies, indeed requires, that people differ in the degree to which they possess moral virtue, and that these differences are both consistent across a range of circumstances and stable across time. If Joe can be trusted in this job, he can be trusted in others. If he can be trusted today he can also be trusted tomorrow, next week, and probably next year too. The objection is that this kind of consistency and stability in people's moral conduct simply does not exist. Joe may be honest and responsible today but dishonest and unreliable tomorrow. He may be a trustworthy and loyal employee in one job but untrustworthy and disloyal in another. How he behaves will depend entirely on the circumstances in which he finds himself at the time and not on any general inclination he has to be virtuous in everything he does.

This chapter explores the concept of moral character, considers some of its possible meanings and concludes that moral character does after all have some reality in people's behavior but that, as with so many disputes between incompatible alternatives, the truth lies somewhere between them. People are, to a significant degree, consistent from one occasion and situation to the next in the moral qualities they display; at the same time, their conduct and integrity are not immune to situational pressures. Consequently, valid assessments of individual differences in moral character are possible and they can serve as useful predictors, for example, of the relative integrity of different individuals in a particular job. At the same time there are limits to the predictability of people's moral conduct, while context and circumstances do also need to be taken into account.

The chapter will examine criticisms in psychology of the concept of moral character, tracing these first to assumptions about the nature of deviance and second to difficulties of measurement. We will then need to consider the relative advantages and limitations of different ways of assessing character. The second part of the chapter examines the evidence in favor of consistency of character and asks how this consistency can best be explained.

There is one further question we need to pose at this point, even if we cannot answer it immediately: How many different kinds of moral virtue are there? In their detailed study of adolescent character, Havighurst and Taba (1949) examined five virtues they believed were distinct from one another: honesty, responsibility, loyalty, courage, and friendliness. One can argue with their particular selection; is friendliness really a moral virtue, for example, and even if it is, is it a more consequential virtue than others not on the list—for example, generosity or fairmindedness? More recently there has been particular interest in the virtue of service to others and to the community (e.g., Aquino & Reed, 2002). For most of this chapter, in order to keep discussion within manageable limits I shall consider just one dimension of character—willingness to abide by rules and standards of social conduct. I take this to include the inclination to abide by those rules, which are often also laws, that proscribe conduct injurious to the person, property, rights, or dignity of others. Breaches of these rules have familiar labels—"assault," "theft," "vandalism," "persecution," "humiliation," "bullying." For the moment, this must serve as a working definition of moral character.

The Psychology of Moral Character—A Historical Introduction

The idea that *Homo sapiens* is preeminently a moral or rule-following animal has become almost a cliché in social science (cf. Wright, 1994). Human societies, so the argument goes, are viable only to the extent that the majority of their members abide by various rules or norms of social behavior most of the time—tell the truth, keep promises, do not betray trusts, return favors, respect the interests of others, defer to legitimate authorities within the group, and so on. Precisely what the standards should be, or how they should be interpreted in particular cases, are matters of endless debate in every known society. But it is also recognized that social rules and the standards of conduct they are intended to embody are not respected by everyone all the time. So the questions arise: Who breaks these rules, when, and why? To understand the answers that psychology itself has produced to these questions, we need to look at a little history, in particular, the history of society's views about crime.

From the late 18th to the late 19th century, theories of crime in Western culture were dominated by the ideas of Jeremy Bentham (1748–1842) and Cesare Beccaria (1738–1794). Both men believed that humans make decisions based on rational calculations of the personal costs and benefits of alternative lines of action. They further assumed that people must be naturally inclined to break rules if the activities these rules forbid are inherently attractive and rewarding. This inclination will be inhibited only if the anticipated costs outweigh the rewards of transgression.

During the 19th century, rates of crime and civil disorder were seen to increase rapidly in the new industrial cities of Europe and America. Social theorists initially made sense of these increases by arguing that the industrial revolution that created these new cities had also swept away the kind of society in which punishment for crime was more certain. This was supposedly a society of small-scale communities in which everyone knew everyone else's business; it was much more difficult under these conditions to break any of the rules without being found out and punished. Within the new industrial cities, by contrast, the conditions of daily life were much more impersonal and anonymous. These conditions made crime a rational choice. They provided more opportunities than ever before to break the rules covertly and secretly, and to remain undetected and unpunished.

There was, however, a flaw in this neat analysis. It required far more lawlessness than was actually the case. The entire population was not after all running riot, committing mayhem, or indulging their lusts while the backs of their neighbors or their rulers were turned. Many people seemed to be keeping to the rules even when transgression could not possibly be detected—in other words, when it would seem to be irrational to do so. The obvious conclusion, to which Sigmund Freud and many others came at the time, was that in matters relating to moral standards, conduct is not under rational control. Furthermore, because no external threat or inducement could be permanently present in the anonymity of city life to discourage these people from the gratifications of misbehavior, purely internal control must be both commonplace and frequently effective. And this internal control must be immune to or independent of reason.

Freud (1930) argued that a mechanism of internal control is created as part of the individual personality during childhood; he called this mechanism the superego. His argument about superego formation is now largely of historical interest. It has been superseded by other theories of moral development, variously emphasizing the methods of discipline and control employed by parents (Hoffman, 1988), processes of conditioning or of imitative learning (Bandura, 1991), or the consequences of cognitive development (Kohlberg, 1984). Textbooks in developmental psychology will describe these theories and discuss their differences. What they may not do is draw any attention to their very considerable similarities. Yet almost all theories, whether neo-analytic, cognitive-social learning or cognitive developmental, accept that moral development is a process in which controls over conduct are internalized and become autonomous. And almost all imply the process is generally successful; only quite abnormal adults lack internal controls and only these pathological individuals consistently violate moral standards.

Social psychological research on deviance seemed, however, to point to quite different conclusions. While developmental theories were predicting that most adults will be well socialized and therefore virtuous, social psychologists set about demonstrating just how fragile and situation-contingent their good behavior can be. Moreover, a common thread runs through this line of argument down to the present day: Individuals will abandon standards of civilized behavior when they find themselves in groups or crowds.

This idea was first promoted by Gustav Le Bon (1895/1947) as an explanation for the civil disorder that afflicted industrial France in the 1800s. He attributed the destructive behavior of mobs to a kind of hypnosis that crowds produce in their members. This and many similar arguments remained, nonetheless, largely speculative interpretations until the 1950s and 1960s. During this period a succession of experiments dramatically demonstrated how readily individuals, when gathered together in groups, can be induced to deny, by word (Asch, 1956) or deed (Milgram, 1964), what is true or good or decent or humane. These studies confirmed, moreover, the powerful influence of the situation on conduct. Circumstances rather than individual character, it seemed, determine behavior. Finally, some social psychologists argued that the presence of a group has this "immoralizing" effect on conduct because it actually increases the individual's feelings of anonymity (e.g., Zimbardo, 1970). In effect, the group, in experimental social psychology, became a metaphor for the city with its impersonal and anonymous quality of life.

Rule Breaking: The Reality of Individual Differences

The thesis of this chapter is that orientation to rules for moral conduct is a personality characteristic; individuals differ in the degree to which they are inclined to uphold or to violate these standards. These differences are generalized in the sense that this disposition applies to moral rules as a broad category, and not just to a limited set of rules. These differences are also quite stable. An implication of this thesis is that criminality is not some special or pathological characteristic but that it is continuous with more moderate levels of rule breaking; it is simply toward the extreme of the continuum and crime is only rare or unusual in the way that very high or low levels of intelligence are rare or unusual.

Many psychologists believe that the idea of moral character has been so thoroughly discredited that it barely deserves discussion. For example, writing in 1976, Walter Mischel concluded: "The data on self-control and moral behavior do not support the existence of a unitary, intrapsychic moral agency like the superego nor do they support a unitary trait of conscience or honesty" (p. 461). This view continues to find strong support (e.g., Doris, 2002; Lapsley, 1996). Mischel's argument, it should be noted, was aimed at a much larger target than the concept of moral character: He was attacking the very enterprise of personality description as traditionally conceived. But by far the strongest evidence for his general case does concern moral character, and it is to the practicalities of assessing character that we now turn.

There have been four principal solutions to the problem of measuring moral character: experimental tests of character, the recorded judgments of law courts, self-reports, and reputational evidence.

Experimental Tests   From the outset, psychologists were attracted by the idea of submitting people to tests of character under the scientifically controlled conditions of the laboratory. But there was a difficulty. Psychologists' theories of deviance told them that the true test of character is to resist temptations and uphold moral standards when there is no external inducement to do so, no possibility of transgression being detected, no sanction if one succumbs, and no reward when one does resist. Of course, not only psychologists have assumed this; it is part of our folklore; our heroes are authentically heroic only as long as their identities remain concealed and thus their motivations impeccably unselfish. Consequently, the fictional prototypes—Zorro, Batman, the Lone Ranger—must wear masks while they go about the business of doing good. But how do you observe the unobservable, or detect the undetectable?

Hartshorne and May (1928), as part of their study of childhood character education, solved the problem of measuring moral character in the following way. They realized it was necessary only to create a convincing illusion for the children being studied that they could transgress without being detected. Children would be tempted to cheat on classroom tests of intelligence, numerical ability, or physical capacity. In every case the individual child under assessment was given the impression that he or she could cheat and get away with it. Thus if any child did not cheat it could only be because he or she had been restrained by internal controls and not out of any concern to secure social approval or to avoid criticism. In fact, of course, the experimenters were able to detect cheating by various ingenious tricks. For example, they ensured that the task could not be solved by honest means or that performance beyond a certain level was highly improbable without cheating, or they surreptitiously recorded true performance levels to check on dishonest reporting of performance.

Their conclusions were surprising to say the least. Children's moral behavior was highly inconsistent. It was seldom the same child who cheated the most on different tests, and seldom the same child who was most honest. Furthermore, the average amount of cheating varied considerably from one test to another; cheating was a function of the situation. Precisely this kind of evidence is what Mischel (1976) and others found so compelling. It seemed to justify the social psychologist's preference for situational explanations of deviance, and by the same token it seemed to rule out explanations of moral behavior in terms of a stable trait of character.

It is unlikely that Hartshorne's evidence can support the conclusions customarily derived from it, for at least five reasons. The first is that the behaviors sampled by the various tests represent rather trivial transgressions, if they can be regarded as immoral at all (cf. Turiel, 1983). They hardly belong in the same league as assaults causing bodily harm, thefts of valuable property, or destructive vandalism. And what is true of trivialities need not be true of more serious transgressions.

A second, related and perhaps more significant point concerns the moral ambiguity of experimentally induced transgressions. The methodology itself places the experimenter in a dilemma. To create conditions under which more serious offences could occur would constitute a form of contributory negligence. In practice, when serious matters are at stake, obstructions are put in the way of rule breaking—precautions to reduce opportunities for transgression. For a person in a position of responsibility to fail to take such precautions would be regarded as both foolish and a little bizarre. The absence of even the most elementary precautions in Hartshorne and May's tasks must therefore tell the children who take them that the experimenter is either foolish or, more likely, does not regard these as serious matters.

A third reason to question Hartshorne and May's conclusions in particular is that the steps necessary to construct an adequate measure of individual differences in honesty were not taken. When others say that Hartshorne and May's data indicate the inconsistency of conduct, what they usually have in mind are the positive but very modest correlations between honesty in one test and honesty in another, an average correlation over all the tests of a little over 0.2. No psychological attribute can be accurately assessed on the basis of a single sample of behavior. At the very least, measures need to be based on the combination or "aggregation" of a number of separate relevant observations. The point is simple but fundamental. Any single act is an imperfect measure of a general trait. Performance of the act may be influenced by the strength of the trait of interest—for example, honesty—but also potentially by a host of other factors that have nothing to do with this trait. The influence of these other factors represents error in measurement at least as far as the act is of interest as a measure of the trait; they are what cause this single act to be an imperfect indicator of the trait. However, if the occurrence of a number of different actions is observed, each of which reflects, albeit imperfectly, the relevant trait, and if at the same time each of these acts is not influenced in the same way by any other factor, then by combining or aggregating these observations, the imperfections of each will to some degree cancel one another out (see chapter 6 of Judd, Smith, & Kidder, 1991). The larger the number of relevant observations combined in this way, the more the effects of error on estimates of the trait in question are reduced.

We have learned that the individual items that together make up a test of, for example, intelligence will not necessarily correlate very highly with any other single item in the test but that the test as a whole can still provide valid and reliable assessments. The low correlations in Hartshorne and May's data are not by themselves evidence against the existence of a general trait of honesty. The crucial test is whether a number of observations, when combined, meet the requirements of a unidimensional scale. Whether these requirements are met can be tested by various forms of factor analysis, and indeed, Burton (1963) was able to show that such a trait could be identified in the Hartshorne and May data. However, the more serious obstacles to the use of experimental tests of character are practical; assessment based on multiple samples of behavior is cumbersome and expensive and researchers seldom have the resources required to undertake them.

However, there is a fourth reason to suspect that Hartshorne and May's study does not provide a good test of the hypothesis that there are individual differences in rule breaking: The concept of moral character, which underlies their tests, may itself be inappropriate. Like many others before and since, these researchers conceived character as private and covert conformity to rules—for example, continuing to work conscientiously even when you are alone and no one could possibly know if you were not working. Consequently their tests were situations confronting a single child with an opportunity to break the rules without being observed. I shall argue later that conformity to social rules per se, whether in private or in public, is the more relevant test of character: Do you, for example, work conscientiously at all, whether anyone else is watching you?

Finally, there is no logical or empirical relation between the truth of the claim that conduct is subject to situational influences and the truth of the claim that conduct varies consistently across individuals. Moreover, the requirements for testing one claim are quite different from those for testing the other (the third point above describes the requirements for testing claims about individual differences in conduct). In effect the person versus situation debate, in the context of moral conduct and more generally, has been based on a false choice (for further discussion of this, see Epstein & O'Brien, 1985; Kenrick & Funder, 1988).

Official Records   One solution to the danger of over-sampling trivial misconduct might be to use the records that are kept of certain kinds of rule breaking and rule breakers, such as the criminal records kept by the criminal justice system. They have been used widely in psychological research, sometimes directly by counting criminal convictions and sometimes indirectly by comparing incarcerated convicted offenders a with unincarcerated individuals at large who are in principle more innocent of illegal or immoral conduct. But criminal convictions have other problems that significantly limit their usefulness as evidence of moral character.

One is that crimes are relatively uncommon and certainly uncommon enough for most people not to have any criminal convictions (though British government statistics indicate that almost one third of 30-year-old males have at least one conviction [see Smith, 1995]. Rates in the United States are if anything even higher). Using officially recorded convictions as a measure of rule breaking would therefore result in a highly skewed distribution of people with scores of zero predominating. This would be quite acceptable if the world really is divided into a small minority (criminals) who routinely break the rules when they get a chance, and a large majority who never do so. As we shall see, however, this is not an accurate description of reality.

Another difficulty is that many things intervene between committing a criminal transgression and being convicted for it, of which detection of the crime is only one. The crime must be reported; the police must decide to take action, and they must then catch the culprit and seek a prosecution; prosecutors must decide to take the case to court; juries must be convinced of the culprit's guilt and judges must deliver a sentence. Convictions represent a small proportion of all the acts that would formally qualify as crimes, and they are likely to be in various ways a biased selection (see Box, 1981, pp. 157–202), albeit toward seriousness and the apparent risk posed by the offender. The common research practice of comparing people who are officially of good character—they are not currently imprisoned for any offence (the careful researcher also checks that they have no *previous* criminal record either)—with those who are currently in prison exacerbates the problem. Incarceration is likely to have psychological effects of its own, quite apart from any psychological peculiarities that may have produced the criminal activity in the first place.

Perhaps the most reasonable view is that criminal conviction represents the extreme of a continuum. As such it can be a useful source of information about rule breaking and rule breakers in general but one to be used with caution and always checked against evidence from other sources.

Reputational Measures   If you want to know about a person's moral character, why not ask some of the people who know this individual? One might regard this as the obvious solution; it is in effect what requests for character references do and it is precisely what reputational measures involve. Parents, teachers, peers, or employers might be asked to rate the individual concerned, either for qualities of character (punctuality, reliability, courage, generosity, and so on) or for the occurrence of specified behaviors (how often this person arrives late for work, gets into fights, does work for charity, etc.).

Despite its simplicity, this solution became unfashionable in psychology for a variety of reasons. First, if the natural reflex of sinners is concealment, there will necessarily be much misconduct about which observers could not know. Second, if Hartshorne and May were correct, there could be no stable core to character that people could make ratings of. This objection appeared more plausible when research in person perception revealed that people can be very unreliable judges of others' character, prone to imagine more consistency than actually exists, and liable to make the world fit their own implicit models of personality (e.g., Cronbach, 1955; Shweder, 1982). Thus, if the method suggested individual differences in character, this was merely an illusion in the minds of perceivers.

It now appears that these criticisms were overstated. When ratings are provided by people who are well acquainted with their targets and when ratings are aggregated from different sources, some of the inaccuracies can be overcome (Cheek, 1982; Funder, 1999; Kenrick & Funder, 1988), and observer ratings specifically of moral conduct or character have been used in some studies (Gold, 1970; Havigthurst & Taba, 1949). Moreover, the fact that reputational measures work at all for assessments of moral qualities tells us something important about the nature of moral conduct.

Self-Reports   Self-reporting relies on people's reporting on their own degree of conformity or nonconformity to a variety of moral standards. If you want to know what rules people have broken and how often, you simply ask them (and in principle you could do the same to assess their generosity, as Rushton, Chrisjohn, and Fekken [1981] have done, though you might perhaps expect people to be forthcoming about their generosity in a way that they would not about their mendacity). But if there are individual differences in rule breaking, do self-reports of behavior represent a good way of measuring them?

Short and Nye (1957) are credited with the first systematic use of this approach to assess conduct. Their inventory included questions about 23 different kinds of misbehavior, including minor crimes, acts of disobedience, and breaches of regulations. Since then self-report measures have become widely used in sociological research, initially to answer questions about the extent of unrecorded crime, but in the longer run as a way of assessing individual deviance (Huizinga & Elliot, 1986). The advantages are obvious. Large numbers of different kinds of conduct can be sampled economically, and the sample need not be limited to trivial misbehavior.

In psychology the method has been far less popular. Objections to its use have included the claim that people cannot be expected to report honestly, accurately, or objectively on their own rule breaking. Quite apart from the natural tendency to conceal one's sins, so the argument might run, there will be serious distortions arising from the sheer fallibility of human memory, distortions quite possibly compounded by defensive needs.

The short answer to this and other objections is that scales based on self-reports of rule violation appear to be able to provide valid and highly reliable measures of actual degree of misconduct. Reliability coefficients between .88 and .96 are common (Singh, 1979); these are high values by the standards of psychological measurement generally. There are also several indications of the validity of self-reports. Incarcerated young offenders obtain much higher scores than their peers who are still at liberty (Emler, Heather, & Winton, 1978). This is admittedly a rather crude test of validity. More direct validation is possible by checking acts that have resulted in convictions against self-reports of these same actions, as in a study by Gibson, Morrison, and West (1970). Another test has been to include direct questions about police contacts and convictions in the self-report. Each of these is vulnerable to the same criticism, however: A person might be expected to be candid about matters that can be checked in official records anyway, while continuing to deny any misdemeanors that have so far remained undetected. To overcome this objection, Gold (1970) attempted to corroborate self-report claims with evidence from respondents' acquaintances. The results were largely comparable. Finally, there is evidence of predictive validity: Self-reports of antisocial behavior predict future convictions (Farrington, 1989).

DISCOVERING AND ACCOUNTING FOR MORAL CHARACTER

Now that we have considered the relative merits of different forms of measurement, what does their use reveal about the basic question—namely, do people differ in moral character in a consistent and coherent way? This section of the chapter examines this and a further question: To the extent that there are such differences, how can we account for them? To answer these questions I will draw on the results of our own research into moral conduct (Emler & Reicher, 1995).

This research has focused on just one period of life: adolescence. There are many indications that adolescents are more likely than any other age group to break social rules. This has led to the speculation that bad character may just be a passing phase in most cases (cf. Moffitt, 1993), a further question for us to consider. Our research program has relied extensively on self-report evidence of conduct as an efficient, cost-effective basis for testing hypotheses about conduct and character. At every point, therefore, it is proper to ask whether findings from this kind of evidence converge with those from other reliable sources.

The Consistency of Conduct

One kind of consistency is generalization: How generalized is the tendency to break or respect rules? Do people who break one kind of rule break other kinds, and conversely, are the people who respect one kind of rule also those most likely to respect other kinds of rule? Hartshorne and May's (1928) answer, as we saw, was no; even in the specific case of cheating, different forms were unrelated to one another. But if appropriate item-selection criteria are applied, responses in different tests are combined so that measures are based on several items, and these measures are then submitted to factor analysis, as Burton (1963) did with the original Hartshorne data, consistency does emerge. Burton found a general factor underlying different measures of honesty that accounted for between 35% and 43% of the variance in test scores.

Our own approach has been to use self-report inventories sampling a large number of different kinds of rule breaking and then to examine relations between admissions of these different kinds. In one study we asked 214 boys, 15 to 17 years of age, about 38 different kinds of misbehavior. We found one general factor accounting for just over 33% of the total variance in responses. In a study of 440 boys and girls, 12 to 15 years of age, a general factor accounted for 31% of variance in responses (Emler & Reicher, 1995).

In a more intensive study of a smaller group ($N = 40$) of 14- to 15-year old-boys we asked in more detail about a larger range of misbehaviors, 68 in all (Emler, Reicher & Ross, 1987). This procedure allowed us to create scales for different categories of misbehavior and then to examine the relationship between these categories. For example, an aggression scale assessed preparedness for and involvement in different forms of violence (e.g., carrying a weapon such as a knife, attacking an enemy, getting into a fight at a sporting event, assaulting a teacher). A vandalism scale assessed activities involving damage to public and private property (e.g., writing on walls with spray paint, smashing windows of empty houses, deliberate littering). Table 14.1 describes the correlations between the scales formed in this way. The relationships are uniformly positive and in most cases strong, suggesting that one form of rule breaking is consistently related to others.

If self-report and experimental evidence converge, what about evidence from official records? Klein (1984) was able to confirm that young people do not show any tendency toward specialization in one particular form of rule breaking—in effect, being of good character in all respects but one. If they have convictions or recorded police contacts for one kind of offense, they tend to

Table 14.1 | Intercorrelations Among Different Forms of
Rule Breaking and Antisocial Behavior

	Aggression	Vandalism	Status	Minor/Nuisance	Drugs
Theft (8 items)	.75***	.77***	.76***	.46***	.48***
Aggression (13 items)		.83***	.66***	.47***	.41**
Vandalism (9 items)			.56***	.52***	.43**
Status offenses (8 items)				.18*	.17
Minor/Nuisance (10 items)					.36*
Drug use (8 items)					

$N = 40$ (boys, ages 14 to 15)

Status offenses = behavior forbidden only by virtue of a person's age, such as drinking alcohol in bars or driving a motor vehicle on a public road.

*$p < .05$

**$p < .01$

***$p < .001$

Source: From "The Social Context of Delinquent Conduct," by N. Emler, S. Reicher, and A. Ross, 1987, *Journal of Clinical Psychology and Psychiatry, 28*, p. 102. Reprinted with permission of the publisher.

have records for others. It seems that there is one general dimension to which most of the common forms of rule breaking are related (see also Gottfredson & Hirschi, 1990).

The self-report evidence helps to clarify certain other questions about this dimension, in particular the types of rule violation that are especially representative of the dimension and those that are less representative. Most representative are various forms of theft, from both individual victims and businesses; attacking other people and using weapons in fights; and damaging both public and private property. Rather less representative for adolescents are smoking, gambling, drinking, using illegal drugs, violating traffic regulations, and staying away from school without permission. This dimension, therefore, is defined most strongly by rule breaking that has victims—both individual and corporate—than by rule breaking that does not. This provides some support for a distinction made by Turiel (e.g., Turiel, 1983; Turiel, Killen, & Helwig, 1987) between moral and conventional transgressions. The former category is defined by the presence of a victim whose welfare or rights are damaged by the transgression; conventional transgressions are transgressions primarily because they violate an arbitrary custom or regulation. Regulations concerning gambling, school attendance, or the legal age for drinking, smoking, and driving a motor vehicle are closer to Turiel's category of conventional rules. The self-report evidence suggests that there is a behavioral dimension defined primarily by willingness to violate *moral* as opposed to other kinds of social rule. However, Turiel's moral/conventional distinction is correlated with seriousness, and this behavioral dimension is also defined by relatively more serious forms of misbehavior, activities normally regarded and treated as criminal offenses. This underlines the point made earlier about the problem of reliance on measures of trivial transgressions in experimental tests of character. Finally, as official records would lead one to expect, but contrary to Freud's (1955) prediction about the more exacting consciences of men, males are more likely to have "bad character" in this sense than females (see also Moffitt et al., 2001).

The other common meaning of behavioral consistency is stability across time. There is a difficulty and an apparent contradiction in the evidence here. Both self-reports and official records indicate that serious rule breaking of the kind we are talking about rises to a peak when youths are about 14 or 15 years of age, levels off, and then gradually declines toward the end of adolescence. So does this mean that moral conduct is not stable across time? The answer would seem to be no in the sense that the disposition to break or respect rules, *relative to others of the same age*, is quite stable. Those most likely to break rules at 11 or 12 are generally those most likely to do so at 14 or 15, and these in turn are most likely to do so at 17 or 18. Therefore, although absolute levels of rule breaking do change with age, rule breaking at different ages will be correlated. Among 12- to 16-year-olds we found correlations in the range 0.42 to 0.84 between self-reports over an 18-month period (Emler & Reicher, 1995). Others have found similar degrees of stability over even longer periods. Farrington (1991) provides some particularly impressive evidence on this point for the stability of a trait he calls antisocial personality and which has close similarities to the present concept of moral character.

There is one other body of evidence relevant to the behavioral consistency issue. It concerns the basic dimensions of personality. Of the five basic and broad dimensions along which, in the view of many researchers, human personality varies—the so-called Big Five (Digman, 1990; Goldberg, 1990)—two, Conscientiousness and Agreeableness, appear to include more specifically moral traits. And the implication is that there are therefore two broad dimensions to moral character, two distinct clusters of moral traits. The conscientiousness cluster includes such traits as reliability and responsibility; the agreeableness cluster includes the traits of kindness, compassion, generosity, and sympathy (McCrae & John, 1992). These clusters emerge from both self-ratings and peer ratings of personality, lending further support to the conclusion that there are stable and generalized traits of character. We have been able to confirm this two-factor solution with respect to the clustering of moral traits in peer-rating studies (e.g., Pedersen, 1996), though it was also interesting to discover that some traits, notably honesty, clustered with neither factor. There is, however, a difference between the research on basic personality dimensions and that on moral conduct. Self- and peer-rating studies of personality typically involve the use of scales at rather general descriptive levels compared to the specific behaviors that are probed by self-report and observer-rating studies of delinquency and antisocial behavior. Further research would be desirable here to compare the results of these different methods. A useful step in this direction is provided by the Krueger, Hicks, and McGue (2001) study comparing results from self-report measures of delinquency and altruism, respectively. They found these two dimensions of conduct to be unrelated, and their independence was further underlined by quite distinct patterns of association with other variables.

To sum up our examination of consistency in character, each of the general views of deviance we considered earlier can now be seen to have overstated its respective case. First, if moral character is a product of childhood socialization, then that socialization does not always work perfectly and criminal misconduct is not confined to a tiny, abnormal minority. Rather, rule breaking is commonplace, and serious crime is perhaps only the extreme of a distribution whose middle range is represented by moderate degrees of rule breaking. A very small minority of the population has committed robbery with violence, whereas many and perhaps the majority have breached the rules in less serious ways at some time or other, and a proportion somewhere in between these extremes of rule breaking have committed minor thefts, assaulted other people, or deliberately damaged others' property.

The implication is that we may not need one kind of explanation for the moral conduct of most people and quite another for the criminal conduct of the few, any more than we need different kinds of explanations for normal and exceptional intelligence, for they are not categorically different. Finally, conduct is not, as some social psychologists have argued, entirely a function of the situation. In situations in which rules sometimes get broken, the same people tend to break them.

Explaining Individual Differences in Character: How Well Do Existing Theories Do?

What can explain this consistency? Many explanations for individual differences in moral conduct attribute bad conduct to some psychological deficit in the individual. Candidates for the identity of the crucial deficit have included weaknesses in superego strength, in capacity to experience guilt, in empathic ability, in self-esteem, in social skills, and in intelligence. In this section I consider two popular explanations that also invoke psychological deficits to explain immoral conduct: Eysenck's (1977) theory of criminality (cf. Hampson, 1988) and Kohlberg's theory of moral development (cf. Smetana, 1990).

Neurotic Extraverts   Eysenck's (1977) theory ingeniously integrates learning processes with genetic factors. Eysenck argues that adult conduct is normally controlled by an internal mechanism based on conditioned anxiety. Anxiety responses to certain stimuli (temptations) are acquired in childhood by a process of Pavlovian or classical conditioning. A small boy is about to draw with his crayon on the living room wall when his mother shouts angrily at him; he steps back in alarm. If she does this often enough in the same circumstances he will automatically begin to flinch every time he approaches a wall with a writing implement.

Conditioned responses of this kind, however, are not equally strong in every individual. And those in whom they are weakest are the ones most likely to act antisocially. The relative strength or weakness of these responses will depend on two things: the extent to which parents provided the appropriate socializing experiences and the extent to which the child is constitutionally conditionable. Eysenck regarded the latter, genetically determined factor as the more significant source of individual differences. This quality of conditionability is reflected in two features of personality: extraversion-introversion and neuroticism-stability. Neurotic extraverts are the least conditionable and so the most prone to antisocial behavior.

The most popular way of testing this hypothesis has been to compare the personalities of incarcerated offenders with those of controls. Support for the hypothesis from such research has been mixed at best (Emler, 1984; Hampson, 1988). Given the problems of interpretation raised by these kinds of comparisons, self-report measures of antisocial behavior should provide a better test. Here the results have been more conclusively negative. In very few studies is a strong relationship reported between antisocial behavior and neuroticism. Extraversion emerges as a significant correlate of misbehavior in some samples of older (late adolescent or young adult) males but in few of younger males and virtually none of the female samples. Our own research confirms this picture (Emler, Reicher, & Ross, 1987).

One other dimension of personality identified by Eysenck is very consistently and strongly related to antisocial and delinquent behavior, both as assessed by self-reports and as indexed by criminal convictions or incarceration (Emler, 1984). This dimension is Psychoticism (Eysenck & Eysenck, 1976). There is some argument, however, as to whether Psychoticism as defined and assessed by Eysenck's own procedures reflects one personality factor or two. Costa and McRae (1995) argue that Psychoticism is primarily a combination of elements of the "Big Five" Conscientiousness and Agreeableness factors. Does this mean that the antisocial, rule-breaking pattern identified in this chapter as the negative pole of a dimension of moral character is in fact the product of a combination of low Agreeableness and low Conscientiousness? It is an interesting possibility. But, as already noted above, the nature of the association between moral conduct and such personality factors, whether assessed by self-ratings or peer ratings, still awaits systematic exploration. We should also be aware that a two-factor interpretation of Eysenck's Psychoticism scale takes us only a little further in the direction of an *explanation* for moral character. As Gottfredson and Hirschi (1990) point out, personality-based explanations for criminality are often only re-descriptions of the behavioral phenomenon.

Deficient Moral Insight   In a highly influential theory, Lawrence Kohlberg (1984) proposed that moral development is much like the development of intelligence. Acting morally means finding solutions to problems in which obligations or interests conflict. Not only are some moral problems more complex and difficult to resolve than others but also the solutions we come up with can be more or less satisfactory. As we develop we construct successively more adequate strategies for solving these problems. Kohlberg argued that this development can best be described as a sequence of steps or stages. Each new stage involves a new moral theory, a new way of reasoning about problems and choosing between competing demands and interests. The first stage is rather simple, inadequate for coping with most moral problems, and it provides very imperfect solutions. The second is a little more complex and it overcomes some of the limitations of the first but it still has many shortcomings. So we go on to construct a third and then a fourth and so on. Kohlberg proposed that there are potentially six stages of this kind, each a more complex and adequate moral theory than the one it replaces.

The number of stages is only a potential because hardly anyone progresses all the way to the sixth stage. Indeed, most adults in Western society appear to have come to a halt after only four or even three (Snarey, 1985). Moreover, just as intelligence develops at different rates in different individuals, so people move through this sequence more or less rapidly. How might this help explain differences in moral character?

Kohlberg himself had little time for the idea of moral character, agreeing with Hartshorne and May that you cannot divide the world into honest and dishonest people. Nonetheless, he also assumed that there would be a connection between stage of moral reasoning and conduct: Higher stages produce better moral decisions, so we should expect better behavior of people who have achieved such stages than of those who have not. In addition, Kohlberg anticipated that the reasoning–action association would become progressively more consistent at each successive stage of development and additionally that the impact of reasoning on action would be mediated by "ego controls." These included such variables as attentional stability or "will" and intelligence.

There is an intuitive appeal to the idea that an individual who lacks insight into the nature of moral obligations will be more likely to violate rules of conduct than someone who grasps the obligations those rules reflect. The theory also suggests an explanation for the age pattern of rule breaking as follows. A considerable degree of external control is still in place for children at the start of adolescence; they are extensively supervised by parents, teachers, and other adults. Well-developed internal control is not yet much needed and its absence has few serious consequences. But as the years pass the external controls slacken. If moral insight develops at different rates in different individuals it may have reached only an early stage in some young people when they are beginning to experience less external control. Are adolescent rule breakers therefore individuals temporarily inhabiting a gap between external controls and internal controls, after the police have departed but before a fully developed conscience has arrived?

Unfortunately, there is as yet no convincing evidence to support this explanation. Most researchers have compared the moral reasoning levels of criminal offenders with nonoffenders of the same age, or they have used some similar criterion such as institutional placement, psychiatric diagnosis, or counseling staff classification. Jennings, Kilkenny, and Kohlberg (1983) reviewed the results from several studies in which this comparison had been made and all showed the predicted negative relation between moral reasoning and these measures of character. More recently, Smetana (1990) identified 35 tests of the relation between moral reasoning and antisocial conduct. Again the great majority revealed the predicted negative association. However, this is less impressive than it seems. The correlations in these studies are never strong (though better behavioral prediction might have been achieved if ego-control measures had also been included, as Kohlberg recommended). But more important, they are potentially contaminated by effects of the formal and public labeling represented by the measures used of conduct or character. On the one hand, young people who have difficulty articulating sophisticated moral arguments may be at greater risk of being negatively labeled by those in authority. On the other, such labeling can form part of a response, such as incarceration, which disrupts their education and consequently their development of moral reasoning powers. And the label itself can become a self-fulfilling prophecy, amplifying any inclination to break rules (Kituse, 1980).

When we compared the moral reasoning of incarcerated adolescent male offenders and controls (Emler, Heather, & Winton, 1978) we found the relationship that Smetana reports; the incarcerated group had lower moral reasoning scores. But when we looked directly at self-reports of delinquency, we found no link with moral reasoning level, either within or between the groups. The absence of any relationship between moral reasoning and self-reported delinquency has been confirmed more recently in a much larger study with more appropriate measures of the independent variable and better controls (Tarry, 2001; see also Aleixo & Norris, 2000).

The Visibility of Conduct and the Nature of Society

Both Eysenck and Kohlberg, though in very different ways, explain variations in conduct in terms of the strength of internal controls. Both therefore accept an assumption deeply rooted in moral psychology that external constraints are insufficient to account for good conduct. The assumption rests on the twin assumptions that (1) rule breaking normally occurs under conditions of anonymity, and (2) such anonymity is readily and widely available in contemporary society. I shall argue that neither of these assumptions is justified.

Conduct, both good and bad, is typically visible and the actor is identifiable. One indication of this is that many forms of transgression are by definition unconcealed, at least from the victim—for example, bullying and other acts of direct aggression. A second indication is that reputational measures of conduct work and they can do so only because people can be identified as the authors of their actions by observers, particularly acquainted observers. A third is that self-reports also work; concealment is apparently not the natural reflex of sinners for they are at least willing to make researchers privy to their past misconduct.

There is, however, a more fundamental reason that most conduct is public knowledge, that observer ratings have some validity, and that it is difficult to conceal deviance. It is that the anonymous society is largely a myth. Despite the tremendous changes brought on by industrialization and mass urbanization, the vast majority of us continue to live in worlds populated by people who know us. Whether we live in small villages or cities, most of the significant business of our lives is conducted with and in the presence of acquaintances, not strangers (Fischer, 1982; Emler, 2000). Furthermore, because so many of the people we know and mix with also know and mix with one another, there is very little of any significance that we do, good or bad, that is not likely to become public knowledge among our acquaintances. This suggests a straightforward explanation for rule following: Good character has social guarantees. People behave well, not just to the degree that they are personally and privately committed to standards they have internalized but because they wish to preserve their good name in the social worlds they inhabit. Why then does anyone still break the rules (see Activity Box 14.1)?

One possibility is that the conditions that make our conduct visible to others are matters of degree. Some people may be socially reclusive by temperament or alternatively socially isolated by circumstances, perhaps because they are homeless or not in full-time education or regular employment, or because they have moved to a new neighborhood or because the neighborhood has a highly transient population. This cannot be the whole story, however. It has now been convincingly and extensively documented that rule breakers are no less likely to have friends or regular social contacts than anyone else (Emler & Reicher, 1995; Giordano, Cernovich, & Pugh, 1986).

Is it possible that immunity to social control is subjective rather than objective, in that rule breakers chronically miscalculate the visibility of their conduct or the damage it will do to their reputations? Or do they instead simply lack the skills needed to construct a good name for themselves? Our own research and other studies so far provide little support for either possibility. The views of chronic rule breakers may differ from those of more conforming peers on some points of detail, but they largely agree about the implications of rule breaking for reputation. And there has still to be an unequivocal demonstration that rule breakers lack any of the skills or insights rule followers possess.

Finally, far from being unaware that their misdeeds will be noticed, we have found that delinquent adolescents actually prefer audiences to witness their accomplishments. We are forced to contemplate the possibility that a reputation for bad behavior is to some degree a deliberate choice on the part of the individual concerned while remaining open to the additional possibility that lack of skill in constructing a good reputation could favor this choice.

THOUGHTS ON PINNING DOWN EXPLANATIONS

It seems we are little closer to explaining moral character. Many promising hypotheses have had to be ruled out or placed for the present in the "not proven" category, but this is no reason for pessimism. We have actually made quite a lot of progress, as should be clear if we briefly take stock. We know that there is a consistent core to character and that it is most directly defined by the way an individual behaves in relation to rules about respecting the person and property of others. Serious violations of these rules are rare but less serious breaches are commonplace. They are also unconcealed. We know that the people in society most likely to break these rules are adolescent boys, and that those who so do are not ignorant of the consequences for their public reputations. The question that remains is why people choose to pursue different kinds of reputations.

In this section I shall sketch out a preliminary answer. It begins with the observation that social life involves extensive regulation of our affairs by various

Activity Box 14.1   Deviance and Attitudes Toward Authority: Self-Concept and Reputation

There is hardly anyone who has never broken a rule and hardly anyone who believes that authorities are perfect in every respect. Both, like so much else in life, are matters of degree. Where do you think you stand on these dimensions? Do you believe that on balance you are more law abiding or honest than most people of your acquaintance, or less? And do you think that your views about authority are more positive or more critical and negative than those of most people you know? Equally important, what do other people think about you, and does their assessment of your conduct and attitudes agree with your own?

This Activity Box contains various questions about misbehavior—some trivial, some less so—and various statements about authority. Make two or more copies and then answer the questions for yourself on one of the copies.

SELF-DESCRIPTIONS

Behaviors: Circle *True* if you have ever engaged in the activity described, *False* if you have never engaged in the activity.

True	False	1. I have torn up or thrown on the floor things belonging to other people.
True	False	2. I have smashed, slashed or damaged things in public places—in streets, movie theaters, clubs, trains, buses, or shopping malls.
True	False	3. I have carried some kind of weapon (e.g., a knife) in case it was needed in a fight.
True	False	4. I have annoyed or insulted strangers in the street.
True	False	5. I have thrown things such as stones at people.
True	False	6. I have driven an automobile or motorcycle while I was under the influence of alcohol or drugs.
True	False	7. I have taken money that was not mine from home with no intention of returning it.
True	False	8. I have obtained money by deception or false pretenses.
True	False	9. I have stolen things from department stores, supermarkets, or other stores while the store was open.
True	False	10. I have had a flight with someone in a public place.
True	False	11. I have switched price tags on items in stores before buying them.
True	False	12. I have deliberately traveled on a train or bus without a ticket or deliberately paid the wrong fare.
True	False	13. I have witnessed an incident in which the law was broken and have failed to report it to the police.

Scoring: To obtain your total score, count the number of times you have circled *True*. An average score for males is around 5. If you are male and your score is 8 or above you are definitely more delinquent than the average student. If it is 2 or less, you are distinctly less delinquent than the average. If you are female, all these values should be halved.

Activity Box 14.1 *(continued)*

Attitudes: For each statement, indicate whether you strongly agree (SA), agree (A), are undecided (U), disagree (D), or strongly disagree (SD), by circling the appropriate letter or letters.

SA A U D SD   1. Laws are made for the benefit of everyone in society.

SA A U D SD   2. The police are often unnecessarily brutal to people.

SA A U D SD   3. Rules in schools and colleges are made for the benefit of the staff, not the students.

SA A U D SD   4. People do treat everyone the same on the whole.

SA A U D SD   5. A lot of laws are not made to help ordinary people but purely to restrict their freedom.

SA A U D SD   6. Most policemen are honest.

SA A U D SD   7. The main purpose of the law is to keep things as they are in a society that favors the rich.

SA A U D SD   8. You should always do what the police tell you.

SA A U D SD   9. It can be okay to break a law if it is to help a friend.

SA A U D SD   10. The police exist to make society a better place for everyone.

Scoring: To find your total score, for questions 1, 4, 6, 8, and 10, score 5 for SA, 4 for A, 3 for U, 2 for D, and 1 for SD; for the remaining questions, score 1 for SA, 2 for A, 3 for U, 2 for D, and 1 for SD. Then add the score across the ten items.

The average score for males is around 24, for females about 26. Scores of 30 and above are distinctly more positive than the average for both males and females, while scores of 18 and below are more negative than the average for males, 22 and below for females.

How did your scores for behavior and attitudes compare? Were they both on the same side of the respective averages? Behavior and attitudes may not always coincide; sometimes people may be critical of authority but not at all delinquent. It would, however, be unusual to be highly delinquent and at the same time to have very positive views about authority.

REPUTATION

This exercise can be developed by asking friends and acquaintances to guess your replies to the two sets of questions. For example, give one copy of the questions to a friend who knows you very well and in whom you often confide and another copy to someone who knows you less well, possibly a recent acquaintance or someone you see infrequently. Ask them to guess how you responded. You might expect the first person to be more accurate—this is certainly what some recent research has shown—but how accurate? And how *in*accurate is the second person? It is unlikely that the responses of either will perfectly match your own scores, but in which direction are the errors and do both make errors in the same direction? Do they make errors in different directions respectively for behavior and attitudes? Overall, do you appear to have a better or a worse reputation than you deserve? Finally, is it possible that someone else's assessment of your character could be more accurate than your own?

authorities, who both make and enforce rules and who issue a variety of instructions and orders. At the beginning of our lives this authority is most likely to be represented to us by our parents, but as we grow older it is increasingly encountered in other, often more impersonal and symbolic forms—teachers and school principals, policemen and other officials of the state, employers and work supervisors. Each of us has to arrive at some kind of accommodation with authority, and there are reasons to believe this starts early, in the family. The kind of accommodation we make has far-reaching and relatively enduring effects on our conduct.

One justification for making this intimate link between accommodation to authority and moral conduct comes from studies of the relation between rule breaking and attitudes toward institutional authorities. In our own research program with adolescents (Emler & Reicher, 1987, 1995; Reicher & Emler, 1985) the correlations we observed between measures of these two variables were so strong and consistent as to suggest not that attitudes predict conduct but that attitudes and conduct are really two facets of the same relationship—namely, the relationship between the young person and authority. The verbal and subjective facet of the relationship is to be found in what young people say and believe about authority, the behavioral facet in how they conduct themselves in relation to the standards that authority supports.

A negative relation with authority, however, not only puts the individual at odds with the requirements of authority, but it can also place that individual beyond its protection. Rule breaking may then become a defensive strategy, providing informal means for settling grievances if formal remedies are believed to be unavailable. It also offers informal protection by virtue of the sort of reputation it does convey, a reputation for being the kind of person whom it is dangerous to victimize or offend. One can see therefore why rule breakers might want their mayhem to be known, particularly to potential enemies. And as might also be expected, they present themselves in personality tests as wild and reckless but also as tough, unemotional, and indifferent to the suffering of their victims.

It would, however, be a mistake to assume that rule breakers are in every respect unpleasant people. Recall here the evidence from peer-rating and self-report studies of personality that converge on the conclusion that Conscientiousness (the moral aspects of which resemble the rule-following/rule-breaking dimension of character) is distinct from Agreeableness (with which generosity and kindness are sometimes associated; cf. also Krueger et al., 2001). Rule breakers may be quite generous, helpful, and loyal to their friends (otherwise it is unlikely they would have any), though their social worlds may be more sharply divided into friends and enemies. If this is so, we should find a strong "relationship" component (cf. Kenny, 1994) in peer ratings of these dimensions among chronic rule breakers. That is, ratings of such qualities as generosity, loyalty, and helpfulness should vary with the relationship between rater and ratee; when raters are on friendly terms with the people they are rating, their ratings will not entirely match the ratings of the same individuals by people who do not like them so well.

As to the greater prevalence of males among the rule breakers, we can see that a positive accommodation to authority competes with several cultural expectations—for independence, assertiveness, toughness—that are stronger for boys than for girls. By the same token the rule breaker's reputation as hard, strong, unemotional, and cruel is less compatible with traditional images of femininity.

We have yet to address one of the most striking features of adolescent misbehavior: It is far more often a collective than a solitary activity. Precisely what this tells us about the causes of misconduct is still unclear, but I incline to the view that people who are disposed to break the rules will do so only when they are in like-minded company (cf. Emler et al., 1987). Company does not make people behave well or badly; it only releases dispositions that are already present and only when the company is similarly disposed.

This may help to make sense of the greater prevalence of criminal misbehavior in adolescence. This period combines an increase in opportunities for criminal misbehavior with an increased probability of finding like-minded company. The latter arises with the move from small elementary schools to large high schools and the tendency of these schools to group young people in ways that are sensitive to their delinquent inclinations. And this brings me to the consequences of character.

Moral conduct as defined in this chapter is closely associated with educational performance. Why should this be? Is it because they are both influenced by a more basic attribute of the person, namely, intellectual ability? There is not the space here to explore this controversial issue in the detail it deserves, but I will mention one difficulty about explaining differences in moral conduct in terms of differences in intelligence. Mean levels of involvement in delinquent misbehavior increase between ages 10 and 14. In absolute terms, intellectual powers also increase over this period; the average 14-year-old is capable of intellectual accomplishments that are beyond the average 10-year-old. It is hard to see why increasing intellectual powers should produce increases in delinquency.

On the other hand, intelligence undoubtedly is related positively to educational attainment, just as delinquency is negatively related. One possibility this suggests is that the young person's orientation to formal authority influences his or her educational career rather than the reverse, and that it is an influence independent of that of intellectual ability. This does make some sense. It is consistent with the idea that doing well at school is not just a matter of being intellectually able. It also depends also on deferring to the authority of teachers, abiding by the various rules of classroom procedure, submitting to the school's routine, and following instructions. More generally it suggests that moral character has consequences for those prospects in one's life that derive from one's educational qualifications. (For a contrary view, that intelligence does play a causal role in antisocial behavior, see Lynham, Moffitt, & Stouthamer-Loeber, 1993; Moffitt & Silva, 1988.)

Two final thoughts: First, almost everyone who has thought deeply about moral questions has recognized that occasions sometimes arise in which the more moral course is to resist authority. To take just two examples, soldiers have been ordered by their superior officers to fire on innocent civilians and employees have been instructed by their bosses to ignore health and safety regulations. About the special qualities of character such resistance requires I have said nothing. I have claimed that an important quality of character is the inclination to follow the rules of social conduct supported by the established authorities in society. Whether those who most persistently defy such authority in the service of their own interests would also prove the most resistant in the face of corrupt or unjust authority we do not yet know. However, there are indications that it is easier to convince others of one's moral failings than of one's virtue. One reason for this, suggested by Skowronski and Carlston (1989), is that behavior that upholds moral standards such as honesty is expected and approved; when it occurs it is therefore more likely to be attributed by observers to situational pressures than to the special virtue of the actor. In contrast, to violate moral standards is almost always to defy social pressures and so explanation for such action is more likely to be located in the actor. To put it another way, our daily lives provide us with few opportunities to provide others with unequivocal evidence of our exceptional virtue but very many opportunities to suggest we are morally flawed.

This brings me to the second thought. Societies are organized to reduce the social costs of interpersonal variability in moral character. How much mischief and mayhem any individual can cause will depend on the degree of access he or she has to relevant opportunities. The character references sought by employers, banks, rental agencies, and others are used to confine such access to those individuals least likely to abuse these opportunities. Likewise, education can be seen as an extended character test, the results—educational credentials—being used to control entry to positions of trust and responsibility (cf. Jencks, 1972). And organizational structures operate to monitor most closely the activities of those whose virtues are most suspect. Conversely, therefore, moral character matters most when conditions allow individuals discretion about how they act. Among the relevant conditions are those in which individuals are in positions of power or authority over others. So it is perhaps not surprising that in elections for political office the moral character of the candidates is of such interest to the electors (Kinder, 1998). But the selection and promotion mechanisms of political and economic organizations are not perfect in this regard, and their imperfections provide dramatic reminders of the costs of failing to estimate moral character accurately (Emler & Cook, 2001).

SUMMARY

Psychologists started to think seriously toward the end of the 19th century about the forces that cause people to behave morally. They were curious as to how people are restrained from transgressing when they are alone, particularly as the mass society of cities seemed to create so much anonymity. The general conclusion, common to a number of theories, was that individuals must be restrained by some form of control internal to the personality. However, the concept of moral character had all but vanished from the psychological literature by the middle of the 20th century, psychologists by then being convinced that people are not distinguishable from one another in terms of any stable moral traits. This accorded with a preference for social psychological explanations of behavior in terms of the characteristics of situations rather than individuals.

One major obstacle to progress in this research area has been the lack of good measures of character. The experimental tests of character, evidence from which had done so much to discredit the very concept of moral character, have a number of limitations, as do such proxies for character as criminal convictions and police records. Alternative methods have consequently grown in popularity, including observer ratings and self-report inventories.

Evidence based on these alternatives now supports the view that there is a stable core to moral character. People do consistently differ in their inclination to abide by rules of conduct. However, the same evidence also raises questions about a number of popular psychological explanations for rule breaking, including those that have attributed it to psychological deficits such as lack of conditioned anxiety, low intelligence, and immaturity of moral insight.

More interesting, it appears that transgressions of the rules are not typically concealed and that most rule breaking occurs in the company of acquaintances. Indeed the very notion that modern society is anonymous and allows many opportunities for covert misbehavior seems to have been in error. This raises the possibility that people are deterred from breaking rules by a concern for their reputation or good name within the communities to which they belong. The intriguing question is then why anyone should deliberately behave in such a way as to create a bad name for himself or herself. A tentative answer is that from relatively early in life some individuals find it difficult to accommodate to the demands of authority, particularly the formal authority encountered in settings like the school. Then they get to know others with the same difficulties and together their opposition is translated into action. They develop an anti-authority ethos and work out informal solutions to the hazards of life in which they see a bad reputation as having certain attractions and advantages.

DISCUSSION QUESTIONS

1. What distinctive research strategies are required to test, respectively, hypotheses about individual differences in character and variations in situations or circumstances upon moral conduct?
2. What are the merits and limitations of alternative options for measuring moral character?
3. How could questions about the number of distinct dimensions of moral character be tested and how could the distinctiveness of the dimensions be validated?
4. Personality and other correlates of conduct: How do we decide whether these correlates contribute to an explanation of individual differences, whether they are merely describing these differences in other terms (or perhaps, more usefully, adding to the detail of description of the differences), or whether they are consequences of the differences?

SUGGESTED READINGS

Colby, A., & Damon, W. (1992). *Some do care: Contemporary lives of moral commitment.* New York: Free Press. A different take on moral character to the one explored in this chapter, emphasizing not respect for the rights of others as embodied in social rules and legal obligations, but exceptional concern to serve and address the needs of others. The book offers a series of case studies of individuals whose lives have been characterized by this kind of exceptional moral commitment.

Emler, N., & Reicher, S. (1995). *Adolescence and delinquency: The collective management of reputation.* Oxford, UK: Blackwell. The authors examine various theories of delinquency that attribute such behavior to the failure of internalized controls. They develop an alternative explanation for individual differences in rule breaking in terms of the different reputational goals that individuals may have, and the origins of these different goals.

Havighurst, R., & Taba, H. (1949). *Adolescent character and personality.* New York: Wiley. An in-tensive study of a group of 16-year olds growing up in a small American city in the Middle West. The research was notable for its use of "reputational" measures of character, ratings provided by a range of people acquainted with the sample, including peers, teachers, and employers. Although the research is many years old it is still valuable because of the near-impossibility at the present of marshaling the same level of resources as were deployed for the intensive data collection of this study.

Doris, J. (2002). *Lack of character: Personality and moral behavior.* New York: Cambridge University Press. The author criticizes the concept of moral character, specifically with respect to its ability to explain conduct. He contrasts this with evidence that conduct is highly sensitive to current circumstances and argues that people typically substantially overestimate the importance of character as a determinant of conduct.

SUGGESTED WEB SITES

http://chiron.valdosta.edu/whuitt/col/morchr/morchr.html
An essay by Bill Huitt at Valdosta State University examines the role of the U.S. educational system in building moral character in students.

http://www.spssi.org/
The web site of division 9 of APA, the Society for the Psychological Study of Social Issues. Here, read more about the impact of moral character on psychosocial problems.

INFOTRAC COLLEGE EDITION SEARCH TOPICS

Moral conduct	Crime	Orientation to authority
Character	Moral reputation	

REFERENCES

Aleixo, P. A., & Norris, C. E. (2000). Personality and moral reasoning in young offenders. *Personality and Individual Differences*, 28, 609–623.

Aquino, K., & Reed, A. (2002). The self importance of moral identity. *Journal of Personality and Social Psychology*, 83, 1423–1440.

Asch, S. (1956). Studies of independence and conformity: A minority of one against a unanimous majority. *Psychological Monographs*, 70 (Whole No. 416).

Bandura, A. (1991). Social cognitive theory of moral thought and action. In W. Kurtines & J. Gewirtz (Eds.), *Handbook of moral behavior and development* (Vol. 1, pp. 45–103). Hillsdale, NJ: Erlbaum.

Box, S. (1981). *Deviance, reality and society.* New York: Holt.

Burton, R. V. (1963). Generality of honesty reconsidered. *Psychological Bulletin, 70,* 481–499.

Cheek, J. M. (1982). Aggregation, moderator variables, and the validity of personality tests: A peer-rating study. *Journal of Personality and Social Psychology, 43,* 1254–1269.

Costa, P. T., & McCrae, R. R. (1995). Primary traits of Eysenck's P-E-N system: Three- and five-factor solutions. *Journal of Personality and Social Psychology, 69,* 308–317.

Cronbach, L. J. (1955). Processes affecting scores on "understanding others" and "assumed similarity." *Psychological Bulletin, 52,* 177–193.

Digman, J. M. (1990). Personality structure: Emergence of the five-factor model. *Annual Review of Psychology, 41,* 417–440.

Doris, J. (2002). *Lack of character: Personality and moral behavior.* New York: Cambridge University Press.

Emler, N. (1984). Differential involvement in delinquency: Toward an interpretation in terms of reputation management. In B. A. Maher & W. B. Maher (Eds*.), Progress in experimental personality research* (Vol. 13, pp. 173–239). New York: Academic Press.

Emler, N. (2000). Social structures and individual lives: Effects of participation in the social institutions of family, education and work. In J. Bynner & R. Silbereisen (Eds.), *Adversity and challenge in the life course in England and in the new Germany* (pp. 62–84). London: Macmillan.

Emler, N., & Cook, T. (2001). Moral integrity in leadership: Why it matters and why it might be difficult to achieve. In B. Roberts & R. Hogan (Eds.), *Personality psychology in the work place* (pp. 272–298). Washington, DC: APA Press.

Emler, N., Heather, N., & Winton, M. (1978). Delinquency and the development of moral reasoning. *British Journal of Social and Clinical Psychology, 17,* 325–331.

Emler, N., & Reicher, S. (1987). Orientations to institutional authority in adolescence. *Journal of Moral Education, 16,* 108–116.

Emler, N., & Reicher, S. (1995). *Adolescence and delinquency: The collective management of reputation.* Oxford, UK: Blackwell.

Emler, N., Reicher, S., & Ross, A. (1987). The social context of delinquent conduct. *Journal of Child Psychology and Psychiatry, 28,* 99–109.

Epstein, S., & O'Brien, E. J. (1985). The person-situation debate in historical and current perspective. *Psychological Bulletin, 98,* 513–537.

Eysenck, H. J. (1977). *Crime and personality.* London: Granada.

Eysenck, H. J., & Eysenck, S. B. G. (1976). *Psychoticism as a dimension of personality.* London: Hodder & Stoughton.

Farrington, D. P. (1989). Self-reported and official offending from adolescence to adulthood. In M.W. Klein (Ed.), *Cross-national research in self-reported crime and delinquency* (pp. 399–423). Boston, MA: Kluwer.

Farrington, D. P. (1991). Antisocial personality from childhood to adulthood. *The Psychologist, 4,* 398–394.

Freud, S. (1930). *Civilization and its discontents.* New York: Norton.

Freud, S. (1955). Totem and taboo. In J. Strachey (Ed. & Trans.), *The standard edition of the complete psychological works of Sigmund Freud* (Vol. 13, pp. 1–162). London: Hogarth Press. (Original work published 1913)

Fischer, C. (1982). *To dwell among friends: Personal networks in town and city.* Chicago: Chicago University Press.

Funder, D. (1999). *Personality judgment: A realistic approach to person perception.* New York: Academic Press.

Gibson, H., Morrison, S., & West, D. J. (1970). The confession of known offences in response to a self-report delinquency schedule. *British Journal of Criminology, 10,* 277–280.

Giordano, P. C., Cernovich, S. A., & Pugh, M. D. (1986). Friendship and delinquency. *American Journal of Sociology, 91,* 1170–1201.

Gold, M. (1970). *Delinquent behavior in an American city.* Belmont, CA: Brooks/Cole.

Goldberg, L. R. (1990). An alternative "description of personality": The Big-Five factor structure. *Journal of Personality and Social Psychology, 59,* 1216–1229.

Gottfredson, M. R., & Hirschi, T. (1990). *A general theory of crime.* Stanford, CA: Stanford University Press.

Hampson, S. E. (1988). *The construction of personality* (2nd ed.). New York: Routledge.

Hartshorne, H., & May, M. A. (1928*). Studies in the nature of character. Vol. 1. Studies in deceit.* New York: Macmillan.

Havighurst, R., & Taba, H. (1949). *Adolescent character and personality.* New York: Wiley.

Hoffman, M. L. (1988). Moral development. In M. H. Bornstein & M. H. Lamb (Eds.), *Developmental psychology: An advanced textbook* (2nd ed., pp. 205–260). Hillsdale, NJ: Erlbaum.

Huizinga, D., & Elliot, D. S. (1986) Reassessing the reliablity and validity of self-report delinquency measures. *Journal of Quantitative Criminology, 2,* 293–327.

Jencks, C. (1972). *Inequality: A reassessment of the effects of family and schooling in America.* New York: Basic Books.

Jennings, W. S., Kilkenny, R., & Kohlberg, L. (1983). Moral development: Theory and practice for youthful and adult offenders. In W. Laufer & J. M. Day (Eds.), *Personality theory, moral development and criminal behavior* (pp. 281–355). Toronto: Lexington Books.

Judd, C. M., Smith, E. R., & Kidder, L. H. (1991) *Research methods in social relations* (6th ed.). New York: Holt.

Kenny, D. (1994). *Interpersonal perception.* New York: Guilford.

Kenrick, D. T., & Funder, D. C. (1988). Profiting from controversy: Lessons from the person situation debate. *American Psychologist, 43,* 23–34.

Kinder, D. (1998). Opinion and action in the realm of politics. In D. T. Gilbert, S. T. Fiske, & G. Lindzey (Eds.), *Handbook of social psychology* (4th ed., Vol. 2., pp. 778–876). New York: McGraw-Hill.

Kituse, J. I. (1980). The "new conception of deviance" and its critics. In W. R. Gove (Ed.), *The labelling of deviance.* Beverly Hills, CA: Sage.

Klein, M. (1984). Offence specialisation and versatility among juveniles. *British Journal of Criminology, 24,* 185–194.

Kohlberg, L. (1984). *Essays on moral development. Vol. 2. The psychology of moral development.* New York: Harper & Row.

Krueger, R. F., Hicks, B. M., & McGue, M. (2001). Altruism and antisocial behaviour: Independent tendencies, unique personality correlates, distinct etiologies. *Psychological Science, 12,* 397–402.

Lapsley, D. K. (1996). *Moral psychology.* Boulder, CO: Westview Press.

Le Bon, G. (1947). *The crowd: A study of the popular mind.* London: Ernest Benn (first published 1895).

Lynham, D., Moffitt, T., & Stouthamer-Loeber, M. (1993). Explaining the relation between IQ and delinquency: Class, race, test motivation school

failure or self-control? *Journal of Abnormal Psychology, 102,* 396–410.

McCrae, R. R., & John, O. P. (1992). An introduction to the five-factor model and its applications. *Journal of Personality, 65,* 175–197.

Milgram, S. (1964). Group pressure and action against a person. *Journal of Abnormal and Social Psychology, 69,* 137–143.

Mischel, W. (1976). *Personality and assessment* (2nd ed.). New York: Wiley.

Moffitt, T. (1993). "Lifecourse persistent" and "adolescent limited" antisocial behaviour: A developmental taxonomy. *Psychological Review, 100,* 674–701.

Moffitt, T., Caspi, A., Rutter, M., & Silva, P. A. (2001). *Sex differences in antisocial behaviour: Conduct disorder, delinquency and violence in the Dunedin longitudinal study.* Cambridge, UK: Cambridge University Press.

Moffitt, T., & Silva, P. A. (1988). IQ and delinquency: A direct test of the differential detection hypothesis. *Journal of Abnormal Psychology, 97,* 330–333.

Pedersen, C. (1996). *Assessments of moral character by self and acquaintances.* Unpublished doctoral thesis, Oxford University, Oxford, UK.

Reicher, S., & Emler, N. (1985). Delinquent behaviour and attitudes to formal authority. *British Journal of Social Psychology, 24,* 161–168.

Rushton, J. P., Chrisjohn, R. D., & Fekken, G. C. (1981). The altruistic personality and the self-report altruism scale. *Personality and Individual Differences, 2,* 293–302.

Shweder, R. A. (1982). Fact and artefact in trait perception: The systematic distortion hypothesis. In B. A. Maher & W. B. Maher (Eds.), *Progress in experimental personality research* (Vol. 11, pp. 65–95). New York: Academic Press.

Singh, A. (1979). Reliability and validity of self-report delinquency studies. *Psychological Reports, 44,* 987–993.

Short, J. F., & Nye, F. J. (1957). Reported behavior as a criterion of deviant behavior. *Social Problems, 4,* 296–302.

Skowronski, K., & Carlston, D. (1989). Negativity and extremity biases in impression formation. *Psychological Bulletin, 105,* 131–142.

Smetana, J. (1990). Morality and conduct disorders. In M. Lewis & S. M. Miller (Eds.), *Handbook of developmental psychopathology* (pp. 157–179). New York: Plenum.

Smith, D. J. (1995). Youth crime and conduct disorders: Trends, patterns, and causal explanations. In M. Rutter & D. J. Smith (Eds.), *Psychosocial disorders in young people* (pp. 389–489). New York: Wiley.

Snarey, J. (1985). Cross cultural universality of socio-moral development: A critical review of Kohlbergian research. *Psychological Bulletin, 97,* 202–232.

Tarry, H. (2001). *Moral reasoning and delinquency.* Unpublished doctoral thesis, University of Oxford, Oxford, UK.

Turiel, E. (1983). *The development of social knowledge: Morality and convention.* Cambridge, UK: Cambridge University Press.

Turiel, E., Killen, M., & Helwig, C. C. (1987). Morality: Its structure, functions and vagaries. In J. Kagan & S. Lamb (Eds.), *The emergence of morality in young children* (pp. 155–244). New York: Academic Press.

Wright, R. (1994). *The moral animal: The new science of evolutionary psychology.* New York: Random House.

Zimbardo, P. (1970). The human choice: Individuation, reason and order versus deindividuation, impulse and chaos. In W. J. Arnold & D. Levine (Eds.), *Nebraska symposium on motivation* (pp. 237–307). Lincoln: University of Nebraska Press.

15 | Culture and Personality

A. TIMOTHY CHURCH

FERNANDO A. ORTIZ

Are there cultural differences in personality characteristics, such as aggressive-ness, dependability, or modesty? This might be the first question that comes to mind when one thinks about the relationship between culture and personality, and it is a question that has long interested psychologists, anthropologists, and lay people. Cross-cultural psychologists have come to realize, however, that we cannot determine whether cultural groups differ in their personality character-istics without first addressing more basic questions about culture and person-ality. For one, we must first determine whether personality traits such as ag-gressiveness and modesty are defined in an equivalent manner, or represented by comparable behaviors, in different cultures. If not, then cross-cultural com-parisons of average levels of personality traits may be like comparing apples and oranges.

An even more basic question is whether the very idea of what constitutes "personality" is the same in different cultures. For example, according to many psychologists, Americans tend to think of personality as internal dispositions of individuals that are relatively stable over time and useful in understanding be-havior across a range of situations. In contrast, some anthropologists and cul-tural psychologists have questioned whether individuals in all cultures think of personality as an "internal package of attributes" or expect such attributes to be as predictive of behavior as social roles, norms, or situational factors are (Cross & Markus, 1999; Markus & Kitayama, 1998; Triandis, 1995). Cross-cultural studies can help to resolve controversies about the nature of personal-ity across cultures.

Other important questions are addressed in cross-cultural studies of per-sonality, including the following: What is the nature of the relationship between culture and personality? For example, does culture primarily influence person-ality or do they both influence or "make each other up"? How can culture and its influence on personality be measured? Do people in different cultures de-scribe themselves and others using personality traits, and if so, are similar traits applied across cultures? Do personality inventories measure characteristics that are relevant for individuals in all cultures or do we need to develop inventories that are unique to particular cultures? Are particular personality traits such as dominance or conscientiousness manifested in a similar manner in all cultures? Can cultural differences in the level or amount of particular traits be detected using personality inventories? What is the impact of culture on other aspects of personality, for example, self-concept, values, beliefs, motives, emotions, and subjective well-being? Often, an underlying issue in cross-cultural studies is the extent to which personality dimensions or processes are biologically based uni-versals or are "constituted" and mediated by culture (Markus & Kitayama, 1998; McCrae & Costa, 1997).

The science of psychology should involve the study of all human beings, not just those in a particular cultural context such as the United States. Cross-cultural studies are important because they enable tests of the universality of psychological theories and concepts and provide a natural experimental "treatment" for studying the influence of culture and ecology (i.e., the physi-cal environment) on personality. The study of personality across cultures can also reduce ethnocentrism—for example, the exclusive focus on one's own cultural group—in the science and practice of psychology, by broadening perspectives on ways to live, value systems, and patterns of personality, behavior, and experience.

HISTORICAL BACKGROUND

Psychologists became interested in cultural differences in the mid-19th century, as illustrated by the publication in Germany of *Zeitschrift fur Volkerpsychologie und Sprachwissenschaft* (Journal for Folk Psychology and Language Studies) and a 10-volume series, *Volker-psychologie* (Elements of Folk Psychology), published by Wilhelm Wundt between 1900 and 1920 (Marsella, Dubanoski, Hamada, & Morse, 2000). In anthropology—but with the participation of psychologists and psychiatrists—a field referred to as culture and personality emerged in the first half of the 20th century and flourished in the 1930s and 1940s before "falling from grace" by 1960 (LeVine, 2001). According to LeVine (2001), most contributors to this field concurred with the following core propositions:

> (a) All adult behavior is "culturally patterned," just as all adult speech is patterned by a particular language; (b) childhood experience, also culturally patterned, has a long-term influence on adult personality; (c) adult personality characteristics prevalent in a community have an influence on its culture, institutions, patterns of social change, and forms of psychopathology. (p. 808)

One important controversy among culture-and-personality theorists involved the degree of correspondence between individual personality and culture. Ruth Benedict (1934), in *Patterns of Culture*, described a close correspondence between cultural *configurations* and individual personality (i.e., culture as personality writ large). Kardiner (1939, p. 237) introduced the concept of *basic personality structure,* defined as "the effective adaptive tools of the individual which are *common to every individual in the society* [italics added]" and Linton introduced the concept of *basic personality type*, defined as "that personality configuration which is *shared by the bulk of the society's members* as a result of the early experiences which they have in common [italics added]" (Kardiner, Linton, Du Bois, & West, 1945, viii). In contrast, Sapir (1956), Wallace (1961), and others placed greater emphasis on individual variability in personality and argued that the impact of culture could differ for each individual in the society. The concept of *modal personality* (e.g., Dubois, 1944) acknowledged the existence, even in relatively simple cultures, of both central tendencies (i.e., the most frequent personality type in the culture) and individual variability.

Bock (2000) and LeVine (2001) noted that efforts during and after World War II to apply the ideas and methods of culture-and-personality studies to describe the *national characters* of people in large, complex nation states such as Russia, Japan, and Germany led to a crisis in the field and its virtual abandonment. A particularly controversial example was the "swaddling hypothesis" put forth by Gorer and Rickman (1949) in their book *The People of Great Russia*, in which they linked the Russian's purported preference for authoritarian leadership under Stalin and the Czars to their having been swaddled (i.e., tightly wrapped in cloth) as infants (Levine, 2001).

Bock (2000) noted a number of questionable assumptions underlying the national character studies, such as the assumption that child-rearing practices could be linked to predictable adult personality characteristics (the continuity assumption). In addition, these studies often characterized the personalities of whole populations (e.g., fanatical and restrained Japanese, authoritarian Germans) while ignoring the considerable individual variability in personality within any cultural group (the uniformity assumption). Many studies exhibited an over-reliance on projective tests such as the Rorschach and Thematic Apperception Test, without sufficient attention to whether the responses to these tests have equivalent meanings or interpretations in diverse cultural groups (the projective assumption). Anthropologists often lost sight of their own potential for ethnocentrism or lack of objectivity, leading to biased descriptions of other cultural groups (the objectivity assumption). Bock (2000) has warned that these same assumptions could threaten current research on personality and culture. For example, there are dangers in assuming that the personality traits measured by current tests (e.g., Extraversion and Conscientiousness) necessarily represent causal entities, and in using mean scores on such tests to characterize and compare entire nations.

Although a number of personality psychologists and psychoanalysts showed an early interest in personality from a cross-cultural perspective (e.g., Freud, 1950; Kluckhohn & Murray, 1948; McClelland, 1961), interest waned during the 1970s and 1980s (McCrae, 2000). Church (2001, pp. 787–788) noted several recent factors, however, that have led to a significant increase in efforts to infuse culture into the study of personality. For one, the concept of personality traits, which had become controversial in the 1960s—as researchers questioned the ability of traits to predict behavior across situations—has been rejuvenated as a result of supportive research (McCrae, 2000; also see chapter 7 in this book). Second, the five-factor model of personality, which comprises the broad dimensions of Extraversion, Agreeableness, Conscientiousness, Emotional Stability (versus Neuroticism), and Openness to Experience (or Intellect), has reemerged as a possible comprehensive and universal model of personality structure (McCrae & Costa, 1997). Third, the elaboration of individualism-collectivism (I-C) as a dimension that may link ecology, culture, and personality has greatly facilitated the growth and conceptual integration of cross-cultural studies (Triandis, 2001), as has the infusion of research on culture and self into mainstream psychology (Markus & Kitayama, 1991; Triandis, 1989).

Other recent factors that have increased interest in the study of culture and personality include the emergence of indigenous or local psychologies in various countries (Enriquez, 1994; Sinha, 1997); the multicultural movement in American psychology, which has addressed identity and assessment issues that are relevant to the study of personality (Dana, 2000); and the refinement of terminology and procedures for addressing conceptual, linguistic, and measurement equivalence in cross-cultural research (van de Vijver & Leung, 1997). Finally, the field of culture and personality has benefited from the increasing globalization of scientific activity, which has made cross-cultural collaboration easier and the extension of psychology across cultural boundaries more imperative. Currently, the study of culture and personality is thriving and being approached from a variety of theoretical perspectives.

ALTERNATIVE PERSPECTIVES ON CULTURE AND PERSONALITY

Definition of Culture

Although culture has been defined in many ways, most cross-cultural psychologists would probably be comfortable with Fiske's (2002, p. 81) definition:

> A culture is a socially transmitted or socially constructed constellation consisting of such things as practices, competencies, ideas, schemas, symbols, values, norms, institutions, goals, constitutive rules, artifacts, and modifications of the physical environment.

That is, culture includes both observable activities and objects (i.e., things outside the individual and in the environment) and symbols, values, and meanings (e.g., shared cognitive meanings in the minds of individuals) (Berry, 2000). Despite some consensus on what constitutes culture, psychologists differ in how they incorporate or treat the cultural variable in their research. A useful approach is to distinguish four perspectives: cross-cultural, cultural, indigenous, and evolutionary (Greenfield, 2000; Shweder, 2000; Triandis, 2000; Yang, 2000).

Cross-Cultural Perspectives

Typical features of the cross-cultural approach include the following: (a) comparisons of multiple cultures in the hope of demonstrating cross-cultural universals or identifying culture-specifics amidst these universals; (b) treatment of culture, or quantitative variables indexing culture and ecology (e.g., aspects of the physical environment), as variables "outside" the individual, which can be used to predict personality and behavior; (c) use of traditional psychometric scales or inventories to assess both culture and personality; (d) emphasis on issues of cross-cultural equivalence of constructs and measures; and (e) a focus on individual differences in personality traits, values, beliefs, and so forth.

Cross-cultural psychologists nonetheless differ in the extent to which they attribute individual differences in personality to biological factors or environmental factors such as ecology and culture. In their Five-Factor Theory, McCrae and Costa (1996) argue that certain *basic tendencies,* including the trait dimensions of the five-factor or Big Five model—Extraversion, Agreeableness, Neuroticism, Concientiousness, and Openness to Experience—are biologically based and independent of culture. These are to be distinguished from *characteristic adaptations* such as personal strivings, attitudes, habits, and aspects of self-concept that are influenced by both basic tendencies and external influences such as culture. Triandis and Suh (2002) share the view of many cross-cultural psychologists who acknowledge the role of biological influences but attribute more of the variability in personality to ecological and cultural factors. Indeed, implicit in much cross-cultural research is an ecocultural model, which postulates a causal sequence from ecology (e.g., the physical environment) to culture to socialization patterns (e.g., child-rearing practices) to personality (Triandis & Suh, 2002).

Accordingly, some cross-cultural psychologists have developed taxonomies and indices of ecocultural or environmental factors such as ecology (e.g., temperature), education (e.g., school enrollment levels), economics (e.g., Gross National Product per capita), mass communications (e.g., radios per 1,000 inhabitants), and population (e.g., rate of population increase) (Georgas & Berry, 1995). Other researchers have related such factors, or value-based indicators of culture, to personality. For example, van Hemert, van de Vijver, Poortinga, and Georgas (2002) found that higher Gross National Product and related economic indices were associated with lower scores on the Lie scale of the Eysenck Personality Questionnaire. This suggested that greater national affluence is associated with less socially desirable responding. Van de Vliert, Schwartz, Huismans, Hofstede, and Daan (1999) found that the prevalence of political violence is greater in nations with warm climates than in nations with cold or very hot climates. They also noted, however, that this temperature-violence relationship might be accounted for by the relatively high masculinity (i.e., assertiveness, achievement orientation) of warm cultures.

McCrae (2001) reported several findings that are consistent with the ecocultural model but also noted that the direction of causality in such studies can be ambiguous. That is, does culture shape personality or vice versa? For example, McCrae (2001) suggested that the relationship he found between Power Distance (i.e., acceptance of inequality in a society) and Conscientiousness might involve culture shaping personality; high institutional emphasis on status and authority might lead to personalities that average higher on order and discipline, both aspects of Conscientiousness. In contrast, the relationship McCrae found between Uncertainty Avoidance (i.e., discomfort with uncertainty and ambiguity in society) and Neuroticism might reflect personality shaping culture; societies with personalities exhibiting higher levels of anxiety and anger (i.e., Neuroticism) might evolve social structures to minimize stress or uncertainty.

Much of the personality research conducted from a cross-cultural perspective has involved the study of traits. Trait psychologists tend to treat culture as an independent variable that may impact the level, expression, and correlates of traits, but not the underlying structure or dimensions of personality (e.g., Barrett, Petrides, Eysenck, & Eysenck, 1998; McCrae & Allik, 2002). Most of this research has involved investigations of the extent to which personality dimensions are the same across cultures and is reviewed later in this chapter. Cultural differences in levels of traits have also been studied (e.g., Lynn & Martin, 1996; McCrae, 2001). However, such comparisons are more controversial because they require prior demonstration of the conceptual and measurement equivalence of the personality scores being compared across cultures.

Cultural Psychology Perspectives

Whereas cross-cultural psychologists tend to treat culture and personality as relatively distinct entities, cultural psychologists emphasize the "mutually constitutive" and deeply intertwined nature of culture and personality (e.g., Cross & Markus, 1999; Heine, 2001). Conceptions of personality and self are viewed as socially constructed (i.e., produced through the shared cognition and experiences of members of particular cultures) and hence variable across cultures. As a result, the existence of universal personality traits is questioned. Indeed, in this perspective, conceptions of personality as "characteristic patterns of thought, emotion, and behavior, together with the psychological mechanisms—hidden or not—behind those patterns" (Funder, 2001, p. 198) are seen as reflecting a Western bias to view personality as "inside" the person rather than as embedded in a network of relationships, roles, and obligations (Cross & Markus, 1999).

Markus and Kitayama (1998) noted an important way in which conceptions of personality and self differ across cultures. The *independent* view of personality, which is described as most prevalent in Western countries, incorporates the following ideas:

1. A person is an autonomous entity defined by a somewhat distinctive set of attributes, qualities, or processes.
2. The configuration of internal attributes or processes determines or causes behavior (i.e., the origins of behavior are in the individual and people are knowable through their actions).
3. Individual behavior will vary because people vary in their configurations of internal attributes and processes and this distinctiveness is good.
4. People should express their attributes and processes in behavior so there should be consistency in behavior across situations and stability over time and this consistency and stability is good.
5. The study of personality is significant because it will lead to an understanding of how to predict and control behavior. (Markus & Kitayama, 1998; p. 69)

In contrast, the *interdependent* view of personality, which is described as most prevalent in Asian, African, Latin American, and many southern European countries, incorporates the following ideas:

1. A person is an interdependent entity who is part of an encompassing social relationship.
2. Behavior is a consequence of being responsive to the others with whom one is interdependent. The origins of behavior are in relationships and people are knowable through their actions within a given social relationship.
3. The precise nature of a given social context often varies so individual behavior will be variable from one situation to another and from one time to another. This sensitivity to social context and consequent variability is good.
4. The study of personality is significant because it will lead to an understanding of the relational and interpersonal nature of behavior. (Markus & Kitayama, 1998, p. 70)

Given this perspective, it is not surprising that cultural psychologists have not focused much on individual differences or traits in their studies. While acknowledging that people in all cultures can fill out personality inventories and rate their "personalities," cultural psychologists suggest that introspecting and reporting on one's personality characteristics is a much more natural task for those with independent conceptions of personality and self (i.e., in individualistic cultures). Instead of traits, personality research in the cultural psychology perspective has focused on the interaction of culture with self content and processes (Heine, Lehman, Markus, & Kitayama, 1999; Triandis, 1989). For example, cultural psychologists have investigated whether spontaneous descriptions of oneself contain more references to internal attributes or traits in individualistic cultures and more references to social roles, relationships, and statuses in collectivistic cultures, consistent with the hypothesized differences between cultures that emphasize independent versus interdependent conceptions of self, respectively (e.g., Kanagawa, Cross, & Markus, 2001).

Indigenous Perspectives

Indigenous psychologists emphasize the need to formulate theory, concepts, and methods that reflect indigenous cultural contexts (Church & Katigbak, 2002a; Ho, Peng, Lai, & Chan, 2001; Sinha, 1997). In the personality domain, indigenous psychologists have often focused on elaboration of constructs thought to be especially salient for particular cultural groups. Examples include the Japanese concept of *amae* (indulgent dependence; Doi, 1978); the Korean concept of *cheong* (human affection; Choi, Kim, & Choi, 1993); the Chinese concept of *ren qin* (relationship orientation; Cheung, Leung, Fan, Song, Zhang, & Zhang, 1996); the Indian concept of *hishkama karma* (detachment; Sinha, 1993); the Mexican concept of *simpatía* (avoidance of conflict; Triandis, Marin, Lisansky, & Betancourt, 1984); and the Filipino concepts of *pagkikipagkapwa* (shared identity), *pakikiramdam* (sensitivity, empathy), and *pakikisama* (going along with others; Enriquez, 1994). Although approximate English translations of these concepts may be possible, the behaviors and situational contexts associated with them may not generalize well across cultures.

Some indigenous psychologists have advocated the development of culture-specific research methods. For example, Filipino psychologists have proposed a number of indigenous methods that resemble the ethnographic methods used by anthropologists. These include various levels of participant observation, ranging, for example, from the relatively unobtrusive *pagmamasid* (general scanning or looking around), through increasing levels of researcher participation and obtrusiveness, such as *padalaw-dalaw* (occasional visits to respondent homes) and *pakikisangkot* (deeper involvement in barrio activities). Other methods involve unstructured (though guided) conversations and discussions, often in a small group context, in lieu of more structured interviews (e.g., *pagtatanoung-tanong*, informal, interactive questioning) (Church & Katigbak, 2002a). Such methods might become necessary should personality psychologists venture into populations with lower literacy levels and little familiarity with standard questionnaires and inventories. Presently, however, indigenous psychologists generally apply standard psychometric scales or inventories, developed, however, in local cultures with culture-specific content (e.g., Cheung et al., 1996; Katigbak, Church, Guanzon-Lapeña, Carlota, & del Pilar, 2002). Indigenous psychologists sometimes relate indigenous dimensions to dimensions identified in other cultures by administering both indigenous and imported inventories to the same sample. This method has been referred to as the *combined emic-etic* (indigenous-imported) or *cross-indigenous approach* (Enriquez, 1994).

Some indigenous psychologists have grappled with the difficulties of translating indigenous conceptions of human existence into new theories, concepts, and methods for personality psychology. For example, we can ask whether personality concepts extracted from Asian religious or philosophical traditions will describe the psychology of lay people in Asia or other societies. Ho et al. (2001) noted that relational constructs such as those cited earlier in this section (e.g., *amae, ren qin, pakikipagkapwa*) are particularly relevant in many indigenous theories. In their view, this suggests the need for a paradigmatic shift in psychology away from *methodological individualism* to *methodological relationalism*, in which the unit of analysis is the person-in-relations rather than the individual personality.

Evolutionary Perspectives

Evolutionary psychologists have much to say about culture and personality. They view the mind as composed of specific *psychological mechanisms,* many of which (1) evolved to solve adaptive problems linked with group living (e.g., successfully attracting mates, negotiating status hierarchies, forming coalitions) and (2) increased survival or reproduction in the ancestral environments of the human species (e.g., Buss, 1996; Hogan, 1996; MacDonald, 1998). Examples include mechanisms underlying mate selection strategies, detection of individual differences in personality traits, detection of cheating and infidelity, fear of strangers or outgroup members, and status striving motives.

Some evolutionary theorists have explained the personality dimensions of the five-factor model in terms of evolved psychological mechanisms. For example, Buss (1996) proposed that all humans have evolved *difference-detecting mechanisms* that enable us to place others along the dimensions of the five-factor model, because these dimensions are important in identifying individuals who will be strategic facilitators of our goals. According to Buss (1996), *strategic trait usage* may also be a cultural universal that evolved as a means to attract mates, friends, and allies and to disparage competitors. MacDonald (1998) proposed the existence of evolved neurophysiological systems in the brain that underlie individual differences in Big Five traits. For example, the cultural universality of the Extraversion dimension and related traits such as sensation seeking and impulsivity, is hypothesized to be the result of an evolved *behavioral approach system* that is designed to motivate us to approach sources of reward (e.g., sexual gratification) that were enduring and recurrent features of the environments in which humans evolved.

Evolutionary psychologists also address the relationship between evolved psychological mechanisms and culture. Unlike many cross-cultural psychologists, evolutionary psychologists are disinclined to view cultural variables, such as individualism-collectivism, or independent versus interdependent self-construals, as causes of personality or behavior. Rather, evolved psychological mechanisms, in interaction with culture, are viewed as ultimate causes (Buss, 2001). For example, Buss (2001) suggests that cultural differences in sexual promiscuity observed in two South American tribes can be explained in terms of the different male-female ratios in the societies. Where there is a surplus of women (e.g., in the Ache tribe), marriages become unstable and partner switching is frequent. Where there is a relative surplus of men (e.g., in the Hiwi tribe), men lucky enough to secure a wife strive hard to keep her and incentives and opportunities for men to switch partners are reduced. According to this sex-ratio hypothesis, men and women in both cultures have evolved psychological mechanisms that address mating strategies, but these strategies are sensitive to, or interact with, local cultural conditions of mate abundance or scarcity to produce cultural differences in personality or behavior.

Evolutionary psychologists have distinguished types of cultural phenomena that may help to integrate different conceptions of culture and personality (e.g., Barkow, Cosmides, & Tooby, 1992; Buss, 2001; Tooby & Cosmides, 1992). *Metaculture* refers to those aspects of culture that are universal because of the shared biology of the human species. *Evoked culture* involves differential or selective activation of universal psychological mechanisms in different ecological contexts leading to cultural differences such as those described for the Ache and Hiwi tribes. *Transmitted culture* refers to cultural phenomena (e.g., new ideas) that are passed among persons within a cultural group, again resulting in cultural differences.

Although the focus of personality research tends to differ in the cross-cultural, cultural, indigenous, and evolutionary perspectives, these approaches may be complementary. Indeed, some attempts to integrate them are now emerging (e.g., Church, 2000; Fiske, 2000; McCrae & Costa, 1996). For example, Fiske (2000) proposed a *complementarity theory*, which integrates the evolutionary and cultural psychology perspectives, and postulates the co-evolution of cultural paradigms or systems and psychological proclivities (mechanisms) that facilitate the learning and transmission of these cultural paradigms.

CONCEPTUAL AND METHODOLOGICAL ISSUES IN CROSS-CULTURAL RESEARCH

The study of personality across cultures involves a number of challenges. These include sampling considerations and various cross-cultural equivalence issues.

Sampling Issues

Sampling Cultures   Researchers have often used samples of convenience for cross-cultural studies based on cost and logistical considerations and the availability of collaborating scientists. This can lead to over-sampling of cultures that are affluent and similar to each other. Random samples of cultures are generally not feasible, but in some studies the number of cultures sampled has been large enough to perhaps approximate representative samples—for example, over 60 in the cross-cultural study of values (Sagiv & Schwartz, 2000), 55 in studies of subjective well-being (Diener, Diener, & Diener, 1995), over 30 in studies of personality trait dimensions (Barrett et al., 1998; McCrae, 2001), and 37 in a study of sex differences in human mate preferences (Buss, 1989). Still, certain regions of the world, in particular Europe, North America, and East Asia, continue to be over-sampled relative to other regions. If one is interested in demonstrating cross-cultural universals, then the diversity of cultures sampled is as important as the number of cultures sampled. Still, the more cultures one samples, the more likely one is to eliminate rival explanations of any cultural differences found.

Cross-cultural researchers often use purposive sampling, which involves the intentional selection of cultures expected to vary along the dimension of primary interest (e.g., individualism vs. collectivism), while attempting to control for extraneous variables (e.g., differences in GNP, religion, climate). For example, researchers have frequently used Hofstede's (1980, 2001) rankings of more than 50 cultures along the dimensions of Individualism-Collectivism, Power Distance, Uncertainty Avoidance, and Masculinity-Femininity to select cultures varying along the desired dimension (see Table 15.1). Other rankings or classifications of national cultures are also available for sampling purposes (e.g., Georgas & Berry, 1995; Schwartz, 1994; Smith, Dugan, & Trompenaars, 1996).

Sampling Individuals   Diversity among persons and subgroups within a culture (e.g., with respect to ethnicity, religion, social class) is often a problem in cross-cultural studies and requires that researchers clearly describe their samples and the subpopulations to whom their findings can be generalized. Unfortunately, there is often a trade-off between representativeness of samples *within* cultures and equivalence of samples *between* cultures. For example, to obtain equivalent samples for between-culture comparisons, researchers often sample college students. However, college students are probably a relatively elite or westernized subpopulation in most cultures. As in the sampling of cultures, purposive sampling can be used to control for extraneous variables (e.g., levels of schooling, affluence). For example, by replicating between-culture differences in both high and low socioeconomic subgroups in each culture, cross-cultural differences in affluence may be eliminated as a rival explanation for any cultural differences found.

Cultural Bias Versus Equivalence

A variety of conceptual and methodological biases can detract from the comparability or equivalence of personality constructs and measures across cultures. Van de Vijver and Tanzer (1997; see also Van de vijver & Leung, 1997) differentiate construct, method, and item bias. *Construct bias* occurs when the definitions or behavioral exemplars of the construct only partially overlap across cultures (i.e., lack *construct equivalence*), complicating cross-cultural

Table 15.1 | Dimensions of Culture

Source	Dimension	Description		Country or Culture Examples
Hofstede (2001)				
	Individualism vs. Collectivism	Valuing loosely knit social relations in which individuals primarily care for themselves and their immediate families versus tightly knit relations in which individuals receive support from larger in-groups (e.g., extended family, clan) in exchange for loyalty.	Ind:	United States, Australia
			Coll:	Guatemala, Ecuador
	Power Distance	Acceptance of unequal power in society.	High:	Malaysia, Guatemala
			Low:	Austria, Israel, Denmark
	Uncertainty Avoidance	Discomfort with uncertainty and ambiguity; valuing of beliefs and institutions that provide certainty and conformity.	High:	Greece, Portugal
			Low:	Singapore, Jamaica
	Masculinity vs. Femininity	Valuing achievement, assertiveness, and material success versus relationships, compassion, and interpersonal harmony.	Masc:	Japan, Austria
			Fem:	Sweden, Norway
	Long- vs. Short-Term Orientation	Fostering future-oriented virtues such as perseverance and thrift versus respect for tradition, "face" maintenance, and fulfilling social obligations.	High:	China, Hong Kong
			Low:	Nigeria, Pakistan
Schwartz (1994)				
	Egalitarianism	Valuing equality, transcendence of selfish interests, and cooperation.	High:	Italy, Spain, Portugal
			Low:	Thailand, Bulgaria
	Hierarchy	Emphasis on fulfillment of ascribed roles and an unequal distribution of power and resources.	High:	China, Uganda
			Low:	Italy, Bosnia, Ethiopia
	Harmony	Valuing harmonious fit in social and physical environments.	High:	Italy, West Germany
			Low:	Israel, Hong Kong, Ghana
	Mastery	Valuing active self-assertion and environmental mastery.	High:	China, India
			Low:	Philippines, Finland
	Intellectual Autonomy	Valuing individual pursuit of own ideas.	High:	Sweden, France
			Low:	Nigeria, Philippines
	Affective Autonomy	Valuing individual pursuit of positive affective experiences.	High:	France, Denmark
			Low:	Nigeria, Ghana
	Embeddedness	Viewing people as embedded in collectives; maintenance of status quo and stable in-group relations	High:	Nigeria, Malaysia
			Low:	West Germany, Austria

(continued on next page)

Table 15.1 | Dimensions of Culture (*continued*)

Source	Dimension	Description	Country or Culture Examples
Smith, Dugan, & Trompenaars (1996)			
	Conservatism vs. egalitarian commitment	Preference for particularistic relations (i.e., favoring one's immediate associates) and ascribed status versus universalistic (egalitarian) relations and achieved status.	Cons: Ex-Yugoslavia, Indonesia Egal: Denmark, USA
	Loyal involvement vs. utilitarian involvement	Preference for family loyalty and sharing of responsibility versus individual responsibility.	Loyal: Singapore, Burkina Faso Util: Ex-Czechoslovakia, Hungary
Chinese Culture Connection (1987)			
	Integration	Valuing tolerance, solidarity, and harmony with others; noncompetitiveness	High: W. Germany, Netherlands Low: India, Bangladesh
	Human-heartedness	Valuing patience, courtesy, and kindness.	High: Japan, Philippines Low: India, Netherlands
	Confucian Work Dynamism	Valuing persistence and thrift versus respect for tradition and protecting "face."	High: Hong Kong, Taiwan Low: Nigeria, Pakistan
	Moral discipline	Valuing restraint and moderation and prudence regarding personal desires.	High: Philippines, S. Korea Low: Zimbabwe, Sweden
Other dimensions			
	High Context vs. Low Context	Characterized by communications in which most of the information is implicit in the context or internalized in the person versus explicitly coded in the transmitted part of the message.	High: Japan, Mexico Low: Germany, USA, Sweden
	Tight vs. Loose	Characterized by explicit and stringent enforcement of group norms versus tolerance of deviations from group norms.	Tight: Japan, traditional Greece, Israel Kibbutzim Loose: Thailand, USA, Kurds

Note: Descriptions of dimensions and country/culture examples based on the following sources: Carpenter (2000); Chinese Culture Connection (1987); Hall (1976); Hofstede (2001); Schwartz (2001); Schwartz (2002); Smith, Dugan, & Trompenaars (1996); Smith & Schwartz (1997); Triandis (1995). Ind = Individualistic; Coll = Collectivistic; Masc = Masculine; Fem = Feminine; Cons = Conservatism; Egal = Egalitarian; Util = Utilitarian.

comparisons. For example, McClelland's (1961) conception of the achievement motive emphasizes individualistic striving for personal goals and thus may be culture-bound. In more collectivistic or group-centered cultures, achievement motives may be more socially oriented, emphasizing group goals, social belonging, and family achievement (Yu, 1996).

Method bias can take three forms: (1) *sample bias* (e.g., cultural samples are nonequivalent on confounding variables such as education level); (2) *instrument bias* (e.g., caused by cultural differences in response biases such as the tendency to acquiesce or agree with items regardless of their content; and (3) *administration bias* (e.g., resulting from communication problems between the assessor and assessee). Finally, *item bias* or *differential item functioning* (DIF) occurs when individuals with the same level or amount of a trait, but from different cultural groups, exhibit a different probability of answering the item in the direction scored for the trait. DIF could result from nonequivalent translation of items, or inclusion of items that are less relevant in certain cultures.

Cross-cultural researchers have devised a number of methods to investigate construct, method, and item bias. To investigate construct bias versus equivalence, researchers have applied statistical procedures (e.g., factor analysis) that examine whether the items or subscales in a personality measure intercorrelate and define the same "structure" or dimensions across cultures (e.g., Paunonen & Ashton, 1998). In studies of method bias, a number of researchers have found that respondents in different cultures use rating scales somewhat differently, causing systematic biases in the mean scores that will be compared across cultural groups (Grimm & Church, 1999). For example, Chen et al. (1995) found that Japanese and Chinese high school students were more likely than U.S. and Canadian students to use the midpoint of 7-point rating scales, while U.S. students were more likely than the other three groups to use the extreme values of the scales (i.e., ratings of 1 and 7). To reduce item bias, cross-cultural researchers emphasize the importance of careful translation (e.g., van de Vijver & Tanzer, 1997) and statistical procedures have been developed to identify items that exhibit item bias or DIF (Camilli & Sheppard, 1994).

Construct, method, and item bias can all detract from the comparability of personality scores across cultural groups. As a result, many cross-cultural psychologists are skeptical about direct cross-cultural comparisons of personality test scores and feel more comfortable investigating the structural equivalence and behavioral correlates of personality dimensions across cultures (Church & Katigbak, 2002b; Poortinga, van de Vijver, & van Hemert, 2002).

The *etic/emic distinction* has often been employed when addressing the cross-cultural equivalence of constructs, theories, and measures (Berry, 1969). The terms derive from the distinction in linguistics between phon*etics* (the study of *universal* sounds in all human languages) and phon*emics* (the study of the *unique* or language-specific meanings associated with particular sounds). *Etic* concepts or measures are universal. *Emic* concepts or measures are culture-specific; they may not be meaningful in other cultures. When researchers transport into new cultures concepts or measures that may not be relevant there, they are applying an *imposed-etic* or *pseudo-etic* strategy by presuming that the concepts or measures are etic or universal. In reality, most concepts are not purely etic or emic, but involve both etic and emic aspects in each culture. For example, Tanaka-Matsumi and Draguns (1997) suggested that depressed affect, lethargy, and somatic complaints may be universal or etic aspects of depression, whereas feelings of guilt may be an emic aspect of depression that is more prominent in Western or individualistic cultures. By identifying those elements of a concept that are shared or universal across cultures, a *derived-etic* emerges (Segall, Dasen, Berry, & Poortinga, 1990).

DIMENSIONS OF CULTURE AND RELATION TO PERSONALITY

Dimensions of Culture

To study the relationship between culture and personality we need to identify and measure dimensions along which cultures can be compared. A number of such dimensions have been identified, primarily in comparisons of entire nations (i.e., "national cultures") (Smith & Bond, 1996). Table 15.1 provides brief descriptions of some dimensions of culture, plus example nations that are high and low on each dimension. Most of these dimensions involve cultural differences in values, derived by statistically analyzing the responses of individuals in many cultures to value-based items. Several researchers have noted that there is considerable conceptual similarity and empirical overlap among the dimensions derived by different investigators, so the different sets of dimensions should not be considered highly distinct or independent of each other (Chinese Culture Connection, 1987; Hofstede, 2001; Smith & Bond, 1996).

The rankings of national cultures on these dimensions can guide the purposive sampling of cultures. However, there are disadvantages in relying solely on such rankings. First, there is significant cultural diversity within most nations, so samples of individuals may not actually differ in the ways expected based on national-level rankings. Second, unless one directly measures the individual-level differences in cultural values that are hypothesized to predict personality variables, one cannot be confident that the value differences are the explanatory variable in the study, as opposed to other variables that differentiate the cultural samples (e.g., religion, social institutions). With this in mind, instruments have been developed to measure dimensions of culture at the individual level, especially individualism-collectivism, which is viewed by many to be the most central difference between cultures.

Measuring Individualism-Collectivism

Triandis (1995) described individualism-collectivism (I-C) as a complex syndrome involving such contrasts as (1) an individualistic sense of self as an autonomous or independent person versus a collectivistic sense of self as more connected to ingroups (i.e., independent vs. interdependent self-construals; Markus & Kitayama, 1991), and (2) priority of personal goals (individualists) versus subordination of personal goals to group goals (collectivists). For Oyserman, Coon, and Kemmelmeier (2002), the core of individualism is valuing of personal independence and uniqueness, while the core of collectivism is duty to one's in-group (e.g., extended family, close friends or co-workers). The concepts of individualism and collectivism have been used to differentiate cultures as well as individuals (when applied to individuals the terms *idiocentric* and *allocentric*, respectively, are sometimes applied; Triandis, Leung, Villareal, & Clack, 1985). Activity Box 15.1 shows a measure of independent and interdependent self-construals that is commonly used to measure the self-construal component of I-C (Singelis, 1994).

The I-C construct has provided the theoretical or explanatory framework for numerous studies of personality (Oyserman et al., 2002; Triandis, 1995). However, the construct and its measures are currently undergoing considerable scrutiny (Bond, 2002; Fiske, 2002; Kitayama, 2002b). Critics have argued that many aspects of culture are too inaccessible to awareness to be measured using self-report. Such measures also falsely suggest that culture is a static entity rather than a dynamic system of meanings, practices, and mental processes. In applying such measures, researchers may commit the *ecological fallacy* by assuming that differences between cultures can be assessed by comparing mean scores on individual-level measures. Furthermore, the construct of I-C may be too broad and distal from behavior to have much explanatory power. Finally, some unexpected cultural differences have been found with these measures. For example, Japanese and Korean samples have not been found to be more collectivistic than North American samples and Latin American samples have not differed from North American samples in individualism (Oyserman et al., 2002). Accordingly, some critics have proposed that such measures be abandoned in favor of participant observation, experience sampling of ongoing behavior, or implicit measures such as projective techniques (Bond, 2002; Fiske, 2002; Kitayama, 2002b). Others continue to believe, however, that traditional self-report scales can be useful, but that they should focus on measuring specific components of I-C (Oyserman et al., 2002).

Individualism-Collectivism and Personality

Despite the ongoing debate over the I-C construct and measures, cultural mean differences in I-C have frequently conformed to expectations and the I-C distinction has been related to a number of personality variables. Oyserman et al. (2002) conducted a detailed meta-analysis of studies done since 1980 and concluded that North Americans are not distinguishable on individualism or collectivism from other English-speaking countries (Australia, New Zealand, and White South Africa). However, North Americans are higher in individualism and lower in collectivism than people in most regions of the world. Above, however, we noted exceptions to this general pattern involving Latin America, Japan, and Korea.

When cultures identified as individualistic and collectivistic have been compared, individuals in collectivistic cultures have exhibited (1) a greater sense of obligation to in-groups; (2) a greater tendency to supplement trait information with information about the situations when making inferences about behavior; (3) a greater emphasis on fulfilling social norms and achieving interpersonal harmony, rather than emotions and self-esteem, in the prediction of life satis-

Activity Box 15.1   **Measuring Independent and Interdependent Self-Construals: An Aspect of Individualism-Collectivism**

Instructions. This is a questionnaire that measures a variety of feelings and behaviors in various situations. Listed below are several statements. Read each one as if it referred to you. Beside each statement write the number that best matches your agreement or disagreement. Please respond to every statement. Thank you.

1 = Strongly Disagree	4 = Don't Agree or Disagree	5 = Agree Somewhat
2 = Disagree		6 = Agree
3 = Somewhat Disagree		7 = Strongly Agree

____   1. I enjoy being unique and different from others in many respects.

____   2. I can talk openly with a person who I meet for the first time, even when this person is much older than I am.

____   3. Even when I strongly disagree with group members, I avoid an argument.

____   4. I have respect for the authority figures with whom I interact.

____   5. I do my own thing, regardless of what others think.

____   6. I respect people who are modest about themselves.

____   7. I feel it is important for me to act as an independent person.

____   8. I will sacrifice my self-interest for the benefit of the group I am in.

____   9. I'd rather say "No" directly, than risk being misunderstood.

____   10. Having a lively imagination is important to me.

____   11. I should take into consideration my parents' advice when making education/career plans.

____   12. I feel my fate is intertwined with the fate of those around me.

____   13. I prefer to be direct and forthright with dealing with people I've just met.

____   14. I feel good when I cooperate with others.

____   15. I am comfortable with being singled out for praise or rewards.

____   16. If my brother or sister fails, I feel responsible.

____   17. I often have the feeling that my relationships with others are more important than my own accomplishments.

faction; (4) greater social anxiety and embarrassability; (e) lower optimism and self-esteem; (5) more indirect and face-saving communication patterns; (6) a greater emphasis on duty-based moral codes, as compared to the individual rights–based moral codes favored in individualistic cultures; and (7) greater preference for equal distribution of resources, over the equity- or merit-based distribution of resources favored in individualistic cultures (Heine, 2001; Oyserman et al., 2002; Triandis, 2001; Triandis & Suh, 2002).

Regarding personality traits, individualists are expected to be more independent, pleasure-seeking, assertive, creative, competitive, self-assured, efficient, and direct, whereas collectivists are expected to be more attentive, respectful, dependent, empathic, self-controlled, dutiful, self-sacrificing, con-

Activity Box 15.1 *(continued)*

_____   18. Speaking up during a class (or a meeting) is not a problem for me.
_____   19. I would offer my seat in a bus to my professor (or my boss).
_____   20. I act the same way no matter who I am with.
_____   21. My happiness depends on the happiness of those around me.
_ _ _   22. I value being in good health above everything.
_____   23. I will stay in a group if they need me, even when I am not happy with the group
_____   24. I try to do what is best for me, regardless of how that might affect others.
_____   25. Being able to take care of myself is a primary concern for me.
_____   26. It is important to me to respect decisions made by the group.
_____   27. My personal identity, independent of others, is very important to me.
_____   28. It is important for me to maintain harmony within my group.
_____   29. I act the same way at home that I do at school (or work).
_____   30. I usually go along with what others want to do, even when I would rather do something different.

Scoring

To obtain your score for independent self-construal add each number (1 to 7) for the independent items (1, 2, 5, 7, 9, 10, 13, 15, 18, 20, 22, 24, 25, 27, 29) and divide by 15. Then, do the same for the interdependent items (3, 4, 6, 8, 11, 12, 14, 16, 17, 19, 21, 23, 26, 28, 30).

Readers should be cautioned that the Self-Construal Scale was designed more for research purposes than for assessment or diagnosis of individuals. The best way for students to use their scores from this Activity Box is to compare their own independent and interdependent self-construal scores to each other to see if they have a stronger emphasis on one of the two types of self-construal or exhibit a more balanced (equal) or bicultural self-construal.

Note. Self-Construal Scale printed with the permission of Professor Ted Singelis, Department of Psychology, California State University at Chico, Chico, CA 95929-0234.

forming, and cooperative (Markus & Kitayama, 1991; Triandis, 1989, 1993). Empirical studies have generally supported these personality implications of I-C between or within cultures (e.g., Bond & Smith, 1996; Hui & Villareal, 1989; Triandis et al. 1985). Regarding I-C and the Big Five dimensions, Mc-Crae (2001) found that individualistic cultures exhibited higher average scores on Extraversion and Openness to Experience. In Estonia, Realo, Allik, and Vadi (1997) found collectivism to be modestly related to Big Five Agreeableness and Openness to Experience (inversely). In U.S. and Hong Kong samples, Kwan, Bond, and Singelis (1997) found that independent self-construals were associated with Extraversion, Conscientiousness, Neuroticism (inversely), and Openness to Experience, while interdependent self-construals were associated with Agreeableness.

Cultural psychologists have successfully applied the I-C distinction in studies of the self. A common method is the Twenty Statements Test (TST), in which respondents answer the question "Who am I?" up to 20 times. Consistent with hypothesized differences between independent versus interdependent self-concepts, researchers have expected to find larger proportions of responses referring to internal attributes (e.g., pure traits) in individualistic cultures (e.g., the United States, Australia) and larger proportions of responses referring to social roles and relationships in collectivistic cultures (e.g., Japan, India). A number of studies have supported these expectations, at least in part (e.g., Kanagawa et al., 2001; Rhee, Uleman, Lee, & Roman, 1995).

There is some TST evidence that the self-concepts of Asians are more context-specific (i.e., change more across situations and roles) than the self-concepts of Americans (Cousins, 1989; Kanagawa et al., 2001). Suh (2000) also found that ratings of one's traits were less consistent across situational contexts for Koreans than Americans, and that consistency was more strongly related to well-being for Americans. These results suggest that East Asians endorse an *incremental* view of the self (i.e., the self as more malleable or changeable), while North Americans endorse an *entity* view of the self (i.e., the self as fixed and stable) (e.g., Heine et al., 2001).

A consistent finding is that persons in individualistic cultures are more likely to exhibit self-enhancement tendencies, including (1) "false uniqueness" effects (i.e., overestimating the uniqueness of their own positive attributes); (2) unrealistic optimism regarding the likelihood of positive (vs. negative) events happening to oneself as opposed to others; (3) self-enhanced evaluations of their personality traits and performance; and (4) more positive statements about oneself (Heine, Lehman, Markus, & Kitayama, 1999). Apparently, individuals with independent selves, for whom internal attributes are more central to identity, are more motivated to identify and enhance internal attributes than are individuals with interdependent selves, who may even show a tendency to self-criticize (Kitayama, Markus, Matsumoto, & Norasakkunkit, 1997).

Some studies support the view that individuals in Asian cultures are less likely than individuals in Western cultures to attribute the causes of behavior to personality traits (e.g., Lee, Hallahan, & Herzog, 1996; Miller, 1984; Morris & Peng, 1994). However, Choi, Nisbett, and Norenzayan (1999) reviewed the evidence and concluded that cultural differences in causal attributions are more likely due to greater use of situational information in Asian cultures than a lesser tendency to infer trait causes. For example, Choi et al. (1999) cited an unpublished study by Choi and Markus in which Koreans and Americans were presented with a description of a murder case in which a high-status person (i.e., a professor) murdered a low-status person (i.e., a graduate student). Respondents were asked to explain why the murder happened. Although the Koreans and Americans did not differ in the amount of trait explanations of the murderer's behavior, Koreans did present more situational explanations than the Americans did.

Kitayama (2002a; Kitayama & Markus, 1999) proposed a *collective construction theory*, which describes how cultural models of the self (e.g., independent vs. interdependent) underlie cultural differences in the primary types of social situations in the culture. These situations then foster or encourage certain psychological tendencies. For example, Morling, Kitayama, and Miyamoto

(2002) were able to show that "influence" situations (e.g., "I talked my sister out of dating a guy I knew was a jerk") are more primary in American culture, whereas "adjustment" situations (e.g., "When I am out shopping with my friend, and she says something is cute, even when I don't think it is, I agree with her") are more primary in Japanese culture. Americans rated themselves as higher in efficacy or confidence primarily in influence situations and Japanese reported greater relatedness to others primarily in adjustment situations. In short, a strong sense of self-efficacy for North Americans and relatedness to others for East Asians may be fostered by the recurrent social situations in the respective cultural groups (Kitayama, 2002a; Kitayama et al. 1997). These studies suggest that cultural differences in the expression of personality may be intimately connected to models of the self and the prevalence of social situations that foster various personality characteristics.

DIMENSIONS OF PERSONALITY AND THEIR MEASUREMENT ACROSS CULTURES

Investigation of personality dimensions across cultures can proceed using imported (imposed-etic) or indigenous (emic) approaches. Table 15.2 summarizes issues to consider when deciding whether to use imported or indigenous instruments. Also, although the etic (universal) versus emic (culture-specific, indigenous) distinction can be useful in discussing constructs and measures, a more descriptive approach is probably to delineate a continuum of levels of test adaptation or indigenization (see Table 15.3).

Imported (Imposed-etic) Approaches

Many researchers have administered translated personality inventories in new cultural contexts. In some cases, items have been modified to make them more culturally relevant (i.e., levels 2 and 3 in Table 15.3). When the item responses have been statistically analyzed (e.g., with factor analysis), the imported personality dimensions are generally found to be well replicated in the new culture (Church & Katigbak, in press; Paunonen & Ashton, 1998). In particular, there is extensive evidence for the cross-cultural generalizability of the five-factor model of personality, as measured by the Revised NEO Personality Inventory (Costa & McCrae, 1992) and by other instruments developed to assess the Big Five dimensions (e.g., Caprara, Barbaranelli, Borgogni, & Perugini, 1993; McCrae, 2001). Even more impressive is replication of the Big Five dimensions using transported inventories that were not originally developed to measure the five-factor model, such as the Personality Research Form (Jackson, 1984) and Nonverbal Personality Questionnaire (Paunonen & Ashton, 1998).

Several points may reduce the significance of these findings, however, or the definitiveness of conclusions about the universality of personality dimensions. First, these studies have not included less literate samples, where alternative assessment methods may be needed. Second, researchers using different inventories, with somewhat different dimensions, have also replicated their

Table 15.2 | Considerations in the Use of Imported (Imposed-Etic) Versus Indigenous (Emic) Personality Measures

1. Efficiency

Although it is probably less time-consuming to translate and adapt an existing measure for use in a new culture than to develop a new indigenous measure, adaptation of imported tests may be less expedient than presumed if researchers conduct the studies needed to evaluate cross-cultural applicability and measurement equivalence. Also, training and resources for the development of indigenous measures may be limited in some cultural settings.

2. Constructs assessed

Imported measures assess constructs of interest to the researcher, and these constructs are often associated with extensive clinical and research data. However, construct equivalence across cultures needs to be demonstrated, and the researcher is more likely to identify culture-specific constructs using indigenous measures.

3. Item content

Even when imported measures assess universal constructs, some proportion of the items may not tap relevant indicators of the construct in the new cultural setting and important culture-specific indicators may be missed. This has implications for how well the construct is represented in each culture (i.e., content validity).

4. Universals versus culture-specifics

Investigators interested in demonstrating cross-cultural universality often favor imported instruments, whereas investigators interested in culture-specifics tend to favor indigenous measures. The use of imported measures may be biased toward findings of cross-cultural comparability, whereas the search for cultural differences may be facilitated by the development of more indigenous measures. Even when searching for universals, the case for universality is probably made more persuasively if researchers first allow indigenous data to structure themselves independently in different cultures, after which cross-cultural links between indigenous dimensions are sought.

5. Ease of cross-cultural comparisons

The use of imported measures facilitates direct cross-cultural comparisons of trait levels, assuming that scalar equivalence can be demonstrated. Trait levels on indigenous measures are not directly comparable, although the comparability of indigenous and imported dimensions can be compared using joint structural or regression analyses. Using Item Response Theory techniques, trait levels can be compared across cultures using sets of items that are only partially overlapping.

6. Development of indigenous and universal psychologies

Although it is short-sighted to uncritically reject imported theories, constructs, and methods, the emergence of indigenous and less ethnocentric scientific psychologies will probably be facilitated by decreased reliance on the importation of Western theories, constructs, and measures and increased focus on indigenous theory, constructs, and methods. Furthermore, it can be argued that the emergence of a more comprehensive universal psychology will result from the integration of indigenous psychologies that are derived with some degree of independence.

Note. From "Personality Measurement in Cross-Cultural Perspective," by A. T. Church, 2001, *Journal of Personality, 69*, p. 983. Copyright 2001 by Blackwell Publishers. Reprinted with permission.

Table 15.3 | Continuum or Levels of Test Adaptation/Indigenization

Imposed-etic	1. Administration of an imported test in a non-native or second language.
	2. Administration of an imported test in literal translation without item adaptations.
Indigenization from without (i.e., outside the culture studied); culture as target	3. Items modified, where necessary, to be more relevant to the new culture.
	4. Psychometric investigations of cross-cultural applicability and equivalence (e.g., local norm development; analyses of reliability, dimensional structure, validity, differential item functioning; differential response styles).
	5. Indigenous items/content developed to assess constructs identified in (primarily Western) psychological literature (content indigenization).
Indigenization from within (i.e., inside the culture studied); culture as source; emic	6. Indigenous constructs identified and assessed with indigenous items/content.
	7. Consideration or incorporation of more culturally relevant response formats and administration procedures (format indigenization).
	8. Consideration of appropriateness of item content, response formats, and administration procedures for diverse indigenous subpopulations (e.g., less westernized or educated individuals).
	9. Investigation of the reliability and construct validity of indigenous measures, including studies using indigenous criteria.

Note: Indigenization-from-without versus indigenization-from-within and culture-as-target versus culture-as-source terminology used by Enriquez (1994). Content versus format indigenization terminology used by Sahoo (1993). Imposed-etic versus emic terminology used by Berry (1969), among others.

From "Personality Measurement in Cross-Cultural Perspective," by A. T. Church, 2001, *Journal of Personality, 69,* p. 984. Copyright by Blackwell Publishers. Adapted with permission.

dimensions across cultures. This indicates that transported inventories facilitate emergence of their embedded structure or dimensions—even if these dimensions are somewhat different from those in other inventories—by incorporating many items that assess the particular dimensions targeted by the instrument. Third, dimensions derived using indigenous approaches sometimes carve up the personality space differently (Church, Katigbak, & Reyes, 1998; Yang & Bond, 1990). Fourth, there is little consensus on the nature and number of more specific personality traits "under" the Big Five. For example, the number of specific traits that are organized under the Big Five domains in various inventories ranges from 10 to 30 (Church & Katigbak, in press). Finally, cross-cultural comparisons of the situational behaviors that measure particular traits have rarely been made. Therefore, we do not know much about whether particular traits are manifested differently in behavior across cultures (Huang, Church, & Katigbak, 1997).

Indigenous Approaches

Lexical Studies   To identify indigenous personality dimensions, researchers in the United States and a growing number of other countries have applied the lexical approach, which assumes that the personality characteristics that are salient in particular cultures will have become encoded in the natural language(s) (Saucier & Goldberg, 2001). Typically, researchers cull from comprehensive dictionaries all terms referring to personality characteristics, then respondents in the culture describe or rate their personality using large and representative sets of these trait terms (e.g., friendly, dominant, sensitive). Statistical analyses are then conducted to identify the dimensions or "factors" that account for the correlations among the rated trait terms.

These procedures have been used in the Czech, Dutch, English, Filipino, French, German, Hungarian, Italian, Korean, Polish, and Turkish languages. Similar studies with representative, but not comprehensive, sets of trait terms have been conducted in the Hebrew, Russian, Spanish, Japanese, and Chinese languages (for reviews, see Ashton & Lee, 2001; de Raad, Perugini, Hebíková, & Szarota, 1998; Saucier & Goldberg, 2001). The key issue in these studies involves the number of lexically based dimensions that can be viewed as universal. Support for the existence of the Big Five dimensions in these cultures has been good, with the Intellect (or Openness to Experience) dimension exhibiting the most cultural variation (Ashton & Lee, 2001; de Raad et al., 1998).

Alternative lexical models have been proposed. In Table 15.4 we match up dimensions from these models that are similar or comparable. Ashton and Lee (2001) suggested that a separate Honesty dimension can be identified in most cultures that is relatively independent of the Big Five dimensions (i.e., a "Big Six" model). A Big Seven model has been derived when highly evaluative terms have been included, comprising dimensions corresponding to the Big Five (but labeled somewhat differently), plus dimensions labeled Positive Valence (e.g., remarkable, extraordinary, and exceptional) and Negative Valence (e.g., stupid, useless, depraved) (e.g., Benet & Waller, 1995). Saucier (2001) noted resemblances between the seven dimensions identified in the Hebrew and Filipino lexical studies, which suggested a Multi-language 7 (ML7) model. Yang and Wang (2002) identified six dimensions that replicated well across Taiwan and mainland Chinese samples and two sample-specific dimensions (Table 15.4 shows the seven Taiwan dimensions). Although these alternative models divide up the personality domain somewhat differently, they also indicate that similar lexically based dimensions are derived in most cultures.

Indigenous Inventories   Indigenous inventories provide a promising, but relatively untapped source of information on the cultural universality versus uniqueness of personality dimensions. A number of inventories developed around the world have included local items, but the items were written to assess Western personality constructs (i.e., content indigenization; level 5 in Table 15.3). An example is the Global Personality Inventory, for which items measuring the Big Five dimensions were contributed by psychologists in 14 countries, but items thought to be specific to particular cultures were eliminated (Schmit, Kihm, & Robie, 2002). Although these inventories may contain items that are somewhat less bound to particular cultures (i.e., *culturally decentered*), this approach is unlikely to reveal culture-specific dimensions.

Some researchers, however, have used more completely indigenous approaches, with local items written to measure local constructs (level 6 in Table

Table 15.4 | Lexically Based Personality Dimensions: Alternative Models

Big Five/Six	Big Seven	Multi-Language 7	Taiwan Seven
Extraversion	Positive Emotionality	Gregariousness	Extraversion
Agreeableness	Agreeableness	Concern for others (versus Egotism)	Agreeableness Other-Orientedness
Conscientiousness	Conscientiousness	Conscientiousness	Industriousness
Emotional Stability (versus Neuroticism)	Negative Emotionality	Even Temper Self-Assurance	Optimism Large-Mindedness
Intellect[a]	Conventionality[a]	Intellect[a]	Competence
Honesty[b]	—	—	—
—	Negative Valence[c]	Negative Valence[c]	—
—	Positive Valence[c]	—	—

Note. See text for explanation of table entries. When two dimensions correspond to the same Big Five dimension they are not double-spaced in the table (e.g., the Multi-Language 7 dimensions of Even Temper and Self-Assurance both correspond to aspects of Big Five Emotional Stability (vs. Neuroticism). [a]The Intellect dimension corresponds closely to Big Five Openness to Experience, but lexical researchers typically use the Intellect label; Conventionality is approximately the inverse or opposite of Openness to Experience. [b]Ashton and Lee (2001) add Honesty to the Big Five dimensions. [c]Positive and/or Negative Valence dimensions emerge when highly evaluative terms are included.

15.3). In some cases, these measures have been validated against locally relevant criteria (level 9 in Table 15.3). La Rosa and Díaz-Loving (1991; see also Díaz-Loving, 1998) developed a Mexican self-concept measure using trait adjectives generated by cultural informants. Interestingly, considerable conceptual overlap seems apparent between the factor-analytically derived Mexican dimensions and the Big Five dimensions as follows: (1) Mexican Affiliative Sociability (e.g., courteous, amiable) and Inter-individual Feelings (e.g., tender, loving) resemble aspects of Big Five Agreeableness; (2) Expressive Sociability (e.g., friendly, communicative) and Initiative (e.g., dynamic, quick, dominant) resemble Extraversion; (3) Emotional States (e.g., happy, jovial) and Emotional Health (e.g., calm, serene) resemble Emotional Stability; (4) the Occupational dimension (e.g., reliable, studious, responsible) resembles Conscientiousness; and (5) the Ethical dimension (e.g., honest, sincere, upright) resembles Ashton and Lee's (2001) Honesty dimension. These indigenous dimensions may carve up the personality space somewhat differently, but they do not appear to be highly culture-specific or unrecognizable to non-Mexicans.

Probably the best evidence for an indigenous dimension adding something new to Western inventories comes from the development of the Chinese Personality Assessment Inventory (CPAI) by Cheung and colleagues (Cheung et al., 1996; Cheung et al., 2001). In a combined etic (universal)–emic (culture-specific) approach, these researchers wrote locally relevant items to measure (1) dimensions believed to be culturally universal (although the dimensions were identified originally in Western literature and instruments) and (2) more indigenous concepts of specific interest to Chinese culture. Examples of indigenous concepts included (1) Harmony: inner peace of mind, avoidance of conflict; (2) *Ren Qing* (Relationship Orientation): adherence to cultural norms of interaction based on reciprocity and exchange of favors; (3) Thrift versus Extravagance: a traditional virtue involving thriftiness versus hedonistic spending; and (4) Face: behaviors that enhance one's face (e.g., pretending to understand a lot, to prevent being looked down upon by others) and behaviors that avoid losing face (e.g., not admitting the mistakes one has made). These are among the scales that identify, in factor analyses of the CPAI scales, an Interpersonal Relatedness dimension that is independent of the Big Five dimensions. Further research is needed to determine whether the Interpersonal Relatedness dimension is unique to Chinese populations. Indigenous test development projects have been rare, so it is not yet possible to draw confident conclusions about the likelihood of identifying personality dimensions that are unique to particular cultures.

AN ILLUSTRATIVE RESEARCH PROGRAM: INDIGENOUS AND CROSS-CULTURAL RESEARCH ON FILIPINO PERSONALITY TRAITS AND DIMENSIONS

We can illustrate indigenous and cross-cultural approaches by drawing on our own personality research in the Philippines, where the indigenization movement (i.e., the development of indigenous concepts, methods, and instruments) has been particularly strong (Church & Katigbak, 2002a; Enriquez, 1994). In terms of the dimensions of culture described in Table 15.1, the Philippines has been found to be (1) very high in Power Distance, Moral Discipline, Human-heartedness, and Embeddedness; (2) very low in Uncertainty Avoidance, Long-term Orientation, Confucian Work Dynamism, Mastery, and Affective and Intellectual Autonomy; and (3c) substantially lower than the United States in individualism (Chinese Culture Connection, 1987; Hofstede, 1980, 2001; Schwartz, 2002). We organize our overview of studies by addressing several questions that are relevant to the study of personality across cultures.

Are Personality Traits Used to Describe or Understand Persons in All Cultures?

In the Philippines, the answer to this question is "yes." For example, we have asked Filipino college students in interview and questionnaire studies to describe the characteristics of Filipinos with healthy or unhealthy personalities. In their responses, respondents often made use of trait terms such as *matulungin* (helpful), *masipag* (industrious), and *masungit* (temperamental) (Church & Katigbak, 1989). Indeed, based on comprehensive lexical studies with the Filipino (Tagalog) language, we have concluded that Filipinos have a large and refined vocabulary for describing personality traits. We culled from a comprehensive Filipino dictionary 6,900 adjectives that can be used to describe aspects of persons (e.g., personality traits, mental abilities, experiential states, social roles and effects; Church, Katigbak, & Reyes, 1996). We then asked trained Filipino judges and large samples of Filipino college students to indicate which terms referred to personality traits or mental abilities. The result was 1,297 such adjectives. By comparing our results with those in other languages, we determined that the number of person-descriptive adjectives in Filipino is roughly comparable in size to that reported by lexical researchers in the German, Dutch, Italian, Spanish, Hungarian, Czech, and Polish languages, but substantially smaller than the English person-descriptive lexicon. On the other hand, whereas more than 80% of Filipino trait adjectives were rated as moderately to very familiar by college-educated Filipinos, about three-quarters of English trait terms are too obscure, ambiguous, or slangy to be useful for personality assessment (Norman, 1967).

Do the Trait Terms in Different Cultures Refer to Similar Personality Characteristics?

To learn whether trait terms in different cultures refer to similar personality characteristics, we asked judges to classify the 1,297 Filipino trait terms, plus a representative list of 1,431 English trait terms compiled by Norman (1967), into a 133-category English taxonomy based on the Big Five dimensions (Goldberg, 1990). We found that Filipino terms could be identified for each of the 133 categories, indicating that the Filipino and English languages make comparable trait distinctions. We also found that the relative sizes of the Big Five domains were quite similar across the two languages. The largest number of terms refers to characteristics in the Agreeableness domain. The Extraversion and Conscientiousness domains were the next largest, and the Emotional Stability (vs. Neuroticism) and Intellect (or Openness to Experience) domains were the smallest. These results suggested that (1) the Big Five domains do a good job of subsuming the various personality characteristics referred to in the Filipino language; and (2) the relative size of the Big Five domains may indicate their relative importance, or at least their degree of refinement, in person description in most cultures (Church et al., 1996). This is not to say that the personality characteristics referred to in different cultures are identical. Most bilinguals can provide examples of trait terms that are difficult to translate across languages. However, the trait terms identified in the languages studied thus far apparently refer to very similar personality characteristics.

How Well Do Dimensions Assessed by Imported Inventories Replicate Across Cultures?

Dimensions assessed by imported inventories apparently replicate well across cultures. We have administered the Revised NEO Personality Inventory (NEO-PI-R; Costa & McCrae, 1992) in the Philippines in both Filipino and English versions (English is a language of instruction in the Philippines) (Katigbak, Church, & Akamine, 1996; Katigbak et al., 2002). A third study, using the

Filipino version, was reported by McCrae, Costa, del Pilar, Rolland, and Parker (1998). In all three studies, the Big Five dimensions were well replicated in factor analyses of the scales of the instrument. That is, the Big Five dimensions provide one acceptable representation of personality structure in the Philippines, although they might not provide the optimal representation.

Can Cultural Differences in Average Trait Levels Be Inferred from Comparisons of Scores on Personality Inventories?

We have conducted three types of studies that raise questions about the legitimacy of direct comparisons of inventory scores across cultures. First, in two studies we have found evidence that Filipinos and Americans respond differently to Likert-type scales. In a study of 16 academic motives (e.g., Thinking Motives, Achieving Motives, Grades Orientation), Church and Katigbak (1992) found that Filipino college students averaged higher than American college students on all 16 scales, possibly because of a stronger acquiescence or agreement response style. Grimm and Church (1999) found that Americans more than Filipinos exhibited a tendency to rate their own personality traits in a socially desirable manner, consistent with greater self-enhancement tendencies.

Second, we found that almost 40% of the items of the NEO Personality Inventory performed differently (i.e., exhibited differential item functioning) in comparisons of Filipinos and Americans (Huang et al., 1997). That is, these items were either (1) less relevant as measures of the intended personality trait in one or the other culture, or (2) endorsed less frequently in one or the other culture by persons who actually have equal amounts of the trait. Eliminating these items resulted in fewer average differences between the scores of Filipinos and Americans on the scales.

Third, we investigated whether NEO-PI-R scores of Filipinos, when compared to American norms, would conform to hypotheses regarding personality differences between Americans and Filipinos. We found rather good agreement between hypotheses derived from the literature and the judgments of bicultural judges who had lived a long time in both cultures. However, the hypotheses received only limited or partial support in the actual Filipino mean profiles. For example, Filipinos, as expected, averaged higher than Americans in Self-Consciousness, Tender-Mindedness, and Compliance, and lower on Excitement-Seeking and Openness to Values. However, predicted higher scores for Filipinos on Warmth, Positive Emotions, Altruism, and Modesty, and predicted higher scores for Americans on Assertiveness, Straightforwardness, Openness to Actions, and Openness to Ideas, were not supported. We considered a number of reasons for this, including the possibility that the NEO-PI-R items, like the items of many personality inventories, are rather context-free. For example, they do not sufficiently take into account the ingroup-outgroup distinction that may be more important in determining behavior in collectivistic cultures such as that of the Philippines. All three sources of evidence considered here lead us to be skeptical about the meaningfulness of direct comparisons of personality scores across cultures.

Do Indigenous Lexical Studies Reveal Culture-Specific Personality Dimensions?

Using the Filipino trait adjectives derived in our lexical studies, we have asked large samples of Filipino college and high school students to describe their own personalities by rating each trait on a 6-point scale ranging from "extremely inaccurate as a description of me" to "extremely accurate as a description of me." Seven indigenous dimensions have emerged repeatedly in these studies (e.g., using factor analysis) and we have labeled them as follows: Concern for Others versus Egotism, Gregariousness, Temperamentalness, Self-Assurance, Conscientiousness, Intellect, and Negative Valence (Church, Reyes, Katigbak, & Grimm, 1997; Church et al., 1996, 1998; Katigbak et al., 2002). In several studies we have correlated scores on these dimensions with measures of the Big Five dimensions and found good one-to-one correspondences between Philippine Concern for Others and Big Five Agreeableness, Philippine Conscientiousness and Big Five Conscientiousness, Philippine Gregariousness and Big Five Extraversion, and, to a lesser extent, Philippine Intellect and Big Five Intellect or Openness to Experience. The Philippine Temperamentalness and Self-Assurance dimensions, although generally most related to Big Five Neuroticism (vs. Emotional Stability), have tended to be related to more than one Big Five dimension. Our lexical results have not supported the need for a distinct Honesty dimension, as in Ashton and Lee's (2001) "Big Six" model. However, the Philippine dimensions do correspond well to Saucier's (2001) Multilanguage 7 model, which derived in part from the Filipino lexical results (see Table 15.4). Indeed, Filipino lexical studies suggest that more than five dimensions, albeit resembling the Big Five, are needed for a comprehensive description of Filipino personality.

Do Indigenous Inventories Reveal Culture-Specific Personality Dimensions?

We have studied this question with several Philippine inventories. Some of the most persuasive support for the Big Five dimensions in the Philippines comes from our factor analysis of the scales of the *Panukat ng Pagkataong Pilipino* (PPP; Carlota, 1985), an indigenous inventory that measures 19 traits considered particularly relevant for Filipinos (Katigbak at al., 2002). Interpretation of the four dimensions or factors identified, and their correlations with Big Five measures, indicated that one dimension was a blend of Big Five Neuroticism and Agreeableness, and the other three dimensions corresponded closely to Big Five Extraversion, Conscientiousness, and Openness to Experience. A few PPP scales (Social Curiosity, Risk-Taking, and Religiosity) overlapped less well with the Big Five dimensions and therefore may be particularly salient, or constructed somewhat differently, in the Philippines. However, these constructs are not unknown in Western cultures.

Another way to determine whether indigenous dimensions add anything unique beyond imported dimensions is to examine whether they increase the accuracy of prediction of important societal criteria beyond that obtained with imported scales alone. We compared the ability of our Filipino lexical dimensions, Carlota's (1985) PPP dimensions, and the Filipino NEO-PI-R to predict self-reported smoking, drinking, gambling, praying, accident proneness, tolerance of homosexuality, and tolerance of extramarital and premarital sexual relations. The indigenous scales did not outperform the imported scales, but they did increase the accuracy of prediction to a modest extent (Katigbak et al., 2002).

We have also developed an indigenous inventory that measures Filipino college students' conceptions of healthy personality (Church & Katigbak, 1989; Katigbak et al., 1996). The inventory items refer to behaviors that the students provided as exemplars of the various healthy personality concepts. Factor analyses of self-ratings on these items resulted in six dimensions, which we labeled Responsibility, Social Potency, Emotional Control, Concern for Others, Broad-Mindedness, and Affective Well-being. Although developed using a different method, these dimensions are similar conceptually to the Filipino lexical dimensions based on trait adjectives. We have also found moderate to strong correlations relating these Philippine inventory dimensions to the Big Five and to the dimensions of Tellegen's (1982) Multidimensional Personality Questionnaire. Thus, none of the Philippine dimensions are highly culture-specific. However, the Broad-Mindedness and Concern for Others dimensions were less related to the Western dimensions, perhaps because of cultural differences in the behavioral exemplars of these two dimensions. The Broad-Mindedness dimension measures openness to different ideas and acceptance of the uniqueness of individuals, themes that resemble Big Five Openness to Experience. However, some Broad-Mindedness items refer to being open to giving, receiving, and learning from criticism, themes that appear absent from the NEO-PI-R Openness to Experience dimension. Similarly, the Philippine Concern for Others dimension contains items that refer to behaviors that are probably more relevant or ordinary occurrences for Filipinos than for Americans (e.g., doing chores for relatives, caring for ill grandparents, giving gifts when visiting a friend, sharing food with friends and classmates).

SUMMARY

Cross-cultural studies of personality examine the influence of culture on personality and the universality versus cultural uniqueness of personality dimensions and processes. In so doing, they address the generalizability of personality theory, concepts, and methods and broaden perspectives on human behavior beyond that which can be achieved in studies of single cultures. The study of culture and personality is thriving, but it needs to avoid the pitfalls or questionable assumptions of early culture-and-personality studies. Alternative perspectives on the study of culture and personality—including cross-cultural, cultural, indigenous, and evolutionary—differ in their treatment of the culture variable and in the focus of their studies, but personality research will likely benefit from each approach and their possible integration. Some unique conceptual and methodological issues characterize the field, including special problems in sampling of cultures and individuals and issues of conceptual and measurement bias versus equivalence.

To investigate the influence of culture on personality, researchers have identified and measured a number of ecological and cultural dimensions that can be used to differentiate cultures. Some of these dimensions, especially individualism-collectivism, have also been used to assess culture-related variables at the individual level. Although the individualism-collectivism construct and measures are vulnerable to a number of criticisms, the construct has been rather successful in organizing, and possibly explaining, a wide variety of findings related to personality and self.

Personality researchers have applied both imported (imposed-etic) and indigenous (emic) measures in the investigation of personality dimensions across cultures and each approach has specifiable advantages and disadvantages. There is good support from both imported and indigenous approaches for the universality of dimensions resembling the Big Five dimensions of Extraversion, Agreeableness, Conscientiousness, Emotional Stability (vs. Neuroticism), and Intellect (or Openness to Experience). However, indigenous studies sometimes suggest cultural differences in the optimal dimensional representation of personality structure and may yet reveal culture-unique dimensions. Direct comparisons of average levels of personality traits across cultures remain controversial, and conceptual and measurement equivalence issues necessitate considerable caution in such comparisons. Research conducted in the Philippines illustrates the cross-cultural and indigenous perspectives in the study of personality traits and dimensions across cultures and has led to conclusions that are consistent with those noted in this summary.

DISCUSSION QUESTIONS

1. Why do psychologists study personality across cultures? Consider the importance of cross-cultural studies for both the science and practice of psychology. What research questions are asked in such studies?

2. Discuss how the cross-cultural, cultural, indigenous, and evolutionary psychology perspectives differ in regard to (1) how they tend to treat the culture variable, (2) the extent to which they anticipate cultural universality versus uniqueness of personality dimensions, and (3) the focus of personality research. Do you think these approaches are complementary or incompatible?

3. Discuss some unique issues of sampling and bias versus equivalence encountered in cross-cultural studies? Do these conceptual and methodological difficulties seem surmountable?

4. For the culture, nation, or ethnic group that you know best, discuss whether you think it would be characterized as high, low, or intermediate on each of the dimensions of culture shown in Table 15.1. Does this discussion suggest any difficulties or cautions in characterizing cultures in terms of such dimensions?

5. Would you describe yourself as an individualist, collectivist, or both (e.g., see Activity Box 15.1)? Do the findings relating individualism-collectivism

and aspects of personality fit your perceptions of your individualistic or collectivistic tendencies?

6. What are the advantages and disadvantages of applying imposed-etic (imported/transported) versus emic (indigenous) inventories in the science and practice of psychology? Do research findings regarding the structure or dimensions of personality tend to differ depending on which approach is used?

7. Why might comparisons of personality trait levels of different cultural or ethnic groups be controversial and need to be made with considerable caution? Take into account both measurement equivalence issues and sociopolitical considerations (e.g., labeling, stereotypes).

SUGGESTED READINGS

Bond, M. H. (1997). *Working at the interface of cultures: Eighteen lives in social science*. New York: Routledge. Fascinating autobiographical accounts written by leading cross-cultural researchers, relating how their personal experiences in different cultures shaped their thinking and research on culture.

Church, A. T. (Ed.). (2001). Culture and personality. *Journal of Personality* [Special issue], 69(6). A collection of articles by experts in the field, who address anthropological, cross-cultural, indigenous, and evolutionary psychology perspectives on culture and personality, as well as cross-cultural methodology and personality measurement.

Church, A. T., & Lonner, W. T. (1998). Personality and its measurement in cross-cultural perspective. *Journal of Cross-Cultural Psychology* [Special issue], 29(1). A high-quality collection of articles, particularly if you are interested in personality measurement across cultures. See also the incisive article by Markus and Kitayama on the cultural psychology approach to personality, contrasting independent versus interdependent conceptions of personality and self.

Lee, Y. T., McCauley, C., & Draguns, J. (1999). *Personality and person perception across cultures*. Mahwah, NJ: Lawrence Erlbaum. Readable chapters on theory and practice, with greater focus on person perception and stereotypes than the other suggested readings.

McCrae, R. R. (Ed.). (2000). Personality traits and culture: New perspectives on some classic issues. *American Behavioral Scientist* [Special issue], 44(1). An engaging set of cross-cultural personality articles with an emphasis on the trait approach, including studies in the Philippines, Malaysia, Hong Kong, South Africa, Russia, and Spain.

Triandis, H. C. (1995). *Individualism & collectivism*. Boulder, CO: Westview. For a thorough and readable review of individualism and collectivism by a leading proponent, this would be a good place to start.

van de Vijver, F. J. R., & Leung, K. (1997). *Methods and data analysis for cross-cultural research*. Thousand Oaks, CA: Sage. Perhaps the best single reference on cross-cultural research methods and data analysis, although technical in spots.

SUGGESTED WEB SITES

http://www.ac.wwu.edu/~culture
Online readings in Psychology and Culture, organized and maintained by the Center for Cross-Cultural Research at Western Washington University. Contains short, invited chapters in all areas of psychology by an international collection of cross-cultural researchers. Refer especially to Unit 2: Conceptual, Methodological, and Ethical Issues in Psychology and Culture, and Unit 6: Measuring Personality and Values Across Cultures.

http://www.iaccp.org
Web site of the International Association for Cross-Cultural Psychology, containing information on cross-cultural research projects, publications (e.g., journals and books), educational resources (course

syllabi, film lists, graduate programs), conferences, plus more.

http://expert.cc.purdue.edu/~qguo/dimensions.html
Created by Xin Meng and Jennifer Guo at Purdue University, this web site contains descriptions of some of the dimensions of culture listed in Table 15.1, as well as additional information such as the rankings of countries on Hofstede's cultural dimensions.

INFOTRAC COLLEGE EDITION SEARCH TOPICS

Culture	Culture and personality	Individualism-collectivism
Cross-cultural	Etic	Independent and interdependent
Indigenous	Emic	self-construals
Cultural psychology	Cultural bias versus equivalence	Personality structure

REFERENCES

Ashton, M. C., & Lee, K. (2001). A theoretical basis for the major dimensions of personality. *European Journal of Personality, 15,* 327–353.

Barkow, J., Cosmides, L., & Tooby, J. (Eds.). (1992). *The adapted mind.* New York: Oxford University Press.

Barrett, P. T., Petrides, K. V., Eysenck, S. B. G., & Eysenck, H. J. (1998). The Eysenck Personality Questionnaire: An examination of the factorial similarity of P, E, N, and L across 34 countries. *Personality and Individual Differences, 25,* 805–819.

Benedict, R. (1934). *Patterns of culture.* Boston: Houghton Mifflin.

Benet, V., & Waller, N. G. (1995). The "Big Seven" model of personality description: Evidence for its cross-cultural generality in a Spanish sample. *Journal of Personality and Social Psychology, 69,* 701–718.

Berry, J. W. (1969). On cross-cultural comparability. *International Journal of Psychology, 4,* 119–128.

Berry, J. W. (2000). Cross-cultural psychology: A symbiosis of cultural and comparative approaches. *Asian Journal of Social Psychology, 3,* 197–205.

Bock, P. K. (2000). Culture and personality revisited. *American Behavioral Scientist, 44,* 32–40.

Bond, M. H. (2002). Reclaiming the individual from Hofstede's ecological analysis—A 20-year odyssey: Comment on Oyserman et al. (2002). *Psychological Bulletin, 128,* 73–77.

Bond, R., & Smith, P. B. (1996). Culture and conformity: A meta-analysis of studies using Asch's (1952b, 1956) line judgment task. *Psychological Bulletin,119,* 111–137.

Buss, D. M. (1989). Sex differences in human mate preferences: Evolutionary hypotheses testing in 37 cultures. *Behavioral and Brain Sciences, 12,* 1–49.

Buss, D. M. (1996). Social adaptation and five major factors of personality. In J. S. Wiggins (Ed.), *The five-factor model of personality: Theoretical perspectives* (pp. 180–207). New York: Guilford Press.

Buss, D. M. (2001). Human nature and culture: An evolutionary psychological perspective. *Journal of Personality, 69,* 955–978.

Camilli, G., & Shepard, L. A. (1994). *Methods for identifying biased test items.* Thousand Oaks, CA: Sage Publications.

Caprara, G. V., Barbaranelli, C., Borgogni, L., & Perugini, M. (1993). The Big Five Questionnaire: A new questionnaire for the measurement of the five factor model. *Personality and Individual Differences, 15,* 281–288.

Carlota, A. J. (1985). The development of the Panukat ng Pagkataong Pilipino (PPP). *Philippine Journal of Educational Measurement, 4,* 55–68.

Chen, C., Lee, S. Y., & Stevenson, H. W. (1995). Response style and cross-cultural comparisons of rating scales among East Asian and North American students. *Psychological Science, 6,* 170–175.

Cheung, F. M., Leung, K., Fan, R. M., Song, W. Z., Zhang, J. X., & Zhang, J. P. (1996). Development of the Chinese Personality Assessment

Inventory. *Journal of Cross-Cultural Psychology, 27*, 181–199.

Cheung, F. M., Leung, K., Zhang, J. X., Sun, H. F., Gan, Y. Q., Song, W. Z., et al. (2001). Indigenous Chinese personality construct: Is the Five-Factor Model complete? *Journal of Cross-Cultural Psychology, 32*, 407–433.

Chinese Culture Connection. (1987). Chinese values and the search for culture-free dimensions of culture. *Journal of Cross-Cultural Psychology, 18*, 143–164.

Choi, I., Nisbett, R. E., & Norenzayan, A. (1999). Causal attribution across cultures: Variation and universality. *Psychological Bulletin, 125*, 47–63.

Choi, S. -C., Kim, U., & Choi, S. -H. (1993). Indigenous analysis of collective representations: A Korean perspective. In U. Kim & J. W. Berry (Eds.), *Indigenous psychologies: Research and experience in cultural context* (pp. 193–210). Newbury Park, CA: Sage.

Church, A. T. (2000). Culture and personality: Toward an integrated cultural trait psychology. *Journal of Personality, 68*, 651–703.

Church, A. T. (2001). Introduction. *Journal of Personality, 69*, 787–801.

Church, A. T., & Katigbak, M. S. (1989). Internal, external, and self-report structure of personality in a non-Western culture: An investigation of cross-language and cross-cultural generalizability. *Journal of Personality and Social Psychology, 57*, 857–872.

Church, A. T., & Katigbak, M. S. (1992). The cultural context of academic motives: A comparison of American and Filipino college students. *Journal of Cross-Cultural Psychology, 23*, 40–58.

Church, A. T., & Katigbak, M. S. (2002a). Indigenization of psychology in the Philippines. *International Journal of Psychology, 37*, 129–148.

Church, A. T., & Katigbak, M. S. (2002b). The five-factor model in the Philippines: Investigating trait structure and levels across cultures. In R. R. McCrae & J. Allik (Eds.), *The five-factor model across cultures* (pp. 129–154). New York: Kluwer Academic/Plenum Publishers.

Church, A. T., & Katigbak, M. S. (in press). Personality structure across cultures: Indigenous and cross-cultural perspectives. In S. Hampson & P. Borkenau (Series Eds.) & A. Eliasz, S. Hampson, & B. de Raad (Vol. Eds.), *Advances in personality psychology. Vol. II*. London: Psychology Press.

Church, A. T., Katigbak, M. S., & Reyes, J. A. S. (1996). Toward a taxonomy of trait adjectives in Filipino: Comparing personality lexicons across cultures. *European Journal of Personality, 10*, 3–24.

Church, A. T., Katigbak, M. S., & Reyes, J. A. S. (1998). Further exploration of Filipino personality structure using the lexical approach: Do the big-five or big-seven dimensions emerge? *European Journal of Personality, 12*, 249–269.

Church, A. T., Reyes, J. A. S., Katigbak, M. S., & Grimm, S. D. (1997). Filipino personality structure and the Big Five model: A lexical approach. *Journal of Personality, 65*, 477–528.

Costa, P. T., Jr., & McCrae, R. R. (1992). *Revised NEO Personality Inventory (NEO-PI-R) and NEO Five-Factor Inventory (NEO-FFI) professional manual*. Odessa, FL: Psychological Assessment Resources.

Cousins, S. D. (1989). Culture and selfhood in Japan and the U.S. *Journal of Personality and Social Psychology, 56*, 124–131.

Cross, S. E., & Markus, H. R. (1999). The cultural constitution of personality. In L. A. Pervin & O. P. John (Eds.), *Handbook of personality: Theory & research* (2nd ed., pp. 378–396). New York: Guilford Press.

Dana, R. H. (Ed.). (2000). *Handbook of cross-cultural and multicultural personality assessment*. Mahwah, MJ: Lawrence Erlbaum.

de Raad, B., Perugini, M., Hebíková, M., & Szarota, P. (1998). Lingua franca of personality: Taxonomies and structures based on the psycholexical approach. *Journal of Cross-Cultural Psychology, 29*, 212–232.

Díaz-Loving, R. (1998). Contributions of Mexican ethnopsychology to the resolution of the etic-emic dilemma in personality. *Journal of Cross-Cultural Psychology, 29*, 104–118.

Diener, E., Diener, M., & Diener, C. (1995). Factors predicting the subjective well-being of nations. *Journal of Personality and Social Psychology, 69*, 851–864.

Doi, L. T. (1978). Amae: A key concept for understanding Japanese personality structure. In R. J. Corsini (Ed.), *Readings in current personality theories* (pp. 213–219). Ithaca, NY: Peacock Publishers.

Dubois, C. (1944). *The people of Alor*. Minneapolis: University of Minnesota Press.

Enriquez, V. G. (1994). *From colonial to liberation*

psychology: The Philippine experience. Manila, Philippines: De La Salle University Press.

Fiske, A. P. (2000). Complementarity theory: Why human social capacities evolved to require cultural complements. *Personality and Social Psychology Review, 4,* 76–94.

Fiske, A. P. (2002). Using individualism and collectivism to compare cultures—A critique of the validity and measurement of the constructs: Comment on Oyserman et al. (2002). *Psychological Bulletin, 128,* 78–98.

Freud, S. (1950). *Totem and taboo.* New York: Norton.

Funder, D. C. (2001). Personality. *Annual Review of Psychology, 52,* 197–221.

Georgas, J., & Berry, J. W. (1995) An ecocultural taxonomy for cross-cultural psychology. *Cross-Cultural Research: The Journal of Comparative Social Science, 29,* 121–157.

Goldberg, L. R. (1990). An alternative "description of personality": The big-five factor structure. *Journal of Personality and Social Psychology, 59,* 1216–1229.

Gorer, G., & Rickman, J. (1949). *The people of Great Russia.* London: Cresset Press.

Greenfield, P. M. (2000). Three approaches to the psychology of culture: Where do they come from? Where can they go? *Asian Journal of Social Psychology, 3,* 223–240.

Grimm, S. D., & Church, A. T. (1999). A cross-cultural study of response biases in personality measures. *Journal of Research in Personality, 33,* 415–441.

Hall, E. T. (1976). *Beyond culture.* Garden City, NY: Anchor Books.

Heine, S. J. (2001). Self as a cultural product: An examination of East Asian and North American selves. *Journal of Personality, 69,* 880–906.

Heine, S. J., Kitayama, S., Lehman, D. R., Takata, T., Ide, E., Leung, C., & Matsumoto, H. (2001). Divergent consequences of success and failure in Japan and North America: An investigation of self-improving motivations and malleable selves. *Journal of Personality and Social Psychology, 81,* 599–615.

Heine, S. J., Lehman, D. R., Markus, H. R., & Kitayama, S. (1999). Is there a universal need for positive self-regard? *Psychological Review, 106,* 766–794.

Ho, D. Y. F., Peng, S. Q., Lai, A. C., & Chan, S. F. (2001). Indigenization and beyond: Methodological relationalism in the study of personality across cultural traditions. *Journal of Personality, 69,* 925–953.

Hofstede, G. (1980). *Culture's consequences: International differences in work-related values.* Newbury Park, CA: Sage.

Hofstede, G. (2001). *Culture's consequences* (2nd ed.)*: Comparing values, behaviors, institutions, and organizations across nations.* Thousand Oaks, CA: Sage.

Hogan, R. (1996). A socioanalytic perspective on the five-factor model. In J. S. Wiggins (Ed.), *The five-factor model of personality: Theoretical perspectives* (pp. 163–179). New York: Guilford Press.

Huang, C. D., Church, A. T., & Katigbak, M. S. (1997). Identifying cultural differences in items and traits: Differential item functioning in the NEO Personality Inventory. *Journal of Cross-Cultural Psychology, 28,* 192–218.

Hui, C. H., & Villareal, M. J. (1989). Individualism-collectivism and psychological needs: Their relationships in two cultures. *Journal of Cross-Cultural Psychology, 20,* 310–323.

Jackson, D. N. (1984). *Personality Research Form manual* (3rd ed.). Port Huron, MI: Research Psychologists Press.

Kanagawa, C., Cross, S. E., & Markus, H. R. (2001). "Who am I?" The cultural psychology of the conceptual self. *Personality and Social Psychology Bulletin, 27,* 90–103.

Kardiner, A. (1939). *The individual and his society.* New York: Columbia University Press.

Kardiner, A., Linton, R., Du Bois, C., & West, J. (1945). *The psychological frontiers of society.* New York: Columbia University Press.

Katigbak, M. S., Church, A. T., & Akamine, T. X. (1996). Cross-cultural generalizability of personality dimensions: Relating indigenous and imported dimensions in two cultures. *Journal of Personality and Social Psychology, 70,* 99–114.

Katigbak, M. S., Church, A. T., Guanzon-Lapeña, M. A., Carlota, A. J., & del Pilar, G. H. (2002). Are indigenous personality dimensions culture specific? Philippine inventories and the five-factor model. *Journal of Personality and Social Psychology, 82,* 89–101.

Kitayama, S. (2002a). Cultural psychology of the self: A renewed look at independence and interdependence. In C. von Hofsten & L. Baeckman (Eds.), *Psychology at the turn of the millennium,*

Vol 2: Social, developmental, and clinical perspectives (pp. 305–322). Florence, KY: Taylor & Frances/Routledge.

Kitayama, S. (2002b). Culture and basic psychological theory—Toward a system view of culture: Comment on Oyserman et al. (2002). *Psychological Bulletin, 128*, 89–96.

Kitayama, S., & Markus, H.R. (1999). Yin and yang of the Japanese self: The cultural psychology of personality coherence. In D. Cervone & Y. Shoda (Eds.), *The coherence of personality: Social cognitive bases of personality consistency, variability, and organization* (pp. 242–302). New York: Guilford.

Kitayama, S., Markus, H. R., Matsumoto, H., & Norasakkunkit, V. (1997). Individual and collective processes in the construction of the self: Self-enhancement in the United States and self-criticism in Japan. *Journal of Personality and Social Psychology, 72*, 1245–1267.

Kluckhohn, C., & Murray, H. A. (Eds.). (1948*). Personality in nature, culture and society*. New York: Knopf.

Kwan, V. S. Y., Bond, M. H., & Singelis, T. M. (1997). Pancultural explanations for life satisfaction: Adding relationship harmony to self-esteem. *Journal of Personality and Social Psychology, 73*, 1038–1051.

La Rosa, J., & Díaz-Loving, R. (1991). Evaluación del autoconcepto: Una escala multidimensional [Evaluation of the self-concept: A multidimensional inventory]. *Revista Latinoamericana de Psicología, 23*, 15–33.

Lee, F., Hallahan, M., & Herzog, T. (1996). Explaining real-life events: How culture and domain shape attributions. *Personality and Social Psychology Bulletin, 22*, 732–741.

LeVine, R. A. (2001). Culture and personality studies, 1918–1960: Myth and history. *Journal of Personality, 69*, 803–818.

Lynn, R., & Martin, T. (1996). National differences for thirty-seven nations in extraversion, neuroticism, psychoticism and economic, demographic and other correlates. *Personality and Individual Differences, 19*, 403–406.

MacDonald, K. (1998). Evolution, culture, and the five-factor model. *Journal of Cross-Cultural Psychology, 29*, 119–149.

Markus, H. R., & Kitayama, S. (1991). Culture and self: Implications for cognition, emotion, and motivation. *Psychological Review, 98*, 224–253.

Markus, H. R., & Kitayama, S. (1998). The cultural psychology of personality. *Journal of Cross-Cultural Psychology, 29*, 63–87.

Marsella, A. J., Dubanoski, J., Hamada, W. C., & Morse, H. (2000). The measurement of personality across cultures: Historical, conceptual, and methodological issues and considerations. *American Behavioral Scientist, 44*, 41–62.

McClelland, D. C. (1961) *The achieving society*. Princeton, NJ: Van Nostrand.

McCrae, R. R. (2000). Trait psychology and the revival of personality and culture studies. *American Behavioral Scientist, 44*, 10–31.

McCrae, R. R. (2001). Trait psychology and culture: Exploring intercultural comparisons. *Journal of Personality, 69*, 819–846.

McCrae, R. R., & Allik, J. (Eds.). (2002). *The five-factor model across cultures*. New York: Kluwer Academic/Plenum.

McCrae, R. R., & Costa, P. T., Jr. (1996). Toward a new generation of personality theories: Theoretical contexts for the five-factor model. In J. S. Wiggins (Ed.), *The five-factor model of personality: Theoretical perspectives* (pp. 51–87). New York: Guilford.

McCrae, R. R., & Costa, P. T., Jr. (1997). Personality trait structure as a human universal. *American Psychologist, 52*, 509–516.

McCrae, R. R., Costa, P. T., Jr., del Pilar, G. Y., Rolland, J.-P., & Parker, W. D. (1998). Cross-cultural assessment of the five-factor model: The Revised NEO Personality Inventory. *Journal of Cross-Cultural Psychology, 29*, 171–188.

Miller, J. G. (1984). Culture and the development of everyday social explanation. *Journal of Personality and Social Psychology, 46*, 961–978.

Morling, B., Kitayama, S., & Miyamoto, Y. (2002). Cultural practices emphasize influence in the United States and adjustment in Japan. *Personality and Social Psychology Bulletin, 28*, 311–323.

Morris, M. W., & Peng, K. (1994). Culture and cause: American and Chinese attributions for social and physical events. *Journal of Personality and Social Psychology, 67*, 949–971.

Norman, W. T. (1967). *2800 personality trait descriptors: Normative operating characteristics for a university population*. Unpublished manuscript, University of Michigan, Ann Arbor.

Oyserman, D., Coon, H. M., & Kemmelmeier, M. (2002). Rethinking individualism and collectivism: Evaluation of theoretical assumptions and meta-analyses. *Psychological Bulletin, 128,* 3–72.

Paunonen, S. V., & Ashton, M. C. (1998). The structured assessment of personality across cultures. *Journal of Cross-Cultural Psychology, 29,* 150–170.

Poortinga, Y. H., van de Vijver, F. J. R., & van Hemert, D. A. (2002). Cross cultural equivalence of the Big Five. In R. R. McCrae & J. Allik (Eds.), *The five-factor model across cultures* (pp. 281–302). New York: Kluwer Academic/Plenum.

Realo, A., Allik, J., & Vadi, M. (1997). The hierarchical structure of collectivism. *Journal of Research in Personality, 31,* 93–116.

Rhee, E., Uleman, J. S., Lee, H. K., & Roman, R. J. (1995). Spontaneous self-descriptions and ethnic identities in individualistic and collectivistic cultures. *Journal of Personality and Social Psychology, 69,* 142–152.

Sagiv, L., & Schwartz, S. H. (2000). A new look at national culture: Illustrative applications to role stress and managerial behavior. In N. M. Ashkanasy, C. P. M. Wilderom, & M. F. Peterson (Eds.), *Handbook of organizational culture and climate* (pp. 417–435). Thousand Oaks, CA: Sage.

Sahoo, F. M. (1993). Indigenization of psychological measurements: Parameters and operationalization. *Psychology and Developing Societies, 5,* 1–13.

Sapir, E. (1956). *Culture, language, and personality: Selected essays.* Berkeley, CA: University of California Press.

Saucier, G. (2001, August). *Going beyond the Big Five.* Invited address presented at the meeting of the 109th Annual Convention of the American Psychological Association, San Francisco.

Saucier, G., & Goldberg, L. R. (2001). Lexical studies of indigenous personality factors: Premises, products, and prospects. *Journal of Personality, 69,* 847–879.

Schmit, M. J., Kihm, J. A., & Robie, C. (2002). The Global Personality Inventory (GPI). In B. de Raad & M. Perugini (Eds.), *Big Five assessment* (pp. 195–236). Seattle, WA: Hogrefe & Huber.

Schwartz, S. H. (1994). Beyond individualism/collectivism: New cultural dimensions of values. In U. Kim, H. C. Triandis, C. Kagitçibasi, S. C. Choi, & G. Yoon (Eds.), *Individualism and collectivism: Theory, method, and applications* (pp. 85–119). Thousand Oaks, CA: Sage.

Schwartz, S. H. (2002). [Country means on value dimensions]. Unpublished table.

Segall, M. H., Dasen, P. R., Berry, J. W., & Poortinga, Y. P. (1990). *Human behavior in cross-cultural perspective: An introduction to cross-cultural psychology.* New York: Pergamon Press.

Shweder, R. A. (2000). The psychology of practice and the practice of the three psychologies. *Asian Journal of Social Psychology, 3,* 207–222.

Singelis, T. M. (1994). The measurement of independent and interdependent self-construals. *Personality and Social Psychology Bulletin, 20,* 580–591.

Sinha, D. (1993). Indigenization of psychology in India and its relevance. In U. Kim & J. W. Berry (Eds.), *Indigenous psychologies: Research and experience in cultural context* (pp. 30–43). Newbury Park, CA: Sage.

Sinha, D. (1997). Indigenizing psychology. In J. W. Berry, Y. H. Poortinga, & J. Pandey (Eds.), *Handbook of cross-cultural psychology: Vol. 1. Theory and method* (2nd ed., pp. 129–169). Boston: Allyn & Bacon.

Smith, P. B., & Bond, M. H. (1996). *Social psychology across cultures* (2nd ed.). Needham Heights, MA: Allyn & Bacon.

Smith, P. B., Dugan, S., & Trompenaars, F. (1996). National culture and the values of organizational employees: A dimensional analysis across 43 nations. *Journal of Cross-Cultural Psychology, 27,* 231–264.

Suh, E. M. (2000). Culture, identity consistency, and subjective well-being. *Dissertation Abstracts International: Section B: The Sciences and Engineering, 60*(9-B), 4950.

Tanaka-Matsumi, J., & Draguns, J. G. (1997). Culture and psychopathology. In J. W. Berry, M. H. Segall, & C. Kagitçibasi (Eds.), *Handbook of cross-cultural psychology: Vol. 3. Social and behavioral applications* (2nd ed., pp. 449–491). Boston: Allyn & Bacon.

Tellegen, A. (1982). *Brief manual for the Differential Personality Questionnaire.* Unpublished manuscript, University of Minnesota.

Tooby, J., & Cosmides, L. (1992). Psychological foundations of culture. In J. Barkow, L. Cosmides,

& J. Tooby (Eds.), *The adapted mind* (pp. 19–136). New York: Oxford University Press.

Triandis, H. C. (1989). The self and social behavior in differing cultural contexts. *Psychological Review, 96,* 506–520.

Triandis, H. C. (1993). Collectivism and individualism as cultural syndromes. *Cross-Cultural Research, 27,* 155–180.

Triandis, H. C. (1995). *Individualism and collectivism.* Boulder, CO: Westview Press.

Triandis, H. C. (2000). Dialectics between cultural and cross-cultural psychology. *Asian Journal of Social Psychology, 3,* 185–195.

Triandis, H. C. (2001). Individualism-collectivism and personality. *Journal of Personality, 69,* 907–924.

Triandis, H. C., Leung, K., Villareal, M. J., & Clack, F. L. (1985). Allocentric versus idiocentric tendencies: Convergent and discriminant validation. *Journal of Research in Personality, 19,* 395–415.

Triandis, H. C., Marin, G., Lisansky, J., & Betancourt, H. (1984). *Símpatia* as a cultural script of Hispanics. *Journal of Personality and Social Psychology, 47,* 1363–1375.

Triandis, H., & Suh, E. (2002). Cultural influences on personality. *Annual Review of Psychology, 53,* 133–160.

van de Vijver, F. J. R., & Leung, K. (1997). *Methods and data analysis for cross-cultural research.* Thousand Oaks, CA: Sage.

van de Vijver, F., & Tanzer, N. K. (1997). Bias and equivalence in cross-cultural assessment: An overview. *European Review of Applied Psychology, 47,* 263–279.

van de Vliert, E., Schwartz, S. H., Huismans, S. E., Hofstede, G., & Daan, S. (1999). Temperature, cultural masculinity, and domestic political violence: A cross-national study. *Journal of Cross-Cultural Psychology, 30,* 291–314.

van Hemert, D. A., van de Vijver, F. J. R., Poortinga, Y. H., & Georgas, J. (2002). Structural and functional equivalence of the Eysenck Personality Questionnare within and between countries. *Personality and Individual Differences, 33,* 1229–1249.

Wallace, A. F. C. (1961). *Culture and personality.* New York: Random House.

Yang, K. S. (2000). Monocultural and cross-cultural indigenous approaches: The royal road to the development of a balanced global psychology. *Asian Journal of Social Psychology, 3,* 241–263.

Yang, K. S., & Bond, M. H. (1990). Exploring implicit personality theories with indigenous or imported constructs: The Chinese case. *Journal of Personality and Social Psychology, 58,* 1087–1095.

Yang, K. S., & Wang, D. F. (2002, July). Are corresponding indigenous and imported basic personality dimensions similarly related to motivation, attitude, and behavior? The Chinese case. In A. T. Church (Chair), *Indigenous and cross-cultural analysis of personality.* Symposium conducted at the meeting of the 25th International Congress of Applied Psychology, Singapore.

Yu, A. B. (1996). Ultimate life concerns, self, and Chinese achievement motivation. In M. H. Bond (Ed.), *The handbook of Chinese psychology* (pp. 227–246). Hong Kong: Oxford University Press.

Stress and Illness | 16

KATHLEEN A. LAWLER

REBECCA L. VOLZ

MARINA F. MARTIN

CHAPTER OUTLINE

Stress is an inherent part of living in a developed, industrialized society. From the external difficulties of life in cities, with crowding, crime, and traffic jams, to the internal difficulties of trying to manage time, maintain quality interpersonal relationships, and sustain a positive self-concept, stress is woven throughout many of our activities from work to family life to recreation. Stress can stimulate and energize our experiences, but it can also undermine our sense of control and render us more vulnerable to psychological and physical ailments. The sources of stress in our lives, our responses to these stressors, and the relationship of stress to illness comprise the major themes of this chapter. In addition, we focus on the role that personality plays in exacerbating or dampening the effects of stress on our health. Two personality factors, hostility and depression, increase the negative effects of stress, while hardiness and optimism are associated with enhanced resistance to stress.

MODELS OF STRESS

Stress is an experience familiar to almost everyone, but it is difficult to define precisely. One common definition, reached by a consensus of researchers, is that stress is a process in which environmental demands tax or exceed the adaptive capacity of an organism, resulting in psychological and biological changes that may place an individual at risk for disease (Cohen, Kessler, & Gordon, 1995). This definition encompasses the three basic areas of stress research, aptly described by Cox (1978): (1) stress as the stimulus characteristics of disturbing or unpleasant environments, (2) stress as a person's response to disturbing environments, and (3) stress as a lack of fit between the demands of the environment and the resources of an individual. Personality plays an important role in all three of these approaches: Some individuals experience more stressful events than others, some individuals experience the same event as more stressful than others, and personality is a major individual resource with which one responds to stress. In reviewing the literature on stress and illness, we shall discuss each of these areas in turn; all are important for a complete understanding of stress and its experience by individuals.

The Environmental Stress Perspective

The earliest focus on the situational factors leading to the experience of stress emerged from the work of psychiatrist Adolf Meyer (Lief, 1948). He was concerned that physicians were attending only to the physical symptoms presented by their patients and ignoring important psychological factors, such as losing a job. He recommended that physicians complete a life chart for each patient, including both major life events and physical disorders and the age at which each of these was experienced, in order to determine an accurate diagnosis of any current condition. This approach was influential and led to the development of the Social Readjustment Rating Scale or SRRS (Holmes & Rahe, 1967), the most popular method of measuring life stress today. This scale, shown in Table 16.1, contains 43 items, each associated with corresponding weights (Life Change Unit [LCU] values), which reflect the magnitude of adaptation required

Table 16.1   Events Listed on the Social Readjustment Rating Scale

Life event	LCU	Life event	LCU
Death of spouse	100	Son or daughter leaving home	29
Divorce	73	Trouble with in-laws	29
Marital separation	65	Outstanding personal achievement	28
Jail term	63	Wife begins or stops work	26
Death of close family member	63	Begin or end school	25
Personal injury or illness	53	Change in living conditions	25
Marriage	50	Revision of personal habits	24
Fired from job	47	Trouble with boss	23
Marital reconciliation	45	Change in work hours or conditions	20
Retirement	45	Change in residence	20
Change in health of family member	44	Change in schools	20
Pregnancy	40	Change in recreation	19
Sex difficulties	39	Change in church activities	19
Gain of new family member	39	Change in social activities	18
Business readjustment	39	Mortgage or loan less than $10,000	17
Change in financial state	38	Change in sleeping habits	16
Death of close friend	37	Change in number of family get-togethers	15
Change to different line of work	36	Change in eating habits	15
Change in number of arguments with spouse	35	Vacation	13
Mortgage over $10,000	31	Christmas	12
Foreclosure of mortgage or loan	30	Minor violations of the law	11
Change in responsibilities at work	29		

Source: Reprinted by permission of the publisher from "The Social Readjustment Rating Scale," T. H. Holmes and R. H. Rahe, *Journal of Psychosomatic Research, 11,* 216. Copyright 1967 by Elsevier Science.

by each event. The events pertain to major areas of significance in the social structure of the American way of life, such as changes in the family resulting from death or divorce, changes in occupation or education, and financial difficulties. Some of these are desirable events, in accordance with American values of achievement and success, while others are negative, but each event requires some adjustment or coping behavior on the part of the individual involved. The weights are derived from the amount of adjustment or change required, as rated by a broad sample of ordinary individuals and not from the psychological meaning or social desirability of the event. An individual checks off all events experienced within a specified time frame, generally the previous six months to two years, and their weighted scores are summed. This leads to a total stress score expressed as a Life Change Unit score.

Since the development of the SRRS, hundreds of studies have examined the relationship between stress and illness. Some of these studies have focused on particular illnesses, such as heart disease or cancer, while others have recorded ill health in general. For example, Rahe (1968) quantified the number of life events for 2,500 Naval personnel, just before they boarded their ships for a six-month tour of duty at sea. He found that men in the high LCU group had significantly more new illnesses and more illness each month of the six-month cruise than did men in the low LCU group.

Stone and colleagues (Stone et al., 1992) examined the relationship of life stress and susceptibility to colds. The rhinovirus infection is one of the most common acute infections, but approximately one third of infected persons do not develop clinical symptoms. After filling out a life events survey, 17 undergraduate students were administered nasal inoculations of rhinovirus (associated with symptoms of the common cold). Seventy percent of the exposed students developed a cold whereas 30% remained healthy. The students who developed colds had three times as many life events as the healthy students. While this study links stress to the artificial inoculation of rhinovirus, few studies have examined stress effects on the naturally acquired common cold. Takkouche, Regueira, and Gestel-Otero (2001) carried out a one-year, prospective study on faculty and staff at a University in Spain. Four dimensions of stress all predicted cold symptoms: stressful life events, perceived stress, negative affect (self-descriptions, such as nervous and irritable), and positive affect (self-descriptions, such as happy and enthusiastic), as measured by the Positive and Negative Affect Scale (PANAS; Watson, Clark, & Tellegen, 1988). The highest quartiles of stressful life events and perceived stress had two to three times the number of colds as expected (incidence rates of 2.0 and 2.8), while the highest quartile of negative affect had almost four times the expected rate (incidence rate of 3.7). These findings support the conclusion that psychological stress, especially when experienced as negative affect, is a risk factor for the common cold, reflecting diminished immune system competence.

Although accepting the principle that stressful experiences may reduce a person's resistance to disease, many scientists have questioned the wisdom of quantifying stressors by using event checklists. As you might expect, for some persons a particular life event, such as losing a job, may be extremely stressful, especially if it occurs in a time of high unemployment and that individual is the sole breadwinner for a family of four. However, for other persons, losing an unsatisfactory job may open a door of opportunity to find something better or to move to a new location. Thus, checklist methods of measuring stressors neglect individual differences in event impact. In addition, several other concerns have been raised about these scales (Rabkin & Struening, 1976), three of which are listed here:

1. Although positive correlations are often reported between stressor LCU level and illness, the absolute magnitude of these correlations tends to be about .30, suggesting that only a relatively small percentage (about 9% or less) of the variation in illness among people is due to the influence of stress.

2. The list of life events generally reflects external stressors, but some items on the list may also be the result of illness. For example, a change in

Figure 16.1 | Daily numbers of sudden deaths related to cardiovascular disease from January 10 through 23, 1994 (January 17, 1994, was the day the earthquake struck the Los Angeles area in California).

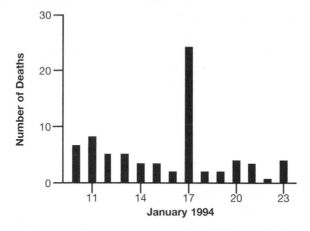

Source: From "Sudden Cardiac Death Triggered by an Earthquake," by J. Leor, W. K. Poole, and R. A. Kloner, 1996, *The New England Journal of Medicine, 334*, p. 415. Reprinted by permission of *The New England Journal of Medicine.* Copyright 1996 Massachusetts Medical Society. All rights reserved.

sleeping habits may be an external stressor brought on by moving to the night shift at work, but it may also be an outcome of illness. Thus, a correlation between life events and illness may be artificially increased by this item contamination.
3. In many studies, illness is documented by visits to a doctor or clinic. Thus, the stress-illness relationship may reflect an association between stressful life events and care-seeking behavior as much as actual illness.

These concerns have led to improvements in the assessment of life events as well as to other models or ways of thinking about stress.

Staying within the environmental stress perspective, some researchers have chosen to examine the health effects of specific stressors rather than a grand tally of different events. These individual events range from common experiences (Engel, 1967), such as life in a large city or divorce, to traumatic events. One of the clearest examples of an association between stress-as-an-event and illness was documented by Leor, Poole, and Kloner (1996). On January 17, 1994, one of the strongest earthquakes ever recorded in a major city in North America occurred in the Los Angeles area of California. This earthquake provided an opportunity to examine the relationship between acute emotional stress and sudden death due to cardiac causes, such as heart attacks or fatal arrhythmias. Based on data collected from the Los Angeles County coroner's office, the number of deaths increased from an average of 35.7 during the seven days before the earthquake to 101 on the day of the earthquake.

Figure 16.1 displays the number of sudden deaths from cardiovascular disease from January 10 to 23, 1994, showing a fivefold increase on January 17.

These deaths did not result directly from earthquake-associated injuries, and they occurred in individuals already at risk of death from heart disease; two thirds occurred immediately or within one hour after the earthquake. Estimating from these data, the researchers concluded that approximately 41% of all sudden deaths may be due to environmental triggers or emotional stress.

Similar findings have been reported in relation to asthma and the World Trade Center attack of September 11, 2001. A telephone survey of Manhatten residents, five to nine weeks after the attack, found that 27% of adults with asthma reported more severe symptoms (Morbidity and Mortality Weekly Report, 2002a). Interestingly, the two strongest predictors of increased symptoms were difficulty breathing because of smoke and debris *and* having two or more life stressors during the preceding year (defined as death of a close family member, serious illness or injury, change in marital status, change in family or work situation, or emotional problems). Even high school and college students who were rapidly evacuated from the World Trade Center area experienced higher levels of depression and post-traumatic stress syndrome in the subsequent four to six months, when contrasted with comparable students more than five miles from the area (*Morbidity and Mortality Weekly Report,* 2002b). Finally, research two years before the attack found that mere exposure to a large, metropolitan area, such as New York City, has important health consequences (Christenfeld, Glynn, Phillips, & Shrira, 1999). Residents of New York City had higher death rates from heart disease (155% of the expected rate), compared to visitors to the city (134% of expected rate) or to residents traveling outside the city (80% of expected rate). While the particular causal factors linked to living in a big city have not been identified, the researchers suggest that exposure to stress is a primary candidate.

More familiar events, such as the divorce of parents, have also been found to predict ill health. Friedman and colleagues (1995) examined a longitudinal sample of gifted California girls and boys, initially studied in 1921. About half of these individuals had died, and the association between psychosocial variables and cause of death could be studied. Adults whose parents were divorced when they were children (before age 21) had a one-third higher death rate than adults whose parents remained married. Similarly, domestic abuse, either sexual or physical, also has long-term effects on health, even after the abuse has ended. A recent study of adult women (Campbell et al., 2002) found that women who had been sexually or physically abused in the preceding four to twelve years now experienced more headaches, back pain, and other chronic stress-related health problems in comparison to a random sample of never-abused women. Finally, women with college degrees who have higher levels of family responsibilities and job strain have higher blood pressure than educated women with lower levels of family and job stress (Brisson et al., 1999). Thus, even in intellectually gifted and generally advantaged individuals, the effects of stress can be *long lasting* and harmful to health.

Despite these associations between environmental stressors and illness, there are still large individual differences. Most of us know people who have endured hardships and even catastrophic events and remained healthy and productive. Clearly, quantifying the stressful nature of an environment cannot tell us which individuals in that environment will remain healthy and which will fall ill. The need to assess individual vulnerability has led to the second model of stress, the response-based view.

Response-Based Views of Stress

In 1956, Hans Selye, in his book *The Stress of Life*, proposed that rather than being a characteristic of one's environment, stress is a nonspecific, biological response of the body to any demand placed on it. He called this nonspecific response the General Adaptation Syndrome. This syndrome or response is an adaptive reaction of the body to environmental events that progresses, with sufficient time, through three stages: alarm, resistance, and exhaustion. The alarm stage represents the initial sympathetic nervous system response to a threat or challenge that mobilizes the body for fight or flight. Our awareness of a pounding heart or sweaty palms as we approach a final exam is a manifestation of the alarm stage. For many short-term stressors, the stress response is experienced entirely as this brief arousal phenomenon. If the stressor takes on a more chronic nature, as in a stressful job—such as air-traffic controller or worker in a hot and noisy factory—our bodies may adapt to the stressor by moving into the stage of resistance. Now the person is functioning reasonably well under the stress, but is doing so at a cost to bodily health, which may ultimately be expressed as high blood pressure, stomach ulcers, chronic headaches, or lower back pain.

According to Selye, the classic signs of exposure to stress, caused by continued pituitary and adrenal cortex activation, are shrunken thymus, spleen, and lymph glands, enlarged adrenal glands, and ulceration of the stomach and gut. With continued exposure to stress, the body finally weakens under the strain of adapting and moves into the stage of exhaustion. This collapse either removes the person from the stressful situation, thereby leading to the possibility of healing, or precedes death. According to Selye (1993), the body's adaptability or adaptation energy is finite. We do not know precisely what is lost, but Selye states that resistance is analogous to "an inherited bank account from which we can make withdrawals but to which we apparently cannot make deposits" (Selye, 1993, p. 10).

Recent response-based theories have further expanded Selye's ideas, especially focusing on the role of chronic, or long-term stress. The body has a variety of systems (the hypothalamic-pituitary axis, the autonomic nervous system, the metabolic system, and the immune system) that continually alter their states in an effort to adapt to surroundings and demands. This process of continual change, in the service of adaptation, is called allostasis (Sterling & Eyer, 1988), and the wear and tear on the body that is the outcome of continual adaptation is called allostatic load (McEwen & Stellar, 1993). This wear and tear occurs in three separate, but related ways: (1) increased magnitude or frequency of the physiological stress response, (2) failure to terminate the stress response quickly and efficiently, and (3) inability to mount an adequate stress reaction. McEwen and Stellar (1993) review the evidence that each of these pathways is linked to illness. Examples of illness associated with increased magnitude or frequency of the stress response are headaches and heart attacks; examples associated with failure to recover to pre-stress levels are high blood pressure, obesity, and Type II (adult-onset) diabetes; and examples associated with inability to mount a sufficient stress response are post-traumatic stress syndrome, chronic fatigue syndrome, and autoimmune or inflammatory disorders, such as lupus.

Pruessner, Hellhammer and Kirschbaum (1999) studied burnout in teachers. Burnout is a syndrome, observed in caregivers, teachers, and hospital staff, that consists of exhaustion, fatigue, headaches, and disturbed sleep. The teachers with high levels of burnout had lower levels of cortisol (a hormone secreted by the adrenal cortex in response to stress) on awakening in the morning, an indication of a reduced ability to respond to stress. In addition, the teachers with high burnout and high stress had twice the number of pain-related complaints and the lowest level of self-esteem. Frequent stress, leading to an increased frequency of stress responses may, over time, facilitate the development of delayed recovery and insufficient stress response mobilization.

Thus, according to McEwen and Stellar (1993), it is important to appreciate that the same body systems that promote adaptation and homeostasis can also cause harm when overstimulated because of frequent or chronic exposure to stress. However, even these newer response-based models of stress fail to address the issue of individual differences in the perception of stress. Why do individuals vary so significantly in the effects of stress on the body? This question has led to a third type of stress model, which attempts to include individual perception as a critical step linking environmental stress to bodily responses.

A Transactional Model of Stress

The environmental model and the response-based model can be fused to present a reasonably complete picture of an individual reacting to a stressful situation. However, they place the individual in a passive role of reacting to the stressors experienced. In addition, they are unable to explain how individuals could differ in response to the same stressful situation. To respond to these issues, several theorists have proposed a transactional model, as in Figure 16.2, emphasizing an individual's perception of the environment as stressful and the selection of a particular strategy or coping response with which to respond (Lazarus & Launier, 1978). In this model, cognitive appraisal of the stressor is more important than the stressor itself: Because humans perceive and evaluate their environments, they also select and shape them, thus contributing to or preventing certain kinds of stress from ever happening (Lazarus, 1990).

The transactional model emphasizes the significance or the meaning of a potentially stressful event for an individual. Lazarus and Folkman (1984) identified two types of appraisal processes: primary and secondary. Primary appraisal is the initial evaluation a person makes to determine whether an event is meaningful and, if so, the degree to which the event is threatening. Secondary appraisal is another evaluative step involving the assessment of coping resources and options. When demands are perceived as potentially threatening, stress may or may not be experienced, depending on the confidence one has in being able to master the demand. Reappraisal is an additional process that per-

Figure 16.2   A biopsychological framework for stress-health interactions.

Cognitive assessment moderates both the interpretation of experience and the selection of an appropriate coping response.

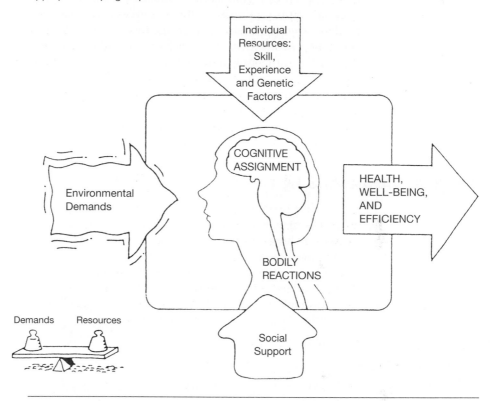

Source: From "The Psychophysiology of Workload, Stress, and Health: Comparison Between the Sexes," by M. Frankenhaeuser, 1991, *Annals of Behavioral Medicine, 13* (1991), 198. Used with permission.

mits one to revise either one's estimate of the stressor or one's resources for coping with it.

Coping with stress can be defined as the thoughts and ways that a person employs to deal with stress. There are two general ways of coping: problem-focused coping and emotion-focused coping. Problem-focused coping strategies are directed at defining the demand, generating solutions, and taking action to reduce, eliminate, or overcome the problem. A student facing the stress of making a failing grade in a class may respond by seeking help from the teacher, studying harder, or joining a study group; these are all examples of problem-focused coping responses. Emotion-focused coping is directed at reducing the level of emotional distress felt, especially when changing the situation is not feasible, such as in the case of the illness or death of a loved one. Emotion-focused coping strategies consist of minimizing the problem or searching for strategies to minimize felt distress, such as talking with friends, exercising, or praying.

To summarize, stress can be thought of as an event in the environment, such as an earthquake. Or, stress can be thought of as a biological response, such as the General Adaptation Syndrome or allostatic load. However, many researchers prefer a model that includes a process of cognitive appraisal: Is this demand important and are my resources a sufficient match? Transactional models provide a useful framework for studying individual differences in the perception of stress, as well as behavioral and physiological reactions to stress. Personality differences may make some individuals perceive stress more readily or even create more stressful events in their lives. In addition, personality differences affect both the selection of coping strategies and the efficacy of their employment. In the next section, we shall examine the role that personality factors play in the stress-illness relationship.

PERSON VARIABLES IN THE STRESS-ILLNESS RELATIONSHIP

Personality psychologists have played a key role in studying the person variables that may moderate the stress-illness relationship. Person variables are defined as a category of constructs that include personality traits, such as extraversion or neuroticism, and also transient psychological states, such as anger or depression. Scheier and Bridges (1995) examined the literature for the person variables most strongly predictive of illness. They found four variables that were strongly related to health outcomes: anger/hostility, depression, pessimism/fatalism, and suppression of emotions.

Personality Traits

In 1987, Friedman and Booth-Kewley examined the published literature on personality traits and illness with a statistical technique called meta-analysis. This technique allows researchers to combine findings from many studies and examine both the consistency and the magnitude of a relationship. They assessed four personality traits: anxiety, depression, anger/hostility/aggression, and extraversion, and five diseases: coronary heart disease, asthma, ulcers, arthritis, and headache. All of these personality factors were associated with coronary heart disease, asthma, and arthritis; depression was strongly associated with headache and ulcers. Taken together, anxiety and depression were most strongly related to all five diseases. They concluded that rather than thinking of specific disease-related personalities, such as a "migraine personality," the associations better support a "disease-prone personality" with the specific disease dependent on physiological or genetic factors.

Friedman and Booth-Kewley (1987) also examined pathways through which personality might lead to illness or health. First, they noted that certain aspects of personality may be the result of disease rather than its precursor. Thus, caution is necessary in considering concurrent measures of personality and illness. Second, personality could lead to disease through poor or unhealthy habits, such as overeating or smoking. Third, there could be a direct link from a personality variable to a physiological mechanism, as we shall see with regard to hostility. Last, a third variable could underlie both the personality factor and the health status. For example, a hyperreactive (increased frequency or magnitude of stress responses) nervous system could lead to both chronic anxiety and coronary heart disease. To the extent that most serious illnesses have a multifactorial etiology, it is important to consider that personality may be linked to illness through all of these pathways: poor health behaviors, physiological responses, and underlying variables.

In a recent paper on long-term predictors of health, rather than illness, Friedman (2000) found that conscientiousness, a personality trait measured by the NEO Personality Inventory, was an important and overlooked factor predicting health. Conscientiousness, or a tendency to be prudent, planful, persistent, and dependable, is not highly related to most personality measures used in health research. However, when assessed in childhood, it predicted survival into middle and old age. This relationship may be due to healthy behaviors, since conscientious children were less likely as adults to smoke and drink. Conscientiousness was also linked to a lower death rate in a group of patients with chronic renal (kidney) insufficiency (Christensen et al., 2002).

In the sections that follow, we will explore research on the single personality variables of anger/hostility, depression, optimism, and hardiness. Suppression of emotion will be examined within the context of anger.

Hostility and Anger

Interest in hostility grew out of earlier work on the coronary-prone or Type A behavior pattern (Rosenman et al., 1975), a complex of aggressive, competitive, and time urgent behaviors that predicted the future development of coronary heart disease. Acute cases of myocardial infarction (heart attack) eight years after the Type A testing were more likely in Type A men, especially when they manifested a readiness to become angry, anger directed outward, and frequent experiences of anger. Attempts to determine which components of Type A behavior are particularly linked to heart disease led to the current focus on hostility and anger (Matthews, Glass, Rosenman, & Bortner, 1977).

Hostility is defined as a cynical attitude toward other people, for example, assuming that they cannot be trusted and will not have the hostile person's best interests at heart. It is often measured by a subset of items from the Minnesota Multiphasic Personality Inventory, described as the Cook-Medley Hostility Index (Cook & Medley, 1954). Several studies have examined the association between scores on this hostility scale during young adulthood and coronary heart disease in middle age. Barefoot, Dahlstrom, and Williams (1983) found that men who had scored above the median on this scale 25 years earlier, when they were medical school students, had five times the incidence of clinical coronary heart disease as those who scored below the median. Other studies have found similar associations (e.g., Barefoot et al., 1987), leading researchers to search for explanations of the path by which hostility might lead to pathology in the cardiovascular system. Williams and colleagues (1980) presented data

Figure 16.3 | Relation of Type A behavior pattern, hostility, and gender to the presence of significant coronary occlusions.

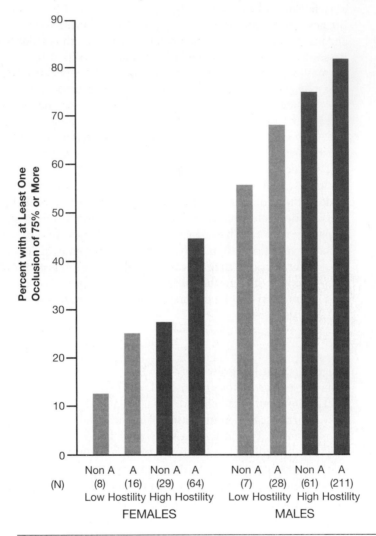

Source: "Type A Behavior, Hostility, and Coronary Atherosclerosis," by R. S. Williams, T. L. Haney, K. L. Lee, Y-H Kong, J. A. Blumenthal, and R. E. Whalen, 1980, *Psychosomatic Medicine, 42,* 539–549. Reprinted with permission.

that began to address this issue. They studied patients referred for diagnostic coronary arteriography (the assessment of blockage in coronary arteries) because of suspected clinical coronary heart disease. As shown in Figure 16.3, the percentage of individuals with at least one artery with 75% or more blockage increased with being male, exhibiting Type A behavior, and having high hostility scores. Thus, hostility reflects an attitude about the world and a behavioral set that is accompanied by structural changes in the cardiovascular system that may ultimately lead to heart attack or stroke.

When confronted with a stressful situation, hostile individuals may be unable to look to others for support because of an inherent lack of trust. In addition, their high level of suspiciousness may heighten the perception of threat, even when none is intended. Furthermore, frequent perception of threat and poor interpersonal skills may lead them to react in an aggressive and confrontive manner, which is accompanied with sympathetic nervous system arousal, such as increased blood pressure and levels of adrenaline (Shekelle, Gale, Ostfield, & Paul, 1983). In fact, the emotional experience of anger has also been linked to high blood pressure and the development of coronary heart disease. Williams and colleagues (2000) studied heart disease rates in 12,986 black and white men and women, enrolled in a prospective study (healthy participants studied initially and assessed for the following six years) on atherosclerosis risk. Each person completed a questionnaire measuring trait anger (Spielberger, Jacobs, Russell, & Crane, 1983,) with items such as "I have a fiery temper" and "When I get frustrated, I feel like hitting someone." There was a linear increase in heart attack and sudden death with increasing levels of trait anger. Further follow-up of these data indicated that a strong, angry temperament (a tendency to quick, minimally provoked, or unprovoked anger) was associated with heart disease risk rather than anger in reaction to criticism, frustration, or unfair treatment.

Anger has also been shown to be a particularly important risk for premature heart disease or disease in individuals under the age of 55 years. Chang, Ford, Meoni, Wang, and Klag (2002) followed 1,055 men for an average of 36 years after the men had attended medical school. The highest level of trait anger was associated with three times the risk for coronary heart disease. Similarly, the progression of heart disease, or artery blockage, over a two-year time period is associated with two predictors: overt expression of anger and low social support (Angerer et al., 2000). Finally, research indicates that even a single angry outburst can be a trigger for a heart attack. In a large population-based study in Sweden, nurses interviewed 660 heart attack cases about their experiences during the preceding 26 hours. In the hour after an episode of anger, with an intensity of at least "very angry" (5 on a 7-point scale, where 5 is "very angry: body tense, clenching fists or teeth" and 7 is "enraged: loss of control, throwing objects, hurting yourself or others"), the relative risk of a heart attack was 15.7 for those with no other warning signals (such as chest pain), an increase of almost 1600% (Moller et al., 1999).

Even the suppression of anger has been linked to risk of heart disease. Assessing blood pressure in 3,000 high school students, Spielberger and colleagues (1985) found a step-by-step increase as scores on a measure of anger increased. Students scoring high on this measure would report that they almost always "control my temper," "keep things in," and "tend to harbor grudges that I don't tell anyone about." Several other studies have shown that suppressing anger, especially when faced with situations of high family strain or high job strain, is linked to increases in blood pressure (Gentry, 1985). This may be due to the unique effects of holding anger inside, but simply the act of concealing any negative emotions appears to entail a physiological cost. When college students were instructed to try to conceal the disgust they felt at viewing slides of gruesome accidents, this general emotional suppression was also accompanied by larger increases in blood pressure (Richards & Gross, 1999).

Depression

In Friedman and Booth-Kewley's (1987) analysis of a "disease-prone personality," the most striking relationships were obtained between depression and illness. Recent research has clearly indicated a causal link between depression and stroke (Jonas & Mussolino, 2000) and between depression and heart disease, but not with cancer (Wulsin, Vaillant, & Wells, 1999). However, depressed individuals do have compromised immune systems, making them more vulnerable to a variety of infectious diseases. Miller, Cohen, and Herbert (1999) examined 32 women with a major depressive disorder and compared them to 32 control women with no history of psychiatric disorder. The depressed women had reduced immune competence, showing a smaller response to a test of immune challenge, as well as greater tobacco and caffeine consumption, less physical activity, and poorer sleep quality. All of these characteristics would lead to poorer health.

Up to one fifth of all patients with coronary heart disease have concurrent major depression. In patients with angiographic evidence of coronary artery disease (the buildup of plaque and consequent obstruction of their arteries), presence of major depression was the single best predictor of a subsequent heart attack in the following 12 months (Sheps & Sheffield, 2001). Thus, depressed individuals are at greater risk for heart disease; one proposed pathway for this association is increased blood pressure responses to stress (Sloan, Shapiro, Bagiella, Myers, & Gorman, 1999). Kathy Light and her colleagues have studied cardiovascular responses to stress in women with mild, depressive symptoms (Light, Kothandapani, & Allen, 1998). They found that mildly depressed women, when asked to give a three-minute speech about a recent personal event that made them angry, had larger blood pressure increases and greater levels of norepinephrine, a stress hormone released into the bloodstream by the adrenal glands, than did nondepressed women. Thus, depressed individuals may react more strongly to stress and may even encounter more stress. While anger suppression was not measured in this study, depressed women may attempt to hide their angry emotions more than women without depression. However, Light et al. (1998) did report a remarkably strong relationship between depressive symptoms and lack of social support (a correlation of $-.82$, $p < .0001$) suggesting that lack of social support may be an important factor linking depression and poorer health.

Carney, Freedland, Miller, and Jaffe (2002) have examined a variety of pathways that may link depression to illness. In addition to the greater magnitude of stress response noted above, they also proposed that depression may affect heart disease by way of antidepressant cardiotoxicity (antidepressant drugs may be harmful to cardiovascular health), poorer health habits, and poorer adherence to prevention and treatment regimens. Future research must focus on delineating the pathways by which depression predicts illness; to the extent that these pathways differ by gender or age, specific intervention or treatment programs may be developed.

Hardiness

Examining the stress-illness relationship often means that investigators search for psychological factors that improve the statistical correlation between stress and illness; for example, the stress-illness correlation would be presumed to be higher for hostile than nonhostile men. However, another and equally important approach is to look for psychological factors that are predictive of good health, especially when a person is under the pressure of a stressful environment. In what kinds of individuals does stress not lead to illness? In an attempt to answer this question, Kobasa (1979) developed the construct of the hardy personality—a composite of three traits that were found to protect a person from the illness-producing effects of stress. The components of hardiness are commitment, challenge, and control. Commitment is defined as one's sense of meaning and purpose in life, encompassing self, others, and work; control is defined as one's sense of autonomy and ability to influence one's own destiny; challenge is defined as one's zest for life that leads one to perceive changes as exciting and as opportunities for growth rather than as threats to security (Maddi & Kobasa, 1984).

Kobasa and her colleagues studied 670 male public utility executives to test her idea that people who experience high levels of stress without falling ill have a personality structure different from that of people who become sick under stress. In a longitudinal study (Kobasa, Maddi, & Kahn, 1982), high-hardiness men who experienced high levels of stress had less illness three years later than low-hardiness men. Similarly, Bartone, Ursano, Wright, and Ingraham (1989) found that hardiness reduced symptoms of distress in survivor assistance officers whose job was to help families of soldiers killed in a 1985 airline crash in Gander, Newfoundland. This study measured hardiness and social support (from work supervisors, family, and friends) in 131 men who were assisting the bereaved families; six months later they measured physical and psychological health. Both social support and hardiness were found to serve a protective function in reducing the distress (such as trouble sleeping, headaches, and trouble concentrating) experienced by these officers as they carried out this difficult assistance. Finally, Williams and Lawler (2001) found that hardiness predicted health in a sample far removed from the middle-class men on whom the original scales were assessed. One hundred black and white women living in poverty were given the hardiness questionnaires, along with measures of stress and illness. Stress was a significant predictor of illness (correlation of .49, $p < .0001$), but hardiness was found to be a significant moderating variable. When experiencing high levels of stress, high-hardy women had significantly lower illness scores than low-hardy women. The effect of hardiness may partly reflect the ways that these hardy women perceived their environments; high-hardy women reported less violence and community stress than low-hardy women, even though they all lived in the same community.

Little research has been conducted to determine the pathways by which hardiness leads to better health. Williams, Wiebe, and Smith (1992) found that hardy individuals used effective, active coping strategies, such as problem-focused coping and seeking social support; in addition hardy persons were more likely to engage in better health practices, such as regular exercise and not using tobacco products (Wiebe & McCallum, 1986). Thus, hardiness clearly predicts health in both men and women. In addition, the idea of defining factors predictive of health, as well as those associated with illness, is an important direction in psychology (Seligman & Csikszentmihalyi, 2000).

Optimism

As with hardiness, optimism reflects a positive set of cognitive beliefs that are associated with good physical health and mental well-being. Scheier and Carver (1985) defined dispositional optimism as the tendency to believe that one will generally experience good rather than bad outcomes in life. They developed a scale to measure this trait called the Life Orientation Test (LOT), as shown in Activity Box 16.1. These researchers hypothesized that successful adaptation to different forms of life stress can be predicted by dispositional optimism, and that optimists will be better able to cope with stress than pessimists.

In an effort to examine the relationship between optimism and physical health, Scheier and Carver (1985) administered the LOT to a sample of undergraduate men and women, along with a physical symptom checklist. Optimism was associated with fewer physical symptoms of illness, both at the time the scale was administered and one month later. Shortly thereafter, another study was conducted to extend the optimism-health relationship beyond self-reported symptoms to more concrete, physical health indices (Scheier et al., 1989). Fifty-one middle-aged men who were undergoing coronary artery bypass surgery filled out the LOT before surgery. Their health was assessed one week after surgery and six months later. The optimists achieved each milestone of physical recovery, such as sitting up in bed, earlier than pessimists. At the six-month follow-up, optimists were significantly more likely to have engaged in vigorous exercise and to have returned to full-time work. Moreover, in spite of this increased activity, optimists were also less likely to have had a heart attack in the six-month interval. At a five-year follow-up, optimists were still more likely to be employed on a full-time basis, and among patients experiencing chest pain, optimists reported less severe pain than pessimists (Scheier & Carver, 1992).

In addition to predicting health among individuals already diagnosed with heart disease, recent research (Kubzhansky, Sparrow, Vokonas, & Kawachi, 2001) indicates that optimism lowers the risk of developing coronary heart disease in a group of healthy older men. More than 1,000 healthy men, with an average age of 60 years, were assessed for optimism and studied for 10 years. In that time, 162 cases of heart disease were found. Optimists had lower levels of fatal heart attacks, nonfatal heart attacks, and chest pain. Even controlling for the use of alcohol and cigarettes, the higher the scores on optimism, the lower the heart disease incidence. These authors concluded that optimism may

Activity Box 16.1   **Test Your Optimism:
The Revised Life Orientation Test (LOT-R)**

Write the number 4 for strongly agree, 3 for agree, 2 for neutral, 1 for disagree, or 0 for strongly disagree next to each statement listed below to indicate the extent to which you personally agree with each item. Try to be as accurate and honest as possible, and try not to let your opinion for one item influence your opinion for other items. There are no correct or incorrect answers.

_____   1. In uncertain times, I usually expect the best.

_____   2. It's easy for me to relax.

_____   3. If something can go wrong for me, it will.

_____   4. I'm always optimistic about my future.

_____   5. I enjoy my friends a lot.

_____   6. It's important for me to keep busy.

_____   7. I hardly ever expect things to go my way.

_____   8. I don't get upset too easily.

_____   9. I rarely count on good things happening to me.

_____   10. Overall, I expect more good things to happen to me than bad.

Scoring instructions:

   Step 1: For items 3, 7, and 9, subtract your score from 4.

_____   Step 2: Add these corrected scores for items 3, 7, and 9, and record the total here.

_____   Step 3: Add your scores for items 1, 4, and 10, and record the total here.

_____   Step 4: Add the totals from steps 2 and 3 to obtain your overall optimism score.

Are you more optimistic or pessimistic than the average person? The mean LOT-R score for over 2,000 undergraduate students was 14.3, with a standard deviation of 4.3 (Scheier, Carver, & Bridges, 1994).

Note: This scale was developed for research purposes and administration to large numbers of persons; thus, one should observe caution in drawing meaning from a particular score.

Source: M. F. Scheier, C. S. Carver, and M. W. Bridges, "Distinguishing optimism from neuroticism (and trait anxiety, self-mastery, and self-esteem): A reevaluation of the life orientation test," *Journal of Personality and Social Psychology, 67,* 1073. Copyright © 1994 by the American Psychological Association. Adapted with permission.

allow individuals to mobilize highly effective coping resources, such as planning and problem solving, which benefit them when facing adversity.

As Peterson (2000) noted in his article, "The Future of Optimism," optimism has been found to predict better morale, problem solving, good health, and longevity whereas pessimism predicts depression, passivity, illness, and higher death rates. Future research must go beyond demonstrating these associations and address the pathways that link optimism and better health. He proposed three: immunological robustness (e.g., rapidity of antibody response to infection), absence of negative mood (such as anger or anxiety), and improved health behaviors (such as exercise and lack of alcohol or drug abuse). A recent study with college students (Mulkana & Hailey, 2001) found that optimists have better health habits in six areas: responsibility for one's health, physical exercise, nutrition, spiritual growth, interpersonal relations, and stress management. Similarly, Brissette, Scheier, and Carver (2002) analyzed the roles of social support and coping in students during their first semester in college. Those who were optimists at the beginning of the semester had smaller increases in stress and depression during the semester and had greater increases in social support. They concluded that optimists are better able to attract social support and have higher quality friendships, which protect them from the stresses and strains of college life. Similarly, Raikkonen, Matthews, Flory, Owens, and Gump (1999) evaluated the effects of optimism on blood pressure during work and nonwork days in a sample of healthy men and women. The adults wore a blood pressure monitor from 8:00 A.M. until 10:00 P.M. on the work days, and from 10:00 A.M. until 6:00 P.M. on the nonwork days, and blood pressure was taken every 30 minutes. Averaged across these intervals, the optimists had lower blood pressure values than the pessimists. The pessimists also reported that they experienced negative mood and negative interpersonal interactions more frequently. Finally, optimists experienced lower blood pressure during a positive mood than during a negative mood; for pessimists, positive moods did not affect their pressure levels. Thus, pessimists appear to experience more stress, which is accompanied by higher ambulatory levels of blood pressure.

Another concern raised by Peterson (2000) was the role of realistic perceptions. Are optimists unrealistically optimistic, and if so, does the discrepancy from reality harm them in the long run? Taylor and colleagues (Taylor, Kemeny, Bower, Gruenewald, & Reed, 2000) examined optimism in men infected with the HIV virus but who were initially symptom-free. This prospective study examined 72 men for six years; at the beginning of the study 37 of them had suffered the death of a close friend or partner within the last year. The bereaved men had more pessimistic expectations about their own health and in fact experienced a more rapid onset of symptoms. Even controlling for initial health, health habits, and mood, positive expectations, even in the face of a negative prognosis, were predictive of better health and delayed onset of HIV symptoms. Taylor et al. (2000) concluded that even unrealistic optimistic beliefs about the future may be health-protective.

SOCIAL AND CULTURAL CONTEXTS OF STRESS

It is essential to keep in mind that the most complex model of environmental stressors, personality dynamics, coping strategies, and biological responses does not exist independently of a social and cultural context (Aneshensel, 1992). A factor that predicts illness in one culture, such as crowding, may not be perceived as stressful in another culture. This is particularly true if the culture has developed clearly structured ways for dealing with interpersonal encounters. Similarly, within any culture, the strongest predictor of health is social status, even in cultures where nationalized health insurance provides medical care for everyone (Marmot, 2001; Diez Roux et al., 2001). First, individuals whose income places them in lower socioeconomic levels are more likely to experience stressful life events and have fewer coping resources with which to respond (such as the time, energy, and knowledge to use library or Internet resources to identify alternative health treatments; or the possibility of turning a job loss into a "creative opportunity"). In addition, people with fewer socioeconomic resources are more likely to experience chronic, enduring stressors, such as poverty, poor working conditions, and crowded apartments, which provide a backdrop for the experiences of acute, short-term stressors or life events. Finally, individuals with lower status are more likely to conclude that they are powerless in the face of life events, a personality dimension that seems to worsen the illness-predisposing effects of the events themselves.

Future models and research investigations of stress and illness need to include the social and cultural contexts as important factors in producing illness or health (Stansfield, Head, & Marmot, 1998; Lynch, Smith, Kaplan, & House, 2000). In addition, future studies need to include two other variables: age and the possibility that stress may be beneficial as well as harmful. Most investigations of stress have focused on young adult and middle-aged adult samples, yet health concerns become increasingly important in older populations. Furthermore, while life change unit scores typically decrease in older populations on questionnaires such as the Social Readjustment Rating Scale (see p. 459), the elderly as a group experience many critical stressors with greater frequency than do other age groups, such as hospitalization, retirement, death of a spouse, and the institutionalization of a family member. It is important to discover the coping strategies and personality traits that permit some individuals to weather these storms with equanimity and perhaps even with growth (Weiss & Bass, 2002).

The idea that stress may lead to positive outcomes reflects the newest area of stress research on the horizon, the notion that stress may offer an opportunity for growth or other potential benefits (Aldwin, 1996; Tennen & Affleck, 1998; Brandtstädter, 1999). While the particular stressful event itself may not be viewed as desirable, having experienced the challenge of job loss, divorce, or a failing grade may lead adults to examine their perception of events and their resources for meeting those demands. Some people report that stress, such as combat experience or a health crisis, had positive benefits for them, such as improved coping skills, enhanced social ties, and changes in values and perspectives. Just as hardiness incorporates a component of challenge in response to stress, facing stressful events may provide an opportunity for personality development and mastery in adulthood. These developmental changes may increase resistance to stress and decrease one's vulnerability to illness.

SUMMARY

Stress is a concept used to describe several ideas. It reflects events to which one must adapt, the adaptive response made by one's body, and any perceived discrepancy between environmental demands and one's coping resources. Early models of stress focused either on an enumeration of life events and their relationship to illness or on a nonspecific response of the body to stress in general. More recent models have focused on cognitive appraisals of environmental demands, selection of coping strategies, and the accompanying responses of the sympathetic nervous system, the endocrine system, and the immune system. Moreover, the process of responding to stressful events is moderated by personality variables. Hostility, anger, and depression have been shown to increase the likelihood of illness, especially cardiovascular disease. On the other hand, hardiness, a composite of feelings of commitment, challenge, and control, arose from the identification of individuals who, although experiencing high levels of stress, remained healthy. A generalized expectancy that social and material resources will be plentiful and that goals can be achieved—that is, optimism—has also been associated with better health and longer life.

Finally, it is important to remember that stress occurs in a particular social and cultural context, which plays a critical role in determining both perceptions of stress and coping resources. The most recent theoretical focus is directed at the possibility that stress may have a positive side. In actively coping with life's difficulties, individuals may improve coping skills and develop enhanced social ties. Furthermore, stress may play a key role in providing opportunities for adult personality growth.

DISCUSSION QUESTIONS

1. What are the strengths and weaknesses of the three models of stress?
2. What are the pathways by which chronic stress might lead to decreases in health?
3. Which personality factors have been linked to coronary heart disease? How are they related to one another?
4. Depression has been linked to a variety of serious illnesses. How can researchers determine whether depression is an antecedent or a consequence of illness?
5. Do positive personality factors, such as hardiness and optimism, relate uniquely to illness or are they merely the lack of negative personality factors?

SUGGESTED READINGS

Aldwin, C. M. (1996). The role of stress in adult development and aging. *The Health Psychologist, 18*, 18–19. A report from the committee on aging and health, American Psychological Association (Division 38), noting the complex relationship between stress and aging.

Engel, G. (1977). Emotional stress and sudden death. *Psychology Today, 11*, 114, 118, and 153. A fascinating article of case study reports linking stress and sudden death by a pioneer in the field of behavioral medicine.

Friedman, H. S., & Booth-Kewley, S. (1987). The "disease-prone personality." *American Psychologist, 42*, 539–555. A readable synthesis of the psychosomatic literature, leading to a novel approach to thinking about personality and illness.

Marmot, M. G. (1982). Socio-economic and cultural factors in ischaemic heart disease. *Advances in Cardiology, 29*, 68–76. An examination of the role of socioeconomic status in health, written by a leader in this field.

Peterson, C. (2000). The future of optimism. *American Psychologist, 55*, 44–55. A thorough review of research on optimism and health.

Scheier, M. F., & Bridges, M. W. (1985). Person variables and health: Personality predispositions and acute psychological states as shared determinants for disease. *Psychosomatic Medicine, 57*, 255–268. A critical review of personality factors related to health and illness.

Sapolsky, R. M. (1998). *Why zebras don't get ulcers: An updated guide to stress, stress-related diseases, and coping.* This book summarizes a wide range of psychological and biological research on the association between stress and health. Relevant chapters focus on the role of depression, temperament, and personality characteristics on coping with stress.

Seligman, M. E. P., & Csikzentmihalyi, M. (2000). Positive psychology. *American Psychologist, 55*, 5–14. This entire issue is devoted to positive psychology, factors that predict optimal functioning and health.

SUGGESTED WEB SITES

www.healthfinder.gov

This site contains a wide variety of health-related information of interest to specific groups such as women, teens, or medical professionals. Current information on depression, drug abuse, and stress is listed under Teens and information about health careers in found under Medical Professionals.

www.apa.org/pubinfo

The Public Affairs office of the American Psychological Association provides current information on health, family, and the mind-body connection. Recent articles featured topics such as shyness, workplace violence, depression, and anger management.

www.stress-management.net/stress-test.htm

At this site you can take an interactive version of the Holmes and Rahe (1967) stress test, as well as download articles on stress.

www.cdc.gov/niosh.stresswk.html

This site, maintained by the Centers for Disease Control and Prevention, contains information about stress at work.

INFOTRAC COLLEGE EDITION SEARCH TOPICS

Stress	Hardiness	Hostility
Optimism	Depression	

REFERENCES

Aldwin, C. M. (1996). The role of stress in adult development and aging. *The Health Psychologist, 18*, 18–19.

Aneshensel, C. S. (1992). Social stress: Theory and research. *Annual Review of Sociology, 18*, 15–38.

Angerer, P., Siebert, U., Kothny, W., Muhlbauer, D., Mudra, H., & von Schacky, C. (2000). Impact of social support, cynical hostility and anger expression on progression of coronary atherosclerosis. *Journal of the American College of Cardiology, 36*, 1781–1788.

Barefoot, J. C., Dahlstrom, W. G., & Williams, R. B. (1983). Hostility, CHD incidence and total mortality: A twenty-five-year follow-up study of 225 physicians. *Psychosomatic Medicine, 45*, 59–63.

Barefoot, J. C., Siegler, I. C., Nowlin, J. B., Peterson, B. L., Haney, T. L., & Williams, R. B. (1987). Suspiciousness, health, and mortality: A follow-up study of 500 older adults. *Psychosomatic Medicine, 49*, 450–457.

Bartone, P. T., Ursano, R. J., Wright, K. M., & Ingraham, L. H. (1989). The impact of a military air disaster on the health of assistance workers: A prospective study. *Journal of Nervous and Mental Diseases, 177*, 317–328.

Brandtstädtler, J. (1999). Sources of resilience in the aging self: Toward integrated perspectives. In T. M. Hess & F. Blanchard-Fields (Eds.), *Social cognition and aging* (pp. 123–141). San Diego: Academic Press.

Brissette, I., Scheier, M. F., & Carver, C. S. (2002). The role of optimism in social network development, coping, and psychological adjustment during a life transition. *Journal of Personality and Social Psychology, 82*, 102–111.

Brisson, C., Laflamme, N., Moisan, J., Milot, A., Masse, B., & Vezina, M. (1999). Effect of family responsibilities and job strain on ambulatory blood pressure among white-collar women. *Psychosomatic Medicine, 61*, 205–213.

Campbell, J., Jones, A. S., Dienemann, J., Kub, J., Schollengerger, J., O'Campo, P., Gielen, A. C., & Wynne, C. (2002). Intimate partner violence and physical health consequences. *Archives of Internal Medicine, 162*, 1157–1163.

Carney, R. M., Freedland, K. E., Miller, G. E., & Jaffe, A. S. (2002). Depression as a risk factor for cardiac mortality and morbidity. *Journal of Psychosomatic Research, 53*, 897–902.

Chang, P. P., Ford, D. E., Meoni, L. A., Wang, N. Y., & Klag, M. J. (2002). Anger in young men and subsequent premature cardiovascular disease: The precursors study. *Archives of Internal Medicine, 162*, 901–906.

Christenfeld, N., Glynn, L. M., Phillips, D. P., & Shrira, I. (1999). Exposure to New York City as a risk factor for heart attack mortality. *Psychosomatic Medicine, 61*, 740–743.

Christensen, A. J., Ehlers, S. L. Wiebe, J. S., Moran, P. J., Raichle, K., Femeyhough, K., & Lawton, W. J. (2002). Patient personality and mortality: A 4-year prospective examination of chronic renal insufficiency. *Health Psychology, 21*, 315–230.

Cohen, S., Kessler, R. C., & Gordon, L. U. (1995). *Measuring stress.* New York: Oxford University Press.

Cook, W. W., & Medley, D. M. (1954). Proposed hostility and pharisaic-virtue scales for the MMPI. *Journal of Applied Psychology, 38*, 414–418.

Cox, T. (1978). *Stress.* Baltimore, MD: University Park Press.

Diez Roux, A. V., Merkin, S. S., Arnett, D., Chambless, L., Massing, M., Nieto, F. J., et al. (2001). Neighborhood or residence and incidence of coronary heart disease. *New England Journal of Medicine, 345*, 99–106.

Engel, G. (1977). Emotional stress and sudden death. *Psychology Today, 11*, 114, 118, 153.

Frankenhaeuser, M. (1991). The psychophysiology of workload, stress, and health: Comparison between the sexes. *Annals of Behavioral Medicine, 13*, 197–204.

Friedman, H. S. (2000). Long-term relations of personality and health: Dynamisms, mechanisms and tropisms. *Journal of Personality, 68*, 1089–1107.

Friedman, H. S., & Booth-Kewley, S. (1987). The "disease-prone personality." *American Psychologist, 42*, 539–555.

Friedman, H. S., Tucker, J. S., Schwartz, J. E., Tomlinson-Keasey, C., Martin, L. R., Wingard, D. L., & Criqui, M. H. (1995). Psychosocial and behavioral predictors of longevity. *American Psychologist, 50*, 69–78.

Gentry, W. D. (1985). Relationship of anger-coping styles and blood pressure among black Americans. In M. A. Chesney & R. H. Rosenman (Eds.), *Anger and hostility in cardiovascular and behavioral disorders* (pp. 139–148). Washington, DC: Hemisphere.

Holmes, T. H., & Rahe, R. H. (1967). The social readjustment rating scale. *Journal of Psychosomatic Research, 11*, 213–218.

Jonas, B. S., & Mussolino, M. E. (2000). Symptoms of depression as a prospective risk factor for stroke. *Psychosomatic Medicine, 62*, 463–471.

Kobasa, S. C. (1979). Stressful life events, personality and health: An inquiry into hardiness. *Journal of Personality and Social Psychology, 37*, 1–11.

Kobasa, S. C., Maddi, S. R., & Kahn, S. (1982). Hardiness and health: A prospective study. *Journal of Personality and Social Psychology, 42*, 168–177.

Kubzhansky, L. D., Sparrow, D., Vokonas, P., & Kawachi, I. (2001). Is the glass half empty or half full? A prospective study of optimism and coronary heart disease in the normative aging study. *Psychosomatic Medicine, 63*, 910–916.

Lazarus, R. S. (1990). Stress, coping and illness. In H. S. Friedman (Ed.), *Personality and disease* (pp. 97–120). New York: Wiley.

Lazarus, R. S., & Folkman, S. (1984). *Stress, appraisal and coping.* New York: Springer.

Lazarus, R. S., & Launier, R. (1978). Stress-related transactions between person and environment. In L. A. Pervin, & M. Lewis (Eds.), *Perspectives in interactional psychology* (pp. 287–327). New York: Plenum.

Leor, J., Poole, W. K., & Kloner, R. A. (1996). Sudden cardiac death triggered by an earthquake. *New England Journal of Medicine, 334*, 413–419.

Lief, A. (Ed.). (1948). *The commonsense psychiatry of Dr. Adolf Meyer.* New York: McGraw-Hill.

Light, K. C., Kothandapani, R. V., & Allen, M. T. (1998). Enhanced cardiovascular and catecholamine responses in women with depressive symptoms. *International Journal of Psychophysiology, 28,* 157–166.

Lynch, J. W., Smith, D. G., Kaplan, G. A., & House, J. S. (2000). Income inequality and mortality: Importance to health of individual income, psychosocial environment, or material conditions. *British Medical Journal, 320,* 1200–1204.

Maddi, S. R., & Kobasa, S. C. (1984). *The hardy executive: Health under stress.* Homewood, IL: Dow Jones-Irwin.

Marmot, M. G. (2001). Inequalities in health. *New England Journal of Medicine, 345,* 134–136.

Matthews, K. A., Glass, D. C., Rosenman, R. H., & Bortner, R. W. (1977). Competitive drive, Pattern A, and coronary heart disease: A further analysis of some data from the Western Collaborative Group Study. *Journal of Chronic Diseases, 30,* 489–498.

McEwen, B. S., & Stellar, E. (1993). Stress and the individual. *Archives of Internal Medicine, 153,* 2093–2101.

Miller, G. E., Cohen, S., & Herbert, T. B. (1999). Pathways linking major depression and immunity in ambulatory female patients. *Psychosomatic Medicine, 61,* 850–860.

Moller, J., Hallqvist, J., Diderichsen, F., Theroell, T., Reuterwall, C., & Ahlbom, A. (1999). Do episodes of anger trigger myocardial infarction? A case-crossover analysis in the Stockholm Heart Epidemiology Program (SHEEP). *Psychosomatic Medicine, 61,* 842–849.

Morbidity and Mortality Weekly Report. (2002a). Self-reported increase in asthma severity after the September 11 attacks on the World Trade Center—Manhattan, New York, 2001. *Centers for Disease Control and Prevention, 51,* 781–784.

Morbidity and Mortality Weekly Report. (2002b). Impact of September 11 attacks on workers in the vicinity of the World Trade Center—New York City. *Centers for Disease Control and Prevention, 51,* 8–10.

Mulkana, S., & Hailey, B. J. (2001). The role of optimism in health-enhancing behavior. *American Journal of Health Behavior, 25,* 388–396.

Peterson, C. (2000). The future of optimism. *American Psychologist, 55,* 44–55.

Pruessner, J. C., Hellhammer, D. H., & Kirschbaum, C. (1999). Burnout, perceived stress, and cortisol reponses to awakening. *Psychosomatic Medicine, 61,* 197–204.

Rabkin, J. G., & Struening, E. L. (1976). Life events, stress, and illness. *Science, 194,* 1013–1020.

Rahe, R. H. (1968). Life-change measurement as a predictor of illness. *Proceedings of the Royal Society of Medicine, 61,* 1124–1126.

Raikkonen, K., Matthews, K. A., Flory, J. D., Owens, J. F., & Gump, B. B. (1999). Effects of optimism, pessimism, and trait anxiety on ambulatory blood pressure and mood during everyday life. *Journal of Personality and Social Psychology, 76,* 104–113.

Richards, J. M., & Gross, J. J. (1999). Composure at any cost? The cognitive consequences of emotion suppression. *Personality and Social Psychology Bulletin, 25,* 1033–1044.

Rosenman, R. H., Brand, R. J., Jenkins, C. D., Friedman, M., Straus, R., & Wurm, M. (1975). Coronary heart disease in the Western Collaborative Group study: Final follow-up experience of eight and one-half years. *Journal of the American Medical Association, 233,* 872–877.

Scheier, M. F., & Bridges, M. W. (1995). Person variables and health: Personality predispositions and acute psychological states as shared determinants for disease. *Psychosomatic Medicine, 57,* 255–268.

Scheier, M. F., & Carver, C. S. (1985). Optimism, coping, and health: Assessment and implications of generalized outcome expectancies. *Health Psychology, 4,* 219–247.

Scheier, M. F., & Carver, C. S. (1992). Effects of optimism on psychological and physical well-being: Theoretical overview and empirical update. *Cognitive Therapy and Research, 16,* 201–228.

Scheier, M. F., Carver, C. S., & Bridges, M. W. (1994). Distinguishing optimism from neuroticism (and trait anxiety, self-mastery, and self-esteem): A reevaluation of the Life Orientation Test. *Journal of Personality and Social Psychology, 67,* 1063–1078.

Scheier, M. F., Matthews, K. A., Owens, J. F., Magovern, G. J., Sr., Lefebvre, R. C., Abbott, R. A., & Carver, C. S. (1989). Dispositional optimism and recovery from coronary artery bypass surgery: The beneficial effects on physical and psychological well-being. *Journal of Personality and Social Psychology, 57,* 1024–1040.

Seligman, M. E. P., & Csikzentmihalyi, M. (2000). Positive psychology. *American Psychologist, 55,* 5–14.

Selye, H. (1956). *The stress of life.* New York: McGraw-Hill.

Selye, H. (1993). History of the stress concept. In L. Goldberger & S. Breznitz (Eds.), *Handbook of stress* (pp. 7–20). New York: Free Press.

Shekelle, R. B., Gale, M., Ostfield, A. M., & Paul, O. (1983). Hostility, risk of coronary heart disease, and mortality. *Psychosomatic Medicine, 45,* 109–114.

Sheps, D. S., & Sheffield, D. (2001). Depression, anxiety, and the cardiovascular system: The cardiologist's perspective. *Journal of Clinical Psychiatry, 662, Supplement 8,* 12–16.

Sloan, R. P., Shapiro, P. A., Bagiella, E., Myers, M. M., & Gorman, J. M. (1999). Cardiac autonomic control buffers blood pressure variability responses to challenge: A psychophysiologic model of coronary artery disease. *Psychosomatic Medicine, 61,* 58–68.

Spielberger, C. D., Jacobs, G., Russell, S., & Crane, R. S. (1983). Assessment of anger: The state-trait anger scale. In J. N. Butcher & C. D. Spielberger (Eds.), *Advances in personality assessment* (pp. 161–189), Hillsdale, NJ: Lawrence Erlbaum.

Spielberger, C. D., Johnson, E. H., Russell, S. F., Crane, R. J., Jacobs, G. A., & Worden, T. J. (1985). The experience and expression of anger: Construction and validation of an anger expression scale. In M. A. Chesney & R. H. Rosenman (Eds.), *Anger and hostility in cardiovascular and behavioral disorders* (pp. 5–30). Washington: Hemisphere Publishing Corporation.

Stansfield, S. A., Head, J., & Marmot, M. G. (1998). Explaining social class differences in depression and well-being. *Social Psychiatry and Psychiatric Epidemiology, 33,* 1–9.

Sterling, P., & Eyer, J. (1988). Allostasis: A new paradigm to explain arousal pathology. In J. Fisher, & J. Reason (Eds.), *Handbook of life stress, cognition, and health* (pp. 629–639), New York: John Wiley.

Stone, A. A., Bovbjerg, D. H., Neale, J. M., Napoli, A., Valdimarsdottir, H., Cox, D., et al. (1992). Development of common cold symptoms following experimental rhinovirus infection is related to prior stressful life events. *Behavioral Medicine, 18,* 115–120.

Takkouche, B., Regueira, C., Gestal-Otero, J. J. (2001). A cohort study of stress and the common cold. *Epidemiology, 12,* 345–349.

Taylor, S. E., Kemeny, M. E., Bower, J. E., Gruenewald, T. L., & Reed, G. M. (2000). Psychological resources, positive illusions, and health. *American Psychologist, 55,* 99–109.

Tennen, H., & Affleck, G. (1998). Personality and transformation in the face of adversity. In R. G. Tedeschi, C. L. Park, & L. G. Calhoun (Eds.), *Posttraumatic growth: Positive changes in the aftermath of crisis.* Mahwah, NJ: Erlbaum.

Watson, D., Clark, L. A., & Tellegen, A. (1988). Development and validation of brief measures of positive and negative affect: The PANAS scales. *Journal of Personality and Social Psychology, 6,* 1063–1070.

Weiss, R. S., & Bass, S. A. (2002). *Challenges of the third age.* Oxford: Oxford University Press.

Wiebe, D. J., & McCallum, D. M. (1986). Health practices and hardiness as mediators in the stress-illness relationship. *Health Psychology, 5,* 425–438.

Williams, D., & Lawler, K. A. (2001). Stress and illness in low-income women: The roles of hardiness, John Henryism, and race. *Women and Health, 32,* 61–76.

Williams, J. E., Paton, C. C., Siegler, I. C., Eigenbrodt, M. L., Nieto, F. J., & Tyroler, H. A. (2001). Anger proneness predicts coronary heart disease risk: Prospective analysis from the atherosclerosis risk in communities (ARIC) study. *Circulation, 101,* 2034–2039.

Williams, P. B., Wiebe, D. J., & Smith, T. W. (1992). Coping processes as mediators of the relationship between hardiness and helath. *Journal of Behavioral Medicine, 15,* 237–256.

Williams, R. B., Haney, T. L., Lee, K. L., Kong, Y-H., Blumenthal, J. A., & Whalen, R. E. (1980). Type A behavior, hostility, and coronary atherosclerosis. *Psychosomatic Medicine, 42,* 539–549.

Wulsin, L. R., Vaillant, G. E., & Wells, V. E. (1999). A systematic review of the mortality of depression. *Psychosomatic Medicine, 61,* 6–17.

The Interface of Personality and Relationships

17

WARREN H. JONES

LAURIE L. COUCH

PERSONALITY AND RELATIONSHIPS

Relationships are not only one of the most important aspects of our lives, but understanding relationships—how they are formed, how they influence a person's life, how they dissolve, what are their benefits and limitations—constitutes one of the basic issues in several areas of psychology. For example, the study of relationships is one of the topics that may be found in various areas of psychology including, for example, clinical, developmental, and social psychology. Increasingly, questions concerning relationships have received research and theoretical attention in these areas.

In this chapter we will focus on the role of personality and individual differences in relationships and the interplay between personality and this broad domain of behavior and experience. We begin by considering why relationships are important in the study of personality and by considering some basic methodological issues including how relationships are conceptualized and studied in psychology. As an overview of the psychological literature on relationships, we next consider factors that often contribute to the emergence of relationships as they develop through stages described as initiation, enhancement, maintenance, and termination. Next we discuss in detail a specific dimension of personality relevant to relationship formation, development, and functioning and one of the most important dimensions in relationship continuation—namely, trust. In particular, we compare and contrast two ways of thinking about trust—trust in human nature or people-in-general, termed global trust; and trust in specific relationship partners, known as relational or partner trust. In addition, we discuss theories and models of trust and relevant research evidence concerning how trust develops as a more-or-less permanent trait of the individual as well as how feelings of trust develop between relationship partners. Finally, we speculate about the possible associations among the varieties of trust proposed in the literature and draw some broad conclusions about personality and relationships and the conjunction of the two.

It is necessary to consider the psychology of relationships more generally before discussing the topic of personality and relationships. Specifically, we need to address issues such as what we mean by the term *relationship*, what is known from previous research about the function of relationships in behavior and experience, and why relationships are considered to be important, especially with respect to understanding personality.

THE PSYCHOLOGY OF RELATIONSHIPS

Definition

We use the term *relationship* to refer to a state of mutual awareness and interdependence between two people; that is, a relationship exists when two people believe a relationship exists and both feel some sort of commitment or emotional bond toward the other. Typically, the bond between relational partners involves attraction and some degree of positive emotion (i.e., liking or love) and commitment ordinarily refers to the intentions to be responsive to the partner and to stay in the relationship. However, it is important to note that the relational bond is not always positive. In addition to love, admiration, and affection, relationships may be based on competition, suspicion, and even hatred. Also, what one considers responsive, under certain circumstances, may be viewed by one's partner as cold and selfish, and even the most solemn pledges of faithfulness are sometimes broken. Thus, relationships can be both rewarding and problematic. Indeed, for many people the very same individuals who provide companionship, warmth, and security in life also are their main sources of stress, conflict, and disappointment. Furthermore, asymmetric relationships are possible, in which one person feels the emotional bond much more than the partner, although presumably these are less common among one's network of companions and intimate partners than those relationships in which both partners experience a mutual bond.

Of course, the length, the degree of commitment, and the type of emotional bond vary considerably across differing relationships. Some of the more commonly studied relationships include the parent-child bond, friendship (especially relationships between same-sex friends), marriage, dating, and other romantic relationships. Additional relationships among "blood" relatives (e.g., siblings, cousins, grandparents-grandchildren), in-laws (e.g., sisters-in-law), blended family members (e.g., stepsiblings, stepparents and stepchildren), and the various relationships that emerge because of other circumstances and activities of life (e.g., supervisor-worker, teacher-student, neighbors) are less frequently studied but also are very important in specific instances.

Personality and Relationships Interface

What do relationships have to do with the phenomenon of personality? Much of what an individual does is related to and dependent upon his or her relationship partners. For example, think for a moment about how much of your time is spent meeting, talking, arguing, sharing, and simply being with your friends and family. Researchers report that among college students about 75% of their waking time is spent with other people (Larson, Csikszentmihalyi, & Graef, 1982). Thus, interactions with others and the relationships that emerge from such interactions are important because of their ubiquity. Furthermore, even when what we are doing is not directly related to a particular relationship, our experiences (and personalities) unfold in the context of our relationships and are shaped by them. Part of what makes a clumsy action or a foolish statement so embarrassing is having someone whose opinion we value observe such awkwardness, for example. Similarly, what creates the joy of an accomplishment? Much of the sense of elation derives from the reactions of one's friends and loved ones to the accomplishment. Thus, relationships make up the social context in which our experience unfolds and this context adds texture and meaning to those experiences.

Also, relationships are important in the study of personality because of their apparent relevance to our adjustment and functioning, topics long at the center of personality psychology. Research indicates that satisfactory relationships are important for people's psychological well-being and that one of the major factors in predicting psychological and emotional health is the quality and status of close relationships. For example, psychologists have known for a long time that one of the best predictors of mental illness among adults is marital status (Hafner, 1986). Generally, single adults are over-represented among individuals undergoing psychiatric treatment and hospitalization relative to their proportion in the population. This does not necessarily mean that marriage is an antidote for psychological dysfunction. It may simply be that those somehow predisposed to mental illness are less likely to marry because of their problems. On the other hand, it does suggest a fundamental link between the ability to relate effectively to other people—as presumably is required for a satisfying and lasting marriage or committed relationship—and vulnerability to the various problems subsumed under the label of mental illness. Similarly, the degree of support one perceives from one's social network also has been shown to be related to one's state of adjustment and well-being (Sarason, Sarason, & Pierce, 1990). *Social support* is the help (e.g., information, advice, money) as well as the sense of belongingness (e.g., companionship and identity) one typically receives from one's social network (e.g., family, friends, romantic partner, neighbors, and other associates with whom one has more-or-less regular contact).

Perhaps the most compelling reason that relationships are important for understanding personality is because the two are deeply intertwined, with each apparently exerting a powerful influence on the other throughout life. As we will discuss later, relationships—especially those in infancy and childhood—are believed to propel and shape the development of personality (e.g., Bowlby, 1982; Erikson, 1964). At the same time, personality processes are seen as guiding the dynamics of relationship development and change. Some psychologists (e.g., Buss, 1994) have argued that the main purpose for the evolutionary emergence of personality in humans was to determine success in social and interpersonal competition (e.g., status in social groups, success in mating). Other theorists have suggested that it makes no sense to speak of personality apart from the interpersonal interactions from which it emerges. Sullivan (1953), in particular, became known for essentially fusing together the ideas of personality and relationships. Sullivan developed a theory of personality asserting that the self-concept (see Baumeister, this volume, chapter 9) forms as a function of the responses an individual receives from others, especially those responses that reflect the consensus regarding the person's identity. This has been called the *looking-glass self*. Sullivan believed that a sense of security from others is the driving force behind personality development and sense of self. More specifically, he suggested that the view a person holds of himself or herself results from a process called *consensual validation*, in which one's view of himself or herself derives from confirmations by intimate others of various features of the individual's personality. According to Sullivan, if your friends and family act as if and talk as if you are calm and even-tempered, for example, then through the process of consensual validation you will come to believe that these traits in part define your unique personality. Finally, and most important, Sullivan suggested that personality is so thoroughly confounded with one's experiences with certain other people in one's life that it does not exist apart from its manifestation in one's interactions with significant others. So, in Sullivan's theory the connection between relationships and personality is more-or-less complete.

Obviously, given the variety of relationships in which people participate, there is considerable diversity in the characteristics that are necessary to describe and account for them. Even so, research suggests that certain interpersonal processes and concepts are applicable across a variety of stages and types of relationships. To introduce these ideas and to describe the course of relationships in general, we next turn to how relationships are To order to discuss these issues simultaneously, we will use the concept of relationship stages. Every relationship may be described as having four logically distinct stages or phases: initiation, enhancement, maintenance, and termination.

Relationship Development and Functions

Initiation   First is the initiation phase during which future relationship partners become aware of each other, meet, interact, become acquainted, and begin to affiliate (e.g., choosing to be together). How and why the participants become acquainted will depend, of course, on a variety of factors, particularly the type of relationship involved. In fact, in some relationships such as those between parents and their children, the initiation phase is quite different from, for example, a friendship or relationship in the work setting.

For many relationships, the initiation phase corresponds to what is called the *acquaintanceship process*. Research indicates that many factors contribute to the determination of the one among all other persons with whom we become acquainted and choose to affiliate. Some of these factors involve characteristics of the person (i.e., the person whose relationships or affiliation we are trying to explain). Illustrations of relevant person characteristics are various personality dimensions such as shyness, sociability, trust, and public self-consciousness. Shyness, for example, refers to the tendency to become excessively self-focused and anxious in the presence of others and sociability is defined as one's level of interest in being with and interacting with other people versus being alone. Research indicates that extremely shy people often avoid interpersonal opportunities that might lead to the development of new relationships and thus they tend to have smaller social networks and fewer friends and they rely more extensively on family members rather than friends for social contact (Jones, Cheek, & Briggs, 1986).

A second set of factors that contributes to the extent of initial affiliation includes characteristics of the other (i.e., the person with whom one chooses to affiliate). One important category here is desirable characteristics illustrated by physical attractiveness, social status, talent, wealth, and pleasant personality characteristics. For example, research shows that people clearly prefer to affiliate with physically attractive individuals as compared to unattractive ones (Feingold, 1991). However, it is also important to note that because such characteristics are desirable for almost everyone, these effects are perhaps moderated by a tendency to select others whose physical and social characteristics are similar to one's own (Byrne, 1971; Lee & Bond, 1996; White, 1980).

Third, characteristics of the situation in which the potential relational partners find themselves also contribute to the likelihood that a relationship will develop. For example, *propinquity* or physical closeness (e.g., living in close proximity) provides greater opportunities for meeting and interacting and thus may contribute to the development of a relationship (Whitbeck & Hoyt, 1994). Also, when one is afraid or in a threatening situation there is a tendency to want to affiliate with others (Kulik, Mahler, & Moore, 1996) either for *social comparison* (to see how others are feeling and coping with the threat) or *fear reduction* (it is comforting to be with others when afraid).

In addition, the tendency to initiate a relationship through affiliation is often based on the interplay or combination of the above factors. For example, there is evidence that similarity between two people on certain key variables such as beliefs, social standing, physical attractiveness, group identification, and so on, is conducive to initial affiliation (e.g., Kupersmidt, DeRosier & Patterson, 1995). Also, when choosing to affiliate under conditions of external threat we typically prefer to affiliate with others who are similar to us or who face similar threats (Kulik et al., 1996).

The illustrations listed above are far from complete and, to complicate matters further, they pertain primarily to certain "voluntary" relationships (e.g., friendships, dating relationships). As noted earlier, some relationships develop as a consequence of other life processes or commitments (e.g., marriage, having children) and this applies to some of one's most important relationships, such as those between parents and children. On the other hand, these factors may influence how even such "given" relationships evolve. For example, characteristics of the child such as having an "easy" or "difficult" temperament may contribute to the parents' effectiveness at raising the child and the relationship they subsequently develop with that child (Buss, 1995).

Enhancement   The second stage of a relationship may be called the enhancement phase. Typically, during this period the participants get to know one another better, often by self-disclosing intimate and private information about themselves. During this stage, participants may become attracted toward each other and, just as important, begin to feel the sort of emotional bond or tie toward the other described earlier. Also, it is during this phase that participants begin to feel and act interdependently and to identify themselves to each other and to other people as a pair, a couple, friends, and so forth.

Mutual attraction between two participants determines the degree of enhancement once two people begin to affiliate with one another, at least in part. Research indicates that many of the same factors that increase the probability of affiliation also, generally speaking, increase *interpersonal attraction*. In addition, other factors such as mutual liking, shared interests, common group affiliations, and in certain relationships, sexual intimacy enhance feelings of closeness, satisfaction, and commitment and thus facilitate the continued development of the relationship. In addition, *self-disclosure* (the process by which participants in a relationship share information and reveal themselves to one another including aspects of their identities, their thoughts, their feelings, and their personalities) has been described as the vehicle through which close personal relationships develop (Derlega, Metts, Petronio, & Margulis, 1993). Research also suggests, however, that disclosures vary according to the type of relationship and what is considered to be appropriate to the situation. Similarly, reciprocity of various kinds—exchanging favors, compliments, invitations—also contributes to relationship development, at least in the early stages. Finally,

attitude similarity, or the degree to which participants agree on important social, political, and religious issues has been shown to be related to attraction toward others and hence the enhancement of relationships (Kupersmidt et al.,
1995). When someone shares your attitudes and values it confirms your view
of the world, which is positively reinforcing, and thereby increases your attraction to that person. Alternatively, when people express attitudes and values that
are discrepant with your own, it implies that you may be wrong. At the very
least, people with differing beliefs are less predictable and less comfortable to
be around and thus you are less likely to form mutually satisfying relationships
with them (Rosenbaum, 1986).

Again, this is not all that can be said about the enhancement of a relationship. For one thing, as noted earlier, some relationships develop beyond the initial stages because of negative influences. More frequently, relationships may
simply "endure" because of circumstances outside the relationship itself (e.g.,
co-worker relationships typically continue to evolve as long as their participants are in the same employment settings). Also, research indicates that there
are limitations on these processes and that they may change over the course of
a relationship. For example, Clark and Mills (1993) have demonstrated that
perfectly reciprocal relationships are viewed as new or superficial and that non-
reciprocal behaviors (i.e., where one partner does more for the other) are seen
as evidence of genuine love and caring.

Maintenance   Except for the passage of time, the third stage of a relationship,
the maintenance phase, is often indistinguishable from enhancement. The primary issue during the maintenance phase is how the relationship develops after
it is more-or-less established. In many cases this stage will be associated with
greater closeness and interdependence. Alternatively, this period in a relationship may involve a loss of interest on the part of one or both participants and
a weakening of the emotional bond on which the relationship was initially established, either suddenly or through a slower process of disengagement.
Again, many factors contribute to what happens during the maintenance phase
(e.g., the development of alternative and competing relationships, physical separation), including factors external to the relationship itself.

In many ways less is known about the maintenance of relationships than
about their initiation and enhancement because research has tended to focus
on these earlier stages. Contrary to what one might think, some research does
suggest that relationships of longer duration such as longer marriages are not
necessarily more satisfying (Kamo, 1993), but it is possible that the timing of
certain life events confounds the interpretation of such data (the ages of one's
children and accompanying child-rearing responsibilities, career changes, etc.).
Also, it has been argued that in romantic relationships the couple must trans-
form the basis of the relationship from one of passionate love (dominated by
sexual desire) to one based on companionate love (emphasizing togetherness,
expressions of concern, affection, etc.)—presumably with moments of passion
interspersed here and there—in order for the relationship to endure (Hatfield,
1988).

One of the more common ways of describing the maintenance phase of a relationship involves theories based on analogies to economic exchange, that is,

the idea that a relationship is built and maintained on the exchange of personal qualities or resources (e.g., Foa, Converse, Tornbloom, & Foa, 1993). One such model—which also is used to explain the earlier stages of a relationship—known as exchange theory suggests that the outcome of the maintenance phase will depend on the participants' respective levels of comparisons for alternative relationships (Drigotas & Rusbult, 1993). Specifically, the theory predicts that a couple will remain together if the ratio of what they obtain from the relationship relative to what they have to give to it is greater than it would be for any possible alternative relationship. Relevant research generally supports this prediction. In any case, it is clear that once developed, relationships remain dynamic processes and, typically, must be enhanced further or they will deteriorate.

Another important process during the maintenance phase is relationship commitment. Commitment refers to a relationship participant's intention to stay in a relationship. Recent research (Adams & Jones, 1997; Adams & Spain, 1999; Johnson, Caughlin, & Huston, 1999) suggests that the architecture of commitment consists of three "nested" motives. First, satisfaction or commitment to the partner denotes commitment based on happiness and taking pleasure from the relationship. So long as a participant is happy with the partner, other forms of commitment are irrelevant. When satisfaction wanes, moral commitment (i.e., the desire to keep one's word or meet one's obligations) may become the salient factor propelling the relationship forward. Finally, barriers to dissolving the relationship (e.g., financial and legal complications, social disapproval) may keep a couple together, but these are relevant only when the participants are no longer satisfied with the partner or morally committed.

Termination   Finally, all relationships come to an end, one way or another—whether as the result of drifting apart, breaking up, running away, getting a divorce, or death. As with the earlier stages, a variety of factors apparently contribute not only to how and when the relationship will end but also to how participants will experience the timing and the type of termination. One of the dominant factors appears to be the length and quality of the relationship before it is terminated. Widows who report having been more satisfied with their marital partners experience more difficulties in adjusting to the loss of the spouse than those who were less satisfied (Stroebe & Stroebe, 1986). Another set of issues contributing to the outcome of the termination phase involves the circumstances of the termination and the behaviors it invokes. One illustration is that widows who "rehearse" what they would do should their spouse die (e.g., thinking about being alone; becoming involved in family finances, auto or home repair, or some other aspect of living that was previously the sole responsibility of the husband) adjust more readily to widowhood than do those for whom the husband's death is an unanticipated surprise (Hansson & Carpenter, 1994).

Research Issues in Studying Relationships

The outline above represents only one account of the development of relationships. A variety of alternative models of relationship phases and stages have been proposed. Levinger and Snoek (1972) described a process in which partners in a relationship progress from zero contact (no awareness of one another) through surface contact (limited and largely independent interaction) to various degrees of mutuality (interdependency). Perhaps the most important consideration to keep in mind about relationship stages is that any attempt to describe them risks imposing relatively static concepts on what is a highly complex and dynamic series of processes. Thus, in such models, stages are typically not described as fixed or absolutely discrete; instead, considerable overlap between phases is envisioned, with one phase often fading imperceptibly into the next.

Also, note that the impact of relevant factors may vary as a function of the stage of the relationship with regard to determining whether it will develop into a deeper relationship. What is considered attractive or even appropriate at one stage in a relationship may be highly undesirable at another. For example, although intimate self-disclosures may be important to enhance ongoing relationships, the same disclosures made shortly after meeting someone may have the opposite effect. In fact, some theories of relationships include descriptions of how the factors that determine relationship enhancement or termination will depend on the extent to which the relationship has developed previously. For example, Murstein's (1987) *stimulus-value-role* theory suggests that the interpersonal qualities exchanged in the development of a relationship begin with the "superficial" stimulus factors (e.g., physical attractiveness) then move to "deeper" value qualities (e.g., attitude and belief similarity), and then finally to how the participants behave or the roles they assume within the relationship (e.g., shared expectations regarding respective roles). Furthermore, because more research is available on the earlier stages of relationships, our models and theories may overemphasize certain features to the exclusion of others. As noted earlier, reciprocity between partners (i.e., each partner making sure that every overture is met with a response of equal value) tends to characterize the earlier stages of relationship development rather than the later stages and is often seen as a characteristic of less intimate relationships (Clark & Mills, 1993). Also, reciprocity may be more typical of some relationships, such as friendship, than it is of others, for example, the parent-child relationship.

Relationships do not develop in a vacuum. The description of relationships presented above focuses on what might be called proximal factors of development. In addition, relationships are also influenced by distal factors. Accordingly, what a relationship is or what it can become depends to some extent upon the biological potentialities and precursors of relationship experience as well as the cultural history and norms of the society in which it unfolds. All human behavior has an evolutionary-biological history. Apparently, people have always lived in groups (Jarvenpa, 1993); and group living not only encourages the development of language and culture, it was likely one of the main evolutionary advantages of humans. Furthermore, different cultures (and different historical periods within a given culture) are associated with varying rules and expectations regarding how relationships should be established, between whom, and so on (Beall & Sternberg, 1995). In Western culture the contemporary system of marital courtship emphasizing choice and love between romantic partners appears to have evolved from earlier family-influenced systems of courtship in conjunction with changes in economics, transportation, and work. For example, the shift from an agrarian to a service-oriented economy, the advent of mechanized transportation (e.g., the bicycle), and more abundant time free from subsistence labor are believed to have shaped contemporary ideas and values regarding romance and courtship (Murstein, 1986).

Finally, there is a highly subjective quality to relationships. What a relationship appears to be and whether a relationship even may be said to exist may be in the eye of the beholder to some extent. One psychologist who has studied romantic relationships has found that when people say they are in love with someone, the person with whom they are in love is as much their image or concept of an ideal partner as it is their partner viewed from the perspective of his or her own self-description (Sternberg, 1987). As a result, one of the most important issues concerning the definition, measurement, and study of relationships is whose perspective on the relationship is being assessed or considered. For example, the researcher may assess the satisfaction of one participant in a relationship by asking him or her or by asking the relational partner. Although naturally there is generally a correspondence between the two levels of satisfaction, they need not be and typically are not identical. Indeed, men are often more satisfied with their romantic and marital relationships than are their women partners (Sternberg, 1987). For this reason it is typically a good idea to try to combine these two perspectives in research, thereby creating what is known as the transactional view of the relationship. In addition, the researcher or any other outside observer has his or her own view of the relationship which in many instances will diverge from that of the participants. It is not uncommon, for example, for observers to hold a negative view of an emotionally tumultuous relationship whereas the participants may express satisfaction with it. The main point here is that what a relationship appears to be will, to some extent, depend on the perspective from which the relationship is measured and studied.

Despite considerable variation in the number, types, and patterns of relationships and despite variations in the pathways by which such relationships unfold, there is a growing consensus among researchers that most people have a deep *need to belong* to others—that is, a need to engage in interpersonal exchanges and a need to feel connected to other people through a variety of relationships (Baumeister & Leary, 1995). However, there is a paradox here. Given a presumably universal motive to engage in relationships (and especially assuming that we really do know a good deal about how successful relationships are formed and maintained), why are relationships so problematic for some people and, at specific times, so difficult for virtually everyone else. In part, the reason may have to do with the phenomenon of trust and this is the topic to which we will now turn.

THE PSYCHOLOGY OF TRUST

Trust is one of the most important factors in the development of relationships. It contributes to whether a relationship will develop at all and how long it will last if it does so. Some authors have suggested that believing that other people are generally trustworthy—hence trusting people in most circumstances—is essential to complex social behavior and functioning (Rotter, 1971, 1980).

Hatfield (1984) has argued that trust is fundamental to all close personal relationships and that people involved in such relationships must believe that their partners will meet their needs and expectations for the relationship in question to be rewarding and satisfying. It has been argued that trust is so essential to relationships, social groups, and social systems that it would not exist apart from interactions among people (Lewis & Weigart, 1985), a point that is similar to what Sullivan (1953) said about personality generally.

Trust is important in this regard because despite the obvious benefits and rewards of interpersonal involvement and relationships there are also numerous risks associated with initiating and engaging in relationships with other people (Jones & Burdette, 1994; Jones, Couch, & Scott, 1997). There is often a kind of tension or contradiction between the differing roles one may assume in a relationship—for example, having legitimate authority over another person may make friendly companionship difficult if not impossible, and parents often struggle with the contradiction between protecting one's children versus encouraging them to become competent, independent, and self-sufficient. An even more common risk is that one's partner (or intended partner) may not reciprocate the feelings of attraction and commitment, at least not in the same ways or to the same degree. Being rejected is an enormously unpleasant experience and is sometimes devastating even when done in as pleasant a manner possible. Also, as relationships develop, there are natural increases in commitment, self-disclosure, and intimacy, each of which increases the risk of potential embarrassment and humiliation should one's partner reveal the secrets one has shared or the intimate details of the relationship. Furthermore, becoming involved with others often results in major changes in lifestyle and identity (e.g., living together, marrying, interacting with others as a couple). Once such changes are made, being betrayed by one's intimate partner risks, at the very least, emotional upheaval, disruption, and inconvenience (e.g., anger, arguments, breaking-up, divorce), and at the worst, alienation and loss of identity.

Trust has been defined and studied in a variety of ways. First, trust may be considered a general tendency or personality trait (stable and characteristic pattern of emotion, behavior, perception, etc.) that suggests how a person will act over time and in various situations. The appropriate term for this characteristic is *trait trust*. Alternatively, trust also may be seen as the immediate experience of feelings, thoughts, and judgments that are occurring at a given moment, thereby defining *state trust*. Second, one may think of trust toward a specific relationship partner or a specific group of people (e.g., one's family), or, by contrast, trust in human nature, or trust in life. Often a correspondence would characterize these two definitions, but discrepancies also can occur. For example, one can imagine the generally distrustful person who nevertheless trusts close friends and colleagues as well as the generally trusting individual who is suspicious of someone who has proved himself or herself unworthy of trust in the past. Third, trust may be described as both a precursor to and as a consequence of the dynamics of close personal relationships. As a precursor, trust is seen as impacting the development or likelihood of a relationship, whereas trust is a consequence when relationship developments lead one to become more or less trusting of one's partner or people in general.

Global Trust

As a personality trait, trust has been studied primarily as it relates to one's experience with people in general. This kind of trust is referred to as generalized, or global trust. Global trust is defined as a generalized expectancy that an individual or group can be relied upon (Rotter, 1971) or the belief that human beings are basically honest (Wrightsman, 1992). One might imagine a continuum of global trust toward humanity or people in general. At one end of the continuum are individuals who are suspicious, wary, and inclined to attribute negative characteristics to others (e.g., dishonesty, manipulativeness, selfishness) and thus are low in trust. At the other end of the continuum are people high in trust who might be described as accepting, inclined to take others at their word, and likely to make positive judgments about people in general as well as specific others. Presumably, most people would fall between these two extremes. People who fall in the middle of the trust continuum might be best described as trusting or not depending on the circumstances, their mood, or the other person whose trust is at issue.

Theories of Global Trust   Erikson (1964) was one of the first to discuss at length the development of a trusting personality. Erikson argued that trust is a basic human attitude that includes a deep faith in the self, in other people, and in one's culture and society. Erikson believed that as a personal identity develops, one passes through stages or crises, the first of which is *basic trust versus mistrust*. Basic trust is defined as a general sense of the correspondence between one's needs and one's world, whereas mistrust is defined as an expectation of danger or an anticipation of discomfort. According to Erikson, trust develops from the attachment bond formed between an infant and his or her primary caregiver(s) during the first year of life. In this conceptualization of trust, two basic manifestations are emphasized: (1) trust of specific other persons (e.g., the caregiver); and (2) trust of life itself. These two consequences correspond roughly to the two environmental sources Erikson believed to be responsible for a child's development of trust: (1) a trustworthy caregiving environment in which the infant develops a sense of mutuality, and (2) a trustworthy social environment from which a sense of the meaning of life emerges. For basic trust to evolve, the infant must come to rely on the dependability of his or her caregivers. Initial trust is the basis for the trusting feelings that develop later in life. Accordingly, if trust is established with the caregiver, the infant will "translate" that experience into other relationships, whereas mistrust or the failure of trust to develop, will develop into subsequent suspicion of people in general.

Similarly, Bowlby (1982; see chapter 5, this volume) formulated *attachment theory* as a theoretical approach to infant-caregiver relationships and this model also provides an account of the mechanisms underlying the development of global trust. Bowlby argued that the relationship between an infant and a caregiver serves a biological function—protection of the attached infant from physical and psychological harm. At birth, humans engage in behaviors that have the consequence of bringing them into closer proximity and interaction with a caregiver and through subsequent interactions, these behaviors come to be preferentially directed toward the caregiver and become integrated into a coherent attachment system. According to Bowlby, activation of the attachment system stems from perceived danger and is deactivated by perceived safety. Perceived danger draws the child closer to the attachment figure and the information gained about the caregiver during these interactions is translated into the child's view of relational interactions and the responsiveness of other potential relational partners. Presumably, information about the lack of reliability of the caregiver may lead to a more permanent effect on the mental representation of the world and significant persons for the child. These cognitive models are continually updated with the new information from each interaction, but because the new information is assimilated into the existing model, one's sense of trust tends to be resistant to dramatic changes. Therefore, the child's worldview and view of others tends to remain fairly stable across time, and in this way, the child's level of trust is developed and remains stable.

Rotter (1967) agreed that trust evolves through interactions with others but also argued that any social agent may influence an individuals' level of trust. This perspective, known as *social learning theory* holds that behaviors or judgments depend, in part, on the expectancy of an individual that a given behavior will lead to a particular outcome or reinforcement in that situation. Accordingly, trust is seen to develop through observation during experiences of positive and negative outcomes with various social agents, such as parents, peers, teachers, and other people encountered in the social world. These experiences are believed to generalize from one social agent or situation to another so that a "generalized expectancy" emerges in which the individual assumes that the words or promises of others can be relied upon—or not—to varying degrees. For example, an individual whose parents, friends, and teachers were consistent and reliable (e.g., true to their word) would develop an expectancy to trust others or a "trusting personality," whereas an individual accustomed to unreliable behavior and broken promises from these significant others would develop an expectancy of suspicion and distrust. Rotter also argued that people may learn trusting or mistrusting expectancies without direct personal experience because others who are trusted may manifest, and hence "model," distrusting or trusting behaviors or attitudes.

Despite their different emphases, these theories share several commonalities regarding the development of global trust, which may be summarized as follows: (1) trust is a precursor of adequate functioning in the social world; (2) trust is (at least partially) acquired through experiences with significant other people; (3) trust is a developmental and ongoing process; but (4) once acquired, trust evolves into a stable, global, or generalized dimension of personality through a process by which experience with other people at one point in development contributes to the capacity to trust at a subsequent point in life. These last two conclusions, in turn, also suggest that individuals vary in their levels of trust as a result of the different experiences they may have had with their relational partners earlier in development. Bowlby and Erikson would argue that differences in trust result from disparate experience with attachment; Rotter would argue that individuals also develop differing expectancies because of different experiences with reinforcements in social situations.

Research on Global Trust   Research has supported the utility of these models and has suggested that the influence of global trust may be seen in many areas of a person's life. For example, trust has been found to be positively related to competitiveness, need for approval, and self-esteem, and inversely associated with negative emotional traits such as suspicion (e.g., Couch, Adams, & Jones, 1996; Rotter, 1967). Research also has suggested that global trust is not identical to what may appear to be very similar concepts including gullibility, social dependence, and naiveté (Rotter, 1967, 1971).

The tendency to trust others is not only essential for social interactions and social structurebut also has been found to be related to constructive problem solving, effective strategies for seeking social and emotional support, better health, and more effective coping under stress (Schill, Toves, & Ramanaiah, 1980). People higher in trust also have been found to be happier and better adjusted whereas, by contrast, low trust has been linked to emotional distress and anxiety (e.g., Schill et al., 1980). People higher in trust are less likely to betray their own relationships, for example, through infidelity (Zak, Coulter, Giglio, Hall, Sanford, & Pellowski, 2002) and more likely to manifest displays of love when the relationship is threatened (Gonzaga, Keltner, Londahl, & Smith, 2001).

As a personality trait, both children's and adults' trust has been consistently related to measures of agreeableness (Sneed, 2002) as well as measures of prosocial behavior, empathic concern, perspective-taking, and benevolent interpretation of partner's behavior (Joireman, Needham & Cummings, 2002). Many of these findings have been observed cross-culturally as well (e.g., Li, 2000).

Because trusting individuals operate on the assumption that people will respond to them and are therefore more likely than others to make their needs known, these individuals may develop a sense of personal control, according to some scholars. In this regard, internal locus of control (i.e., the belief that one has some control over important outcomes in one's life) has been found consistently to be positively correlated with generalized trust (Rotter, 1971). Not surprisingly, individuals higher in trust have been found to lie, cheat, steal, betray, or conceal their attitudes from others less than those scoring lower in trust (Couch et al., 1996; Couch & Jones, 1997; Rotter, 1980). Furthermore, trust has been found to be positively related to characteristics of the individual as perceived by others. For example, persons higher as compared to lower in trust are more likely to be seen as attractive, trustworthy, and having common sense, and they also are more likely also to be liked by others (e.g., Rotter, 1980).

Despite its idealistic connotation, global trust likely refers to more than just what people say in response to statements on a questionnaire. For example, self-report measures of global trust have been compared with behavioral indices of trust, such as falling backward with the expectation of being caught (Cash, Stack, & Luna, 1975), with the finding that people who describe themselves as higher in trust are more likely to behave in a trusting manner that those lower in trust. In another study, trust was associated with depending on others' promises in laboratory games (Schlenker, Helm, & Tedeschi, 1973).

The relevance of global trust is that at least a modicum of trust in life, in society, and in human nature appear necessary for individuals to face the interpersonal challenges and risks of daily living (e.g., meeting new people, starting new relationships). In this sense trust might be considered a necessary prerequisite for almost any interpersonal undertaking, especially those involving others who are strangers or who are different. Research on global trust also emphasizes that trust in human nature is not only associated with people's willingness to undertake new social endeavors, as might be considered self-evident, but it is associated with social skills and happiness as well.

Relational Trust

By contrast with the generalized nature of global trust, relational trust involves an emotional bond between specific individuals and the confidence or sense of security that allows an individual to face the uncertainty of the future with a specific person (Rempel, Holmes, & Zanna, 1985; Lewis & Weigart, 1985). It reflects a concrete and immediate belief in (or confidence about) the fairness, honesty, and positive feelings of a specific relational partner (Holmes, 1991; Lazelere & Huston, 1980; Rempel et al., 1985). The feelings of trust in a close relational partner often are expressed as a belief that he or she will not criticize, embarrass, or hurt the individual emotionally (Johnson-George & Swap, 1982). Consequently, the expression of trust has the effect of strengthening the bond between the two individuals, making the relationship in question stronger.

Time and experience with the relationship are required for relational trust. During the initiation stage of romantic love, for example, it is generally agreed that the issue of trust is overshadowed by the powerful absorption of the individual into the love experience. In this regard, Holmes and Rempel (1989) describe trust in the early stages of love as tantamount to a naive expression of hope. Eventually, however, as relational partners become increasingly intimate and committed, expectations develop based on the behavior of one's partner. In other words, as the relationship progresses, and as the risks of participation in the relationship also increase, relationship partners develop new feelings about their partner's reliability. These expectations are presumably based largely on the partner's behavior in the relationship. As a result, relational trust is often described as dynamic (i.e., it may change considerably over time) and emergent, meaning that it arises from the relationship, specifically from the continuing interactions between the relational partners (Holmes, 1991; Rempel et al., 1985).

Theories of Relational Trust   The idea that relational trust grows from one's past experience with a specific relationship partner, or with similar relationships, is frequently cited in the literature and is the beginning assumption for most theories of the determinants and consequences of relational trust. For example, what is called the component model of relational trust assumes that trust in the partner develops through three phases, or types of trust, over the course of a relationship (Rempel et al., 1985). The phases are called predictability, dependability, and faith. According to the theory, trust is based initially on predictability or consistency of the partner's behavior. This is the most concrete and specific level of trust. If one's partner is predictable over time and one benefits from and comes to have confidence in that predictability (e.g., the partner is responsive), then trust may shift to dependability, which is a more abstract judgment about the partner's behavior and intentions toward the relationship. Finally, these judgments and expectations may eventually evolve into a kind of trust in the partner's ultimate fidelity and responsiveness, called faith, which extends beyond current circumstances, time, and partner behavior.

This model of trust assumes that its development requires taking interpersonal risks such as relying on the partner's word, engaging in intimate disclosures, and sacrificing present rewards for future gains. Also, although attributing characteristics to the partner (e.g., dependability) is assumed to be based on the partner's behavior, it still requires a positive inference to be drawn and ultimately a risk on the part of the individual who chooses to trust his or her partner. In any event, the component model suggests that reassurance of the partner's fairness and caring develops through stages eventuating in a faith in the partner and the relationship despite any uncertainties about the future.

As previously noted, several theories of relationships are based on an economic analogy and are generally referred to as social exchange theories (e.g., Foa et al., 1993). In this type of approach, each partner may be thought of as needing to barter with the other for his or her trustworthiness. Specific behaviors and symbols (e.g., gestures of sharing) become evidence of the partner's trustworthiness and play a role in trust building. Because people care about relationships in which they have made investments of time, caring, and emotional commitment, interpersonal exchanges with the relationship partner are seen as evidence that the partner also cares about the relationship and wants to maintain it. In this view, trust builds incrementally and developmentally through a series of gradually increasing investments (e.g., symbols of good faith and fairness) in the relationship. If one's partner enacts the expected relational behaviors and symbols (e.g., attentiveness, sharing, expressions of affection) trust continues to develop throughout the relationship, and the individual learns that his or her expectations will be met. On the other hand, the failure of the partner to reciprocate or "exchange" such investments is likely to be taken as an indication that the partner is untrustworthy and therefore not to be trusted.

According to the appraisal process model of relational trust (Holmes, 1991; Sorrentino, Holmes, Hanna, & Sharp, 1995), people assess and interpret their relationships in conjunction with their level of trust. Those high in trust tend to see positive events as confirming their decision to trust whereas negative events are given little weight in decision making. Similarly, those low in trust give more weight to negative events that confirm their inclination not to trust and they view positive events as less important. Thus, both individuals high and low in trust are "certainty oriented" because they apparently prefer to view their partner's behavior as consistent with their own preexisting expectations about which they feel certain. In this way, people filter information about their partners based on their own level of trust. In a sense, those with moderate levels of trust are in an awkward position in a relationship because they are less certain about whether to trust their relationship partners. For the person of intermediate or moderate trust, each piece of information gathered through interaction with the partner is potentially important and may be weighed more-or-less equally with all other information. One of the implications of this is that for individuals of moderate trust, any single event takes on an elevated significance for the relationship. Evaluation of one's partner and the quality of one's relationship are especially likely to occur as partners are "getting to know one another." During this phase conflict is more likely to occur and the role of trust in determining the subsequent course of the relationship is likely to be greater (Lazelere & Huston, 1980).

There is an underlying similarity to these models and theories despite their differences. Most obviously, all of these approaches assert that (1) trust develops out of the interpersonal exchanges between partners in a given relationship; and (2) both as it develops as well as throughout the course of the relationship, the partners' sense of trust at one point in time contributes to the subsequent nature of the relationship by encouraging greater (or lesser) trust, or by virtue of the certainty with which the actions of the partner may be interpreted. Taken together, these theories also imply that relational trust is both a contributor to and a consequence of the development of a relationship. In other words, a certain amount of trust (or at least naive hope) is necessary for a relationship to get underway, but it is only through the consistency and responsiveness of the relational partner that one is able to reach a more substantial and presumably more satisfying level of trust. Similarly, the descriptions of global trust and relational trust may be seen to converge on this point, at least theoretically, as we will discuss below.

Research on Relational Trust   Research confirms that relational trust plays a key role in various types of relationships. For example, assessments of trust have been found to be related to the positive aspects of children's and adolescents' peer relationships (Rotenberg, 1991) and the formation of young adults' intimate relationships (Lazelere & Huston, 1980). Also, the value of friendship appears to be directly related to the level of trust an individual experiences within the relationship as indicated by studies in which trust was found to be related to both ideal friendship preferences and actual friendship choices (Rotenberg, 1991; Rotenberg & Pilipenko, 1984). Similarly, parent-child relationships also have been found to be satisfying to the degree that each participant trusts the other (Komarovsky, 1974).

In particular, the study of romantic relationships demonstrates the importance of trust in a partner and this is one of the areas of research in which the concept is most frequently applied (Holmes & Rempel, 1989; Holmes, 1991). For example, relational trust has been found to vary with the length, degree of satisfaction, and commitment (i.e., importance of the relationship to an individual and his or her intention to remain in it) of romantic relationships (Lazelere & Huston, 1980). Moreover, researchers have also found that as self-disclosure and intimacy increased in a relationship, partners' trust for one another also increased.

In more recent research, patterns of attributions were observed to differ in married couples based on their levels of trust. Rempel (2001) found that even after the influence of relational satisfaction was removed, statements made by high trust married couples were more likely to emphasize positive parts of the couple's relationship, whereas couples with moderate and low levels of trust focused more on negative explanations for relational events.

As is often the case in the study of personality, relational trust appears to belong to a cluster of dimensions, each of which has been shown to facilitate or inhibit the quality and success of relationship experiences. For example, people in romantic relationships who were higher in relational trust scored lower on measures of relationships problems, such as jealousy, loneliness, suspicion, betrayal, and anger (e.g., Couch et al., 1996). Trust has been directly correlated with styles of loving that are thought to be positive and adaptive (passionate love, friendship love, etc.) and inversely correlated with styles that appear problematic (e.g., desperate love, game-playing love; Couch, 1994). Attributions of honesty (Lazelere & Huston, 1980) were found to be related to higher trust in one's relational partner and to predict positive behavioral outcomes such as constructiveness in marital communication (Doherty & Ryder, 1979) (see Activity Box 17.1).

Divergent Perspectives on Trust

So which view of trust is the correct one? All of the approaches described above have some merit and they are not as divergent as they might initially appear to be. For example, as suggested above, at least some degree of global trust is likely necessary for individual growth and development and necessary, in particular, for an individual to undertake new relationships outside the family of origin or initial social network. Once a relationship is under way and mutual expectations for reliability develop, a more specific kind of trust (i.e., relational trust) emerges. With time and increasing intimacy in the relationship, people are generally motivated to protect their emotional investment. If the partner is responsive and also expresses love, caring, and understanding, both relational and global trust are reinforced.

Because people have contact and experiences with a variety of others, however, global and relational trust are typically not interchangeable concepts. Imagine, for example, someone who is generally trusting toward others, but who is nevertheless wary of some untrustworthy person, or the characteristically suspicious individual who, despite it all, has developed a close and trusting relationship with one particular person or group of people. Consistent with these speculations, a recent study (Couch & Jones, 1997) indicated moderate but statistically significant correlations between measures of global trust and measures of relational trust (i.e., average rs of about .40).

Similarly, it seems reasonable to suppose that shabby treatment, hostility, and rejection not only undermine an individual's faith in the specific relational partner whose behavior could be characterized as such, but collectively and over time such experiences would likely result in a jaded and cynical view of both people and relationships. Interestingly, research on interpersonal betrayal (e.g., lying, infidelity, physical and emotional abuse, telling secrets), not only supports the expectation that the frequency of betrayals and one's level of trust

Activity Box 17.1	**Measuring Global and Relational Trust: The Trust Inventory**

Please indicate the extent to which each of the following statements applies to you using the following response format: 5 = *Very true of me* OR *strongly agree*; 4 = *True of me* OR *agree*; 3 = *Sometimes true* OR *undecided*; 2 = *Not true of me* OR *disagree*; 1 = *Very untrue of me* OR *strongly disagree*. If a question involves the term "partner," it refers to your current romantic partner (or a specific past romantic partner if you are not currently romantically involved with anyone).

____ 1. I tend to be accepting of others.

____ 2. My relationships with others are characterized by trust and acceptance.

____ 3. Basically I am a trusting person.

____ 4. It is better to trust people until they prove otherwise than to be suspicious of others until they prove otherwise.

____ 5. I accept others at "face value."

____ 6. Most people are trustworthy.

____ 7. It is better to be suspicious of people you have just met, until you know them better.

____ 8. I make friends easily.

____ 9. Only a fool would trust most people.

____ 10. I find it best to accept others for what they say and what they appear to be.

____ 11. I would admit to being more than a little paranoid about people I meet.

____ 12. I have few difficulties trusting people.

____ 13. Basically, I tend to be distrustful of others.

____ 14. Experience has taught me to be doubtful of others until I know they can be trusted.

____ 15. I have a lot of faith in the people I know.

____ 16. Even during the "bad times," I tend to think that things will work out in the end.

____ 17. I tend to take others at their word.

____ 18. When it comes to people I know, I am believing and accepting.

____ 19. I feel I can depend on most people I know.

____ 20. I almost always believe what people tell me.

____ 21. My partner makes me feel safe.

____ 22. My partner makes me uncomfortable.

____ 23. I do not worry that my partner will leave me.

____ 24. I am skeptical that relationships ever work out.

____ 25. I believe in my partner.

____ 26. In relationships, I tend to be alert for the possibility of rejection or betrayal.

____ 27. I am sure about how my partner feels about me.

____ 28. I am doubtful that my partner will always be there for me if I need him or her.

(continued)

Activity Box 17.1 *(continued)*

_____ 29. I tell my partner that I trust him or her completely.

_____ 30. Relationships will only lead to heartache.

_____ 31. I am rarely ever suspicious of people with whom I have a relationship.

_____ 32. I am afraid my partner will hurt me emotionally.

_____ 33. I am afraid my partner will betray me.

_____ 34. I generally believe what my partner tells me.

_____ 35. I never believe my partner when he or she tells me how he or she feels about me.

_____ 36. I feel that I can be myself in the presence of my partner.

_____ 37. I am certain about how my partner feels about me.

_____ 38. It is dangerous to "let your guard down" with your partner.

_____ 39. I am sometimes doubtful of my partner's intentions.

_____ 40. When my partner is with others, I worry that he/she will not be faithful.

The items above make up the Generalized Trust Scale (a measure of global trust) and the Partner Trust Scale (a measure of relational trust) of the Trust Inventory developed by Couch (1994). The scales have been found to be reliable (e.g., coefficient alphas of .91 for the Generalized Trust Scale and .91 for the Partner Trust Scale), and the scores were highly correlated with appropriate measures of personality and relationship qualities. For example, the Generalized Trust Scale was positively correlated interpersonal warmth, a general liking for people, and gregariousness, and negatively correlated with shyness and suspicion, whereas Partner Trust was associated with feelings of love, relational satisfaction and commitment, self-disclosure, and passion, and negatively related to game-playing in relationships and loneliness (Couch, Adams, & Jones, 1996; Couch & Jones, 1997).

To determine your Generalized Trust score, reverse the responses that you gave for items 7, 9, 11, 13, and 14 (that is, 1=5, 2=4, 4=2, 5=1), and then sum your responses to items 1–20. To determine your Partner Trust score, reverse the responses that you gave for items 22, 24, 26, 28, 30, 32, 33, 35, 38, 39, and 40 as described above, and then sum your responses to items 21–40.

Based on a sample of 175 college students (Couch, Adams, & Jones, 1996), the mean score for Generalized Trust was 71.3, and the standard deviation was 11.4. Consequently, scores above 83 might be considered especially high for Generalized Trust, scores from 60 to 82 might be considered average Generalized Trust, and scores of 59 and below might be considered low Generalized Trust.

Among a sample of 167 college students (Couch, Adams, & Jones, 1996), the mean score for Partner Trust was 73, and the standard deviation was 13.7. Consequently, scores above 87 might be considered especially high for Partner Trust, scores from 60 to 86 might be considered average Partner Trust, and scores of 59 and below might be considered low Partner Trust. It is important to remember, however, that results from questionnaires and other psychological instruments always should be interpreted with caution.

Source: From "The Assessment of Trust Orientation" by L. L. Couch, J. M. Adams, and W. H. Jones, *Journal of Personality Assessment, 67,* pp. 302–323. Copyright © 1996 Lawrence Erlbaum Associates, Inc. Used with permission.

are related, but they are related in more than one way (Jones et al., 1997). As one might expect, people who report that that they have been more frequently betrayed by their relational partners tend to score lower on measures of both global and relational trust. In addition, people who score lower on measures of global and relational trust tend to report that they have betrayed their relational partners more frequently as well.

CONCLUDING REMARKS

Relationships and personality refer to complex interpersonal and psychological processes that involve the full spectrum of human behavior and experience. As a consequence, any effort to draw broad conclusions regarding their correspondence necessarily omits considerable qualifying detail and thereby runs the risk of misleading by over-simplification. Nonetheless, a few concluding comments are in order. First, most pertinent theories, to varying degrees, emphasize that the mutual influence of personality and relationships is dynamic and interactive; each influences the development and outcome of the other. As discussed earlier, trust and other relevant personality dimensions contribute to relationship formation and change, whereas success or failure in love and friendship reinforces trust or suspicion as characteristic ways of seeing life and people.

Second, much research in personality has focused on the role of early parent-child relationships in the formation of personality. For example, the degree of attachment between an infant and the caregiver or the responsiveness of the caregiver are seen as significant factors in the child's development of a trusting view of the world. Although the impact of the early caregiver-child bond is usually described as substantial, subsequent relationships during childhood, adolescence, adulthood, and old age also may contribute to the development of personality organization and structure (e.g., identity, emotional and cognitive styles, motives, adjustment). Thus, although the degree to which relationships influence personality may well "narrow" over the span of a lifetime, especially as personality assumes consistency, each stage of life presents its own unique interpersonal needs and challenges. Put another way, the infant-caregiver relationship may determine the most basic level of trust-mistrust as Erikson (1964) suggested, but adolescent friendships, falling in love, work relationships, marriage, being a parent oneself, and so on are experiences that also contribute to one's trust in others.

Third, what a person becomes as reflected in personality also clearly plays a major role in the quality and quantity of relationships in which one engages. In adolescence and early adulthood the importance of an individual's interpersonal traits (e.g., sociability) and social emotions (e.g., shyness) for acquiring friends, courtship, and marriage has been extensively documented. Less obviously, the personality and behavioral tendencies of the infant also may determine, in part, the vigor and effectiveness of parental caregiving and nurturance.

Fourth, although numerous personality dimensions have been related to important relational outcomes, it is possible that the personality dimensions critical to relationships are organized into a structure that resembles the major stages of relational development and change. In other words, personality dimensions that facilitate or inhibit meeting people for the first time or talking to strangers and the like differ to some extent from the dimensions that facilitate or inhibit psychological and sexual intimacy, self-disclosure, and long-term commitment. The need to get along with others while also striving to get ahead in a competitive social environment seems to be an inherent dilemma in the domain of relationships and this may be precisely where personality traits and tendencies make the greatest difference in the nature and quality of experience. In this regard, few if any personality dimensions have been shown to be as strongly or as extensively related to assessments of relationship satisfaction and effectiveness as the dimension of trust.

Finally, research and theorizing on the interface of personality and relationships will, of course, continue and may result in the modification of at least some of the ideas and conclusions presented in this chapter. This is as it should be. It is unlikely, however, that future conceptions will diminish the apparent importance and centrality of personality and relationships to a broader understanding of human experience. It is also unlikely that the concept of trust will become any less useful as a conceptual tool in explaining relationships as society becomes more diverse or the world becomes smaller and more interdependent.

SUMMARY

An interpersonal relationship may be defined as a state of mutual awareness in which participants feel an emotional bond toward one another. People participate in a variety of relationships formed in different interpersonal settings. Understanding relationships is necessary for understanding personality because relationships (1) are central and important to life and provide the context in which experience occurs; (2) play a role in adjustment and health; and (3) contribute to the development of personality and, in turn, are strongly influenced by personality traits and processes. Relationships may be described as developing through four phases: initiation, enhancement, maintenance, and termination. The factors that determine the nature and quality of a relationship vary as a function of phase and the type of relationship and include characteristics of the person, characteristics of the partner in the relationship, and characteristics of the situation in which the relationship is formed. In studying relationships several methodological and conceptual issues warrant attention including (1) arbitrary distinctions between stages, (2) generalization of factors appropriate in one stage to another stage, (3) the impact of factors that typically are not measured in psychological studies, and (4) the potential importance of perspective in determining the outcomes of research studies.

An important personality dimension in the study of relationships is trust, which has been conceptualized in various ways. First, generalized or global trust refers to trust in human nature or people in general. Most theories of global trust suggest that it develops from the certainty and responsiveness of the infant's experience with the caregiver. Trust thus develops into a trait or generalized expectancy that shapes judgments and interactions with others, and trust operationally defined in this way has proven to be a predictor of important psychological qualities such as self-esteem, adjustment, and happiness. By contrast, relational trust refers to the trust that emerges for a specific relational partner and develops from and contributes to the relationship itself. Theorizing regarding relational trust tends to assume that trust is malleable and changes throughout the course of a given relationship, but that it may also shape the relationship in question. Most believe that the various models of trust and, in particular, the global versus relational trust conceptualizations are essentially complementary rather than contradictory. Conclusions focus on the integral connection between personality and relationships, especially as illustrated by the concept of trust.

DISCUSSION QUESTIONS

1. In your view, what are the costs and benefits of trusting others?
2. Are there situations in which even those high in trust would be wary of trusting others?
3. In the chapter, specific attention was paid to trust one has in a specific romantic partner or romantic relationship. How might trust be demonstrated in other types of relationships, such as in work relationships? When one has trust for a dear friend or work colleague, is it a manifestation of global trust or a unique form of relational trust?
4. What does it feel like to trust or distrust another? How can trusting and distrusting be shown behaviorally?
5. In close relationships, how is trusting a relational partner different from relational satisfaction?
6. Besides trust, what other personality traits play a role in the experiences of interpersonal relationships? Are these traits most important in the development of relationships, their maintenance, or both? Which personality traits may play a role in relationship dissolution?

SUGGESTED READINGS

Couch, L. L., & Jones, W. H. (1997). Measuring levels of trust. *Journal of Research in Personality, 31,* 319–336. This article presents empirical evidence comparing different types and measures of trust, including global versus relational trust. The article also outlines a differential conceptualization of trust (i.e., global, relational).

Holmes, J. G. (1991). Trust and the appraisal process in close relationships In W. H. Jones & D. Perlman (Eds.), *Advances in personal relationships* (pp. 57–106). London, U.K.: Jessica Kingsley. This chapter is perhaps the best overview of theories and research (prior to 1990) regarding trust. Also, this essay introduces and explains the appraisal process model of trust.

Jones, W. H., Couch, L. L., & Scott, S. (1997). Trust and betrayal: The psychology of trust viola-

tion. In R. Hogan, J. Johnson, & S. R. Briggs (Eds.), *Handbook of personality psychology* (pp. 466–482). New York: Academic Press. The literature on trust is considered along with research on betrayals of relationships or what are termed violations of trust. In particular, this chapter compares and contrasts research and theory on trust and betrayal.

Sorrentino, R. M., Holmes, J. G., Hanna, S. E., & Sharp, A. (1995). Uncertainty orientation and trust in close relationships: Individual differences in cognitive styles. *Journal of Personality and Social Psychology, 68,* 314–327. The role of uncertainty in trust formation and change is investigated in this article. Three laboratory experiments that explore this issue are presented.

SUGGESTED WEB SITES

http://www.personalityresearch.org/papers/cardillo.htm

This site features scholarly student papers and responses about how interpersonal relationships play a role in personality development.

http://www.iarr.org

The International Association for Relationships Research. This web site provides information about this scholarly society for interdisciplinary research in interpersonal relationships. The site also provides information about journals and other publications in the area of interpersonal relations.

http://www.socialpsychology.org

The Social Psychology Network. This web site provides links to information about and contact information for people who are researching close relationships (as well as other areas of social psychology), and it also provides links to research laboratories that emphasize research on personality and close relationships.

http://www.geocities.com/research93

This web site is entitled "Close Relationships & Personality Research Website." It provides links to several online research studies on the topics of personality and close relationships.

http://www.russellsage.org/programs/proj_reviews/trust.htm

The Russell Sage Foundation Project on Trust. This site provides information about ongoing interdisciplinary research on trust in many contexts. Links to working research papers are provided.

http://www.georgetown.edu/mcallister/research/trustdistrust.pdf

This theoretical paper presents a view that trust is a multidimensional experience comprising simultaneous possibilities for trust and distrust.

INFOTRAC COLLEGE EDITION SEARCH TOPICS

Relationships

Functions of relationships

Relationship development

Global trust

Relational trust

REFERENCES

Adams, J. M., & Jones, W. H. (1997). The conceptualization of marital commitment: An integrative analysis. *Journal of Personality and Social Psychology, 72,* 1177–1196.

Adams, J. M., & Spain, J. S. (1999). The dynamics of interpersonal commitment and the issue of salience. In J. M. Adams & W. H. Jones (Eds.), *The handbook of interpersonal commitment and relationship stability* (pp. 165–179). New York: Plenum.

Baumeister, R. F., & Leary, M. R. (1995). The need to belong: Desire for interpersonal attachments as a fundamental human motivation. *Psychological Bulletin, 117,* 497–529.

Beall, A. E., & Sternberg, R. J. (1995). The social construction of love. *Journal of Personal and Social Relationships, 12,* 417–438.

Bowlby, J. (1982). *Attachment and loss: Attachment* (Vol. 1, 2nd ed.). New York: Basic Books.

Buss, A. H. (1995). *Personality: Temperament, social behavior, and the self.* Boston: Allyn & Bacon.

Buss, D. M. (1994). *The evolution of desire: Strategies of human mating.* New York: Basic Books.

Byrne, D. (1971). *The attraction paradigm.* New York: Academic Press.

Cash, T. F., Stack, J. J., & Luna, G. C. (1975). Convergent and discriminant behavioral aspects of interpersonal trust. *Psychological Reports, 37,* 983–986.

Clark, M. S., & Mills, J. (1993). The difference between communal and exchange relationships: What it is and is not. *Personality and Social Psychology Bulletin, 19,* 684–691.

Couch, L. L. (1994). *The development of the Trust Inventory.* Unpublished master's thesis, University of Tennessee, Knoxville.

Couch, L. L., Adams, J. M., & Jones, W. H. (1996). The assessment of trust orientation. *Journal of Personality Assessment, 67,* 302–323.

Couch, L. L., & Jones, W. H. (1997). Measuring levels of trust. *Journal of Research in Personality, 31*, 319–336.

Derlega, V. J., Metts, S., Petronio, S., & Margulis, S. T. (1993). *Self-disclosure*. Newbury Park, CA: Sage.

Doherty, W. J., & Ryder, R. G. (1979). Locus of control, interpersonal trust, and assertive behavior among newlyweds. *Journal of Personality and Social Psychology, 37*, 2212–2220.

Drigotas, S. M., & Rusbult, C. E. (1993). Should I stay or should I go? A dependence model of breakups. *Journal of Personality and Social Psychology, 62*, 62–87.

Erikson, E. H. (1964). *Childhood and society* (2nd ed.). New York: Norton.

Feingold, A. (1991). Sex differences in the effects of similarity and physical attractiveness on opposite sex attraction. *Basic and Applied Psychology, 12*, 357–367.

Foa, U. G., Converse, J., Jr., Tornbloom, K. Y., & Foa, E. B. (Eds.). (1993). *Resource theory: Explorations and applications*. San Diego, CA: Academic Press.

Gonzaga, G. C., Keltner, D., Londahl, E. A., & Smith, M. P. (2001). Love and the commitment problem in romantic relations and friendships. *Journal of Personality and Social Psychology, 81*, 247–262.

Hafner, R. J. (1986). *Marriage and mental illness*. New York: Guilford.

Hansson, R. O., & Carpenter, B. N. (1994). *Relationships in old age*. New York: Guilford.

Hatfield, E. (1984). The dangers of intimacy. In V. J. Derlega (Ed.), *Communication, intimacy, and close relationships* (pp. 207–220). Orlando, FL: Academic Press.

Hatfield, E. (1988). Passionate and companionate love. In R. J. Sternberg & M. L. Barnes (Eds.), *The psychology of love* (pp. 191–217). New Haven, CT: Yale University Press.

Holmes, J. G. (1991). Trust and the appraisal process in close relationships. In W. H. Jones & D. Perlman (Eds.), *Advances in personal relationships* (2nd ed., pp. 57–106). London: Jessica Kingsley.

Holmes, J. G., & Rempel, J. K. (1989). Trust in close relationships. In C. Hendrick (Ed.), *Close relationships* (pp. 187–220). Newbury Park, CA: Sage.

Jarvenpa, R. (1993). Hunter-gatherer sociospatial organization and group size. *Behavioral and Brain Science, 16*, 712

Johnson, M. P., Caughlin, J. P., & Huston, T. L. (1999). The tripartite nature of marital commitment: Personal, moral, and structural reasons to stay married. *Journal of Marriage and the Family, 61*, 160–177.

Johnson-George, C., & Swap, W. (1982). Measurement of specific interpersonal trust: Construction and validation of a scale to assess trust in a specific other. *Journal of Personality and Social Psychology, 43*, 1306–1317.

Jones, W. H., & Burdette, M. P. (1994). Betrayal in close relationships In A. L. Weber & J. Harvey (Eds.), *Perspectives on close relationships*, (pp. 243–262). New York: Allyn & Bacon.

Jones, W. H., Cheek, J. M., & Briggs, S. R. (Eds.). (1986). *Shyness: Perspectives on research and treatment*. New York: Plenum.

Jones, W. H., Couch, L. L., & Scott, S. (1997). Trust and betrayal: The psychology of trust violation. In R. Hogan, J. Johnson, & S. R. Briggs (Eds.), *Handbook of personality psychology* (pp. 466–482). New York: Academic Press.

Joireman, J. A., Needham, T. L., & Cummings, A. (2002). Relationships between dimensions of attachment and empathy. *North American Journal of Psychology, 4*, 63–80.

Kamo, Y. (1993). Determinants of marital satisfaction: A comparison of the United States and Japan. *Journal of Social and Personal Relationships, 10*, 551–568.

Komarovsky, M. (1974). Patterns of self-disclosure of male undergraduates. *Journal of Marriage and the Family, 36*, 677–686.

Kulik, J. A., Mahler, H. I. M., & Moore, P. J. (1996). Social comparison and affiliation under threat: Effects on recovery from major surgery. *Journal of Personality and Social Psychology, 71*, 967–979.

Kupersmidt, J. B., DeRosier, M. E., & Patterson, C. P. (1995). Similarity as the basis for children's friendships: The roles of sociometric status, aggressive and withdrawn behavior, academic achievement and demographic characteristics. *Journal of Personal and Social Relationships, 12*, 439–452.

Larson, R., Csikszentmihalyi, M., & Graef, R. (1982). Time alone in daily experience: Loneliness or renewal? In L. A. Peplau & D. Perlman (Eds.), *Loneliness: A sourcebook of current theory, research and therapy* (pp. 40–53). New York: Wiley-Interscience.

Lazelere, R. E., & Huston, T. L. (1980). The dyadic trust scale: Toward understanding interpersonal trust in close relationships. *Journal of Marriage and the Family, 42,* 595–604.

Lee, R. Y-P., & Bond, M. (1996). *How friendship develops out of personality and values: A study of interpersonal attraction in Chinese culture.* Unpublished manuscript, Chinese University of Hong Kong.

Li, D. (2000). A study of the factors influencing the prosocial behavior of children. *Psychological Science (China), 23,* 285–288.

Levinger, G., & Snoek, J. D. (1972). *Attraction in relationship: A new look at interpersonal attraction.* Morristown, NJ: General Learning Press.

Lewis, J. D., & Weigart, A. (1985). Trust as a social reality. *Social Forces, 63,* 967–985.

Murstein, B. I. (1986). *Paths to marriage.* Beverly Hills, CA: Sage.

Murstein, B. I. (1987). A clarification and extension of the SVR theory of dyadic pairing. *Journal of Marriage and the Family, 49,* 929–933.

Rempel, J. K. (2001). Trust and communicated attributions in close relationships. *Journal of Personality and Social Psychology, 81,* 57–64.

Rempel, J. K., Holmes, J. G., & Zanna, M. P. (1985). Trust in close relationships. *Journal of Personality and Social Psychology, 49,* 95–112.

Rosenbaum, M. E. (1986). The repulsion hypothesis: On the nondevelopment of relationships. *Journal of Personality and Social Psychology, 51,* 1156–1166.

Rotenberg, K. J. (Ed.). (1991). *Children's interpersonal trust: Sensitivity to lying, deception, and promise violations.* New York: Springer-Verlag.

Rotenberg, K. J., & Pilipenko, T. A. (1984). Mutuality, temporal consistency, and helpfulness in children's trust in peers. *Social Cognition, 2,* 235–255.

Rotter, J. B. (1967). A new scale for the measurement of interpersonal trust. *Journal of Personality, 35,* 651–665.

Rotter, J. B. (1971). Generalized expectancies for interpersonal trust. *American Psychologist, 26,* 443–452.

Rotter, J. B. (1980). Interpersonal trust, trustworthiness, and gullibility. *American Psychologist, 35,* 1–7.

Sarason, B. R., Sarason, I. G., & Pierce, G. R. (Eds.). (1990). *Social support: An interactional view.* New York: Wiley.

Schill, T., Toves, C., & Ramanaiah, N. (1980). Interpersonal trust and coping with stress. *Psychological Reports, 47,* 1192.

Schlenker, B. R., Helm, B., & Tedeschi, J. T. (1973). The effects of personality and situational variables on behavioral trust. *Journal of Personality and Social Psychology, 25,* 419–427.

Sneed, C. D. (2002). Correlates and implications for agreeableness in children. *Journal of Psychology, 136,* 59–67.

Sternberg, R. (1987). Explorations of love. In W. H. Jones & D. Perlman (Eds.), *Advances in personal relationship* (Vol. 1, pp. 171–196). Greenwich, CT: JAI Press.

Sorrentino, R. M., Holmes, J. G., Hanna, S. E., & Sharp, A. (1995). Uncertainty orientation and trust in close relationships: Individual differences in cognitive styles. *Journal of Personality and Social Psychology, 68,* 314–327.

Stroebe, W., & Stroebe, M. S. (1986). Beyond marriage: The impact of partner loss on health. In R. Gilmour & S. Duck (Eds.), *The emerging field of personal relationships* (pp. 203–224). Hillsdale, NJ: Erlbaum.

Sullivan, H. S. (1953). *The interpersonal theory of psychiatry.* New York: Norton.

Whitbeck, L. B., & Hoyt, D. R. (1994). Social prestige and assortive mating: A comparison of students from 1956 and 1988. *Journal of Social and Personal Relationships, 11,* 137–145.

White, G. L. (1980). Physical attractiveness and courtship progress. *Journal of Personality and Social Psychology, 39,* 660–668.

Wrightsman, L. S. (1992). *Assumptions about human nature: Implications for researchers and practitioners* (2nd ed.). Newbury Park, CA: Sage.

Zak, A., Coulter, C., Giglio, S., Hall, J., Sanford, S., & Pellowski, N. (2002). Do his friends like me? Predictors of intimate relationships. *North American Journal of Psychology, 4,* 287–290.

Disorders of Personality: Diseases or Individual Differences?

18

JAMES E. MADDUX

CLARE E. MUNDELL

The study of personality is in many ways the study of how people deal with the changes and challenges that are a natural part of human life. Therefore, the study of personality is in many ways the study of psychological adaptation and adjustment. Of course, we cannot fully understand adaptation and adjustment without also understanding maladaptation and maladjustment— that is, what goes wrong in our attempts to deal with change and challenge, and why things sometimes go wrong, as they so often do. Thus, the study of personality would be incomplete without an exploration of the dysfunctional aspects of human life. Almost every chapter of this book deals to some extent with the abnormal or maladaptive aspects of personality. This chapter, however, deals with the issue more explicitly. To begin, consider the following descriptions:

> Sue is a 20-year-old college sophomore. She has been called "shy" all her life. She has never had more than one or two close friends, and these usually have been people who are very shy like her. She rarely initiates conversations with others and rarely goes out on weekends, except maybe for a movie now and then, often in the daytime by herself. She almost always arrives for class just before it starts and leaves immediately when it ends to avoid having to talk to her classmates. Recently, she dropped a class when she learned that one of the required assignments was a group project. She wants friends very badly and does not like being so shy, but, as she tells her parents, she "just can't help it." She avoids other people because she feels so inadequate around them and is very sensitive to any sign that others do not approve of her or do not like her. As a result, she has had only one close female friend, Pam, who saw some of Sue's good qualities and was very persistent in trying to build a friendship with her. Sue, of course, constantly worries that Pam became her friend only out of pity. Although Sue is attractive, she has never been on a date. She gets invitations to go out from men now and then, but she always becomes anxious and says she is busy.
>
> Joe is a 40-year-old furniture mover. He has been married for three years but has always suspected that his wife married him for reasons other than love, although when pressed for a reason he simply says, "Because women just can't be trusted." Although he is a good provider and a loyal husband, he worries constantly that his wife may be having an affair, despite the absence of any evidence of infidelity. For the first year of their marriage, his wife did not work, and he suspected that she was using their home to see other men. She took a job to relieve Joe's fear, but now he suspects she is having an affair with a co-worker who called one night to check on the time of a meeting the next morning. He searches through her belongings almost every day for evidence of her infidelity and questions her angrily if she arrives home from work a few minutes later than usual. At his own place of work, whenever he sees people talking, he assumes they are either talking about his wife's affairs or plotting against him in some way. He trusts no one, not even his friends and family members. He rarely confides in others about these fears because he is afraid they will use what he says against him in some way. He reacts strongly to insults and typically bears grudges for perceived insults from others.

Both Sue and Joe show patterns of thinking, feeling, and behaving that we might call *personality disorders*. Some psychologists and psychiatrists would say that Sue has an *Avoidant Personality Disorder* and that Joe has a *Paranoid Personality Disorder*. Others would say that Sue and Joe are simply displaying extreme variations of relatively common concerns—shyness, jealousy, and distrust of other people's motives. On the one hand, Sue and Joe cannot possibly be happy with their lives. On the other hand, they have thoughts and feelings and display behaviors that many people show from time to time, some more so than others. You may know people who sometimes express the concerns and behaviors shown by Sue and Joe, yet who most of the time are fairly well-adjusted people. Do people like Joe and Sue have disorders that are similar to diseases, or are they just different from the rest of us in the frequency and severity with which they experience and express otherwise common concerns, emotions, and behaviors?

The goal of this chapter is to address this difficult question by providing an overview of some important general issues in the study of the abnormal, maladaptive, or "disordered" side of personality. The most important principle guiding this chapter is that the normal or adaptive aspects of personality do not differ in kind or type from the abnormal or maladaptive aspects of personality; they differ only in degree. Because we assume continuity between normal and abnormal personality, we believe that the study of personality disorder is not the study of subject matter that is distinct from what is covered in the other chapters of this book. Instead, it is the study of the same subject matter from a different perspective, that of the clinical psychologist, psychiatrist, or other mental health professional interested in enhancing adjustment and reducing disorder in people's lives. Thus, we draw on material from previous chapters and ask you to make connections between what you have read in those chapters and what you read in this chapter.

This chapter addresses four important and controversial questions in the study of disordered personality. First, what is a personality disorder and how is it different from so-called normal personality? Second, how are personality disorders similar to and different from other types of psychological problems? Third, is it better to think of personality disorders as diagnostic categories or as extreme points on a dimension or continuum of individual differences? Fourth, are there different types of personality disorders that can be accurately distinguished from one another, the way we can distinguish different kinds of diseases?

To a great extent, these issues and controversies center on the definition and conceptualization of personality disorder in the *Diagnostic and Statistical Manual of Mental Disorders* (usually called simply "the *DSM*"), the "official" manual of diagnostic categories for psychological and psychiatric disorders. First published by the American Psychiatric Association in 1952 and now in a revised fourth edition (*DSM-IV-TR*; American Psychiatric Association, 2000), the *DSM* is used by mental health professionals all over the world. Although the study of disordered personality predates the *DSM*, it was the appearance of personality disorders as a separate set of diagnostic categories in the third edition of the *DSM* in 1980 (*DSM-III*) that ignited the explosion of interest in disordered personality by clinicians and researchers. For this reason, much of what we have to say begins with what the *DSM* says about personality disorder.

Although we focus to a great extent on the *DSM* and controversies surrounding it, we do not provide detailed descriptions of the "official" *DSM*

Table 18.1 | *DSM-IV-TR* Personality Disorders

Name	Major Feature
Antisocial Personality Disorder	disregard for, and violation of, the rights of others
Avoidant Personality Disorder	social inhibition, feelings of inadequacy, and hypersensitivity to negative evaluation
Borderline Personality Disorder	instability in interpersonal relationships, self-image, and affects, and marked impulsivity
Dependent Personality Disorder	submissive and clinging behavior related to an excessive need to be taken care of
Histrionic Personality Disorder	excessive emotionality and attention seeking
Narcissistic Personality Disorder	grandiosity, need for admiration, and lack of empathy
Obsessive-Compulsive Personality Disorder	preoccupation with orderliness, perfectionism, and control
Paranoid Personality Disorder	distrust and suspiciousness such that others' motives are interpreted as malevolent
Schizoid Personality Disorder	detachment from social relationship and a restricted range of emotional expression
Schizotypal Personality Disorder	acute discomfort in close relationships, cognitive or perceptual distortions, and eccentricities of behavior

Source: Reprinted with permission from the *Diagnostic and Statistical Manual of Mental Disorders, Text Revision*, copyright 2000, American Psychiatric Association.

personality disorders. Such descriptions can be found in the *DSM-IV-TR*. Table 18.1, however, provides a list of the *DSM-IV-TR* personality disorders and a brief description of the core features of each. You should keep in mind, however, that very little research supports the validity of these categories—that is, the extent to which they accurately describe reality.

ABNORMALITY, MALADAPTIVENESS, AND DISORDER

So far, we have used both the normal-versus-abnormal contrast and the adaptive-versus-maladaptive contrast in describing disordered personality. Although many people treat these two contrasts as if they were the same, we do not believe that they are. We treat *normal* and *abnormal* as purely statistical terms. *Normal* refers to that which is relatively average or typical, and *abnormal* refers to that which is somewhat atypical or different from the norm or the average. Thus, *abnormal* refers to statistical deviation from the norm or average. A frequently asked question is, How far from the average must a person's behavior or personality deviate before it is considered abnormal?

There is no clear answer to this question. The answer depends on who is asking it and who is answering it. There is no hard and fast line between normal and abnormal psychological functioning and personality, just as there is no hard and fast line between short and tall when we talk about the height of human beings.

Adaptive and *maladaptive* refer not to statistical averages and deviations from those averages but to the effectiveness or ineffectiveness of a person's behavior. If a behavior "works" for the person—if the behavior helps the person deal with challenge, cope with stress, and accomplish his or her goals—then we say the behavior is more or less adaptive. If the behavior does not help in these ways, or if the behavior makes the situations worse instead of better, we say it is more or less maladaptive. If a person usually behaves effectively, we say he or she has an adaptive personality; but if the person usually behaves ineffectively, we say he or she has a maladaptive personality, a disordered personality, or a personality disorder.

Normality and adaptation often go hand in hand, and statistical deviation and maladaptiveness often go hand in hand, but this is not always the case. Having an IQ of 60 is both statistically deviant and maladaptive in most of the ways we measure maladaptiveness. An IQ of 140 is just as statistically deviant as an IQ of 60, but it is not maladaptive. Shyness is very common and therefore is statistically normal, but shyness is almost always maladaptive to some extent, because it almost always interferes with a person's ability to accomplish what he or she wants to accomplish in life and relationships.

When we use the term *personality disorder*, we are referring to personalities that are much more maladaptive than adaptive and much more maladaptive than the personalities of most other people. Such personalities are also statistically deviant or abnormal, and most personalities that are extremely deviant statistically are also maladaptive, but not always. In talking about disordered personality, however, we are more concerned with maladaptiveness than with statistical deviance.

As we noted previously, the distinctions between normal and abnormal and between adaptive and maladaptive are, at best, fuzzy and often arbitrary. Very few human behaviors are in and of themselves either normal or abnormal or either adaptive or maladaptive. Even behaviors that are statistically rare and therefore abnormal will be more or less adaptive or maladaptive under different conditions. The extent to which a behavior or behavior pattern is adaptive or maladaptive depends on a number of factors, such as the goals the person is trying to accomplish and the social norms and expectations of a given situation. So-called normal personality involves a good deal of occasionally maladaptive behavior, which you can find evidence for in your own life and the lives of friends and relatives. In addition, people given official personality disorder diagnoses by clinical psychologists and psychiatrists often get along just fine in life and do not always behave in disordered ways. Finally, there is an infinite number of "shades of gray" between the black and the white or normal, healthy personality and officially disordered personality.

For these reasons, we assume that normal, abnormal, adaptive, and maladaptive are points on a continuum, not different types or categories of behaviors or personalities. Thus, we view the "official" personality disorders defined by the *DSM* as continuous with normal personality. A clear distinction between normal personality and disordered personality simply does not exist. Just as we cannot find on a thermometer a line that separates "hot" from "cold," we cannot find on our measures of personality a line that separates normal from abnormal, adaptive from maladaptive, or "ordered" from "disordered." Likewise, just as one person finds a room a little too warm and another person finds the same room a little too cool, so will people (including clinical psychologists and psychiatrists) differ in their judgments of the adaptiveness or maladaptiveness of someone's personality. Although we would probably agree on the most extreme cases of maladaptive or disordered personality, in many other less clear cases, we might disagree. For these reasons, to say that a behavior or a personality is abnormal, maladaptive, or disordered is not to state a fact but to offer an opinion.

Finally, we do not use the term *disorder* in the way it is used in medicine— that is, we are not referring to a collection of symptoms that has an identifiable cause somewhere inside the person. We do not intend for *disorder* to mean *disease*. By *disorder* we simply mean that the person's behavior creates disorder in his or her life and the lives of other people.

A BRIEF HISTORY OF THE CONCEPT OF DISORDERED PERSONALITY

The notion that some people display enduring and pervasive styles of behaving, thinking, and feeling that are largely maladaptive or dysfunctional has been around for a long time and did not originate in 1980 with *DSM-III*. Millon provides an interesting history of the notion of personality disorder (Millon, with Davis, 1996). He notes that conceptions of personality and personality disorder go back to the ancient Greeks and Romans. More recent conceptions, however, have had a greater influence on contemporary views of disordered personality. These include the ideas of two of the most influential people in the history of psychiatry and psychology, Emil Kraepelin and Sigmund Freud. Kraepelin, the father of psychiatric diagnosis, wrote about disordered personality in the eighth edition of his textbook of psychiatry in 1913. Freud, the father psychoanalysis, was concerned with the role of unconscious defense mechanisms (unconscious strategies for warding off anxiety) in the development of maladaptive *character types*, another term for personality. The ideas of both of these thinkers and many others are described in detail by Millon (Millon, with Davis, 1996). Essentially, the idea that people can display not only behaviors and emotions that are maladaptive but entire personalities that are maladaptive has been around for centuries.

The study of personality disorders as distinct diagnostic categories began in 1980 with the publication of the third edition of the *DSM* (*DSM-III*). *DSM-III* formally introduced and defined personality disorders as part of the distinction between what it called *Axis I disorders*, or clinical syndromes, and *Axis II disorders*, or personality disorders. Although not specifically defined in the *DSM*,

Axis I clinical syndromes are groups of related symptoms (problems or complaints) that form an identifiable pattern and that lead a person to seek professional help. These clinical syndromes include such problems as anxiety, depression, and eating disorders—serious problems that are usually the source of considerable concern and distress. Axis II personality disorders are long-standing and maladaptive styles of relating to other people that may cause distress but usually not enough distress to prompt people to seek professional help under most circumstances. The *DSM* assumes that personality disorders have a much greater duration than clinical syndromes, although this idea has been challenged, as we will see a little later. The difference between Axis I and Axis II is similar to the distinction, made by Leary in chapter 1, between a state (a current, short-lived reaction to the immediate situation) and a trait (a tendency to experience a particular state).

The appearance of personality disorders as a distinct set of diagnostic categories was a milestone in psychiatric diagnosis. For better or for worse, these new disorders gained tremendous attention from clinicians, theorists, and researchers, so much so that within seven years (in 1987), a new scientific journal was founded that was devoted to the study of these new disorders, the *Journal of Personality Disorders*. In addition, 1988 saw the formation of the Society for the Study of Personality Disorders. Since then, research on the *DSM* personality disorders has burgeoned, as evidenced by hundreds of journal articles and numerous books and book chapters. In addition, every textbook in abnormal psychology now contains one or two chapters on the personality disorders defined and described by the *DSM*. The *DSM*'s influence cannot be overstated. Without the *DSM-III*, disorders of personality would not have received the attention from personality and clinical psychologists that they have in the past two decades. In fact, most of the research we present deals with the controversies raised by the *DSM*'s assumptions about the nature of abnormal or maladaptive personality.

WHAT IS A PERSONALITY DISORDER?

Defining *personality disorder* is difficult because we need to agree on definitions of both *personality* and *disorder*, two concepts that have been the topic of considerable debate for most of the history of psychology and psychiatry. We cannot even begin to explore these debates in a short chapter such as this one. In chapter 1 of this book, Leary defines personality as "the system of enduring inner characteristics of individuals that contributes to consistency in their thoughts, feelings, and behavior." We agree that personality should be viewed as enduring consistency in thoughts, feelings, and behavior, although we question the notion that this consistency should be attributed largely to "inner characteristics" because it seems to downplay the importance of learning and situational influences. Nonetheless, "enduring consistency" is the key concept. As we noted previously, we use the term *disorder* not to refer to a disease-like entity but simply to note that an individual's behavior causes disorder in his or her life and the lives of others.

One of the most important questions to consider is whether personality disorders are real disease-like entities (such as cancer or diabetes) or simply what we call *social constructions*—abstract concepts that we construct or build jointly because they help us make sense of a confusing world or serve social goals, such as helping us decide whom to call "healthy" and whom to call "sick." In fact, one of the important social goals that the *DSM* serves, for better or for worse, is that it helps professionals and nonprofessionals decide who is normal or healthy and who is abnormal or sick. (This issue is discussed in some detail in Barone, Maddux, & Snyder, 1997, chapter 14; see also Maddux, 2002, and Szasz, 1974.) We begin, therefore, with the definition of *personality disorder* that comes from the source that has been most responsible for the recent interest in this topic.

According to the *DSM-IV-TR*, "A Personality Disorder is an enduring pattern of inner experience and behavior that deviates markedly from the expectations of the individual's culture, is pervasive and inflexible, has an onset in adolescence or early adulthood, is stable over time, and leads to distress or impairment" (p. 685). Among definitions of psychological disorders, this is a pretty good one. First, it meshes nicely with the definition of personality provided in chapter 1 of this volume; it defines personality as an enduring and pervasive pattern of inner experience and behavior. Second, its conception of disorder is consistent with most other definitions in its reliance on the extent to which the individual is experiencing distress or is impaired in some manner. As with any definition of a psychological disorder, this definition leaves unanswered the question of just how much someone must be distressed or impaired before we will say that this person has a disorder. But this problem plagues all definitions of psychological disorders, so we cannot be too critical of the *DSM* on this point in its definition of personality disorder.

The *DSM*'s definition, to its credit, also indicates that psychological deviation and disorder can be identified only by comparing someone's behavior to social and cultural norms. In our opinion, this definition does not stress sufficiently the cultural and interpersonal aspects of personality and personality disorder; nor does it sufficiently stress the idea that personality and disorder are social constructions and not disease-like entities. But otherwise, it is a pretty good definition. The problems, however, lie not with the *DSM*'s definition of personality disorder but with what it implies about the nature of disorders of personality by taking the next big step of dividing maladaptive personality into disease-like categories of specific personality disorders. Here is where it goes astray in some important ways, which we discuss later in detail.

We cannot emphasize too strongly the idea that personality disorder is not illness. Personality is a certain patterning or consistency in your cognition (thinking), emotion (feeling), and behavior (doing) as observed by yourself or others. Personality is not something inside you that makes you think, feel, and behave in certain unique ways; personality *is* the certain unique way you think, feel, and behave. Adaptive personality consists of patterns of cognition, emotion, and behavior that are relatively effective in the pursuit of important goals and in coping with challenge and stress. Likewise, maladaptive or disordered personality consists of patterns of cognition, emotion, and behavior that are ineffective and often counterproductive. Maladaptive patterns that lead to the label *personality disorder* are not symptoms of underlying psychological illness or disease. There is not a condition inside the person called a personality disorder that makes the person behave, think, and feel in maladaptive ways. As Millon has stated, a personality disorder is not the result of "some 'foreign' entity or legion that intrudes insidiously within the person to undermine his or her so-called normal functions" (Millon, with Davis, 1996, p. 9). Therefore, a personality disorder is not something you *have* the way you might have a disease; it is something you *do* (and think and feel), as well as something someone else observes or experiences.

> Disorders of personality are not medical entities. . . . [They are] problematic styles of human adaptation [characterized by] an unsatisfying sense of self, a problematic way of expressing thoughts and feelings, as well as a troublesome manner of behaving and relating to others. (Millon, with Davis, 1996, p. vii)

> [P]ersonality disorders are not disorders at all in the medical sense. Rather, personality disorders are . . . varied styles or patterns in which the personality system functions maladaptively in relation to its environment. (Millon, with Davis, 1996, p. 86)

Therefore, understanding personality disorders means identifying what the maladaptive patterns are and in what situations they occur, not diagnosing "mental illnesses" lurking inside the person. Referring to a person's psychological problem as a *personality disorder* simply provides a description of the problem—and only in very general terms. Likewise, diagnosing someone as having a specific *DSM* personality disorder only names the person's difficulties; it does not explain them (see Activity Box 18.1).

MAJOR FEATURES OF DISORDERED PERSONALITY

People who are considered to have personality disorders display some important features or problems. First, they have great difficulty getting along with other people and report a history of disruptive relationships with family, friends, and co-workers. They have great difficulty regulating or controlling their own behavior. They may have goals that are maladaptive, and they may go about trying to attain their goals in maladaptive ways. More often than not, they are not distressed about their own behavior, but other people with whom they live, work, or otherwise interact often become very upset about their behavior. Second, they have difficulty learning from experience. Although their behavior constantly causes problems for them and others, they rarely change, and if they do change, the change is usually temporary. Third, a point related to the second, they usually do not accept responsibility for their own behavior and problems and typically blame other people when things go wrong. This tendency to blame others is probably one reason they do not learn from experience and do not change their behavior. To have some motivation to change your behavior, you need to see your behavior as a problem. As long as you believe that everything that goes wrong in your life is someone else's fault, you have no reason to change what you think, feel, and do.

Activity Box 18.1   When Do Differences Become Disorders?

In this chapter we state that a personality disorder is personality that is much more maladaptive than adaptive and much more maladaptive than the personalities of most other people. We argue that an assessment of the adaptiveness of a behavior cannot be made adequately without taking into account the situation in which the behavior occurs. In addition, we assume that adaptive behavior and maladaptive behavior are not qualitatively different from one another. Rather, we assume that each of us displays a variety of behaviors that vary in their degree of adaptiveness, depending on how well our behavior helps us accomplish our goals for that particular situation. In other words, our behavior and our personalities do not fit neatly into one of two categories—adaptive and maladaptive.

This exercise may help clarify this issue for you. Following is the *DSM-IV* description of Avoidant Personality Disorder, which, as we said at the beginning of the chapter, might be applied to extremely shy Sue. While reading this definition, ask yourself how the *DSM-IV* conceptualization meets the two assumptions noted in the previous paragraphs—that the situation is important in accounting for behavior and that adaptiveness and maladaptiveness are on a continuum.

AVOIDANT PERSONALITY DISORDER

A pervasive pattern of social inhibition, feelings of inadequacy, and hypersensitivity to negative evaluation, beginning by early adulthood and present in a variety of contexts, as indicated by four (or more) of the following:

1. Avoids occupational activities that involve significant interpersonal contact because of fear of criticism, disapproval, or rejection.
2. Is unwilling to get involved with other people unless certain of being liked.
3. Shows restraint within intimate relationships because of the fear of being shamed or ridiculed.
4. Is preoccupied with being criticized or rejected in social situations.
5. Is inhibited in new interpersonal situations because of feelings of inadequacy.
6. Views self as socially inept, personally unappealing, or inferior to others.
7. Is unusually reluctant to take personal risks or to engage in any new activities because they may prove embarrassing.

Do you know anyone who is "avoidant" at times? Maybe you yourself have been "avoidant"

Fourth, people who display personality disorders do not fare well in psychotherapy for all of the above reasons. The main reason for this difficulty is that they bring their maladaptive interpersonal styles into the therapy session. They have difficulty establishing a close and trusting relationship with the therapist. Therapists experience them as difficult people for the same reason that other people do. They tend to blame other people for their problems and usually do not accept personal responsibility for the difficulties in their lives and their relationships. For this reason they are more interested in talking about how other people need to change than about how they need to change. The final reason they are difficult therapy clients is that their problematic patterns are both chronic and pervasive. They have been practicing their problems for a long time, and they practice them in many different situations. Such well-established patterns by nature are very difficult to alter. For these reasons, psychotherapy with these people is long and difficult and usually not very successful.

Millon describes three other features of a personality disorder, all of which are related to the person's difficulties in coping with challenge and stress, espe-

Activity Box 18.1 *(continued)*

at one time or another. Go through each of the *DSM-IV* criteria for Avoidant Personality Disorder. Think about a shy person you know—perhaps even yourself—and compare that person's behavior to each of these criteria. Which criteria seem to fit the person? For each criterion, think about the person in various different situations and decide to which situations the criterion applies. For example, is the person preoccupied with being criticized or rejected in all social situations or just in those where he or she may have to talk to a stranger or person of rank or authority? Does the person view himself or herself as inferior to others in all ways at all times or just when he or she is with certain people (such as strangers, professors, older people, and persons of the opposite sex)?

How many of the criteria matched your person in most situations you could think of? The *DSM-IV* implies that disordered personality is evident in a "variety" of situations. But this exercise has probably shown you that a person's behavior may change greatly as situations change. A person may be avoidant in some situations but not in others. Even people who meet all of the criteria for Avoidant Personality Disorder are usu-

ally not avoidant in all situations. How many different situations define a "variety"?

Now consider how many of the criteria the person you have in mind meets in most of the situations you can think of. In order to receive a diagnosis of Avoidant Personality Disorder, an individual must meet four of the criteria listed. How many of the criteria did your person meet? Would you say that someone who meets three of the criteria is more similar to someone who meets four of the criteria or more similar to someone who meets none of the criteria? The person about whom you are thinking may display some avoidant behaviors, but unless he or she meets enough of the criteria to be diagnosed as having a "disorder," the *DSM-IV* categorical system implies that he or she is not very different from someone who displays no avoidant behavior at all. Again, if you were a therapist, what would you find more useful to discuss with your client—which of his or her behaviors are maladaptive in which situations or whether he or she has a "disorder"? Which do you think would be easier for a therapist to help a client change: specific behaviors that are maladaptive in specific situations or a "personality disorder"?

cially in dealing with other people (Millon, with Davis, 1996). These features help us understand how these patterns become so well learned and rigid, how they are maintained, and why they are so difficult to change. These features are tenuous stability, adaptive inflexibility, and a tendency to foster vicious circles.

Tenuous stability refers to emotional fragility and lack of emotional resilience in response to stress. Painful emotions (anxiety, sadness, anger) are a normal part of life that we all experience in response to stress, and there are certainly differences among so-called normal people in their emotional fragility under stress and their ability to return to normal after a stressful experience. The person displaying a personality disorder does not hold up well under stress and has trouble "bouncing back" or returning to normal after a stressful experience.

Adaptive inflexibility means that the person displaying a personality disorder has relatively few effective strategies for relating to other people, achieving life goals, and coping with stress and uses these few strategies rigidly in situations for which the strategies are inappropriate. In other words, people displaying a personality disorder, compared to most of the rest of us, have far fewer ways of getting along with other people, dealing with the problems that arise at times in all relationships, getting what they want from life, and dealing with stress. In addition, because they have so few strategies for dealing with life, they often use the wrong strategy in the wrong situation. They keep trying the same thing over and over again, even though it does not work, because that is all they know how to do. Because they never try anything new, they never learn anything new, and the more they practice the few strategies they have, the more automatic these strategies become, and the more they rely on them despite their ineffectiveness.

Vicious circles are perhaps the most interesting and maladaptive features of people displaying personality disorders. A vicious circle is a situation that starts out bad and gets worse the more a person tries to cope with it or resolve it. Once it gets going, it keeps going around and around without getting anywhere, as if the person were on an unpleasant psychological merry-go-round where he or she keeps ending up at the same difficult place but cannot find a way to get off. Even worse, each time the person goes around, that difficult place becomes more and more stressful. A vicious circle is also like quicksand—the more the person struggles to get out, the deeper he or she sinks. In a psychological vicious circle, however, the quicksand is of the person's own making. In talking about vicious circles, we are talking about how personality disorders are maintained—how they are self-perpetuating.

The vicious circles created by people displaying personality disorders are the result of their ineffective and rigid coping strategies. In so many cases, people's basic beliefs about themselves and other people lead them to attempt to cope with stress, resolve interpersonal problems, or protect themselves from expected harm in ways that not only do not solve the problem but usually make the problem worse than if they had done nothing at all. What starts out as a minor and ordinary problem or disagreement between two people becomes a major problem when the person's limited and ineffective strategies for solving interpersonal problems add fuel to the fire of the conflict. The individual who creates vicious circles has a knack for "making mountains out of molehills." The person then uses the fact that the problem got worse as evidence that his or her problematic and distorted beliefs about himself or herself and other people are indeed correct.

Personality in general is self-perpetuating for a number of reasons that we can mention only briefly. One reason is that your beliefs about yourself and other people and the beliefs that others hold about you are formed early in your life and become *self-fulfilling prophecies*. By this term we mean that the beliefs you and others have about your personality are a set of expectations about what you will think, feel, and do in certain situations. Research has demonstrated that we tend to behave in ways that are consistent with our own and others' expectations. We automatically strive for a kind of consistency in the way we think, feel, and behave. People also behave toward us in ways that encourage us to behave in ways consistent with their expectations.

An example of a common vicious circle is shyness or social anxiety, such as displayed by Sue, whom we described at the beginning of the chapter. Shyness, of course, is a common experience, and many normal, healthy people are somewhat shy at times. We are not saying that shy people have a personality disorder, although the *DSM-IV-TR* does describe an Avoidant Personality Disorder that is essentially an extremely maladaptive form of shyness. Even mildly shy people, however, create for themselves a kind of vicious circle. Shy people usually believe that other people will not like them or will reject them. For this reason, they often experience anxiety in social situations or even while thinking about an upcoming social situation. Too often the shy person copes with this anxiety by avoiding situations in which he or she feels shy, such as parties or gatherings. If the shy man enters a social situation, he may stand around waiting for others to initiate conversation, or he may see a group of people talking but not make an attempt to enter the conversation. Also because he looks uncomfortable, other people may be reluctant to talk to him, since people tend to experience anxiety in the presence of an anxious person. Thus, because of the man's own passive behavior and discomfort, no one talks to him. He may then decide that other people really are unfriendly or that he is not attractive to the others. If someone does attempt to engage him in conversation, he may feel and appear anxious and not give much in return in the conversation. As a result, the otherwise friendly person who initiated the conversation moves on to someone else. The shy person then uses this as evidence that people will indeed reject him.

By avoiding social situations, the shy person also deprives himself or herself of the opportunity to work on overcoming shyness by learning a few social skills and by learning to be less anxious around other people. In addition, the more a shy person avoids and otherwise "acts shy," the more the person and others will label him or her as a shy person. Such labels, of course, tend to be self-fulfilling prophecies, because people treat us in ways that bring out in us the behavior they expect from us. Our labels for ourselves have the same effect. In this way, the shy person's avoidance, which is a strategy for coping with shyness, not only fails to reduce the shyness but helps maintain it and may even make it worse over time.

The workings of the vicious circle also can be seen in the behavior of extremely distrustful people, especially people—such as Joe the furniture mover—who are so distrustful of others that they are labeled "paranoid" or even as having a Paranoid Personality Disorder. We assume that the general tendency to trust or distrust other people is a dimension of individual difference along which we can all place ourselves. In addition, our trust of others will wax and wane as situations change, especially as the people in those situations change. Thus, we do not have to pose the existence of an entity called a paranoid personality disorder to understand the self-fulfilling nature of distrust. The process, however, is more vivid in more extreme cases of interpersonal distrust, as explained by Fenigstein (1996):

> Because of the general expectation that others are against them or are somehow trying to exploit them, paranoid persons tend to be guarded, secretive, and even vigilant, constantly looking for signs of disloyalty and malevolence in their associates. These expectations are easily confirmed: The hypersensitivity . . . turns minor slights into major insults, and even innocuous events are interpreted as harmful or vindictive. As a result, a pernicious cycle is set in motion whereby expectations of

treachery and hostility often have the effect of eliciting such reactions from others, thus confirming and justifying the paranoid's initial suspicion and hostility. (p. 242)

In both of these examples, the person's attempt to deal with the problem and ward off danger not only is ineffective but also makes the problem worse and helps to maintain it over time. The more the shy person practices being shy and avoids, and the more the paranoid person practices thinking distrustful thoughts and behaving in a hostile manner toward others, the worse their problems become. This is the essence of the vicious circle.

CAUSES OF PERSONALITY DISORDERS

We assume continuity between normal and disordered personality. Because of this continuity, we also assume that the factors that determine the development of normal or adaptive personality also determine the development of abnormal or maladaptive personality. For this reason, asking "What causes personality disorders?" is the same as asking "What causes personality?" Because many of the other chapters in this book are devoted in one way or another to the causes of personality in general, they are concerned also with the causes of abnormal or maladaptive personality. We agree with Theodore Millon, whose ideas shaped the *DSM*'s conceptualization of personality disorders, that "personality pathology results from the same forces that are involved in the development of normal functioning" (Millon, with Davis, 1996, p. 13). Thus, our view is that there are no conditions called "personality disorders" that need a set of explanations that are different from those offered for so-called normal personality. Also, as we will discuss later, the available research suggests that the categories the *DSM* calls personality disorders are not really different in kind from other major categories of psychological problems (such as mood disorders and anxiety disorders). Thus, we believe that personality disorders are not special conditions for which we need to offer causes that are different from the causes offered for other types of psychological problems.

In trying to find the causes of abnormal or maladaptive personality, we look instead to what we know about the development of personality in general. Whatever forces are involved in the development of normal personality are also involved in the development of abnormal or disordered personality (see chapter 5, this volume). The most we can say is that disordered personality, like all personality, is the product of the complex interaction of genetic predisposition on some relatively small number of dimensions or traits (such as intelligence, social extraversion, emotionality) and learning experiences. (See Coker & Widiger, in press, and Livesley, 2001b, for a discussion of biological and genetic factors involved in several *DSM* personality disorders.) Not surprisingly, culture plays a major role in the development of personality (Triandis & Suh, 2002) and in definitions of normal and abnormal (disordered) personality (Alarcon, Foulks, & Vakkur, 1998).

Cause is not the same as maintenance. To ask about the causes of personality is usually to ask about historical events and biological factors that explain how a person got to be the way he or she is today. To ask about maintenance, however, is to ask a somewhat different question—not how the person got this way, but how the person manages to stay this way—how the person's patterns of thinking, feeling, and doing, which we call his or her personality, are self-maintaining or self-perpetuating. In other words, maintenance refers to how these patterns keep themselves going, even though they are so often maladaptive and ineffective. We discussed how personality disorders are maintained in the section on vicious circles. Keep in mind, however, that not even the tendency to be self-perpetuating distinguishes disordered personality from normal personality, because personality of any kind is to some extent self-maintaining.

TREATMENT OF PERSONALITY DISORDERS

Treatment of psychological problems of any kind is a complex issue, and we could not begin to do it justice in this chapter. More important, however, to discuss "treating" a disorder we must first assume that there is some distinct condition or disorder to treat. But our basic contention, once again, is that the personality disorders are not distinct conditions that have distinct causes. For this reason, they do not require treatments that are different in kind from the treatments that have been proven effective in treating other maladaptive patterns of thinking, feeling, and behaving. We agree with many others that the patterns of thinking, feeling, and behaving that we call personality disorders are more difficult to change than many other maladaptive patterns (such as a phobia). We do not believe, however, that they are more difficult to change because they are a special type of problem differing in quality from other dysfunctional patterns; instead, we believe they are more difficult to change because they are, by definition, more enduring, pervasive, and habitual than other problems. Any problem behavior that has been "practiced" by a person for many years and in most situations of that person's life will be more difficult to change than a problem that is of briefer duration or is more situation-specific. In a sense, a problematic pattern is called a personality disorder because it is extremely difficult to change. (See Liveslcy, 2001b, for detailed chapters on various approaches to the treatment of personality disorders.)

PROBLEMS WITH THE OFFICIAL VIEW OF PERSONALITY DISORDER

Now that you have a better idea of the characteristics of disordered personality, we will tackle the issue mentioned previously—the problems with the official *DSM* conception of disordered personality. As we noted, the problem lies not so much with the *DSM*'s conceptual definition of personality disorder (an enduring and dysfunctional pattern of inner experience and behavior) as with its attempt to define specific categories of personality disorders.

The *DSM* is based on a *categorical model* of psychological adjustment and maladjustment. The *DSM*'s categorical model makes three basic assumptions about disordered personality (Livesley, Schroeder, Jackson, & Jang, 1994). First, personality disorders are qualitatively different from normal personality. Second, personality disorders are qualitatively different from Axis I disorders such as depression and anxiety disorders. Third, personality disorders are qualitatively different from each other—that is, they are distinct syndromes or conditions. We will examine the research that has investigated each of these three assumptions. As you will see, this research supports an alternative to the categorical model for understanding personality disorders—the *dimensional model*.

A dimensional model of personality disorders assumes, as we stated earlier, that normal/adaptive and abnormal/maladaptive personality lies on a dimension or continuum and that there is no clear line between normal/adaptive and abnormal/maladaptive. Thus, the dimensional model sees personality disorders as differing quantitatively, not qualitatively, from normal or adaptive personality. Another word for *dimension* is *trait*—something about people's psychological or behavioral characteristics that we can measure and on which people will show individual differences (see also chapter 7, this volume). From the dimensional approach, personality disorders are simply extreme and maladaptive variations of the same traits or dimensions that appear among so-called normal, well-adjusted people. Most dimensional approaches are based on either traditional trait theories of personality, on biological theories of personality, or on empirical research. The *DSM*'s categories of personality disorders, however, are based on neither theory nor research. Instead, they were developed over several decades from the collective clinical experiences of psychologists and psychiatrists—from clinical "folk wisdom," as Lorna Benjamin (1996) says.

Certainly folk wisdom should be heeded to some extent and may be a good place to begin. Science is better, however, and the vast majority of the scientific studies that have examined the categories-versus-dimensions issue support the dimensional model of personality disorders. The following sections present some of this research, addressing each of the *DSM*'s three assumptions.

Distinction Between Normal Personality and Personality Disorders

A categorical approach assumes that personality disorders are qualitatively distinct from normal personality—that is, they differ from normal personality in kind, not in degree. If an individual meets a certain number of criteria for a particular disorder, then that person receives a diagnosis for the disorder. If the person meets fewer criteria than the threshold, then he or she does not receive a diagnosis for the disorder. For example, in order to receive the diagnosis of Histrionic Personality Disorder, an individual must show "a pervasive pattern of excessive emotionality and attention seeking," as indicated by at least five of eight specific criteria (for example, displaying rapidly shifting and shallow expression of emotions; discomfort in situations in which the person is not the center of attention). If the person meets five of the criteria, a diagnosis is made; if he or she does not, a diagnosis is not made. This model assumes that a disorder is an either-or phenomenon, similar to a physical disease such as tuberculosis, whose presence or absence can be determined by a medical test. According to this *medical model* of disease, a person either has tuberculosis or does not. Likewise, the categorical model of personality disorders assumes that a person either has a disorder or does not—there is no in-between.

Most of the research, however, suggests that there is no qualitative distinction between normal and abnormal personality. It suggests, instead, that people with personality disorders display extreme and maladaptive variants of normal, adaptive personality traits. Research on personality structure and biological correlates of personality is reviewed in following sections and sheds light on this aspect of the categories-versus-dimensions debate.

One way of examining the issue of whether a dimensional or a categorical approach is more appropriate for distinguishing normal personality from personality disorders is to compare a group of individuals who meet the criteria for *DSM* personality disorders with a group of individuals from the general population. Specifically, we want to know whether the personality traits, or dimensions, of the "normal" group and the "disordered" group fall into clusters at either end of a continuum of severity, or if they are evenly distributed along the continuum. In this type of study, a large group of people are given tests of various personality dimensions that are associated with personality disorders. If the group's scores on any given dimension are continuously distributed form low to high, meaning that scores fall at all points on the continuum of severity, then we can assume that a dimensional model best describes personality disorders. If, on the other hand, scores fall into two groups, one at the low end of the distribution and one at the high end (called a bimodal distribution), then we can assume that a categorical model applies.

In one such study (Livesley, Jackson, & Schroeder, 1992), researchers used one hundred personality scales to measure personality dimensions in a combined sample of individuals from the general population and individuals who were receiving treatment for a personality disorder (*DSM-III-R* criteria) at a hospital psychiatric clinic. Consistent with a dimensional model, this study found that individuals fell at various points along a continuum of disorder; none of the distributions of any of the one hundred personality scales administered was bimodal. In addition, the personality test scores of who met the *DSM-III-R* criteria and those who did not overlapped considerably. Some individuals without a diagnosed personality disorder actually showed more personality disorder features than did some people with a diagnosed disorder. A related method for looking at the dimensionality issue is to compare the personality traits of individuals who meet different numbers of criteria for a personality disorder. For example, we might compare individuals meeting the minimal number of criteria for a personality disorder with individuals meeting either more or fewer than the minimal number of criteria. One such study (Widiger, Sanderson, & Warner, 1986) found that individuals who met the minimum of five criteria for Borderline Personality Disorder (characterized largely by extreme emotional instability and identify confusion) were more similar on a personality inventory to people meeting fewer than the minimum number of criteria than to individuals meeting more than the minimal number of criteria. In this case, individuals diagnosed with Borderline Personality Disorder who met only the minimum number of criteria were more similar to people without the diagnosis than to other people who received the diagnosis. This finding suggests that there is no clear line past which people can legitimately be said to "have" a personality disorder. (See also chapter 7, this volume.)

A third way that researchers can determine whether personality disorders lie on a continuum with normal personality is to determine whether personality in a normal population has a different "structure" from personality in individuals diagnosed with personality disorders (Livesley et al., 1994). By structure, we do not mean a physical entity in the brain; rather, we are referring to the patterns of co-occurrence of traits—the ways that various traits cluster together. If individuals with personality disorders display different clusters of traits from individuals without personality disorders, then the categorical model would be supported. Research on this question has found that the structure of personality of people with personality disorders does not differ from that of people without personality disorders. For example, in the study by Livesley and his colleagues discussed earlier (Livesley et al., 1992), the same 15 personality dimensions were found to describe the structure of personality for both a normal population and a group of individuals diagnosed with personality disorders (Livesley et al., 1992). Those who were diagnosed with personality disorders simply manifested these traits to a more extreme and maladaptive degree. These findings support the dimensional model. Numerous other studies since have produced results largely consistent with these earlier studies (Coker & Widiger, in press; Livesley, 2001b).

Research on the biological components of psychopathology also supports the dimensional model of personality disorders. Several theories (for example, Cloninger, Svrakic, & Przybeck, 1993; Siever & Davis, 1991) propose that biological mechanisms may predispose individuals to display both personality traits and personality disorders. According to these theories, both personality traits and maladaptive personality characteristics are influenced by neurochemical systems in the brain, and different systems correspond to different traits and maladaptive behaviors. Some research supports this idea. For example, in one study, prisoners who had committed violent crimes and would probably be diagnosed as having Antisocial Personality Disorder (characterized in part by impulsive behavior and lack of remorse for wrongdoing) showed disruptions in the serotonin system (Brown & Linnoila, 1990). The authors of this study concluded that "some form of impulsivity, disinhibition, or dyscontrol is the behavioral variable linked to low levels of [serotonin] rather than antisocial acts in and of themselves" (p. 34). Persons diagnosed with Borderline Personality Disorder, a disorder also characterized by impulsive behavior, have demonstrated similar serotonin disruptions (Siever & Davis, 1991). This research suggests that differences among people along some personality traits or dimensions—impulsivity, for example—may be rooted in differences in biological mechanisms. This is not surprising because it is only logical to assume that biological differences among people, especially differences in the brain and nervous system, will result in differences among people in their patterns of thinking, feeling, and behaving. This research does not suggest, however, that the particular clusters of these traits that make up each *DSM* personality disorder have distinct biological causes. As Marvin Zuckerman (1995) has said, "We are not born as extroverts, neurotics, impulsive sensation-seekers, or antisocial personalities, but we are born with differences in reactivities of brain structures and levels of [biochemical] regulators" (pp. 331–332).

Genetic research also appears to support a dimensional model of personality disorders. A great deal of research has demonstrated that many personality traits are influenced by genetic factors (see chapter 3, this volume). Genetic variations can explain between 30% and 60% of the personality trait variations among individuals (Carey & DiLalla, 1994; Zuckerman, 1995). One study found preliminary evidence that the relative contribution of genes is similar in normal personality and personality disorders (Livesley et al., 1994), suggesting that they are more similar than different. More research remains to be conducted in this area.

It is clear from the research presented in this section that the first assumption of a categorical model such as the *DSM*—that normal personality is qualitatively different from maladaptive or disordered personality—is not valid (see also Widiger, Verheul, & van den Brink, 1999, and Livesley, 2001a). But what about differences among the various *DSM* disorders? Even if we assume that normal personality and personality disorders lie on a continuum of dysfunction, it is still possible that there may be certain categories of personality disorder that lie at the severe end of the continuum and are qualitatively distinct from one another. For example, from the research presented earlier, we could argue that Borderline Personality Disorder is defined by extreme scores on a particular group of personality dimensions that are also found among normal people. But is Borderline Personality Disorder distinct from other personality disorder categories defined by the *DSM*? A related question is whether the personality disorders are qualitatively different from Axis I disorders. For example, is Borderline Personality Disorder distinct from Major Depressive Disorder?

Distinction Between Axis I and Axis II Disorders

According to the *DSM-IV-TR*, disorders to be reported on Axis I are *clinical* disorders, such as mood disorders or eating disorders, and other conditions that may be a focus of clinical attention. Personality disorders, along with mental retardation, are reported on Axis II. The rationale for separating the two axes is that such a distinction "ensures that consideration will be given to the possible presence of Personality Disorders and Mental Retardation that might otherwise be overlooked when attention is directed to the usually more florid Axis I disorders" (p. 28). This rationale implies that (1) these axes must be handled separately because they represent two distinct types of disorder, and (2) they must be handled separately because their distinctiveness is often overlooked. Another possibility, however, is that the disorders are not truly distinct and that the reason one is often "overlooked" at the expense of the other is that they overlap so much (Widiger, 1989). For example, if the criteria for diagnosing two disorders are very similar, then the clinician probably will give a client a diagnosis for only one of the disorders. The clinician who does this is not necessarily "overlooking" anything.

One conceptualization that supports the view that no true distinction exists between Axis I and Axis II disorders is the *spectrum model* (Akiskal, 1981; Siever & Davis, 1991). A spectrum model assumes that Axis I and Axis II disorders are on a continuum of disorder and that many of the personality disorders are maladaptive outgrowths of Axis I disorders. As Millon (Millon with Davis, 1996) explains, "personality disorders and Axis I conditions may be seen as developing from the same constitutional soil and therefore as existing on a continuum" (p. 18). In the spectrum model, this "constitutional soil" refers to some biological mechanism that predisposes an individual to the Axis I condition, which may then be amplified into a personality disorder. Other models similar to the spectrum model also propose a connection between Axis I and Axis II disorders. For example, in what Millon calls the *vulnerability model*, personality is viewed as the psychological equivalent of the immune system. If the personality is not operating efficiently, Axis I disorders, such as depression or anxiety, can result. The *complication model* is a reversal of the vulnerability model—personality disorders can result from the psychological stress brought about by an Axis I disorder.

All of these models support the existence of some relationship and continuity between Axis I and Axis II. Millon (Millon with Davis, 1996) argues that any of these models might apply to different individuals. Research on the distinction between Axis I and Axis II disorders provides some support for the existence of a continuity between disorders classified on the two axes, suggesting that they are not two different kinds of disorder.

Several areas of research lead to questions about the validity of placing so-called clinical syndromes and personality disorders on separate axes. The first area is the etiology, or cause, of a disorder (Livesley et al., 1994). Historically, what are now called Axis I disorders were believed to be biological in origin, while what are now called personality disorders were viewed as learned patterns of thinking, feeling, and behaving resulting from exposure to adverse environments. It has become clear, however, that both Axis I disorders and personality disorders result from the interaction of biological and environmental causes. For example, the dopamine system is associated both with psychotic symptoms in schizophrenia (an Axis I disorder) and psychotic-like symptoms in Schizotypal Personality Disorder (an Axis II disorder). In addition, schizophrenia-related personality disorders are actually more prevalent than schizophrenia among relatives of people with schizophrenia (Siever & Davis, 1991). These findings imply that schizophrenia and Schizotypal Personality Disorder may be represented by the same biological vulnerability; as Siever and Davis (1991) put it, "schizophrenia may represent only the tip of the iceberg of the schizophrenia related disorders" (p. 1650). Findings such as these undermine the argument that Axis I disorders (clinical syndromes) and Axis II disorders (personality disorders) have different causes.

A second way to examine the distinction between Axis I and Axis II disorders is to examine the stability of the disorders over time (Livesley et al., 1994). Part of the *DSM-IV-TR* definition of personality disorder is that it is an "enduring pattern of inner experience and behavior" (APA, 2000, p. 686). Thus we would expect personality disorders to be more stable than the clinical syndromes. Evidence suggests, however, that many personality disorders are unstable over time and that some clinical syndromes, such as schizophrenia or dysthymic disorder (a disorder characterized by chronically depressed mood lasting for two or more years), are considerably stable over time. Thus, temporal stability alone cannot distinguish Axis I from Axis II disorders.

A third way to examine the distinction between Axis I and Axis II is to examine the overlap between Axis I disorders and Axis II disorders. One way of doing this is to examine *co-morbidity*, or the frequency with which specific Axis I and Axis II disorders are diagnosed for the same person. If a specific Axis I disorder is commonly diagnosed along with a specific Axis II disorder, the dual diagnosis may reflect some common thread running through the disorders that indicates that they are not truly distinct. One area in which the co-morbidity issue has received a great deal of attention is in the relationship between depression (an Axis I disorder) and Borderline Personality Disorder. According to one author, as many as 74% of individuals diagnosed with Borderline Personality Disorder also meet the diagnostic criteria for Major Depressive Disorder (Widiger, 1989). Also, at least one study found that individuals diagnosed with Borderline Personality Disorder scored higher on average on a depression inventory than did a comparison group of people diagnosed with an Axis I major depression disorder (Akiskal, Yerevanian, Davis, King, & Lemmi, 1985). (See also Zanarini et al., 1998a.)

Much of the Axis I and Axis II co-morbidity can be explained by the overlap in diagnostic criteria. In the case of Borderline Personality Disorder, for example, one of the criteria is "chronic feelings of emptiness" (APA, 2000, p. 710), which may overlap with the Major Depressive Episode (Axis I) criteria of feelings of worthlessness and diminished interest or pleasure in activities. One of the criteria for a manic episode of what is called Bipolar Disorder, which is on Axis I, is "inflated self-esteem or grandiosity" (p. 362), while one of the criteria for Narcissistic Personality Disorder is that the individual has "a grandiose sense of self importance" (p. 717). Also, the personality dimension of neuroticism—excessive susceptibility to anxiety and depression—is associated with Borderline Personality Disorder but is also a prominent feature of Axis I anxiety disorders. Thus, just because a person meets the diagnostic criteria for two different *DSM* categories we need not conclude that the person *has* two different disorders. Cats and dogs have many overlapping features—four legs, two eyes, two ears, sharp teeth, and fur. Thus, a cat will meet most of the most important "diagnostic criteria" for the category "dog," and vice versa. But this does not mean that a cat is both a cat and a dog or that "catness" is "co-morbid" with "dogness."

In general, research strongly indicates that "[t]here do not appear to be fundamental distinctions between personality disorder and *all* other mental disorders of the kind that would warrant a major distinction between them" (Livesley, 2001, p. 29), such as the distinction DSM makes between Axis I and Axis II.

Distinctions Among the Personality Disorders

The categorical approach assumes that each personality disorder represents a distinct group of people who differ qualitatively from people in other personality disorder categories. Such an approach might be useful when an individual fits into only one category and when the category is fairly exhaustive in describing that individual. For personality disorders, however, neither of these conditions holds. Research demonstrates that very few individuals meet the criteria for only one personality disorder.

Studies that have examined the overlap among the personality disorders have found that most people are given more than one personality disorder diagnosis (Widiger et al., 1991). The more common finding is that people are given more than one personality disorder diagnosis. In one study, individuals were given an average of four personality disorder diagnoses (Skodol, Rosnick, Kellman, Oldham, & Hyler, 1991). Widiger and his colleagues (Widiger et al., 1991) concluded from several studies that about 95% of people given a Borderline Personality Disorder diagnosis will be given at least one other personality disorder diagnosis. (See also Zanarini et al.,1998b.)

This overlap can be explained in several ways (Widiger et al., 1991). The first possibility is that some common underlying etiology links more than one personality disorder. For example, the same biological vulnerability might predispose an individual to develop either of two personality disorders, depending on environmental forces influencing the person. A second possibility is that one disorder causes the other. A third and more likely reason for high rates of comorbidity—one we discussed when we examined the overlap between Axis I and Axis II disorders—is that the criteria necessary to make a diagnosis are often quite similar for the different personality disorders. For example, one feature of Borderline Personality Disorder is "affective instability due to marked reactivity of mood" (APA, 2000, p. 710). This feature is similar to the Histrionic Personality Disorder feature "displays rapidly shifting and shallow expression of emotions" (p. 714). Also, the Borderline Personality Disorder feature "impulsivity in at least two areas that are potentially self-damaging" (p. 710) is similar to the Antisocial Personality Disorder feature "impulsivity or failure to plan ahead" (p. 706). Once again, cats and dogs have many features in common, but that does not mean that a cat also has "dogness" or that a dog also has "catness."

DIMENSIONAL MODELS: AN ALTERNATIVE TO CATEGORIES

The categorical model to understanding disordered personality simply does not hold up well to scientific and logical scrutiny. The dimensional approach, however, fares considerably better. Most dimensional approaches to personality are statistical models that use mathematical methods to identify the basic dimensions of personality. They are based not on theory but on empirical research. Several dimensional models have been proposed (for example, Cloninger, 1987; Eysenck & Eysenck, 1985; Livesley et al., 1992; Millon, with Davis, 1996; Siever & Davis, 1991; Tellegen, 1993). The best-known and best-researched dimensional model, however, is Costa and McCrae's (1992) five-factor model (see chapter 7, this volume). This model is rooted in a technique called lexical analysis, in which all the words that describe personality traits in a particular language are identified and studied (Coker & Widiger, in press). Lexical analysis is based on the assumption that if a personality trait is found in a particular culture, the language of the culture will have a word for it. If all of these words are identified, then an analysis of their relationships will shed light on patterns of personality. In 1934, Louis Thurstone analyzed 60 English language adjectives describing various aspects of personality and found that they could be reduced to five basic factors. Since Thurstone, several researchers have replicated this finding, and there is general consensus that five factors or dimensions can best describe personality. Costa and McCrae (1992) labeled these five factors neuroticism versus emotional stability, introversion versus extraversion, closedness versus openness to experience, antagonism versus agreeableness, and conscientiousness versus undependability. These are often referred to as "the Big Five." Each of these can be differentiated further into various *facets* or subdimensions (Costa & McCrae, 1992).

Several decades of research indicate that the five-factor model is extremely useful for describing normal personality. Only recently, however, has the five-factor model been applied to personality disorders. Thomas Widiger (1993a) is one of the most vocal proponents for conceptualizing personality disorders from the perspective of the five-factor model. He believes that various combinations of four of these five factors (excluding openness to experience, to be discussed later) can be used to describe each *DSM* personality disorder and can provide descriptions that are more complete than those provided by *DSM* diagnostic criteria (Coker & Widiger, in press; Lynam & Widiger, 2001). For example, an individual with a Borderline Personality Disorder (see Table 18.1) can be described as high in neuroticism, high in extraversion, low in some facets of agreeableness, and low in some facets of conscientiousness (Coker & Widiger, in press). The Antisocial Personality Disorder (see Table 18.1) can be understood as maladaptively low in agreeableness and conscientiousness (Coker & Widiger, in press)

Widiger (1993a) believes that the five-factor model adds precision to diagnoses. For example, he cites the difficulty in distinguishing between Avoidant Personality Disorder, which is characterized by extreme fear of social rejection, and Schizoid Personality Disorders, which is characterized by extreme social indifference. The criteria for these disorders are fairly similar. Widiger argues, however, that the avoidant person is anxious, self-conscious, and vulnerable, whereas the schizoid person is not. In addition, the two patterns differ on some aspects of introversion. Avoidant and schizoid people are low in warmth and gregariousness, but the schizoid person is characterized by low positive emotions, while the avoidant person is characterized by low assertiveness.

Wiggins and Pincus (1989) found that the personality disorders could be explained using the five dimensions in the five-factor model. The extraversion-introversion dimension can differentiate Histrionic and Schizoid Personality Disorders; people with Histrionic Personality Disorder exhibited extreme extraversion, while those with Schizoid Personality Disorder displayed extreme introversion. The neuroticism dimension correlated with Borderline Personality Disorder and Passive-Aggressive Personality Disorder, which was in *DSM-III* but is not in *DSM-IV-TR*. Neuroticism, however, was a component of many other personality disorders when combined with extremes on other dimensions. The agreeableness dimension was associated with Dependent and Paranoid Personality Disorders; extremely high agreeableness characterized Dependent Personality Disorder, and extremely low agreeableness characterized Paranoid Personality Disorder. Extremely high conscientiousness was associated with Compulsive Personality Disorder. Finally, openness to experience was associated with Schizotypal Personality Disorder, although this relationship was weak.

Some studies using factor analysis have found that personality disorders can be described by using only four factors, not five (Hyler & Lyons, 1988; Kass, Skodol, Charles, Spitzer, & Williams, 1985). Widiger (1993b) believes the four factors found in these studies correspond to four of the five dimensions in the five-factor model. He believes that the fifth factor of the five-factor model—openness to experience—may not be relevant to personality disorders but may be related to self-actualization or mental health. In addition, the measures used in these studies may not have been sensitive enough to tap into extreme variants of the openness factor (Widiger, 1993b).

Together, these studies strongly suggest that a dimensional model, as exemplified by the five-factor model, is more useful for understanding disordered personality than is the categorical model, as exemplified by the *DSM* (see Costa & Widiger, 2002 for more detailed discussions).

THE *DSM* REVISITED

If there is so little evidence for the validity and utility of the categorical model and so much evidence for the validity and utility of the dimensional model, then why spend so much time and effort attempting to describe the categories using dimensions? If so much research strongly suggests that a dimensional model is more accurate for conceptualizing personality disorders than a categorical model, why has the *DSM* stayed with the categorical model? Some researchers (such as Costa & McCrae, 1992; Widiger, 1993b) have advocated that we eliminate use of these categories altogether and start from scratch by redefining disordered personality from a dimensional perspective. In fact, a work group of personality disorder researchers considered several changes that would have incorporated into the 1994 *DSM-IV* some of the knowledge gleaned from the research on personality dimensions (Widiger & Sanderson, 1995). One suggestion was to present an alternative dimensional model in an appendix to *DSM-IV*, but disagreement on which of the many dimensional models to present prevented this change. Another recommendation was to include clear and precise rules for rating the severity of a disorder in addition to the criteria for diagnosing the disorder. For various reasons, including concerns about the reliability of assessing dysfunction when a person has more than one personality disorder diagnosis, the work group rejected this suggestion as well. Several other changes were considered, but the only change implemented was the inclusion in the introduction of a brief discussion of the limitations of the categorical approach, including an acknowledgment that dimensional models "increase reliability and communicate more clinical information" than a categorical approach (APA, 1994, p. xxii).

A short discussion of dimensional models is included in the Personality Disorders section of the *DSM-IV-TR*, but the remainder of the *DSM-IV-TR* remains based entirely on a categorical model. The reasons outlined in the *DSM-IV-TR* for retaining the categorical model have little to do with its validity as a way of conceptualizing disorders. Rather, its authors argue that dimensional descriptions of disorder are "much less familiar and vivid than are the categorical names" and that there is "as yet no agreement on the choice of the optimal dimensions to be used for classification purposes" (APA, 2000, p. xxxii). The *DSM-IV-TR* does allude to an eventual transition to a dimensional model in stating that "it is possible that the increasing research on, and familiarity with, dimensional systems may eventually result in their greater acceptance both as a method of conveying clinical information and as a research tool" (APA, 2000, p. xxxii). Many personality disorder researchers believe it is simply a matter of time before the weight of scientific evidence exceeds the weight of tradition and the *DSM* adopts a dimensional approach.

SUMMARY

This chapter has examined some important questions and controversies in the study of the abnormal, maladaptive, or disordered aspects of personality. Our basic premise is that disordered personality is continuous with so-called normal personality—that there is not a clear point of division between normal and abnormal personality or between adaptive and maladaptive personality, just as we cannot designate a clear division between "hot" and "cold" on a thermometer. A disordered personality or a personality disorder, therefore, is continuous with normal personality and results from the same interaction of biological predisposition and life events that explain normal personality development.

A personality disorder is an extremely maladaptive pattern of thinking, feeling, and behaving that appears to occur across many situations and that appears to endure over time. We say "appears to" because we have to acknowledge the idea that personality and personality disorder are not things but are social cognitive constructions—abstract concepts that people agree on because they find them useful. For this reason, personality disorders are not diseases; they are differences, although often extreme differences. Nor are they conditions inside people that explain how and why some people behave in extremely maladaptive ways under many conditions and over long periods of time. Personality disorder diagnoses, therefore, are descriptions of people's problems, not explanations.

The interest in personality disorders has increased greatly since they were first defined as a separate category of psychological disorders by the *DSM-III* in 1980. As noted earlier, the problem lies not in the *DSM*'s definition of a personality disorder. It lies in the practice of putting personality disorders in a separate category from other psychological problems and then dividing them into subcategories. This practice makes several questionable assumptions about the nature of disordered personality: (1) that personality disorders are qualitatively different from normal personality, (2) that personality disorders are qualitatively different from other disorders such as depression and anxiety disorders, and (3) that personality disorders are qualitatively different from each other (i.e., distinct syndromes or conditions). We examined the research on each of these assumptions and concluded that this research does not support them. Instead, our conclusion was that research supports the idea that personality disorders are maladaptive variants of normal personality traits, not qualitatively distinct pathological conditions or categories. We also believe that research indicates that personality disorders are closely related to other kinds of psychological problems such as anxiety and depression. Finally, the *DSM* personality disorders probably are not anywhere close to being as distinct from one another as the *DSM* categories imply. Progress in understanding the maladaptive aspects of personality probably will not come from continued efforts to refine diagnostic categories of limited validity and utility such as those found in the *DSM*. Instead, the future of the study of disordered personality probably rests in the hands of theorists and researchers interested in the dimensional approach to understanding normal and abnormal personality.

DISCUSSION QUESTIONS

1. One of the most difficult problems in studying personality disorders is defining the term *disorder*. What are some of the different ways in which this term can be defined? What are the pros and cons of these different definitions?
2. What are the strengths and weaknesses of the *DSM*'s definition of personality disorder?
3. What are the major differences between the categorical and dimensional approaches to understanding personality disorders? What are the advantages and disadvantages of each approach?
4. What is a "vicious circle" and how does it help us makes sense of disorders of personality? How can this concept be applied to other psychological problems such as depression and anxiety disorders (e.g., phobias)?
5. In your opinion, what accounts for the relatively weak influence that the research on personality disorders has had on the *DSM*?

SUGGESTED READINGS

Benjamin, L. S. (1996). *Interpersonal diagnosis and treatment of personality disorders* (2nd ed.). New York: Guilford. In this book, Lorna Benjamin, one of the leading theorists and researchers on psychotherapy for people with personality disorders, presents a model for the assessment and psychotherapy of personality disorders that focuses on changing the maladaptive interpersonal behavior that characterizes each of the *DSM-IV* personality disorder categories.

Clarkin, J. F., & Lenzenweger, M. F. (Eds.). (1996). *Major theories of personality disorder*. New York: Guilford. This edited volume presents a collection of comprehensive reviews of five theories of personality disorders—cognitive, psychoanalytic, interpersonal, evolutionary, and neurobiological—by noted experts such as Aaron Beck, Otto Kernberg, Lorna Benjamin, Theodore Millon, and Richard Depue.

Costa, P. T., & Widiger, T. A. (Eds.). (2002). *Personality disorders and the five factor model of personality* (2nd ed.). Washington, DC: American Psychological Association. This edited text provides excellent chapters on a wide range of topics concerning theory and research on the use of the five-factor model in defining and understanding disorders of personality.

Costello, C.G. (Ed.). (1996). *Personality characteristics of the personality disordered*. New York: Wiley-Interscience. This edited book takes a step back from the *DSM* to focus on the specific features or symptoms of personality disorders. Costello insists that the tremendous overlap in the diagnostic criteria of the *DSM-IV* personality disorder categories demands that we treat these criteria as dimensions of individual difference, not as symptoms of discrete disorders or syndromes, the approach we advocate in this chapter. Experts summarize the research on the normal and pathological aspects of these dimensions, including aggressiveness, emotional instability, impulsiveness, dependency, and paranoia.

Livesley, W. J. (Ed.). (2001). *Handbook of personality disorders: Theory, research, and treatment*. New

York: Guilford. A comprehensive, up-to-date handbook edited by one of the leading researchers of personality disorders. Probably the best place to start for those desiring an in-depth look at theory and research on personality disorders.

Millon, T., with Davis, R. D. (1996). *Disorders of personality: DSM-IV and beyond* (2nd ed.). New York: Wiley-Interscience. In this encyclopedic text (over 750 pages), Theodore Millon—the "father" of the *DSM*'s personality disorder categories—and Roger Davis summarize practically everything that has ever been written about personality disorders, both before and since *DSM-III*. Millon and Davis cover history, theory, diagnostic issues, development, assessment, and treatment, faithfully (although not uncritically) following *DSM-IV*'s categories.

SUGGESTED WEB SITES

www.isspd.org
International Society for the Study of Personality Disorders (ISSPD). ISSPD was formed in 1988 following an international conference on personality disorders in Copenhagen, Denmark, in order to "stimulate, support, and exchange scholarship, clinical experience, and research results in the field of personality disorders" (quote from web site). The *Journal of Personality Disorders* has been an official publication of the ISSPD since 1989.

www.guilford.com/periodicals/jnpd.htm
Journal of Personality Disorders. This quarterly publication is the major scientific outlet for theory and research on the diagnosis, assessment, etiology, and treatment of personality disorders. The journal

was founded by Theodore Millon and Allen Frances in 1986 and, as noted above, became an official publication of the International Society for the Study of Personality Disorders in 1989.

//pdf.uchc.edu
Personality Disorders Foundation. This relatively small organization of personality disorder theorists and researchers was founded in 2000. Its stated mission is to "Attain significant progress in the research and treatment of severe personality disorders; Advocate for policies and funding necessary to achieve these advances; To gain national exposure aimed at educating the public about, and destigmatizing the diagnoses of, personality disorders" (quote from the web site).

INFOTRAC COLLEGE EDITION SEARCH TOPICS

Personality disorder	Vicious circle	Co-morbidity
Categorical model	*Diagnostic and Statistical Manual*	
Dimensional	*of Mental Disorders*	

REFERENCES

Akiskal, H. S. (1981). Subaffective disorders: Dysthymic, cyclothymic, and bipolar II disorders in the "borderline" realm. *Psychiatric Clinics of North America, 4,* 25–46.

Akiskal, H., Yerevanian, B., Davis, G., King, D., & Lemmi, H. (1985). The nosologic status of bor-

derline personality: Clinical and polysomographic study. *American Journal of Psychiatry, 142,* 192–198.

Alarcon, R. D., Foulks, E. F., & Vakkur, M. (1998). *Personality disorders and culture: Clinical and conceptual interactions.* New York: John Wiley.

American Psychiatric Association (APA). (1994). *Diagnostic and statistical manual of mental disorders* (4th ed.). Washington, DC: American Psychiatric Association Press.

American Psychiatric Association (APA). (2000). *Diagnostic and statistical manual of mental disorders* (4th ed., text revision). Washington, DC: American Psychiatric Association Press.

Barone, D. F., Maddux, J. E., & Snyder, C. R. (1997). *Social cognitive psychology: History and current domains*. New York: Plenum.

Benjamin, L. S. (1996). *Interpersonal diagnosis and treatment of personality disorders* (2nd ed.). New York: Guilford.

Brown, G. L., & Linnoila, M. I. (1990). CSF serotonin metabolite (5-HIAA) studies in depression, impulsivity, and violence. *Journal of Clinical Psychiatry, 51(4)*, Suppl., 31–41.

Carey, G. & DiLalla, D. L. (1994). Personality and psychopathology: Genetic perspectives. *Journal of Abnormal Psychology, 103*, 32–43.

Cloninger, C. R. (1987). A systematic method for clinical description and classification of personality variants. *Archives of General Psychiatry, 44*, 573–588.

Cloninger, C. R., Svrakic, D. M., Przybeck, T. R. (1993). A psychobiological model of temperament and character. *Archives of General Psychiatry, 50*, 975–990.

Coker, L. A., & Widiger, T. A. (in press). Personality disorders. In J. E. Maddux & B. A. Winstead (Eds.), *Psychopathology: Contemporary theory, research, and issues*. New York: Erlbaum.

Costa, P. T., Jr., & McCrae, R. R. (1992). The five-factor model of personality and its relevance to personality disorders. *Journal of Personality Disorders, 6*, 343–359.

Costa, P. T., & Widiger, T. A. (Eds.). (2002). *Personality disorders and the five factor model of personality* (2nd ed.). Washington, DC: American Psychological Association.

Eysenck, H. J. Y., & Eysenck, M. W. (1985). *Personality and individual differences*. New York: Plenum.

Fenigstein, A. (1996). Paranoia. In C. G. Costello (Ed.), *Personality characteristics of the personality disordered*. New York: Wiley.

Hyler, S. E., & Lyons, M. (1988). Factor analysis of the *DSM-III* personality disorder clusters: A replication. *Comprehensive Psychiatry, 29*, 304–308.

Kass, F., Skodol, A. E., Charles, E., Spitzer, R. L., & Williams, J. B. W. (1985). Scaled ratings of *DSM-III* personality disorders. *American Journal of Psychiatry, 142*, 627–630.

Livesley, W. J. (2001a). Conceptual and taxonomic issues. In W. J. Livesley, (Ed.), *Handbook of personality disorders: Theory, research, and treatment* (pp. 3–38). New York: Guilford.

Livesley, W. J. (Ed.) (2001b). *Handbook of personality disorders: Theory, research, and treatment*. New York: Guilford.

Livesley, W. J., Jackson, D. N., & Schroeder, M. L. (1992). Factorial structure of traits delineating personality disorders in clinical and general population samples. *Journal of Abnormal Psychology, 3*, 432–440.

Livesley, W. J., Schroeder, M. L., Jackson, D. N., & Jang, K. L. (1994). Categorical distinctions in the study of personality disorder: Implications for classification. *Journal of Abnormal Psychology, 103*, 6–17.

Lynam, D. R., & Widiger, T. A. (2001). Using the five-factor model to represent the personality disorders. *Journal of Abnormal Psychology, 110*, 401–412.

Maddux, J. E. (2002). Stopping the madness: Positive psychology and the deconstruction of the illness ideology and the *DSM*. In C. R. Snyder & S. J. Lopez (Eds.), *Handbook of positive psychology*. New York: Oxford University Press.

Millon, T., with Davis, R. (1996). *Disorders of personality: DSM-IV and beyond*. New York: Wiley-Interscience.

Siever, L. J., & Davis, K. L. (1991). A psychobiological perspective on the personality disorders. *American Journal of Psychiatry, 148*, 1647–1658.

Skodol, A. E., Rosnick, L., Kellman, H. D., Oldham, J. M., & Hyler, S. E. (1991). Development of a procedure for validating structured assessments of Axis II. In J. Oldham (Ed.), *Personality disorders: New perspectives on diagnostic validity* (pp. 41–70). Washington, DC: American Psychiatric Association Press.

Szasz, T. S. (1974). *The myth of mental illness: Foundations of a theory of personal conduct* (Rev. ed.). New York: Harper & Row.

Tellegen, A. (1993). Folk concepts and psychological concepts of personality and personality disorder. *Psychological Inquiry, 4*, 122–130.

Thurstone, L. L. (1934.) The vectors of mind. *Psychological Review, 41*, 1–32.

Triandis, H. C., & Suh, M. (2002). Cultural influences on personality. *Annual Review of Psychology 53*, 133–160.

Widiger, T. A. (1989). The categorical distinction between personality and affective disorders. *Journal of Personality Disorders, 3*, 77–91.

Widiger, T. A. (1993a). Conceptualizing a disorder of personality from the five-factor model. In P. T. Costa & T. A. Widiger (Eds.), *Personality disorders and the five-factor model of personality* (pp. 289–309). Washington, DC: American Psychological Association.

Widiger, T. A. (1993b). The *DSM-III-R* categorical personality disorder diagnoses: A critique and an alternative. *Psychological Inquiry, 4*, 75–90.

Widiger, T. A., Frances, A. J., Harris, M. Jacobsberg, L. B., Fyer, M., & Manning, D. (1991). Comorbidity among Axis II disorders. In J. Oldhan (Ed.), *Personality disorders: New perspectives on diagnostic validity* (pp. 165–194). Washington, DC: American Psychiatric Association Press.

Widiger, T. A., & Sanderson, C. J. (1995). Toward a dimensional model of personality disorders. In W. J. Livesley (Ed.), *The* DSM-IV *personality disorders* (pp. 433–458). New York: Guilford.

Widiger, T. A., Sanderson, C., & Warner, L. (1986). The MMPI, prototypal typology, borderline personality disorder. *Journal of Personality Assessment, 50*, 540–553.

Widiger, T. A., Verheul, R., & van den Brink, W. (1999). Personality and psychopathology. In L. A. Pervin & O. P. John (Eds.), *Handbook of personality: Theory and research* (2nd ed.). New York: Guilford.

Wiggins, J. S., & Pincus, A. L. (1989). Conceptions of personality disorders and dimensions of personality. *Psychological Assessment, 4*, 305–316.

Zanarini, M. C., Frankenburg, F. R., Dubo, E. D., Sickel, A. E., Trikha, A. Levin, A.,& Reynolds, V. (1998a). Axis II comorbidity of borderline personality disorder. *Comprehensive Psychiatry, 39*, 296–302.

Zanarini, M. C., Frankenburg, F. R., Dubo, E. D., Sickel, A. E., Trikha, A. Levin, A., & Reynolds, V. (1998b). Axis I comorbidity of borderline personality disorder. *American Journal of Psychiatry, 155*, 1733–1739.

Zuckerman, M. (1995). Good and bad humors: Biochemical bases of personality and its disorders. *Psychological Science, 6*, 325–332.

Credits

This page constitutes an extension of the copyright page. We have made every effort to trace the ownership of all copyrighted material and to secure permission from copyright holders. In the event of any question arising as to the use of any material, we will be pleased to make the necessary corrections in future printings. Thanks are due to the following authors, publishers, and agents for permission to use the material indicated.

Chapter 3, p. 72: From "Resolving the Person-Situation Debate," D. C. Rowe, in *American Psychologist,* Vol. 4, No. 31, pp. 218–227. Copyright © 1997 by the American Psychological Association. Adapted with permission. **p. 77:** From "Personality Similarity in Twins Reared Apart and Together," by T. J. Bouchard et al., in *Journal of Personality and Social Psychology,* Vol. 54, p. 1035. Copyright © 1988 by the American Psychological Association. Adapted with permission. **p. 80:** Based on *The Authoritarian Personality* by T. W. Adorno et al. Copyright © 1950 by the American Jewish Committee. Reprinted by permission of HarperCollins Publishers, Inc.; and from *Measures of Personality and Social Psychological Attitudes,* ed. J. P. Robinson et al., reprinted with permission from Elsevier. **p. 82:** From "Familial Studies of Intelligence: A Review," by T. J. Bouchard, Jr., and M. McGue, 1981, *Science, 212,* Figure 1, p. 1056. Copyright 1981 by the American Association for the Advancement of Science. Reprinted with permission of the authors and publisher. **p. 84:** From "Synchronies in Mental Development: An Epigenetic Perspective," by R. S. Wilson, 1978, *Science, 202,* p. 942. Copyright 1978 by the American Association for the Advancement of Science. Reprinted with permission of the publisher.

Chapter 5, p. 134: Adapted from Hazan and Shaver (1987). Used by permission.

Chapter 6, p. 174 (top photo): From Veroff, J., Atkinson, J. W., Feld, S. C., & Gurin, G. (1960). "The Use of Thematic Apperception to Assess Motivation in a Nationwide Interview Study." *Psychological Monographs,* 74(12), Whole number 499.

Chapter 7, p. 199: Adapted from Costa and McCrae (1985). Reproduced by special permission of the Publisher, Psychological Assessment Resources, Inc., 16204 North Florida Avenue, Lutz, Florida 33549, from the *NEO Personality Inventory-Revised,* by Paul Costa, and Robert McCrae, copyright 1978, 1985, 1989, 1992 by PAR, Inc. Further reproduction is prohibited without permission of PAR, Inc.

Chapter 10, p. 287: Allan Fenigstein, Michael Scheier, and Arnold Buss, "Public and Private Self-Consciousness: Assessment and Theory," in *Journal of Consulting and Clinical Psychology, 43,* 522–527. Copyright © 1975 by the American Psychological Association. Reprinted by permission.

Chapter 11, p. 319: From "The Desirability of Control" by J. M. Burger and H. M. Cooper, *Motivation and Emotion, 3,* Table 1, pp. 384–385. Copyright © 1979 Kluwer Academics/Plenum Publishers. Reprinted with permission.

Name Index

McEwen, B. S., 463, 464
McFadden, S. H., 375, 379
McFann, H. H., 164
McFarlin, D. B., 261, 264
McGee, R. O., 374
McGue, M., 79, 82, 85, 404
McGuffin, P., 103
McGuire, C. V., 252
McGuire, S., 373
McGuire, W. J., 252
McKinley, J. C., 345
McLean, J. E., 339, 340
McNamara, W., 180
McNeil, P., 323
McWard, J., 313
Meacham, J. A., 249
Mead, G. H., 284
Meadows, S., 371, 383
Mecca, A. M., 259
Medley, D. M., 467
Mednick, A. A., 18
Meehl, P. E., 50
Meissner, P. B., 282
Mendelsohn, G. A., 212
Meng, X., 451
Meoni, L. A., 469
Merikle, P. M., 221
Merton, R. D., 344
Merz, J., 286
Mesquita, B., 368, 369
Messick, S., 11
Metalsky, G. I., 378
Metter, E. J., 206
Metts, S., 486
Meyer, A., 458
Miles, C. C., 345, 346, 360
Milgram, S., 396
Miller, D. C., 337
Miller, E. M., 356
Miller, G. A., 168, 296
Miller, G. E., 470
Miller, J. B., 128
Miller, J. G., 438
Miller, N., 145, 338
Miller, R. S., 366, 367, 370, 379, 380, 382, 383, 384, 385
Miller, S. M., 313, 314
Millon, T., 512, 515, 517, 520, 526, 528, 533
Mills, J., 487, 489
Milne, A. B., 293
Mineka, S., 379
Mischel, W., 137, 162, 268, 284, 378, 379, 396, 397
Mita, T. H., 226
Mitchell, J. E., 357
Miyamoto, Y., 438

Miyazaki, A. D., 325
Mockler, C., 30
Modigliani, A., 380, 382
Moffitt, T. E., 374, 402, 404, 413
Mohr, D. M., 250
Moller, A. P., 356
Moller, J., 469
Monat, A., 313
Montemayor, R., 250
Moore, P. J., 486
Mora, F., 166
Morash, M. A., 272
Morf, C. C., 256
Morin, A., 302
Morling, B., 438
Morris, M. W., 438
Morrison, S., 401
Morse, H., 422
Motti, F., 130
Mount, M. K., 59
Mueller, E., 146
Mulkana, S., 474
Mullen, B., 299
Mundell, C. E., 507
Murphy, D., 337
Murphy, S. T., 224
Murray, C., 88
Murray, H. A., 13, 18, 171, 423
Murstein, B. I., 489, 490
Musante, L., 321
Mussolino, M. E., 470
Myers, A. M., 350
Myers, M. M., 470

N
Nanni, C., 315
Nasby, W., 293
Nash, M. R., 217, 221, 234, 237, 239, 243
Natsoulas, T., 282
Nauta, W. J. H., 110
Neale, J. M., 226, 378
Neale, M. C., 82
Needham, T. L., 494
Neisser, U., 221
Nesselroade, J. R., 83
Newcomb, M. D., 314
Newman, L. S., 231
Ng, M. T., 317
Nichols, P. A., 255
Nichols, R. C., 81
Niebuhr, R., 310
Nisbett, R. E., 220, 225, 226, 243, 368, 438
Nitschke, J. B., 118
Nix, G., 300
Nolen-Hoeksema, S., 292

Noller, P., 151, 378
Norasakkunkit, V., 438
Nordlie, J. W., 223
Norenzayan, A., 438
Norman, W. T., 195, 198, 445
Norris, C. E., 408
Nowicki, S., 317
Nozyce, M., 375
Nurius, P., 168
Nuttin, J. M., 226
Nye, F. J., 401
Nystedt, L., 286

O
Oakman, J. A., 323
Oatley, K., 370
O'Brien, E. J., 399
Odbert, H. S., 195
O'Gorman, J. G., 106
Okamura, L., 323
Oldham, J. M., 528
Olds, J., 165
Oliver, M. B., 340
Oliver, P., 24
O'Malley, P. M., 260
Oniszcenko, W., 374
Ortiz, F. A., 420
Ostendorf, F., 53, 384
Ostfield, A. M., 469
Oswald, F. L., 60
Owen, M. J., 103
Owens, J. F., 474
Oyserman, D., 434, 435, 436
Ozer, D. J., 60

P
Packard, M. G., 102
Palys, T. S., 168
Parekh, I., 108
Parke, R. D., 137
Parker, C. P., 285
Parker, W. D., 446
Parrott, W. G., 383
Passini, F. T., 198
Pastorelli, C., 315
Patrick, C. J., 379
Patterson, C. P., 486
Paul, O., 469
Paulhus, D. L., 43, 211
Paunonen, S. V., 433, 439
Pavlov, I. P., 99
Peake, P. K., 379
Pearson, K., 67
Pedersen, C., 404
Pedersen, N. L., 64, 83
Pellowski, N., 494
Peng, K., 438

Subject Index

A

Ability tests, 44
Abnormal personality, 510–511, 522–525
Abnormal traits, 86–87
Achievement motive, 172–173, 175–176
   autobiographical memory and, 180–181
   career choice and, 173, 175–176
   desire for control and, 322–323
Acquaintanceship process, 485
Actualizing tendency, 138
Adaptive inflexibility, 517–518
Adaptive personality, 511, 514
Administration bias, 433
Adolescents
   attachment patterns of, 133
   attitudes toward authority, 412, 413
   collective misbehavior among, 413
   delinquency among, 87, 402–405, 409, 413
   false-self behavior in, 140
   identity crisis in, 272
   rule breaking by, 402–405, 412–413
   self-concept development in, 250
   self-esteem of, 258
   See also Children
Adopted children
   Galton's study of, 67
   IQ studies of, 85
Adult Attachment Interviews (AAI), 133
Adult personality tendencies (APT), 149
Adults
   attachment patterns in, 133–135
   hypnotic age regression of, 233–242
   self-esteem of, 258–259
Affect intensity, 376–377. *See also* Emotions
Affective autonomy, 431
Affective awareness, 316

Affective chronometry, 115
Affective reactivity, 109–116
Age regression, 233–242
Aggregation principle, 49
Aggressive behavior
   authoritarianism and, 15
   heart disease and, 469
   self-esteem and, 260
   sex differences in, 337–338
   sociocultural studies of, 147
Agreeableness, 6, 199, 404, 406, 494, 530
Alcoholism, 87
Alleles, 68
Allelic association, 74
Allocentric individuals, 435
Allostatic load, 463
Alpha activity, 111
Altruistic behavior, 90
American Medical Association (AMA), 238
American Psychiatric Association (APA), 86, 195, 346, 509
American Psychological Association (APA), 346
Amnesia
   posthypnotic, 229–230
   source, 228
Anal stage, 126–127
Anger
   heart disease and, 467–470
   power motive and, 176
   suppression of, 469–470
Anterior activation asymmetry, 110–116
Anthropology, 422
Antisocial personality disorder, 510, 524, 528, 529
Anxiety
   attachment patterns and, 130–132
   causal inferences about, 193–194
   emotional temperament and, 373, 374
   perceived control and, 313
   physiological measures of, 100
   social, 286

Anxious/ambivalent attachment, 134–135
Anxious/avoidant attachment, 130–131
Anxious/resistant attachment, 131–132
Appraisal of stressors, 464–465
Appraisal process model of trust, 496–497
Approach tendencies, 373
Art of Travel, The (Galton), 65
Assessing personality. *See* Personality measurement
Assessment center, 35–36
Association studies, 74–75
Attachment patterns, 129–135
   adult intimacy and, 133–135
   emotional experience and, 375
   global trust and, 492–493
   internal working models and, 132–133
   styles of attachment and, 130–132, 375
Attachment theory, 129–135, 492–493
Attention-deficit hyperactivity disorder (ADHD), 87
Attitude Interest Analysis Survey, 345
Attitude similarity, 487
Attributions, 170, 497–498
Augmentation/reduction studies, 107–108
Authoritarianism
   family correlations for, 80–81
   research on, 14–15
   sex differences in, 338
Authoritarian parents, 141
Authoritative parents, 141
Authority
   accommodation to, 412, 413–414
   attitudes toward, 410–411, 412, 413
Autobiographical memory, 180–181
Avoidant personality disorder, 508, 510, 516–517, 529
Awkward uncertainty, 383